Nicholas Wall

London 1970.

AN ECCLESIASTICAL HISTORY OF ENGLAND

THE VICTORIAN CHURCH

AN ECCLESIASTICAL HISTORY
OF ENGLAND
General Editor: J. C. Dickinson

THE VICTORIAN CHURCH

BY

OWEN CHADWICK

PART II

ADAM & CHARLES BLACK
LONDON

FIRST PUBLISHED 1970

A. AND C. BLACK LTD
4, 5 AND 6 SOHO SQUARE LONDON W.1
© 1970 OWEN CHADWICK

SBN 7136 1020 4

PRINTED IN GREAT BRITAIN
BY R. & R. CLARK, LTD., EDINBURGH

PREFACE

PARAGRAPHS from Chapter I were published in a supplement to *Colloquium* (Auckland 1968).

I have again to acknowledge the gracious permission of Her Majesty the Queen to make use of material in the Royal Archives.

The National Trust gave leave for extracts from the Hughenden Papers; the Duke of Wellington for the use of Stratfieldsaye Papers.

My thanks to the librarians or archivists of the University Library at Cambridge; the Leeds City Library and the Brotherton Library at Leeds; the British Museum and the superintendent of its newspaper repository; the Bodleian Library; the Lambeth Library; Nottingham City Library; the Borthwick Institute at York; the Northamptonshire Record office; the Norfolk and Norwich City Library; Trinity College, Cambridge, and Balliol College, Oxford; the trustees of the Broadlands Archives; the Oratory at Birmingham, and especially Father Stephen Dessain; Pusey House; Canon R. Cant, in charge of the archives of York minster, and Mrs. J. Varley at the Lincolnshire archives; Mr. Harry Carter, archivist of the Oxford University Press; Dr. Anne Worden; and the Reverend R. J. C. Gutteridge.

CONTENTS

CONTENTS

CHAPTER I

SCIENCE AND RELIGION

I. DARWIN AND THE CONFLICT

MORE educated Englishmen doubted the truth of the Christian religion in 1885 than thirty years before. And in 1885 many persons, whether they doubted or affirmed, blamed 'science' for this change in opinion. Some of them talked as though 'science' alone was responsible. And among those who blamed science, some fastened upon the name of Charles Darwin as the symbol, or centre, or intellectual force, of an entire development of the sciences as they came to bear upon the truth of religion. One schoolboy, George Macaulay Trevelyan, born in 1876, accepted (as he afterwards believed) the truths of the Christian religion in his nursery until the age of thirteen when he learnt that 'Darwin' had disproved the Bible, and then the fabric of Christian doctrine instantaneously fell away in ruin.[1]

This was what men believed. And if we attempt to test their belief against the evidence, we meet the special difficulty of intellectual history, that we can with hesitation judge the true effect of articulated opinion even on a single mind and then only if that mind is analytical and capable of expressing itself, while here we are asked to judge the effect of such opinion upon the half-conscious axioms of society.

Why, for example, did men hesitate to be clergymen of the Church of England? Men always hesitated before taking orders if they found it difficult to accept the tenets which they must teach as officers of that church. The question arises whether more of those who contemplated taking orders shrank back by reason of doubt. Though the evidence on such a point must be haphazard and unsatisfactory, we shall see how some of the evidence points to a social cause rather than an intellectual cause of such hesitation; except at

[1] Trevelyan, *Autobiography*, 23.

certain moments of intellectual crisis, as at the time of the law suits over the Bible in 1861–5, or the arguments over *Lux Mundi* in 1890 to 1892. More educated men doubted the Christian faith, for more Englishmen were educated.

When therefore we seek to analyse the part of 'science' and especially of Darwin in this momentous change, we must first recognise that science (using that word in the English sense to mean the natural sciences) was one aid to unsettlement in a more general unsettlement of minds, and that it remains to be seen how important or unimportant it was to that unsettlement; not in common belief, for everyone agreed that science unsettled, as they listened to the speeches of prime ministers, divines, biologists or physicists, who told them of the incompatibility between science (as now) and religion (as now); but in reality. At the end of the century it was more difficult to believe in life after death than fifty years before— or at least more people said that it was difficult. No one has yet been able to analyse what (if anything) the natural sciences had to do with this difficulty. In this shadowy land none can determine how philo-sophical beliefs, or beliefs about the external world, affect religious faith. In some minds those beliefs powerfully affected the nature of faith or non-faith, in other minds beliefs about the external world could be altered or reversed without any effect whatever upon religious faith in its citadel of the soul. Roman Catholic doctrine became for the agnostic more difficult at the end of the century than at the beginning. And the numbers show that educated men found it just as easy to be Roman Catholics.

The Christian church taught what was not true. It taught the world to be 6,000 years old, a universal flood, and stories in the Old Testament like the speaking ass or the swallowing of Jonah by a whale which ordinary men (once they were asked to consider the question of truth or falsehood) instantly put into the category of legends. Many educated Christians ceased long before 1860 to believe in a universal flood or Jonah's whale or the 6,000 years of world history. But quiet men in pews knew nothing of these matters and were untroubled until they met the question in a newspaper, a pamphlet, an agitator or a friend. This governed everything. The churches taught something that could no longer be believed, and therefore all the other teaching of the churches fell into question. But how it was found or felt to be untrue, whether by history or natural science or philosophy or moral feeling, that was a secondary question, more difficult to answer, and varying from mind to mind.

The unsettlement of faith about the Bible in 1861–5 was directly caused by historians, or those who posed as historians in dealing with the texts of the Old and New Testament. It was not caused by Darwin, who published his *Origin of Species* in 1859. In one aspect the unsettlement was due not to the natural sciences but to the advance in historical study of ancient texts. In another aspect these students of ancient documents probably could not have written as they did unless they wrote in a climate of opinion already formed by natural scientists and by philosophers. Geology disproved Genesis. Most educated Christians did not mind that geology changed their understanding of Genesis chapter i, or narrowed the area of land covered by the flood. But whether they minded or not, the world understood how geology contradicted Genesis. 'Science' and 'Religion', it was soon being said, had opposed conclusions. From 1864 the controversy between 'science' and 'religion' took fire. The *Times* newspaper first wrote a leading article upon the subject in May 1864. And whether this was a conflict between science and religion or between historical study and accepted views of the Bible, hardly mattered to the public. They called the challenge to Biblical inspiration by the name 'science'. Some scientists were cross that they should be loosely accused of antagonism to religion and that their reputation should so be lowered without just cause. But the public seized on the single incontrovertible truth. Geology contradicted Genesis, and men said that after all the Bible was untrue.

We must distinguish between science when it was against religion and the scientists when they were against religion. Science was a growing body of knowledge which formed conclusions about the external world, as for example about its age, contrary to the conclusions commonly accepted hitherto on the basis of documents which were also the basis of the prevailing religion. The scientists were but men, and some of them were religious and some of them were not. This is a distinction essential to our understanding of what happened. If a scientist attacked Christianity, the public (after it accepted the axiom that 'science' was in conflict with 'religion') instantly inferred that the scientist attacked Christianity because he was a scientist. But it was not so, or was not always so. Scientists were also men, and there might be many other reasons why a man

should assail religion, for example that he was in revolt against his
father who was religious. Wallace in his middle years assailed
Christian orthodoxy. As he was one of the founders of the doctrine
of natural selection, men might easily infer that his science led him
to assail orthodoxy. But it was not true. For Wallace assailed
orthodoxy before he knew anything about evolution. His science
simply offered him new arguments to strengthen the old.

This axiom, lodged in the public mind after 1864, that science and
faith were in conflict, had a related consequence. If a scientist
attacked religion, he might claim that he attacked it because he was
a scientist. But sometimes, even where his science may be assumed
to have contributed something to his posture of antagonism,
the attack was not based upon his scientific knowledge. Huxley
wrote many articles against Christianity, especially during the years
after he ceased to take an active part in scientific research. He
assailed the story of the Gadarene swine. Because Huxley was or had
been a scientist, men easily inferred that he represented 'science' in
assailing the story, when the truth was that a man, who was also a
natural scientist, was against the Gadarene story. John Tyndall
attacked the doctrine of miracle in the Bampton lectures by J. B.
Mozley. Because Tyndall was becoming prominent as a physicist
and geologist, it was easy to assume that he represented the natural
sciences in his criticism. But the arguments which he used against
Mozley did not arise out of his scientific training, for they were the
strong arguments of an amateur philosopher, and came rather from
the reason than from the empirical examination of nature. In May
1889 Professor Flower of the Natural History Museum complained
indignantly to the Dean of Windsor about this misunderstanding.
He said 'it is very hard and very unfair that, because Huxley and
Tyndall happen to be scientific men of the first order, and happen
also to be opposed in some sense to the truths of religion, scientific
men generally should be ticketed as though they belonged to the
same school of thought. . . . Both Huxley and Tyndall were anti-
religious in a dogmatic sense long before they had made any mark
in science, and . . . their views on these subjects cannot therefore
be regarded as the legitimate outcome of scientific thought and
scientific knowledge.'[1]

Thus the historian need not be impressed when he finds scientists

[1] Bell, *Davidson*, i, 154.

who attacked religion, until he can discern why they attacked religion. The changing picture of the world was more important than the arguments of any hostile writer, whether scientist or not, in planting the axiom of conflict into the public mind. Geology contradicted Genesis, and the Bible was not (in all its parts) true, and if man had not been created in the way that Genesis taught, whence came he? Was it possible that those few despised authors who said that man was descended from apes were right after all?

To this growing sense of conflict between faith and reason Darwin contributed a little before 1864 and a lot afterwards.

Between the publication of the *Origin* and the publication of *The Descent of Man* in 1871 the doctrine of evolution became axiomatic, or probable, or tolerable, to many educated Englishmen. How they were persuaded of its scientific truth is less important than that they were persuaded, for most of them were incapable of testing the evidence or following closely the argument. By 1871 the theory that man developed out of lower forms of animals was more probable than any other theory, not only to most of the scientists but to many educated members of the general public. It was still confessed, especially by the scientists, to have many improbabilities and vast gaps in the evidence. But the theory was nevertheless more probable than any other because no other theory existed. Genesis had gone, and descent from lower animals was the only theory in the field. Evolution conquered because it was the only explanation with any evidence whatever. Some have thought it paradoxical that Darwin should have made evolution probable by the very narrow theory of descent solely by natural selection, as it appeared in the first 1859 edition of *The Origin of Species*, and that he then withdrew little by little from his exclusive reliance upon natural selection as the way in which development occurred. He retracted a vital part of that theory which accustomed men to think evolution to be a likely truth. But the public accepted the doctrine of evolution for a bigger reason than the simple probability established by Darwin, namely that, if they did not, their mental picture of the origins suddenly became an intolerable blank; unless like Mr. Gladstone they accepted upon religious and non-scientific grounds, and despite the historians, an idea of creation still extracted from the book of Genesis.

The planting of the axiom in the public mind—that science was against religion—is shown by those scientists who were Christians.

By the seventies society found it surprising, or striking, when they found a devout scientist. Faraday, or Sir George Stokes, or Kelvin, or Lister, or Asa Gray, or Bonney, or Pritchard, became exhibits— here is a scientist who is a Christian—how remarkable! When the physicist Clerk Maxwell died, the preacher after his funeral said that he would not use the occasion to point out the harmony of science and faith in their great man. But the preacher's very device, in the pulpit at Cambridge, shows that Clerk Maxwell was indeed an exhibit.

The extant evidence about late Victorian scientists seldom bears out this new assumption by the public. We may allow for the circumstances that in late Victorian England a man's influence might still be a little diminished in some circles if he were known to be agnostic; and truly agnostic men are seldom confident enough about their opinions to broadcast their difficulty. We may allow for the circumstance that we shall know if a man was strongly for religion and might not know if he cared for none of these things. But we find a fair number of leading scientists quietly practising their faith in church or chapel. And even more, we continue to find that old axiom or feeling, which Darwin seemed to have demolished in himself, that scientific study can lead upwards towards God. Faraday felt it; Kelvin never doubted it; the most eminent among Victorian medical men, from Sir James Paget to Sir Ronald Ross, were marked for their piety; and the long tradition from Sedgwick through Jeans and Eddington to Sir Alister Hardy continued to be an important, though seldom a representative, group among the students of the natural sciences. Professor Flower of the Natural History Museum told the Dean of Windsor in 1889 that he knew no evidence to suggest more unsettlement of faith among the profession of scientists than among the profession of (say) barristers.[1]

But we cannot judge this change in opinion by its effect upon the scientists. For they were educated men, and if they were told that 'science disproved' religion, they knew that it did not. Most of them jettisoned belief in the historical information of Genesis before they knew about evolution. Sir Charles Lyell remained a practising Anglican all his days, and if someone had said to him that Darwin

[1] Bell, *Davidson*, i, 154; for the religion of scientists, *inter alia*, cf. *Memoir of Sir George Stokes*, i, 78; J. E. B. Mayor, *Cardale Babington*, 1895; *Life of Clerk Maxwell*, etc.

proved the Bible untrue, he would not have assented, for his own geology helped both to create the intellectual situation in which Darwin became probable and to produce the conflict between geology and Genesis. The level at which we must judge this is not at the level of the Kelvins or the Galtons or Huxleys, nor even the philosophers or publicists like Leslie Stephen or John Morley, who claimed to base their opposition to Christianity partly (but only partly) upon the advance of science. We must keep in our minds the schoolboy who at the age of thirteen discovered that 'Darwin' had proved the Bible untrue.

Consider first the attitudes of the scientists to these matters and then the attitudes of the divines.

In 1864 the arguments of the historians about the truth of the Bible reached a climax in the question whether a man who on historical grounds disbelieved the book of Genesis, or other books of the Bible, could be nevertheless a clergyman. As it had already entered the mind of the public that geology—and now evolution —stood against the truth of the Bible, and as Huxley was declaring this in a loud voice, some religious men blamed 'science' for this controversy, or (more precisely) accused scientific men of misusing their science. Accordingly Herbert MacLeod, of the Royal College of Chemistry in Oxford Street, conceived the idea of collecting the signatures of scientists to a declaration, which expressed 'sincere regret that researches into scientific truth are perverted by some in our own times into occasion for casting doubt upon the truth and authenticity of the Holy Scriptures. . . . We cannot but deplore that natural science should be looked upon with suspicion by many who do not make a study of it, merely on account of the unadvised manner in which some are placing it in opposition to Holy Writ.'

This declaration was signed by 716 persons, thirty-eight of whom were students at the Royal College of Chemistry, and other names upon the list looked 'queer' to some of the scientists. It caused resentment to many good men who regarded it as a new test, a hitherto unknown shibboleth, a fortieth article of religion, and encountered ridicule as well as hostility from those who disliked it. They said that only sixty-two Fellows of the Royal Society out of 600 signed, only nineteen out of the 166 writers in *Philosophical Transactions*, and that the list was notable for the names which did not appear on it—Darwin, Faraday, Daubeny, Hooker, Lyell, Owen, Playfair, Roget, Tyndall, Whewell. But a few of those who refused to sign it declared that they refused not because they could not sign it, but because they would not force this shibboleth upon others. Herschel took this view, and in reply to a request for his signature Professor Daubeny regarded the suggestion as unwarrantable that men of science beyond other men were liable to the charge of infidelity and thought it better to pass over the accusation 'in silent contempt', for the real attacks upon the Bible in late years proceeded not from the scientists but from an Anglican bishop in Africa (Colenso) who was not 'addicted to the study of nature'.[1]

Therefore a number at least of those who did not sign it nevertheless believed it. And among those who signed it were some famous names, Sedgwick, Brewster, Challis, Gosse, Clerk Maxwell. The declaration continued to be quoted, even as late as 1880, as a sign that scientists generally believed the truth of the Bible and that those who did not believe were exceptional. The nature of the declaration hardly warranted this use.

Seven years later a relative of Darwin, Francis Galton, no friend of the churches, who helped to found the application of statistical methods to society, started to apply his mind to certain assumptions about the place of religion in society. The methods, as we shall see, were not yet well established, but their results were interesting. In 1873 he applied statistics to 'the causes which operate to create scientific men', including their heredity and religious background.[2] In the following year he published *English Men of Science: their nature and nurture*, after sending out a questionnaire to all persons whom he regarded as established scientists, and receiving 126 replies. Of these 126 men, eighty-eight, or seven out of every ten, said that they were members of one of the established churches. Of the remaining thirty-eight the most numerous category was of no church; and then, in this order, established church 'with qualification', Unitarian, 'Nonconformist', Wesleyan, Roman Catholic, Bible Christian. Galton (p. 135) expected 'dogmatism' to have a more deterrent effect than his answers showed. 'One would have thought that the anathemas from the pulpits against most new

[1] Daubeny, *Misc.* iv, 130–3; Herschel in *Athenaeum*, 17 September 1864; Graves, *Life of W. R. Hamilton*, iii, 618–21; *Times*, 20 September 1864.
[2] *Fortnightly Review*, 1873, i, 345.

scientific discoveries . . . must have deterred many; and, as I have already shown, few of the sons of clergymen are on my list.' Nevertheless, in answer to the direct enquiry, 'Has the religious creed taught in your youth had a deterrent effect on the freedom of your researches?', 'I am met with an overpowering majority of negatives', for seven or eight said *no* to each one who said *yes*. (No deterrent effect 39; none, with emphasis, 12; none, with reasons, 14; good effect, not bad, 8.)

The value of numbers such as these is not easy to determine. Galton's axiom—that he expected religious dogmas to deter men from scientific discovery and was surprised that they seemed not to —was an important feature, perhaps the most important feature, of the Victorian conflict between religion and science, and so powerful an expectation in the minds of some scientists as to turn otherwise scholarly men into belligerents.

This conflict between science and religion comprised two oppositions of different kinds: first, conclusions of natural science opposed (or held to be opposed) to accepted teaching of the churches, as for example that the world was more than 6,000 years old, or that the doctrine of evolution made the doctrine of special creations unnecessary, or that the doctrine of natural selection showed an element of purposelessness in the physical process, or that man had risen and not fallen, or that nature was so uniform as to make miracles unthinkable; and secondly, the need for science to claim a sovereign independence in the physical sphere. What mattered to some scientists was not that their conclusions might look opposed to conventional theology—for they could modify their conventional theology and continue to be religious—but the assertion (if it were asserted) that they must not reach those physical conclusions, because the way was barred by evidence from a non-physical source. In earlier days the works of God and the word of God so spoke in harmony that the enquirer felt no incongruity in drawing evidence from either source. But since the development of geology, and the contemporary advances in history, they no longer spoke in harmony and the enquirer could not rightly enquire unless he treated physical evidence as the only justification for conclusions about the physical nature of the world.

At the end of June 1860 the British Association met in Oxford, and on the Saturday of the meeting Professor Huxley clashed with

Bishop Wilberforce over the theory of evolution. This clash became the symbol of the entire Victorian conflict: empirical and instructed professor versus ignorant, rhetorical and obscurantist bishop. It did not become that symbol until near the end of the Victorian age, for though it was talked about privately, it did not become great matter of public interest until the publication of Darwin's biography (1887) and still more of Huxley's biography (1900). To write Huxley's life his son sent round seeking reminiscences, and much of the evidence, on which was based the later picture of the scene, he collected thirty-five years after the event. When the biographer of Samuel Wilberforce published his account of the scene, in the year before Darwin died,[1] he mentioned how the speech of Wilberforce in the museum made a great impression on the audience, and drew 'from a certain learned professor the retort, "I would rather be descended from an ape than a bishop."' Naturally the biographer and son of Wilberforce presented the scene in a manner unfavourable to Huxley, but could not have represented it thus if it were already the notorious symbol of clash between science and religion.

A small number of letters from eye-witnesses survives. It is clear that the speech of J. D. Hooker, and not the speech of Huxley, made the big impression on the audience in countering the bishop's arguments for the perpetuity instead of the evolution of species. It is clear that the bishop's arguments (which he seems to have learnt from Professor Owen) were genuine and formidable arguments, but that he also used a rhetoric which some members of the meeting felt to be flippant and unfitting (Hooker thought that he ridiculed Huxley 'savagely') and therefore caused them to excuse Huxley his retort. It is not clear precisely what the bishop said to rouse Huxley's wrath, nor what precise words Huxley used. It appears certain that however ill his eloquence, Wilberforce intended to appeal to moral feeling, especially to Victorian feeling about ladies. Even if it be supposed that we males are descended from apes, is it conceivable of woman with all her gentleness? Intending, as it seems, to call human feeling to his aid, he put the argument in the crude and absurd form, almost with a direct address to Huxley—he heard it said that Huxley did not see that it mattered whether his grandfather was an ape and asked whether he would be willing to trace his descent through his grandmother. The accounts of Huxley's retort

[1] Ashwell-Wilberforce, 1881, ii, 451.

are various. Huxley's own description of the meeting,[1] which he
carefully recorded to correct wilder reports, as that he had said that
he would rather be an ape than a bishop, records the sense of his
speech thus: ' "If . . . the question is put to me, would I rather have
a miserable ape for a grandfather or a man highly endowed by
nature and possessed of great means of influence and yet who
employs these faculties and that influence for the mere purpose of
introducing ridicule into a grave scientific discussion—I unhesi-
tatingly affirm my preference for the ape." Whereupon there was
inextinguishable laughter among the people.'

In later legend the clergy were hostile to Huxley. The contemporary evidence has a different picture, and understandably, for
in 1860 Bishop Wilberforce had not won that stature which he
acquired ten years later. Huxley reported: 'You can't think how
pleased all his confrères were. I believe I was the most popular man
in Oxford for full four-and-twenty hours afterwards.' A few friends
of Huxley suspected that he harmed his own cause by this kind of
controversy.[2]

Huxley, then, did not knock down Wilberforce's arguments with
a bludgeon, for his retort attacked rather the tone and rhetoric than
the arguments, and contemporaries were agreed that the man who
answered the arguments was Hooker. But concealed beneath the
little drama the freedom of the scientist was at stake. Wilberforce
appealed not only to the evidence of pigeons, but to the evidence
of moral feeling or sentiment. Moral feeling was indeed evidence
for the philosopher or the divine. But it could not be brought into
the scientific argument over the descent of man. The scientist could
not allow this non-physical evidence to intrude into his enquiries.

Because other theologians directly blamed 'the scientists' for the
argument over faith, a few scientists felt like Daniel in the lions' den
or pictured themselves as warriors summoned to do battle for the
liberty of the human reason. The Roman Catholic Church made
a particular contribution to this feeling of oppressive dogma, for
just then, partly for the intellectual reasons present also in English

[1] Huxley to Dyster, 9 September 1860, Huxley collection at Imperial College.
[2] E.g. Dean Liddell, cf. Rolleston to Huxley, undated 1860, Imperial College. For
contemporary evidence: eye-witnesses; Letters of J. R. Green, 41–42; Huxley, Life
of J. D. Hooker, i, 525; Huxley's letter to Dyster; Athenaeum, 1860, ii, 18–19; Rolleston to Huxley, 9 July 1860, Imperial College; Lyell, who was not there but in
Oxford, Life of Lyell, ii, 335. Later evidence: Life of Huxley, i, 259 ff.; Life of Darwin,
ii, 321; Tuckwell, Reminiscences of Oxford, 51–54.

society but partly also for political reasons of reaction against
Italian liberalism, the Papacy happened to be passing through a
phase of thought and conduct which resisted innovations in politics
or in scholarship if the scholarship touched religion. In the same
year 1864 when the English scientists issued their declaration, the
Pope issued the encyclical *Quanta Cura* with its appended syllabus
of errors. Even in Protestant England papal policy was taken to be
typical of ecclesiastical resistance to the liberty of the human mind.
Men reminded each other of Copernicus, and of the condemnation
of Galileo, and past attempts at a vain authority over science.
Huxley, who had the advantage of a brilliant style, eloquence of
speech, and an attractive personality, constituted himself the champion of radical Darwinism, and liked to pretend that the opposition
to Darwin was theological. At first much of the opposition to
Darwin's theory came from scientists on grounds of evidence, not
from theologians on grounds of Scripture. Huxley's way of defending Darwin was to assert that opponents were non-scientific, and to
identify them with theological 'prejudice'. He formed a picture in
his mind of science advancing through the ages, clad in shining
armour, embattled against the dark and dismal ranks of theologians.
'Extinguished theologians', he declared,[1] 'lie about the cradle of
every science as the strangled snakes beside that of Hercules.' For
Huxley it was science versus orthodoxy, science versus a semi-
barbarous Hebrew cosmology, day versus night.

The most belligerent of the few belligerent scientists was John
Tyndall. He came from Ulster, a great climber in the Alps, a
physicist and an authority on glaciers. From about 1865 Tyndall
constituted himself the hammer of theology wherever it impinged
upon physical nature—prayers for a good harvest, prayers against
epidemics, miracles, prayers for the sick. In 1874 the British Association met at Belfast and found it natural to invite Tyndall to be their
president. Tyndall made a presidential address which became famous
over Europe. He appeared to claim two things: first, matter has
what he called the promise and potency of all life; and secondly,
that the scientists would wrest from religion the whole realm of
cosmological theory. This address gave offence. When he published
it, he added a preface that he did not want to trample on religion,
that on the contrary the facts of religious experience were as valid

[1] *Westminster Review*, April 1860, p. 556.

as any other facts. But he warned religion off all physical areas of enquiry. In popular opinion this address at Belfast may be considered the high point of this conflict. Tyndall did not claim that science could solve problems in all areas of human life. But that was what some intelligent men thought the address to claim.

One other illustration of aggression. Galton applied statistics to the efficacy of prayer. Average age of the upper classes when they die: members of royal houses, 64·04; clergy, 69·49; lawyers, 68·14; English aristocrats, 67·31; medical men, 67·31. Yet everyone prays for the sovereign and royal family.

The divines found this mode of argument aggressive because Galton, proceeding from allegedly physical evidence, assaulted a non-physical statement or aspiration, and identified prayer with a physical cause like treatment by electric shock.[1]

Science, Huxley believed, advanced against religion and we shall see that Christian leaders of the sixties made sufficient pronouncements to make plausible this belief. Historians of the late fifties and sixties, like Buckle and Lecky, sought to illustrate the moral growth of Europe as reason conquered superstition. Lecky was an able and learned man, and his book of 1865, *A History of the rise and influence of Rationalism in Europe*, influenced the historical picture of a generation of educated readers. An American scientist, J. W. Draper, tried to do for science and religion what Lecky was to do for reason and superstition, and was less well equipped than Lecky for the historical task. In 1864 Draper published *The Intellectual Development of Europe* and in 1875 *A History of the Conflict between Science and Religion*. He identified Christianity not only with the Roman Catholic Church, but with the right wing of the contemporary Roman Catholic Church. History consisted in the light of science entering the dark rooms of Catholic orthodoxy. Copernicus and Galileo—the opposition to these theories was for Draper characteristic of the attitude of religious men towards the progress of science. When religious men signally contributed to the progress of science, Draper did not mention it. When the Pope contributed to the progress of science, as with the calendar, Draper did not

---

[1] Eve-Creasy, *Tyndall*, 91–92; 125–6; 168–9; *Fortnightly Review*, N.S., i. 645; Galton in *Fortnightly Review*, N.S., xii (July–Dec. 1872), 125ff.; but he said that the article was written years before; *Spectator*, 24 August 1872; *Contemporary Review*, October 1872, three papers, two by Tyndall and one by M'Cosh of Princeton; CCR (Leeds), 1872, 114 ff.; G. J. Romanes, *Christian Prayer and General Laws*, 1874.

mention it. As a contribution to history the book was worth little. As a contribution to the intellectual atmosphere of that age, the book was powerful. It represented two mysterious entities, called Religion and Science, struggling for the mastery. It was a tract, not a history.

Shortly afterwards A. D. White, the president of Cornell university, delivered a lecture called *The Battlefields of Science*. It was published next day in the *New York Tribune*. It then grew into a little book, called *The Warfare of Science*, published in 1876 with a preface by Tyndall. Then it was further expanded, year by year, until the big work appeared in 1896, called *The Warfare of Science with Theology*. It was republished as lately as 1955.

White was better equipped than Draper for the purpose. Forming his original opinions from the study neither of science nor of history, but from the historical philosophies of Buckle and Lecky, he wanted the world to have more religion and not less. His declared purpose was to strengthen religion as well as science. It may be doubted whether the book achieved this end. He was not one-sided like Draper, in that he confessed how religion often fostered or encouraged science. But he also aimed to prove that religious interference with science always harms both religion and science, and and that all untrammelled scientific investigation in the end helps religion as well as science. Such a thesis, though not perhaps easy to demonstrate, is easy to illustrate from history. White illustrated it at length. And yet the philosophy of scientific light versus religious darkness hung about the book, more subtly than in Draper but still pervasively. Nothing illustrates more dramatically the Victorian sense of conflict, and the axioms in the public mind, than the influence of these endeavours to stretch the present conflict backwards into the past, as a permanent condition of human progress.

Huxley, Tyndall, Galton and Draper were the spearhead of scientific aggression against Christianity. But aggression was not, and never has been, typical of scientists; and there is no evidence that more scientists than of other classes of the educated ceased to practise religion because of inner disagreements between their reason and their religious axioms. Nevertheless, to understand the force of the conflict, and therefore the anti-religious pull of the natural sciences in that age, we need examples of individuals whose scientific studies led them away from religion. These are difficult to find. The scientists who stood against religion had seldom been known to practise it, and the scientists who were already religious usually continued to practise religion while they altered their philosophy of religion. Religion was of the heart and conscience, and was often unaffected by any change of attitude towards the external world. But where religion had been appropriated as bearing 'truths' about the external world, the demolition of these 'truths' hurt the religion of which they seemed to be an integral part. And in the sixties and seventies many Christian preachers and theologians continued to talk as though Christianity indeed provided truths about the physical world. On 22 August 1868 the *Pall Mall Gazette* criticised Hooker, who as president of the British Association made a sharp speech about the then opposition between religion and science, and declared that as the two subjects were on different planes, there could not be opposition between them. 'Religion is your opinion on one set of subjects, science your opinion upon another set of subjects.' Even Darwin called part of this article 'monstrous'.[1]

Therefore it should be possible to find minds whose scientific study led them away from religion. This is not easy to do, for the intelligence of no man is an island, and it is conjecture to distinguish intellectual development from the influence of heredity and environment. But three scientists (at least) show signs, in the course of their intellectual development, of being led away from religion, in part by that intellectual development: W. K. Clifford, G. J. Romanes and Charles Darwin himself.

When Francis Darwin came to write the life of his father, he had at hand the autobiography which Darwin wrote for his family, and this contained passages on his view of religion. Francis Darwin wanted to publish the autobiography intact, and believed it to be a scholarly duty to do so. His sister Henrietta thought that some of these passages were so strong that they would offend the public or lower her father's reputation; and the argument between brother and sister waxed warm until Francis found that his mother agreed with Henrietta, and therefore agreed to omit the objectionable passages

[1] Darwin to Hooker, 8 September 1868; *More Letters*, i, 308-9.

when he published the biography. Darwin's granddaughter Lady Barlow published the complete autobiography in 1958 and the suppressed passages add little to what was already known, though Darwin spoke rather more strongly against the doctrine of hell.

Charles Darwin was the son of Robert Darwin who was a physician and not a religious man. His mother died when he was a small boy. It therefore might have been predicted that this boy would grow up with a mind at least neutral towards religion. It was not so. His father believed that men ought not to worry their children about these matters, and concealed his lack of faith from his son. When Charles left Edinburgh his father, seeing him no scholar, proposed that he should take holy orders. Charles asked his father for time to consider, 'as from what little I had heard and thought on the subject I had scruples about declaring my belief in all the dogmas of the Church of England; though otherwise I liked the thought of being a country clergyman. Accordingly I read with care *Pearson on the Creed* and a few other books on divinity; and as I did not then in the least doubt the strict and literal truth of every word in the Bible, I soon persuaded myself that our creed must be fully accepted.' So he went up to Christ's College and read Paley with much delight, saying later that he was 'charmed and convinced by the long line of argumentation'.[1] At Christ's he met one of the remarkable men of that generation, John Stevens Henslow.

Henslow was the professor of botany in Cambridge. He was a fellow of Darwin's college, and soon also the rector of a large country parish, Hitcham in Suffolk. He was a delightful person and quickly saw something in Darwin which Darwin's father had not seen, that this young man had gifts which nobody had drawn out. They started to walk together every day. There is no doubt that Darwin owed to Henslow his love of science and his start in scientific enquiry. He wrote that looking back he did not think Henslow was himself a great scientist in the sense of being an original thinker, but still he was a capable scientist and a lovable and godly man.

'He was free from every tinge of vanity or other petty feeling; and I never saw a man who thought so little about himself or his own concerns. His temper was imperturbably good, with the most winning and courteous manners; yet, as I have seen, he could be roused by any bad action to the warmest indignation and prompt

[1] *Autobiog.* 57, 59.

action. . . . Henslow's benevolence was unbounded, as he proved
by his many excellent schemes for his poor parishioners. . . . My
intimacy with such a man ought to have been and I hope was an
inestimable benefit.'[1]

Darwin admired Henslow as a scientist, as man, as clergyman. The
letters between Darwin and Henslow have been published by Norah
Barlow (1967). He always looked back to Henslow with gratitude.
It is important in the history of our subject. Darwin later ceased to
be a religious man. But he retained all his life a respect for good
religion where it could be found, and part of this may be due to the
debt which he owed both in science and in humanity to his first
teacher, Henslow.

Through Henslow he became the naturalist on board H.M.S.
Beagle and spent five years sailing round the world. In that famous
journal of the voyage of the *Beagle* some see signs of a thinking mind
which was beginning to be dissatisfied with the axioms of the
religion in which he had been brought up, at least by school and
university if not by home. They are signs more of a thinking mind
than of discontent. Afterwards it was not the problems of the natives
of Tierra del Fuego and their development, nor the creatures on the
Galapagos Islands, which gave him qualms. It was rather what he
heard about Hindu gods and about other revelations. These were
what first troubled his mind.

Then he came back to England and married his cousin Emma
Wedgwood. Emma was another Christian person. His father
advised him not to tell his wife that he was having troubles about
religion, and said that he had known marriages disturbed by hus-
bands rashly telling their wives such things. But Darwin was one
of the most transparent characters in the world. It was impossible
for him not to tell his wife the true state of his mind, and at first she
was troubled.

It is therefore almost certain that intellectual difficulties had something to do with Darwin's slow withdrawal from religion.

We may attribute something in Darwin to the influence of
heredity; and something to his withdrawal from almost all life
that was not the life of his family; and something to intellectual
questioning derived from knowledge which did not arise out of
scientific studies, like an elementary knowledge of comparative

[1] *Autobiog.* 65–66.

religion. But Henslow and his wife were two anchors to Christian practice. To the one he owed his vocation and to the other his happiness. Despite these anchors he withdrew little by little from religion. Probably therefore one important reason was intellectual. The history of his mind after 1859 strengthens this probability.

During the three years after his return from the voyage of the *Beagle* (1836–9) he gradually came to believe that he could trust the Old Testament no more than the sacred books of the Hindus, and looked at the widespread existence of false religion. He did not lose his theism, but lost a belief in Christianity as the special revelation of God. He disliked giving up his belief, and tried to imagine evidence which would convince him again, as the discovery of new manuscripts at Pompeii or elsewhere which should confirm the truth of the gospels. 'But I found it more and more difficult, with free scope given to my imagination, to invent evidence which would suffice to convince me.' The disbelief came slowly over him, so slowly that in retrospect he could not remember finding it painful.[1]

The nature of the evidence which he imagined as possible if he were to be convinced—new manuscripts to confirm the truth of the gospels—shows that in the late thirties the prime source of his diquiet was less the scientific enquiry than the historical criticism of the Old and New Testaments.

In July 1842 we have a draft of the plan which was later to appear as *The Origin of Species*. Two things are clear from this draft. First, the idea of evolution by natural selection was already present as something which he could not prove but for which he would seek to collect evidence. Secondly, in this plan for proving evolution part of his motive was the old desire of the Bridgewater treatises to find design in the world. He wanted to reduce the number of accidents and inexplicable oddities. The growing body of evidence in biology appeared to be producing more and more apparent accidents. If you can only find a law to explain what was hitherto inexplicable, then these apparent accidents can be brought into the total pattern and purpose of the universe. In this first draft he wanted to remove what was 'derogatory' as he said 'to the creator'. In this there was a curious continuity with the science proving religion in the eighteenth century.

[1] *Life of Darwin*, i, 309.

As he came to work out his theory this aspect of his work fell away. But in *The Origin of Species* appeared places where the attitude came through. He placed on the title page a quotation from Bacon's *Advancement of Learning*, that we need to advance in the study both of God's word and of God's work, both in divinity and in philosophy. At the end, in one of the last paragraphs, he wrote a rather beautiful passage about the Creator impressing his laws on matter and breathing life into the original forms. When he wrote the *Origin* he still believed in God. He was not a Christian, as the men of 1859 understood the word Christian, but at least when he wrote the book he was a theist.

In the years after 1859, this belief in God began to waver more and more. From the moment when his book was published there were two different schools of thought. Some said that Darwin helped religion and others said that Darwin overthrew religion. Asa Gray, the head of the Herbarium at Harvard, made himself Darwin's champion at a time when Darwin had no other champion in the United States. And Asa Gray was a devout Christian man. All his life Asa Gray continued to maintain that by thus introducing law into the development of the species Darwin strengthened the argument of design. He wrote letters to Darwin trying to persuade him that he had indeed strengthened the argument from design. On the contrary, Huxley believed that this development of the evolutionary theory was the strongest possible weapon which could be wielded against religious faith. Darwin had shown a natural explanation and his theory was more than half-way to making the creation an unnecessary hypothesis.

Darwin's mind showed charming humble hesitations, almost stammerings. At first he was unsure whether he had strengthened purpose or whether he had thrust it aside. He tended to agree with people. The Duke of Argyll came to him and they talked of the orchids. Argyll said that it was impossible to look on nature's wonderful contrivances without seeing that they were the effect and expression of mind. Darwin looked at him hard, and said, 'Well, that often comes over me with overwhelming force; but at other times', and he shook his head vaguely, 'it seems to go away.' Karl Marx tried to dedicate to Darwin the English translation of one of his books, and Darwin's letter of refusal is interesting. He did not say, I would not like it if a person dedicated such a book to me. He said, members of my family might not like it. The older he grew the more the sense of purpose and therefore the theism faded away from his mind.

He was one of the rare persons in whom the scientific development of the mind can be shown with probability to have affected the religious outlook. Whatever else in the family history contributed to Darwin's mind on religion—for no man is 'a pure scientist'—the intellectual process of discovery was part of that which led him away from religion.[1]

Darwin's mind was in no sense philosophical or systematic. He seemed to feel that he had been forced to contemplate chance in the universe, as with the variation of the fantail pigeon, and therefore could no longer have the same sense of an eternal providence. He destroyed, for himself, as well as for some others, the old argument towards God from the designs evident in nature.

To this humble undogmatic student came feelings rather than philosophical inferences; a feeling that there was meaninglessness in the world; a feeling that the problem of pain was sore upon theism; a feeling that his argument weakened the appeal to design and the doctrine of special creations. This last feeling assailed, not religious faith, but the contemporary theology in which that faith was expressed. The Christians could jettison the doctrine of special creations without any sense of loss. But it was not easy to disentangle faith from its contemporary expressions in theology, nor to separate religion from the logic of apologists for religion.

What was true of Darwin's heart did not affect the minds of all his contemporaries. To the end of his life he believed that Asa Gray and Charles Kingsley were right in denying incompatibility between theism and the doctrine of evolution.[2] The conflict arose less because the theory of evolution was made probable, than because it was sometimes denied not upon scientific grounds but upon theological. The conflict was not ultimately over the theory of evolution, or over any other scientific theory, but over the freedom of the scientist to be a scientist.

Darwin helped the adjustment of English minds to new truth because he, who became the symbol of the conflict, had almost no

[1] For this whole question, see F. Darwin, *Life of Charles Darwin*, i, 304ff.; C.U.L. Darwin Papers, 139 (12).

[2] Cf. his letter to J. Fordyce, in CUL Darwin papers 139 (12); published by Fordyce in his *Aspects of Scepticism* (1883); part printed in F. Darwin, i, 304.

pugnacity. In his background was the Reverend Dr. Henslow, at his side was a Christian wife, and his personality lacked all wish to demolish religion. He was a direct, humble and reverent seeker after truth.

W. K. Clifford was an unusual mathematical genius. As an undergraduate and just after he was a devout and ascetic Anglo-Catholic, so devout that men commented. As a young Fellow of Trinity College in Cambridge he began to study Darwin and Herbert Spencer. His nature experienced a bouleversement, or conversion, and he became the leading spirit of a little group of Darwinian enthusiasts. Natural selection would provide a new system of ethics. From 1871 he was professor of applied mathematics at University College, London. Here he published a series of essays painful to religious men.

To Clifford's bouleversement science unquestionably contributed. It is possible to say no more than that, for the evidence is not plentiful. Probably other ideas besides science contributed. For if the change was purely an intellectual process, it is surprising to find such emotion after it. He hated Catholicism, and his departure from it, if not without temporary pain, felt to be liberation of spirit as well as mind.

Romanes was a devout evangelical undergraduate. Soon after his degree in 1870 he read Darwin's books, which made an extraordinary impression upon him. He wrote, and published (1874), a defence of Christian prayer against the criticisms of Tyndall and Galton. The essay showed no sign of hesitancy in belief. But, soon after, Charles Darwin was attracted by the scientific interests of the young Romanes and wrote him a friendly little letter. The letter began a friendship, on the side of Romanes a discipleship. By 1875, perhaps even by 1874, the very year in which his defence of prayer was published, he concluded that Darwinism disproved Christianity. He settled down to write a book destroying all the arguments for belief in God. The book was published in 1878, after a delay and without the author's name, under the title *A Candid Examination of Theism*. Darwin was not sure that he had made out his case. His case was that all judgments must be based on sound reasoning, that all sound reasoning was scientific, that since scientific reasoning gave no ground for theism, there were no grounds for theism and theism must be renounced.

Romanes did not welcome this conclusion. His mental struggle fascinates because his heart regretted and resented the conclusion to which his mind drove him. He made no attempt to conceal the agony of his loss. He became a sceptic out of duty to truth, but nothing made him like the duty. 'Forasmuch', he wrote, 'as I am far from being able to agree with those who affirm that the twilight doctrine of the "new faith" is a desirable substitute for the waning splendour of "the old", I am not ashamed to confess that with this virtual negation of God the universe to me has lost its soul of loveliness. . . . When at times I think, as think at times I must, of the appalling contrast between the hallowed glory of that creed which once was mine, and the lonely mystery of existence as now I find it —at such times I shall ever feel it impossible to avoid the sharpest pang of which my nature is susceptible.'[1]

Romanes is of special importance because Biblical and historical criticism, which to most men was more important than Darwin, seems to have played no part in his mental development. No doubt the history of his mind cannot be separated from the intellectual climate of that age, and no doubt the reason which led him owed as much to logic as to science. But his conflict illustrated in its naked form the conflict of science and religion. A deeply religious scientist, with no desire to shed religion, believed that his science forced him to shed it. There was indeed anti-religious power in science, amid the environment of those years.

In a battle between heart and head, the heart has resources likely in the long run to prove too strong for the head. Romanes was poetic and musical; admired the novels of Charlotte Yonge; enjoyed the company of intelligent clergymen as well as the company of intelligent agnostics; and was married to a wife who saw no reason to shed her faith. The rival tugs of religion and science would not allow Romanes to rest. In 1883 he began a slow stormy voyage back towards faith. He wanted faith, but would not have faith till he saw it to be reasonable. R. W. Church, Henry Scott Holland, P. N. Waggett, Aubrey Moore and Charles Gore had some superficial part in bringing his mind back towards the reasonableness of theism. He finally achieved a faith only during the last year or two before his premature death in 1894. But he left notes

---

[1] *A Candid Examination*, 114. For Romanes, *Life and Letters*; for Clifford, see the memoir by F. Pollock, preface to Clifford's *Lectures and Essays*.

for a book which was to refute his *Candid Examination of Theism.* By his instructions his widow gave the unfinished notes to Gore, who published them (1895) as *Thoughts on Religion.* To the last his intelligence continued to feel the scientific pull towards agnosticism. But his heart brought him to think that there were other roads to truth than that of scientific intelligence alone.

It was not simply a victory of heart over head. His scientific mind had become less dogmatic. And his philosophical mind was helped by the new liberal divinity which he now met. In *Thoughts on Religion* (p. 155) he declared his belief that the intellectual standing of faith was stronger now than quarter of a century before, when it looked as though it must be demolished, by Darwin from without, and by the Biblical critics from within.

2. EVOLUTION AND THE CHURCHES

In the year 1896 Frederick Temple became Archbishop of Canterbury. Twelve years earlier he delivered the Bampton lectures at Oxford, on *The Relations between Religion and Science.* These lectures assumed evolution as an axiom. It was not therefore surprising that his elevation to the most senior see should cause a protest. But the protest came from an unusual quarter. A clergyman named Brownjohn had resigned his parish because he accepted evolution and held it an impossible belief for a clergyman of the Church of England. Brownjohn appeared at Temple's confirmation in Bow church to lodge a protest against the faith of him who was nominated to be archbishop. The vicar-general overruled the protest.

This trivial little incident may be taken to mark the final acceptance of the doctrine of evolution among the divines, clergy and leading laity of the established church, at least as a doctrine permissible and respectable in an eminent clergyman. For no one who disbelieved evolution, and thought it incompatible with the faith of a Christian bishop, lodged a protest. For a decade or two after 1896 some members of the Church of England, especially among the evangelicals, and nearly all official members of the Roman Catholic Church, and most of the simple worshippers among the chapels of the poor, continued to know nothing of evolution or to

refuse to accept it on religious grounds, that is, on their faith in the
inspired truth of the Old Testament. To the end of his life (1900)
the evangelical Bishop Ryle of Liverpool believed in the physical
information of the Old Testament. But for two decades before 1896
the acceptance of the doctrine among educated Christians, while far
from universal, was both permissible and respectable. Some more
conservative divines sought to distinguish an acceptance of the
evolution of animal species, which they regarded as permissible for
a Christian, from an acceptance that man was part of the process
of evolution. In 1885 Bishop Ellicott of Gloucester and Bristol,
who was a good theologian, issued a charge to his diocese in
which he condemned the doctrine that man was part of the evolutionary series. Even then the charge was regarded in many
quarters as old-fashioned, and when in the year before Bishop
Frederick Temple of Exeter delivered his Bampton lectures and took
evolution for granted, no one commented. And yet in 1884–5 a
bishop who allowed evolution in his pulpit was still just worthy of
mention in the newspapers. In December 1885 Bishop Magee of
Peterborough accepted evolution in a sermon at St. Mark's in
Peterborough, and the occasion was considered news by the press.
Two years before Charles Gore, the first principal of Pusey House,
heir to the ideals of the lately dead Pusey, accepted evolution in a
sermon at Oxford and only one or two correspondents complained
in the newspapers. As late as 1888 J. W. Burgon was writing of
the *absurdity* of the Darwinian theory of the origins of man, but
his advocacy was not able to commend his argument. Therefore
the reception of the view, among more educated Christians, that
evolution and Christian doctrine were compatible, can be dated
to the twenty-five years from 1860 to 1885. We can mark its
stages.

During the sixties, and especially after the publication in 1871 of
Darwin's *Descent of Man*, which tried to explain the evolutionary
growth of man's higher qualities, a large number of religious men
probably regarded Darwinism as a menace both to Christian faith
and to the social order. It is easy to find comments of this nature
in the press, from the most famous of newspapers to the denominational magazines.[1] It is easy to find famous clergymen who at the
Church Congresses of the sixties took up in their speeches posi-

---

[1] Many instances in Alvar Ellegård, *Darwin and the General Reader*, 99ff.

tions that in a few years would be derided as obscurantist.[1] Arch-deacon Denison rose at the Church Congress of 1867 to denounce the claim of science to equality with the Bible as a road to truth, saying, 'Those who accept the Bible do not investigate truth, they receive it';[2] and though he got cries of *no! no!*, he was also greeted with loud cheers. In 1865 churchmen founded the Victoria Institute, 'to investigate fully and impartially the most important questions of philosophy and science, but more especially those that bear upon the great truths revealed in Holy Scripture, with the view of defending these truths against the opposition of science falsely so-called'. Though some of the founders were warm against Darwin, the institute gathered support and began to do good work.

To understand the conservatism of the sixties, which would later be called by many Christians and which was then called by Huxley obscurantism, it must never be forgotten that at the same time men were arguing over the historical evidence for the truth of the Bible. They were afraid of losing the Bible, and with it the evidence for the future life, the motive for right conduct, the ethical standards of civilised society. The Darwinians were on the side of those who attacked the truth of the Bible; and so at the extreme the *Family Herald* (20 May 1871)[3] asserted 'Society must fall to pieces if Darwinism be true'. Nor at that date did the scientific evidence for the truth of the Darwinian theory look so probable as it later came to look. The conservatives afterwards appeared more obscurantist than they were because the theory became more established as a scientific theory. They defended the Bible against a hypothesis which they could still with reason call 'speculative'.

Nevertheless, the speech of Archdeacon Freeman at the British Association of 1869 can hardly be defended. And the height of the conflict was marked by some strong antipathies. Hooker kept denouncing the ignorance of the clergy. In the choice of applicants for a lectureship in botany at St. Bartholomew's hospital (1866) a clergyman turned out to be the best candidate, but some of the governors of the hospital were averse to the choice of a clergyman and preferred him not to be recommended to them.[4] Such illiberal

---

[1] E. B. Birks and Dr. Baylee at Norwich in 1865, CCR, 1865, 190 ff.; Archdeacon Freeman in the Anthropology section at British Association, Exeter, 1869, G, 69, 961, an astounding paper.
[2] G, 67, 1115; CCR, 1867, 206.   [3] Ellegård, 101.
[4] *Life of Hooker*, ii, 57; *Memoirs and Letters of Sir James Paget*, 233.

opposition would have been unthinkable only ten years before. It
is a sign of the widening gap, or of the sensation that the gap was
widening.

At the other extreme stood the few who welcomed Darwin on
religious grounds; some, like Asa Gray or Charles Kingsley, because
Darwin reduced the number of inexplicable things in the universe
and therefore pointed towards a design; others, like R. W. Church
or Frederick Denison Maurice, because it was proper to welcome
this evident search for truth and they saw nothing incompatible with
God's goodness; and still others because they were pained by the
gymnastics of those who in the name of religion sought to reconcile
geology with Genesis, and saw evolution as a liberation from
intolerable divinity. In *Omphalos* (1857) Philip Gosse, who was
quite a good scientist and a devout Plymouth Brother, posed the
question whether at the creation of the world that which came to
exist came to exist bearing in itself the signs of growth, or birth.
Adam had not been born—did he have a navel? The trees in the
garden of Eden had not grown, did they when cut down show
rings which displayed growth? He suggested that the course of
nature is circular and that God in creating must have created at some
point by breaking into the circle and therefore there were indeed
trees with rings though they had not grown and man and woman
with the signs of birth though they had not been born. This kind of
speculation displeased some who thought about their doctrine of
God, and Darwin came among them like a preserver of Christian
doctrine from what was unintentionally blasphemous. If they disbelieved evolution, they were left with more difficult problems
about God-in-nature than if they believed it.

The liberal divines found it easy to welcome Darwin, and the
new science generally, because they did not need to defend the
literal inspiration of the Bible. Darwin's theory favoured those
historians who did not believe all the historical information of the
Bible, and this was the chief reason why conservatives shrank away.
But as the liberal divines did not themselves believe all the history
in the Bible, they had no need to fear on this score. On the personal
plane Kingsley and Arthur Stanley did good work in keeping in
touch with the leading scientists, and Stanley became the private
pastor of that hammer of orthodoxy Professor Tyndall.

Meanwhile the great school of moderate theologians held their judgement in suspense; welcoming scientific advance if it could be shown to be well-founded, too cautious to hail every new theory as a revelation, perceiving a present disharmony between their faith and the tendencies of physical knowledge, not yet discerning how to reconcile that disharmony, but confident in the God of truth and therefore content that the way of reconciliation would one day appear. Bishop Tait of London was eminent among them. Dr. Pusey and his disciple Liddon were both moderates in the field of physical science, unexpectedly, for they led the resistance to the new history of the Bible. A majority of the Anglican clergymen who thought about these matters awaited further light hesitantly, neither denouncing the Darwinians nor throwing themselves into the belief that evolution was a new revelation.

The *Guardian* newspaper recorded the advancing opinions of intelligent and moderate high churchmen. During 1867 it began to defend the clergy from an imputation, first made by F. W. Farrar,[1] that the clergy as a class were the enemies of science. They were entitled to be critical when scientists stepped outside their field and pronounced on ethics or metaphysics where they had no special qualifications. In 1868 the *Guardian* talked of Darwin's 'brilliant genius and patient research'. A few months later it commended the tenth edition of Lyell's *Principles* where he declared (at last) his adherence to Darwin. In 1871 it printed a letter from Archdeacon Freeman in which he called Darwinism the most easily refuted sophism of the day and then printed a reply from T. G. Bonney, the Cambridge geologist, that though Darwinism was only a hypothesis it was a more probable hypothesis than Freeman's. Its reviewer was critical of Darwin's *Descent of Man,* but believed that evolution would soon be as axiomatic as the law of gravity, and accepted the necessity that man was part of the evolutionary process. 'Nor is there any reason why a man may not be an evolutionist and yet a Christian. That is all that we desire to establish. . . . Evolution is not yet proved, and never may be. But . . . there is no occasion for being frightened out of our wits for fear it should be.'[2]

Henceforth there could be only one solution. Two other incidents marked the way towards the year 1885, when the question looked to be settled finally.

---

[1] *On Some Defects in Public School Education,* 1867; answered by John Hannah, *Contemporary Review,* 1867, vi, 1ff.   [2] G, 68, 952; 71, 681, 714, 937.

In 1874 T. G. Bonney published a book called *A Manual of Geology*. The book's importance consisted in the publisher, the S.P.C.K., an official publishing house of the Church of England. It was not without protest. An attempt to unseat two members of the publishing committee failed and S.P.C.K. continued to publish Bonney's book.

Darwin died in 1882 and expected to be buried at Down. Huxley considered briefly the possibility of burial in Westminster abbey and dismissed it, confident that the request would be refused. Canon F. W. Farrar said to him, 'we clergy are not all so bigoted as you suppose', and elicited an application.[1] So Darwin was buried in Westminster abbey with Christian rites, Huxley and Hooker and Wallace among the pallbearers, Dr. Bridge's anthem *Happy is the man that findeth wisdom*, and an excellent sermon on the following Sunday from that most humane of bishops Harvey Goodwin of Carlisle. A few protesters complained that the funeral was unfitting, a Roman Catholic writer talked of 'the giving of that which is holy to the dogs'. But the churches generally took a national pride in the decision, and were thankful that they could honour, and be grateful for, such a quest for truth even though it cast them into disarray. The general committee of the memorial fund[2] included not only Galton, Hooker, Romanes, Tyndall and Herbert Spencer, but the Archbishops of Canterbury and York and the Bishop of London. The Tractarian leader Liddon was invited to serve on the committee but refused. His reason was interesting: that his master, Dr. Pusey, would not like it.

Towards the end of the century Darwin's friend Asa Gray told the Bishop of Rochester that looking back on the progress of thought in England and America, 'he could not say that there had been any undue or improper delay on the part of the Christian mind and conscience in accepting, in such sense as he deemed they ought to be accepted, Mr. Darwin's doctrines'. But some leaders in the churches, including Cardinal Manning, still denounced those doctrines as false and unscientific.[3]

Six years later the school for the blind at Liverpool applied for a faculty for mosaic glass in its chapel; with the light of the world

---

[1] *Life of Farrar*, 109.   [2] Darwin Papers, 140/5.
[3] Talbot of Rochester in CCR, 1896, 152. For Manning, cf. his letter of 14 April 1889, in *Do we Believe?*, 1905, 153-4.

in the centre, and men or women deriving inspiration from him. Among the men appeared Charles Darwin. In granting the faculty, the chancellor commented that some might doubt whether Darwin should be there; but 'we have long ago satisfied ourselves that natural science, as represented by Darwin, is not contrariant to revealed religion; and it is a wholesome thing to be reminded that "every good and perfect gift cometh from above, from the father of lights". Darwin's remains were honoured with a funeral in Westminster abbey, and I am not prepared to say his name is out of place.'[1]

The phrases of evolutionary biology could be made to sound religious.

Henry Drummond was of the Free Church of Scotland and devoted his life to evangelistic preaching of a revivalist type. But it was revivalism of a rare language. He became professor of natural science at the Free Church College in Glasgow. Already as a student (1870–1) he welcomed natural selection as 'a real and beautiful acquisition to natural theology' and *The Origin of Species* as 'perhaps the most important contribution to the literature of apologetics' to have appeared in the nineteenth century. Teaching science to students on weekdays and religion to working men on Sundays, he found that the one overflowed into the other. Applying the idea of laws of nature on weekdays, he began to apply them on Sundays, and published in 1883 *Natural Law in the Spiritual World*. If Herbert Spencer could use the laws of nature to order social theory, why should they not be used to order the equally intangible realm of the spirit? The book was a series of parables between the natural world used to show forth the world of the spirit. As Drummond did not think of them as parables, but real applications of the same law to the realm of nature and to the realm of grace, he alienated all philosophical readers by confusion of language. (Hort to Ludlow, 22 February 1886: 'a quite singularly muddle-headed book')[2]. It is a sign of the Victorian state of mind, under the impact of the natural sciences, that the book was enormously successful. Its success was partly due to its purely religious side, to Drummond's ability to

[1] G, 03, 4.
[2] *Life of Hort*, ii, 340; Criticism of Drummond, especially by T. C. Finlayson, *Biological Religion*, 1885; and A. T. Lyttelton in CQR, Jan. 1885, 392–410; cf. John Kent, *From Darwin to Blatchford*, 20ff.

write movingly about the realm of grace. But its success was also
due, at least a little, to its use of scientific jargon like biogenesis, and
to its illustrations drawn from Darwin or Spencer, and its manifest
assurance that science aided the religious understanding of man's
predicament. His readers were 'not now concerned whether Drummond made out a case. . . . It was enough for them that they
encountered a teacher who expounded, defended and enforced
their deepest religious experiences upon what appeared to be the
dominant intellectual methods of their generation.'[1] When ten
years later Drummond published a similar book, *The Ascent of Man*,
it won nothing like the same applause, and partly for the reason that
the Victorians, having passed the worst battles of their conflict
between science and religion, no longer needed this kind of
devotional writing.

The theologians were busier with the consequences of Biblical
criticism than the consequences of the natural sciences. But the
acceptance of evolution affected their fundamental attitudes.

Unless they were Roman Catholics committed to a form of
Thomism they slowly dropped natural theology, that is, they ceased
to argue towards the existence or qualities of God from a contemplation of nature. The old arguments continued for a time, and
for a time were still respectable.[2] But whether Darwin strengthened
or demolished the argument from design, that argument became
impossible to use in the old form of Christian apologetic. If they
used the argument from design, they used it in some form hard to
recognise, as in Henry Drummond's notion of natural law. They
looked out upon the world and saw pattern, or providence, or a
beauty which was not merely the wildness caused by an infinite
succession of accidents. But they were no longer quite sure—or,
even if they were sure, their public was no longer sure—that they
perceived this pattern or beauty unless their soul or conscience was
already in a state capable of perceiving it. Though men who matriculated at Cambridge university still needed to pass an examination
on Paley's *Evidences*, Paley's argument from design became irrelevant to any late Victorian theology that mattered. The first shadow
of the knowledge of God seemed to lie in the heart or the conscience, not in nature; and only after God was apprehended through

[1] G. A. Smith, *Drummond*, 44–45, 214.
[2] Buckland's Bridgewater treatise was reprinted in 1869 with applause.

feeling or through moral judgment did nature become evidently sacramental of his being.

On this matter the great divide came after the Bampton lectures (1865) of J. B. Mozley entitled *On Miracles*. The book is the last statement, by a great English Protestant theologian, of a world of divinity which henceforth vanished except in the scholastic manuals. Mozley's fundamental axiom was the need to 'prove' Christianity, as Paley once proved it; and the internal evidence of heart and conscience can supply no 'proof' to the reason. Miracles are needed to 'prove' the truth of the revelation which they accompany. They are the form of external evidence that is left now that it is no longer safe to use the external evidence of nature.

It is a watershed in Christian thought. Though Mozley's book reached a fifth edition in 1880, no divine of the first rank could ever again argue the case as Mozley argued. For their new historical knowledge made them shrink from basing the revelation of God upon documents which without doubt contained historical truth but no one could yet say how much truth; and secondly, the acceptance of evolution made them shrink from singling out special acts of God as alone worthy of the epithet *supernatural*. In throwing away the idea of a sequence of special creations, they looked rather to see God in the process, God not only as the creator but as the sustainer, not only as transcendent above and detached from his world but as immanent within the world and within its development. Therefore they did not wish to base revelation upon miracle, but saw the miraculous as part of, a consequence of, the revelation. How do we know that the revelation is indeed a revelation of God? Not, as Mozley said, by its miracles, but by the character of Christ and his effect upon mankind, by its correspondence with the highest moral aspirations of the soul, by the direct apprehension of the divine in so many members of the human race. Nearly all the English theology of the later nineteenth century was 'immanentist'; talked as often of God within the world as of God above the world; dwelt more upon the incarnation of the word in Christ and less upon the atonement wrought by Christ; and (like Coleridge and Maurice) based its ultimate claim upon the religious experiences of men. History contributed as much as science to this change of thought. But we cannot doubt that the enormous impulse which Darwinism gave to ideas of process helped to turn the Christian divines towards these characteristic attitudes of liberal divinity.

For a century and a half the civilised world had not expected miracles to happen. Historical knowledge separated the miracles of the New Testament as a special case, warranted by an over-whelming event, from the subsequent miracles of saints or the miracles alleged in heathen religions. When Newman wrote of the scriptural miracles (1826) he wrote assuredly and was read with respect, when he defended ecclesiastical miracles (1842) he wrote tortuously and was read with opprobrium. But after historical criticism began to treat the Biblical documents like other documents, the evidence of scriptural miracles began to lose its unique quality. The doubtful expectation began to apply as sceptically to Biblical miracles as to ecclesiastical. And meanwhile scientists talked much of the 'uniformity of nature', and regarded every physical breach in a generally observed law as a doubtful event which required further physical explanation. 'The declining sense of the miraculous', as Lecky called it in 1863, was pushed further into decline by Darwin and the public acceptance of evolution. By removing special creation of species, Darwin removed the need for very numerous interferences with physical laws.

Huxley was far too able to claim that science could disprove any miracle. He confessed the contrary. The evidence for miracle was historical, and rested upon witnesses to whom science, which worked by induction, had nothing to say. Yet 'the laws of nature' of which the scientists so often talked, looked like unalterable parts of the design of the universe. Some philosophers tended to con-vert 'hitherto unvarying' into 'invariable'. The liberal theologian Baden Powell gave up miracles, so far as they could be said to be violations of 'the laws of nature', during the fifties. Though 'science' could not disprove a single miracle, men who talked of the miracu-lous began during the sixties to look anti-scientific. Extraordinary and unaccountable things were confessed to happen. The incurably ill were cured. But the scientist preferred to call such events inexplic-able rather than to call them supernatural. Liberal theologians slowly accepted the old doctrine of Hume, republished by Mill, that no evidence could prove a miracle to a man who did not already believe in God. Retaining all the belief that God acted in the world, they slowly became agnostic on whether some acts were breaches in 'the laws of nature', and refused to follow James Mozley in basing faith upon the evidence for miracle. All that the evidence could do was to prove the event to be wonderful, and it was faith which saw through wonder to the hand of the divine.

One other consequence of evolution was the rise of scientific anthropology. As soon as it was accepted that man had a pre-history before Genesis, the study of primitive man began. Since the pre-historians could hardly study civilised man in his primitive condition, they needed to study the primitive tribes in various parts of the earth, on the axiom that the development of these cruder societies might be found in part parallel to what could be postulated of an earlier development of civilised society. The acceptance of evolution coincided with, and was helped by, the sudden development of sea-transport and empire which enabled travellers to reach more remote peoples and to bring back a mass of new evidence. Their conclusions sometimes outran the evidence, for they partly depended on narratives by amateurs, and scientific work in the field did not begin until almost the end of the century. And in that flood-tide of evolutionary theory they rested upon two axioms that were not, and could not be, verified; that all societies develop through parallel stages, and that the developments are in general for the better, so that if a society is more primitive it is earlier. Upon these axioms they produced many fertile ideas and some misleading speculations.

In the middle-sixties the anthropologists confronted religious men with a new kind of conflict—the fall of man versus the rise of man. Members of the churches who abandoned the story of Adam and Eve as legendary were already engaged in freeing the doctrine of original sin from its reference to an alleged event of history and in seeing it more as bias towards evil by heredity and social environment. The anthropologists did no more to Christian thinking than to stimulate or hasten this work of turning history into parable. After 1875 Victorian churchmen showed little sign of being perturbed by researches into primitive cultures, and were more likely to welcome than to repudiate E. B. Tylor's speculative search for the origins of religion in primitive animism. Tylor was a humane scholar. But the *Anthropological Journal* of the middle sixties contained strange matter. If all societies developed in parallel, did all pass through a stage of cannibalism? A succession of orthodox

V C.–2 *a*

writers, from Archbishop Whately downwards, seized upon the inconsistencies and unverifiable nature of the axiom that societies always developed upward and drew attention to societies which developed downward. They contended that civilisation was primitive and that barbarism was the consequence of fall. Their strongest argument observed that no society was known to raise itself in the scale of civilisation except by coming into touch with a higher society; and therefore the higher society must be original. They adduced the retrospective yearnings after an earlier golden age to be found among many savage societies, and the opinion of African travellers that some backward peoples were then growing more backward. The theory was attacked by many students from Lubbock downwards, but gave way less to new evidence or new arguments than to the general acceptance of evolution among educated men. By 1875 it became a piece of litter from the past of science.[1]

The early science of psychology had little effect, if any, upon religion in England. Troubled souls do not seem to have consulted their pastors after learning that the functions of the brain *might* be brought under laws of empirical observation. They were disturbed neither by the mental philosophy of Bain nor by Herbert Spencer's *Principles of Psychology* (1855, much extended 1870-2). Boyd Carpenter's Hulsean lectures of 1878 proclaimed that psychological enquiries were useful to religion. New work in this field first touched the theologians when William James studied the psychology of conversion in his Gifford lectures of 1901-2, *The Varieties of Religious Experience*.

Science contributed to the unsettlement of the educated English mind by its general issues; by pushing men towards more scepticism over evidence for the miraculous; by giving the ordinary man the uncomfortable feeling that somehow, he knew not how, science favoured a materialistic philosophy of life, though no scientist known to fame was a materialist; by giving the historians their chance to treat the documents of the Bible as historical texts; and by first proving that parts of the Bible were myth. In the private papers of Henry Drummond on the Christian side, or Huxley on the agnostic side, perturbed correspondents lamented their loss of

---

[1] Whately, *On the Origin of Civilisation*, 1854; reprinted 1861 in *Misc. Lectures*, 26–59; J. Lubbock, 'On the Origin of Civilizations' in *Proc. Brit. Association*, 1867, ii, 118–25; Argyll, *Primeval Man*, 1869; *Contemporary Review*, 1869, xi, 164; *Journal of the Victoria Institute*, i, 1867, 189–96, etc.

faith and attributed its loss to *science*. We need, however, to be sure that when they refer to *science* they mean natural sciences. Some of those who attributed loss of faith to *science* meant that *history* deprived them of their confidence in the inspiration of the Bible.

In the pews, no doubt, continued to sit large numbers of worshippers who never heard of Tylor, were indifferent to Darwin, mildly regretted what they heard of Huxley and, if they thought about it at all, knew that their faith rested upon moral considerations inaccessible to the physical sciences.

In 1900 men talked as though the conflict was over. The difficulties in the minds of the young were not scientific. A nonconformist of 1900 testified that his questioning young no longer assumed a conflict between science and religion, and that if they asked him about intellectual difficulties they often asked him about the textual criticism or the authority of the Bible.[1] Some sighed that the conflict no longer raged, for peace was established because religion had abandoned, or was abandoning, an ancient claim to give truths about the physical world. Those who sighed, preferred a territory where two sides competed for a no-man's-land, to a territory where each side was left in possession of its own domain without influence upon the other. Some philosophical divines were left with a sense of dissatisfaction, at this division of the world into compartments, which they bequeathed to the twentieth century.

2. COMPARATIVE RELIGION

The study of religion was not quite new but it made such advances in the nineteenth century that its impact upon western thought was new. Charles Darwin and Beatrice Webb both found the first shaking of their Christian axioms because their eyes were open to Indian religion. By 1847 it was worth the labour of Frederick Denison Maurice to publish a short series of sermons called *The Religions of the World*; not describing those religions in a way that their adherents would accept, but seeking for truths underlying the various forms in which men expressed their worship. On the one side ease of communication and the political development of Indian empire allowed a rapid increase in public knowledge and therefore public sympathy. On the other side Christian thinkers, finding that

[1] Charles Booth, vii, 118-19.

they could no longer stand on mere argument, as from miracle or from prophecy, sought a new basis by examining the nature of religious experience. They could not examine religious experience if they contemplated Christian experience alone. Like Jowett and all who were under the influence of either Plato or Hegel, Maurice wanted to say that the religious aspiration in man is natural to man, and therefore universal even if unrecognised. The evidence of other religions became suddenly more important to Christian divines.

The two different sources of interest are represented in the two very different men who created the modern English study of comparative religion: Brian Hodgson and Friedrich Max Müller.

Hodgson was the British resident in Nepal from 1833 to 1843. There he collected many Buddhist manuscripts. From his endeavours four hundred Sanskrit manuscripts passed into the libraries of Calcutta, Paris and the British Museum. Students who used his work regarded him as the founder of the scholarly study of Buddhism.[1] He otherwise received hardly any public recognition.

Max Müller on the contrary received a recognition so extensive as to surprise posterity. A German from Dessau, he was brought to England under the patronage of the Chevalier Bunsen, and settled in Oxford during 1848 to translate the *Rigveda,* of the first importance among the hymns of the Brahmins. The *Rigveda* was published in six volumes between 1849 and 1874, and meanwhile he also published (1859) a *History of Ancient Sanskrit Literature.*

In the election of 1860 for the Sanskrit chair at Oxford, the electors chose Monier Williams as against Max Müller partly because some suspected the religious views of Max Müller, but even more because he was a foreigner and they thought that Oxford chairs should go to Englishmen trained at Oxford. But Pusey, who had no natural sympathy with Max Müller in religion, worked hard to secure his election. Pusey's reasons illustrate the slow growth of scholarly ideals in the Victorian age. He had a missionary ideal before his eyes. We need to know the religious mind of those whom we wish to convert. No one can tell us that better than Max Müller. Pusey regarded the translations of the Vedas as 'the greatest gifts which have been bestowed on those who would win to Christianity the subtle and thoughtful minds of the cultivated Indians'.

[1] Cf. W. W. Hunter, *Life of B. H. Hodgson,* 1896.

'Your work', he told Max Müller,[1] 'will form a new era in the efforts for the conversion of India.'

Between 1879 and his death Max Müller edited and published *The Sacred Books of the East*, completed afterwards in fifty volumes. Dean Liddell of Christ Church helped to persuade the Oxford university press to bear part of the expense; and though a few society folk gossiped that Max Müller meant to discredit the Christian religion, this was not the view of the many eminent Anglicans, including Pusey, who gave their patronage to the plan. He was accused in 1886[2] of omitting objectionable parts of *The Sacred Books* in order to represent eastern religions in a more favourable light. But the light was inside Max Müller. He did not intentionally misrepresent, but saw all humanity in the light of German romanticism and philosophical idealism. And his translations made *The Sacred Books* far better known among Hindus than ever before. He helped India to rediscover its own religious foundations.

The public interest in the mid-Victorian age was a curious mixture of genuine interest for its own sake, and religious interest, either for the sake of missions or for the sake of religious apologetics. Max Müller came at the end of his life to seem to the public like the archetypal dryasdust, the Germanised don practising unread scholarship for the sake of scholarship. If the public had been right, Max Müller would not have become so famous. He wanted to make men discern the values in other religions, especially for the sake of their own religion. His youth in the heyday of German idealistic philosophy led him to see the high religions of the world in terms of varied manifestations of a single principle. He believed that in their original form most religions were free from the 'corruptions' which later entered them; that nearly every religion contained sufficient truths to enable those who sought God to find him in their hour of need; and that no one could know what Christianity was who did not know other religions.[3] Max Müller's later work was not of permanent value. But certainly he did more than anyone of his age to widen the views of educated men on the nature of religion, even if his notions on that nature were imprecise and were not always

---

[1] Pusey to Max Müller, 2 June 1860; *Life of Max Müller*, i, 237–8.
[2] By Bishop Copleston of Colombo, *Life of Max Müller*, ii, 194–5; again in 1895 by T. M. Lindsay.
[3] Cf. his speech at the Philosophical Hall, Leeds, 7 March 1865; *Life of Max Müller*, i, 300.

to be confirmed in subsequent study. He was essentially a linguist, and advance in the study of religion could hardly proceed far without the help of the anthropologists, who were themselves not yet equipped to give much help.

The rival Monier Williams was as good, though not as far-ranging, a scholar as Max Müller. If Pusey believed that Max Müller's election would help Indian missionaries, Monier Williams equally believed in a direct connexion between his professorship and missionary work. His inaugural lecture was entitled *The Study of Sanskrit in relation to missionary work in India*. Apart from translating later Sanskrit documents, he published several works intended to open to the English the knowledge of Indian religion, both Hindu and Buddhist.[1] He would always wax angry if he heard Hindus described as *heathen*, and humorously would say that he was 'half a Hindu'. He created the Indian Institute at Oxford.

The attitude did not sink deep into English life. Yet it fitted other mental habits of that age. The vicar of Rochdale (J. M. Wilson) quoted in the pulpit (1894) a saying from the Vedas, 'Those who honestly worship other gods, involuntarily worship me'; and a working weaver, as he went out of church, thanked the vicar for the quotation and said that he had been reading one of Max Müller's books.[2] By the nineties the comparative study of religion, however unscientific in its attitudes, became a little force in public education. And some people felt that their *Christian* life was deepened by reading Max Müller's translation of non-Christian literature; not usually by the grateful sense that Christianity was a purer thing than what they read (though we find that reaction also), but by feeling that they understood more sensitively the grandeur of God and of his revelation of himself in different times and places. Westcott looked for a new understanding of St. John's gospel and of Christian mysticism to proceed out of Indian thought.[3]

A Russian traveller named Notovitch published a *Life of Christ* which, as he claimed, was dictated to him by the priests of a Buddhist monastery in Kashmir while they nursed his broken leg. Because of ethical resemblance between Buddhism and Christianity,

[1] Especially *Hinduism*, 1877; *Modern India and the Indians*, 1878; *Religious Thought and Life in India*, 1883; *Buddhism*, 1889.

[2] J. M. Wilson to Max Müller, 16 January 1894; *Life of Max Müller*, ii, 311.

[3] For Christian views of this matter, see especially John Wordsworth, *The One Religion*, 1881; Boyd Carpenter, *The Permanent Elements in Religion*, 1889.

the idea grew up among the unscholarly that Christ might have been influenced by Buddhist doctrines. Notovitch brought evidence that during the hidden years of his life Jesus studied Sanskrit and Pali and the Vedas in India, and that the history was written down upon scrolls now preserved at Lhasa, by Jewish merchants who came to India soon after the crucifixion. Enquiries at the monastery enabled Max Müller to produce evidence that the monks possessed no Life of Christ and that they had nursed no one with a broken leg for at least half a century.[1] Arguments like these, though nothing to do with the progress of scholarship, illustrated in a dramatic way the new sense of the reality of non-Christian religion.

[1] Max Müller, *Works*, xviii, 182.

CHAPTER II

HISTORY AND THE BIBLE

I. TEXT AND TRANSLATION

THE study of the text of the Greek Testament had not stood still during the seventeenth and eighteenth centuries. It is enough to mention the names of Walton and Mill, of Wettstein and Bengel and Griesbach. Griesbach, who died in 1812, collected many more manuscripts on his journeys. But the end of all this study was largely to support the received text as a text admittedly variant from the unknown original in certain details, but as good a text as could be found. Lachmann's edition of the New Testament 1831, with a much extended edition in two volumes in 1842 and 1850, summarised all this work. Nothing more could be done without further investigation of the ancient manuscripts.

In the Vatican library there was known to be an excellent manuscript. But in the forties and fifties the authorities at the library did almost as much as they could to prevent anyone getting at this manuscript. At the beginning of the forties Tischendorf devoted himself to the manuscript tradition. He went to Paris and succeeded in deciphering the Codex Ephraemi (edition of New Testament, 1843). In May 1844 he visited the monastery of St. Catherine on Mount Sinai and saw enough fragments to realise the possibility of a treasure there. With the Tsar's help he found the Codex Sinaiticus in 1859 and was permitted to carry it to St. Petersburg. It remained there until the British government of 1933 bought it from the Russian government for £100,000. In 1862 Tischendorf published a good folio edition. Four years later he at last persuaded the Vatican authorities to allow him a fortnight, three hours a day, at the Codex Vaticanus. Under these conditions he published a not fully satisfactory edition in 1867.

Meanwhile the Englishman S. P. Tregelles was performing work which in a different way was as valuable as that of Tischendorf.

For a time a member of the Plymouth Brethren, and later in life a presbyterian, he lived on a small income and devoted himself from 1838 to the study of the text. With the aid of various journeys to collate manuscripts, he began publishing a critical text of the New Testament from 1857. It appeared in sections until in 1870 he suffered a stroke while revising the last chapters of the book of Revelation. He left important material for prolegomena which were published after his death by Fenton Hort and A. W. Streane (1879). European scholarship came to think the works of Tregelles almost as important as the discoveries of Tischendorf.

By the early fifties the extent of the problem was plain to the students of New Testament Greek. About 1850 Scrivener, an Anglican incumbent, devoted himself to the question, and in 1861 published his *Introduction to the criticism of the New Testament*, which reached a fourth edition in 1894 and continued thereafter to be much used by students. In 1853 two young Cambridge men, Hort and Westcott, agreed to work together to produce a revised text of the Greek New Testament. It took them a long time, for reasons which will appear. The text of Westcott and Hort was at last published in 1881, though it was circulated privately for ten years before.

To distinguish the earlier manuscripts was far from easy, for the nineteenth century resembled the early Middle Ages in the production of forged documents. Letters were the usual products, including twenty-seven by Shakespeare. But archaeological evidence was profitable and relatively easy to manufacture, and the information about Christian origins could be drastically altered by a single discovery. During 1868 the black basalt stele known as the Moabite stone was discovered in the desert to the east of the Dead Sea and supported the historical information in the Book of Kings. In 1883 Moses Shapira, a shopkeeper in Jerusalem of Slavonic extraction, offered to London a new manuscript of the book of Deuteronomy, written on parchment in the characters of the Moabite stone, said to be discovered in a dry cave to the east of the Dead Sea. At first the English Hebraists were inclined to trust this manuscript, though some of the evidence which pointed to a later date for Deuteronomy had vanished and Moses did not record his own death. But a Palestine surveyor told them that no manuscript could survive in those caves, and after careful examination Ginsburg, the expert of the British Museum on the Moabite Stone, pronounced it to be a forgery. Shapira shot himself in a hotel at Rotterdam. Though it is certain that the manuscript which Shapira proffered was not the original text of Deuteronomy, it needed the finding of the Dead Sea Scrolls more than half a century later to raise qualms whether Shapira might indeed have brought a genuine manuscript.[1]

Tischendorf did not escape this difficulty. The so romantic discovery of Sinaiticus raised doubts. Constantine Simonides, already celebrated as a Greek scholar of doubtful methods, said that the manuscript was modern and claimed to have written it himself in a monastery on Mount Athos. His expertise in calligraphy was sufficient to make the claim possible. He produced a witness who had seen him writing it. The English scholars avowed their belief in the antiquity and genuineness of Sinaiticus. Simonides published other fragments, including verses of gospels and epistles with quite unusual readings, and colophons tending to prove the apostolic origin of the text. There was a fragment of early Christian chronology from a stone at Thyateira, fragments of St. Matthew's gospel written in A.D. 48.

To distinguish the genuine Moabite stone from spurious archaeological pieces, or the genuine Greek text of the second-century *Shepherd* of Hermas, which Simonides first saw on Mount Athos, complicated the difficult tasks of Biblical scholarship, and contributed to the air of uncertainty, and even of unpopularity, which hung about the enterprise.[2]

Whatever view was taken of the new evidence, it was clear that Codex Vaticanus and Codex Sinaiticus were of high importance. Westcott and Hort believed that an agreement between Vaticanus and Sinaiticus must conquer other evidence, and based their text upon this view. But if the new text were taken out of the austere pages of the Greek editions, and given an English clothing, and placed on lecterns, and read in homes at family prayers, what would

[1] *Times*, 10–27 August 1883; *Punch*, 8 September 1883; Sir Walter Besant, *Autobiog*, 162–4; J. M. Allegro, *The Shapira Affair*, 1965.
[2] For Simonides, C. Stewart, *Memoir of Simonides* (1859); Prothero, *Henry Bradshaw*, 92–99; J. A. Farrer, *Literary Forgeries.* Of course, some forgeries delayed no scholar a moment; in 1900 an American published (*The Archko Volume*) Jewish documents containing a conversation between Gamaliel and Joseph, alleged to have been found in the mosque of St. Sophia, with two reports by Caiaphas; and a report by Pilate's wife from the Vatican. A respectable English publishing house consented to be the agent in London, and M. R. James took the trouble to expose it, G, 1900, 403.

be the consequences for English religion as well as for English literature?

The reading of the Bible in private and public lent a sacredness to the King James version. In a passage which became so famous as to be quoted or misquoted in Parliament and out of it after its author was lost to view, Frederick Faber called the beauty of that version one of the strongholds of Protestantism in England.[1] 'It lives on in the ear like a music that never can be forgotten; like the sound of church bells, which the convert hardly knows how he can forgo. . . . It is part of the national mind, and the anchor of the national seriousness. . . . It is his sacred thing, which doubt never dimmed and controversy never soiled.' Edward King talked of the Bible casting its pool of light upon the next place where the foot must step. Ruskin believed that he gained his taste in literature because his mother made him learn passages from the Bible.

> Throw thou no shadow on the sacred page,
> Whose faults, if faults, are sanctified by age.

Scholars were more and more aware of faults, whether in text or in the English of the translators. After 1840 the probable text of the Greek, as supposed by the more careful students, began rapidly to diverge from the actual text which the men of King James translated. And the question, what if anything should be done about it, was a problem for religion as well as for scholarship. Nothing but rewriting would satisfy the scholars. But most Englishmen, it has been said, would have preferred a committee to rewrite Shakespeare.[2]

Until 1856 this question was argued only among the experts. All the experts were for caution. Some wanted correction of as few inaccuracies as possible, others wanted correction wholly according to the new evidence. But in 1856 the debate suddenly appeared in the open. Any great advance of scholarship catches at last the public imagination, which sees it in simple terms. And this advance proceeded far enough by 1856 for it to become propaganda for orators or pamphleteers who wanted to beat the churches. You base yourselves on the Bible!—and yet everyone now knows that

[1] Faber, Prefatory essay, 116, to the *Life of St. Francis of Assisi*, in the Oratorian series of lives of saints, vol. xxv, 1853; Ruskin, *Praeterita*, i, 1899, 44ff.
[2] Hemphill, 26.

the text on which you base yourselves is not what was written. A
sense of insecurity about the Biblical text began to enter some in-
expert minds. Moreover the quest for new evidence was romantic.
Tischendorf with his basket of old papers in a monastery cell was a
dramatic character, and the argument on whether the Sinai manuscript was fabricated did not lessen the drama. By 1856-8 the debate
on whether the Bible should be translated anew ceased to be hidden
among the scholars and became popular.

The churches did not want a new translation. They were afraid
of losing sacred words as well as beautiful poetry. The King James
version was a bond uniting all the churches except the Roman
Catholic, as beloved by the dissenters as by the Anglicans, uniting
the English overseas, and the Americans with the English at home.
No plan for an official new translation could have succeeded which
did not propose to make as few changes as possible. The language
was confessed not to be the language of everyday speech. But as the
architecture of a church is better, so it was argued, if it transcends the
architecture of a cottage, so the aspirations of Christian worship
required a language which lifted men out of everyday speech into
poetry, while the simplicity of Elizabethan English rendered it
intelligible.

The problem of the scholars was to persuade the Convocations
of the Church of England that something should be done. The Convocation of York was not so persuaded and refused to join a plan
for a revised translation. They allowed that errors should be recti-
fied, but were unwilling to forward a plan to rectify. The Convocation of Canterbury was persuaded by a committee, headed by
Samuel Wilberforce, on 3 May 1870. They contemplated no new
translation of the Bible, or any alteration of the language, 'except
where in the judgment of competent scholars such change is necessary'. They recommended that the style of the King James version
should be followed in any changes. The resolution to translate was
not adopted without a protest from Bishop Christopher Wordsworth of Lincoln. 'Beware lest by altering the text of the authorised
version of the Bible, you shake the faith of many', and especially of
the poor.[1]

On 14 June 1870 Buxton moved in the House of Commons that
the queen should be invited to pray the president of the United

[1] *Chron. Convoc.*, 1870, 222.

States to join with her in appointing a commission to revise the King James version. His motive appeared to be less to secure a good translation than to prevent Convocation from increasing its influence, for many members of Parliament still regretted that Convocation had been allowed during the fifties to revive. (Dean Stanley agreed with this view, that the work would be better done by royal commission than by a committee appointed by Convocation;[1] for this was the procedure adopted by King James.) Buxton thought that if they left the work to Convocation they seemed to recognise the assembly as the governing body of the established church. Gladstone replied that the government would be unwise to spend public money on an undertaking which could be better done in private hands; that he saw no objection to Convocation acquiring authority if it did useful work; and that the president of the United States would be surprised to receive such a request in a sealed envelope, and might feel that his co-operation was excluded by the American constitution.

Convocation went ahead to select its translators. The selection and its consequences almost halted the project.

The Scriptures, argued some, were the possession of the Catholic Church. It was felt so strongly that this revision was by Christians for Christians, that some wanted to see the resolution framed to exclude Jewish scholars from co-operating with the committee for revising the Old Testament.

The authorised version of 1611 was made by Anglicans alone. It could not be said that in 1870 the Church of England lacked good scholars, either in Greek or Hebrew. It had (men claimed) the best scholars in Europe for this purpose. You cannot translate without your doctrinal axioms affecting nuances in your rendering. The church is the guardian of Scripture. This revision should again be an Anglican revision. So argued conservative students of the Bible like Christopher Wordsworth, Bishop of Lincoln.

To the contrary, it was contended that scholarship did not depend upon religious profession. The sole duty of the revisers was to get the best text possible and then say what it meant. We need not orthodox men but experts in the history of words. Therefore Jews should freely be invited to help with the Hebrew of the Old

[1] *Chron. Convoc.* 5 May 1870, 342; Hansard, ccii, 100.

Testament, and non-Anglican scholars to help with the Greek of the New Testament.

But even if it were allowed that Greek experts among non-Anglicans were very few, there was a practical or diplomatic reason for inviting some. The King James version was sacred not only in the Church of England. It was the Bible of English free churchmen and of the United States. If this future revised version were to become as acceptable as the authorised version, representatives from these other bodies should be invited to share in the work.

After debate and voting, Convocation decided (5 May 1870) to accept this last argument and to invite non-Anglican scholars.

The revisers were selected by a committee. They were not so widely representative as had been hoped. Newman was invited to represent the Roman Catholics but declined. Jowett, the professor of Greek at Oxford, was not invited. A Unitarian, Dr. Vance Smith, was invited (by a majority of one mistaken vote on the selecting committee, for old Bishop Ollivant of Llandaff was deaf and meant to vote on the other side) and on Stanley's invitation joined the other revisers in receiving holy communion at Westminster abbey on 22 June 1870. The presence of the Unitarian at holy communion displeased many people, and prevented the revisers from having among their members Dr. Pusey; and Bishop Samuel Wilberforce their original chairman, who did not resign but did not attend meetings; and Bishop Thirlwall of St. David's who resigned in order to stop the bishops from retracting the invitation to the Unitarian. If they had retracted the invitation they would also have lost the services at least of the Cambridge scholars Westcott and Hort and Lightfoot.

But the translators who accepted were rich in the best English scholarship: an eminent nonconformist scholar like Moulton (it was a new recognition of the distinction of scholarship among nonconformists); Scott of the famous Greek lexicon; Kennedy, the professor of Greek at Cambridge.

The chairman of the New Testament committee was quiet Bishop Ellicott of Gloucester and Bristol. Of the 407 meetings of the committee Ellicott attended 405. Scrivener and Hort were almost always there. The weight of textual knowledge lay with Scrivener, Hort and Westcott, Scrivener being often in disagreement with the other two. The weight of linguistic knowledge lay with Scott,

Westcott, Lightfoot, Moulton, Milligan and Ellicott. But the company was a friendly harmonious group, untroubled by its varied denominations.[1]

Its expenses—travelling, maintenance, printing sheets—were considerable. Several members spent large sums from their pockets. They appealed to the public, and the public gave little. In March 1873 they sold the copyright to the university presses of Oxford and Cambridge, who eventually paid £20,000 in the way of expenses. The queen's printer, who shared in the privilege of publishing the authorised version, thought the scheme too doubtful commercially.

A difficulty at once presented itself. The scheme was only acceptable because it was conservative. Though the revisers were ordered to make as few alterations as possible, they had co-opted men who had not designed the scheme and disliked it. Westcott, Hort and Lightfoot were nothing like so conservative as the scheme, and only accepted it because they could get no better[2]. Ellicott was identified by the public with a conservative plan, which he recommended in print. Westcott knew that inside Ellicott there was a wish for something more.[3]

Round the table sat several scholars of European standing. They had been told to change only what must be changed in the opinion of eminent scholars. These men were confronted with a task which to them seemed to demand much more change than any of the designers had expected. They were determined men because their ideals of scholarship were at stake. They must reconstruct the text, and render it literally. Westcott, Hort, Lightfoot, Moulton, Milligan had no use for a revision that was not thorough. At one of the first meetings Lightfoot made a powerful speech against tinkering.[4]

The conservatives among the revisers were relatively weak. Stanley, whom everyone knew to be a notorious radical in ecclesiastical politics, surprised by extreme conservatism about the authorised version.[5] Dean Merivale attended only nineteen meetings until he felt the changes to be rash[6] and retired from the battle. He disliked the method. It may have been Merivale who said, 'I was invited to

[1] *Memoir of W. F. Moulton*, 103–4.
[2] *Life of Hort*, ii, 135–6; Westcott to Hort 29 May 1870, *Life of Westcott*, i, 390.
[3] Westcott to Hort, 7 July 1870, *Life of Westcott*, i, 393; Hemphill, 46.
[4] Ellicott, *Addresses*, 99; Hemphill, 67.
[5] *Life of Hort*, ii, 137.
[6] *Autobiog.*, 389–90, 395.

translate and was expected to construe'.[1] Archbishop Trench
suffered injury when crossing the sea and ceased to come.

Thus the company departed far from the scheme which Convocation intended when it created them. The task took hold of
them, it became a duty, the original terms of reference became
largely irrelevant. Ellicott had prophesied an average of one change
for each verse, a prophecy which alarmed some of his colleagues.
The revisers ended with 36,000 changes, or four and a half to each
verse. One of the more conservative revisers, David Brown, said
that an itch of change took possession of the company.[2]

Two members of the committee had the singular advantage that
they had been working on a text of the New Testament for sixteen
years before 1870. In 1870 (gospels) and 1871 (epistles) Westcott
and Hort privately printed a text for the use of the revisers. It was
not published till the very day of 1881 when the revised version was
published. But the other revisers were not overwhelmed by it.
They finally accepted 64 places where they preferred Westcott and
Hort to other texts.

This inseparable pair were very different men. Westcott, regius
professor of divinity at Cambridge from 1870, was a Christian-
Platonist mystic who meditated upon the words of the Greek
Testament, until they seemed shafts of light from heaven. His
attitude to a New Testament word was academic, in the sense that
every possible equipment must be used in determining its meaning.
What interested him, however, was the doctrinal use of the separate
Biblical words, and he loved each word as an individual.

Afterwards it came somehow to be understood that Westcott
was very influential in the choice of readings. Ellicott much later
told a friend why this was not true. Westcott would take up time
in the meetings weighing the pros and cons of a reading or a translation; and then when they came to the voting, he retreated into a
corner of the room and refused to vote. But it is surprising, and one
wonders if Ellicott may not have been exaggerating a little in self-
defence. When Westcott was a canon of Peterborough he was
found pertinacious on committees, knowing his mind and strong to
persuade the committee to do what he wanted.[3] It is also certain

---

[1] *J. B. Lightfoot*, reprint from QR, 43–44.
[2] Blaikie, *Brown*, 222; Hemphill, 71, 75.
[3] Cf. A. S. Farrar to W. Sanday, 18 October 1901, Sanday MSS, iii, 264; G. W. E.
Russell, *Selected Essays on Literary Subjects*, 93–4.

that Westcott (perhaps like every other translator in such work) could not wholly approve the result. 'How terrible some things look now that all is unalterable' he wrote to Hort when the revision was finished. 'Yet I think that the work is very fair, and it will do good.'[1]

Hort's mind was harder than Westcott's, less devotional and more critical. He was unusual in combining almost total inability to publish with extreme fluency in letters and in speech. A horror that he might mislead afflicted him and prevented him from leading at all in print. But in conversation he was different. He had articulate views on every subject and words welled up within him so that he could not keep silence. When he came with his black skull-cap and his taut manner to the revisers' table, he could not but speak. An unfriendly critic afterwards accused him of talking for three years out of the ten years during which the revisers sat. He was not only persistent, but a formidably equipped and scrupulously accurate student of the text. The dry light of his mind lit up every kind of detail and variant. The gift unfitted him to be a commentator. If his notes on the New Testament word *faith* are compared with those of Lightfoot, the one is obscure where the other is intelligible. Lightfoot presented it so clearly that the reader might fear too simple a view, Hort saw so many nuances that the end was still dark.[2] It was said of him that he looked through the microscope, not only when it was necessary, but even when he needed a telescope. But a gift or habit which hampered a commentator or historian was of utmost value to a textual critic and philologist.[3]

Lightfoot was not a textual critic in the sense of Hort but a historian. Yet he was the greatest scholar in the Jerusalem Chamber, and his cautious utterances were weighty beyond all others. Of the merits of the new translation in contemporary scholarship there could be no question. But Lightfoot was responsible for one axiom in the venture which was a mistake. He held that the same Greek word should be translated, wherever possible, by the same English

[1] C.U.L. Add. MSS 6597, 609; Westcott to Hort 12 July 1880.
[2] For Westcott, see the separate Westcott lectures by D. H. Newsome, C. K. Barrett, Henry Chadwick, Owen Chadwick and G. F. A. Best; A. C. Benson, *Leaves of the Tree*; A. R. Vidler's Westcott lecture in *F. D. Maurice and others* (1966). There are delightful descriptions in the memoirs of the time: see especially *Letters of William Bright*, 347, and G. F. Browne, *Recollections of a Bishop*, 238, a charming story of how he travelled with Westcott to Lightfoot's funeral.
[3] Cf. G, 1899, i, 466.

word. A reflexion upon the act of translating any language suggests that this axiom is neither necessary nor desirable. It was accepted by the revisers and had important consequences.

The revised version of the New Testament was finished on 11 November 1880 and laid before the Convocation of Canterbury on 17 May 1881.

Its reception by the public ranged from moderate gratitude to coolness. A twentieth century familiar with every variety of modern translation still experiences stabs of disappointment at the loss of hallowed words or familiar poetry. It can hardly imagine the extent of disappointment on the first occasion when men encountered such changes. On the one hand every serious student confessed it to be a help to private study, and statesmen saw how useful it was as antidote to the allegations of the soapbox that the Bible did not represent the original text. The examiners of the Cambridge examination for holy orders that autumn set the question (p. 19) 'Illustrate historically the tendency in all ages to attribute to translations of the Scriptures the divine authority which is proper only to the original'; and Westcott was one of the examiners. On the other hand, if the Bible was to be read in church—that is, if it was a liturgical book as well as a historical—it would need more than scholarship. It would need to conserve what was sacred to prayer, and what was imperishable in the literature of the English language. Its style, as well as its accuracy, must commend itself to the listener. And since some of the beauty in the King James version was the beauty of familiarity, no style could instantly commend itself. No one then argued, as was often argued eighty years later, that the shock of novelty brought strong to the soul passages which were remote because Elizabethan. But in 1881 Englishmen still expected the Elizabethan language to be familiar, whereas in 1961 some of them expected Elizabethan language to be almost as unfamiliar to the people as the Latin vulgate.

The revisers had been ordered to use Elizabethan English. They obeyed. They added to the total number of peradventures, howbeits, aforetimes, to uswards. But they maintained the simplicity and the cadences where they could, and despite the difficulty of translating by committee the language was on the whole adapted to its purpose. Criticism fastened upon the loss of words or phrases which every schoolboy used in prayers. Underlying was a truly

important debate, whether the Bible was historical or also liturgical; that is, whether it was in some sense the possession of the
church as well as the possession of mankind. For centuries the
church called the sacred place at Jerusalem by the name *holy
sepulchre*; and whatever the translators called it, the church would
continue to call it the holy sepulchre. There ought if possible to be
agreement between the usage of the church and what was read from
its lecterns. Then were translators right to substitute *tomb* or *grave*
merely because sepulchre was a word not in use apart from this
sacred context? The centuries called the thief at Calvary *the penitent
thief,* and nothing would stop Christians calling him *the penitent
thief.* What induced the revisers suddenly to name him the penitent
robber? Did they seriously suppose that Christians would call him
the penitent robber?

In the Lord's Prayer were words familiar to every English Protestant. For centuries they had borne the burden of worship in the home.
The revisers altered the order—*as in heaven, so on earth*—why?—it
seemed no plainer. They removed the doxology *For thine is the
kingdom* . . . because the manuscript evidence of St. Matthew did not
support it. Under Lightfoot's guidance they changed *deliver us from
evil* to *deliver us from the evil one,* because the Greek could mean
either and Lightfoot held the balance of probability to favour the
masculine gender and not the neuter. If this was (on balance) the
verdict of contemporary scholarship, then the scholar should know
it in his study. But if this was an aspiration of Christian worship, why
should the revisers narrow the prayer to Satan instead of the whole
range of evil? Should Christians accept the loss merely because 'on
balance' the scholars of the time preferred that meaning?

The same criticism was directed towards other passages: notably
the song of the angels at Bethlehem, *on earth peace among men in whom
he is well pleased.* At Christmas children were going to use the old
language whatever the translators said—were they not, on manuscript probability, prising the Bible away from the church? In the
greatest poem of the New Testament, and one of the most beautiful
in the English language, the thirteenth chapter of 1 Corinthians,
though I speak with the tongues, they laid rough hands upon *charity* and
put in *love.* No one used *charity* to mean *love*—except the church to
mean God's love. And if it were argued that *charity* might be mis-
understood to mean *almsgiving*, it was replied that love was often

used to mean other things less desirable than God's love. Why were the revisers seeking to do to the Elizabethan St. Paul what they would not have dared to do to Shakespeare?

So said the moderate critics. Their spokesman was Christopher Wordsworth, Bishop of Lincoln. At his diocesan conference in October 1881 he made the sensible suggestion that competent authority should incorporate the best readings of the revised version in the margin of the authorised version, and allow the clergy to read the margin if they preferred; and then, when people were accustomed, to incorporate the improvements in the authorised version. For the moderate critics confessed that there were improvements even for the worshipper: the change of *damnation* into *judgment*, the alteration of the erroneous statement that *the love of money is the root of all evil*, the conversion of *Take no thought for the morrow* into *Be not anxious*.

That the decision was right to maintain the Elizabethan tradition, whatever alterations were demanded by scholarship, was shown by other attempts of the time to render the original into modern English. F. W. Farrar paraphrased *That thou doest do quickly* as 'Thy fell purpose is matured, carry it out with no more of these futile hypocrisies and meaningless delays.'

The less moderate assailants usually had another motive. They still feared that the Biblical critics were allied with the sceptics or those who held lax views of inspiration. The new version sacrificed the ending of St. Mark's gospel in deference to a (still hypothetical) theory of the manuscripts. It removed the Trinitarian text of the three witnesses in the epistle of St. John.

The spokesman of the extreme conservatives was J. W. Burgon, the Dean of Chichester.

Burgon was an original. An impulsive and imaginative lover of the human race, lively and passionate, utterly lacking in self-consciousness, full of humour and never for a moment dull, with a simple faith united to real ability, Burgon devoted his life to maintaining the Church of England exactly where it stood about 1850. In an age of change such conservatism meant that he was engaged in perpetual resistance to every variety of alteration, whether in thought, ritual or administration. He was a controversialist who lost influence because he was an extremist, and gained some of it back because his personal attacks were lightened by honesty and by the humour which kept breaking in. His enemies called him a clerical mountebank, and once in the House of Commons he was denounced as a jocose fanatic.[1] But the *Times* (10 October 1889) was very unjust when it called him an ecclesiastical Don Quixote doubled with an academical Sancho Panza. His *Lives of Twelve Good Men* is one of the delightful books of the nineteenth century, because his liveliness was married to affection. He was probably more scorned than any other distinguished clergyman of the Victorian age, and he elicited a warmth of friendship which found expression after his death in the noble west window of the Jesse tree in St. Mary's at Oxford.

In October 1881 Burgon launched the first great onslaught upon the scholarship of the revised version in an article in the *Quarterly Review*. He followed this with a second article on the revisers' English (January 1882) and a third article (April 1882) on the textual theory of Westcott and Hort. These articles were extended and reprinted in a single volume of 1883, *The Revision Revised*.

The onslaught was lively and comic and readable. If Burgon weakened his influence because he defended what was indefensible, he also knew a great deal and knew the weakest points to attack. Hort's theory of how the received text was formed—by a conscious process of revision by eastern divines of the fourth and fifth century—was improbable in itself, had no evidence to support it, and has not been sustained by later scholarship. Burgon enjoyed himself displaying the improbabilities. Westcott and Hort (so later scholars have agreed) put too much faith in the agreement of the two great manuscripts Vaticanus and Sinaiticus, at the expense of other early evidence especially from the Fathers; and Burgon enjoyed himself displaying the resulting improbabilities. The revisers' English was the point easiest to attack. It was indeed a weakness in Westcott that he thought the revised version to have preserved the beauty of the authorised version.[2] Burgon had a happy time with the English language. He saw clearly enough that Lightfoot's principle—translate the same Greek word by the same English word—led sometimes to fatal results, though he did not know the principle to be Lightfoot's. Interspersed among these shafts was abuse of Westcott and Hort, especially Hort. The most

[1] Hansard, ccxxix, 1744, 12 June 1876.
[2] Cf. Westcott to Hort, 1 April 1882, CUL Add. MSS 6597, 657.

sarcastic passages did not reach the printer because they were struck
out in proof by a friend of Burgon.[1] But imagination can hardly
encompass what the vanished passages said. In the passages which
survived Hort was represented as an ingenious theorist of extraordinary views, an excellent and honourable man who preached
moonshine. The pair were called two irresponsible scholars of the
university of Cambridge, two misguided men possessed of a weak
superstition about Codex Vaticanus.[2] Burgon did not think that
the authorised version was perfect. He wanted it altered. But he
believed neither in the theory on which the text was constructed,
nor in the final product of an English by committee. The Church
of England was being deprived of her heritage, the beautiful and
familiar cadences which were hallowed to the religious conscience.

Hort, who was chiefly assailed, believed that Burgon must be
answered. Lightfoot advised him against an answer. Westcott
enjoyed extracts from Burgon read to him at breakfast by the Archbishop of Canterbury, and thought that violence answered itself.[3]
Westcott and Hort sold unexpected numbers of their introduction
to the text of the New Testament because Burgon attacked it. Two
of the revisers, Ellicott and Archdeacon Edwin Palmer of Oxford,
composed an answer to Burgon, but it could not sell like Burgon's
book. For what Burgon wrote was what many men wished to be
persuaded on other grounds than those of scholarship.

When Burgon was dying a most Christian death, he confessed
that he had no merit of his own before God—and then, with a gleam
of the old fire, said that one thing consoled him, 'I have been
enabled to crush the revised version of the New Testament, so that I
believe it will never lift up its head again.'[4] Good judges, like Bishop
Durnford of Chichester, believed that Burgon had done more than
anyone to prevent the new version from becoming widely read in
the churches. Even Ellicott, who held the first article of the
Quarterly Review in contempt, confessed anxiously that the article
was having much effect in the provinces. If it had not convinced,
it made men doubtful.[5] By 1890 the revised version was said to

---

[1] Goulburn, *Life of Burgon*, ii, 335.
[2] e.g. Burgon, *The Revision Revised*, vii, xxx, 177, 276, 325, etc.
[3] Lightfoot to Hort, 14 November 1881; Westcott to Hort, 4 February 1882;
CUL Add. MSS. 6597, 637, 649.
[4] Goulburn, *Life of Burgon*, ii, 291, 404.
[5] *Memoir of W. F. Moulton*, 100.

be hardly selling. But the situation was complicated. Gladstone expressed the difficulty well when he said, 'You will sacrifice truth if you don't read it, and you will sacrifice the people if you do.'[1] In the *Expositor* for October 1892 Walsham How said that the revised version was not popular and was comparatively neglected. The accounts of the Oxford university press show that he had reason. In the year ending 31 March 1889 the press sold 694,684 copies of the King James version, with or without the apocrypha, and 24,594 copies of the revised version. The highest year for the revised version, after the first great rush, was 1892 (54,419; King James version, 722,326); and by 1902 the figures were authorised version 774,785 and revised version 13,574. An enquirer of 1901 thought the revised version to be more used among nonconformists than among Anglicans.[2]

There was a legal difficulty. Suppose that a vicar wished to read the revised version from his lectern, could he do so lawfully? The King James version was 'authorised'. The highest legal authority in the land, Lord Chancellor Selborne, stated in a letter to Bishop Wordsworth (*Times*, 3 June 1881) that there was no legal authority to warrant the reading of the revised version in church. Investigation into the events of 1611 suggested more doubt about the sole legality of the authorised version. But though many used it in texts for sermons, few incumbents liked to take it to their lecterns until at least it was authorised by Convocation. And for a long time the Convocations refused to authorise it. The Old Testament was published in 1885, and was a more conservative revision, with changes which did not trample upon Christian feelings and familiarity. But still approval lagged. At last in 1899 the bishops of the Convocation of Canterbury approved the revised version for lecterns, and good old Bishop Ellicott came to be grateful after all his patience. The House of Laymen (1901) would not go quite so far, and voted for its 'occasional employment . . . where, in the interest of more accurate translation, it is desirable'.

Lightfoot said in the York Convocation on 3 April 1883 that the outcry was much less than he expected. Some believed by 1897 that Christians were more free now, than when the new version

[1] G, 90, 717; E. B. Ottley quoting Gladstone at the London diocesan conference.
[2] Stock press lists, kindly communicated by Mr. Harry Carter, archivist of the Oxford press. See A. F. Buxton's speech in the Canterbury House of Laymen, 8 May 1901.

appeared, from superstitious reverence for familiar words. Others, but a diminishing number, still believed that this attachment to familiar words was in no way superstitious, and that the beginning of a divide between church and King James version was a disaster for English religion.

Meanwhile the printing trade had engaged in its mechanised revolution and changed all the possibilities of popular education, including the production of cheap Bibles. The cheap Bibles of the eighteenth century had never been printed in large numbers and often used such shoddy paper as to be in places illegible. The new stereotyping process allowed increase of accuracy with successive editions. The British and Foreign Bible Society, founded in 1804, at once began to use the new methods for producing large numbers of Bibles cheaply. The Oxford press began to mechanise in 1834, the Cambridge press between 1838 and 1840.[1] The Oxford press became the biggest producer of Bibles in the world, rising from an average of about 127,000 Bibles and prayer books a year in 1780–1790, to well over a million a year in 1860. The English privileged printers were helped in this production by the American market, the expansion of Victorian missions, and the energy of the British and Foreign Bible Society. The ordinary poor man once afforded his 'family Bible' only by buying it in separate instalments, and for the first half of the century the possessions of the poor, or the gifts of the parish visitor, were more likely to be gospels, or epistles, or new testaments, or even single gospels. In 1836–8 Charles Knight published in parts the Pictorial Bible, of which the illustrations must have governed many Victorian ideas on dress and customs in old Palestine. John Cassell's *Illustrated Family Bible* (1859), with more than a thousand illustrations, sold 300,000 copies a week in 1d numbers.[2] During the sixties paper became at last cheap, as well as good, by the use of wood-pulp and esparto-grass, the prices continued to fall, and more of the poor were able to buy and the parish visitor was able to distribute more copies. In 1864 the British and Foreign Bible Society, which made a practice of selling below com-

[1] M. H. Black, 'The Printed Bible', in Greenslade (ed.), *Cambridge History of the Bible*, ii, 467–8.

[2] M. H. Black, in Greenslade, 469; S. Nowell-Smith, *The House of Cassell*, 1958, 57; cf. *The Holy Bible*, with 200 engravings by S. O. Beeton, 1861–3.

mercial rates, was able to sell a Bible at 6*d*., and then in 1884 a New Testament at 1*d*., which sold eight million copies by 1903.[1]

The right to print was confined by the Bible patent to the three presses, the queen's printer, Oxford and Cambridge. The language of the patent gave them the right to print all Bibles and versions —'all and singular Bibles and New Testaments whatsoever in the English tongue, or in any other tongue whatsoever, of any translation with notes or without notes'.[2] But the privilege was frequently infringed by private enterprise, and from early in the nineteenth century, if not before, the privileged printers were resigned to confining the privilege to the King James version. But on 17 July 1839 the Scottish patent expired and was not renewed. Though Sir James Graham said that the patent was the only way to preserve accuracy, Lord John Russell replied that not to renew the patent was to lower the price of the Bible. Scottish printers could now print under licence from the Lord Advocate's board, and began occasionally to compete for the English market with the English privileged presses.[3] The argument for not renewing the Scottish patent, if well-founded, appeared to apply to the English patent which expired in 1860. A select committee of the Commons took interesting evidence, which did not always sustain the theory that free competition meant less expensive and equally accurate Bibles. The committee recommended that the patent be not renewed, but to reach that decision it needed the casting vote of its chairman Edward Baines, who was famous for the strength of his views on the subject. The patent was nevertheless renewed in 1860 during the crown's will and pleasure.[4]

2. THE STUDY OF THE OLD TESTAMENT

Until the sixties the Bible had not received accurate examination. Most of England assumed without enquiry that the Bible was still true as history, even if educated England was abandoning the precise accuracy of the earlier parts of Genesis. But once a lack of accuracy was conceded, the historians must attempt to determine the extent of error or of myth, the reliability, the dating, and the authorship

[1] M. H. Black, 471.   [2] PP, 1859, 2, v, 403.
[2] Hansard, xlvii, 1104; xlviii, 140; Anderson, *Annals of Eng. Bible*, 615.
[4] Under the demise of the crown act, 1911, the patent ceased to need renewal; M. H. Black, 472.

of the various books. By 1860 the examination of the Biblical text had proceeded far enough to make scholars aware that a multitude of new questions opened before the enquirer. It had not proceeded far enough for any student to determine with conviction or with evidence what the results would be, even in their outlines. Twenty-five years later the scholars were widely agreed, and were changing the way in which men looked at the Old Testament.

It happened slowly. Law-suits over the opinions of Bishop Colenso of Natal in the sixties were succeeded in the seventies by law-suits over the opinions of Professor William Robertson Smith in Scotland, and therefore the subject was often kept as controversial in the public mind. These controversies made many people sure that they did not believe what their fathers believed, but brought little agreement about what was true, and wise men shrank from publishing on the subject until they could see their way with more light. Therefore the process was slow.

The agenda of the annual Church Congress is a useful guide to the time when subjects became of widespread debate in the Church of England. The critical study of the Old Testament first appeared on the agenda at the Reading Church Congress of 1883. Its appearance there distressed some people. But it was late in the day. Educated laymen were freely treating parts of the Old Testament as legendary. Remarks which an earlier generation might have thought shocking appeared in conversations. An Oxford undergraduate went to study law with an Oxford don and was asked whether he believed in the Bible. When the undergraduate said that he did, the don said, 'Surely you cannot believe in those silly stories about the flood, and the ark, and Balaam's ass speaking, and Jonah's being preserved alive in the fish. Nobody believes them now, they are all given up.' The undergraduate said that he had come to study law and not divinity.[1]

[1] Goulburn, *Life of Burgon*, ii, 182. Arthur Stanley, *Lectures on the History of the Jewish Church* (3 parts, 1863, 1865, 1876), popularised Ewald, whose *History of Israel* was translated 1867–74. In 1861–5 Abraham Kuenen published at Leyden an investigation into the origins of the books of the Old Testament, and Colenso published in 1865 an English translation of the first part of this work, on the Pentateuch and the book of Joshua. In 1875 appeared the article 'Bible' in the new edition of the Encyclopaedia Britannica, an article written by Robertson Smith in which he accepted the composite character of the books of Moses and the pseudonymous character of Deuteronomy. He was ejected in 1881 from his professorship at the Free Presbyterian College in Aberdeen. His *Religion of the Semites* (1889) became the standard history of religious development in the Old Testament.

Nobody believes them now? Few, perhaps, in Oxford. But in little Lincolnshire villages men went in their old ways, troubling their heads little, content with their worship and still accepting what their fathers accepted. They were being taught by clergy whose education lay twenty years behind and not all of whom had read books since they were educated. Criticism was vaguely associated with infidelity and feared. The year 1883 was late indeed for the subject to come upon the agenda of the Church Congress, but its lateness did not mean that most ordinary men and women were ready for it.

In 1885 was published an English translation of Julius Wellhausen's *Prolegomena to the History of Israel*, of which the original was published in Germany in 1883, based upon an early version of 1878. With this book the famous Graf-Wellhausen thesis of Hebrew origins, which held the field for so many years, was under discussion. At Christ Church Driver advised his colleagues to read it. Liddon accordingly read it and disliked it,[1] confident that Wellhausen's theory would go into limbo with its predecessors. But the younger divines were less confident than Liddon. E. S. Talbot, warden of Keble College and one of the best of the younger Tractarians, also read Wellhausen and began to believe that he might be right. By 1887 the Anglican mind was at last thinking hard about the Old Testament. Several of the scholars imparted into their utterances a harsh or rebellious tone. Wellhausen's book was marred by a tone which did not depend upon the contents. Cheyne, the Oriel professor of Holy Scripture at Oxford, was beginning to be careless or to think it good to shock.

Between 1860 and 1900, therefore, the new historical knowledge brought widespread agreement in the main study of the Old Testament, so widespread that it began to penetrate the mind of many educated people. This change was due not only to German criticism and to English scholarship but to the general growth of a historical consciousness and a more comparative attitude to early sources. The historian E. A. Freeman, who was a good Anglican, said that he held, and saw nothing in the doctrine of the Church of England to hinder him from holding, 'that a great part of the early Hebrew history, as of all other early history, is simply legendary. I never read any German books on those matters at all, but came to the conclusion simply from the analogies supplied by my own historical studies.'[2]

[1] Stephenson, *Talbot*, 54.   [2] Stephens, *Freeman*, i, 345, cf. ii, 412.

The Lincolnshire archives contain the notebook of withdrawals from a clerical library, maintained continuously through the century. This notebook allows us to compare the books which the clergy of the deanery withdrew in the first four years of Queen Victoria's reign, with the books which they withdrew at the end. So far as we may judge by the withdrawals, hardly any of the clergy studied the Old Testament at the beginning of the reign, and only one or two at the end of the reign. But if they read at all on the subject, the books which they read came from different worlds. In 1839–42 they read Sharon Turner's *Sacred History*, a long account of the creation and deluge with all natural history thrown in to illuminate. In 1898–1900 they read R. L. Ottley's *Aspects of the Old Testament* (1897). The most important of all changes was the reversal of the respective positions of the law and the prophets. In earlier studies the law was central and the prophets derivative, in later studies the prophets were central and the law derivative; and as part of this change the books of Deuteronomy, Numbers and Leviticus were dated several centuries later than in the earlier chronologies. Ottley assumed that the earlier narratives of Genesis were poetical and not historical, that the legend of the fall was concerned with the character and not the origin of human sin, that the Old Testament shows a gradual evolution of the idea of God from polytheism through tribal Gods to a national God and then to monotheism, that the psalter was a hymn-book collected over different centuries, and that prophets did not predict but spoke to their own time as inspiration moved them. So far as the clergy took their picture of what happened from Sharon Turner in 1838 and Ottley in 1897, little was common to the two pictures. Perhaps this made less difference than might be expected, partly because at both ends of the century they read the value of the Old Testament in its relation to the New Testament, and partly because at both ends of the century they hardly studied the Old Testament; or not at least in comparison with their studies of the New Testament and the history of the Church.[1]

3. THE STUDY OF THE NEW TESTAMENT

The unsettlement of scholarship—and also of the public mind—was greater over the New Testament than over the Old, partly

[1] Smith's *Dictionary of the Bible*, 1863, is an intermediate stage between Sharon Turner and Ottley. This still discusses the measurements of the ark (s.v. Noah,

because it touched the centre of Christianity, and partly because the principal European scholars in the field took a view of the dating and provenance of the documents which removed them further from the events which they described than afterwards proved to be the case.

History demanded natural explanations as imperiously as science. To the historian it was no explanation of the crusades to say that they were inspired. History, to remain history, must seek a natural explanation of prophecy in the Old Testament. And since nothing could be exempt from this law, history must also seek a natural account of Jesus.

The sixties saw the first serious attempts at a biography of Jesus. The later Middle Ages wrote lives of Christ, but they were harmonies of Scripture and legend woven together for the purpose of devotion and meditation. The Reformation, like the early church, avoided all such endeavours. For the Scripture gave a single life in four shapes, and beyond the Scripture no man might safely go. Then in 1835 Strauss published his *Life of Jesus*. The title was a sign of the new age which European intelligence now entered. But the book was not a biography of Jesus such as a historian might require. It was partly an investigation of sources, and partly a theological contemplation of the consequences. The *Life of Jesus* by Strauss was too theological to be historical.

The attempt to describe Jesus as a human person could not fail to startle. In the nature of his task, a biographer seemed compelled to strip the person not only of his halo but of his otherness. Historical understanding depends in part upon the idea of a common humanity, upon showing that a modern man, given the background of ideas and the circumstances, could have acted in a way not so unlike the character whom he seeks to understand. Therefore the new biographers of Jesus could not set to work without an air of familiarity repugnant to Christian feeling. They needed to show the likeness to ourselves more than the unlikeness. They caused a shock greater

---

J. J. S. Perowne), thinks Deuteronomy entirely Mosaic, and Exodus, Leviticus, Numbers to a great extent Mosaic, and holds itself precluded by the New Testament from believing Jonah to be a legend (s.v. Jonah, H. Bailey). But it allows that the flood was only of the Euphrates valley, that the story of the fall can be taken as an allegory, that the six days of Genesis 1 are six periods, that the Pentateuch (though in bulk Mosaic) did not attain its present form until after the exile, that Genesis contains different older documents brought together by a single editor.

in degree than Milman caused when he called Abraham a sheikh, but it was a shock the same in kind.

The first signs of what was happening appeared in the accounts of tourists in the Holy Land. By this spring he taught. Upon this lake he was in danger. Upon the rock beneath this church he was slain. The pilgrim to the sacred places was almost as old as Christianity. In the fifties of the nineteenth century—with the railways bringing the Mediterranean passage near—the Palestine of the first century became more alive because it became more like the Palestine of the nineteenth century. The picture of the carpenter's shop by Millais, *Christ in the House*, exhibited at the Academy in 1850, caused the artist to be criticised for irreverence. Posterity has seen the picture as among the more reverent and beautiful productions of the pre-Raphaelite school.

To attempt a biography of Jesus, other than a harmony of the gospels, was impossible until the doctrine of inerrancy was abandoned and the Biblical scholarship of the nineteenth century determined the main questions over documents. It was also impossible afterwards, but that was not yet known.

In 1863 appeared the first effective biography, by the French writer of genius Ernest Renan.

Renan was a Breton who prepared to take orders as a Catholic priest. He never got as far as being a sub-deacon and by the age of twenty-two rejected important Catholic doctrines. He was influenced by the German philosophers and by Strauss. Meanwhile he became one of the leaders of Semitic scholarship. His use of the Talmud added depth to the study of the New Testament. Though he lost his orthodox faith, Catholicism continued to fascinate him. In a famous epigram, he declared[1] that to write the history of a religion, it is necessary to have believed it—otherwise we should not understand; and it is necessary to have ceased to give a total assent to it, for total assent is incompatible with the historian's detachment. This was a way of claiming that Renan alone fulfilled the conditions needed to write a life of Jesus.

The book was written in the East, while on an expedition to Palestine on behalf of the French government. It conveyed the air of a romantic Palestine, a land flowing with milk and honey. It had the strength of a fair view of the gospels. Unlike his predecessors

[1] *Life of Jesus*, ET, 34.

who aimed to hammer Christianity and undervalued the Christian sources Renan accepted the probability that St. Mark's gospel was indeed written by Mark the friend of St. Peter; that St. Matthew's discourses are in substance a reliable record of what was said; that St. Luke was the friend and fellow-traveller of St. Paul. He would not allow to St. John the same value (except in the account of the Passion) but believed that all four gospels were of the first century. Renan's analysis of the sources was fair.

Fifty years later such an approach would hardly have caused so great a stir. But Renan described a man; and in that generation the compliments of the historian were as offensive as the abuse of the rationalist. An original genius; a great soul; a superior person; an incomparable artist; a lovable character; an idyllic and gentle nature—this was not the language of reverence. Renan gave an idealised picture both of Palestine and of Jesus. Palestine was a land of noble peasants, the fields gay with lilies, the little children smiling, nature gentle and beautiful. Galilee was the land of the turtledoves and the crested larks. Jesus was a sweet and enchanting person—in the English translation he kept appearing as 'charming'. Christianity was a pastoral idyll, and the portrait thus painted owed much to Renan's wish. The Christianity which Jesus meant to teach was a pure worship, without priests or liturgies or external customs or a church.

And round this wonderful person gathered legends, especially the stories of miracles. This was not to be regretted. Round every powerful person the legends gather, and 'nothing great has been established which does not rest upon a legend'.[1]

Like any biographer who tried to write a biography with the aid of such materials, Renan needed to use his imagination. He used his imagination with sympathy, and yet its use allowed free scope to his private view of what religion ought to be. In such circumstances he was sometimes willing to make up his mind more quickly than the evidence allowed.

It was said that no Protestant could have written it, that it could only have been written by an ex-Catholic. It was the infidelity of incense, not the infidelity of whitewashed walls.[2] There is justice in the charge. But the power in it did not only derive from the art of

[1] ET, 186–7.
[2] e.g. J. B. Paton, *A Review of the Vie de Jésus of M. Renan*, 1864.

writing, the charm, the workmanship, the sense of beauty. It contained much truth, as later scholarship accepted it. Whether or not it could only have been written by a Catholic, the portrait had affinities with the Jesus of liberal Protestantism at the end of the century.

In France the book sold 60,000 copies in the first few months. The English translation did not sell so widely, and only a small number of antidotes were published in England. But 'the quest for the historical Jesus' began in earnest.

At the end of 1865 appeared an anonymous life of Jesus, published by Macmillan, under the title of *Ecce Homo*. It was the first attempt by an English author.

The book went through seven editions in seven months, and won a surprising attention from the informed reviewers. Rumour ascribed it to all sorts of authors—Newman, Whewell, A. P. Stanley, Jowett, Archbishop Thomson of York, R. H. Hutton the editor of the *Spectator*, Tennyson, the Duke of Argyll, Gladstone and Louis Napoleon.[1] H. B. Swete and R. H. Hutton aided the discovery of the true author in November 1866.[2] It was J. R. Seeley, then the professor of Latin at University College, London.

Patently the book came from the pen of a writer far above the average. Though not disfigured by such occasional shocks as Renan liked to administer, and obviously the work of a serious and engaged mind, *Ecco Homo* was a lesser book than that of Renan. It gave the impression of being written by an amateur in the subject, writing to satisfy his mind, rather by an author thinking aloud than an author publishing after he thought. Without the crisp mastery of Renan, it yet had the impressiveness of a man grappling with the sceptic within himself and coming at last to faith.

The title misled. Unlike Renan, Seeley was not interested in seeking out the person of Jesus. He eschewed all enquiry into documents. The book was neither a biography nor a portrait of a man. It was a study of the foundations of Christian morality. This, said Seeley, is what Christian goodness has been in the world and this is how it was founded. Christ is portrayed as the moralist, almost as the new

---

[1] Cf. A. P. Stanley's review in *Macmillan's Mag.*, June 1866, 134–42.
[2] H. B. Swete, *A Remembrance*, 17. Swete always spoke of the book with respect: Elliott-Binns, *Religion in the Victorian Era*, 185.

Moses, who founded a society whereby his moral principle should serve the nations. Within this context the historian in Seeley hinted at the part of Christianity in developing western civilisation, the spiritual commonwealth within the secular commonwealth.

The power of the book was its freshness. Hostile critics of Christianity declared that if you stripped away the interpretations of the church and went new to the sources you would find a different Christ from the person whom the churches presented. Seeley stripped away the interpretations. His language was unfamiliar, his approach unique. But going back to the documents, he declared the overwhelming impression which he received, as though to say that this was how the course of history was changed. Seeley's Christ was less alive as a person than Renan's Christ. But Renan achieved his three dimensions by a liberal use of the imagination. Seeley's Christ was stronger, more austere. And many readers felt that the consequences of Christ were more easily attributable to one of the stature which Seeley described than to one with the charm so beloved by Renan. A worker in the East London slums like Samuel Barnett found in *Ecce Homo* a foothold for faith and action, and the biographies of others show how it touched them when they were young.[1]

Some writers imagined that *Ecce Homo* raised a storm comparable with that aroused by *Essays and Reviews*. It was rather interest than a storm, an interest not diminished by the anonymity and the quest for the author. The impression of storm was largely caused by a single sentence of Lord Shaftesbury. At the annual meeting of the Church Pastoral-Aid Society in May 1866 Shaftesbury declared in passing—it was nothing to do with the matter of the speech—that the book was the 'most pestilential book ever vomited, I think, from the jaws of hell'. The phrase was reported and became famous. Seeley afterwards calculated that Shaftesbury's utterance was a singular piece of good fortune, selling 10,000 copies and putting £1,000 into his pocket; and Shaftesbury later lamented privately that he had been the means of putting money into the pocket of an infidel and of helping the circulation of an evil book.[2] But it was not typical. Of course the book suffered several unfriendly reviews. A writer in *Fraser's Magazine*, perhaps the editor James Anthony

---

[1] *Life of Barnett*, ii, 6; E. A. Abbott; W. R. Inge (Adam Fox, 57); Hastings Rashdall (Matheson, 79).   [2] Shaftesbury's *Diary*, 1 October 1869.

Froude, damned it as giving the impression of being written by a sheep in wolf's clothing. 'The skin is the skin of the rationalist wolf, but the voice is the voice of the tamer and more orthodox animal.' Some reviewers attacked it for avoiding the criticism of the texts, others for avoiding theology. But unfriendly reviews do not make a public controversy. Representatives of every school welcomed it. The *Fortnightly Review* declared it to be the most important book to appear for a quarter of a century, A. P. Stanley greeted it with enthusiasm in *Macmillan's Magazine*, but others besides broad churchmen valued it. The nonconformist press was fair. The Tractarians were friendly, Gladstone[1] thought that it should lead men towards faith, the high church *Guardian* received it as a great book. And though the *Record* cried its condemnation, some evangelicals approved. Shaftesbury himself was nonplussed when he asked an evangelical clergyman for his opinion. The clergyman said that the book excited his deepest admiration, and did not hesitate to add that it had conferred great benefits upon his soul. The book was confessed to be a fragment. It treated the New Testament from one side only. But as a partial account many valued it. Newman, in the *Month* for June 1866, attacked the author severely for publishing before he had thought through his material, and yet praised it as a remarkable book. Both Gladstone and Tait, men of widely differing opinions in religion, thought the critics unreasonable.[2] A counter-book by Joseph Parker called *Ecce Deus* was rather a supplement than a reply.

Renan's quest was taken up by various non-Christian or semi-Christian pamphleteers. Sir Richard Hanson, then chief justice of Australia, published a sober dry book *The Jesus of History* (1869). Thomas Scott, an ex-Roman Catholic, published from Ramsgate between 1862 and 1877 some 200 pamphlets of a liberal or free-thinking variety. He persuaded a variety of authors to write for him, from Samuel Hinds the former Bishop of Norwich, and Vansittart Neale the former Christian Socialist, to Newman's Unitarian brother Frank. Among the pamphlets appeared *The English Life of Jesus* (1872), said to be in part written by Colenso's biographer G. W. Cox. There was now a necessity for a life of Jesus written for ordinary Christian. Bishop Ellicott's *Historical Lectures on the of our Lord* (1860, sixth edition 1876) served the purposes of study

---

[1] *Good Words*, 1868, 33.   [2] Add. MSS., 44330, 41.

but made no attempt at a complete biography. The best life before 1874 was written by Archbishop Thomson of York as the article 'Jesus Christ' in Smith's *Dictionary of the Bible*. But being an article inside an encyclopaedia it was never well known.

The gap was filled, satisfyingly to many Victorians, by the publication in 1874 of the *Life of Christ*, by F. W. Farrar. The publisher first offered the work to a divine (possibly Harold Browne) who resigned from it when he became a bishop. Farrar's life became the best-selling biography of the later Victorian age. He read widely and at least used the work of German critics, and the early labours of the Cambridge scholars Lightfoot and Westcott, and the new textual knowledge. He was uncontroversial, making no efforts to confute the critics. The life was written by a man of faith for men of faith. And yet there was more than a hint of Ludolph the Carthusian and the devotional biography of the later Middle Ages. It contained not only narrative but meditation on the narrative, and material for prayerful study. He copied Renan in using the colour of Palestine, which like Renan he found smiling and idyllic. He was criticised by the conservative for casting doubt on demons, and on the story of the coin in the fish's mouth. He was criticised by everyone for expanding the simplicity of the gospels into what he thought was style. *Jesus wept* was enlarged and became, 'As he followed them, his eyes were streaming with silent tears.' These criticisms meant only that someone had to do what Farrar did and that no one could do it perfectly. For the task was in the nature of the case impossible. And if it was too rhetorical, it was also vivid, alive and religious.

Renan pointed to the importance of the Jewish documents in understanding the New Testament. In 1883 Alfred Edersheim, a Jew who was an Anglican clergyman, used this material from the Talmud in publishing *The Life and Times of Jesus the Messiah* in two volumes. Edersheim had more learning, and more dry light than Farrar. But the work was heavy, and used only by students. And by this date the impossibility of the task was beginning to be recognised. The *Guardian* review of Edersheim began, 'It would be well if, for a time at any rate, an end could be put to these attempts to write "Lives of our Lord".' And yet the Christian attitude to Jesus subtly changed as the historical consciousness developed. They were no longer distressed at realism about his humanity. Forty years after Millais exhibited his picture of *Christ in the House*, devout men could not understand what the fuss had been about when it first appeared.[1]

The German universities attained something nearer to academic detachment than the English, and contained more chairs of divinity. Many of the important advances were made by German professors. Most of them were free of any desire to defend verbal inspiration, which they saw to be indefensible. Therefore, earlier than in England, they began to investigate each book of the Bible as an ancient historical document which required to be put into a social context.

These German critics were excellent scholars. But some of them, in the excitement of new discovery, must be confessed to have built extravagant theories upon narrow foundations. De Wette, Baur, Schwegler, Hitzig, Volkmar, Lagarde—the list of powerful but viewy names might be extended.

Of these Germans, the most legendary in England were Ferdinand Christian Baur (died 1860) and his disciples in the Tübingen school. According to this school the New Testament arose from the conflict between Peter and Paul, between Gentile and Jewish Christianity; a conflict which was slowly resolved into the synthesis of the second century which is Catholic Christianity. Every document of the New Testament was written as part either of the controversy or of the compromise; and the theory therefore required late dates for most of these documents. Baur thought that the gospel of St. John could hardly be written till A.D. 150.

Baur was slow to become known in England. Liddon regarded the Tübingen school as a 'desolate waste',[2] and devoted some notes to confuting it. Lightfoot occasionally referred to it from 1865 onwards. But the readers of Baur were rare enough. Men learnt of him rather from his opponents than from himself. Some regarded him as obsolete by 1869.[3] 'Do you consider,' Earl Stanhope asked the fellow of an Oxford college in 1871, 'that the works of the school which is known as the Tübingen school are extensively read in Oxford?' 'No,' replied Mr. Appleton, 'no theology of any school is much read at Oxford.'[4] Appleton exaggerated, for the philosopher T. H. Green at Balliol read Baur during the sixties and

[1] Cf. G, 86, 99.
[2] Prothero, *Life of Stanley*, ii, 169. In 1863 R. W. MacKay published *The Tübingen School and its antecedents*.
[3] Pattison, *Suggestions*, 165.   [4] PP, 1871, ix, 281.

reached the conclusion that Christianity should be freed altogether from its basis in history. During the seventies translations of Baur began to appear. A poor translation of the first volume of the second edition of Baur's *Paul the Apostle* appeared in 1873; a translation of his *History of the Early Christian Church* in 1878.[1] Baur began to be read in English just as his work ceased to count in European scholarship.

During the sixties, and even seventies, the English had to choose between the Tübingen school or an English scholarship too conservative to be credible. As lately as 1884 an able young nonconformist from Oxford university knew no theories about the New Testament but either old-fashioned orthodoxy or Tübingen.[2] The crying need was a school of critical scholarship. Such a school must be conservative in conclusions or it would have no influence over the minds of the English churches, and so academic in method that it would treat the German critics fairly and be respected by English enquirers. The creation of such a school depended not only upon the appearance of the right men, but upon the possibility that, in the state of the evidence, detached academic enquiry could issue in satisfyingly conservative conclusions; or, more simply, that the evidence must be strong enough in reality, and not only by dogmatic axiom, to bear the weight put upon it. The principal founder of the new English school was Joseph Barber Lightfoot, since 1852 Fellow of Trinity College, Cambridge.

When William Richmond painted Lightfoot (1889) he said that it was the most interesting subject that he had ever had. His body was little and crooked, his head very big and like a gargoyle. The artist also found his subject to be a character of the most delightful kind. Yet Lightfoot had a reputation for being excessively shy with individuals. Men compared him to a very gentle mastiff, or to the cherub with the face of an ox, or a Newfoundland dog, dumb but affectionate.[3] He never said much in conversation. His letters convey information in the shortest form, and among the extant mass of them it is rare to find any disclosure of a state of mind. And this terseness helped to make the quality of the commentaries on the Bible. There was not a word to spare. The exegesis explained what needed to be explained and no more.

[1] The original of *Paul* was 1845; second edition by Zeller, 1866–7. The original of the *History* was 1859, third edition 1863, and this was the edition translated.
[2] R. F. Horton, *Autobiography*, 84.
[3] Stirling, *Richmond Papers*, 374; Benson, *Leaves*, 189; Eden-Macdonald, 35–36.

His temperament was stable, his constitution sturdy. He worked hard without hurry or perturbation. His standards of historical scholarship were new to Cambridge, new to England in that generation. The Germans had created new standards of critical history, and Lightfoot helped to create these standards in English scholarship. A man immersed in books, he had nothing in him of the book-worm or pedant. He was wholly unassuming, his mind tranquil and balanced. A learned and sensible mind combined with so gentle a soul to make an ornament to English learning and Christian divinity. A younger friend, who usually saw men with a critical eye, said that he passed through life 'very much as Mr Greatheart accompanied the pilgrims, loving the work he was sent to do, with an amused tenderness for the young and weak, a sturdy self-confidence that was neither rash nor egotistical, and a very practical dexterity in dealing with the giants who encumber, now as then, the road to the city of God'.[1] 'I feel very confident', he wrote in the preface to his first commentary (*Galatians*, 1865), 'that the historical views of the Tübingen school are too extravagant to obtain any wide or lasting hold over the mind of men.' But his commentaries were not controversial. *Philippians* appeared in 1868, *Colossians* and *Philemon* in 1875. He was much helped by his use of German critics of Baur like Albrecht Ritschl.

This moderate school of scholarship headed by Lightfoot was given a fillip in 1874 by the publication of an anonymous book, *Supernatural Religion* (two volumes 1874, third volume 1876). This was a destructive attack upon the documents of the New Testament and was bolstered by references to numerous and rare German authorities. The book placed the four gospels and Acts towards the end of the second century. It was acclaimed as learned by most of the reviewers, and John Morley in the *Fortnightly Review* (xvi, 504ff.) was enthusiastic. The author was rumoured to be Bishop Thirlwall, who had just resigned the see of St. David's in May 1874, and died on 28 July 1875. Some rejoiced that a great and learned bishop had been converted to free-thinking.

Lightfoot was angered by the rumour that it was Thirlwall, now defenceless, blind and dying at Bath. The author declared that he had prepared this attack on Christianity for many years. Yet Thirlwall had been preaching and confirming and ordaining. Thirlwall's

---

[1] Benson, *Leaves of the Tree*, 211.

fair name was in question. Lightfoot was also angered by attacks in the book on the scholarship and good faith of his friend and colleague Westcott.

The articles in the *Contemporary Review* (1874–5) wherein Lightfoot assailed *Supernatural Religion* were the only polemics which he wrote. The book was not difficult to demolish. Its vast footnotes turned out on inspection to be in part a sham, a parade of learning, proving little to do with the points for which they cited. Lightfoot showed by examples that the author had no equipment for the task which he had undertaken. But *Supernatural Religion* was demolished not only because the author did not know all that he seemed to know. He wrote his history of ancient Christianity in a world of scholarship which had just vanished, where Tübingen reigned and Peter fought with Paul for the soul of Catholicism. The study of ancient history had passed beyond that phase, and turned to befriending an early date for more of the books of the New Testament. The Tübingen school found it necessary to give a late date, not only to the books inside the New Testament, but to writings just outside the New Testament like Clement and Ignatius. In 1873 Theodore Zahn published his defence of the seven epistles of St. Ignatius; and though he diminished his influence by adopting untenable positions on other subjects, and by ferocity towards opponents, his view gathered steady support among German students. In 1885 Lightfoot published the first edition of his *Apostolic Fathers* and the argument almost ended. The first epistle of Clement and the seven epistles of Ignatius were accepted as letters of A.D. 90–120; and the establishment of the early date had its effect on the whole chronology of early Christian documents.

Supernatural Religion went on selling up to 1905, but only as propaganda. It ceased to count with serious students. Its demolition did something to restore confidence in the substantial authenticity of the New Testament.[1]

Up to the end of the century and after, many English Christians believed that they had good grounds of history and not of piety, for thinking St. John to have written St. John and St. Matthew to

[1] Acton writes an estimate of Seeley (Figgis and Laurence 1(1917) 172) which takes it for granted that he is the author of *Supernatural Religion*; a letter to Gladstone of 1895: cf. H. Chadwick, *The Vindication of Christianity in Westcott's Thought*, 27. The author W. R. Cassels was an Indian merchant who retired from Bombay after 1865, and died in 1907.

contain certain matter written by St. Matthew. The first century character of the documents was established, with the exception, as most allowed, of the second epistle of St. Peter.

In the study of the Old Testament, to compare a book of the earlier part of the reign with a book of the later was to compare two different worlds. But this was not nearly so true of the New Testament. A life of Christ written in 1905 was extraordinarily like the same life written in 1863. The 1863 life[1] was distinguished from predecessors of many centuries only because it knew more of the manuscript tradition, as for example that the story of the woman taken in adultery was not found in early manuscripts of St. John's gospel. The 1905 life[2] sat more loosely to the sources, allowed that some stories might be repeated twice in different places (as, for example, that the temple was cleansed once and not twice), agreed to the possibility that some stories of miracle might be legendary, and began with the adult ministry, relegating the nativity-stories to the end as 'supplemental matter', though believing them to contain evidence from Mary. The differences were not trivial; but in the light of all the intervening diligence, hunts for manuscripts, philology and textual criticism, comparative religion and every kind of voice uplifted whether sane or eccentric, the similarity was more remarkable than the difference. He who studied the Old Testament in 1897 could hardly use the equipment of 1863 with profit. He who studied the gospels in 1897 could still gain much from the equipment of 1863. For the sources were proved after all to be of the first century, and no one had made any new discovery in literature or archaeology of sufficient weight to change men's ideas.

In the thirty-five years after 1860, therefore, the churches needed to discuss whether these new views which the scholars put forward were permissible for a Christian man. But all churches took enlarged views of what their laymen might believe and even say. What caused suffering, and the possibility of schism, was the question whether a clergyman, or Roman Catholic priest, or minister of one of the nonconformist denominations, might believe, or (still more) teach, these new views and still remain a public officer of his church speaking in its name.

---

[1] By W. Thomson, s.v. 'Jesus Christ' in Smith's *Dictionary of the Bible*.
[2] W. Sanday, *Outlines of the Life of Christ*.

For the difficulty was not only intellectual. Students could not sit down to their desks with eyes only upon their books. Upon the Bible seemed to hang the nature of the society in which they lived. It was the guardian of the home. They could not conceive a world in which the Bible was found to be 'untrue', or was cast from the table or bedside. They confronted an enquiry of which no one knew the end. Whether they were responsible or irresponsible, they knew that their enquiries would have consequence beyond the academic quest for truth about the past.

Therefore, responsible Christian scholars hesitated to publish. They were not sure where they were going. They did not want to unsettle faith unnecessarily. And as the problems became more and more known, this reluctance to publish left an uneasy atmosphere. A lot of informed people knew that parts of the Bible, especially the Old Testament, needed to be looked at in a different light. But no one said so, except the pamphleteers or extreme divines whom sensible and moderate men were accustomed to disregard.

Those who wished to speak out had therefore a motive which was not only an academic motive. They felt the uneasiness about them. Some of them knew educated men whose faith was unsettled or lost because they still thought it necessary to a Christian to believe in a universal flood. In these circumstances it was natural that the first utterances should shock; and also natural that one or two of those who first spoke wanted to shock; and natural that some of those best qualified to speak refrained from speaking.

Religious men could not watch this process of scholarship with indifference. Whatever touched the Bible touched their souls. It was Christian to accept new knowledge when it was knowledge. But it was not Christian, nor even sensible, to throw away the truth of some story dear to the memory because a German guessed that it could not be true. And they noticed that these new theories of scholars who claimed to be Christian resembled the theories which anti-Christian critics had been saying, without evidence, since the days of Voltaire. They observed that some of the new opinions, like those of Baur, were formed, not only upon the evidence, but upon philosophical axioms to which evidence was made to conform. The English churches were inclined at first to reject the new knowledge as baseless fabrications of unChristian minds; even if those minds claimed to be Christian, and even if those minds belonged to clergymen or pastors authorised by one of the churches.

The opposition was put succinctly by Pusey in his commentary on the book of Daniel (1864). 'The critics' say that Daniel is of the second century because it prophesies events which happened in the second century. The only evidence is not evidence but an axiom, that miraculous prophecies cannot happen. The Christians hold that miracles can happen. 'The critics' do not. That is the only difference. The evidence is better for the traditional date than for the second century. The opposed conclusions depend on rival axioms and not on evidence.

Moreover they felt a gulf widening between the religious use and the academic study of the Bible. The Bible was intended to save men's souls. Its historical investigation might or might not lead to results true in scholarship but men's souls were still in need. In his poem *Christmas Eve* (1849) Robert Browning went in a dream to a German lecture room and listened to a dry professor dissecting the gospels, and found there nothing which concerned his pursuit of the vision of God. The same feeling was often expressed during the sixties and seventies:

> From bondage to the old beliefs
>   You say our rescue must begin
> But I want refuge from my grief
> And saving from my sin.[1]

Until about 1888–92 the churches as a whole were not reconciled to Biblical criticism and paid little attention to the new scholarship. Meanwhile some of their members paid much attention. And the question arose whether they had the right, within the churches, to teach what they were coming to regard as the assured results of scholarship. As late as 1901 a meeting at Cardiff of the National Council of Evangelical Free Churches cried down Professor Rendel Harris when he mildly referred to the origins of the book of Genesis.[2] As late as 1902 Bishop Handley Moule of Durham appeared as the writer of the commendatory preface in a book which contained little but sweeping denunciation of the Biblical critics.[3]

For conservatives felt it (at least) doubtful whether a man could be a loyal Christian and believe that Deuteronomy was not written

[1] *Life and Letters of Alfred Ainger*, 104.   [2] G, 02, 422.
[3] Sir Robert Anderson, *The Bible and Modern Criticism*, 1902.

by Moses and Daniel not written by Daniel. This feeling was made articulate in the finest Bampton lectures of the century: *The Divinity of Our Lord,* by H. P. Liddon; delivered at Oxford in 1866, published in 1867. Pusey had summoned him to his vocation, to dam the speculation on the Bible. The lectures contained a sustained effort to refute Renan, Baur and Strauss. But they contained more: an attempt to prove that since Jesus believed Moses to be the author of the Pentateuch, or David to have written Psalm 110, or Jonah to have lived in the whale, therefore anyone who did not believe these three facts would convict his Lord of error and therefore could not be a loyal Christian. Edition after edition showed how the public valued these lectures as the most cogent defence of traditional belief. It was a new expression of the old *Either-Or* of Newman or W. G. Ward; either you must believe all or you will end by not believing. Either you must believe all the Old Testament to be true or you cannot truly believe in Christ. These lectures were the best defence of conservative Victorian religion.

Then, if it were disloyal, how should a man be a clergyman and teach such opinions about Genesis or Deuteronomy or Jonah?

The Church of England was the earliest of the churches to concede that such a thing was possible. For it was connected with the State.

4. ESSAYS AND REVIEWS

In the middle fifties two Anglican clergymen, Jowett of Balliol and Frederick Temple, agreed that the reticence on the subject of the Bible was unhealthy. They agreed to collect writers who would publish a volume to encourage free and honest discussions of Biblical questions. They stipulated that nothing should be written inconsistent with the obligations of an Anglican clergyman.[1] H. B. Wilson, formerly one of the tutors who assailed Tract XC, and now rector of Great Staughton in Huntingdonshire, edited the volume and collected seven authors. Hort and Stanley both refused to contribute, apparently because they thought the plan premature. Max Müller agreed to contribute but fell out. The seven who sent essays were H. B. Wilson, Temple, Rowland Williams, vice-principal of St. David's College at Lampeter, Professor Baden Powell, Mark Pattison, Jowett and C. W. Goodwin of Cambridge (the only

[1] *Life of Temple,* i, 223.

layman). Of the seven authors four (Wilson, Rowland Williams, Baden Powell and Jowett) were already notorious for publishing unwelcome books of divinity.

Like all collections of essays, this collection varied in quality. The method invited superficial treatment. An author had space to hint or speculate or pass quickly, not to examine with mature and extended reasoning. Frederick Temple sent a university sermon of no particular importance, based upon Lessing's famous little piece on the education of the human race. Rowland Williams gave an appearance of scholarship in a discussion of Bunsen's Biblical researches, but his tone conveyed a flippant air. C. W. Goodwin sent an essay which said that the origins of the world taught by science could not be reconciled with the origins of the world taught by Genesis, and therefore that we should not expect information about physics from the first two chapters of Genesis; and since many educated men (clergymen or laymen) accepted this as an axiom by 1860, the essay was of little importance. H. B. Wilson was no penetrating thinker, and his essay on the National Church bore signs of being superficial.

But the three essays of Baden Powell (on the study of the evidence of Christianity), Mark Pattison (on tendencies of religious thought in England) and Benjamin Jowett (on the interpretation of Scripture) show a different depth of penetration. Baden Powell's essay, which ruled out miraculous interventions whether as evidences for revelation or (by implication) in themselves, said in brief compass what he said more fully in his earlier series of volumes. Mark Pattison's essay was the best single study in the book, a brilliant survey of thought in the earlier eighteenth century, so good as to be used by students a hundred years after it was written. Jowett's essay is also a remarkable piece of writing, but remarkable in quite a different way from that of Pattison. Pattison's mind was more coherent and dry and compelling, Jowett's more affectionate and more religious.

If Pattison's essay is discounted as historical, certain leading ideas appear in several of the writers.

First: a gap has opened between Christian doctrine and the real beliefs of educated men. People conceal this gap. They conspire to keep silence. But they are uncomfortable with its inward awareness. It is time to speak and begin reconciliation between Christianity and the modern mind (Williams, Wilson, Baden Powell, Goodwin, Jowett).

Second: all truth is of God. Therefore be not afraid of any sane investigation of truth, whether by geologist or by historian (Temple, Williams, Baden Powell, Jowett). He who is afraid is guilty of high treason against the faith.

Third: do not tie the truth of Christianity to the maintenance of the exact truth of a detailed record of events. Parable, myth, legend, poetry give religious truth, even if the event which the parable describes did not happen (Williams, Wilson, Jowett).

Fourth: do not prove the truth of revelation by the traditional method of citing miracles and prophecy. The truth of revelation is known in its moral impact. If miracles are received, they are received because revelation reveals them. The truth of the revelation of God does not hang upon miracles, but the truth of miracles hangs upon the revelation of God (Williams, Baden Powell, Jowett—and implicitly perhaps, the historian Pattison).

Jowett's essay was unique; at once reverent and disturbing. It was reverent because it was inspired with religious affection for the Bible and for the person of Christ. Yet there was something complex, at times almost tortuous. For inside Jowett two persons strove for the mastery. One was the Platonic philosopher, the other the textual critic of Greek. The Platonic philosopher wanted to see the ideal truth embodied behind the external word, and desired men to look not to the letter but the spirit. The textual critic wanted to go straight to the text of Scripture, strip it of traditional interpretations, see it in its historical context, and discover a single meaning. The critic took men to the letter, the philosopher urged them to rise above it. In consequence this long and powerful essay, for all its fragmentary beauty, left the reader in doubt how he ought to pursue the truth of religion. Sometimes (for example pp. 365–8 of the 1860 edition of *Essays and Reviews*) Jowett left the reader with a helpless sense that he could not get truth out of Scripture by any method whatever. Yet 'interpret the Bible like any other book' and there is a single meaning to be found. But the churches and the theologians have often failed to find it. When interpreted like any other book, the Bible will be found to be unlike any other book. And the essay ended with a noble aspiration towards the love of truth.

One other passage of the book caused surprise. It was an Anglican doctrine that the Bible was the word of God. Was it then possible for an Anglican clergyman, as well as a deist, to hold these critical views of Biblical narrative? Wilson pointed out that the sixth article of the thirty-nine articles, which defined Anglican doctrine, did not define any doctrine of inspiration. The sixth article, he wrote (p. 175), 'contains no declaration of the Bible being throughout supernaturally suggested . . . nor the slightest attempt at defining inspiration'.

The book was important because it was written by clergymen. If laymen had written it, it would have fallen dead from the press. Bishop Wilberforce said that the writers could not 'with moral honesty maintain their posts as clergymen of the established church'.[1]

The essayists must be confuted, lest the public be corrupted. But they could not be confuted, partly because they were elusive in their working, and partly because they happened to be (in general though not in detail) right. Therefore the question came to be, whether such opinions were possible in a clergyman and a teacher in the English church. Everyone agreed that a clergyman was limited in what he might say in the name of the church, limited by the Prayer Book and the thirty-nine articles. If the critics were extreme in their doctrine of the collective responsibility of the essayists, they demanded that all five should resign their office; five, because Baden Powell died during 1860 before the argument began, and was beyond the reach of critics. If they were moderate or sensible in their doctrine of responsibility, they exempted Temple from the demand for resignation, because his essay was generalised and religious; exempted Pattison, because his essay contained nothing to which anyone but the captious might object; exempted Jowett, however they disliked it, because he was a professor of Greek and not of divinity and his office difficult to assail and his essay confessed to be religious. Therefore the demand that all six clergymen should resign or be expelled, quietly turned into a demand that two clergymen should be expelled, Rowland Williams and H. B. Wilson. And among more moderate men the same demand was coupled with a desire that the more 'innocent'— Temple, Jowett, Pattison—should jettison their colleagues by some public utterance and prove that they did not hold the opinions that were reprobated.

On 12 February 1861 Archbishop Sumner of Canterbury issued

[1] QR, 1861, 302.

a general declaration on behalf of the bishop. The bishops were unanimous. From a young evangelical like Pelham of Norwich or a devout Tractarian like Hamilton of Salisbury to scholarly and old-fashioned liberals like Hampden of Hereford or Thirlwall of St. David's, the bishops were unanimous. They could not understand, said Sumner, how clergymen could consistently hold such opinions and honestly subscribe the articles of the Church of England.[1]

The only way to stop heretical teaching, or to prove that it was heretical, was to prosecute it in the courts. Prudence hesitated before such a prosecution. Archbishop Sumner was no friend to the book, but did not believe in prosecution. His experience of ecclesiastical courts, especially over the Denison case, made him aware of their clumsiness. And the supreme court was the judicial committee of the privy council, largely composed of lay lawyers. Whatever the instincts of lawyers over ritual innovation, their attitude to doctrinal language was always in favour of toleration. Doctrinal definitions were not hard rules easily tested in law-courts, and lawyers were likely to put upon the language that interpretation which was most favourable to the accused person. Sumner told a deputation at Lambeth (13 March 1861) that 'ecclesiastical courts are so encumbered by forms and technicalities, that it is very doubtful whether it would be wise to appeal to them'.[2] He preferred answers, declarations, statements, to clear the church. Among the bishops who agreed with him was Bishop Turton of Ely, in whose diocese H. B. Wilson held his living, and whose consent was therefore necessary to any prosecution of Wilson.

But the arguments for prosecution were grave. The doctrinal authority of the church was in question. Was it not the Catholic faith, held everywhere and always and by every Christian, that the Scripture was inspired in all its parts? Not to prosecute appeared to confess that the Church of England had no authority to prevent heresy from being taught in its pulpits. The Church of England needed vindicating from the charge that as a church it lacked authority. This charge was being made openly. Canon Christopher

---

[1] The bishops' declaration referred not to *Essays and Reviews* formally, but to general denials of the atonement or Biblical inspiration, as mentioned in an address from a rural deanery in Dorset. But in the date of issue it was evident what they meant; and they intended a censure on *Essays and Reviews*. Through the rest of his long life Temple never quite forgave Tait of London for joining the censure.

[2] *Times*, 14 March 1861.

Wordsworth of Westminster abbey stayed in Rome during 1862 and heard Manning talk to several cardinals about the Anglican predicament. 'The Church of England', he said, 'sits in her chair mute and confounded.'[1]

Rowland Williams was beneficed in the diocese of Hamilton of Salisbury, the only true Tractarian on the bench, devoted and prayerful. For a month or more Hamilton tormented himself on the question whether to prosecute or no. Though not worldly-wise, he had eyes open to dislike the ecclesiastical courts. With the utmost reluctance he concluded at last that he must prosecute. He remembered his duty to banish error, and believed that his conscience had no alternative. The clergy of his diocese pressed him to act. 'I am bound', he told his archdeacon on Whit Monday, 'to endeavour to show that the Church of England does protect her members against such false teaching.'[2]

The decision gave satisfaction to a powerful little group. Few other people approved of it. It kept the book before the public eye, perhaps for years. And memories of the Gorham case of 1849–50 or the Denison case of 1853–8 did not encourage those who hoped for victory in the courts. In both these cases a clergyman under a charge of heterodoxy was allowed to continue in his living, partly because of the ecclesiastical courts, and partly because the judges held for a liberal interpretation of theology. In English law offence against orthodoxy must be glaring to be offence. Therefore the prosecution might fail. And if it failed, the failure might be a disaster greater than the book itself. Thus many persons who shared Hamilton's opinion of the book believed nevertheless that his decision was wrong.

In January 1862 Bishop Turton of Ely, who refused to prosecute H. B. Wilson, allowed a rector in his diocese to institute proceedings.

On 25 June 1862, the dean of arches, Stephen Lushington, gave judgment in both cases. This judgment of Lushington at once took an extreme importance for the established church, and therefore for other churches afterwards.

The question, he declared, was not whether Rowland Williams contradicted the Scriptures, or the doctrines of the ancient church, or the consensus of learned Anglican divines. The sole test which the

---

[1] *Chron. Convoc.*, 1864, 1798–9.
[2] Hamilton to Archdeacon of Dorset, *Times*, 23 May 1861.

court could apply was compatibility with, or contradiction of, the legal formularies of the establishment: articles, liturgy, canons. All questions not plainly decided by those formularies must be held to be open questions, on which a clergyman may teach as he thinks fit. It was possible that in a book like *Essays and Reviews* there might be much for Christian men to censure, and yet that the law would not reach it.

Dr. Rowland Williams declared at his ordination that he unfeignedly believed all the canonical Scriptures of the Old and New Testament. What was meant by this belief? Lushington held that the belief must be limited. The books of the Bible were numerous, varied and ancient; parts of vital import, parts of obvious allegory, parts historical and less sacred. The church has nowhere defined inspiration. Therefore the belief professed at ordination must be limited to belief that the holy Scriptures contain everything necessary to salvation, and that to that extent they have the direct sanction of God. A critic might declare that a verse or verses ought not to be in the Bible, and not render himself liable. But to maintain that a whole book ought not to be in the Bible would contravene one of the articles of religion.

Upon these axioms Lushington held that Rowland Williams had contradicted the articles of religion. To describe the Bible as 'an expression of devout reason' violated the articles declaring it to be God's Word written. To declare that 'propitiation' meant establishing peace in the hearts of men, and that justification meant a sense of divine favour, violated the articles. In the parallel case of Fendall *v.* Wilson, Lushington condemned Wilson for denying inspiration and eternal punishment, but rejected the majority of charges. He suspended both from their benefices for one year.

This judgment was the most momentous single judgment of that series which enabled Anglican clergymen to adjust their teaching in the light of modern knowledge. For although the dean of arches condemned both Wilson and Williams on momentous points, the traditional mind of churchmen was startled by the liberties (or errors) which Lushington sanctioned. A clergyman might freely deny the genuineness of any book of the Bible if he did not deny the divine authority; might deny that any prophecy in the Old Testament was Messianic; might interpret all historical narratives as parable, poetry or legend. Rowland Williams sang a hymn of victory on the liberties of the Church of England. 'No clergyman', he wrote,[1] 'will again be prosecuted in England for refusing to misrepresent the origin of the book of Daniel and of the psalms, for abstaining from distortion of Hebrew prophecy, and from calumny of the Hebrew race. Hence literary misrepresentation is so far checked, that although bishops will still make it a passport to their favour, they can no longer enforce it by law. Glory be . . .'

An appeal lay to the judicial committee of the privy council. Not even the most sanguine believed that the committee would be more severe or precise than Lushington. The question rather was whether it was likely to uphold even his condemnations.

Lushington's judgment posed the problem of the modern church in a stark form; the problem which plagued all the churches during the sixties and seventies. Part of the traditional teaching of the Christian churches was being proved, little by little, to be untrue. Therefore the churches must jettison, and must seek to jettison, while they preserved that which was meaningful inside the obso-lescent language. But the hallowing instincts of religion cast a halo of reverence upon whatever was associated with the conscience. It was true that the book of Daniel was not written by the prophet Daniel. If true, it was essential that clergymen be not prosecuted for stating it. Yet if a clergyman stated it rudely and irreverently he might be harming the consciences of simple people in a matter more profound and more momentous than the academic debate on the authorship of an ancient book. And it was also a question whether, if a clergyman were able to teach something so contra-dictory to common Christian axioms, he could be stopped from teaching anything he liked. Yet the churches, if they were anything but clubs, had a message of truth for the world. If they had a message of truth, they must be able to control what their representatives taught.

In the sixties and seventies the issue of this difficulty depended upon the differences of church government among the various churches. If the church had a strong government—the Roman Catholic church, the Wesleyan Methodist Conference—it could control its teachers absolutely, expel them if they vacillated, and hurl defiance at the contemporary mind. If the church had a weak government—the Congregationalists, Anglicans—it could not rein

[1] *Daily News*, 28 June 1862.

its teachers so tightly, and must allow room for individual conviction of truth. A series of privy council judgments during the
sixties proved that the Church of England allowed its teachers far
more room than even Sir Stephen Lushington expected in his
judgment on Rowland Williams. To conservatives of that age the
weak government, with tangled jurisdictions, crossfire of law-
courts, elastic articles, felt a disadvantage. As strong conservatives
of the thirties cast envious eyes at the Church of Rome because it
was so hostile to Whigs of politics, so strong conservatives of the
sixties cast envious eyes in the same direction because Rome was so
hostile to liberals of dogma. From its eminence posterity prefers the
personal qualities of Pusey or Manning to the personal qualities
of Rowland Williams or Wilson. Yet even posterity allows that in
these strange and unlooked-for circumstances of faith, the weak
governments did more good than the strong to Catholic Christianity.

The judicial committee of the privy council heard the case of
Williams and Wilson in June 1863 and delivered its judgment on
8 February 1864. The majority (Lord Chancellor Westbury, Lords
Cranworth, Chelmsford and Kingsdown, and Bishop Tait of
London) cleared Williams and Wilson. What they taught was not
inconsistent with the formularies of the Church of England. The
minority (Archbishop Longley of Canterbury and Archbishop
Thomson of York) dissented in main part from the judgment. Each
of the archbishops published a pastoral letter explaining his dissent,
and received much gratitude, including a memorial with 137,000 lay
signatures. Tait received many sad or critical letters, including one
from Gladstone.[1]

Since prosecution failed, the church must clear itself by declarations.

The Convocation of Canterbury had earlier considered the book
but postponed its decision while the case was in the courts. The
history of Convocation showed precedents for censuring books,
though the precedents were seldom encouraging. On 19 April 1864
Bishop Wilberforce brought the book before the upper house.
Two months later a 'synodical condemnation' of the book was
carried in both houses; in the lower house by only 39 votes to 19
(total number of members 149), in the upper house by 8 votes to 2.
The two dissenting bishops were Tait of London and Jackson of

[1] Cf. Davidson-Benham, i, 318–19ff.

Lincoln. Thirlwall of St. David's would certainly have joined the minority if he had attended. But the number of bishops who failed to attend showed that the activities of the Convocation were not so representative of the clergy of England as they wished to appear.

Meanwhile Pusey and Denison and others, Tractarian and evangelical in alliance, caused a declaration to be signed. It declared that the Church of England was Catholic in maintaining 'without reserve or qualification' the inspiration and divine authority of the Bible, and in teaching that the punishment of the 'cursed' and the 'life' of the righteous is everlasting. This declaration was signed by 10,906 clergymen, or under half the clergymen in England and Ireland.[1]

Such a declaration or synodical condemnation was necessary to relieve minds. They must show that the church possessed a true authority in spiritual things. They must prove to their critics and their people that the church was not at the mercy of uncomprehending latitudinarian lawyers, Gallios like Lord Chancellor Westbury. The bishops were assailed by some of the best among their own advisers, and received letters from simple troubled parishioners. Either clear the conscience of the church or we must leave it. Pusey regarded the judgment as the greatest crisis through which the Church of England had ever passed. He cared much for souls, and souls would be destroyed if the fear of hell were dismissed. A bishop like Wilberforce believed that something must be done if the church was to be held together.

For a leader like Tait of London, the course of action was a calamity. The intelligent mind of England was troubled. It would not be less troubled by semi-authoritative declarations. Tait continued to think it folly to have published *Essays and Reviews*, folly for Stanley to have written in defence of it. But the intelligent laymen of England were being alienated from the faith by measures taken in panic. He looked round in despair at the bench of bishops, and saw only Thirlwall of St. David's as the one hope of preventing a breach between the authorities of the church and intelligent men. Through these years Tait gained a national stature. He acquired with some evangelicals and some Tractarians an unpopularity which

[1] Statistics in *Chron. Convoc.* 1864, 1663; total clergy 24,805. F. D. Maurice was prominent against the declaration. The *Record* was more disturbed that Professor William Selwyn of Cambridge refused to sign the declaration on the grounds that passages in the Bible are of human origin.

remained with him for the rest of his life. But the educated laymen of England began to see him as a strong, sensible and moderate man.

Neither Wilberforce nor Tait were theologians, though for all his busy life Wilberforce read more theology than Tait. Tait was not against Wilberforce because he had more carefully considered the reigning doctrine of inspiration. Wilberforce put his loyalty to the church above his loyalty to the nation; or rather, thought that his highest loyalty to the nation lay in his allegiance to the church. Though no Tractarian in the narrow sense, he accepted the Tractarian doctrine of the independence of the church from the state. He saw the Church of England as the Catholic Church within the nation. Tait, throughout his life, saw the Church of England as the national church. Its duty to the nation came before its duty to Catholicism, or rather, its highest duty to Catholicism lay in its duty to the nation. Towards the nation it must seek to be as comprehensive as possible. Therefore he had no desire for new doctrinal definitions, nor declarations, nor condemnations for heresy. Tait's mind and conduct showed how the establishment made for comprehension and for liberality. It so happened, during the difficult years of Biblical criticism, that liberality was one of the principal needs of the Church of England.

Friendly pressure sought to persuade the 'innocent' among the essayists to do something to clear their names by somehow dissociating themselves from Williams and Wilson. This particularly weighed upon Temple; partly because Rugby school would suffer if its headmaster allowed the stigma to rest. Tait publicly called upon Temple and Jowett for a declaration that they were not responsible for every word of the book.[1] Temple was offended by the demand, and asked Tait to forget that they were friends. He regarded such a declaration as disloyalty to colleagues. With his eye on the parents of his boys, however, he agreed to publish a volume of sermons which he had preached in the chapel of Rugby school and showed him as a teacher of Christian faith.

The demand was renewed in 1869, and the controversy over *Essays and Reviews* given its appendix. In 1868 Gladstone became prime minister for the first time, and England had a Tractarian as prime minister.

[1] *Chron. Convoc.*, 28 February 1861, 460.

Gladstone was conservative, though not narrow, about the Bible. But he was now a Liberal in politics, and held that all the schools of thought within the Church of England should be represented upon the episcopal bench. Temple was a Liberal in politics, in an age when eminent Liberal clergymen, though more common than in the days of Melbourne, were still uncommon. He was also a liberal in divinity. But his character and religion made him a liberal respected by some who were far from his theological opinions. In October 1869, as part of a complex balancing of episcopal appointments, Gladstone nominated Temple to the see of Exeter. It was one of the nominations of the century after 1829—the others being Hampden to Hereford in 1847 and Henson to Hereford in 1917—which caused a public campaign of protest.

The campaign was less powerful in 1869 than in 1847, partly because Temple was a bigger man than Hampden, and partly because churchmen trusted the prime minister who was nominating. At bottom the reason was the same. Hampden might well be orthodox but the university of Oxford voted that he was not, and he refused to clear his name. Temple was probably orthodox, but he contributed to a book which was condemned in Convocation and refused to clear his name. A man is known by the company which he keeps.

When Gladstone informed Tait of the nomination, he confirmed that he expected trouble. But he accompanied this with a literary twinkle which seemed not to expect much of it. He got more trouble than he wanted. In one other respect the Temple nomination resembled the Hampden nomination. It united political opposition to religious opposition. Gladstone had just passed an act to disestablish the Irish church, and Temple approved of the deed. The enemies of Temple included some who were enemies not of Temple as a divine but of Gladstone as a politician. Gladstone consciously performed an act of state which his master Peel regarded as an error in the exercise of patronage; making from political motives an appointment which could be resisted on religious grounds by those who wanted to resist it on political grounds.

From his hermitage at Christ Church Dr. Pusey (10 October 1869) addressed an enormous letter to the *Guardian*. He thought that the nomination raised the possibility of bishops being a curse to the church, and surpassed 'in its frightful enormity anything which has been openly done by any prime minister'. He believed disestablishment to be the only remedy.

At Exeter Temple succeeded Phillpotts. In one respect it was easy to succeed Phillpotts, for in his last years the old champion became too chair-bound to be in touch with his clergy. But in the diocese were disciples of Phillpotts, and strong in resistance. The demand that Temple should clear himself of *Essays and Reviews* arose again, in a form more difficult for Temple to refuse, from the clergy of the diocese where he would serve. Some took down *Essays and Reviews,* re-read the essay, and were puzzled to seek for whatever was supposed to be objectionable. And some high churchmen discovered to their surprise that the main organs of high church opinion refused to stand behind Dr. Pusey. The *Guardian,* representing Tractarians like R. W. Church[1] and politically devoted to Gladstone, thought the campaign a grievous error. Still more surprising, the *Church Times,* organ of the more extreme Tractarians, dissented from Pusey's condemnations, and thought the selection of Temple more objectionable because he was a schoolmaster than because he was an essayist. It recalled the quarrel on Hampden's appointment to the see of Hereford, and reminded its readers how Hampden turned into the most harmless of prelates. Temple's opinions it declared to be at least as orthodox as those of Tait, now Archbishop of Canterbury; of whom confessedly its opinion was not high.[2] But some 200 of the 1,000 clergy in the diocese of Exeter signed a memorial urging the dean and chapter to vote against the nomination. They would have been greatly relieved if Temple had spoken. He was besieged with requests, public and private, and even by his friends was blamed for 'taciturnity'.

But Temple would not speak. He would make no declaration other than that required by law. He would not narrow the limits of belief in the Church of England by confessing that men had a right to satisfy themselves on his orthodoxy other than by his readiness to subscribe the articles. He said so, uncompromisingly, in a letter to a Devon newspaper.

If Temple would not speak, his friends tried to speak for him. E. W. Benson and W. C. Lake both wrote to the press, confident from personal knowledge that Temple did not share the opinions

---

[1] Cf. *Life and Letters of R. W. Church,* 182, 184.
[2] CT, 15 October 1869.

of the other six essayists. Evidence was given that Temple advised his sixth form not to read *Essays and Reviews*. Even Tait allowed a private letter of this kind to be published. It will be observed that all Temple's leading defenders were confident that he would dissociate himself from *Essays and Reviews* if he could. No one took the line that Temple had nothing of which to repent. On the contrary, they were sure that he was penitent, and his difficulty was only that he could not say so. If he spoke now, he would open himself to the sneer that he would do for preferment what he would not do for truth.

On 11 November 1869 in Exeter Cathedral the dean and twelve others, including Archdeacon Phillpotts son of the bishop, voted for Temple. The sub-dean and five others voted against. A protest at the subsequent confirmation in Bow church was a fiasco. But the protest at Temple's consecration was far from a fiasco. Several bishops were determined that Temple should speak before he was consecrated. If he did not speak, might there not be a new edition of *Essays and Reviews* with the name of the Bishop of Exeter on the title-page? On 21 December 1869, in a fog-girt Westminster abbey, the service of consecration was delayed while four bishops entered protests against consecrating Temple until he should have cleared his name. The contents of *Essays and Reviews* were no longer relevant. One of the protesters, Selwyn of Lichfield, confessed that he had not read *Essays and Reviews* and had no intention of reading it. The consecration would set aside a solemn act of Convocation, and so weaken doctrinal authority in the Church of England.[1]

Tait thought that Temple ought to speak after consecration, when he could no longer be accused of speaking for the sake of preferment. But he did not speak. And by the end of the year sober men feared that the Church of England was near to schism. If a division occurred it would be fundamentally on the question whether modern biblical criticism was lawful for clergy of the Church of England.

The schism did not happen. The sudden arrival of a mass of new knowledge placed strain on every ecclesiastical structure; as in the

[1] The four were Ellicott of Gloucester and Bristol; Atlay of Hereford; Selwyn of Lichfield; Wordsworth of Lincoln. It was announced that four others agreed: Ollivant of Llandaff; Campbell of Bangor; Claughton of Rochester; Magee of Peterborough; Wilberforce had been invited to be one of the consecrators and refused to take part.

Renaissance, so in the nineteenth century. The new knowledge of the sixteenth century produced widespread division among the churches. The new knowledge of the nineteenth century produced extraordinarily few divisions: a little schism in Natal, for a reason parallel to the reason for the threatened schism over Temple's part in *Essays and Reviews*; a schism among the French Protestants; a parallel and substantial division over ecclesiastical authority among the Roman Catholics of Germany after 1870; troubles among the Protestant churches of the United States. But the Christian Church was able to endure these tensions without unbearable stress. Biblical criticism complicated the internal lives of all the churches, but seldom divided them.

A month and a half after his consecration Temple acted at last. To the Convocation of Canterbury on 9 February 1870 Archdeacon Denison introduced a gravamen against Temple. The motion was comfortably lost in the lower house. A few minutes after it failed, Archdeacon Freeman of Exeter announced that Temple's essay would not henceforth be allowed to appear in any edition of *Essays and Reviews*. The announcement was received with loud cheers.

The withdrawal of Temple's essay caused alarm among liberals of every hue. Matthew Arnold, most extreme of lay divines, agreed with Temple that not all the essays handled religious matters in a becoming spirit, and approved the withdrawal of the essay.[1] But some liberals objected warmly to the act as a betrayal. And conservatives alarmed Temple by claiming that he meant more than he intended. Temple was said to have condemned the other writers in *Essays and Reviews*, or to have retracted what he wrote in his own essay. Temple was perturbed by these inferences. He was compelled to make a further public statement, which took away half or more of what he had given. He had not, he said, intended the withdrawal as a condemnation of the other writers. 'I did feel certainly that the publication of one essay amongst others was a thing which might be allowed to Frederick Temple but which was not therefore to be allowed to the Bishop of Exeter.' The opposition was vexed by the withdrawal of the withdrawal, but thankfully accepted this last sentence as sufficient, and the battle ended. A little attempt to prevent Temple becoming vice-president of S.P.G. (18 February 1870) failed.

[1] *Letters of Matthew Arnold*, ii, 28.

V.C.-4

To allow legend in the Bible horrified good men, especially those good men who wanted the church to declare the whole truth which it had received. To allow legend in the Bible was necessary to those who studied the question with open eyes. The ensuing conflict could only avert division by compromise. The conservative insisted that the church must not be committed to allowing legend in the Bible, and therefore that Temple must either withdraw or be prevented from becoming a bishop. The liberal insisted that the problem had arrived to stay with the church and that a liberal divine must be consecrated unconditionally. Temple's conduct, though open at the last moment to the charge of clumsiness, achieved both objectives, and quietened scruples on every side. Although he was a bishop, the Church of England was in no way committed to the belief that a bishop might lawfully allow legend in the Bible. Yet in fact the Church of England now had a bishop who did not think clergymen wrong if in a reverent search for truth they allowed legend in the Bible; a bishop who would be prepared to ordain candidates whose intellectual departures from the older standards were as wide as any departure found in *Essays and Reviews*. Lord Shaftesbury[1] called it the turning-point in the ecclesiastical and theological history of England.

Bishop Colenso of Natal was consecrated, not without protest, in 1853. He undertook a translation of the Bible into Zulu, and employed Zulu assistants. He liked his Africans and sought to learn from them. They began to perplex him with questions. While they were translating together the story of the flood, one of his Zulus asked, 'Is all that true? Do you really believe that all this happened thus?' Colenso knew enough recent geology to be forced to confess to himself that he did not believe it. But he temporised; for he would not say so outright to the Zulu, lest he cast discredit on the general truthfulness of the Bible. Later he was much perturbed when his Zulu expressed moral revulsion against a brutal command of ancient Hebrew law (Exodus 21, 20–1).[2]

In 1861 Colenso published a commentary on Romans. He professed to be a disciple of Maurice but made Maurice's thought simpler, more unqualified, cruder than Maurice could allow. The matter of the commentary was not important; except that it plainly

---

[1] *Diary*, 13 December 1869.   [2] *The Pentateuch critically examined*, I, vii, 9.

held lax views of Biblical inspiration and formally withdrew the belief in eternal punishment which he publicly professed before his consecration to be bishop eight years before.

His metropolitan was Bishop Gray of Cape Town. Gray was a son of that Bishop of Bristol whose palace was burnt during the Reform riots of 1831. He became a vicar in County Durham and in 1847 accepted the invitation to be the first Bishop of Cape Town. He was a moderate Tractarian and a strong Tory, of bulldog courage, generous and unsubtle, with energy so unbounded as to make him liable to overwork. He knew what was Christian faith and what the church taught, and was determined to keep heresy out of the Church of England.

The two men were symbols of the old world and the new. And it is symbolic of so much in Victorian church history, that the old looked fairer than the new.

Colenso was a writer of text-books on arithmetic. He had been brought up to believe that every detail of the Bible was true, and never questioned it; more, he had been brought up in an atmosphere of that peculiar Biblicism, where men calculated the tonnage of the ark. He had some Hebrew and German, but otherwise no equipment for tackling the critical problems of the Pentateuch. He went quickly, beginning his studies on the Pentateuch after he read *Essays and Reviews*. The works of a very few German divines, conservative and critical, were sent out to Natal. His *Pentateuch* was produced from these and his arithmetic. He had no sense of history, no idea how to criticise documents, no wide reading, and no profundity of mind.

The first part of the *Pentateuch* is the strangest of books. Nearly all of it is based upon the statistic that the Israelites had 600,000 armed men between Egypt and the invasion of Canaan. Upon the basis of this figure Colenso proved from climate, and sanitary arrangements, and food supply, and flocks and herds, the impossibility of some of the things which were recounted. He proved, or said that he proved, that one man's reading could be heard by two million persons, even with the many babies crying; that six men had 2,748 sons; that each priest was compelled to eat 88 pigeons daily. These and similar calculations were reported with an air of solemnity. It was the ancient school of biblical calculation topsy-turvy, used to confute and not to prove.

His methods were wholly unimportant except so far as they played into the hands of the conservatives. Conservative critics cheerfully jettisoned the figure of 600,000 as a scribal slip and so ruined Colenso's book. The affair of the Zulu assistant afforded jests about the bishop who went out to convert the heathen and came back converted by the heathen. But the conclusion was more important than the method which attained it. However oddly or naively he reached the judgment, here was a bishop of the Church of England claiming to be a bishop while he held that the Pentateuch was in parts unhistorical, and a compilation of different sources. He declared like the Essayists that Anglican doctrine must be broadened if it was to meet intelligent men. The essential truth of the Bible did not depend upon the historical truth of all its narratives.

For this opinion Rowland Williams and H. B. Wilson were already being prosecuted. Anglican affection for bishops combined with the crudity of Colenso's book and general alarm to make it seem imperative to remove Colenso from being a bishop; preferably by persuading him to resign, but if that failed by deposing him. Colenso began by believing that he ought to resign because he could not in conscience use the language which the Church of England ordered him to use. But in June 1862 Lushington as dean of arches, though suspending Williams and Wilson, acquitted them on the charge of denying the inspiration of the Bible. This judgment allowed Colenso to believe that he taught nothing disallowed to a loyal Anglican; and when it was upheld and extended by the judicial committee of the privy council, he was sure, not merely that he need not resign, but that he must stay in order to prove the liberty which the Church of England permitted.

On 17–21 November 1863 Bishop Gray held a synod of the South African bishops in the Cathedral at Cape Town. On 16 December Gray delivered judgment, deposing Colenso from the see of Natal and prohibiting him from exercising the office of a clergyman in the province of South Africa. Colenso was given until 16 April 1864 to retract. The synod formally declared the independence of the church in South Africa, not from the English formularies to which it was bound, but from the interpretations of these formularies given in the English courts. In England the Convocation of Canterbury condemned *Essays and Reviews* though the courts acquitted it. But in England the church was established, in South

Africa it was not. Therefore Gray claimed the right to depose Colenso for his heresies.

Colenso appealed to the privy council against the synod; that is, not the judicial committee as constituted for ecclesiastical causes, but in its civil capacity. He appealed as a citizen of the empire who was wronged. On 20 March 1865 the judicial committee held that the proceedings of the synod were null and void. The question of whether Colenso was in error of doctrine never came before the privy council. Gray absolutely refused to allow the question of Christian doctrine before a secular court.

The memory of the Gorham case was vivid among some church-men. The issue of the Gorham case left them regarding the judicial committee as nothing to do with the Church of England. By this belief they saved their conviction of the Catholicity of the English church. Never would they recognise any judgment of the judicial committee as binding the church. Gray was wholly of this mind. He thought the judicial committee a secular court, as nothing to do with the church, a court which understood nothing of Christian doctrine, and had policy as its sole function. Never would he take Colenso thither. Gray's intransigence perhaps eased the progress of the Church of England towards comprehension, though this was not his intention. For Colenso was never tried in an English court for heresy. Bishop Tait believed that if he had been tried for heresy he would have been convicted.[1] His case was determined only on the question whether he still had a valid right to his work and his stipend, and therefore whether he had been deposed from his see by a valid court. The theological question was not determined.

No one wanted Colenso back in Natal. Even those many who sympathised with him had little wish that he should return. But Colenso resolved to return. The determination was not least among the evidences that he was an unsuitable person as bishop. Under the prevailing conditions a return to Natal could only mean strife, schism, damage to the congregations. Colenso believed that for the sake of intelligent Englishmen he must prove it possible to hold his views and be a bishop. He toyed with an offer to be editor of a Biblical commentary, but at last returned to Natal. He was delayed for a few months by a resolution of the managers of the colonial bishoprics fund not to pay his stipend. In the light of the judgment

[1] Davidson-Benham, i, 362; Hinchliff, *Colenso*, 101.

by the judicial committee they could not hope to succeed. They delayed him for two more months until he forced them to pay his stipend. He landed in Durban in November 1865, three and a half years after he left it, was greeted by a crowd of welcoming but not very Anglican laity, and made a strange fighting speech about how we need 'the scientific and theological help of Parliament'. He stood for the maintenance of the queen's supremacy in South Africa, and appealed to the loyal feelings of settlers, that Gray was breaking the link with the mother-church and mother country. Gray pronounced the sentence of greater excommunication; which was read by the dean in the cathedral at Pietermaritzburg on 5 January 1866. A series of unedifying scenes ensued when Colenso took possession of the cathedral.

Gray wished the Church of England—that is—the Convocations —to declare support for his excommunication. At the Convocation of Canterbury in June 1866 Samuel Wilberforce proposed a formal declaration that the Church of England was not in communion with Bishop Colenso but was in communion with Bishop Gray. The meaning of this must be condemnation of Colenso for his opinions; but which of his opinions would not be stated. The world would understand it to be a declaration that the clergy of the Church of England refused to allow a man at once to hold ministerial office and allow parts of the Bible to be legendary. Tait and Thirlwall succeeded in changing the resolution into the simple positive statement that the Church of England was in communion with Bishop Gray, and made no definition about Colenso. Therefore the next step was to persuade the bishops in England to provide a new bishop for Natal, for the act would demonstrate the opinion that Colenso was not Bishop of Natal. Gray tried to get Colenso condemned by the first Lambeth Conference of September 1867. He achieved a condemnation not by the conference but in a private paper circulated among the bishops at the conference.[1]

[1] A. M. G. Stephenson, *The First Lambeth Conference, 1867*, 1967, proved that Colenso was far from being the main reason for the summoning of the conference; though one of the important causes was the involvement of the colonial bishops in doctrine after the *Essays and Reviews* judgment and Colenso. The most important papers for the Natal schism and the origins of the Church of South Africa are Burdett-Coutts papers and Tait papers at Lambeth; Macrorie papers at S.P.G. archives; Gray papers in Bishopscourt archives, Cape Town; Colenso papers in Campbell Library, Durban and Natal Archives, Pietermaritzburg; cf. also Hinchliff, *Colenso* 180ff.; Hinchliff, *The Anglican Church in South Africa*, pp. 27–110.

The first candidate selected for the see of Natal refused. On 26 October 1866 a small majority of clergy and representative laity in Natal elected W. J. Butler, the famous Tractarian vicar of Wantage. On 18 November 1867, advised by Archbishop Longley, Butler finally declined the offer. Gray then invited W. K. Macrorie, the vicar of Accrington in Lancashire. The English bishops preferred not to consecrate him, because they could not legally do so, and he was at last consecrated in Cape Town in January 1869.

The little Natal schism was one of the very small number of divisions created among the Christian churches by the influx of Biblical criticism.[1]

It is not easy to determine whether it advanced or retarded the right of clergymen to treat parts of the Bible as unhistorical. That right was legally achieved for Anglican clergymen by the judgment of the judicial committee in 1864 on the two writers of Essays and Reviews. The Colenso case made no difference to that legal right. If Tait was correct in thinking that Colenso would have been condemned if he had been charged for doctrinal error before a valid court, then Gray's refusal so to charge him aided the liberals; for Colenso continued to be Bishop of Natal in the eyes of the law, however he might be a heretic in the eyes of many churchmen. But in such a matter there was a wide difference between a legal consequence and a psychological consequence. The conflict between Colenso and the organs of tradition during the sixties helped to produce that sense of alienation between faith and reason which we have observed as helping to generate the conflict between science and religion. Scientists like Lyell and Darwin subscribed towards Colenso's legal expenses. Lyell even spoke for Colenso from a platform. To them he strove for liberty of mind and the majority of English bishops looked as though they stood for obscurantism. 'I distrust all theologians', wrote the botanist Hooker on 19 May 1863. 'I had thought that all educated clergymen had long ago abandoned the verbal, literal, inspiration of the Bible, e.g. the wor-

[1] Colenso, who was supported by a minority ever growing smaller and was in financial difficulty because, though he had the endowments, he had little aid from England, died 20 June 1883, after courageously seeking to secure justice for Zulus in the courts. See Hinchliff, Anglican Church, 106ff. On Macrorie's resignation (10 June 1891), Archbishop Benson of Canterbury sent A. H. Baynes to be bishop of both groups. He did not succeed in reuniting the Colenso congregations, but by 1901 there were only two Colensoite clergy. The parishes slowly became associated with the Church of South Africa, though traces of the schism may still be discerned.

ship of the letter, the Genesis creation, the flood, Tower of Babel, etc., etc., etc., plus much more of the Mosaic narrative; but this is either not so, or the educated ones hold their tongues. . . .'[1]

The Colenso case broadcast doubts about the history of the early Old Testament, not only among scientists. A timber merchant told Walsham How that the Old Testament contained things that none could believe. He calculated the size and weight of the ark for himself.[2] Colenso's arithmetic was a method which some laymen copied.

But wise heads among the liberal divines believed that the Colenso case delayed the time when legitimate criticism became acceptable. In the later stages of his Pentateuchal criticism Colenso used Kuenen's work and wrote sensibly and usefully. His translations of Kuenen made advanced work available in English. Some minds were comforted that a man with such views was still the legal Bishop of Natal. Then he defended the Zulu people against exploitation, and this conduct did more for his reputation than the best of his Biblical scholarship. For as a critic he was judged not by the later portions, but by the first part and by his calculations. He was judged also by the outrages which occurred in the cathedral at Pietermaritzburg. For a time therefore, for all his courage and clarity, he associated Biblical criticism with conduct not worthy of a Christian bishop. Lightfoot feared that the result of Colenso's book would be to discredit reasonable enquiry and divide the church into warring parties.[3] Hort, whose opinions were quite as advanced as those of Colenso, and who had far more learning, was asked in 1884 to sign a memorial praying for a pension on the civil list for Colenso's widow. The language of the petition based Colenso's claim partly on his services to Biblical literature. Hort refused to sign. He thought that Colenso's writings contained material of permanent value, 'in the midst of much that will not bear investigation.' But these merits, such as they were, seemed to Hort outweighed by 'the discouragement which the cause of progressive Old Testament criticism in England has sustained through the natural revulsion against the manner in which he has represented it'.[4]

To say that it was *legal* to call the Pentateuch partly unhistorical

---

[1] *Life of Hooker*, ii, 58.   [2] Walsham How, *Lighter Moments*, 128.
[3] Lightfoot to Tait, 19 November 1862; Davidson-Benham, i, 338.
[4] *Life of Hort*, ii, 312.

was one thing. To say that it was *acceptable* was another. A clergyman who approved such opinions might still find himself suspect to his brother clergy, or unlikely to receive the preferment which was otherwise his due. It was believed that H. M. Butler remained as headmaster of Harrow longer than was natural because he notoriously befriended Colenso. Biblical criticism did not become respectable among the clergy because it became legal. Some denied that the legal judgment bound the Church of England. No one can understand the impact of *Lux Mundi* in 1889 who does not recognise that the case over *Essays and Reviews* won only quarter of a battle.

5. THE ACCEPTANCE OF BIBLICAL CRITICISM BY THE CHURCHES 1887–95

Educated laymen heard of Tübingen and discussed Colenso. Their attitudes towards Genesis were not governed by what they heard from the pulpit. They could see no difference in their faith if Jonah were fiction instead of fact, and the theory fitted their contemporary knowledge. The new historical study reached the pews before it reached the pulpit, but only the pews of educated men, who were more common in the Church of England than other churches but far from being confined to the Church of England. The occupants of the pulpits were likewise educated, but some of them had religious reasons for believing the new knowledge to be false, and others of them, who perfectly understood that the Bible contained legend, refrained from saying so out of respect to the majority in their congregations, knowing that they could only disturb minds and believing that their work was to build up the religious life of these congregations; with which the date or authorship or authenticity of a book in the Bible had nothing to do.

Yet in one area silence was impossible, the land of public apologetic. You might show, as Lightfoot showed, that Tübingen erred, but you were still left with a problem. It was easier to demolish the fancies of Old Testament critics than to persuade ordinary men that the story of Jonah was true. And at the level of the working man, the atheist pamphleteer or orator knew his business and asked more riddles than the question about Cain's wife. In the eighties it became imperative, for religious reasons, that silence should no

v c.–4 a

longer be kept, lest Christians might be accused of supposing that to be a Christian you must also believe that an ass spoke. And the religious student of the Old Testament, who understood the new knowledge, could not divorce his new understanding from his religion. A teacher at a theological college might abstain in the pulpit but he could hardly abstain if he lectured about the Old Testament to future ministers. Charles Gore, who started to teach the Bible to ordinands at Cuddesdon in 1880, did not conceal what he thought of the criticism of Genesis, and said, 'I hope some day to be able to say this publicly.'[1] Bishop Moorhouse of Manchester preached a sermon to the British Association in Manchester cathedral of which one of the canons said, 'I think much the same as you do, but I dare not say it. You would have been burnt for such a thing in the olden days. They can't do anything to you now except turn you out of your bishopric.'[2] An educated priest, consulted by troubled enquirers about their difficulties over reason versus faith, must say that their trouble was (at least in part) unnecessary. Gore found himself consulted by anxious souls and discovered that if he said what he thought with frankness, they were helped. 'Where you have found a certain method spiritually effective and useful, and you believe it to be quite orthodox, it seems impossible to refrain from saying it.'[3]

By 1887 the silence was broken, not by the pulpits but because the matter gained an important place in public discussion.[4] An intelligent nonconformist journal, the *Expositor* (editor, William Robertson Nicoll), a journal designed for the ministry, allowed a fairly free discussion of the difficulty. T. K. Cheyne introduced the subject, for the first time, to a Church Congress in 1883, but it did not reappear on the agenda, nor produce a tense debate, till the Church Congress of 1888; and this year, late for such an appearance on the agenda of a Church Congress, shows that at last the subject was unavoidable for ordinary churchmen. But it was still unacceptable, or at least very unpopular. When R. F. Horton, Congregational minister at Hampstead, published that year a little

---

[1] Prestige, *Gore*, 38.

[2] Rickards, *Moorhouse*, 168–70; the sermon summarised in *Manchester Guardian*, 5 September 1887.

[3] Gore to Liddon, autumn 1889, Prestige, *Gore*, 103.

[4] R. F. Horton first became interested in Biblical criticism by the publication of the revised New Testament, *Autobiog.* 84; Willis B. Glover, 177.

book called *Inspiration and the Bible*, some of his congregation left
and the Baptist Union cancelled an invitation to preach.

The awkward transition was suddenly made far easier by an
unpredictable turn of events: the breaking of the silence by those
who after the Roman Catholics might be expected most warmly
to disapprove the breaking, the younger leaders of the Anglo-
Catholic party.

The founders of the Oxford Movement were opposed to 'rational
theology'. They wanted to declare the truth whether the people
hear or forbear, and the truth was revealed in the Bible as understood by the primitive and undivided church. Of the founders only
Newman was interested in the relation between the revelation and
philosophy, as he used his powerful intelligence to undermine
confidence in the natural reason. But if a later Tractarian accepted
a theory of evolution because of Darwin, or a theory of Hebrew
origins because of Driver or Wellhausen, he also accepted that the
natural reason influenced religious understanding. Science or history
could provide truth of such a kind as to affect our attitude to the
revelation which we have received. In the realms of science and
religion on the one side and Biblical history on the other, the
younger Oxford Tractarians began to look for such a reconciliation between faith and reason as their religious forbears would have
suspected. For such an attempted reconciliation they needed two
pre-conditions. They needed that sufficient confidence in the documents of the New Testament which was being provided by Lightfoot and Westcott. And they needed a philosophy which, unlike
the philosophies of Mill or Mansel, could contribute to a spiritual
view of life. In the new Oxford they found such a school of
philosophy; and they looked up to a non-Tractarian, half-Christian
leader, T. H. Green of Balliol College.

Green was a solitary, brooding mind. He became a Fellow of
Balliol in 1860 and for a time fell under the influence of Jowett.
By 1861 he sat loose to orthodox religion. About that time, perhaps
through Jowett's edition of St. Paul, he discovered F. C. Baur and
the Tübingen theory. He translated (1863) for himself a third of
Baur's first volume on the origins of the Christian church. He did
not question Baur. His mind was more that of a philosopher, not
that of a historian. He lectured to his pupils on various parts of the
New Testament, taking the material straight out of Baur and other

German students, and gained a reputation for destructive views on the evidence in the New Testament.[1]

As a philosopher he was concerned with religion. He felt himself to be a philosopher because he was a religious man. His philosophy sought for faith. Baur disclosed to him that this faith must be independent of all historical enquiry or evidence. Every man has God in him, and his faith is his awareness of God and his endeavour to realise his unity with God. It has no connexion with historical events except as symbols. Yet Green habitually used language which closely resembled the language of Christian orthodoxy. His soul was a naturally devout soul, the sincere and thinking man of religion who believed that criticism destroyed the gospel narrative. In the seventies he was one of the forces in the life of the university. They found him rather inarticulate in person and tough in message. They did not take to the jargon of Hegelian philosophy. But some of them had a sense almost of revelation; as though Green dispersed the cloud of materialism threatened by Herbert Spencer, and enabled them to see moral and spiritual being at the centre of human life.

The chief link between the Tractarians and Green was Henry Scott Holland of Christ Church. Green could not quite approve of Holland's ordination; but Holland felt that he owed the development of his soul to Green's person and philosophy. One who owed so much to Green could not see rational theology as Liddon saw it. Like Liddon, Holland read his Strauss and his Renan with disapproval. But the disapproval was accompanied by more questioning and less certainty. His whole being was gay, a bubbling optimist by nature as well as by faith. Liddon admired and liked him but warned him from time to time against the facile adoption of new intellectual methods.

Around stood other pupils of Green who could not share his Christianity, especially his close friend R. L. Nettleship. And there were others who could, like Talbot the warden of Keble College, Aubrey Moore and J. R. Illingworth and Charles Gore, Fellow of Trinity College. The group met every year in what they called the 'holy party' to discuss theology. It was a new vocabulary, for we cannot imagine any other Tractarian forbears except Hurrell Froude calling a serious meeting the 'holy party'. Though externally they

[1] Nettleship, *Memoir*, 136.

seemed to sit more lightly to their religion, some were still of the hair-shirt.[1]

The collection of essays called *Lux Mundi* was edited by Gore and published in November 1889. It had been refused by the Oxford university press because, as Gore believed, the conservatives among the delegates thought that it would 'open the floodgates'.[2] Its tone differed from the tone of *Essays and Reviews*, for its attitude was more reverent. The authors of *Lux Mundi* stood, said the preface, not as guessers after truth, but as servants of the Catholic Church who had received the revelation of God and wished to interpret it in such a way that the modern generation could understand it. They wrote, 'with the conviction that the epoch in which we live is one of profound transformation . . . and certain therefore to involve great changes in the outlying departments of theology'. They wanted the church, while standing firm in the truth given, to enter into the apprehension of the new social and intellectual movements of each age, and give its place to all new knowledge. Ten of the essayists were Oxford men, one (Lyttelton) was at Cambridge but formerly a tutor of Keble.

The essay which gave most offence was Gore's own essay on 'The Holy Spirit and Inspiration'. It simply declared that inspiration is compatible with the opinion that Jonah and David are rather dramatic narrators than history. He used the term *myth*. A myth is not a falsehood. It is an apprehension of faith by a child or a primitive people, a faith not yet distinguished into the constituent elements of poetry and history and philosophy. And if Christ was ignorant of the authorship of David or the Psalms, that is because he became man and shared the conditions of human life.

Liddon regarded *Lux Mundi* as the betrayal of everything for which Pusey and the Tractarians stood.

In truth, Liddon's own line of defence made the real difficulty. In his Bampton lectures he based the infallibility of the Old Testament upon the infallibility of Christ. The conservative defence against Colenso and Wellhausen rested upon a central act of Christian faith, the person of Christ. Those who attacked *Lux Mundi* continued this apologetic. Gore, they said, was teaching that Christ taught error. Hence the argument became anxious, caused

[1] Cf. Paget, *Holland*, 164; *Life of Illingworth*, 34; Prestige, *Gore*, 33.
[2] Prestige, *Gore*, 99.

turmoil among ordinands and Methodist ministers and the older Anglican clergy. If Liddon's great *Either-Or* were justified, then the head of Pusey House indeed abandoned everything for which Pusey stood. By April 1890 the attack pressed upon the charge that Gore endangered belief in the divine nature of the Lord. But the general attitude to the Old Testament was in question; whether it could be accepted that prophecy did not predict; whether inspiration could be maintained if the Bible was admitted to contain legend and pseudonymous books. The general unsettlement over the Old Testament was given a focus.

Therefore the years from 1889 to 1892 were the high point of argument within the Church of England, and the Free churches also, over the inspiration of the Old Testament. And if, after all the scholarship of the last thirty years, and the reverent nature of *Lux Mundi* compared with *Essays and Reviews*, and the men concerned, it seems strange that the controversy should come so late, it should be remembered that hitherto the criticism of the Old Testament was generally associated with extremists, with *a priori* assumption against the miraculous and probably against revelation, and therefore did not divide the church. It was different when good Christian worshippers divided on the point. The controversy was fierce because Gore brought it to the centre, instead of the circumference, of Christian opinion. He claimed the right as an *orthodox* man to hold beliefs which had been regarded as unacceptable, however they might, thanks to the establishment, be legal.

Liddon began the attack with a sermon in St. Paul's cathedral on 8 December 1889, afterwards printed under the title *The Worth of the Old Testament*, and restated his *Either-Or*. The attack was joined by such old-fashioned high churchmen who still survived, like Archdeacon Denison (who said '*Essays and Reviews* and Colenso's book were as nothing to the depths of its injury and wrong'), stern young high churchmen like Darwell Stone (then the principal of Dorchester missionary college), evangelical bishops like Ryle of Liverpool and Ellicott of Gloucester and Bristol and Hervey of Bath and Wells, and a few moderate men of influence like Bishop Maclagan of Lichfield. On Whitsunday Liddon preached another *Either-Or* sermon, also printed afterwards, in St. Mary's at Oxford. At the periodical meetings of Convocation, and at the annual meetings of the English Church Union, Denison kept pressing for action against the book. He, a founder member, resigned from the English Church Union because it refused to act. The affair was complicated by the public press and the right of everyone to join the argument, from T. H. Huxley downwards. The Canterbury diocesan conference in July 1890 cheered a colonel who supported the proposition that criticism of the Old Testament is incompatible with Christianity. In September 1890 Liddon died, and gave a handle to speakers who without evidence accused *Lux Mundi* of killing him.[1] 'Is the Pusey House', asked Denison, 'the Pusey House still?—or has it not become another house?'[2] 'It remains that the name be given up by the trustees as representing what has become an unreality.' The trustees of Pusey House discussed whether Gore should cease to be principal. As late as October 1891 Bishop Ellicott denounced Gore, with quotations though not with name, in his charge to his diocese.

Gore was defended by all the liberals. But defence by the liberals was often more harmful than helpful to Gore. It renewed the fears that Gore must be equated with Wellhausen or Colenso. Events caused some hitherto silent to speak, and the broad extent of support for Gore slowly became known. Professor Driver preached a sermon in Christ Church on 31 August 1890 in which he declared for the critics; and though one member of the congregation was aghast that this was Pusey's successor and comforted his mind at home by getting down Pusey's commentaries from the shelves,[3] men respected Driver's gentle, cautious, dispassionate scholarship. In 1891 he published the *Introduction to the Literature of the Old Testament*, with Wellhausen's theory but with a tone far removed from that of Wellhausen. Professor Herbert Ryle of Cambridge spoke to the same cause. And his utterance helped Gore less because of his scholarly reputation than because he was the son of one of Gore's strongest opponents, the Bishop of Liverpool. Professor Sanday at Oxford likewise helped because he was calm and moderate and religious. But the best of all defences came from Bishop Edward King of Lincoln. For King was regarded as a Tractarian saint. He

---

[1] e.g. Captain Parker at the meeting of the English Church Union connected with the Hull Church Congress of October 1890. In June 1890 a remarkable Oxford pair to be in harness, Liddon and Jowett, were given honorary degrees by the university of Cambridge. The undergraduates gave Liddon the more enthusiastic reception. Liddon left £1,000 in his will to Pusey House.

[2] G, 90, 2061.   [3] Cf. G, 90, 1418.

was known to be an affectionate disciple of Pusey and to be a conservative in theology, and no evangelical ever loved his Bible more
than King. He urged the church to approach *Lux Mundi* with
sympathy, patience and consideration.[1] At his diocesan conference
of October 1891 he appealed for gentleness with intellectual doubt,
and got cheers. He invited Gore to conduct the retreat for his clergy
in Lincoln cathedral that autumn.

Gore helped his own cause by publishing a new preface to the
tenth edition of *Lux Mundi* (13 August 1890) in which he apologised
if he seemed to suggest Christ's fallibility as a teacher. In 1891 he
gave the Bampton lectures on the Incarnation, explaining what he
meant by the 'self-emptying' of the divine under the conditions of
human life. The Church of England, and other churches, were
fortunate in Gore. It was necessary to the strength of the churches
in England that the high church movement should accept the rights
of critical scholarship. They would only do so if they were led by
theologians in whose faith and practice, as well as theology, they
had confidence. Gore did more than any other single person to
carry the high churchmen into the modern age, and so released new
energies.

By the end of December 1891 the cause was safe. On 16 December
thirty-eight men published a declaration on holy Scripture. They
believed its historical truth and repudiated and abhorred all suggestions of fallibility in the Lord, in respect of his use of the Old
Testament. It was signed by several men who had rendered great
service to the Church of England during the last forty years, partly
high churchmen, partly evangelical: Goulburn, Denison, W. J.
Butler, T. T. Carter, Dean Gregory of St. Paul's cathedral. They
did not carry informed support with them. A liberal like Hort was
pleased at the declaration, because he thought that it would do much
good in the sense not desired by the authors.[2]

Unsettlement of mind continued for some years. The theological
students of Methodism were much unsettled in mind during 1891–
1892.[3] Wesleyan Methodism did not really start to change rapidly
until 1893 when the stalwart Benjamin Gregory was replaced as
editor of the Wesleyan Methodist Magazine. The Primitive Methodists,

---

[1] In a sermon at St. Barnabas, Pimlico, 11 June 1890.
[2] Hort to Westcott, 29 December 1891: *Life of Hort*, ii, 435.
[3] *Memoir of W. F. Moulton*, 220.

though not without opposition, appointed in 1892 A. S. Peake to be tutor at Hartley College, though his critical opinions were already known.[1] In all the evangelical colleges, whether Anglican or nonconformist, the students were divided for many years into those who were conservatives and those who were not. Some Anglican ordinands at Cambridge were dismayed when they studied theology and were reported as asking, 'If this, or even part of it, is true, what are we to believe?'[2] At Cuddesdon, where formerly Gore taught, hardly a sign of unsettlement appeared. Many held to their old beliefs but ceased to regard those who held the new as unworthy of the name of Christian. At the Birmingham Church Congress of 1893 the eccentric monk Father Ignatius Lyne launched an immoderate public assault upon Gore, and at the Exeter Church Congress of 1894 Lyne fiercely assaulted Driver who sat in the seat of Pusey. Some observers believed that Father Ignatius' attack on Gore was even more important than *Lux Mundi* itself in drawing the attention of the average churchman to the problem.[3] Members of the English Church Union made repeated efforts to get the union to condemn Gore. A lay member asserted in 1894 that if the members were allowed a free vote a large majority would vote to condemn Gore. But they never were allowed such a poll. Their president, Viscount Halifax, and a majority of the council were determined that it was not the business of the union to make doctrinal definitions.

The Congregationalists had little difficulty, for several of their leading ministers (Dale, Clifford, Horton, Fairbairn, Archibald Duff) had not concealed their opinions, even though the affair of *Lux Mundi* allowed them to speak more openly; and they had their Liddon in the conservative champion Alfred Cave. The Presbyterians had little difficulty, for their leaders were in close touch with the arguments in Scotland over Robertson Smith. But among Anglicans and nonconformists there remained a gulf between the intellectual leaders and the congregations. Wise leaders saw how a revolutionary like Cheyne caused alarm, and delayed the slow acceptance of the new knowledge. Robertson Nicoll wrote in 1897 that 'the new truths should dawn on the church as gently as the sunlight, and I am not at all sure but that heretics ought to be burnt. I

[1] Willis B. Glover, 211–12. [2] Foakes Jackson, ap. CCR, 1890, 408.
[3] E. A. Knox, *Reminiscences*, 151.

mean the fellows who make a big row and split their churches.'[1] Even Paget, one of the contributors to *Lux Mundi*, afterwards argued that the shock which they caused had done damage and that they should have moved more quietly,[2] and ought not to allow a cheap edition. Scott Holland humorously confessed the sin. The authors should walk in white shirts into Piccadilly with Archdeacon Denison whipping them 'at each corner, and good Tractarians throwing rotten eggs'; but, when they got home, they should decide to publish the cheap edition. If some were unsettled, others found relief in the debate. They were glad not to be troubled further about Balaam's ass or Jonah's whale. Their doctrine of God seemed to them more Christian when the earlier doctrines of Jehovah were seen to be faulty so far as they were partial. They felt more free to worship with mind as well as heart. Nearly all the intelligent young men stood behind Gore, who by the end of 1894 exerted more influence in the Church of England than most of the bishops. That autumn there was wide applause when the crown set its seal of approval by nominating him to be canon of Westminster. When Gore was made bishop in 1901, a fierce protest forced a postponement of the consecration, but the protest was of a few fanatics and could not be compared with the protest of 1869 against Temple.

The opinions of the authors of *Essays and Reviews*, or most of them, became acceptable as well as legal. This was not true either of the Roman Catholic Church, or of many individual nonconformist, and some individual Anglican, congregations.

The difficulty of adjustment was least for the students of text and history. They wrote a new kind of commentary, and at once made all earlier commentaries obsolete, though far more obsolete on the Old Testament than on the New. The difficulty was greater for preachers and teachers. Several of the most famous preachers in England—Liddon, Spurgeon, Joseph Parker of the City Temple— were among the stern opponents of what happened. The parish priest was accustomed to preaching sermons out of the Old Testament. Archdeacon Bather was a country parson and disciple of Maurice. He welcomed *Lux Mundi* with gratitude, but then found difficulty, and even distress, in adjusting his mind and his sermons to the consequences. He carefully read the new commentators, Sanday, H. E. Ryle, Driver and A. F. Kirkpatrick—and by 1893

[1] Darlow, *Nicoll*, 160.   [2] Gore, *Prestige*, 123–4.

was ready to preach five sermons on the Old Testament.[1] But the clergy needed books on the subject of inspiration—that by Sanday (1893) was widely used. The old sermon needed proof-texts, the new sermon could use the text only in its context, and young preachers were in danger of failing to deliver anything from the pulpit because the words which they had to deliver felt less absolute. Old books of sermons became as obviously dated as the commentaries on the New Testament, unless they were sermons (like those of Liddon or Newman) possessing the intangible quality of not dating. Curates found it more difficult to use old printed sermons without substantial rewriting if the sermons were to sound credible and not remote. The churches knew that they had a message for the world but hesitated a little on what the message was or how to express it, and that hesitation was reflected in curates' sermons. Bishop Moorhouse of Manchester, though strong for the Biblical critics, urged his clergy to keep the critical questions out of their sermons. If they wanted to teach their parishioners Biblical criticism, they should do it by lectures and not by sermons.[2] Many said that questions of date or authorship were irrelevant to religion, and the pulpit was no place for such dry learning.

Not all country congregations approved of the new teaching which they received from the pulpit. Critics in one such parish said that the parson did not believe the Bible, or spoke of parsons who tore the Bible to shreds.[3] One lady left the church for the chapel, though she gave the ostensible reason that the vicar was a socialist. In Rochester Professor Cheyne held a canonry and as Cheyne's scholarship about the Old Testament grew more and more un-balanced during the nineties, the citizens of Rochester were not indifferent. There was a moment when the streets of Rochester carried placards about 'the canon's latest blasphemy' and about Jonah being a fable.[4]

The change in the training of clergy can best be seen by setting down examination questions of the fifties and nineties:

About 1855 (Cuddesdon College: the examiners included Liddon):

What did Adam lose at the fall and how far was that which he

[1] G, 1905, 1528. [2] Rickards, *Life of Moorhouse*, 153-4.
[3] *Commonwealth*, 1913, 202.
[4] A. S. Farrar to Sanday, 26 June 1893, Sanday MSS, iii, 248.

lost unrestored in or exceeded by the grace of the Redeemer? Show the extreme importance of determining the exact conditions of the Paradisiac man and the thoughtless levity of treating this and kindred questions as 'speculative' etc.

State the rationalistic theory based on the two names of God (Elohim and Jehovah) used in Genesis, and show that this theory is uncritical.

In 1891 the Cambridge examination for holy orders, though not negative, was silent on criticism, and even by 1901 the examiners demanded no knowledge of the truly controversial parts of the subject. But the theological tripos of 1891 already posed the question in this form: 'State generally the grounds on which modern critics resolve Genesis into its component documents.'

The catalogue of the clerical library in the Lincolnshire archives enables a comparison of shift in balance between what the clergy read in 1840 and in 1898. Just a few withdrawals are common to both ends of the reign—Newman *On Justification*, Maurice's *The Kingdom of Christ*—and whereas they took out the *British Magazine* and the *Tracts for the Times* in 1839 they took out the *Church Quarterly Review* sixty years later. But the differences are remarkable. In 1838–41 far the commonest book to withdraw was a book of systematic theology, or a study of Christian doctrine. In 1897–1901 far the commonest book to withdraw was a commentary on the Bible. Demolishing the verbal inspiration of the Bible had the effect of making its expositors need more equipment for the study of the text. In 1838–41 they hardly ever withdrew a commentary on a book of the Bible (an exception in Tholuck on Romans and on St. Paul), in 1897–1901 they commonly did so, Westcott on St. John or Perowne on the Psalms or Farrar on St. Paul, or Godet's commentaries, or Sanday on Romans. They used the commentaries neither of Lightfoot nor of Ellicott, though they took out Westcott's *Lessons of the Revised Version*; and the tone of the commentaries was in general conservative. The earlier generation read Keble's edition of Hooker, the later withdrew neither Keble nor Hooker; in sermons, the earlier used those of van Mildert and even Launcelot Andrewes, the later more commonly used Liddon. The earlier generation studied rather more church history, especially the history of the Reformation (using

Soames, Blunt, d'Aubigné), where the later generation hardly looked at history; and in church history the later generation had begun to study the history of the Oxford Movement. Hardly anyone at either end of the reign, in this corner of Lincolnshire, took out a book on the philosophy of religion. The later clergy often read the lives of the saints in the collection of Sabine Baring-Gould, a type of reading not represented in the earlier period, and another sign of how the Oxford Movement altered the Church of England.

The Bible became a more difficult book for laymen. Formerly they went to the simple text, now they seemed to need a commentary to understand it. Not a few people were so disturbed by the argument of the early nineties that they ceased to find pleasure or comfort reading their Bibles. Some, said an experienced director of souls,[1] made the discomfort an excuse for giving up the reading. As it was seen no longer as the words of God but as containing the word of God, the exercise seemed to require more activity of mind by the reader. They could no longer know the Bible by knowing only the Bible.

Textbooks changed more slowly. Even Oxford university press republished as late as 1896 a manual for Biblical study which took no notice of the new knowledge.[2] A *Cambridge Companion to the Bible* (1893) was more up-to-date. Even the best schools took time to change their mode of teaching. During the nineties the headmaster of Rugby felt a need to consult the local suffragan bishop on whether he should introduce his sixth form to the commentary on Isaiah by George Adam Smith. The headmaster felt a difficulty because the commentary assumed that the book of Isaiah contained two different prophets.[3] He hesitated before communicating knowledge which might still cause a parent to complain. Gore was asked how to teach the Old Testament to schoolboys and replied, 'You can only be candid, candour is always best.'[4] Sunday school teachers went on teaching the Bible as they were taught to teach it, even in a congregation where the minister was advanced in his knowledge of the Bible.[5] For some years after *Lux Mundi*

---

[1] Edward King, *The Love and Wisdom of God*, 193.
[2] Elliott-Binns, *English Thought*, 190.
[3] E. A. Knox, *Reminiscences*, 174. Even Pusey thought faith was unaffected if there were two prophets in Isaiah; cf. Pusey to Cheyne, Bodleian Library, MSS. Eng.Lett. E.28/18.   [4] Prestige, *Gore*, 71.
[5] Leslie Peake, *A. S. Peake*, 229–36; Willis B. Glover, 136–7.

there was a gap between the Bible of home and children and the Bible of sixth form and university. The passage from the one to the other forced the young man to do what the churches corporately needed to do during the last forty years of the nineteenth century. Yet it was not so easy for the schoolboy of 1910 as for the schoolboy of 1885 to open his eyes at the age of thirteen and realise that 'Darwin' had disproved the Bible.

Though Christianity was a historical religion, it was far from certain that the detailed research of scientific history had any more to do with religion than the researches of the natural scientists. Yet the natural sciences influenced history, and the advance of history changed the Christian picture of Christian origins. To say *the word of God is in the Bible*, instead of *the word of God is the Bible*, was important to the way of presentation, the structure of dogmatic theory, the logical systems in which men framed the understanding of their faith. But it made less difference to religion than might have been expected, for though earlier centuries professed that *the Word of God is the Bible*, they had always acted and lived by the proposition *the Word of God is in the Bible*. Some said—and it was often claimed afterwards—that the more Catholic parts of Christendom met the new knowledge more easily than the Protestant parts, because Catholic minds lived by the Bible-in-the-church, whereas the Bible only was the religion of Protestants. Such a claim might have a justification in logic, but it can find small claim to support from the historical evidence of what happened, for the Church of Rome was the slowest of all the churches in England to adopt the new knowledge into its teaching. And the smallest Protestant group, even when it claimed to live by the Bible only, lived in fact by the Bible-in-the-church.

Scientific history caused one change of outlook, or presentation, of the first importance to the churches. History could not work upon the evidence about Jesus without treating him as a man and assuming that he was a man. The 'quest for the historical Jesus' issued inevitably from scientific history. The human Christ became more real to the world, and especially to the churches, in the later nineteenth century. For the churches he spoke the word of God, revealed the word of God, was the word of God. But always he revealed through his humanity. Though we must not exaggerate the change, for Christian doctrine had always insisted upon the humanity, later Victorian churchmen understood the childhood, the temptations, the agony in the garden of Gethsemane, even the suffering on Calvary, better than generations of their Christian predecessors.

CHAPTER III

DOUBT

THE religious question of the last forty years of the century is the appearance of 'unbelief'. This does not mean that before 1860 all men believed. In the early Victorian age, as in the eighteenth century, lived atheists and agnostics. Most of them were of the working-class, but some of them were eminent minds like John Stuart Mill. The difference after 1860, and especially after 1870, is nevertheless marked. Churchmen worried more. Their presentation of Christianity was affected by the existence of intelligent agnostics. They believed the number of agnostics to be growing. They began to treat agnostics with more respect in general society. And the whole question of belief or unbelief was so common in public discussion as to force the minds of the educated young—more and more numerous after 1870—to find a faith for themselves, and no longer to inherit serenely the faith of their parents. In the vigorous spring of Victorian energy all religions flourished as never before. And since fervent anti-religion was a form of religion, this also advanced, as Roman Catholics or Anglicans or Methodists advanced.

Victorian opinion registered the eighties as the time when this argument was at its most agonising. In the early seventies bishops would warn their people against unbelief, but they still regarded the unbeliever as rare though dangerous. In the nineties all parties were agreed that the argument grew cooler, that unbelief was less aggressive and faith more serene. In 1888 a bishop declared that you found unbelief everywhere, in your club or your drawing-room. You might hear it from the lady next to whom you sat at dinner. You found it lurking in the newspaper, or the novel. You found parents who watched their children saying their prayers at their knee, and wondered what would happen when the child went away to school or university, or asked themselves 'What will my innocent daughters think when they imbibe the poison of infidelity from the first novel they borrow from the circulating library?'[1]

[1] Magee of Peterborough, CCR, 1888, 261.

Why were the eighties worse than the nineties? In 1880 a majority of the electors of Northampton chose Charles Bradlaugh as their member of Parliament. He was an avowed atheist. To take his seat in Parliament he must take an oath upon the faith of a Christian. Therefore his election presented the constitutional question whether in a Christian country an atheist could be a member of the House of Commons. But Bradlaugh was also a radical, and a champion of working-men. The electors of Northampton continued to return him though he was not allowed to take his seat. His championship of the worker was more important to the electors than his lack of faith. It took six years of struggle before Bradlaugh was allowed (1886) to take his seat. Those six years came near to identifying the rights of the atheist with liberty. They also brought the existence of the atheist, and his rights as a citizen, continually before the public mind. Everyone debated Bradlaugh. The subject of atheism was prominent to the minds and conversation of Englishmen.

Bradlaugh was the simplest reason why unbelief was more talked of in the eighties than in the nineties. His conduct could be observed, discussions to which he gave rise could be followed. But other and subtler moods, more intangible, more difficult to value by historical evidence, made the eighties worse for Christianity than the nineties.

What was true of the conflict between science and religion was true of the wider conflict between reason and religion. Christians were adjusting their divinity to new knowledge and new times. This adjustment was slow and painful. In the early sixties a young man like Leslie Stephen thought that he must either believe every word of the Bible or not be a Christian. Even in the early sixties many clergymen did not believe in this stark alternative. During the seventies and eighties new views of the Bible became steadily commoner among Anglicans and nonconformists. But most of them refrained from proclaiming these new opinions loudly. They went quietly and reverently, lest they disturb a faith simpler than their own. As was afterwards said of Fenton Hort, they were like prophets prophesying into their waistcoat pocket. Therefore most Christians looked conservative in divinity during the eighties. Most preachers continued to assume that a real fish swallowed Jonah. Either you believe what the church has always believed, or you are guilty of unbelief—Pusey died in 1882, but the old alternative was still powerful after his death. In the nineties everyone could see that more educated Christians did not believe every word of the Bible and still confessed themselves to be Christians. The choice between faith and reason was no longer so clear.

The atmosphere of the nineties was more mellow. As the scientist achieved his freedom and did not need to be aggressive like Tyndall, the atheist and agnostic achieved their freedom. They ceased to be so impassioned. They went their way, neglecting religion, critical of the churches, but without expressing the fury and ardour which sometimes marked the mid-Victorian agnostic. The later agnostic claimed the respect due to sincerity, and sometimes gave in return the respect due to the sincerity of the religious mind.

Bishop King of Lincoln added a further answer to the question why things grew better for Christians instead of worse. He argued that Oxford philosophy of idealism changed the intellectual background of the age; that philosophers like Mill and Spencer were hostile to Christianity while T. H. Green and the idealists befriended it. Spencer had more than hinted that all mind could be explained in terms of matter. The idealists declared that matter must be explained in terms of mind. Bishop King thought that Green allowed men to believe again in a soul. Whether or not King was right in attributing such consequences to the Oxford idealist school, Herbert Spencer looked a less eminent philosopher in 1900 than he looked in 1870. After Spencer died, some asked that a memorial be placed in Westminster abbey; and the dean was able to doubt that Spencer was not of sufficient eminence as a philosopher to be worthy of this national tribute.

Consider two contrasts: one between the historians Lecky and J. B. Bury, a second in literature between the passionate anti-Christians of the sixties and the mellower anti-Christians of the nineties.

Lecky's *History of the rise and influence of the spirit of Rationalism in Europe* (1865) exercised wide influence partly because its author was an exceptional writer and partly because it was history that perfectly fitted the age of conflict between reason and faith; an account of reason slowly conquering superstition in society, victorious over magic and witchcraft and religious persecution, promoting tolerance and causing dogma to decline. The book was immensely powerful, and to the end of the century and beyond stirred the general reader or the young historian towards a rationalising view of the historical development of rationality in antagonism to religion or at least to some forms of religion. But forty years later the climate of opinion was markedly different. For in 1913 Professor J. B. Bury of Cambridge published a book which in atmosphere is reminiscent of Lecky: *A History of Freedom of Thought*, a little volume in the Home University Library. This volume was received with astonishment. Though it came from an eminent historian, it looked like an anachronism: 'a ghost', said Scott Holland, 'out of the dead ages'. 'We feel as if the last girl in a hobble skirt had suddenly donned a crinoline, and had taken us back into the lost hoops of mid-Victorian days.'[1]

Why an anachronism? Because no one any longer believed in progress in the way in which the mid-Victorians believed it. They no longer believed that churches had always resisted the advance of learning, nor perhaps that the relentless advance of reason could save society. In reading Bury they almost felt that they stepped back into the sixties when the Vatican proclaimed resistance to the modern world, and when Mazzini told the Fathers of the first Vatican Council that *their* dogma was fall and redemption while *our* dogma is God and progress,[2] and when men must still fight for the liberty of their mind.

The second contrast is of literature. We have seen the hatred which the scientist W. K. Clifford threw against Christianity during the seventies. At some deep level of the soul Christianity touched him where it hurt most, and he reacted. As Lecky or Buckle saw reason liberating the race from its prison, so Clifford abandoned Christianity and liberated his soul.

You can find eminent minds with the same kind of hatred during the sixties and seventies. A Fellow of King's College, Cambridge, Bendyshe, was described as 'a raging and devoted atheist at whose talk God trembles on his tottering throne'.[3] The writer best known to that age, and most regretted by Christians, was the son of Earl Russell, Viscount Amberley. He published *An Analysis of Religious Belief* in 1876, with a comparison of the religions of the world. Here again came that bitterness, though in less readable prose, which appeared in Clifford. A more interesting and unusual state of mind appeared in the poet Swinburne. He was not a popular poet to his

[1] *Commonwealth*, 1914, 3.   [2] *Fortn. R.*, 1870, i, 736.
[3] Swinburne, *Letters* 2, 4.

contemporaries, and the anti-Christian passion was known to few. It was evident in his published verse, but its extent only became evident in the modern edition of his letters. Both Amberley and Swinburne were children of religious parents. Earl Russell was a strong latitudinarian in religion. Swinburne started as a high Anglican, and to the end of her life his mother hoped that he might return to the faith of his childhood.

When Swinburne lost faith, he did not just drop it, but moved into a time of hating the Christian religion. The causes of this conversion lie deep in the need of his tormented psyche, in which varieties of sexual licence felt for a time to be a necessity of his very existence. The mental process is still far from clear, despite the six-volume edition of the letters. Part of the feeling resembled the conviction of Clifford (and later, in much more reverent form, of the young G. M. Trevelyan) that Christianity fettered the development of personality and that atheism liberated. But in Swinburne this was far from being the only strand in the conversion. God may be a 'human figment' but in *Atalanta in Calydon* he is *supreme evil* by the way in which he causes men mockingly to suffer. For a period of his life, especially round 1865 and 1866, God, despite his non-existence, was a cruel ruler of the world. This atheism fought God because he was powerful and not because he was a dream. In some of his moods Swinburne wanted to kill God; and killing God was not the same as telling mankind that they had invented him:

> Him would I reach, him smite, him desecrate,
> Pierce the cold lips of God with human breath,
> And mix his immortality with death.
>
> *(Anactoria)*

At first his anti-theism was enmity to a moral ideal opposite. As his mind developed, positive ideals began to affect it. One such ideal came through his friendship for Mazzini and admiration of the Italian republicans. They stood for liberty against the church. His moral ideal stood for liberty against the Christian God. His original sense of liberty, which was little more than licence for himself, was elevated into a cry for the liberty of humanity. Free man from kings and priests and he will rise to be himself. In *Hertha* the soul of humanity is identified not only with God but with liberty. Freedom is the holiest name of the soul.

In 1869 he tried to help the anti-Catholics of Italy in their fight
against the papacy, by composing a *Hymn of Man*: as he called it in
idea, a *Te Hominem Laudamus*, 'to sing the human triumph over
"things"—the opposing forces of life and nature—and over the God
of his own creation, till he attains truth, self-sufficience and
freedom'.[1]

In Swinburne is manifest a reason for anti-Christianity which is
not a reason of the head. He, and men like him, felt Christianity
to be a fetter upon human life.

> It was for this, that men should make
>   Thy name a fetter on men's necks,
> Poor men's made poorer for thy sake,
>   And women's withered out of sex?
> It was for this, that slaves should be,
>   Thy word was passed to set men free?[2]

Rather as men of the Renaissance turned away from the medieval
ideal of flight from the world, some mid-Victorians revelled in
humanity and its possibility in this world, and turned away from
Christianity as pallid or thin—

> Thou hast conquered, O pale Galilean,
> The world has grown grey from thy breath
>   (*Hymn to Proserpine*)

In this mood religion felt incompatible with a gay apprehension of
the world.

Swinburne's *Poems and Ballads*, which appeared in 1866, suffered
savage criticism as immoral from a non-Christian moralist like John
Morley. And yet it fitted the mood, not of the time, but of some
people in that time. They wanted to break through the rigorous
conventions of the Victorian middle-class, to throw off restraints
upon gaiety, to lose the sense of guilt in romantic passion, and
Swinburne led them in lyrical melodies.

Perhaps some of this was a sensitive and aesthetic expression of
the reaction against 'puritanism' which was so evident in the later
Victorian age. Macaulay held up puritanism to unjust scorn in his
history. The younger generation wanted to relax the restraints
of thier elders about theatres, dancing, Sunday and marriage.

[1] Swinburne, *Letters*, 2, 37.
[2] *Before a Crucifix*, *Poetical Works*, ii (1925), 147.

Even a man of mild religion like Matthew Arnold considered that the young thought of the religious world as 'sombre' or 'narrow'.[1]

Swinburne lived into the twentieth century, and mellowed in his attitude to Christianity. There were special reasons for his mellowness, especially in that he passed under the partial care of Watts Dunton. At the end he gave instruction to Watts Dunton that he was not to have a Christian service at his funeral. And yet there were sides of Swinburne which did not agree with this hatred of Christian fetters. He loved little children, thought the saying of Jesus about children to be the most divine of all divine words and thoughts, and admired Matthew Arnold's attempt at a rational Christianity in *Literature and Dogma*. He read the *Guardian* regularly. One of the fairest hymns of John Mason Neale, *Jerusalem my happy home* (published 1865), aroused his affection because it understood the mingling of sweetness with bitter gall. His approach to nature was religious. Though Swinburne was anti-Christian, he cannot be said to be anti-religious. Probably he was more afraid of a father-god than of theism, or identified theism with fatherhood. He did not reject the possibility of survival after death.[2] In his earlier and more tragic and more poetic phase he allowed Benjamin Jowett to help him at Balliol College and in Scotland. Nothing in Jowett's life was more compassionate than his pity and aid towards Swinburne.

The changing face of English (and European) religion is shown by the partial acceptance of Swinburne by religious men, before the end of the century, on the ground that great art cannot corrupt. In 1906 *Atalanta in Calydon* was staged at the Crystal Palace, with the approval of a ladies' church newspaper.[3] The Victorians did not know of the excess and aberration in Swinburne's earlier behaviour. But anyone could see the trend of his poetry to be anti-theistic, and to glorify man in a way more appropriate to an advocate of progress than a believer in original sin. Victorian churchmen disapproved of Swinburne. And yet beauty was a gift of God, and a man whose verse lifted men up to beauty might be said in some unknown manner to be lifting them towards God even when the verse assailed God. So at least argued a few men and women, touched by the doctrine of art for art's sake. The doctrine appeared in some of

---

[1] Cf. M. Arnold, *Letters*, ed. Russell, ii, 220; a letter of 25 March 1881.
[2] *Letters*, 3, 14; 4, 201; 6, 40 and 237.   [3] G, 06, 1003.

Swinburne's obituaries, and caused a protest to be delivered against
the obituaries in the pulpit of Canterbury cathedral.

Something was here of Hellenism; either of the love of ancient
Greece, as in Swinburne; or of the idealising of the Renaissance, as
in John Addington Symonds or Walter Pater.

All forms of orthodoxy were associated with an austere view of
self-restraint. It would be too Catholic to call this spirit ascetic, and
too Calvinist to call it puritan, but it believed with monk or puritan
that goodness was to be found through the discipline of the self.
The belief was such a truism that no one could subvert it. It was
associated with a belief in original sin. But as orthodoxy became
less rigid, the moral purpose of man began to be seen less in the
restraint than in the development of the self. At Oxford the new
philosophers after T. H. Green saw ethical theory in terms of self-
development. But the divide was not in theory, for Christianity
was agreed on the need for self-fulfilment, and all men agreed that
self-restraint was indispensable to self-fulfilment. And yet to some
men the restraints associated with religion made religion look sombre.

Swinburne was the most brilliant among a group who wanted to
throw off Christianity in some part because they wanted to throw
off Christian moral standards or the feelings of guilt which these
standards generated in their souls. Such men were sometimes the
children of religious parents. George Eliot was different in kind as a
non-Christian. She had no desire whatever to cast off moral standards. In moral endeavour she was as earnest as any Christian, even
(in some respects) as puritan as any puritan. Though she lived for
some years with a man who was not her legal husband, the act was
not felt to be an aggressive act of self-emancipation. For the serious
non-Christians—George Eliot, John Morley, Leslie Stephen and
the like—the problem was morality. The morals of their society
were based upon religion; or, if they challenged, as most of them
did, that there was a connexion of cause and effect between the
religion and the morality, at least it might be said that in the public
mind morality was associated in idea with religion. If the religion
declined, as they hoped, the decline brought danger that the public
morality would decline, which they did not hope. They needed to
find for themselves, and to make plain to their public, why the fall
of religion would not lead to the fall of moral standards. The

natural basis of ethics became the most important question of the philosophic schools, and every eminent philosopher at Oxford or Cambridge attempted it. Leslie Stephen, though no professional philosopher, attempted it with a sense of responsibility as a leading agnostic. And George Eliot attempted it in novels.

In the social context of the later Victorian age, the difficulty of preaching moral life without religion was great. It was the achievement of George Eliot that she succeeded in clothing the platitudes so that hope and despair could be felt in personality. She articulated the vague feelings of the age. Some treated her books with a reverence never before given to a novel. 'She is the first great *godless* writer of fiction that has appeared in England.'[1] Previous novelists, sitting lightly or seriously to religion, gave the moral standards, without which no serious novel could exist, an eternal reference, and saw life through a light which was Christian.

Most Victorians found substitutes for religious morality nebulous or unintelligible, so far as they were abstract and theoretical. But the replacement of *serve God* by *serve society* was intelligible to everyone. And yet a sort of religious attitude survived in the ethical language even of those who, like George Eliot, ceased consciously to give their moral judgments a religious reference. The novels contained high moral aspiration and a devotion which was transferred from God to man without always losing the phrases specially appropriate to God. Men and women went to offer up their sufferings, and yet the 'offering' ceased to be a gift to a person.

Some Victorian readers found the moral earnestness of George Eliot, when they perceived its full relation, repugnant or pallid; lacking joy and lacking humility. But the fact which her novels represent is of the first importance in the history of English society. Morality and religion were seen to be not necessarily inseparable. The perception was not true of most of Victorian society. At the end of the century Henry Sidgwick wrote that for most men, in the foreseeable future, religion and morality would always be linked. But a growing number of intellectuals began to imagine the possibility of morality without religion. One of the sub-plots of Mrs. Humphry Ward's novel *Robert Elsmere* is the story of how an ex-vicar, who ceased to call himself Christian, and a devout wife whose faith was unshaken, suffered in their marriage for a time but

---

[1] Mallock, 158.

at last came through to trust in each other again, by divorcing their moral unity from their religious opinions. The wife, wrote Mrs. Ward when the conflict was over (iii, 322), had 'undergone that dissociation of the moral judgment from a special series of religious formulae which is the crucial, the epoch-making fact of our day'.

Some people said, discard religion and morality remains untouched. That was the view of a very small minority. To most people the old truth that unbelief causes immorality appeared as obvious as ever; and the careers of a Swinburne or a George Eliot did nothing to dispel their conviction. Sceptical old Mark Pattison thought that its partial truth could not be denied. Yet when preachers attacked unbelief or doubt because it tended towards a lower standard of behaviour, they sometimes came under criticism. Bishop Ellicott of Gloucester and Bristol, as early as 1864, allowed in a charge to his diocese that some doubt was 'honest', but believed that three-quarters of the doubt was immoral or worldly or corrupt. He was blamed for 'railing' at the sinner even by some high churchmen.[1] On 6 March 1881 John Wordsworth delivered the first of his Bampton lectures at Oxford and chastised the unorthodox, examining the moral causes of unbelief; and afterwards found himself the object of a critical pamphlet called *Unbelief and Sin*, by Mrs. Humphry Ward, who sat in his audience.[2]

At Cambridge Henry Sidgwick was the living disproof of the doctrine that unbelief always caused sin. Everyone found him in conduct Christian; some thought him a sort of agnostic saint. And Sidgwick troubled himself over the relation of unbelief and sin. He was sure that as a matter of theory unbelief need not cause a lowering of moral standards, at least as it appeared in an individual. He was also sure that in a land where religion and morality were inseparable, the decline of the one was certain to lead to the decline of the other. He would never attack religion lest he injure the society in which he lived. It even became a delicate question of conscience for him how far it could be right to speak out; he must say what he thought if he were asked, and yet he must not trample upon the scruples of others.

As early as 1877 the *Nineteenth Century* published a symposium

---

[1] Ellicott, *Charge*, 1864, 62ff.; G, 64, 984.
[2] Trevelyan, *Mrs. Humphry Ward*, 33; Mrs. Ward, *A Writer's Recollections*, 167-8.

entitled *The Influence on morality of a decline in religious belief.* The
contributors ranged from Huxley to Dean Church of St. Paul's.
But the general effect of the symposium, from ultramontane to
positivist, was agreement with Sidgwick that religion was powerful
in morality and that a decline of religion would mean a decline in
standards of behaviour; and that while this truth did not invariably
apply in individuals, it applied in society. James Martineau contributed a strong plea for the moral sense as wholly independent of
religion, but even he declared that philosophy must pass into worship
if it was to become powerful. Only W. K. Clifford refused to admit
the connexion. If society discarded religion, it discarded 'a source of
refined and elevated pleasure to those who can hold it',[1] but left
its morality untouched. The symposium agreed that some atheists
were good men. But these good atheists had been educated in a
Christian society and perhaps as Christians. We cannot judge the
moral impact of atheism only from such individuals. The symposium also agreed that society could not continue to pretend that
falsehood was true merely because the falsehood raised moral
standards. Some critics of the symposium challenged the axiom that
religious belief was declining. More men, it was admitted, confessed unbelief. But fifty years before it had been a totem belief, a
habit. The change, some argued, was not a decline in religious
belief but a disclosure of the true facts.

Some religious men consoled themselves. Perhaps the agnostics
were in God's providence. Perhaps they overstressed, even absurdly
overstressed, the tendency of science to make for materialism. Perhaps they exaggerated the influence of matter in the realm of conscience and of spirit, in order that the inevitable failure might show
mind to be the source of nature and not nature the source of mind.
Men were led to a new knowledge of the world and of themselves;
and such an advance must be accompanied by one-sided exaggeration of the gain thus made. Perhaps God was withdrawing himself
a little from mankind so as to help them grow out of more primitive
and anthropomorphic ideas about him. Was God blinding men to
himself that they might find him the more truly? 'There is a
scepticism', wrote R. H. Hutton, 'which is of God's making, in
order that we may see how many of the highest springs of human

---

[1] *Nineteenth Century,* 1877, 356.

life are founded in trust.' And if they were disciples of Frederick Denison Maurice, as were so many of those whose minds grappled with the agnosticism of the later Victorian age, they asserted that God was revealed not only in the Bible but in all the experience of the secular world, even when that experience looked for a moment hostile to God. There were men in whom, and circumstances where, denial of God was more religious than an easy faith.[1]

Richard Holt Hutton (1826–97) was the son of a Unitarian minister and himself trained for the Unitarian ministry but never became a preacher. Becoming no longer at home among his people he came under the influence of F. W. Robertson and Frederick Denison Maurice, and so passed into the Church of England. Maurice showed him that a man might be an Anglican without holding the doctrines of everlasting punishment or vicarious atonement. In 1861 Meredith Townsend bought the *Spectator* and made Hutton joint editor and co-proprietor. Hutton turned the *Spectator* (1861–97) into the most revealing guide to the progress of the English mind. The paper became important to the theologians. The *Spectator* was never more influential among educated men than when Hutton edited it. He had a fount of sympathy which enabled him to penetrate to the best in the religious outlook of men with whom he disagreed. He was a modern liberal Anglican who loved and respected Newman; a Maurician able to seize upon the main lines of Maurice's thought, and present them without the obscurity (though sometimes without the profundity) of his master. He who wants to understand Maurice does well to read Hutton. The power of Victorian churches, and the concern of educated Victorians with the fundamental questions of human life, is not illustrated better than by the wide influence of Hutton's *Spectator*. Its enemies said that it was addressed to 'a public sheltered in leafy rectories and in the snug villas of rich nonconformists from the headlong decisions and rowdy activity of the world'. That is only a harsh way of stating a well-merited compliment. The *Spectator* had nothing cheap or catch-penny. It concerned itself with truth, and tried to set each view, political or literary or religious, in a context above the moment. It was said that Hutton did for Victorian journalism what Gladstone did for Victorian politics.[2]

---

[1] Hutton, *Aspects*, 14–15, 314.
[2] Hogben, 39, 47; *Saturday Review*, lxxxiv, 1897, 306.

Hutton stood for the rightful place of science and criticism in helping man to apprehend God as spirit. He was a liberal with no desire to shock but, on the contrary, every desire to conserve. The world was sacramental and he was incapable of believing it to be nothing but the product of chance and matter. He was a liberal keenly conscious of the peril that liberals would chip away the Christian gospel until it was no longer Christian, and reserved his rare severities for men like Matthew Arnold. His mind was profoundly religious and at the same time open. He was sure that Christianity could no longer be based on the evidence of miracle, and yet that the irruption of God into the world was miraculous.

Hutton's mind is a noble illustration of a new Christian attitude towards Victorian unbelief. It was sympathetic because it knew what it was about. No educated Christian could fail to feel the disruption, caused by new knowledge, to the faith of his childhood. Such men understood doubt because they experienced it within their own faith. The old-fashioned denunciation of doubt began to look ever more old-fashioned. To call doubts 'emanations from hell' did not help in the environment of 1884; nor would a Hutton have agreed that it was always true. When Dr. Pusey's *Spiritual Letters* were published in 1899, they showed all the holy man's reverence for the poor, simplicity of heart and life, and perseverance in prayer. But the advice to souls of another generation astonished readers, because it assumed so whole-heartedly that unbelief was always due to sin and recommended men even to 'extirpate curiosity'.

Hutton and his like reproached the agnostics. Sometimes they diagnosed the cause of agnosticism as a failure of nerve. Minds, it was said, would no longer engage truth with passion. They confined themselves to their corner of knowledge, and then rested anxiously or cynically, in a few watery axioms. Life was becoming exciting enough, and they had no time left over to be other than weary about their higher interests. The best minds were concerned in scholarship or science or history, and found in these disciplines the satisfaction which their predecessors found in metaphysics. Hutton was inclined to blame Matthew Arnold for the attitude of his lament that he could neither believe with the Carthusians nor rejoice with the (alleged) leaders of western progress:

> Wandering between two worlds, one dead,
> The other powerless to be born,
> With nowhere yet to rest my head,
> Like these, on earth I wait forlorn.

Schlegel once asked the poet Thomas Moore what would happen if a man conscientiously published a book expressing unbelief. Moore replied, 'As to the man I don't know; but I know how the man would be received, and I should not like to be in his place.' The conversation was recalled and contrasted[1] with the social situation of the mid-Victorian age. The word *atheist*, it was true, was not respectable. It had a ring of revolution and of immorality. Men avoided calling themselves by so suspect a name. At the beginning of the twentieth century G. K. Chesterton said that it was not quite respectable to be an atheist. But men could call themselves agnostics, or even non-theists, perhaps anti-theists, without suffering some disadvantage. In 1869 was founded *The Metaphysical Society*, a group to discuss problems of philosophy and ethics. It included a formidable agnostic in Huxley, and a formidable Roman Catholic in W. G. Ward, and equally acute though less argumentative minds like Henry Sidgwick or James Martineau or Gladstone; not to say the unusual juxtaposition of Archbishop Manning and Archbishop Thomson of York.[2] Even in the seventies some were surprised that these men did not need to carry their intellectual disagreements over into their social communications. The Society was thought to be a rare example of such tolerance, and not everyone believed it right thus to sit down at a table with the most eminent sceptics of the day.

Another mark of a changing world was the difference in obituaries of non-Christians. The *Guardian* was the most intelligent weekly among the churches. It began to write fair and charitable and appreciative notices of agnostics; not only of a Darwin, which was to be expected, nor of a Henry Sidgwick which might almost have been expected, but of hammers of the churches like John Stuart Mill or Leslie Stephen. Such mutual tolerance was likely only in the world of scholarship, as in the Metaphysical Society and at the universities, or in the world of intelligent Londoners. The habit did

[1] CCR, 1877, 50.
[2] Picture of *Metaphysical Society*, by R. H. Hutton in *Nineteenth Century*, August 1885, 177–96; A. W. Brown, *The Metaphysical Society*, 1947. The society dissolved itself in 1880.

not prevail in the drawing-rooms of Herefordshire or the parlours of Lancashire. And yet the change was astonishing. Bishop King of Lincoln, most devout of the heirs of Newman and Pusey at the end of the century, a strong conservative, habitually referred to Thomas Hill Green in language of the highest praise. Green's view of the New Testament, gathered from Tübingen, was abhorrent to King's mind. But King could see that this hardly Christian philosopher perceived something of the first importance to the churches. Praise of such a man by an eminent Tractarian would not have been possible forty or even thirty years before.

Another mark is the admiration which some devout men (though by no means all) showed for some undevout authors. Robertson Nicoll, who was a stout nonconformist, greatly admired the novels of George Gissing.[1] George Eliot as a novelist commanded the affection and respect of many who abhorred her moral and religious principles. They admired these writers as in former ages they would have admired a good craftsman, whether or not he was religious.

Wherever the memory of Frederick Denison Maurice was powerful, the disciple was willing to learn from the agnostics. According to Maurician doctrine all men are children of God by virtue of their humanity. All have apprehended little fragments of so great a truth, and seek to express what they have seen among the shadows. Therefore we must listen to the word of God even from him who tells us that there is no God, to see what side of the truth he has been able to apprehend. Many of the Anglican and nonconformist thinkers who came towards the agnostics with sympathy were intellectual sons of Maurice. And Dean Stanley, though in a different context, exercised something of the same ministry. We have seen how he cherished links between Christianity and some of the leading scientists. So we find him at work among the agnostics; presenting Christianity in such a way as to meet their difficulty; rendering himself liable to the charge that the Christianity which he presented was no longer Christianity; ever going out to meet them with affection; ever eager to emphasise all the non-ecclesiastical elements in Christianity, and to undervalue the Christianity of order and tradition. Annie Besant, on her way towards being a notorious atheist, wanted pastoral ministry for her dying mother. Dean Stanley came to her bedside and gave it, and

---

[1] *Life of Robertson Nicoll*, 99.

remained in the books of Mrs. Besant as a shining exception among a class of men whom she saw as her enemies.

Ought an agnostic to be encouraged to go to church? The question was argued in 1882.[1] The answer was agreed. Of course he should. We all confess our ignorance in so high a mystery. One orthodox writer imagined an Anglican clergyman saying, 'Come then, brother agnostic, thy agnosticism spreads . . . over a wider field than mine; or maybe thy self-consciousness has magnified, or distorted it; yet worship with me, and thou wilt be doing thy duty, not only to thy neighbour, but to thy God, who knows thee well, little as thou knowest, or anyone knows, of him. Thy knowledge will grow of thy reverence, and thy reverence will grow with thy knowledge. Thou art not far from the kingdom of God.'

In all ages growing minds have moved away from or into religion as they grew. In the twenties and thirties Blanco White was a Roman Catholic who became an Anglican and then a Unitarian. In the sixties and seventies we can observe this sort of career more frequently than in the past. Napoleon said that everyone ought to continue in the religion of his upbringing, and the great majority of English Christians continued to profess the faith, and attend the denomination, of their childhood. But we observe more movement than formerly. Bagehot said, 'A man is not bound to be of the same religion as his grandmother, though if he has a grandmother Lois, it may be as well that he should be.'[2] Thomas Arnold, son of the headmaster, was an Anglican who became a doubter and then a Roman Catholic and then an Anglican and finally a Roman Catholic. Such a career is not so unique as it would have been a short time before. Mrs. Annie Besant had psychological reasons for throwing off Anglicanism and was not afraid of change. She became a disciple of the Tractarian Liddon, then of the broad church Anglican Stopford Brooke, then of Voysey the Unitarian, then of Bradlaugh the atheist, and finally of Madame Blavatsky the theosophist. William Edward Addis was a Presbyterian, then a Roman Catholic priest, then a Presbyterian minister, then a professor at a Unitarian College, and finally an Anglican incumbent. Such voyages are evidence of the intellectual and religious unsettlement of the mid-Victorian age.

Nothing is more illuminating than to follow the course of one

---

[1] *Nineteenth Century*, January 1882, 73–77, L. Greg; G, 82, 68.
[2] Darlow, *Life of W. R. Nicoll*, 374.

distinguished and sensitive mind: Beatrice Potter, who after marriage became Beatrice Webb. The evidence is available because she had a habit of long and anxious introspection, was discriminating and articulate, and recorded her meditation in her diary, which began in 1873 at the age of fifteen.[1] Her father was a Unitarian and her family attended no particular church; and yet her father regularly attended parish churches and received communion, sampling famous preachers every Sunday when in London. All important literature was so welcome in that household, that the girls could freely read Rousseau or Augustine, Comte or Renan. Beatrice Potter was determined to find a faith for herself. 'It is no sin to doubt', she wrote in her diary when she was sixteen, 'but it is a sin, after you have doubted, not to find out to the best of your capability why you doubt. . . . I must make a faith for myself, and I must work, work, until I have.' Soon her extraordinary moral earnestness perceived the help that orthodox religion might be to her in living, and for a short time she decided it a pity that she was not brought up to believe doubt a crime. At a boarding school in Bournemouth she was confirmed and became a communicant, though she felt repulsion from the doctrine of atonement ('Probably I completely misunderstand it'). At eighteen the London season swept away her orthodox Christianity. She still thought it beautiful, but felt it as a chain to her mind. An elementary knowledge of eastern religions helped this sense of emancipation. She could not believe in scientific materialism, but ceased to believe that Christianity was the only alternative. A friendship with Herbert Spencer caused her to subscribe for a few years to what was then known as the Religion of Science, which fitted her moral and unpoetic soul, with its faith in progress and in man. The *Meditations* of Marcus Aurelius replaced *The Imitation of Christ* as her book of devotional reading. In 1879 she was reading all Comte, and Buckle about the same time. Six years later she threw overboard the Religion of Science. 'It is impossible for a woman to live in agnosticism', and the experience of her mother's death in 1882 confirmed her religious quest as authentic. She did not return to Christianity as she understood Christianity. She returned to religion. 'Religion is love; in no case is it logic.' In the strain of finding herself, she wrote afterwards, 'it

---

[1] MS. diary at the Library of the London School of Economics: summarised in *My Apprenticeship*.

was the habit of prayer which enabled me to survive, and to emerge relatively sound in body and sane in mind'.

Tennyson was unusual among the minds in difficulty because the doubt came to him as he contemplated the vastness of the universe, the rolling forces of the centuries, little men living their brief day, 'insects of an hour'. This was not usual among the Victorians, because they seldom cared much about mere physical bulk or an infinity of material space or time, except in so far as it raised the problem of meaning and purpose. Tennyson succeeded in battling through to retain his sense of design, but he never ceased to stumble until the final act of faith in *Crossing the Bar*. This perpetual stumbling contributed to his enormous influence among the later Victorians, whose minds themselves faltered, and who were helped more by these hesitant doubting acts of faith than by any amount of assurance or clarity of mind. So it was with Browning's verse. Both the nature of the late Victorian hesitation, and its reverence before a perhaps divine mystery, is illustrated by the religious power of these poets. When Matthew Arnold attempted to strip the mystery and restate a modern Christianity in a series of prose volumes, few Victorian churchmen were attracted towards his proposals, and the books were not influential as theology, for they looked only like a stage on the road to agnosticism and there seemed little reason to stop half-way. But Tennyson and Browning reached upwards in a perplexity and yet a reverence before the greatness which they could not define.

Many laymen of the churches were the educated men of England. They accepted Darwin, and learnt a smattering of knowledge about eastern religions, and ceased to believe that Moses wrote the book of Genesis. Therefore the attitude of the men in the pews slowly altered.

What the man in the pew thought within is a subject on which the historian finds it difficult to get reliable evidence. An educated layman in 1904 accused the clergy of living in a dream, and said roundly that the number of laymen of his generation who sincerely believed in 'a large proportion' of the doctrine was not very great and was decreasing.[1] But, again, much depended on the circle and

[1] Sir M. E. Grant Duff at the annual meeting of the Churchmen's Union for the advancement of liberal religious thought, G, 04, 1093.

v.c.–5 *a*

the society in which a man moved. Well into the twentieth century speakers at church meetings who asserted conservative views of the first Biblical story received applause from many laymen and lay-women. Those who went to church meetings were not in all respects typical of those who sat in the pews. But probably in this they were representative. The ordinary worshipper was slow to adapt his mind to Biblical criticism. And a son of the parsonage, Cyril Alington, was at school at Marlborough College which he left in 1891. In retrospect he declared that in the later Victorian age religion was so 'unruffled' that it was taken for granted. No one at school discussed religion. No one objected to compulsory chapel. There was a sixth form atheist, but 'his ministrations were decidedly half-hearted'.[1] At Harrow in 1892–3 George Trevelyan was the sixth form agnostic and felt himself to be a solitary.

But an occasional layman was introspective and wrote down his thoughts. About the turn of the century one began to keep a diary of his reflexions after going to church. He published parts of this in 1904, without naming author, under the title *The Diary of a Church-goer*. The author proved later to be L. H. Courtney, formerly a distinguished member of Parliament, later Lord Courtney of Penwith. A weekly churchgoer in Chelsea who was an intimate of John Morley could not be a typical man in the pew. But his diary was widely read, and men spoke of it with respect, and were some-times glad that the Church of England could still house so unorthodox and yet so reverent an enquirer.

He was vexed that some preachers on the Old Testament needed to defend dubious characters, like the morality of Jacob in his deceit. He knew clergymen who assumed that Genesis was un-historical and that it did not matter to religion. This was not his usual experience of clergymen. He did not like some passages which he was supposed to say or sing—the cursing psalms, the creeds; and if the clergyman had the Athanasian creed he sat down. He took a very human doctrine of the Christ, though all the time hesitant and puzzled and undefined. And being thus unorthodox, able only to admit fragments of the creeds, discarding some prayers as false, he asked himself whether his churchgoing was a mockery and a sin. 'We go to church and we enter into an atmosphere of calm. The distilled wisdom of the ages is about us. The oldest narrations of

---

[1] Alington, *A Dean's Apology*, 24, 27.

human history are read in our hearing. . . . The sense that we are at
one with the singers of countless generations is an uplifting. Paul's
exhortations stimulate our courage. In the teaching and the passion
of the gospels we follow the way of perfect life which leads to
victory over death. . . . So I remain a churchgoer, though it may
be that my proper place is in the outermost court of the Gentiles.'
It was a very human view of churchgoing. But he went, and week
by week. Curiously he was more severe on the clergy than on himself. As he attended services 'without visible protest', had he any
right, he wondered, to criticise clergymen who conducted services,
yet felt or believed as he? Yet he did criticise them—unless they
could believe the reality and truth of what he called 'the central acts
of worship'. He seems however to have met few such clergymen.
The majority of those under whom he sat were too conservative for
his taste.

Other evidence shows that the wider, or sometimes vaguer,
opinions of the laity sometimes surprised clergymen. A group of
ladies went to be instructed in divinity and astonished Archbishop
Benson of Canterbury when he discovered that they doubted
whether St. John wrote the fourth gospel, doubted how much we
could know of the life of Jesus, and did not accept the doctrine of
the personality of the Holy Spirit.[1]

The churches therefore faced the question what limits they would
place upon the teaching of their authorised ministers. The layman
in his pew was allowed wide opinions, and however agnostic in his
mind, if he could make Christian worship meaningful to his soul,
who should blame him? But the priest or pastor in his pulpit stood
under authority. He was a man entrusted with a message and must
declare what he was commissioned to declare. The educated layman
might cheerfully think that the story of Jonah and the whale was a
legend. But the clergy also were educated. It was inevitable that some
of them thought that the story of Jonah and the whale was a legend.
The question now arose, whether a priest and pastor was entitled
to express such an opinion when he was speaking in the name of
the Christian church. And if the answer were reached, as we have
seen that it was reached, that he was so entitled, what other departure
from received tradition might be lawful and honest? If the churches

---

[1] *Life of Benson*, ii, 299; Elliott-Binns, *English Thought*, 363.

refused to permit their ministers to speak their private minds, they raised a barrier between educated clergy and educated laity, deterred educated men from seeking to be priests or pastors, prevented the new knowledge from influencing the churches, made sermons distant from the interest of men's minds, and conducted religion towards a corner of the world. But they could not permit their ministers to speak their private minds with absolute freedom, for they must be sure that Christianity was being taught and not some substitute for Christianity. They must not lay themselves open to the mocking charge which Disraeli is said to have addressed to Arthur Stanley, who told him that the Athanasian creed should be omitted from the Prayer Book—'Mr. Dean, no dogmas, no deans.'[1]

The layman of the Church of England was not committed to any particular doctrine except that he must be able to make the words of the liturgy real to his mind and conscience. The clergyman of the Church of England solemnly undertook to teach in accordance with the thirty-nine articles of religion and the Book of Common Prayer. If he could be proved to have taught the contrary, he could be suspended or removed by the proper court.

Ever since Newman's *Tract XC* the nature of subscription had been discussed. Arthur Stanley wrote a powerful pamphlet in favour of relaxing the terms. It was alleged in the House of Commons (9 June 1863) that bishops already made a point of allowing candidates to make their subscription as general conformity and not as detailed phrases.[2] 'Press these subscriptions in their rigid and literal sense', said Stanley, 'and . . . there is not one clergyman in the church who can venture to cast a stone at another—they must all go out, from the greatest to the least, from the archbishop in his palace at Lambeth to the humblest curate in the wilds of Cumberland.' Moreover the forms of subscription were complex and narrow. 'I do willingly and from my heart subscribe to' and acknowledge 'all and every the articles' 'to be agreeable to the word of God'.

Not without uneasiness—for fears were expressed that if the terms of subscription were relaxed, the church would find clergymen teaching that Genesis was a myth—a royal commission was appointed early in 1864 to consider the terms of subscription. The convincing argument was the predicament not of divines like the

---

[1] *Memoir of Lord Tennyson* ii, 232.   [2] Buxton, Hansard, clxxi, 580.

authors of *Essays and Reviews*, but of the ordinary parish clergyman who must read the burial service, 'in sure and certain hope of eternal life', over persons for whom he might have no such hope. The clerical subscription act of 1865 passed with extraordinary ease. The royal commission was almost unanimous. In a strong body only Keble's squire Sir William Heathcote refused to sign the report. Nearly everyone welcomed its recommendations. 'I assent to the thirty-nine articles of religion, and to the Book of Common Prayer . . . I believe the doctrine . . . as therein set forth, to be agreeable to the Word of God.'

Some people held that the new form bound the consciences of the clergy as strictly as the old. Others, including some members of the commission, believed and afterwards claimed that the assent was now general instead of particular.

The change was a relief to consciences. It enabled some scrupulous persons, who could not have taken orders under the old system, to take orders under the new. There was a difference between the conscientious attitude and the legal attitude. Few clergymen, whatever they taught, were in danger of prosecution because their sermons or books contradicted the articles of religion. For them it was a question of conscience. If they took a severe view of their general assent, posterity does not learn the fact; for the historian seldom learns of him whose mind doubted whether to be ordained, and only learns of him who was ordained and afterwards doubted. If they took a broad view of their duty, they sometimes claimed publicly that this was justified, in order that their example might help others who were troubled in mind. Arthur Stanley put he widest possible interpretation on the clerical subscription act. The justification for this broad view lay less in the act than in certain legal decisions; especially the judgment over *Essays and Reviews*. Perplexed men, who wondered about the question of good faith— like one lay schoolmaster of whom we hear—were referred to the judgment in the case of *Essays and Reviews*.[1]

Authorities, and among them the lawyers, could not take so general a view of the assent under the new act. Subscription still committed the subscriber to all, and all included the parts. The words must be interpreted very precisely and therefore tolerantly. The judicial committee was accused by Bishop Gray and others of

[1] See G, 97, 204, 275.

being so tolerant that anyone could teach anything he liked within the Church of England. But the behaviour of the judicial committee did not correspond to this accusation. In 1862, before the act was passed, it removed from office on a charge of heresy in his published sermons, Mr. Heath, vicar of Brading in the Isle of Wight. In 1871, after the act, it removed from office on a charge of heresy in his book *The Sling and the Stone*, the vicar of Healaugh near Tadcaster, Charles Voysey. He was convicted of denying that Christ was a sacrifice; of denying original sin; of asserting that justification by faith is contrary to the teaching of Christ; and of holding large passages of the New Testament to be spurious, not on grounds of critical enquiry but merely because they did not commend themselves to his taste.

It was clear that not everyone could teach what he liked within the Church of England. But henceforth it was for the most part left to the conscience of the individual. If he could assent to the articles in a general sense, he was usually permitted to assent.

Another security for traditional doctrine remained; a more important safeguard than the courts. The bishop had the duty of satisfying himself that the ordinand, or clergyman entering his diocese, was sound in the faith.

This duty was performed variously according to the bishop. Over the ordinand or the curate the bishop held an absolute veto. Over the incumbent he must respect the rights of the patron who presented a man to a living. Bishop Phillpotts had not been upheld in the courts when he challenged the orthodoxy of Gorham. But from time to time bishops refused to accept presentees because they were sure that the candidate could not rightly receive authority to teach on behalf of the church. In 1893, for example, Bishop Stubbs of Oxford refused to accept the nominee of a patron to the benefice of Steeple Claydon because he was certain that his duty as bishop compelled him to refuse. Gore, when he became Bishop of Worcester, demanded and at last secured the resignation of a clergyman whose opinions he believed to be incompatible with the office of an incumbent in the Church of England.

The bishops were seldom confronted with the difficulty over ordained men, partly because the clergy were conscientious and resigned if they doubted themselves, and partly because the broad church party was slow in growth, at least until after *Lux Mundi*. In

London and in the universities there were broad churchmen headed by Dean Stanley. In the country dioceses they were hard to find. In 1873 W. H. E. McKnight, who disliked the name of broad churchman but took a wide view of subscription and defended *Essays and Reviews*, believed himself alone among the clergy of his neighbourhood. Six years later a correspondent said that he was probably the only broad church clergyman in North Wiltshire.[1] The movement never became popular among either clergy or laity.

A commoner case was that of the clergyman who resigned his office because he could no longer teach what he had solemnly undertaken to teach. A few men resigned because they took an exceptionally narrow view of their obligations. S. D. Brownjohn resigned his parish because he accepted the theory of evolution, at a time when many instructed clergymen already accepted the theory of evolution. Leslie Stephen resigned his orders, according to his own exaggerated account, because he could not believe in a universal flood, and at a time more than forty years after Canon Buckland taught that they must jettison belief in such a flood. But this picture of his own mind was a caricature. He did not lose his faith because he could no longer believe in a universal flood. His feelings revolted from reading a lesson or a liturgy where a universal flood was somehow assumed to be true though many of the worshippers had their reservations.

The resignation which caused most stir in the mid-Victorian years was that of Stopford Brooke.

Irish by origin, Brooke was a London preacher who became famous in 1865 when he published the life of F. W. Robertson of Brighton. The book was important in the development of the broad church school. It was a drama of the intellectual conflict of the age. In October 1865, when it was published, the argument was raging between an incredible Christian orthodoxy and a scientific or philosophical materialism. The life represented this conflict within a single soul of twenty years before. Robertson's secret soul was observed, battered by the contending forces, introspective and morbid and agonising, and at last rising triumphant with the banner of a liberal Christianity. Whether this conflict was wholly within Robertson, or whether the particular form of it was rather in his biographer, may still be a matter for argument. In understanding

[1] *Recollections of McKnight*, 231, 255.

Robertson, as in understanding Manning, we must be careful to read what he said himself and to distinguish it from the inferences made by the biographer. Robertson exercised far more influence dead than alive.[1]

By 1880 Brooke was sure that he did not believe in miracles. His mind was decided. He could not think it right or loyal to stay in a church whose doctrines were founded upon miracle. He hoped to show that he was no less a Christian. Bishop Jackson of London believed that in this state of mind Brooke was right to leave. Brooke announced his secession in August 1880. He did not thereby lose his proprietary chapel. Some twenty families ceased to attend but their places were soon taken and the chapel was again full. He continued to use the Prayer Book, omitting the creeds and making his own collection of hymns.

Not everyone thought that he was right to go. H. R. Haweis, who was then attaining a reputation as an advanced broad church-man, declared in a letter to the press that the secession was an anachronism.[2] A month after Brooke's secession Stanley declared that the subscription intended by the act of 1865 exacted only 'a slight and colourless adhesion' to the general doctrine of the Church of England.[3] He thought that Brooke was wrong to go. But Stanley and Haweis were unusual. Many more churchmen believed that any honest man who reached that state of mind ought to go with Brooke. Most people respected his integrity. Brooke was not in a state of private doubt. If he disbelieved miracle he must declare the disbelief to his people. If it was truth, the truth must be spoken, and the people shown that their faith did not depend on belief in the miraculous.

Brooke never joined the Unitarian denomination, in a formal sense. He would often consent to preach in Unitarian chapels, but held a little aloof.

We have seen the tension of mind afflicting some who were

[1] Queen Victoria read the sermons, towards which she was directed by reading Brooke's book. After his curacies Brooke's only ecclesiastical positions were as minister to two proprietary chapels—St. James York Street 1866–75, Bedford chapel in Bloomsbury 1875–95. Chaplain to Queen Victoria 1867–80. The queen suggested his name (among others) for a canonry of Westminster in 1875. The *Life of Robertson* directed some evangelicals to wider opinions in theology, e.g. Boyd Carpenter, later Bishop of Ripon—cf. *Life of Boyd Carpenter*, 314.

[2] *Daily News*, Jacks, i, 327.

[3] 18 September 1880; G, 80, 1258: letter to *Northern Echo*.

losing their faith and with it what they felt to be the best in themselves. They could not believe what they had believed since childhood. Yet if they abandoned their belief they felt untrue to their
inmost feelings. If this afflicted laymen, it afflicted clergymen
more. The clergy must teach the faith. Men like Brooke felt that
they were asked to utter words which they could not make their
own. They believed that the church had much truth in it, and
was necessary to the moral condition of society, and was wrapt
with their own conscience. If they left it, they left its borders, as
they believed, narrow. If they stayed in it and continued to teach,
they might have a chance of widening the borders and so saving
their posterity from the tension which they experienced. About
1884 a clergyman lay dying of disease, with a clear mind, but the
mind discovered itself to be in reverent agnosticism. He was sure
that agnosticism was an abyss. He summoned a liberal divine,
Edwin Abbott, to his bedside, and told him that he had so moved
because he had been 'taught to believe too much when young'. He
urged, almost besought, Abbott to do something to 'give young
men a religion that would wear'.[1]

The only way to give men a religion that would wear was by
adjusting the accepted statements of the churches, or the accepted
understanding of the statements of the churches. Abbott, who was a
disciple of Maurice and friend of Seeley, saw no reason to leave the
Church of England. He wanted to allow the possibility that a man
who disbelieved miracle could not merely be a member but hold
office in the Church of England. To this end he published in 1886
an anonymous volume entitled *The Kernel and the Husk: Letters on
Spiritual Christianity*. It was dedicated 'to the doubters of this
generation and the believers of the next'. The title meant that young
men began by believing a great deal too much. As their mind grew,
they tried to strip religion of its unnecessary husk. But their teachers
would not allow them to do so. Their teachers told them to swallow
all or they could swallow nothing. In this *either-or* they were forced
to swallow nothing, and so lost the kernel so precious to themselves
and the world. But Abbott confessed that the difficulty was not
only in the teacher. It was in the mind itself. Many minds were so
constituted that 'at present' acceptance of miracle seemed a necessary
basis for acceptance of Christianity. He did not wish to shake that

[1] Abbott, *The Kernel and the Husk*, 1886, vi–vii.

faith where it was not shaken. But where it was shaken—where a young man said that he could not be a Christian because he could not accept miracle—he wanted to deny that there was a necessary connexion between the two.

The tone of the book was reverent. Though Abbott was not known to be the author, he was a force in the City of London school where he was headmaster. The stripping of what he regarded as 'husk' did not silence his gospel. The strength of the book lay in its pastoral motive—how can I save faith for someone who is conscientiously or constitutionally incapable of believing in miracle?

But the last section gave especial offence. Whatever latitude might be allowed to a layman—and many people believed that no such latitude should be allowed to a layman—nearly everyone thought that a clergyman of these views, who must sign the articles and use the Prayer Book and represent the faith of the church, could not with honesty remain a clergyman. They thought that such a religion was not the old religion restated, but a new religion, if it was religion at all. The last letters in the book argued the contrary. Is it a mark of novelty, he asked, to accept Jesus of Nazareth as the word of God incarnate?

But even a member of the church must profess the apostles' and Nicene creeds during the liturgy. Abbott did not deny that the language might be strained. But he said that no one could be committed to every utterance in a congregational liturgy. We need not watch out for verses of hymns which our intellect rejects. What matters is the total attitude in worship. In detailed phrases every layman must be allowed his right to understand poetry as poetry and old story as metaphor.

A minister who signs the articles? Abbott claimed a right of general assent given by the clerical subscription act of 1865. But he must read the prayers? Abbott confessed uneasiness. He confessed that a man was liable to be haunted with the fear that he might be two-faced. He understood the meaning of words in one sense and his congregation in another. His scruples would be removed only if a metaphorical interpretation were generally admitted to be permissible. Many people already used such interpretation with the Athanasian creed. The freedom of ministers was increasing rapidly. 'Stay where you are', he advised doubting clergymen. He used to advise ordinands of his mind to wait a while before offering themselves for ordination; to wait until they need not conceal their opinions. Now the hour had come when they must go ahead, and frankly tell the bishop, and be ordained if he would ordain them. And the bishop would need to satisfy himself that the young man would be reverent and tender towards the faith of his congregation.

This view of the clergyman's office and language was shocking to many. On Trinity Sunday 1887 Charles Gore, regarded by Tractarians as heir to the mantle of Pusey and Liddon, denounced the book from the pulpit of Oxford university. If men could enter the ministry and yet regard its truths as open questions, Christianity was threatened at its foundations. It was a new casuistry—'oh for one hour of Pascal . . .!' Let the conscience of men awake. At the Shrewsbury Church Congress of 1896, when he was Canon Gore of Westminster abbey, in 1902 and again in 1903 when he was Bishop Gore of Worcester, and as late as 1913 when he was Bishop Gore of Oxford, he made himself the mouthpiece of the large body of clergy and laity who believed that insincerity, if not dishonesty, was inevitable in what Abbott and men like him proposed.

Nor was it only the conservative Christian who felt like Gore. Those who deserted Christianity because they identified it with old orthodoxy felt little sympathy for men who did not desert Christianity because they did not identify it with old orthodoxy. The gravest judgment against the broad church school was pronounced by the philosopher Henry Sidgwick. For Sidgwick was a reverent and sympathetic person, a soul who in almost any other age would have been *anima naturaliter Christiana*. And he commanded that public respect for integrity which lent power to his moral judgment on this precise issue. He resigned his fellowship at Trinity College in Cambridge because, though a layman, he needed to profess himself a member of the Church of England and could no longer. In these earlier years he took a rigorist view of the ethical question, almost as if a man might never join in any public pronouncement unless he agreed *ex animo* with every word. As Sidgwick matured, he mellowed. On 24 November 1895 he delivered a lecture to the West London Ethical Society. Here he confessed that the churches were, in the foreseeable future, the great agencies for moral good in society. Therefore good men think that they ought to cling to the churches if they can, seeing that separation from their church would be a greater evil than a more or less suppressed disagreement with some doctrines which it taught. The age recognises that thought must be free and independent. The churches respect integrity and freedom of mind. So long as a man only feels doubt or suspense of judgment, so long as his judgment is not negative, he is justified in remaining within his church. No one can withdraw from a church as he can from a club, since he is held by sacred ties; and in some respect the agreement of feeling and moral judgment is more important than the agreement of the intelligence. Sidgwick used to think that a member of the Church of England must withdraw from membership if he could not literally believe all the apostles' creed. He thought so no longer. The greatest possible latitude must be granted, and may on ethical grounds be granted. But, at the end of his lecture, Sidgwick conceded no such liberty to the minister. The liturgy forced the minister to use public words which he did not mean. This was an offence to good faith. There was an 'inexorable moral barrier' against the efforts of a generation of English liberals to open the ministry to 'men of modern ideas'. The work of liberating religion cannot be done within the Anglican ministry.[1]

Though the deeply Christian Gore and the deeply agnostic Sidgwick might agree, the view of others depended on the conscience of the individual. Some honest men found it offensive to make public professions while reserving the right to give them a private and metaphorical interpretation. Though it is not easy to see what evidence was available to prove it, many people believed that numbers of men were prevented from taking orders by the necessity for professing that Jesus had no human father. We know of one at least who felt this barrier to an ordination which he otherwise wished, the future Cabinet minister C. F. G. Masterman;[2] who suspected moral obliquity in himself because he could not believe what the church taught, and yet found something in his mind that barred and was not moral obliquity. Others were said to be deterred because in the service of ordination they were asked whether they 'unfeignedly' believed all the canonical Scriptures of the Old and New Testaments. It is easier to find general statements that men were deterred than to find evidence from individuals who were so deterred.

[1] *International Journal of Ethics*, vi, April 1896, 273–90.
[2] Lucy Masterman, 27–31.

Others on the contrary were willing to take orders though their judgment on miracle was doubtful or even negative. They had no intention of being hypocrites. They were not accepting stipends by saying something that they did not believe. But they were content to leave the responsibility with the church, that is, the person responsible for ordaining them, that is, the bishop.

In the year 1888 the problem was brought before the general public in an important novel: *Robert Elsmere*, by Mrs. Humphry Ward, granddaughter of Dr. Arnold of Rugby.[1]

In every feeling and sympathy she was Christian, emotionally and tenderly Christian. But Tübingen and Matthew Arnold and Mark Pattison and T. H. Green made it impossible for her to believe in miracle. (Notice that science had nothing to do with it.) And therefore, like Arnold but unlike Pattison, who said that he wished to follow her but could not, she had a sense of two Christianities struggling for the allegiance of man; the Christianity of the past, with its Calvinism and austerity and relics of past ignorance, and the Christianity of the future, with its freedom and love of creation and consecration of the intellect. She observed the sense of travail in T. H. Green, how his integrity seemed to demand the sacrifice of stories which were associated with his high ideals. She determined to portray the struggle in a novel, and the three volumes of *Robert Elsmere* were the result.[2]

The novel was an intellectual feast, not reading for the common man. But it portrayed with beauty and understanding the drama and the agony in the mental plight of a clergyman losing faith.

Elsmere was a country vicar, devoted to his people and beloved by them. He had been taught by T. H. Green at Oxford and revered him, but found nothing incompatible in the union of Christianity with discipleship of Green. In his country parish he worked away at the history of the earlier Middle Ages, and his study of the lives of the saints and other sources forced him to

[1] She was the daughter of that Thomas Arnold who became a Roman Catholic and helped Newman in Birmingham. She somehow resented Newman because she held him vaguely responsible for the troubles of her family. At Oxford she was befriended by Mark Pattison, J. P. Trevelyan, 19, 21; was helped by *Ecce Homo*, 33. Her husband, T. H. Ward, was a Fellow of Brasenose who in 1881 left Oxford to become a leader-writer on the *Times*.

[2] J. P. Trevelyan, 63; cf. *Elsmere*, ii, 317. The characters were afterwards identified by her: the Squire was modelled on Mark Pattison; Henry Grey on T. H. Green; Langham on Amiel; Trevelyan, 51. There is, however, a suspicion that Walter Pater may have served as part-model for Langham.

contemplate the growth of historical legend, especially the rise of miracle-stories. Then the squire of the parish, a curmudgeon of encyclopaedic learning and anti-Christian opinions, converted Elsmere to the belief that miracles do not happen.

To resign his parish, Elsmere believed, was necessary. He could not go on as a pretender and a hypocrite. Neither mind nor soul would feel clean if he continued. But Mrs. Ward truly understood the agony. Elsmere was married to a devout evangelical whose faith was unshaken, and the religious disagreement raised a barrier sufficient for a time to shake the marriage. He saw his parishioners let down by his departure, their moral and physical well-being in decline, his usefulness gone. And he still believed in God with as much assurance as ever. Broad church clergymen told him that it was ridiculous to give up excellent work because he ceased to believe in miracles which were of little importance to religion. Even T. H. Green (ii, 315), who approved the decision, warned him that many men held his opinions and still did admirable work in the Church of England. Elsmere would have none of it. 'Imagine standing up Sunday after Sunday to say the things you do *not* believe. . . . Nothing would induce me to preach another Easter day sermon to a congregation that have both a moral and a legal right to demand from me an implicit belief in the material miracle!' He retired to work among secularists in the east end of London, and founded a new religion there, suitable for the modern working man, just before his death.

Mrs. Ward believed that Elsmere was right, that a Christian for whom truth was a divine obligation could do no other in his circumstances; that the broad churchmen lacked 'elementary frankness' (iii, 52). But the effect of the novel was not always quite what she intended. Some readers respected Elsmere's integrity, while they regarded the decision as wrong-headed in the circumstances.

The case of Elsmere was not confined to fiction. A man was ordained about 1887, and held a small country parish. About 1901 he could not affirm as once he affirmed. He had a wife and family, and no means to support except his parish. His sermons were excellent, and he was a faithful pastor to his people. He was careful never to say a word which might distress or unsettle. He went to consult a friend on whether he should resign. The friend afterwards put the question in this rhetorical form, expecting and giving the answer *no*.

'Is he to resign his living, to give up the excellent work he is doing, to reduce his family to beggary, as a sacrifice to the opinions he now holds, which, in course of time, may give way, with "more light", to a happier state of things?' Why, in the complicated intellectual circumstances of the day, treat *doubt* as equal to *unbelief*?[1]

Jowett expressed the difficulty in his laconic way. 'Although we are in a false position in the church, we should be in a still more false position out of the church.'[2]

Such opinions were not typical. Until 1914 the great majority of Anglicans, lay or clerical, believed it right for a clergyman to resign if he suspended judgment upon, still more if he denied, all miracles. H. M. Butler, liberal though non-theological Master of Trinity College and a stout defender of Bishop Colenso, wrote privately that he must resign from being a clergyman if he ceased to believe in the two great miracles of the New Testament.[3] And this opinion was shared not only by clericals but by anti-clericals. It was said in 1887 that Oxford university, whether it were clerical or anti-clerical, did not believe that a man had a right to be a clergyman and hold such opinions.[4]

In these troubled states of mind, much responsibility rested upon the individual bishop, for the bishop had an absolute right to refuse to ordain. Conscientious ordinands, with scruples over miracle, discussed it with the bishop. Of course most ordinands had no scruples to discuss. And some conscientious ordinands with scruples did not discuss them with the bishop, believing that their conscience was their own concern. One man who suspended judgment on all miracles was ordained in 1885 and did not tell his bishop. He believed in the Incarnation, in the Church of England as the truest interpretation of the Gospel, and he earnestly wished to serve as a minister. He considered the question, and did not feel it right to throw the responsibility upon another.[5]

But in the last quarter, and especially in the last ten years, of the century, a growing number of ordinands had scruples to discuss with the bishop. The candidate would go to the bishop and declare

---

[1] G, 02, 1829.
[2] Jowett to Florence Nightingale, 4 December 1873, Balliol College MSS.
[3] Butler to Rashdall, 24 April 1914; Graham, *The Harrow Life of Dr. Butler*, 344.
[4] E. Hatch to Boyd Carpenter, 8 May 1887; Major, *Life of Boyd Carpenter*, 156,
[5] G, 03, 101-2.

his difficulty. He wished to be ordained though he could not literally accept all the language of the church. Such men believed that there was now a sufficient common understanding in the church to warrant a man in treating the language, of which he was doubtful, as poetic or allegorical. Their right to do so was publicly defended by bold spirits, from Arthur Stanley downwards.

Some bishops would then refuse to ordain. But during these years a slowly growing number of bishops was willing to ordain. The bishop would find out whether the candidate truly wished to believe and teach what God had revealed, and what the church was commissioned to teach, doubtful though he might be of the precise limits of that revelation, and convinced though he was that some statements, hitherto believed to be part of the revelation, were of no significance in religion. Some bishops took the view that in a time when new knowledge of Christian origins was coming so fast they must be very tender with the scruples.

About 1875 a lay master of Rugby school, J. M. Wilson, sought ordination from Bishop Philpott of Worcester. Wilson admired Frederick Temple when Temple was headmaster of Rugby. Observing the moral tone of the school declining under Temple's two successors, he determined to take orders as a counterweight. But when he reached Philpott he felt bound to tell the bishop that he rejected the doctrine of verbal inspiration and accepted the general results of higher criticism; that he rejected the miracles of the Old Testament and rejected some miracles of the New Testament; that he held the virgin birth to be unproved and inconsistent with the perfect humanity of Christ. Bishop Philpott asked about the resurrection; and Wilson replied that he did not find the evidence for bodily resurrection to be sufficient to prove. He said that of course he would not think it right to proclaim these opinions publicly.

Philpott refused to ordain him.

In 1879 Wilson became headmaster of Clifton College, a position which made it imperative to take orders. Clifton lay in the diocese of Gloucester and Bristol. Wilson knew that Bishop Ellicott held to verbal inspiration. He was afraid that Ellicott would also refuse him. He therefore applied to his master, Bishop Frederick Temple of Exeter, and wrote down his views in a letter.

Temple replied with a letter which approved his abandonment

of verbal inspiration. He declared that question now (1879) settled among scholars, and that by prudence Wilson could preach without hurting the faith of strict believers. He accepted Wilson's general agnosticism on miracles, provided that Wilson did not feel it a duty publicly to deny and denounce it.[1]

For the first time, so far as is known, a bishop accepted for ordination an Anglican who held a suspended judgment about all physical miracles, even the most central in Christian tradition; on the understanding that he would refrain from disturbing the faith of others by public statement.

In the last fifteen years of the century Frederick Temple was not the only bishop. Lightfoot, after he became Bishop of Durham, ordained at least one young man who told him that he was agnostic on the virgin birth.[2] But some bishops who accepted such men were far from welcoming their own decision. Lightfoot was evidently uncomfortable, and his successor at Durham, Westcott, was equally uncomfortable. A young deacon in the diocese of Durham realised, as he approached his priest's ordination, that he could not say the words in their literal sense. He approached Westcott, and had more than one interview, which left an ineffaccable memory of Westcott's kindness. Westcott finally said that it was his duty to say that his views were not illegal in a minister of the church, and that he was free, if he chose, to continue his work. The deacon saw that this amounted to a promise to ordain him priest. But he said that he could not in conscience go forward to ordination. Westcott said words to this effect: 'Of course you cannot. I could not, either. I only wish that others who share your views would take your course.' Evidently the problem perplexed the consciences, not only of ordinands, but of the most tolerant of bishops.

In the seventies Frederick Temple was unusual in his conduct. Thirty years later more bishops were of his mind. A London clergyman in 1902 went so far as to assert that hardly a bishop would now refuse to ordain such men.[3] He was wrong. When challenged, Bishop Winnington-Ingram of London made a public declaration that such men would not be ordained in the diocese of London. In 1906 Frederick Temple's son William sought ordination from

---

[1] Wilson's *Autobiog.*, 99–102, 127n.
[2] The young man was probably Hastings Rashdall; cf. *International Journal of Ethics*, vii, 158; and *Times*, 15 November 1902.
[3] G, 02, 1707; 1670.

Bishop Paget of Oxford, telling Paget that he could not unquestion-
ingly assert the truth of the two great gospel miracles. Paget refused
to ordain him. But Archbishop Davidson believed that Paget's
judgment was wrong, and himself ordained Temple two years
later. Bishop G. F. Browne of Bristol, an intelligent and liberal
man, was as firm in the matter as Bishop Winnington-Ingram.
Bishop Gore of Worcester would not ordain such men. Nor would
old Bishop Ellicott, who outlived Queen Victoria's reign as Bishop
of Gloucester. Bishop Harmer of Rochester not only would not
ordain but dismissed an examining chaplain who disagreed. Conservatives believed that the broad churchmen had no gospel. They
were thought not to know what they believed, their sermons were
suspected of turning towards mere ethics or mere literature or social
reform, they could not declare a message from the pulpit because
they were so unsure of their message. In *Robert Elsmere* Mrs. Ward
drew a picture of a broad church clergyman who was perpetually
engaged in self-contradiction and lack of frankness and half truths.
Yet one of J. M. Wilson's sermons at St. Paul's persuaded the
barrister Cosmo Gordon Lang that Christian faith was compatible
with intellectual honesty.[1]

The question remained whether a man who held these doubting
opinions could become a bishop. On intellectual and pastoral
grounds J. M. Wilson was an obvious person for such a work.
Bishop Boyd Carpenter of Ripon used his influence with the crown
to secure Wilson or someone like him as a bishop, but without
success.[2] Wilson was at last offered the see of Sodor and Man in
1907 but declined it as too old.

Not until 1917 was a clergyman, identified in the public mind
with the right of men to be ordained though they did not accept
miracles, nominated to a see; and the fight to prevent Henson
becoming Bishop of Hereford was like the fight to prevent Temple
becoming Bishop of Exeter. The fight of 1869 wished to prevent a
man becoming a bishop though he believed in the right of Biblical
students to accept some matters as legendary. The fight of 1917
wished to prevent a man becoming a bishop though he believed in
the right of Biblical students to accept even the most important
miracles of the New Testament as in part legendary. Each of the
fights succeeded thus far: it extracted from the candidate for the

_____
[1] Wilson, *Autobiog.*, 116.   [2] Bell, *Davidson*, 152.

bishopric a partial retraction from the position taken up by his more extreme colleagues.

The judgment of the individual bishops could not be subjected to laws. Much depended on the candidate, on whether his attitude was reverent and truth-seeking, and whether the bishop thought him to be intending to teach Christian truth.

Here was a gulf between the religious feelings of most churchmen, lay or clerical, and the practice of a comparatively small number of clergymen. It caused no distress so long as it was treated with reverence and hesitancy. Throughout the reign of Queen Victoria it was so treated. Evidently the difference was great between J. M. Wilson and Stopford Brooke, though both held opinions which many thought incompatible with the profession of Christian minister and some thought incompatible with Christianity. For Wilson had a personal doubt, a suspense of judgment. He did not mean to disturb other men's souls by inflicting upon them his inner uncertainties. Stopford Brooke believed that he must show men how their faith did not rest upon evidence about miracles; and therefore must proclaim his doubt or negation to the people. But sooner or later, the circumstances being what they were, some men would claim the right to do within the Church of England what Stopford Brooke thought that he could only do in honesty by resigning from the Church of England. Then an argument must ensue, continuous with the arguments of the later Victorian age, and arising out of the attempt to adjust Christian knowledge and Christian profession to the new knowledge or new axioms of the nineteenth century. The argument continued through the first thirty-eight years of the twentieth century.

The recitation of the creeds was the principal difficulty. Those who were ordained with a suspended judgment on miracles must use the creeds like hymns, or like the thirty-nine articles. They were a general assent to the faith of the church, and did not commit the worshipper to accepting literally every word.

That religious man but agnostic mind Henry Sidgwick pleaded more than once that the apostles' creed be dropped from the liturgy of the church. The church should reach outward to anyone whose heart agreed even though his mind dissented from its language. Even if a majority of worshippers wholeheartedly receive the words of the creed, they ought to refrain from imposing the formal profession of that creed upon the minority who would like to share in their worship but cannot subscribe to all their doctrines. A man may join in the poetry and devotion and ethical power of the church without feeling committed to historical statements which he does not believe. But if these statements are presented to him formally as an expression of fact, his conscience is given 'the maximum of offence'. The creed was a statement of prose more suitable to an appendix or manual of instruction. It was out of place in worship. So argued Sidgwick.

Yet the broad churchmen never proposed to remove the apostles' or Nicene creeds from the liturgy. This was proposed or demanded by laymen on the fringe, like Sidgwick or Mrs. Humphry Ward.[1] Jowett caused the apostles' creed to be disused in the services at Balliol College. But no responsible churchman proposed that the two creeds be either dropped or modified. Liberals like Rashdall or Abbott valued historical continuity and found little difficulty in the use of creeds as poetic statements of truth. To the heirs of the Tractarians the creeds were indispensable as summaries of the faith of antiquity. Both the leading dogmatic theologians of the *Lux Mundi* group thought that no one should be ordained who doubted the historical information of the creeds. In the uncertainties of faith in the sixties and seventies and eighties worshippers came to value the creeds as a 'solid rock'[2] amid the quicksands of speculation. In an age when the theory of evolution looked menacing, *I believe in God the Father Almighty, Maker of heaven and earth* was a moral assertion as well as a metaphysical. If the worshipper was an articulate defender of traditional orthodoxy, he became determined not to sacrifice a word of those expressions by which ancient Christianity stated its convictions. Richard Holt Hutton, a liberal and lay divine, wrote that 'the recitation of the creed is an act of intellectual adoration, in a day when the intellect is the source of some of our deeper troubles'.[2]

[1] Mrs. Ward wrote a celebrated letter to the *Times* with this proposal, *Times*, 5 September 1899. The letter received negative answers but it shows how 'comprehension' in the Church of England was allowing Mrs. Humphry Ward to move back into the Anglican fold. In *Robert Elsmere* (1888) she believed that salvation must come by leaving the church. After 1899 she believed that salvation must come by staying inside the church and changing it. This decision was made finally explicit in a novel of 1911, *The Case of Richard Meynell*.

[2] Hutton, *Aspects*, 3–5.

Throughout the later Victorian age general opinion in the churches never recognised the right of men to recite the apostles' creed without believing in its literal truth. But general opinion nevertheless changed in subtle ways. Christian opinion accepted the duty of sincerity as a fundamental duty of religion. In an age of unsettlement they became readier to be tolerant of unsettled minds who wanted to believe what God revealed even if they were not always sure what that was. In the seventies they were almost unanimous that a man who wanted to be a clergyman, but could not believe the virgin birth, ought not to be a clergyman. By the nineties they were less unanimous.

This change was illustrated in the novel *Sunningwell*, published by Warre Cornish in 1899. The book was an enchanting description of the various clergy in a little cathedral close of the seventies, the high, the low, and the broad; all treated with sympathy, and with a theological consciousness which made the novel more understanding and less readable than the Barchester novels. The hero of the book was the broad church canon, who also held a living in the town. He was a humane and honest man, an excellent pastor, and conservative in his habits. But he could not believe all the apostles' creed. He had no wish to remove the creed from public worship; partly because it was a symbol of unity through the ages, and partly because he feared its replacement—old formulas allow liberty, new formulas bind. When he was asked why he did not leave the church, he said that he and his like were 'standing in the doorway, as it were, to prevent the door being closed in the face of questions which call for answer, not exclusion; and that to go out would be to betray a trust' (p. 263). He valued the establishment because it brought lay pressure to bear and prevented the exclusion of himself and his friends.

But in the novel it did not prevent his exclusion. An argument at a meeting caused him to preach a fatal sermon in the cathedral pulpit. He found himself notorious, and people believed him dishonest. The bishop asked him to resign his living, though not his canonry. And yet the quiet assumption in the novel is that such things happened in the seventies when science and criticism battered at the doors; but that they probably could not happen now. The novel witnesses to a slow and silent change in some Anglican opinion over thirty years.

In 1871–3 and again in 1900–5 attempts were made to get the recitation of the Athanasian creed abolished, or at least rendered voluntary. This was not from the same motive as the rare proposals to do the same to the apostles' or Nicene creed. For those who doubted miracles preferred the Athanasian creed to the other two. Haldane, Bethune-Baker, Max Müller[1] thought the Athanasian creed the best of all creeds. This opinion was suspected of being paradoxical, Max Müller's vicar even thought it playful. For this was the one creed which many wanted abolished or omitted.

The Prayer Book ordered the Athanasian creed to be recited thirteen times in the year. Many clergymen never recited it, partly because their parishioners could not understand it, and partly because they disliked its verses of damnation. The creed was more used in the sixties than the seventies, but even in the sixties many clergymen never heard it. The Ritual Commission of 1869 recommended that its use be made voluntary. Encouraged by Archbishop Tait of Canterbury, the question of abolishing its compulsory use, or of diminishing the number of days when it must be recited, was debated in Convocation and the press. For nearly three years the argument was warm. But it was soon clear that opinion in Convocation would sanction no such proposal. Bishop Hamilton of Salisbury said repeatedly that he would resign his bishopric if the creed were touched.[2] Liddon told Archbishop Tait that he would retire into private life even if the number of days was diminished. By the nineties all this was changed. Liddon's successor Gore was the leading advocate of the proposal to make its recitation voluntary. It is one outward sign of the changing Tractarian mind. And yet, in an age of doubt, some men held fast to the Athanasian creed, as so many held to the apostles' and Nicene creeds. When the incumbent of a London church invited preachers too unorthodox for the curate's mind, the curate used to sit in the sedilia fuming and relieved his feelings by muttering the Athanasian creed.[3]

[1] *Life of Max Müller*, ii, 438; G, 03, 660.
[2] Malan, *Life of Malan*, 144.
[3] Adderley, *In Slums and Society*, 113; the church was St. Mark's, Marylebone Road, the curate G. R. Woodward, famous in connexion with plainsong and carols.

CHAPTER IV

THE VILLAGE CHURCH

I. THE COUNTRY PARSON

In 1860 the idea of a village church was still embodied in some
country parishes. The squire was in his pew, his friend the parson
in his stall, respectable farmers in pews, and on benches the labourers
in smock frocks, delicately embroidered at front and back, their
wives often in scarlet flannel shawls. The men sat passive, not
following in books, some unable to read, but silent with a stolid
attentiveness, not liking to be absent because of the squire or the
farmer or habit, but in no way sorry to be there, men without
hostility and with quiet acceptance. A preacher of 1852 at Lydiard
looked out from his pulpit and saw mostly snow-white smocks,
here and there a blue smock with a pattern in white thread on the
breast; each male with a red pocket-handkerchief; two or three
farmers in black coats, and women in dresses of various colours.[1]
Of course there were parishes with squire indifferent or non-
Anglican, or with parson despised by the village, or with chapels
so strong that the labourers' benches were sparsely filled. And the
country church of the north, or Wales, or Cornwall, was far different from the country church of the home counties. But when one
intelligent woman saw the title of Kingsley's poem, *The Bad Squire*,
she thought it an anomalous title.[2]

In some country parishes this time-honoured structure continued
to the end of the century and beyond.

There was an opinion that the worst squire was the townsman
newly rich and attempting to be countrified.[3] The relatively small
squire was thought to be better for the village than the great landowner. Wide interests made for small knowledge of a single parish.
The man who owned a few hundred or a thousand acres of the
parish and lived there did more good than a rich and absent grandee.

[1] *Recollections of McKnight*, 182–3.
[2] Dorling, *Dora Greenwell*, 100.   [3] Jessopp, *Trials*, 36.

151

All through the Victorian age villagers, and their vicars, were fortunate if they possessed such a resident of education and public spirit. At Benenden in Kent the rate of illegitimacy fell from 5 to 1 per cent between 1864 and 1894, and the parson attributed this largely to home life made possible by the care of his squire for the people's housing.[1]

Sometimes the 'squire' might be the local manufacturer. At Darley Abbey, the population of 1,000 contained no one but workers in the paper mill and cotton mill and their families. The family (Evans) which owned both mills, owned every house in the village. Each tenant must agree that every young man and woman in his house should attend Sunday school till the age of eighteen. There was no public house in the village. About 1875 a week-night Bible class had 120 women and 70–80 men. The wife of the perpetual curate conducted a Sunday afternoon Bible class for about 60 factory girls.[2] The difficulty with such a church structure was its dependence on one or two powerful laymen or laywomen, and it was weak if the village ran into labour troubles. Only a year or two later we hear that the religion of the village was in a 'sad plight' on account of the number of 'backsliders'. But the Evans family continued to take generous care of the village into the twentieth century.

When 'lay readers' came in, from the end of the sixties, they were useful in mission rooms of remote hamlets, and we know of several Anglican squires who allowed themselves to be used in this way. At Fineshade abbey in Northamptonshire the squire's house was two miles from the nearest church and he found that in winter no one went to church; so he fitted up a room above the stables and got the bishop to license him as a lay reader.[3]

In some parishes the old squarson continued throughout the reign. Burrell Hayley became rector of Catsfield in Sussex, married the daughter of Sir Andrew Pilkington, K.C.B., and moved out of the rectory into Catsfield Place. His house became a centre for the surrounding clergy, his generosity helped to build parsonages in neighbouring parishes, he knew all his parishioners intimately, and was rector for thirty-seven years (1843–80).[4] At the other end of the

---

[1] CCR, 1894, 280.
[2] Dawson, *Hannington*, 113, 153; W. L. Chivers, *Darley Abbey*.
[3] CCR, 1887, 86.   [4] G, 80, 308.

country Christopher Bird became vicar of Chollerton in Northumberland, where he succeeded his father in 1867, and remained for twenty-nine years till death. He did not marry, and used his wealth to help the Central African Mission, or the new and struggling diocese of Newcastle, built schools, restored the church, and privately helped clergymen in distress or their widows. He was regarded affectionately as 'prophet priest and king' among his people.[1]

In 1851 George Martin accepted the almost inaccessible moorland Cornish parish of St. Breward and remained thirty-one years. He arrived with a new wife at a village with no school, a tumbledown parsonage, a leaking church which did not always have services. He left a flourishing school, a restored church, a reasonable house. He was regarded by his brother-clergy as a holy man, and laboured under the perpetual sense of being a failure.

Akin to the squarson was the younger brother of the squire, working with him hand in hand. The younger brother of Lord Lyttelton, William Henry Lyttelton, became rector of Hagley in Gloucestershire and remained thirty-seven years (1847–84). He had no training for the ministry except a degree from the university of Cambridge, and thanks to the patronage system became rector at the age of twenty-seven. He never felt part of any church movement, but was rugged to the last in his individuality, broad in his doctrinal views, comfortable in his attitude to the good things of creation. The one man whom he regarded as influencing his mind was Frederick Denison Maurice. To the later nineteenth century such a man seemed more lay than clerical. He had a zest about his pastoral work, a straightness and purity of mind, a merriment which did not destroy reverence. He taught science in his parish school and eagerly welcomed the progress made by the scientists. His occasional raids into the wider ecclesiastical world were received with alarm.[2] His niece up at the hall recorded that it never occurred to them that church matters were the province of the clergyman and not the squire. They were the province of the whole family.[3] Yet things changed. The pews and gallery disappeared. The church was restored (1858). Soon there were daily services, later holy com-

[1] G, 97, 10.　　　　　　　　[2] G, 84, 1172.
[3] Memoir prefaced to *The Life of Man after Death*, 1893, xiv. For a portrait of Lyttelton, *Life of Alfred Lyttelton*, 10–14.

munion every week, sermons in a surplice, and finally a surpliced choir. He encouraged a custom which only became common in England in the third quarter of the century, that of relatives decking the graves with flowers, so that his churchyard began to seem more like a garden. Yet he was a John Bull who greatly disliked alterations in church. He had no use for the study of history, which he called *Byegones*.

The churches would have felt different to a stranger returning after thirty years. The picturesque smocks were going out in the fifties. Already in 1860 a maker of smock-patterns complained that hardly anyone now bought a smock. The last smocks disappeared quickly in the sixties, and the scarlet shawls with them. A few older men wore smocks into the seventies. The cheap town suit became Sunday best for the labourer, if he had a Sunday best. It looked much uglier. But the smock became a badge of something unwanted, almost a sign of childlike status. Sudden changes in dress were important psychologically. The labourer in his smock expected to go to church. The labourer in his cheap black suit did not, though not merely because he affected a new costume.

The later Victorians discussed why the village church declined. They also discussed why the village declined, and the church declined (where it declined) primarily because the village declined. But that was not the only reason. A growing social consciousness in the labourer, leading to a political consciousness in the labourer, helped the process as much as the depression of agriculture or the lure of the city.

The old order represented village life as at best a family, each member worshipping in due order, and at worst a hierarchy of classes. But the town labourer was organising himself to better his condition. At the end of the sixties the articulate representatives of the labourer, seeing how their wages needed to be raised, began urging them to organise themselves. To organise was in one aspect to unite against the employer. And in the country the employer was more visible and more personal than in the towns. The unions of the agricultural labourer, if conflict came, ruined the family atmosphere of those villages which still possessed a family atmosphere. For it was a more direct confrontation than in the town; a battle between three or four employers and nearly everyone else in the little society.

At a meeting of Warwickshire labourers, a Primitive Methodist preacher, Joseph Arch, who was a labourer at Barford, made a revivalist speech which raised him to the leadership of a movement. The strikers were helped by publicity given in the press, especially in the *Daily News*. On 29 March 1872 they founded at Leamington the Warwickshire Agricultural Labourers' union. It spread speedily, and was soon a National Agricultural Labourers' union, with a membership of nearly 100,000 at the end of 1872.

The country clergy were not naturally against agricultural unions. One or two of them helped to found such unions. The vicar of Leintwardine helped to found a union which used firm but respectful language to landlords, claimed 30,000 members, and had a dissenter as secretary and twenty clergymen as vice-presidents. At Halberton in North Devon Edward Girdlestone led the labourers' campaign for better wages.[1] But these circumstances were new. How unaccustomed were the churches may be judged by a scene at the Leeds Church Congress of 1872. There Bishop Fraser of Manchester caused a sensation at the working men's meeting by defending the right of agricultural labourers to their union, and even extolling the moderation of Joseph Arch. He declared that all *rational* clergymen wanted to see the labourer better off. The speech, which received an ovation, was the more sensational because it was not typical of bishops. Bishop Magee of Peterborough denounced outsiders who interfered between farmer and tenant, and Bishop Ellicott of Gloucester told the annual meeting of the Gloucestershire Agricultural Society that unions were 'iniquitous' combinations, which disturbed the peace of the English countryside. He advised farmers not to throw the union agents into the horsepond. At a great meeting in Exeter Hall to support the labourer, the only bishop on the platform was the Roman Catholic Archbishop Manning.

Arch seized upon such remarks and used them. For the country clergy found the peace of their parishes disturbed, and many of them sided with the landowner. The first utterances of the Agricultural Labourers' union contained abuse of the clergy. The union represented the clergy as part of the landowning system which held the labourers in subjection. The parsons were the slaves of rich

[1] Wagner, 150, 153–4; E. Selley, *Village Trade Unions* 36ff.; Heath, *The English Peasantry*, 158.

patrons. The parsons, said a later labouring pamphleteer, keep preaching to people how to die. 'Horrid mockery to teach men how to die, I say teach them how to live, and make their lot happier here on earth, living in this world is a certainty. . . .'[1]

The anti-clerical campaign received impetus in May 1873. Two county magistrates at Chipping Norton convicted sixteen women of trying to intimidate blackleg labourers, brought in to replace strikers, and sent them to prison for a week or ten days. Both the magistrates were local rectors. The imprisonment was raised in the House of Commons.[2] The women were released and made a triumphal entry into their village of Ascott-under-Wychwood, with a speech by Arch. Through the summer and autumn of 1873 the labourer was learning from those whom he regarded as his friends, that the parson oppressed the poor.

It was not true that the parson oppressed the poor. Amid the suspicion or armed neutrality there were many parsons whom the labourers would never conceive as enemies. But something in the relationship was suddenly awkward. The Anglican vicar was often an educated man of the upper middle class. 'Few will doubt', said the socialist clergyman Llewelyn Davies, 'that the Church of England greatly needs the help of divine grace to preserve it from an undue reverence for station and property.'[3] And in the country parish the predicament of the vicar might be embarrassing. If he was privately convinced that the demands of the labourers were just, could he say so? If he said so, he might earn a temporary popularity among the tenants. Quite a number of parsons helped the unions. For a time the editor of the union journal was a loyal Anglican churchman. Dr. Percival, President of Trinity College in Oxford, E. A. Freeman the historian, W. H. Fremantle of Balliol College were among the eminent Anglicans who gave a general favour to Arch. But the parson's usefulness in the parish, his capacity for almsgiving, his free access, the decoration of his church or effectiveness of his school, often depended on alliance with the squire or the farmers. The parish was divided in bitterness, and a clergyman helped most if he tried not to take sides. Girdlestone in Devonshire

---

[1] *The Position of the Agricultural Labourer in the Past and in the Future*, 1885, 43.

[2] The affair hastened the decline in numbers of clerical magistrates: 1873, 1,043; 1906, about 32; PP, 1873, liv, 35; 1906, xcix, 623. On 18 June 1873 Hinde Palmer and Locke King introduced a clerical justices disqualification bill; withdrawn 29 July.

[3] CCR, 1873, 33.

left an unhappy parish and destroyed his own usefulness, after his campaign to raise the labourers' wages. The wisest bishops advised their clergy to be neutral in the struggle. And yet the lot of the neutral, blamed by both sides, was sometimes as hard as the lot of the partisan. For a time some labourers even suspected the parish alms. Arch himself felt horror at the parson's power over parishes through charity.[1] And if lies were spread in the parish, they harmed the community, and the parson could not but contradict. If lies against the parson were spread, he could hardly help estrangement from the unions.

In most parts of the country where the battle was fought the evidence suggests that the chapel did not gain what the church lost. The labourer stopped going to any place of worship. But we still need a lot of local evidence.

In 1874 the unions suffered defeat over a Suffolk and Norfolk strike, and membership fell rapidly. A year or two later English agriculture started to decline, labourers were dismissed, the unions lost power. But the inheritance of the conflict was left in many parishes. Union men would not come to church. Standing on a Norfolk village green, Arch is said to have told a crowd that 'the church belongs to the rich men'. The union men occasionally attended Easter vestries, to get the meeting adjourned to a time when labourers could attend, and elect a union member as church-warden, on suspicion (real or pretended) that parochial charities were being managed corruptly. In visitation returns of the seventies the incumbent sometimes answered a question about hindrances with some reply like this from Kibworth Beauchamp of 1875, on why fewer artisans came to church: 'to prevalent neglect of religious observance in lower classes, and to recent political agitation among artisans and labourers'.

The change in attitude of labourers, in areas where there was trouble, was much remarked within a short space of time. They exchanged courtesy to the parson for rudeness. Augustus Jessopp was a curate in Cambridgeshire during the fifties, then a distinguished headmaster and then an incumbent in Norfolk during the eighties. He was pained by the contrast in manners between his earlier parishioners and his later.

In the end of the eighties men still talked of the 'hostility' between

---

[1] Arch, *Autobiography*, 341.

country labourer and village parson.[1] The question of the rural labourer's vote kept the argument political during the eighties. The new national schools enabled the labourer to read the pamphlets which identified the parsons with landlords—'it is no wonder that the churches are almost empty in country places on a Sunday, when men get up in the pulpit, and tell them to be contented with their lot in life, as it is the lot in which God has placed them'.[2] In the middle eighties the 'secularist lecturer' began to affect villages. We hear of a 'secularist shoemaker' who settled in a village and gave lectures on Sunday. A woman who heard him said, 'He's put everything in a new light. Why, I always used to have my children baptised and sent to church. But now I see I've been all wrong, and if I'd twenty children I wouldn't let one of them go near the church.' The town labourer was closer to the country labourer than he used to be. On club day at Cheriton in Hampshire the members walked to church headed by a band from a nearby town. One of the band said to an artisan, 'But we're not going *into* church. We know better than that. You can go in if you like; you believe in God, and all that sort of thing, but we don't.' The country artisan produced a Bible from his pocket, and said that the book was enough for him. The secularist would not have been heard unless the labourer were in a mood to hear. A village parson in Devonshire on his way to church saw a group of loafers and invited them to go with him. They said, 'No, and you wouldn't go unless you were paid for it.'[3] Augustus Jessopp, rector of the little parish of Scarning in Norfolk, who understood villagers better than most men, wrote in 1892 that the peasants of the countryside were morose and discontented.[3] He also thought that the parson was slowly winning back the respect which he lost in the seventies. The town orator in the village sometimes caused more sound than influence. Labouring friends of the parson were known to console him after some orator's visit, telling him that it was only the orator's way and no one should take it too seriously. And the alleged surliness varied not only between county and county, but between village and village. Only a few miles away from the Norfolk village where Jessopp, most delightful and cheerful of men, met scowls, the son of the squire had no sense whatever

---

[1] Cf. 'Hodge and his Parson', by Arnold Taylor, *Nineteenth Century*, xxxi, March 1892, 359.
[2] *The Position of the Agricultural Labourer in the Past and in the Future*, 1885, 45.
[3] CCR, 1894, 278; G, 92, 1536-7.

that the poor of the parish imagined anything but the proper ordering of society into classes.[1]

The evangelical J. C. Ryle believed that they would be wrong to attribute the decline only to contemporary circumstances. He was convinced that they were at last paying the penalty for years of bad management in country parishes. In 1851 Suffolk recorded a high rate of church-going and chapel-going. Thirty-five years later Ryle, who lately left a Suffolk parish to become Bishop of Liverpool, launched an immoderate onslaught upon the country parishes, declaring them to have taken the place of cathedrals as the weakest part of the church. He said that in an immense proportion of rural parishes the church was unpopular, its services not valued, churchgoers were outnumbered by chapelgoers, the nonconformist minister was thought a safer guide to heaven than the clergyman, most of his parishioners voted in an election on the opposite side to the parson. Why? The Church of England was at last reaping its rural harvest of pluralities and non-residence, of miserable borrowed sermons and locked churches.[2] This onslaught by Ryle caused much discussion, and it was agreed to be exaggerated or at least far too sweeping. And though he attributed the ills to the legacy of the eighteenth century, it was hard not to connect his feelings with the circumstance that agricultural strife was recently fierce in Suffolk.

The country churches were not empty on a Sunday. But they were less full. The clergy, at least, believed that they were less full, and we have small reason to doubt. Samples taken in the visitation returns of Lincolnshire parishes during the episcopate of Edward King, between 1886 and 1907, show a surprising steadiness of church and chapel life in the country. Much more work is required on different areas and counties. But the clergy at least of some areas were no doubt right in their sense of discouragement. And the reason was not only, probably not mainly, the movement of rustic politics. The village began that long process of decline which continued until the coming of the bus and of electric power. The peasant was a little more morose, though he was too inarticulate to know it, because his world was sliding.

[1] Lawrence Jones, *A Victorian Boyhood*, 69.
[2] CCR, 1886, 118–20; the Reverend R. M. Robertson Stone has kindly communicated to me statistics of communicants in a number of Norfolk churches during the last ten or more years of the century. They do not suggest any marked change in the total picture, though naturally much change up or down in individual parishes.

Every institution in the village declined, as the young moved into the towns in search of higher wages or city lights. The shopkeeper lost customers, the village tailor was forced out of business by the town manufacturer of ready-made suits, the agriculture of the country slid down towards ruin and with it everything that depended on agriculture for support—the revenue of colleges at the university, the rents of the squire, the glebe of the parson, the tithe of the ecclesiastical commissioners. In 1887 the tithe-owner got £87 8s. 0d. for a nominal £100 of tithe. The total loss to the clergy—that is, the total payment lower than what they were expected to receive by the tithe commutation act of 1836, was £388,265.[1] In 1892 they got £75 18s. 0d. for a nominal £100. Some land in Lincolnshire or Essex went out of cultivation. Census returns showed how the cities grew at the expense of the villages. A good country parson took much trouble in commending young people to town parishes, and some found jobs in towns for their emigrating girls.

The squire lost rents. Income fell, perhaps he could no longer afford to live in the great house, and he or his son sought the town and new ways of prosperity. The landowner resided less upon his land, his hall was shut for months of the year. The decline of the Anglican squire was bad for the parish, bad for the rural church, bad for the parson. The old patriarchal system had demerits if the patriarch were selfish or irresponsible, but where it worked it was the strength of the English countryside. Some observers thought that labourers' cottages were less well repaired in the nineties than in the seventies, their sanitation worse, their supply of water poor. The more enterprising of the young labourers moved out, and the level of intelligence in the village was lower, just in the age when literacy became universal. The money of the city, through the commuter or the weekend cottage, was not yet pouring back into the village.

None should blame the country parson that his lot was harder. His parishioners, often, were fewer. His income fell with the depression of the times. His squire, perhaps, moved out, leaving him the one resident to whom the poor could go for help. The demand of charity upon his purse grew as his purse grew shorter. To continue for years at a post where the numbers of worshippers fell from year to year did not raise the spirit of the parson. In the eighties and nine-

[1] CCR, 1887, 122.

ties bishops were troubled over the depression and discouragement of the country parson. The clergy on the whole got better. The people on the whole got fewer. The men especially got fewer. They got fewer at the nonconformist chapel in the village as well as at the church. The children came, being sent, but the young moved out or did not come. 'My congregation', said a vicar sadly, 'is waiting for me in the churchyard.'[1]

Such at least was the melancholy picture presented to the church at large. If it is analysed, much variety is found from parish to parish. Some country parishes were dead in 1860 and flourishing in 1890. Part of the melancholy arose from memories or imaginations of the past. Those who could remember how in the days of early Victorian revival sixty working people attended Wooler church each weekday for daily service (curate W. M. H. Church) were inclined to blame a degenerate posterity. But the later Victorians would have been guilty of dreaming if they supposed most village churches to be like Wooler. Such statistics as can be found seldom bear out the melancholy of the age. And perhaps the mood forgot the recent past. One old clergyman, C. W. Furse, heard a discussion on the plight of the country parish and reminded the meeting that when he was a boy in North Devonshire it was not uncommon for parishes to lack any resident vicar or curate, that the only services of Sunday evening were nonconformist, and that of his five teachers in the art of riding to hounds, three had been beneficed clergymen.[2]

Walsham How, who was one of the best country clergy before he became a bishop, got statistics from the chapels as he was leaving his Shropshire parish. He found two results which worried him: first, the proportion of men to women was much higher at the chapels; and secondly the number of *male* communicants, at church and chapels put together, was very small.[3]

The village which had a fine pastor still attended its church during the eighties. Kibworth Beauchamp had about 1,550 people in 1885. It had a vigorous incumbent, E. A. Knox, the later Bishop of Manchester. Its church contained 500 seats and was filled every Sunday evening. It also had an Independent chapel and two Methodist chapels, each of which prospered sufficiently to support its own minister. All four places of worship had flourishing Sunday schools. In 1890 Wolsingham had a population of 2,500 of which

[1] G, 99, 1268.   [2] CCR, 1894, 291.   [3] CCR, 1880, 94.
V.C.—6 a

1,000 were nonconformists. Yet the Anglican choir numbered forty
to fifty, with twenty-five to thirty boys. Another northern village
with a population of 1,600 over twenty square miles had 187 communicants at Easter 1888. Kenn in Devonshire had 187 communicants at Easter 1894 out of a population of just over 800, but was
confessed to have a country priest of rare quality.[1]

Censuses, such as they are, do not show this standard of village
life. But they often show large congregations in the country. On
5 February 1882 a count was held in the districts round Cheltenham.
It gave these results:

Charlton Kings	Anglican	1,184
	Nonconformist	363
Leckhampton	Anglican	1,642
	Nonconformist	65
Prestbury	Anglican	529
	Nonconformist	76
Swindon	Anglican	131
	Nonconformist	nil

Total attendants: 3,995
Total population: 9,055

Well over 40 per cent of the inhabitants of these districts attended
church or chapel that Sunday. In the figures of percentages of
Easter communicants to population of 1906 the rural southern
dioceses, headed by Herefordshire, topped the list, while Newcastle,
Liverpool, Birmingham and Durham sat at the bottom. Yet the
clergy could see congregations dwindle. One vicar reported that his
morning congregations used to be 50 or 60 and were now 20 or 30;
that the farmers used to come twice a Sunday and now came two or
three times a month.[2] No one could judge the importance of such
evidence unless he knew more about both vicar and parish. Evening
services usually remained well attended. Yet everyone seemed to
agree that the countryman of the eighties and nineties retained a
diminishing sense of the duty of attending public worship. It

[1] E. A. Knox, *Reminiscences*, 119ff.; Kibworth Beauchamp Visitation articles,
Northamptonshire archives; CCR, 1888, 145; 1890, 586; 1894, 278.

[2] G, 99, 1071. A Bath journal published the statistics of attendants at seventy
villages round Bath. Some of the villages had no chapel. The total attendances
(Anglican and Nonconformist) on 20 November 1881 came to about 39.84% of
the total population. Cf. *The Church, the Census and the People*, by a priest of the
Church of England, 1882.

depended on the part of the country. Round Penzance in the nineties the churches were still empty but the chapels were still full.

Some talked of 'secularism'. They said that their flock had lost the axiomatic sense of a future life, and therefore going to church felt less useful or practical. Some talked of the growing inability, even of countrymen, to walk far; perhaps due to railways, perhaps to bicycles, perhaps to new habit. About 1883 they built a large parish church in the centre of a village with a widely scattered population. A year or two later they built 200 cottages, a walk of some ten minutes from the church. A few years later they found that the community of cottages felt too far from the parish church, and a demand was heard for a 'mission church' to serve the cottages.[1] If the mission church was built, it was difficult to serve it adequately, except with the help of an untrained lay-reader. Its existence diminished the numbers and weakened the music of the parish church, and prevented the parish church being the social or religious focus of that scattered population. If they did not build the mission church, a nonconformist chapel quickly appeared. These mission churches seem first to have started in Lincolnshire, where every hamlet had its dissenting chapel. Henry Mackenzie, later suffragan Bishop of Nottingham, claimed to have built the first in the parish of Tydd St. Mary, which was twelve miles long, about 1857, and in South Lincolnshire he was known as the father of 'mission-houses'.[2] Rather than have a mission-house a strong vicar might even move his church. In 1884 the rector of Edgefield in Norfolk, seeing that his village was in one place and his church in another, removed the building almost stone by stone to a site on the glebe near the people, leaving behind an octagonal tower and an old churchyard.[3]

The conduct of services in Anglican mission-chapels raised a problem. After 1865 the needs of the town, especially London, created the office of lay reader, and the pastors of the country were quick to see his utility. Little hamlets now got chapels of the size and cheapness of a nonconformist chapel, which in such hamlets were normally served by lay preachers. But the Anglicans were suspicious of laymen taking services in churches. Some believed it illegal. The man in the pew found it irreverent. In the earlier

[1] G, 98, 1581.
[2] The Tydd St. Mary Fen mission church was sold in 1948 to become a workshop. Cf. Alwyn Peel, *A Short Guide to the Parish Church of Tydd St. Mary* (1965); CCR, 1872, 41, 79.   [3] B. Cozens-Hardy, *Norfolk Archaeology*, xxxiii, (1965), 493.

Victorian age, if a layman under the direction of his incumbent took some service in a cottage, conservative laymen were inclined to imagine that he must be a dissenter, or on the way to become a dissenter.[1] About 1863 the curate of a country parish fell suddenly ill while the bell was ringing for service and asked an educated layman to take it in the schoolroom. The layman read part of morning service and a sermon by Dr. Arnold. The vicar then wrote to the curate on this 'illegal parody', and next week, when the archdeacon on his horse met the layman, he recalled the Israelite who sacrilegiously put out his hand to touch the ark.[2] By the early seventies the attitude vanished or was vanishing, though inside the church building it remained as strong as ever, and even in 1870 it was exceptional to find a layman reading the lessons at morning or evening prayer. The Anglicans gladly accepted lay help in Sunday school and Bible class, and in outlying mission rooms it was not always easy to distinguish between a Sunday school and a service for adults. In 1872 Ely (Bishop Harold Browne) was the first diocese outside London to start training laymen for this work.

The laymen were not allowed to preach or take services in consecrated buildings. They were found preaching in the open air or in churchyards, or visiting public houses on Saturday evenings, or holding prayers in kitchens or living-rooms, or holding Bible classes in cottages. In 1876 the Lincoln diocesan conference took a new step by voting that 'under certain circumstances' they might conduct services in a church. Bishop Wordsworth of Lincoln did not sanction such services. The readers were not at first numerous. In 1883 (in twenty dioceses alone, in others they did not yet exist) the Church of England had about 684 readers.[3] They were a useful supplement to the work of the parson, so useful that at last they became indispensable. Bishop Frederick Temple of London took the step in 1891 of licensing them to preach in consecrated buildings except at the statutory services; but the sermon at the end of evening prayer was included in this permission, because the Prayer Book made no provision for it. By 1904 they were allowed to preach in consecrated churches in only four dioceses, and Lincoln was not one: London, Rochester, Salisbury, Hereford. But twenty years before they were indispensable to the working of many parishes.

[1] Cf. CCR, 1872, 171; Cadman's memory.
[2] CCR, 1888, 151.   [3] C of E YB, 1883, 122

About 1881 a Protestant visitor to the Roman catacombs was shown the inscription *lector* and asked why the Protestants did not preserve this primitive order of ministry. The visitor simulated surprise, and replied that the staff of most well-organised English parishes included a reader.[1]

To bring in laymen did not necessarily mean a wider social grade, not at least in the country. The first lay readers were required to possess education before the diocese could reconcile itself to their preaching. The Bishop of Salisbury asked one of his eminent churchmen, Earl Nelson, to become a reader. Nelson replied that he would only do so if some of every grade of society became readers.[2] Laymen as Sunday school teachers or in other forms of pastoral work were common and often highly organised. This was especially true in Lancashire and Yorkshire, where the particular tradition of adult Sunday schools had long accustomed the laymen to take their share in the parish. In 1872 the town clerk of Louth in Lincolnshire (Falkner Allison) collected a large body of navvies every Sunday afternoon and preached them a sermon. To bring laymen into little country parishes did not mean, contrary to expectation, that the parson was less needed. If the layman was good at the work, he generated among the people a need for clergymen.[3]

Some talked, no doubt rightly, of the disappearance of any sense among the employed that they ought to attend the church of their employer. And not all observers believed that this disappearance was a loss to true religion, even if it was a break in the social unity of the village.

Some talked of the recruitment of the country parson. The newer country parson was a town-bred man. The Victorian age made more educated men, as well as labouring men, town-bred. And the best churchmen cried of the needs of the towns, and persuaded the enterprising and devoted young priest into the slums. 'I hope', said an archdeacon of 1893 to a young man who had got a country benefice, 'you are not going to rust out in that country living.' 'Oh no, I am going to walk into the town and work there four days a week.'[4]

The country scholar-parson still had leisure. At Embleton Mandell Creighton wrote his great history of the papacy. At Crayke

[1] G, 06, 8.   [2] CCR, 1872, 76.
[3] CCR, 1872, 194; CCR, 1886, 308.   [4] CCR, 1893, 219.

in Yorkshire Edward Churton made a serious contribution to the study of Spanish literature. At Warkworth in Northumberland R. W. Dixon wrote the standard Tractarian history of the English Reformation. At Navestock in Essex Stubbs acquired that mastery of English medieval sources which helped to create the English school of history. At Broadwindsor, despite a mind which lacked critical sense, Caesar Malan became one of the English authorities on the study of oriental languages. At Melplash in Dorset Samuel Johnson, vicar from 1881 to 1905, built himself an observatory with his new vicarage, and became an authority in astronomy. Not that such studies always helped the work of the parish.[1]

Learning was less common than formerly, because after 1871 few Oxford or Cambridge dons needed to be ordained for their fellowships, and from about the same time they did not need to resign their fellowship if they married. Though less common than in the early Victorian age it was still common enough to make more than an occasional country vicarage into a house of learning. But it was now possible only for those with a comfortable benefice or with private means. And the hours of leisure available for men without desire to study began to seem too long. As early as the seventies a country doctor said that the great disease which afflicted the mass of country clergy was want of work.[2]

In the last decades of the century the country parson was less universally a countryman in habit and interest, and young men were said to be harder to find in country parishes. The village began to look like a harbour of rest for a man who gave his best years to the town. Men could not judge whether such an urban history prevented the parson being on terms with his farming labourer. Some thought that the town parson was inclined to underestimate the conservatism of the countryman, as over ritual change, or that he might introduce quavers or intonings suitable to town choirs but not so marriageable to a harmonium. The town-bred parson was occasionally accused of preaching sermons above the heads of his country congregation. But the country-bred parson did the same; as Julius Hare used to preach high intellectual food for an hour to the sleeping rustics of Hurstmonceux, or as Professor Henslow

[1] 'To hear that there Reverend of ours in the pulpit you might think we was all right. But bless you, he ain't same as other folk. He do keep a horoscope top o' his house to look at the stares and sich.' Jessopp, *Trials*, 38–39.
[2] CCR, 1893, 219.

used to preach abstractions in too loud a voice to the villagers of Hitcham. The most learned clergyman in England, Mark Pattison, sometimes took duty in village churches during the summer months, but we are told that his ministrations were not 'well adapted' for the purpose. One good country parson said, 'I defy anyone not to be over the heads of half his congregation, if he is to preach sense at all.' The countryman was said to prefer a difficulty in understanding to being talked down to.[1] And some very intelligent town-bred parsons perhaps underestimated their parishioners. Mandell Creighton, who was a donnish country vicar at Embleton in Northumberland for nine years, is reported to have defined the difference between a Russian peasant and an English peasant thus: one swears and gets drunk and goes to mass, the other swears and gets drunk and does not go to mass.[2] This did not perfectly represent Creighton's attitude to his flock. At the other extreme was R. W. Randall, who succeeded H. E. Manning as vicar of Lavington, one of the wonderfully attended Tractarian village churches, with many communicants out of 600 people in the year that Manning became a Roman Catholic; and Randall declared in his old age that he had seen no saintliness of life that ever exceeded the deep religion of the English peasant, and that sometimes when he was giving them communion he wanted to kneel down and kiss their horny hands.[3]

The country parson had advantages denied to his predecessors— higher standards of reverence, more education among the people, more friendship with dissent. But the bishops worried over him. He was depressed; partly because village life decayed, and partly because his income ceased to be adequate.

Statisticians argued over the stipends of the clergy. It was agreed that they fell, but men debated whether they fell in real terms. The parson of the eighties and nineties had no doubts.

Forty years before, there were 6,000 beneficed clergymen. By 1887 there were more than 13,000. More than a third of these benefices had incomes of less than £200 a year, and half of them had incomes of less than £300 a year. By the standards of rural nonconformist pastors this was comfort. But the rural parson was given a big house and expected to keep a gentleman's style. The

[1] DNB, xliv, 63; G, 02, 787.
[2] Adderley, *In Slums and Society*, 93.   [3] CCR, 1894, 290.

worst sufferers were the parsons whose income depended mainly on glebe. In the worst years they could not find tenants to farm the glebe. If they tried to farm it themselves the result was usually calamitous, especially if they were town-bred.[1] Poorer incumbents occasionally helped themselves by market-gardening or breeding poultry, but everyone regarded this sort of work as beneath them. In the early and mid-Victorian years some incumbents helped themselves by keeping a few pupils, in the kind of little society portrayed so charmingly by Trollope in *Dr. Wortle's School*. Some little vicarage schools continued to the end of the century and after. But the rapid growth of boarding schools made the country incumbent no longer indispensable as an aid to the secondary education of the gentry, and some of the later country incumbents had not the academic resources of those who earlier kept school.

Incumbents in the diocese of Lincoln or Peterborough or Southwell fell into distress because their income depended so largely on glebe, and a few of them lost for a time up to three-quarters of their nominal income. Most incumbents were preserved from distress because they possessed private incomes. But the possession of private income mattered more, and could affect parishes in unexpected ways. An incumbent with money gave generously in alms. If he was succeeded by an incumbent without money, the alms were no longer possible, and the parish estranged.

In the nineties the value of tithe was about 25 per cent below par or a little higher. It was calculated that the average incumbent was half as well off at the end of the reign as he was at the queen's accession; that the average income of an incumbent in 1837 was about £500 and in 1897 was £246. (The average net value differed according to the diocese: (in 1901) from London £429, Liverpool £342, Rochester £341, to Hereford £196, Llandaff £194, Bangor £188 and St. David's £171.[2]) But this figure was misleading. For the figure of £500 for 1837 was achieved by counting all the pluralists. Curates did much of the work in 1837, and then the curate's average stipend was £81, plus a house if the incumbent did not reside. The average stipend of a curate in 1893 was £145. But more than that, many parishes looked after by curates in 1837 were looked after by incumbents in 1897. The statistics of falling income

[1] Cf. H. P. Thomas, *The Church and the Land*, 1887, 7ff.
[2] G, 01, 1639; 97, 743; 98, 1933.

were therefore as misleading as statistics sometimes are. Nothing, however, was misleading about the depression in agriculture. The income of the clergy depended upon land. In 1837 land was a profitable, in 1897 an unprofitable, investment.

Between 1885 and 1905 the Easter offering, used as a gift to the parson, and hitherto rare enough in practice, spread rapidly through the country churches and some town churches.[1] By 1905 nearly half the parishes of the country were said to give the Easter offering to their parson. The early Victorian parson would have been surprised at the development. Not till after the turn of the century did Inland Revenue awake to the relevance of these gifts.

So the country parson was sometimes melancholy. He came from his college or his town parish, and found that he settled in a deteriorating countryside among slow-moving minds and with insufficient income. In the last decades of the century men talked much of the *loneliness* of the country clergy, how they lack hope and need encouragement, of the *stagnation* of the rural parson. It was in the eighties that someone, doubtless a country parson, defined a country parson as a spiritually-minded vegetable.[2] The young fellow of a college in 1840 expected to marry a wife and go into a country living where he stayed for the rest of his life. The parishioners liked the parson who baptised them and married them and buried them, and neither expected nor wanted him to move. The bishops discovered during the nineties that they needed to move the country parson for his own sake and that of his people, for stimulus and encouragement. And in the moment that clergy and bishops accepted the doctrine that many men needed to move after ten or twelve years, they began to criticise the patronage system and the parson's freehold because these prevented mobility. The first formidable assaults by Anglicans upon the parson's freehold came at the end of the eighties.[3] The freehold gave a man such security that he could say what he liked to his parishioners whether they would hear or whether they would forbear. It enabled him to be prophet or saint, lover of incense or hammer of bishops. It enabled him to neglect his work and yet survive, or denounce his

[1] In certain parishes the Easter offering had long continued for historic reasons. The vicar of Great Yarmouth sat in his study every day in Easter week to receive gifts in lieu of tithe on fish.
[2] First reference known to me CCR, 1888, 584.
[3] *Nineteenth Century*, xix, 1886, 514 (Jessopp); CCR, 1888, 149.

squire for sin and yet survive. But it made it difficult for him to change his work to what he needed when he needed. The freehold was designed to suit the old-fashioned marriage for life between a country parson and his people. But now the people's sons were mobile, and often it was good for the parson to move. The freehold, still a precious right to the incumbent, became a discomfort to those who cared for the welfare of incumbents.

In the nineties, then, they talked of lonely clergymen, stick-in-the-mud clergymen. This was new talk. It must not be supposed that early Victorian clergymen were never stagnant like some late Victorians. The late Victorian bishops were more active bishops. They knew their clergy better. They started to see what could be done to rescue failures. The new talk issued from greater pastoral care, as well as from increased isolation. And yet there may well have been more sense of loneliness; through the decline of the village and of income, the removal of other educated men, the urban background of many vicars. The village parson was to be saved by his car. No village parson of the Victorian age possessed a car.[1]

In 1903 a man revisited a country district south of the Trent, which he had not seen for thirty years. He tried to contrast the district as he knew it in 1873 with the district then. He thought the archdeacon less grand and more human, more of a parish priest, perhaps also more commonplace. A few scholarly incumbents still enjoyed composing Latin verses, but seem to have gained less credit for their scholarship. Fewer incumbents had been fellows of colleges. The clergy seemed more equipped in technique, more earnest and willing, but somehow less easy in society, less like ordinary gentlemen, more likely to go to a tennis party than to walk across the stubble with the farmer's shooting party. The big vicarage showed little signs of neglect. The gardens had an air of decay, and evidently the incumbent who once had a coachman and a gardener had now but one man. Hardly a vicarage had a carriage-and-pair. About the same time the university clubs in London noticed a shortage of clerical candidates, which was attributed to the eco-

---

[1] It was in 1890 that the story circulated of the country vicar who told his bishop, 'My Lord, I have not been absent from my church for a single Sunday for forty years', and who was surprised when the bishop replied 'Poor people!' CCR, 1890, 601. Doubtless *ben trovato*. But Bishop Frederick Temple was capable of such a retort.

nomies of the country parson, and the university cricket match at Lord's, which used to be called the parson's match because of the number of clerical coats, seemed to attract fewer.[1]

The Ecclesiastical Commissioners were beginning to keep an eye on the size of country vicarages, and the expected size was restrained by the standards of the recent past but still commodious. Their minimum requirements soon after the end of the reign were three reception rooms and five bedrooms. But at last they kept a watch on the rich incumbent who built with his private money and made life difficult for his poor successor and his poor successor's wife.

Despite the town suits and the town manufacturers the village still felt self-contained, to the end of the reign. One little sign. Very few churches of the countryside thought it worth while to put up a sheet in the porch with hours of services. The villagers knew and no one else would come. The first such sheets appeared at the end of the nineties, for the sake of wandering holiday-makers on bicycles. They were still quite rare early in the twentieth century.

It throws light upon the Victorian parish to compare the instructions given to clergymen early in the reign with those given at the end. These comparisons cannot easily make allowance for differences between authors and temperaments. Yet the difference in tone, as well as the continuity, may tell us something.

Some of the guidance is common to early and late. He can do nothing if he is not a good man. He must be a man of prayer and of his Bible. His reading outside the Bible must be wide. He must know his people by visiting them in their homes, especially when they are sick. The opportunities afforded by baptism and marriage and death must not be neglected. The work of the parish priest, helping them to Christian ideals of conduct, teaching them how to understand the place of worship and sacrament in their lives, comforting the old in trouble and helping the young to rise to their chances, turning a collection of men and women into a community —all these appear in the books whether early or late. The essence of the work was unchanging.

For the early Victorian age I select J. J. Blunt's book *The Duties of a Parish Priest*, first published in 1856, so much read that it was given a fourth edition in 1861, after which it began to look obsolete; and R. W. Evans, *The Bishopric of Souls*, first published in 1841, given a

[1] G, 03, 1935; 06, 1145.

fifth edition as late as 1877, valued by such a man as J. B. Lightfoot, and declared to be a 'great' book as lately as 1904. Blunt was professor at Cambridge after many years as a country curate and rector. Evans was a fine vicar in Westmorland for thirty years. Both men were strong Anglicans, neither Tractarian nor evangelical. Both books are charming. Evans's book is the more sensitive and warmhearted, because less donnish.

We notice first, what will not be true of such books in later Victorian England, that these two popular handbooks for the work of the clergy were written by men whose only parochial experience lay in country parishes. Both writers assumed that they should aim at country clergymen as the typical clergymen of the Church of England. Both writers assumed that the men for whom they wrote were well educated at a university. Blunt even assumed that most of them were likely to be sons of clergymen. Both writers assumed that the parishioners were mostly rustics. The parson on his walks passes turnip fields or orchards, sheafs of corn and henroosts, old women with bundles of sticks and old men heaving feeble legs over a stile. Both writers assume the clergyman to be the best informed man in the parish. Evans (p. 17) wrote openly of the pastor's advantage in his 'superior education and station in society'. Blunt expected that the only book known to most of the parishioners would be the Bible, and recommended (p. 165) that clergymen should not waste time in sermons by quoting simple texts at length, because so many of his people would know them from memory. The authorised version is the only English version. Evans made it the model of a preacher, not only in religion, but as the pure well of English undefiled, the language of poor as well as rich.

The parson is able to spend much of his time—at least all his mornings—on reading because the sermon is his most important act. It is the only place where he speaks to the whole parish. A few hostile persons do not come, a few bitter men shut their doors against him, a few louts and their loutish girls watch idly as their betters walk to church, but nearly all the parish comes to sit beneath his word. The sermon is the great moment of teaching. It needs his best endeavours, and therefore a lot of his time. Both expect him to be a learned man to read and study the Hebrew and Greek texts of the Bible; to have read the Greek and Latin Fathers in the original; to be familiar with the original documents of the English Reformation. Neither of them had much use for commentaries. Blunt is not even aware that this course is not likely to be achieved by everybody. Evans is keenly aware, and full of lamentations. Neither of them wanted clergymen to read the little religious books of the day.

Blunt's people joined in his worship rather as spectators than participants, and his parson must do all he can to make them a congregation instead of an audience. Blunt disclosed that people complained of the length, formality and tediousness of the prayers.

He never suggested that the Prayer Book might need amendment. That was not the attitude of the forties and fifties. They saw salvation in more precise obedience to the Prayer Book. The prayers are tedious because the people refuse to join in, not because they are too long or too outmoded. Get the people to join in and the tedium vanishes. Blunt paid much attention to rubrics; how to interpret them, how to act if they are doubtful, how to revive them without offence of innovation if they have lapsed by time. Authority meant much to him. To keep within the parish boundaries; to trespass on no other man's parish; to discourage dissent; to obey the canons of 1603 if they are not manifestly obsolete; to speak in the name of the Church of England the full doctrine of the Church of England— these are a foundation of the ideal of his parson.

Evans's parson is a state officer as well as a church officer. He is the man upon whom rests the responsibility for the moral behaviour of the little society. The people will not become a community without him. 'In building up spiritual society, he also by the way builds up civil, and becomes a most useful source of information to the ruling powers' (p. 24). He must know each as a person. 'Be not too fond of statistics' (p. 35). 'The statistic clergyman . . . can seldom be an efficiently working clergyman. He is too much of a theorist.' He is like a man who carries about a catalogue but never reads a book.

Both writers wanted a village school, controlled by the parson. It is the remedy for ignorance and the vestibule of his church. According to Evans (p. 154) it received little support from the middle-men of the congregation, the shopkeepers and the farmers. 'Sometimes they are opposed to it, but in most cases doggedly indifferent.' But both men regarded the school as the most powerful and excellent organ of parish work and village life. Evans even recommended the parson to flee into it for shelter in times of vexation, for the sight of its encouragements will restore his spirits and hopefulness (p. 157).

They were both for simplicity of life. But Evans deplored one luxury on which Blunt was silent. 'The modest old parsonage is fast disappearing' (p. 192). In its place rises a mansion where the parson may entertain the gentry of the neighbourhood, and which is not to be maintained merely upon the income of the living. He deplored clergymen who went to theatres, or played cricket, or attended balls, or went out shooting or hunting. The parson must be indifferent to criticism if he advocates political programmes on disinterested grounds, and yet must abstain from all vulgar and worldly means of promoting his political cause (p. 221). He should not be like the dissenters in introducing politics into the pulpit.

Neither of them approved of bazaars. Blunt regarded them (and the 'quadrille band') as a distasteful mode of raising money for the church. Evans regards a bazaar in a darker light as a vanity fair.

Turn now to the end of the century and to the same kind of book written for a new generation. I select *Apostles of the Lord* (1901), by W. C. E. Newbolt, who was a Tractarian canon of St. Paul's cathedral; and *Cambridge Lectures on Pastoral Theology* (1903) by the broad churchman J. M. Wilson, vicar of Rochdale and Archdeacon of Manchester.

Both wrote for the clergyman in cities. Newbolt even warned the clergy (p. 43) against the belief that only work in cities was worth doing. He found it necessary to state that this was the happiest profession of all the professions—despite. For the clergyman in Newbolt is up against society. He is unpopular as a member of a class though not as a parson. Everywhere the sick and the leper lie about his path. Little bands of apostolic men launch themselves against sin rampant. Their life is hard, their stipend small. Newbolt found no need to warn the clergy against personal luxury, nor against building over-large vicarages. The parson goes out amid a roaring secular society. His danger is that he may take his colour from that society. Newbolt therefore lays more emphasis than either Blunt or Evans upon the withdrawn nature of the clergyman's religious life. The parson of Blunt or Evans needed to be a prayerful man (Evans greatly disliked the newfangled word *prayer-ful*) because he must bring his people before God. Newbolt's parson needed to be prayerful so that the world could not rush in upon his heart and rule it. He spent more time in deepening the religious life of the select and faithful men and women, the communicants' guild. His daily offices of prayer, and his sacrament, are so regular and frequent that the peril is not neglect but familiarity. He needs, or at least uses, retreats and quiet days more than his predecessors, to withdraw from the noise and business. Though still (hypotheti-cally) a well-read man, Newbolt's clergyman is a less learned man. He regards commentaries with suspicion, but for a different reason. Blunt suspected commentaries as a substitute for first-hand critical study. Newbolt suspected commentaries as too intellectual an aid to Biblical study, for the rightful study of the Bible was the study of the heart, on the knees. Newbolt did not however approach the dictum of the slum priest Robert Dolling that he never read books because he had better things to do with his time.

Newbolt had a warning for the clergy which Blunt and Evans hardly uttered. They are not to hunt preferment. It hardly seems to have occurred to the assured Blunt or Evans that this might be a danger. Their clergymen are content with their lot and expect to continue in it. Newbolt expects clergymen to want to change their work, and is thereby afraid of worldliness creeping into them. New-bolt doubted the propriety of balls, hunts, theatres, shooting, dinner parties (p. 153). But he wrote that 'we have not improved the con-dition of the clergy in the parishes, by merely substituting tennis or croquet for hunting as a regular and constant occupation of clerical time'.

Wilson's book was much less typical, as broad churchmen were themselves much rarer. It is less donnish than Blunt's and yet the most intellectualist of the four books. All the permanent qualities are there. The pastor is a messenger of God to the people. And yet he must not act with the air of authority possible to Blunt or Evans. He is talking to educated people or half-educated people, at least to people who place his mind on no pedestal. He must teach what the church sends him to teach, and yet he must never say, 'The church teaches', implying that this alone is a sufficient ground of truth. Wilson's parson does more arguing with his parishioners. The idea (though not the word) of a 'discussion-group' is prominent in his pastoral work. He cannot expect them to know the Bible. Though he still ought to be (where possible) a well-read man, neither Wilson nor Newbolt suggested the Fathers or the Reformation divines. Wilson's reading outside the Bible was primarily in philosophy or in social issues—the Webbs on trade unions, or Rowntree on poverty, or Sidney Webb on socialism, or Holyoake on the co-operative movement, or Charles Booth on London life. He must lead his people to find religious dynamic for the reforming of society. Though he is a preacher, he must never become a dogmatist in the wrong sense. He must speak of the most sacred truths of Christianity with diffidence, humility, reverence, and must respect the argument even of those who deny them. He should clear away their illusions of what Christianity means, for example by teaching in the pulpit the legendary nature of parts of Genesis. He will find many men who accept Christ but not the Christian creed. These he must respect, and seek to include among his people.

Blunt and Evans were not bitter against dissent, but they wanted in the kindliest way to end it, not by union but by conversion. Wilson did not want to hurt it at all. There was no discomfort whatever between his church congregation and the dissenting congregation. They respected each other. The opinions which divided them were inessential compared with the truths which united them.

More of Wilson's flock did not come to church. But those who came, enjoyed it. They found warmth, life, beauty, comfort. They did not complain, like some of Blunt's, of the cold formality of the prayers. They were not nearly so attached to the words of the authorised version, partly because they knew it less, and partly because the archaisms of the seventeenth century felt now to be a barrier.

Many illustrations of village life may be found in the annals of village clergymen. In these samples which follow, we remember that each parish was unique and no parish typical, and that the people of whom we hear are not the discreditable (unless exceptionally discreditable), nor the ordinary, but those who came to be admired for quality or act by their neighbours.

Arthur Roberts, though a pupil of Keble at Oriel, was an evangelical who became rector of Woodrising in Norfolk in 1831, and died there fifty-five years later. He became famous because he published seventeen volumes of village sermons, which were widely used in country pulpits and parochial devotion, and for his frequent letters to the *Record*. We know of one neighbouring clergyman who looked upon him with reverence, as a light of gospel truth in Norfolk. He was never offered preferment, and never known to regret his tiny sphere. He hardly went out of his church to preach away, taught a Bible class in his kitchen on Sunday evenings, and three times a week taught in the village school. The children of his parish were renowned for their good grounding in Scripture. When there was an eclipse of the sun, he was on holiday and heard his own sermon on the subject preached at two different churches.[1]

It will be observed that some country clergymen still retained the custom of preaching other people's printed sermons. Newspapers published sermons for them to use. But the intellectual unsettlement of the age, or the natural passing of the generations, made older sermons impossible to use. The Anglican formularies encouraged the preaching of the *Homilies* of the English Reformation, and therefore the *Homilies* would be published in edition after edition. It is striking that the last year of publication for these purposes was 1859.

Bartholomew Edwards, rector of Ashill in Norfolk, was a great rider to hounds in the earlier part of the century, and an excellent judge of a horse. When it came to be felt that hunting was unfitting for clergymen, he gave it up. He was absent from his parish church on three Sundays between 1859 and 1889, when he died within nine days of his hundredth birthday.

Robert Elrington was vicar of Lower Brixham in Devon for thirty-four years (1855–89) (second in succession to Lyte, the author of *Abide with me*). He rebuilt his church into one of the grandest on the coast, made a new vicarage and a school, was chairman of the local board, was said to have dealt almost single-handed with a cholera epidemic in Brixham, and broke his health in a similar epidemic of scarlet fever.

Barrington Mills lived in his Suffolk village of Lawshall in a room that looked like a cabin, and was often seen on the quay at Harwich in blue jersey and sou'wester, for his pleasure was sailing. He got an average of thirty communicants on Sunday in a village of 770.

[1] R, 1886, 892, 928. Sermon preached on the day of the sun's eclipse, 15 May 1836, *Village Sermons*, ii (1841), 127ff; Norfolk visitation Returns.

On Ascension day he used to get 40–50 communicants at 4 a.m. in their working clothes. He took eight boys out of the school to sing mattins at 10 a.m. every weekday. He liked the eastward position but did not quite think that the rubric agreed, and so adopted what was called the north-east position. While he was on holiday he sent home a cartload of fish to his parishioners three times a week. He was never heard to preach outside his church, nor to invite another preacher to it. Five days in each week he spent four hours visiting.[1]

John Sharp became incumbent of Horbury in Yorkshire as soon as he became priest in 1834. Men offered him other work but he stayed at Horbury until 1899, sixty-five years. He joined the Oxford Movement, and from all the neighbourhood men travelled to see the sight of a surpliced choir. He got rid of pews after a lawsuit in which he paid the costs by selling most of the furniture in the vicarage. He built two other churches. But his main work was the House of Mercy, for the reclaiming of penitent women, which he aided Mrs. Sidney Lear in founding.

Here is a northern vicar of a less respectable kind. George Bayldon was the vicar of Cowling for over forty years (1850–94). His church was built in 1839 in a village almost run by nonconformists, with a strong Wesleyan Methodist chapel. Bayldon was a scholarly man, said to know more than nine languages. He published a dictionary of the Icelandic language, and a history of the Christian church in verse. A dissenter afterwards described the church thus: the village liked him because he was liberal in politics, friendly to nonconformists, and a teetotaller. When he began he was the only man in the village to take a daily newspaper. There was no congregation at all, no Sunday school, no choir. One of the aisles was used for sitting hens. The bell-ringer, a character of notoriety in the village, kept his pigeons in the belfry. Bayldon would go to the vestry, watch from the window to see if anyone came, and if one or two came he might give them a short service with a text and perhaps a few comments on it. If the bishop complained that he had no confirmation candidates, he went round the chapels, got the young to prepare themselves, and took them to the confirmation at Skipton. In his latter years he stopped living in the parish, but came over on Sundays in case anyone came to church. The parish greatly respected him.

[1] G, 99, 211; 89, 374; 97, 167; Lawshall Visitation Returns (Ely Records).

He was succeeded in 1894 by a vicar J. N. Lee. He was a high Tory, and his idea of duty was more positive. On occasion he needed the protection of the police, and once lost his windows through stone-throwing, and once a bullet came through the window of his study. The village did what they could to make him feel uncomfortable. But he settled down, turned from Toryism to being a radical in politics, and for the first time Cowling church had a prosperous congregation.[1]

Ritualism in the Victorian age was chiefly a difficulty of the towns. The great law-suits over ritual, with one exception, concerned town priests. This did not mean that country parishes were always untroubled by arguments over ceremonial. Archdeacon Denison ran into a famous parish contest over ritual at East Brent, and we find traces of the argument in many country parishes. The Tractarians wanted to make the worship of little churches less bald, to teach reverence by eye as well as word, and to deepen the sacramental sense of their people. Their changes encountered suspicion or hesitation from the countrymen. But often they acted with tact, and if they were good pastors, as many of them were, they at last reached a time when the parish trusted them and let them do more or less what they liked.

James Skinner was a famous ritualist, formerly of that scene of London controversy, St. Barnabas, Pimlico. He was celebrated as a Tractarian writer in moral and spiritual divinity, as a director of souls, as a conductor of retreats. In 1861, because of deplorable health, he accepted the vicarage of Newland near Malvern, which had thirty-six families, but which had not had a resident clergyman for about forty years. In 1861 the sacrament was celebrated seven times; in 1862, twenty-three times; in 1867 daily, always with communicants. He first got them to like to decorate the altar, then adopted linen vestments at Christmas 1867 and was given a full set of coloured vestments for Easter 1868. Neither bishop nor parishioners opposed the innovation; and indeed Bishop Philpott of Worcester, who was a Palmerston bishop and no high churchman, always treated Skinner with kindness and encouragement. The old wooden church was taken down as much too small, and a new one consecrated. Under the wills of the former Earl Beauchamp

---

[1] Snowden's *Autobiography*, i 30–32. But Bishop Longley's notes on the parish (1847–56, Brotherton Library) show a Congregation of 40–70 and a Sunday school of 25–50.

and his first wife, almshouses were built, and free places for singing
boys at a school, and the music must have been among the best in
any English country church. On Sundays the new church was
always crowded, and only parishioners were allowed to take their
seats until the bell stopped. It was a parish dear to those who looked
back upon Keble and Hursley as the authentic country parish of
the English tradition; blue-cloaked pensioners moving in procession
to daily prayers in the church, the vicar in his cassock and cape,
the lawns and elms and archways, one of the little Victorian jewels
created by the Oxford Movement. The trustees of the advowson
made opposition. Skinner battled on against terrible health and the
death of his only child, conducting retreats, writing letters of
counsel, trying to found a school of moral divinity in the Church
of England, until resignation in 1877.[1]

J. C. Atkinson, son of an evangelical vicar in Lincolnshire, went
in 1847 to be vicar of Danby at the heart of the Cleveland
moors, and held the parish until his death in 1900. Nine years before
his death he published a pleasant book, *Forty Years in a Moorland
Parish*, which made Danby one of the famous Victorian country
parishes. Atkinson considered the question, how the parish was
different during his forty-four years, and came to some interesting
answers. Deep down, he thought that little changed; though the
parson now wore black trousers instead of drab breeches and the
people wore broadcloth instead of inherited leather, the changes
were more outward than inward. There was no more class feeling
at the end than at the beginning, because in this Yorkshire dale
everyone was equal when he came and everyone was still equal.
The villagers had better cattle and better horses, spoke less in dialect,
could read, brought many more newspapers into the place and were
able to sign their names when they married. There were no eagles
now on the moors, and no dog-whipper appointed for the church.
The village was less remote, communications quicker, the outside
world nearer. The vestry met in the inn when he arrived, and they
still met in the inn, for the church was nearly two miles from the
homes of most of the people, but now they kept the pipes and beer
until after the meeting. The language at weddings was less earthy.
When he arrived the only religion in the valley that mattered was
that of the Wesleyan Methodists and Primitive Methodists. They

[1] M. Trench, *James Skinner*, 2nd ed., 202ff.; J. Hunt, *Newland* (unpublished).

still mattered, but he hoped that the parish church mattered too. Fewer births were illegitimate. Altogether he thought the 'ostensible' standard of morality and manners to have risen markedly, and attributed this rise to the great improvement in the cottages, so that men and women no longer slept mixed together in shed-like dormitories. Villagers took their hats off when they went into the church now, and even his predecessor as vicar kept his hat on in church except at times of service. The linen in church was cleaner, the floor swept, the altar cared for. The old man himself moved away from his evangelical background into the school of Maurice and Kingsley and F. W. Robertson. One of his yeomen brought him Colenso on the Pentateuch, and said that he did not much care for it but perhaps it was worth looking at it and the vicar could keep it. Atkinson, at least in the eighties, used from time to time to touch in the pulpit on the suggestions of agnostics and free thinkers, and found his parishioners interested. But he bothered himself or his people little enough with the progress of the world's thought. And, looking back, he could not see that his parish or people altered during the Victorian age so markedly as his questioners seemed to expect them to have altered.

The list of interesting incumbents of villages could go on for many pages. The work bred remarkable men.

2. THE VILLAGE CHAPEL

The Wesleyan Methodist chapels were often in towns, and unless the squire was one of the rare Roman Catholic squires, there were no Roman Catholic chapels in the villages. If a Roman Catholic lived in a village, he was regarded as odd and though he might be respected for his life or piety was not accorded the same tolerance as was accorded to Primitive Methodists or Strict Baptists, and men looked to see how he would behave on 5 November.[1] In the north the nonconformist chapel usually occupied the village before the church, and was often stronger. Primitive Methodists and Baptists were village denominations. Lincolnshire had hardly a village without its chapel. In Buckinghamshire in 1887 over 60 of the 78 chapels of the Baptist Union were sited in villages.[2] The little chapel was viable in tiny and remote hamlets, with a congregation of anything

[1] Cf. Champneys, *Patmore*, i, 353-4.   [2] PP, 1888, xxxv, 399-401.

from fifteen to fifty. It was a little lay democracy which might need grants of money from some central fund and visits from neighbouring preachers but was content with the utmost simplicity of building, liturgy, management, music and preaching. The layman had more responsibility, and more sense of it, than at the parish church, partly because at the parish church he would expect to be guided by his betters, and partly because as yet the parish church had no constitutional means of giving a Christian, as distinct from a secular, responsibility to the layman; except so far as those laymen with the right to do so chose the incumbent.

The ministers who looked after rural chapels were usually from simple homes. Though the nonconformist minister of good education was common in the towns, he was not in such plentiful supply as to warrant stationing him in the country unless he had a special attrait in that direction. Occasionally we find rural ministers with a fascinating background of experience, like Edward Stallybrass, Congregationalist pastor at Burnham Market 1858–70, who earlier lived an extraordinary career as the first Protestant missionary in Mongolia.[1] They were unostentatious men. The obituary notices of rural Independent pastors conjure a charming little world of remote chapels. 'D. Griffiths . . . was admitted to the communion of the church at Siloam chapel, and there he commenced preaching. He studied for some time under the Reverend J. Jones, of Horeb. About twenty years ago he settled in the neighbourhood of Llantrissant, Glamorganshire, to work at his trade as a carpenter, and joined the church at Bethel chapel in that town. In 1866 that church called him to the pastorate. . . . There he laboured with a degree of usefulness and general acceptance to the day of his death, 15 September 1884. He was a quiet and blameless man, and serviceable in the small sphere which he occupied.'[2] Occasionally a pastor lived on into the later Victorian age who could remember being rabbled by a village mob early in his life, like John Allen, the pastor at Chudleigh for forty-two years.[3] Their fathers, if not themselves pastors, were usually small farmers, or shopkeepers, or stonemasons, or carpenters or the like. The nonconformist bodies (in the later years of the century they preferred the name nonconformist to the old and once proud name of dissenter) suffered no shortage of ministers. Even at

[1] CYB, 1885, 230; Gilmour, *Among the Mongols*, 1883, 38ff.
[2] CYB, 1885, 198.   [3] CYB, 1885, 174ff.

the end of the century, when the leaders of the Church of England complained loudly of decline in number of vocations, the non-conformists uttered no such complaint. Sometimes a congregation took a good man already in the congregation and invited him to lead them and were able to give him at least an equal stipend, and certainly no lower status, than the place in the village which he already occupied. In 1901 it was calculated that 22 per cent of the Congregational ministers in England and Wales had no college training.[1]

The relations between the parish church and the chapel varied according to persons and circumstances. The chapel congregation tended to move in its own social circle apart from religion. We hear of little religious controversy. A rector near Oswestry said, 'I make it a principle never to speak to dissenters about religious matters. But I have a very good garden with a southern slope, and I send them baskets of early vegetables, and by this means I have brought several over to the church.'[2] Anthony Trollope's finest ecclesiastical novel, *The Vicar of Bullhampton* (1870), described how a squire, angry with his incumbent, allowed a dissenting chapel to be erected at the vicarage gates, and this kind of social difficulty was more prominent in villages than religious difficulties. There is evidence even in 1895 that this division in villages could generate friction.[3] The children were the only principal rub, for the non-conformist chapel often had the better and sometimes the only Sunday school, while the parish church almost always had the only day school. There is a little evidence that chapels were stronger where the village was divided into freeholds and thus the villagers were not dependent on a single landowner. But we need much more evidence before we can judge the consequences in church affairs of these differing tenures of land.

In parts of the north, and in Cornwall, and most of Wales, the chapel was the dominant institution. At Treorky in the Rhondda valley the pastor from 1869 was William Morris, a doctor of divinity from Bucknell university in Pennsylvania. It was the chief social centre of the area, and about half the seats were rented like pews. About 200 out of the 250 members of the Rhondda choral society were members of the chapel, and used its vestry and

---

[1] *British Weekly*, 17 January 1901, 374; quoted Tudur Jones, 324.
[2] Walsham How, *Lighter Moments*, 37.   [3] Cf. CCR, 1895, 445.

its organ as their headquarters. Miners used it for industrial meetings, friendly societies for their work. It had an excellent system of district visitors to administer charity. From the congregation groups went out to be the nucleus of new Baptist chapels in the neighbourhood—an English-speaking chapel in Treorky (1869), new churches at Cwmparc (1874) and Moriah (1875) and Ainon (1896). To the end of the century the Sunday school taught Welsh grammar, because until lately Welsh was not used in Welsh schools. On social matters relations between this chapel and the local Anglican parish at Cwmpark were excellent, and on religious matters they kept silent and apart.[1]

In *Lark Rise* Flora Thompson described how as an Anglican child in Oxfordshire she would be occasionally allowed by her disapproving, agnostic father to visit the Primitive Methodist service, held on Sunday evenings in the cottage of one of the three nonconformist families. Most of the Methodists also attended church until the arrival of an Anglo-Catholic curate. A few villagers not Methodists attended the Methodist meeting, glad to have somewhere to go on Sunday evenings. They sang Moody and Sankey's hymns without accompaniment, had extempore prayer with local history— 'old Mr. Barker telling God that it had not rained for a fortnight and that his carrot bed was getting mortal dry'. Sometimes members stood up to testify their sins or their conversion. The travelling preacher was usually a farm labourer, or small shopkeeper, with few exceptions uneducated, and at one sermon the child burnt with shame to hear the mess the preacher made of it, and at another, by a shop assistant from a near-by town, with oiled hair and perfume, she and the congregation dismissed him as a *poseur*. But the simple labouring preacher and his word came through to her as more genuine, and more direct to God, than what she heard in church, even though she preferred the church service, and she admired the lives of the little group of Methodists.[2]

If the country incumbent was a sensible man, the village continued to recognise him as a leader of the community, for the squire so often was not there. Dissenters were often happy to pay their

[1] PP, 1910, xv, 284ff.
[2] Flora Thompson was born 1877 at Juniper's hill near Brackley, and the church which she describes was that of Cottisford, where she was educated at the village school. Cf. *The Periodical*, xxxi, 1956, 213.

tokens of respect. The relations between church and chapel in the village were usually better. The end of church rate ended the main source of controversy between church and chapel; and after the burials act of 1880 there was only the school to divide, and the school seldom divided the village. The loosening of doctrinal standards among the laity of both church and chapel introduced a friendly haze, unless the incumbent were Anglo-Catholic or the chapel Strict Baptist. 'We're all going to the same place', the squire and charitable nonconformist countryman would say by the end of the century, 'so long as we get there, it does not much matter which way we go.'[1] The old habit whereby dissenters attended the parish church after or before their own service survived in some places throughout the reign, and we find a few parishes, especially in the north, where the dissenters helped the incumbent in his parish duties and taught in his Sunday school.

As the old issues which once divided the village faded away into the past, usually by concession on the part of the established church, the political grouping of the village often retained a relation to the church on one side and the chapel on the other. After the general election of November 1868, for example, Gladstone attributed the failure of the Liberal party in the English countryside to the political endeavours of the country clergy; and, being Gladstone, added that he was glad to find their influence to be still so strong.[2] On the other side one of Disraeli's colleagues told him that at Christchurch in Hampshire the nonconformist minister drove the newly franchised labourers to the polls in support of the Liberal cause.[3] While each side exaggerated the power of church or chapel over votes, a relation between the political grouping of the village and its religious grouping continued in many places. In *Felix Holt* (1866) George Eliot used the circumstance as one of the foundations for a novel. It was not an invariable rule that the political activities of the 'church group' tended to the Tory party. We know of several country clergymen who, like Mandell Creighton in his remote Northumberland parish, spent their time trying to make the Liberal party respectable in an unpromising environment. Probably the majority of country parsons undertook no political activity, some on principle

---

[1] J. M. Wilson, *Pastoral Theology*, 161; cf. G, 02, 787.
[2] *Letters of Queen Victoria*, 2nd series, i, 563.
[3] Malmesbury to Disraeli, 24 November 1868; Hughenden Papers, B/XX/HS/157.

and some because they were not interested. The ballot made such activity no longer public. In remote Danby Atkinson abstained from all political activity until his principles disappeared when a candidate came forward whom he had known and loved since childhood.[1] In his little parish in Shropshire John Allen abstained on principle from voting at all, for forty-five years and more.[2] Moments of stress could make even country clergymen break their rule of not preaching politics. We know of a conventional country parson, who normally avoided these subjects but astonished people by preaching fiercely against the Liberals at the general election in 1886.[3]

3. THE VILLAGE SCHOOL

All experts in parochial life agreed upon the importance of the village school. This usually owed its creation to the parson or the squire. Most village schools were Anglican schools, at least in name, throughout the century. As higher standards prevailed after 1840, the government gave money in return for a management committee and the right of inspection. A few parishes refused to accept either a management committee or the right of inspection, and preferred to do without the money from government. But most parsons and parishes accepted the money and the conditions.

In 1870 Forster's education act created a national system of education. It used the denominational schools and required a board school only where need could be shown to exist. In some parts, especially in dissenting Wales, boards were created which included schools for country parishes. But in most country districts of southern and central England the Anglican school was adequate in its accommodation, or could without difficulty be made adequate. The philosophy beneath the act of 1870 contended that schools of a denomination were suitable for the children of parents from any other denomination. The secular instruction was secular and nothing compelled the parent to send his child to the religious instruction. In the towns this philosophy broke down from time to time, especially in the rare cases where the only school available was a

---

[1] Atkinson, *Forty Years in a Moorland Parish*, 17.

[2] *Chron. Convoc.*, 1880, 90.

[3] Flora Thompson, *Lark Rise*, chapter xiv; a charming picture of the village church before the late Victorians changed it.

Roman Catholic school. In the English countryside it worked reasonably. Most dissenting parents were happy to send their children to the village school and did not mind that it was Anglican. They were happy not to withdraw their children from religious instruction though it was Anglican, for they formed but vague notions of any difference between non-Anglican teaching of religion and Anglican teaching of religion, a difference not often evident to instructed observers and very seldom evident to the simple parishioner who, perhaps by ancestry, worshipped at the dissenting chapel.

The denominational school of the countryside found it easy to maintain the required standards only if the vicar or the squire or the farmers had means and inclination to help with money. If these sources of money were wanting or reluctant, the village school could become poor; especially because it could not easily pay an adequate stipend to the teacher. If they could not afford a reasonable stipend they secured ineffective teaching and a constant sequence of teachers as their men or women looked out for a more remunerative place. The church training colleges produced a supply of effective teachers who were more and more drawn into board schools in towns, instead of church schools in the country. Herefordshire was an Anglican county with Anglican village schools, many of which seem to have been good or adequate. But at the poor village of Upper Sapey, seven miles from Bromyard, the school account was always overdrawn, the teacher always changing, children came two and a half miles over shocking roads. The standard varied according to the area and the parish. During the eighties evidence was offered that the rural schools in Somerset provided a high standard of religious education. Plenty of evidence suggests that after as before 1870 the country clergy were the men who cared most and did most to educate the poor in their parishes.[1] A few stiff men resented the compulsory introduction of the conscience clause by the act of 1870 into Anglican schools, which caused Archdeacon Denison to resign from the National Society in May 1870. But the old argument over the conscience clause faded during the seventies, especially when so tiny a handful of dissenters chose to take advantage.

The strong leaders of nonconformity in the towns disliked the denominational school of the village because it was so commonly

[1] PP, 1887, xxx, 645.

Anglican. Some nonconformists of the village genuinely felt grievance. But for the most part the grievance was felt not so much by village nonconformists as on their behalf by articulate nonconformists of the towns. Looking round for arguments to attack the denominational system, they found importance in the rural schools.

The conscience clause, if unpopular with some high Anglicans and some Roman Catholics, was seldom or never violated. The examples quoted to prove such violation turned out on enquiry to be irrelevant. In 1884 several boys of the Church of England school at Kidlington near Oxford absented themselves to attend the Sunday school treat of the Free Methodist chapel. The schoolmaster flogged them for playing truant, and the case was taken up as though it was a violation of the conscience clause.[1]

The more serious charge was made that rural nonconformist parents were afraid to take advantage of the conscience clause. That so few parents withdrew their children from religious instruction needed explanation. It was confessed that religious indifference had something to do with it. Observers suggested that in some places parents did not know that they had the right to withdraw their children. The facts were remarkable. In the Lutterworth union there were 29,000 children at school. All the schools were Anglican except one, which was a board school. 25 per cent of the children attended nonconformist Sunday schools and presumably had nonconformist parents. Yet only twelve children were withdrawn from religious instruction.[2] Nearly all nonconformist parents cheerfully sent their children to be taught religion in schools connected with the Church of England. And observers agreed that the schools succeeded in communicating no more than the simplest truths of Christianity and that if they taught 'churchmanship' it did not get through to the children.

But the nonconformist leaders had a charge. They were particularly severe on the system if they were leaders among the Primitive Methodists or the Baptists, for both these denominations possessed many chapels in the villages. In many villages of Buckinghamshire the nonconformist Sunday school contained more children than the Anglican Sunday school, yet the nonconformist parents did not withdraw their children from the religious instruction given in the day school of the Church of England. The charge

---

[1] PP, 1887, xxx, 33; 1888, xxxv, 397.　　　　　　　[2] PP, 1888, xxxv, 405.

was made that this was not due simply to ignorance, nor to indifference, nor to contentment with the religious teaching given by Anglicans. It was due, the charge went, to fear; fear by nonconformist parents that their child would be subjected to inconvenience if he alone failed to attend the religious instruction.

The Anglicans argued that the fear, if it existed (which inspectors confidently denied), was imaginary. If a man did not hesitate to go to chapel in a small and largely Anglican village, he would hardly hesitate before the lesser act of singularity in sending his child to school a few minutes late. The fact was, that the grievance existed only for people of very decided opinions against the establishment. If twenty nonconformist families in a village had withdrawn their children, all would have been easy. But most nonconformist villagers did not feel this decided objection to the village school, and were happy. There the one or two nonconformist families, who objected on principle, suffered a real difficulty, that they would make their child unique in the eyes of his fellows. This difficulty existed equally in a big town, and applied to the religious teaching of board schools as of denominational schools. A member of the school board at Huddersfield withdrew his daughter on principle from religious instruction. The headmistress went to him and begged him to let her come back. She said she was so sorry for the child sitting in a classroom by herself.

In all the country (1887) there were more than two million children on the registers of Church of England schools. Only 2,200 children were withdrawn from the whole of religious instruction, and only 5,690 more when the catechism was being taught. The secretary to the Wesleyan education committee said that teachers with an experience of twenty or thirty years had never known a withdrawal. A few Roman Catholics asked. A few Jews asked to withdraw from lessons on the New Testament, though not usually from lessons on the Old.

'You give them Christian instruction?' 'Yes, we give them Christian instruction.'
'You give them Protestant instruction?' 'Yes, we give them Protestant instruction.'

But the statistics were a tribute to the fair manner in which most teachers imparted their religious teaching.

One difficulty was weightier than the reluctance of parents to use the conscience clause. It concerned the teaching profession. To enter the profession they must become pupil-teachers. To become pupil-teachers they must be employed in a school. A nonconformist might therefore find more difficulty in entering the teaching profession in a rural area. In the diocese of Oxford (1885) there were only 72 board schools, while there were 604 schools of the Church of England, thirteen of the Wesleyan Methodists and twelve of the Roman Catholics. Therefore an Anglican candidate in the diocese of Oxford had a better chance of acceptance as a pupil-teacher than had a nonconformist.[1]

The forward and logical among nonconformists wanted a national system of state education, either with religion excluded or with a religion taught in the undenominational manner provided by the act of 1870. The Wesleyan Conference of 1873 wanted to solve the rural difficulty more moderately, not by abolishing the denominational schools but by providing board schools in all parts of the country. In some villages there was a real fight over a school board, and where it occurred, it could be fierce because fought within a smaller group of people. On 15 December 1877 the school board of Stansfield in Suffolk revised the time-table and struck out religious instruction, substituting grammar and geography; the chairman meanwhile protesting the gross indecency of the proceeding.[2]

Probably the rise or rather the development of the teaching profession after 1870 tended to weaken a little the old link between the parsonage and the cottage of the schoolmistress. The village teacher was better trained, more conscious of independent standards, less tied to his or her post. The weakening of the old link is probable on the face of it. Evidence is hard to come by. Archdeacon J. P. Norris of Bristol, a veteran with a long career of public education behind him, conceived the time between 1849 to 1862 to be a time of advance and enthusiasm in the teaching profession which he did not find to be so marked in the seventies and eighties. In those earlier years he was government inspector of schools in Cheshire and Staffordshire and Shropshire; and he could remember how often the school would be visited, how keen the interest of squire's family or clergyman's family or millowner's family, in his memory

---

[1] PP, 1888, xxxv, 398–401; 410–11. [2] PP, 1878–9, lvii, 437.

a gentle and civilising influence surrounding the school and its teacher. He remembered how the pupil-teachers would come up to the hall or the parsonage to be taught singing or the piano or botany from the daughters at the hall and religious instruction at the parsonage. He did not find quite the same interest now.[1] But he was an old man looking back, and moved into a city from a district where most schools were rural.

A few country parishes settled the religious difficulty by a harmony between churchmen and dissenters in management. Bishop Thornton in Yorkshire had a Roman Catholic school and a national school side by side. The parish laid a voluntary rate, and gave the Roman Catholic rate to the Roman Catholic school and the rest to the national school. At Worlaby in Lincolnshire the vicar presided over a group of managers representing both Anglicans and nonconformists. The Anglican school at Clayton near Bradford employed a nonconformist as the assistant teacher in order to satisfy nonconformist parishioners. Such alliances were sometimes achieved under the pressure that without them a school board might be formed.

The steady rise in the standard of the profession ought to have meant that religion was better taught in the schools. The improvement was impossible to test, and not everyone agreed that religion was better taught after 1875 than before 1865. Schools and buildings, it was sometimes argued, increased faster than the number of good teachers. Some who had most right to speak about the quality of teaching in the old denominational schools warned the reformers of the seventies and eighties that they should not underestimate that quality. On the whole, however, men agreed that better training of teachers meant better teaching of religion. The village Sunday schools found their children more knowledgeable about the Bible, and like Sunday schools of the town no longer needed to teach the three Rs but could teach only religion. Certainly those who argued for the beauties of the earlier system needed to encounter the evidence of earlier inspectors' reports couched in strong language of condemnation.

The Sunday school of the village decreased in importance. It lost its function as an educator of other things besides religion. And it was not so important to teach Biblical history to the children if they

[1] PP, 1887, xxx, 136, 182, 189.

would be taught it, and taught it better, at the day school. The better trained teachers of the day school were now seen by children or parents to contrast with the untrained teachers of the Sunday school. The Sunday school had a great place in the social and religious history of England, but after 1870 it fell inevitably into a slow decline. What it could do best was also done elsewhere. On the other hand its standards were raised. Charlotte Yonge was a Sunday school teacher at the age of seven, and by the seventies that was seen as improper.[1]

4. MOTHERS' UNION

The country parish had few organisations but a Sunday school, though more clubs of various kinds were brought into being during the last quarter of the century. The movement of organisations was normally from town to country. But in one important case the movement was reversed. The Mothers' Union began as a parish organisation in a little country town, and spread outwards into the diocese until at last it conquered the parishes of the country.

Mary Sumner (*née* Heywood) was the wife of George Sumner, son of old Bishop C. R. Sumner of Winchester. In 1876 she created a meeting for cottage mothers and lady mothers in her husband's parish of Old Alresford. Despite the social gulf the mothers were to join in a group with the object of arousing parents to a sense of responsibility for the religious upbringing of their children. The members signed a card, and were 'enrolled'. It proved to be so successful in the parish that the Sumners created a similar union for men.

It remained the organisation of a single parish for nine years. The Church Congress at Portsmouth in 1885 held a meeting for working women, which was packed. Bishop Ernest Wilberforce of New-castle was the speaker, but turned to Mary Sumner and insisted that she speak. It was the time when Josephine Butler was agitating, and prostitution was much before the public mind. Mary Sumner lost her nervousness, and appealed to them as mothers to raise the national character. 'Those who rock the cradle', she said, 'rule the world.' The meeting gave her an ovation.

Accordingly in 1887 Bishop Harold Browne of Winchester made

[1] Coleridge, *Yonge*, 95.

the union a diocesan organisation, and commended it to every parish. Soon it spread to other dioceses, first to Lichfield, Exeter and Hereford, where the wives of the three bishops were all friends of Mary Sumner. She was a great organiser and aimed to show women how they could mould the rising generation. The *Mothers' Union Journal* began in 1888 and by 1890 had a circulation of thirteen thousand quarterly. Mary Sumner gained Charlotte Yonge to the cause, and though Miss Yonge's presence on platforms was awkward and embarrassed, her name was the most powerful which could have been gathered.

From 1893 there was a national organisation with a central committee, formalised as the Central Council in May 1896. They began to exercise pressure on social legislation—laws about prostitution, or divorce, or temperance, or education, or infant life insurance, or the registration of domestic servants. They wanted the divorce act of 1857 repealed but had no chance of success. They were more powerful in resisting those who desired to make divorce easier. They were not in the least influenced by the Christian Socialists. Mary Sumner was an aristocratic philanthropist like Lord Shaftesbury. She was a great and gay lady; taking cold baths daily; refusing to have a telephone, or (when they came) a motor-car, or smoking in her house. She thought herrings were food for cats and was astonished to be offered them at a vicarage. She was determined to make the mothers of England care about their children, instead of leaving them to the nurse if they were rich and to the street if they were poor. And despite her early ignorance of working-class mothers, she was wholly without patronage. The cottage mother and the mother of the great hall met in the same meeting and undertook the same duty. There was a difficulty about the card. For working mothers it had a clause about not sending children to the public house, a clause thought not suitable for mothers in the great house. The membership by 1912 was 278,500, nearly all mothers of the working class.[1]

5. THE CHURCH COUNCIL

The old vestry remained part of the civil, as well as the ecclesiastical, administration of the village. Every citizen had the right to

[1] Joyce Coombs, *George and Mary Sumner*, 81–91, 103, 106, 183–8.

sit in it and elect churchwardens, and churchwardens might still be nonconformists or even non-Christians. The churchwarden still retained vestigial duties as a civil officer. The parson retained a more than nominal place as the civil as well as ecclesiastical president. He was *ex officio* the chairman of the vestry, which dealt with much in the village that had nothing to do with the church. The minute book of the vestry at Holt in Norfolk shows the vestry, during the year 1855, ruling on water supply, sanitation, the appointment of constables and overseers and the survey of the highway, the church accounts, the gas inspectors and church rate. At other times the Holt vestry concerned itself with whether certain orphan children should be chargeable to the parish, whether the street should be widened and macadamised, a new organ, the site of the railway station, and whether the west gallery of the church should be dismantled.

In the village the old union of sacred and secular was not to appearances a dream of the past. And in some villages that union was strengthened during the years after 1860. The new provisions in education, the enforced conscience clause, and the better training of teachers allowed the village school to flourish as never before, and in continued union with the parson and the church. One sign of this strength was the building of village halls. As the standards of the village rose, and especially of the women who were not content with the public house, there became a crying need for a hall where might be held the manifold social evenings of the village, from concerts and smoking to a village library and lectures on Shakespeare, and which could also be used for vestry meetings or Sunday school or confirmation class. A high proportion of these village halls were build by the initiative of the vicar or squire or leading church folk, though the nonconformists of the village gave generously or spent freely at a bazaar. A return of 1894, perhaps not exact, showed that only 1 in a 100 were built before 1850; 9 per cent of the total were built between 1850 and 1860, 22 per cent between 1860 and 1880, 48 per cent between 1880 and 1890, 20 per cent between 1890 and 1893,[1] and by 1890 the hall became, like the school, an indispensable equipment of any well-run country parish. The hall was usually regarded as a church hall, but was used for the secular functions of the village. Charlotte Yonge, most conservative of

[1] Hansard, 1893, xxi, 187.

ladies, believed despite her conservatism that the village youths and lasses found it more difficult to be religious in her early days than in her later, because they used not to have the modern outlets for harmless recreation, and in the old days a lad who sought innocent pleasure needed to abstain from almost all pleasure.

The functions of vestry and churchwardens were most manifest at the meetings for laying a church rate to repair the church or maintain the churchyard. While church rate became unenforceable in the towns, it continued unchallenged in many country parishes. In 1868, stimulated by Gladstone, Parliament at last abolished church rate, allowing the 'levy' of a voluntary church rate. Many town parishes were already living on subscriptions or collections, and noticed no change. Many country parishes at first noticed little change. The rate continued to be laid, and parishioners continued to pay. In some country parishes this voluntary rate continued for many years. It was occasionally shaken in little parishes by the sudden reluctance of corporate landowners, some of whose representatives objected. The voluntary church rate at the little parish of Ketteringham, near Norwich, was first disturbed by the railway company whose line ran through the parish. The voluntary church rate at Little St. Mary's in Cambridge was first disturbed because members of the university discovered that the Fitzwilliam Museum, in the parish, paid the rate. (In some urban parishes a compulsory rate continued for a time under the authority of local acts of Parliament. The last compulsory rate was levied in St. Marylebone in 1899.[1]) Holt regularly levied a church rate till abolition, though not without a little opposition and once after a poll. Then on 29 October 1868 the vestry met to consider how to support the fabric of the church and maintain divine worship; and minuted that whereas 'churchwardens have no longer power to enforce the payment of church rates, it is not desirable at present to attempt to provide the requisite funds by means of a voluntary rate; but that, instead thereof, the churchwardens be requested to raise such funds as they can by means of annual subscriptions, to be supplemented if necessary by an evening collection in a church once a month, and should the funds so raised prove insufficient that then a collection be made in church every Sunday evening'. By 1894 every church in the north was said to have a

[1] S. Walpole, *Twenty-Five Years*, ii, 337.

weekly collection, but a fair number in the south still refrained.[1]

The predictions that historic village churches would collapse if church rate ended do not seem to have been fulfilled. Some country clergymen said that they did better by collections than formerly by the rate. A vicar in Derbyshire said that the rate used to raise £30 or £40 and his church was always in debt, whereas the offertory always covered expenses and to spare—'I ask and have.'[2]

The vestry in the village was perhaps an anomaly. It came to be seen as more anomalous when its duties increased in complexity. A series of acts of Parliament interfered with its activities, in sanitation, roads, lighting, workhouses, constables. The government of the village became subject to a variety of other authorities, the spheres of which overlapped. As the villages declined with the agricultural depression, their primitive sanitation or housing became matter of increasing public concern, and critics sometimes blamed the vestry for its inefficiency. The parson had a right to the chair, and not all parsons, it was said, were noted for their aptitude in business. The final impetus to this desire to reform the vestries was given after the enfranchisement of the agricultural labourer. The labourer could help to return a member of Parliament. But in his village he could probably exercise no influence at all on its management. For even if the squire was non-resident or exercised little influence—and if the squire was a good man he still exercised much influence—the government of the village might largely be controlled by the vicar, appointed by the patron, and two church-wardens, one of whom was appointed by the vicar. Moreover, when it came to a vote, the labourer's vote counted less; for the vestry still voted under the system of plural votes, whereby he with more property had more votes. And yet the 'control' was an illusion. For the real government of the village now lay with other authorities, the union, the county council, the highway board, the burial board, perhaps the school board. Vestries, said the president of the local government board, are 'decrepit survivals of former days. . . . They have the form but not the power of local government; they do not possess the confidence of the rural population; and they are in the main useless and obstructive. They do not meet at convenient hours. . . .'[3]

---

[1] CCR, 1894, 612.   [2] CCR, 1878, 241.
[3] Hansard, 1893, x, 687. The civil parish was not invariably identified with the ecclesiastical parish. In 1893 there were about 15,000 civil parishes, of which not more

Therefore from 1886 every Liberal, and some Conservatives, thought it time to create a 'secular' parish council, with each voter possessing a single vote, and so to attempt to restore responsibility for local government of the village. The act of 1894 provided for an elected parish council in villages over 300 people, grouped other villages, abolished plural voting and substituted poll by ballot. The churchwardens ceased to be overseers, the parson was no longer chairman, nor even a member unless elected. This act was on the whole welcomed by the authorities of the church. But in its passage through Parliament it aroused much feeling. Critics described it as 'a bill for the spoliation of the Church of England', and on the other side liberationists rejoiced that the bill was a subtle way of disestablishing the Church of England. Guinness Rogers went into Shropshire and said that he regarded the bill as a 'first step to disestablishment'.[1]

The bill provided that charities should be transferred to the control of the new parish council, but that 'ecclesiastical charities' should remain with the vestry as at present constructed. But when was a charity 'ecclesiastical'? Suppose that a testator left money on trust to the vicar and churchwardens to give coals to poor Anglicans, that was ecclesiastical. But suppose he left the money to the vicar and churchwardens to give coals to the poor, was he leaving his money to the church, or to the village? Had he named the vicar and churchwardens as his trustees because they were the ecclesiastical officers of the village or because they were the secular? The government took the view that such general bequests of 'dole charities' (which some reformers thought demoralising and wanted to abolish) were secular bequests, and their management should be transferred to the parish council. The government had evidence of a certain suspicion among villagers of the management of parochial charities, a suspicion of ecclesiastical favouritism. Perhaps they were not so sanguine as to think that any way of giving a selective dole

---

than 10,000 had the same boundaries as the ecclesiastical parish (Hansard, 1893, x. 681). The civil parish was the district for which a poor rate could be laid, the ecclesiastical parish was the district in which the parson had rights and duties to the residents. In the seventeenth century some outlying villages of the north, mostly in Northumberland, Durham, Yorkshire, Lancashire and Cheshire, were separated for civil but not ecclesiastical purposes from the mother-parish. Then in the nineteenth century the authorities used the various church-building acts to subdivide the ecclesiastical parish but left the civil intact.

[1] Hansard, 1893, xviii, 71.

would command a universal assent, but they thought that it would command more assent if in the hands of a duly elected body. The view roused much anxiety over hard cases. In 1886 Rebecca Michelmore of Ashburton left £1,000 on trust to the vicar and church wardens to divide the income between thirteen poor men and thirteen poor women. She left another £1,000 to the minister and stewards of the Wesleyan chapel to divide between ten poor men and ten poor women. The bill took over the first trust but not the second.[1]

Secondly, was the parish hall secular or ecclesiastical? It was a place of meeting, not confined to Anglicans, used for confirmation classes but also for concerts. Was it managed by vicar and churchwardens as secular officials or as ecclesiastical? Was it true that a clothing club was wholly secular? A transfer of parish halls was widely felt to be unjust. As the bill left the Commons it provided that such halls should be ecclesiastical charities if erected during the last forty years entirely by the denomination. We have seen that some 99 per cent of the existing parish halls were erected since 1850, and therefore the rule of forty years covered nearly all of them; though it secularised, for example, a large parish room of 1831, built by two Anglicans on a site given by a third Anglican, with vicar and churchwardens as trustees, and with access only through the churchyard.[2] The provision was still held to be unjust. It looked impossible to prove that most of the halls were erected entirely by the denomination. The vicar organised an appeal, invited subscriptions, allowed a bazaar; and nonconformists subscribed to the appeal or spent freely at the bazaar. The House of Lords got the provision altered. The hall must have been erected (not *entirely* but) *mainly* by the denomination.[3]

From the early middle ages the country parson was at the hub of parish business. Henceforth he was no longer *ex officio* a member of the council. In most parishes of the country the parson continued at the hub of parish business. He was now there because it was partly his job, or because he was a good man and an educated man,

---

[1] Hansard, 1893–4, xxi, 30–31.   [2] Hansard, 1893–4, xxi, 37.

[3] Closed churchyards—in the years after the burials act of 1880 health authorities closed a number of country churchyards—could be handed over to the parish council and then maintained out of the rates. The church authorities were opposed to this plan and tried to discourage clergymen from handing over their closed churchyards. The incumbent did not lose his freehold in the churchyard by handing it over. But he felt it to be hallowed ground which surrounded his church, and did not like a 'secular' authority to diminish his responsibility.

not because he had a right. The transition was not difficult, though in circumstances it could be awkward. At Welney in the fens the new council elected as chairman the church schoolmaster. With the support of the meeting he called the rector, formerly chairman, to order. Next day the rector dismissed him from school and from harmonium. The dismissal was afterwards withdrawn.[1]

The removal of the secular business left the vestry without a life. The vestry at Holt, which used to meet several times a year, began meeting once a year to elect a churchwarden and to receive the vicar's nomination of the other churchwarden. Ever since the abolition of church rate the country incumbent became a more personal and powerful ruler within his church. The village ceased to pay money except by gift, therefore the village unless church-going ceased to mind what the vicar did to the church. Some observers were inclined to blame very individual restorations or furnishings on this inability of anyone to control the incumbent. The removal of the secular business forced the Church of England to remake its parish constitution.

Legally the vestry was untouched. It still consisted of all the ratepayers, and the churchwardens need not be Anglicans. Plural votes presumably still existed. The vicar was *ex officio* chairman. There was no known means of removing a churchwarden for mis-conduct, and no process by which a churchwarden could resign. The vestry could partially control vicar and churchwardens in the spending of money from church rate but not in the spending of money from the offertory. A mother-church had a vestry which included the ratepayers in all the district parishes carved out of its boundaries, and yet the duties of that vestry concerned only the ecclesiastical matters of the mother-church. It was a little symbol of so much constitutional change of the nineteenth century; the state prising apart secular from ecclesiastical, and then leaving the ecclesiastical to be remedied confusedly. How difficult was the problem was shown when in 1893 Archbishop Benson of Canter-bury publicly deprecated the suggestion that only members of the Church of England might become churchwardens.[2]

[1] G, 94, 1986.
[2] Bishop Talbot of Rochester (7 February 1895) said that if they asked for such a law they 'would be doing more to reduce the Church of England to a denomination or a sect than we should by almost any other step that we could take' (Hansard, 1893, xviii, 10; *Chron. Convoc.*, 1894–5, 83). Bishop Temple of London agreed. Many good

The local government act gave an impetus to an existing but vague movement to create 'voluntary church councils' in each parish.[1] The ruridecanal conference of Burford West, in the diocese of Hereford, asked Convocation to make a scheme for the constitution and conduct of 'church vestries', and suggesting that only Anglicans should have a place in such vestries. This pressure existed from the late sixties, and during the seventies bills to create such councils came to Parliament. They all failed because they had an anti-ritual tang, rousing a suspicion that they were designed to control the parson in worship, and because they made all parishioners, and not only worshippers, the electorate. Lord Sandon's bill of 1871, for example, allowed a majority of the elected council to resist all changes in the existing customs of the church.

More profitable was the formation of voluntary church councils. As early as 1871 Bishop Browne of Ely encouraged every parish to have such a council.[2] This movement was slow to proceed, for not everyone could see why such a council might be useful, and some expected it to be only obstructive.

Evidence kept coming in that the vestries, freed of their secular inheritance, began to be useful in the Christian work of the parish. Some observers thought that the standard of churchwarden began to rise. In the forties and fifties a public-spirited squire like Sir John Boileau of Ketteringham preferred to be churchwarden himself. But in the days when churchwardens were little local officials, the kind of man who was selected as churchwarden varied. The new freedom was found to emphasise the religious character of the churchwarden. Men talked in an unheard-of way about church-

---

Anglicans believed it to be the national duty of the church to allow non-Anglican ratepayers to vote, and to be able to elect any citizen as a churchwarden. So the nation preserved its interest in the church and the church its responsibility to the nation. A committee of the Canterbury Convocation wanted to recommend that all churchwardens should be Anglicans but did not like to do so lest it precipitated a 'very dangerous' argument in church and state (cf. *Chron. Convoc.*, 1894–5, 50–51, 59); and the Lower House of Convocation refused to pass a resolution which moved in that direction.

[1] Such councils existed legally 'for the care and enlargement of the church or chapel and all matters relating thereto' in some parishes created under one or other of the church building acts; cf. 59 George III, cap. 134; and *Chron. Convoc.*, 1895, report no. 288, 4; and in some (but only some) of these parishes, under the act 6 and 7 Victoria, cap. 37 (section 17), churchwardens must be members of the Church of England. Pressure began to build up that the constitution of new parishes should be made universal among the parishes of England.   [2] CCR, 1871, 192.

wardens being after all spiritual officers and not secular. The incumbent needed representative Anglican laymen about him, and was discouraged only by a fear that the national mission of the church might be weakened.

Archbishop Benson was formerly Bishop of Truro where he did good by persuading the Cornish nonconformists that despite their nonconformity they were still members of the Church of England. Therefore he wished to retain the church council elected by all the parish, but this was quite out of touch with the opinions of the country clergy and their congregations. Then he died and Temple became archbishop. On 13 May 1897 the bishops resolved to encourage every incumbent to form a parochial church council with churchwardens, sidesmen, and elected councillors who should be male communicants; to be elected on a franchise of residents who declared themselves members of the Church of England. (The election of sidesmen was obsolete, though men who helped with the alms were often called sidesmen loosely; the office was more common in the north.) The councillors must be male. But it was soon pointed out that nothing in law prevented women from becoming churchwardens, and therefore it was illogical to exclude women otherwise from the vestry. It was discovered that the diocese of Salisbury in 1897 contained two churchwardens who were women. The county of Surrey contained more. Some regret was expressed at the discovery that at Great Staughton in Huntingdonshire both the churchwardens were female. 1,100 ladies petitioned Convocation regretting that the councillors must be male. The Canterbury Convocation, already in a world where some women sought the secular franchise, reaffirmed that the elected members of parochial church councils (unless churchwardens) must be male.[1]

What would the church council do? The bishops conceived it as administering finance and joining with the incumbent in church work; and advising him on matters 'on which he thinks it expedient to consult them'. This last phrase was due to Archbishop Temple. The archbishop did not wish the council to restrict the freedom of the incumbent. He conceived it as like the assistant masters of Rugby school, useful to advise, but not sharing in the decision.

Many vicars believed that they must rid the Church of England of a sense that the affairs of the church were not the business of

[1] *Chron. Convoc.*, 1897, 212ff.; 1898, 123ff.

laymen, and formed such councils. They were voluntary bodies, and
had various constitutions. Everything depended on the vicar. Many
of the councils remained, as before these discussions, groups of
leading laymen summoned privately by the vicar, and were not
constituted by election. Where they were elected, some allowed
women and others not, some allowed non-resident members of the
congregation and others only residents, some allowed ratepayers,
some those who said that they were Anglican, and some those who
had been confirmed. But there began to be links between the
parochial church council and the diocesan conference. By the death
of Queen Victoria a representative system existed in embryo,
whereby a country (or town) congregation could send its elected
representative to be consulted in the diocese at large.

6. THE CHURCHYARD

Until 1880 the churchyard was a rural problem. At least, politicians and journalists in towns said that it was a rural problem.
They declared that it maintained the irritation between church and
dissent in the village. Churchgoers and chapelgoers in some villages
denied that it irritated. But for a decade it became a national
argument.

It was not a town problem, for between 1852 and 1870 towns
provided themselves with cemeteries under the burials act, and in
the towns also were dissenting or Roman Catholic burial grounds.
Occasionally someone would assert that the difficulty also afflicted
parishes in the northern manufacturing towns. But nearly everyone
agreed that it was largely a rural predicament.

As the only school in many villages was an Anglican school, and
some dissenters objected, so the only burial ground in many villages was the churchyard of the parish church. Everyone who died
in the village had a right to be buried there, unless he died excom-
municate, or unbaptised, or by his own hand. A body cast up on
the shore was presumed to be baptised and possessed the same right.
But the right to be buried in the churchyard meant also the right
and indeed the duty to be buried with the funeral service in the Book
of Common Prayer, read by the incumbent or his deputy. And not
everyone who died in the village wished for the funeral service of
the Church of England. Lincoln, the largest rural diocese of England,

had in 1876 634 dissenting chapels, 48 cemeteries, and 546 churchyards. The difficulty was worst in Wales. Anglesey was said to be
the most nonconformist county in Wales, and had not a single
cemetery. It was a Welsh M.P., Osborne Morgan, who kept bringing bills to the House of Commons.

No one could diagnose the precise extent of the trouble. Most
country clergy thought it slight. Most nonconformists, they said,
loved the Anglican service, and often preferred it when they had a
choice. Wesleyan Methodists, when they conducted funerals for
themselves, often used a largely Anglican service. Thomas Jackson
the patriarchal Wesleyan leader was quietly buried with the Prayer
Book rite. The Roman Catholics were not a difficulty, partly
because they were rare in the country, and partly because their
funeral rite was the mass and they were content to be silent at the
grave. And if some nonconformists had conscientious scruples
against the service, many clergy allowed them to hold their own
service in the house and to bury in the churchyard with their own
minister presiding but in silence. Some clergy—perhaps in the early
seventies not very many, to judge by votes and petitions on the
issue—were willing to invite the nonconformist minister to do it,
or not to enquire into what happened at the grave. This was winking
at illegality. But, as tolerant old John Allen said, a clergyman is not
always bound to keep a watchful eye on his churchyard.[1] And under
these conditions of nonconformist contentment with the Anglican
rite, and flexibility by country parsons, most country parishes had
no trouble. The Lincoln diocese, an obvious place for trouble
because the rural parishes were many and nonconformity was strong,
had no reported trouble for those twelve years after 1868 while the
national argument raged.

Yet it might be presumed that far more nonconformists were
troubled than allowed to appear by protest. Tait saw in the wilds
of Cumberland a procession of dissenters singing hymns that
echoed off the hills as they bore the body, until they reached the
gate of the churchyard. The sudden silence at the churchyard
gate disturbed the archbishop's memory.[2] An old-fashioned Wesleyan minister, who did not like to be called dissenter, retired to a
northern sea-coast town and was there buried in the churchyard as

[1] *Chron. Convoc.*, 1876, 87, 16 February 1876.
[2] Hansard, ccxxix, 1876, 623.

he would have wished. The Anglican incumbent was a stranger to him, though he lived a stone's throw from the church, and the crowd of Methodists round the grave felt a sense of coldness, when those who ministered to his illness must be silent.[1] Those who held that a real grievance existed were wont to say that it was not a grievance which mourners were likely to voice at so sacred a moment.

But whether or not it was true that many nonconformists felt a grievance, what disturbed everyone were the isolated cases of rigidity; of Thomas Chamberlain, vicar in Oxford, insisting that his curate read the Prayer Book over a Baptist mother[2] who had already buried six children in silence; of the altercation between a curate and a Primitive Methodist superintendent by a grave at Dore in Derbyshire.

An irrelevant case happened unfortunately to complicate the argument. At the village of Owston Ferry in Lincolnshire the youngest daughter of the Wesleyan minister died at the age of seven. Her father wanted a tombstone in the churchyard with an inscription that she was the daughter of the 'Reverend H. Keet, Wesleyan minister'. The vicar objected that in a churchyard one might not describe a Wesleyan minister as Reverend, and was supported by his bishop, Christopher Wordsworth. Keet went to court, and after losing in both the lower courts won an undefended victory in the judicial committee (1876) that the tombstone might lawfully call a Wesleyan minister Reverend. The Owston Ferry case was irrelevant to the law of burial. But happening in those years when Osborne Morgan pressed burial bills in Parliament, it offered ammunition to every assailant of the Church of England and persuaded the Methodist Conference and some other nonconformists that the established church was rigid.

Whether or not, therefore, the ordinary nonconformist of the village felt a grievance, enough material existed to argue about grievance in Parliament; and to argue successfully, for by 1876 it was evident that the Conservative whips could not much longer hold the party to vote against Liberal bills about burial. A body of Anglican leaders headed by Bishop Temple of Exeter, the most radical of the bishops as Wordsworth was the most conservative, believed that nonconformists, even if they had no personal grievance

[1] G, 80, 765.   [2] Hansard, ccxxvii, 1876, 1367.

and even if they maintained silence, still felt the Church of England to act less kindly about burials than was fitting to a great Christian church.

The clergy were reluctant but willing to allow silence in the churchyard. They were cheerfully willing to compose short services, with words from Scripture, to which no nonconformist could object. They were willing to allow hymns by the grave. What they were not willing to do was to allow nonconformist ministers to officiate in their churchyards. In 1880 15,500 clergymen petitioned against this proposal. And if three-quarters of the clergy signed a petition, they must have approached unanimity. It could be expected that Archdeacon Denison called this proposal the destruction of the Church of England. But the intransigent included men whom at first sight it was surprising to find there. J. C. Ryle, who loved nonconformist ministers like brothers, wrote a burning pamphlet called *Shall we surrender?* This needs explaining.

To the country clergy the plan came as mere politics. In their parish they found no discontent. But away in London politicians, in their quest for issues, were not content with disestablishing the Irish church and abolishing church rate and weakening Christian education, but must now seek to rob the church of its churchyards. To the country clergy this was political and not religious dissent. The arguments which applied to the churchyard—that it was for the benefit of the nation—might apply equally to the church building. Sir Wilfrid Lawson went down to Carlisle and told a meeting that getting hold of the churchyards was only the first step to getting hold of the churches. The clergy did not forget what Lawson said.

This ground was consecrated. If others came in to officiate, might you find an atheist denouncing eternal life? Might you find a rabid dissenter denouncing the parish church or its incumbent or his religion? Might you find fanatical sects misbehaving? The clergy were genuinely afraid of men desecrating their quiet memorials. Bishop Wordsworth produced evidence that at a funeral in Upchurch a sect called the Peculiar People disturbed the churchyard by long continuance of ranting and stentorian hymns.[1] This was sacred ground, 'God's acre'. And when Wordsworth was criticised for saying that they might not hand over such ground to

[1] Hansard, ccxxix, 1876, 634.

heretics and schismatics, he rejoiced to disclose that he used almost the exact words of St. Ambrose of Milan in the fourth century. Moreover, there was injustice. If an Anglican was buried in a Roman Catholic or Quaker burial-ground, he must be buried with Roman Catholic or Quaker rites. Parliament was forcing on the Church of England what it would not force on other denominations.

Many would have liked to solve the difficulty by doing in the country what was done in the towns: creating non-church cemeteries in the villages on the rates. The proposal was not practicable on grounds of expense and of reason, even though an incumbent or two, like the vicar of Waterbeach, opened part of the glebe for the purpose. And a number of country clergymen were not sure that they wanted this to happen. They suspected that the village would be more divided if it did happen.

In 1880 the Tractarian lord chancellor (Selborne) of the new Liberal government with a Tractarian prime minister introduced and carried into law a burial bill framed on more considerate lines than those framed earlier by Osborne Morgan. Relatives might give notice to the incumbent that the deceased would be buried without the Prayer Book service; and the services at the grave might be whatever the relatives think fit provided they are Christian and orderly. No one could give an address which brought into contempt the Christian religion or members of or ministers of any other denomination.

The act settled the entire question. No difficulty ensued, nothing untoward or irreverent occurred. That stout country parson Archdeacon Denison said that he would not register non-Anglican burials and one eminent incumbent resigned his living in order not to serve under the new law. The first funeral under the act was conducted by the Baptist minister of Penge in the churchyard at Beckenham and gathered a company of interested spectators.[1] The only legacy apart from peace was a sense among some country clergy that they were abandoned by the bishops; for Canterbury, York, London, Carlisle, Exeter, Manchester, Oxford and three

[1] G, 80, 1253, 1473. Selborne's act was 43 and 44 Vic., cap. 41. Some clergy disliked clause 10 which compelled them to act as registrars for funerals not conducted by themselves. But the act also empowered them to use the burial service at funerals not in consecrated ground, and with the consent of the bishop might use a service not that of the Prayer Book if requested by the relatives, though the material of the service must be drawn from the Prayer Book and the Bible. For evidence of discontent at the act, P. T. Marsh, 261–2.

Welsh bishops voted in favour, while only seven bishops joined
Wordsworth of Lincoln in voting or pairing against the second
reading.

7. PATRONAGE

More than half the advowsons of the Church of England and
Wales and a higher proportion of country livings were still in
private ownership. The members of the Church of England generally approved the system. A few Anglican parishes had incumbents
elected by the congregation, and no one liked the system or admired
its results. Responsible and devout bishops were convinced that to
this system the Church of England owed the breadth of opinion
among the clergy, their freedom and independence of thought.
When in 1874 patronage was abolished in the Church of Scotland,
the abolition gave rise to discussion in the Church of England. A
select committee of the House of Lords, secured by Bishop Magee
of Peterborough, formally recommended that private patronage
was of great value and deprecated any attempt to supersede it.
Frederick Temple, who saw a few scandals concerning patronage
in the diocese of Exeter, nevertheless believed that private patronage was exceedingly desirable; that the upper classes thus became
officers of the church, and nearly all of them went about their duties
with care and responsibility.[1] That amusing country incumbent
Augustus Jessopp, it was true, wanted patronage abolished altogether, and a body of trustees in each parish, representing landowners, ratepayers, worshippers and the bishop, with the duties of
managing the property and appointing or dismissing the parson.[2]
M. H. Close is said to have resigned the living of Shangton in
Leicestershire (1857) owing to 'scruples as to the propriety of holding
a benefice under lay patronage'.[3] Such a radical view was rare. Most
articulate Anglicans, lay or clerical, held the peculiar excellence of
their church to rest in the independence of the parson and the
variety of means by which he was appointed, so that they avoided
colourless clergymen nominated by uniform committees.

Of patronage that was not private, the evangelical and Anglo-
Catholic trusts were little criticised except occasionally for partisan
attitudes, and plainly sought to choose good men, and were always

[1] PP, 1874, vii, 304, 382.   [2] Nineteenth Century, xix (1886), 507ff.
[3] DNB. It is the only case of such scruples known to me.

concerned for the pastoral welfare of the parishioners. The patronage of the universities, and of the colleges at Oxford and Cambridge, encountered a measure of criticism. The university appointment was conducted with candidates and a poll, and had some of the disadvantages of popular election. The colleges were bound by custom to offer the living to the senior fellow in orders, who might or might not be an appropriate person. After the fellows ceased to be obliged to take holy orders, this custom faded quietly or was consciously abandoned. The Anglican patronage of the university paradoxically improved as the university became less Anglican. The universities remedied the defects of popular election, partly as their livings became less desirable to candidates in the agricultural depression, and partly by securing (1899–1900) committees or boards to appoint. But they made efforts before. The select committee of 1874 received impartial evidence that Cambridge made two model appointments to the parish of East Retford.[1]

Yet by the seventies everyone admitted that private patronage was not working well and needed more than a little reform.

Patronage grew out of a world in which the squire owned the parish, perhaps built the church, and needed a clergyman of whom he approved, and therefore retained the advowson as the right to appoint. Good men believed into the seventies that this was the best of all systems. But all through the nineteenth century the process went on by which the land of the parish was separated from the advowson of the parish. On the death of a squire the estate might be divided among the heirs, and sooner or later the advowson might become separated from the land. Once the advowson was no longer attached to the parish, it became a potential investment, and the patron might have no interest whatever in the parishioners' welfare. A large Suffolk estate (that of Mr. Anguish, later of Lord Sydney Osborne) was united to seven advowsons. When the property was sold in the open market, all seven advowsons were sold separately.[2]

The advowson, once in the market, entered a world where market rules prevailed. Since the advowson included the right to present to an income of so much a year for life, it had a market value. But since the person who could be given the income was restricted—he must be in priest's orders in the Church of England—

---

[1] PP, 1874, vii, 458–9.   [2] PP, 1874, vii, 449.

the right had no value to investors in search of mere gain, and this
was a safeguard against abuse. Moreover many livings were under
£200 a year—known to laymen as 'starvation livings'—and bishops
had difficulty in filling them. Though nonconformists could not see
how it was right that the choice of a pastor was bought and sold,
especially in open market and at auction, few Anglicans objected to
the sale and purchase of advowsons, until the last quarter of the
century. The municipal corporations act provided for the sale of
the numerous corporation livings while no one complained and
archbishops approved. In 1863 Lord Westbury, who as lord chancellor was responsible for filling some very poor livings and found
the task difficult, secured an act of Parliament permitting the sale of
some, for the sake of increasing their income, and few objected. So
pure a reformer as John Keble wholeheartedly approved.[1] As late
as 1874 Lord Harrowby defended the sale of advowsons, and even
of the next presentation to a living, on the ground that in this way
'mercantile' men secured an interest in the church for one of their
children.[2] Squires used to provide for younger sons in this way, but
the new wealth of the country lay in industry and business, and it was
desirable (so ran the old-fashioned argument) that these new magnates should be able at once to help the church and provide for their
sons. 'There are many men now', said Sidney Godolphin Osborne
in 1874, 'who have the greatest ambition to have their sons in the
church who a few years ago would never have thought of having
them in it.'[3] The Lords committee of 1874 defended the sale of
advowsons on the ground that the alternative was rigid inheritance,
and the right would be worse exercised if it descended willy-nilly to
people who did not want it than if it were bought in the market by
people who wanted it. The rector of the little parish of Dean in
Cumberland bought the advowson to his own living, his nephew
was then enabled to succeed him and became an excellent parish
priest and later archdeacon. In 1878 one-ninth, that is 753, of the
total livings in private patronage (6,228) had clergymen who were
not only the incumbent but also the patron; and 599 more had an
incumbent with the same name as the patron or the incumbent was
said to be trustee for the patron.[4]

[1] Keble, *Letters of Spiritual Counsel*, 3rd ed., 72.
[2] PP, 1874, vii, 379.   [3] PP, 1874, vii, 437.
[4] PP, 1880, xviii, 116; approximate figures: CCR, 1886, 50.

Round the general administration of private parsonage, most of which was conducted honourably and responsibly, hovered the black sheep of the country parsonage.

The main abuses were these:

First, a patron wished to sell an advowson and get a good price. He could not legally sell the advowson while the living was vacant. He would appoint a very elderly clergyman, obviously soon to die.

Secondly, a patron could sell not only the advowson but the next presentation or any successive number of presentations to the benefice.

But most of the trouble concerned clergymen who bought advowsons in order to present themselves to livings. It was useless to buy the next presentation, for then the purchaser could not legally (under statute of Queen Anne) present himself; he must invest more money and buy the advowson outright. This provision was, however, evaded with the aid of the less reputable agents. This was simony, the purchase of a spiritual office, but was not easy to prove.

Fourthly, in the days of the squire, the bond of resignation was customary. The squire had a son whom he wanted to occupy the living. But the son perhaps was still at school, and not yet in holy orders. Therefore the patron would present a clergyman to the living, and the clergyman would give a bond of resignation, that is, he would legally covenant with the squire to resign the living in favour of the young man. This was still common in country parishes in the early Victorian age, and it worked.

But in the later Victorian age it worked less well. The squire and his family were less stable in the parish. The intellectual unsettlement of the age, and the opening of the world of business to the sons of squires, meant that fewer wished to take holy orders. And in the underworld of the countryside we hear of seamy stories; of the possibility that a patron might go to an incumbent and say, 'How much will you give me if I do not enforce my bond?'

Fifthly, various dealings connected with the trade came to light. Auctions were advertised in the *Ecclesiastical Gazette* and in the circulars of those agencies of which all good men disapproved. But their negotiations were conducted in secrecy, and few scandals saw the light. There must have been more than we know. One clergyman at least, who engaged in dubious transactions, sought to withdraw and was blackmailed by the agent, who threatened to expose his conduct to the bishop.[1]

A clergyman bought an advowson which would soon be vacant. When he became the incumbent, he found that the glebe was full of brick earth. As he was both patron and incumbent, no one could stop him selling the brick earth. He then resold the advowson, and went to the bishop to resign his living. The bishop, now aware of what was happening, refused to accept the resignation. Accordingly the clergyman bought another living far away, and therefore vacated the brick-earth living automatically.[2]

These abuses were rare, and more rarely known. The list of advowsons for auction always gave a weapon to nonconformist critics. But perhaps the system would have continued unchallenged for longer, on the ground that all modes of appointment are liable to exceptional failures and that this mode on the whole worked well, had it not been for pressure from two different directions: the bishop, and the parishioners.

The active bishops of the second half of the century were not content. Frederick Temple had experiences in the diocese of Exeter which caused him, not to disapprove private patronage which he thought excellent, but to press vehemently for changes in the law, wanting to end all sales of advowsons and to strengthen the power of the bishop in refusing unsuitable men. Bishop Magee had experiences in the diocese of Peterborough which caused him to lead reform in both Parliament and Convocation.

The only protection against abuse lay with the bishop. The bishop had the duty of satisfying himself that the patron's candidate was worthy. But the only way in which he could satisfy himself that the candidate was unworthy was by refusing to institute and allowing himself to be prosecuted in the courts; which cost much money from the bishop's pocket, and drew the attention of newspapers to scandal in the church. The abuse on which bishops felt strongly was their duty to accept an ancient clergyman, physically broken, perhaps in his eighties, incapable of looking after the parish, and obviously nominated by the patron with the sole object of getting the living vacant so that the patron could present himself. Most bishops did not see what could be done. But agents were apt to avoid certain dioceses for such transactions. So long as Henry

[1] PP, 1874, vii, 359.   [2] PP, 1874, vii, 347-8.

Phillpotts was Bishop of Exeter, they avoided the diocese of Exeter, for they knew that this doughty fighter would fight them to the end if he smelt something improper, whatever the cost to his pocket, however unfavourable the publicity, and whatever the inadequacy of his own legal standing. From similar reasons agents also liked to avoid the diocese of Chichester while Gilbert was the bishop.[1] Their favourite kind of living was a 'donative', that is a benefice which historically had been a personal gift, and where even now the new incumbent did not need the approval or institution of the bishop. The owner of a donative in the diocese of Peterborough forbad Bishop Magee to hold a confirmation in his church, but the case was probably unique.[2] Every proposal for reform included the abolition of donatives.

Meanwhile the parishioners received more education and became more articulate. The system took no notice of the wishes of the parish, and need take no notice (but usually did take notice) of the needs and welfare of the parishioners. In the seventies was reported a growing distaste on the part of parishioners for clergymen who had been bought into their livings, and a sense of humiliation among parishioners when they found that the advowson of their church was to be sold at auction above their heads.[3] As voluntary church councils began to appear, the laity of more and more country churches at last began to express opinions on these matters. By 1895 feeling was roused, and the annual failure of a benefices bill roused irritation and was one of the main ingredients of the church reform movement at the end of the century. In the nineties responsible and moderate churchmen condemned the system in terms which few but nonconformists would have used forty years before. 'There is no other church in Christendom', said the very practical lawyer, Lewis Dibdin, 'which has to plead guilty to a condition so humiliating.' The right of a clergyman to buy an advowson and present himself became ever more offensive, and partly because the number of transactions began to rise. For as they declined in real value the advowsons became cheaper to buy, and a clergyman need only borrow £1,000 or £1,500 to secure a reasonable house and a meagre but permanent livelihood. The attacks of liberationists did not slacken, and in 1896 the *Liberator* devoted a special column under

[1] PP, 1874, vii, 372–3.   [2] PP, 1874, vii, 355.
[3] PP, 1874, vii, 381, 437.

the title *The Soul Market*. 'We all, or nearly all,' said Dibdin, 'feel the sting and shame of the thing.'[1] Bishop Ryle of Liverpool, who never minced words, talked about selling souls like a flock of sheep or drove of pigs. He wanted to abolish all sales of livings. But most people did not want to abolish purchase of patronage. They wanted to abolish the purchase by a clergyman of a cure of souls under the cloak that he only bought patronage.

Some people felt a difficulty; that the system of private patronage attracted much money from donors into the parochial system of the Church of England, and that some country parishes were kept going only with this assistance. Weaken private patronage by reform and you gravely diminish the support for the religion of the countryside. At last a Conservative government passed the benefices act of 1898, which ended sales by auction, except when the advowson was held in conjunction with the land of a manor of not less than 100 acres within the parish; made the dubious financial transactions into invalid agreements; and abolished bonds of resignation.

The provisions of the benefices act were good but did not content the reformers. Transfer of advowsons in 1899, 76; in 1900, 71—but many of these transfers were wholly innocent.[2]

Patronage, like the freehold, caused difficulty for reformers who wished to rationalise manpower. The towns grew and could not get enough clergy, the villages emptied and kept the same number of clergy. In the nineties began the first discussions on amalgamating country parishes so that men might be found for the towns, a hankering after an end to the one man–one parish ideal imposed by the Whig reformers of the eighteen-thirties. It looked contrary to reason that one pastor should have 150 people and another 8,000. Yet the existing system found many defenders, from the Bishop of Worcester downwards.[3] The English village was argued to be such that a man must live in it if he was to minister rightly, and that no man could be true pastor to another community where he was

---

[1] CCR, 1896, 181–6.

[2] The further reform of the system awaited the further self-government of the Church of England after 1919. An amending act of 1923 prevented a clergyman-patron from presenting himself and abolished the sale of advowsons from two vacancies in the benefice after 14 July 1924 (again exempting the advowsons appended to land in the parish), and where the advowson was sold before the second vacancy allowed the parochial church council the right to acquire it. Another act of 1931 allowed the parochial church council to exercise a measure of influence in the choice of its new incumbent. Halsbury, 268–75.   [3] CCR, 1888, 555.

non-resident. In 1894 W. Awdry the vicar of Amport near Andover produced a scheme for rationalising the parishes of the Andover deanery. Andover town had one priest to every 1,738 inhabitants or 1,267 acres. The other 22 parishes round had 24 priests, or one priest to every 331 inhabitants or 2,360 acres. His scheme made twelve men look after the 22 parishes, with a higher average income, and a capital saved of £85,000 as well as twelve clergymen released for further work. He argued that the population was decreasing and that the bicycle allowed effective ministration in more than one village, but confessed that Sunday services would be more infrequent and that the clergyman would become only as accessible as the country doctor. He hoped that all the patrons would consent because the value of their patronage was less than it used to be.[1] No one did anything, or could do anything. Bishop Wordsworth of Salisbury contemplated similar schemes for reorganisation but found patronage too high an obstacle.

The notion of the rural parish still largely conditioned the thinking of the Church of England. It could hardly do other when they remembered Richard Hooker and George Herbert and John Keble. Men did not like to dismantle arrangements which in circumstances had proved that so noble an ideal was practicable.

The novelist *par excellence* of the country parish was Charlotte Yonge, whose mind was formed by Keble and Hursley. She had no romantic nostalgia for smocks or illiteracy, and was sure that religious life, certainly moral life, in villages improved in many respects during the reign. Like Keble she lived a quiet retired life. Her best portraits were of poor curates, or occasionally of a squarson, but her interest was the life of the upper classes in the village and the good or evil which they could do to the poor. The social gulf was never crossed. She marked the slow decline in the status of the country clergyman. She disliked popular preachers, lasting work was deeper and less showy. Her model clergyman, Wilmot in *The Daisy Chain*, was very poor as a speaker but exemplary in his pastoral duties. She described idle or not good clergymen, but they were always of 'the old school', and she never allowed a bad clergyman or a broad churchman into her pages. Her laymen must be quiet churchmen or they were likely to come to the turf and debts

[1] CCR, 1894, 605-7.

if they were the son of the house, to steal if they were servants. *The Heir of Redclyffe* (1853) did as much for the moral idealism of the educated classes as any book of the reign. She edited the *Monthly Packet* (1851–) as suitable Christian reading for cottage homes, and her series of *Langley Tales*, moral novels about Langley village which was her own village of Otterbourne, can profitably be studied for the development of village schools and people. As one of the true creative novelists of the nineteenth century, with two or three of her books ranking among the best Christian novels of any age, she was in one respect a channel for the most powerful influence which shy and reserved John Keble exercised upon the Victorian churches. In the world of the eighties and nineties she grew out of place, her mind could not adapt to democracy or Biblical criticism or emancipated women. Her books continued powerful, for a few people seem to have wished to exclude them from schools, but by 1900 nearly all the ladies who read her were said to have silver in their hair.

Keble's personal influence experienced something of the same rise and decline. If a man quoted *The Christian Year* among a group of churchmen in the sixties or seventies, several of those present could have finished the stanza. In the nineties it was observed that the younger no longer knew it like their elders, though families continued to recommend it, like the collect, for Sunday reading. In the memory of many Victorian Anglicans Hursley remained the ideal of a country parish, where a humble man quietly ministered for long years without expectation of worldly reward.

In a very few country churches the custom whereby the congregation approached and knelt round the altar at the words *Draw near with faith* in the communion survived till the end of the century. The increased number of communicants made it inappropriate and it vanished rapidly in the middle years of the century.

Even in the last decade of the century we find occasional violence against pews. The enemies of pews continued their fight, but less vigorously, partly because the contest was won, and partly because they lost their big argument. They said that if all seats were free the labourer might come to church and they were proved wrong.

In the last twenty years of the century critics were still pressing that more country churches should remain unlocked during the day.

About 1883 appeared the first lists of past vicars hanging on the walls of country churches. These were encouraged by Archbishop Benson, who conceived them as a sign of the continuity and Catholicity of the Church of England, stretching back into the Middle Ages. This was certainly in the mind of the vicar of Great Yarmouth when he erected such a list.[1] The first boards for hymn numbers, starting as numerals of painted tin hung on pins, appeared a few years later, and by about the end of the century churches were adopting boards with sliding numbers.

The habit of placing artificial flowers in glass cases on graves began in the last decade of the century and caused such offence that some incumbents sought to prohibit it.

The 'typical' country church, not very high and not very low, at the end of the reign would have differed from the 'typical' country church at the beginning of the reign. Probably the chancel was now thrown into the main worshipping area, and contained a choir. The chancel might have been raised on a step. Some choirs, but not many yet if they were surpliced, contained women. The village of Skelton-in-Cleveland had a surpliced choir of women by 1887 but Dr. Liddon denounced this sort of innovation as grotesque.[2] The pews looked different. There was a verger, but not a clerk to lead responses, and the service was much more congregational and musical, accompanied by an organ, but even in the eighties we find complaints that village congregations are still backward to sing. The font was now universally of stone or brass instead of, as often earlier, plaster or crockery. There was now a lectern and in the aisle perhaps a litany desk. The seats were arranged so that the clergy-man led prayers sideways to the congregation instead of facing them. The altar and its appurtenances, including in many cases the sanc-tuary rails, were additions of the reign. Many more country churches had one or more stained glass windows. Most of them acquired after 1868 collection plates or bags. Some had a new-built vestry, and others, though fewer, a lych-gate.

The first breaches in clerical black came in remote country parishes. The curate of Martinhoe in Devonshire (1874) wore stout nailboots, yellow breeches, yellow gaiters, short black jerkin, and an 'ecclesiastical waistcoat buttoning up at the side'. When he visited a parish in Essex he found it a great bore to wear black

---

[1] George Venables, CCR, 1885, 129.   [2] G, 1887, 1408.

clothes and a top hat. Both the laity and the clergy were conservative in these matters. An Oxford rector, confronted with his curate in a Tyrolean hat and light waistcoat, took him gently to the tailor and ordered him a dark waistcoat and tall hat on his own account. Young country vicars in the eighties raised some eyebrows among their older colleagues by appearing in felt wide-awakes instead of tall hats.[1] The black coat remained a long frock-coat in towns for the whole of the reign, and the short black coat was associated with dissenting ministers who preferred to look more like laymen. But by the end of the century some country clergymen, especially the younger, jettisoned the frock-coat for a short black coat, and occasionally defended the innovation by reminding the critic that they needed to use a bicycle. The short black coat moved from country to town, for town priests also needed bicycles. Black of some sort remained necessary for Anglican, Roman Catholic and Methodist ministers until after the queen died. The Roman Catholics wore the dog collar almost without exception before the Anglicans achieved that uniformity. Many old-fashioned Anglican clergy wore the white tie into the twentieth century and it never altogether died out. But among Anglican high churchmen it was quaint before the end of the century. In the photographs of Cuddesdon theological college the last white tie appeared in 1883. If a clerical collar was worn, black was always worn with it. The first case known to me of a collar without black is of 1899, and the culprit was remarked on holiday in Scotland.[2]

[1] *Life of Hannington*, 89; Knox, *Reminiscences*, 76; Jessopp, *Trials*, 63–4.
[2] G, 99, 976.

CHAPTER V

THE TOWN CHURCH

I. NUMBER OF WORSHIPPERS

THE population of England (without Wales) in 1861 was nearly nineteen millions. In 1901 it was over thirty and a half millions. It grew by nearly three millions in each decade. All this increase went into the towns. In 1851 the people who lived in the country were roughly as many as those who lived in the town. Fifty years later more than three-quarters of the people of England and Wales lived in towns.

As the towns grew bigger, the land in the centre became valuable and was used for shops and offices. The people moved outwards in two stages: first, the middle-class who preferred to live in villas among the suburbs, and later, at the end of the century, the working men who were cleared out and found cheap estates in the suburbs. The bicycles, and the introduction of working-men's trains, speeded this second evacuation. All cities had too many churches near the centre and too few at the circumference. This was true of nonconformist churches as well as Anglican. The rate at which it happened varied greatly between one big town and another.

For two or three decades before 1900, men discussed how to use the emptying churches in the city of London. In Leeds or Huddersfield or Halifax they did not discuss the problem because the great old parish church of the centre still held many worshippers, though more of them now came from a distance. But the reconstruction of English town life forced the churches to reconstruct. They must build churches in the suburbs. And the more they built churches in the suburbs, the weaker would be the churches at the centre. The need must be met by all denominations. Wesleyan Methodist or Congregationalist chapels, mostly dependent on middle-class support, must move outwards with the middle class. All denominations were confronted with an enormous task of finding new sites, constructing new buildings, finding new staff, and deciding what to do with buildings now ill-sited.

Between 1871 and 1881 the increase of population was 14·36 per cent. It was calculated roughly that the Church of England needed to find a parish church—that is, not a church to which a man went, but a church to which he could go if he wanted—for between 300,000 and 400,000 every year, and that these people increased the number in those parishes which already had too many people for one clergyman to look after. Half the increase went to parishes where the church was sufficiently well placed, and where the vicar only needed a curate or another curate. But for the remainder the Church of England, so it was estimated, needed about seventy new parishes and ninety-seven new clergymen every year. And meanwhile the population of numerous country parishes decreased, and the population at the centre of cities decreased; yet no denomination could easily move the minister of the rural district or the minister of the city church.

And yet they did create many more parishes, build many more churches and chapels, and find many more clergymen. The attempt to keep pace with so rapidly rising a population, and the measure of success which the churches achieved, is the generous achievement of Victorian Christianity.

We must distinguish between the numbers of worshippers in an absolute sense, and the numbers in relation to the growth of the population. Between 1860 and 1890, perhaps between 1840 and 1900, all denominations possessed a sense that they took part in a great movement of religion. If the congregations declined in little country churches, in central city churches, in slum churches where the middle class moved away, other congregations in towns flourished, and every year more of them. If they built a new church or chapel in a suburb it might not be full, perhaps might never be full; but it nearly always flourished. All denominations could count the growth in the number of churches, of members, of pastors. They could see Christianity to be advancing. If statisticians pointed out that the number of persons in the country rose faster per cent than the number of worshippers, that disturbed them little, and spurred them to fresh exertion. Conscious of an enormous task ahead of them, they were confident in their progress towards meeting the demand. They saw an alienated working class, a ferment of

controversy about the truth of religion, a science popularly believed
to be hostile to religion. And still the exertions increased, the organisations multiplied, and the number of worshippers rose. This
was the public impression represented in the organs of public
opinion, or in the judgment of individuals as disclosed in their
letters, speeches, autobiographies. The impression needed testing
by statistics. So far as they were able to test it, the statistics confirmed, modestly at least, the truth of what they supposed to be
happening.

In judging the decline of the Church of England, not in absolute
numbers, but in relation to the total population, we must remember
the number of immigrants; for Englishmen had usually been
members of the Church of England, and the Roman Catholic
Church in England was transformed by the influx of Irish immigrants. In 1861 there were 601,634 Irish living in England, nearly
two-fifths of them in Lancashire and Cheshire; in 1861 6·7 per cent
of all Liverpool was Irish, in 1891 9·1 per cent. After 1861 the decline
in the rate of Irish immigration was continuous. The proportion
of persons born in Scotland rose steadily at every census. In 1851
the number of persons who were born in Ireland and lived in
England was four times as many as the number of persons who
were born in Scotland and lived in England. Fifty years later the
proportion was three Scotsmen to every four Irishmen. Towards
the end of the century the striking figures were those of immigrants
from countries not Ireland nor Scotland. At the 1901 census more
than two hundred thousand persons were born in Europe, one-
third of them in Russia or Russian Poland, for the Tsarist government was uncomfortable to the Jews in Russia. Plainly such immigrants would seldom join one of the existing denominations of
English religious life, and yet would affect the pattern of religious
life in the big towns, especially in London.[1]

Accurate statistics are not easy to find. The most obvious source
of nearly reliable statistics is the return to government on the
changing number of marriages in different churches.

The figures mark the steady rise in civil ceremonies, the steady
decline in the proportion, of the total number, held in Anglican
churches, though the actual number of Anglican marriages was on
the whole rising slowly (1844: 120,009; 1874: 150,819; 1904:

[1] PP, Census 1901, lviii, appendix A, 143, 149, 281.

For every 1,000 marriages (England and Wales)[1]:

	Church of England	R.C.	Other Christian Denominations	Jews	Civil Marriages
1844	907	17	49	1	26
1854	840	49	61	2	48
1864	782	48	87	2	81
1874	747	40	106	2	105
1884	707	43	116	3	131
1894	686	42	119	5	148
1904	642	41	131	7	179

165,519); the rapid rise of Roman Catholic marriages in the forties, coinciding with the greatest period of Irish immigration, and then their fall during the sixties and seventies, presumably due in part to re-emigration and still more to assimilation of Irish immigrant families into the English population—even the total number of Roman Catholic marriages fell (1864: 8,659; 1869: 7,231; 1874: 8,179); and the steady rise of nonconformist marriages.

Total civil marriages: 1844: 3,446; 1864: 14,611; 1874: 21,256; 1884: 26,786; 1894: 33,550; 1904: 46,247.

These marriages suggest that through the Victorian age England grew much more secular and a little more nonconformist and much less Anglican. Such a judgment has obvious truth. But when we come to examine such other figures as we possess, this broad picture needs important qualification. For example, in 1837 most nonconformists were still in the habit, formerly compulsory, of being married in a parish church. Yet they were no less nonconformist. The rise in nonconformist marriages (per cent) did not mean only that the nonconformist proportion of the population was rising. It meant primarily a change in marriage custom. The number of marriages in registry offices did not mean that that proportion of the population was anti-Christian or secularist. Other reasons, besides an attitude to religion, caused young couples to use the registrar.

While Anglican marriages were (per cent) falling, Anglican baptisms rose relatively as well as absolutely. The figures are wholly reliable neither before 1900 nor after. But certainly in 1900 the percentage of Anglican baptisms was rising slowly (1885: 623 in each thousand live births; 1895: 641 per thousand; 1902: 658 in each

[1] *Facts and Figures*, 3, 57.

thousand; 1907: 678; 1912: 672; 1917: 705)[1]. No doubt this increase of baptisms reflected a rising Anglican population. It is likely also to be a sign of the energy and efficiency which marked the later Victorian clergyman.

For the Anglican influence on society, the number of confirmations is important. But we must beware of attributing too much to the increase. The railways and the increased activity of bishops and a larger number of bishops and the use of suffragans and assistant bishops, as well as the greater energy of pastors, made confirmation nearer to being universal among churchgoers than it was fifty years before, even among regular churchgoers.[2]

	Males	Females	Total
1872	48,272	69,580	117,852
1877	63,840	97,715	161,555
1881	70,573	106,210	176,783
1886	84,212	125,421	209,633
1891	84,947	129,584	214,531
(1911	101,206	142,824	244,030)

The 1911 figure is approximately 35·8 per thousand males aged between 12 and 20 years, or 318 for a thousand males aged 15, and 49·5 per thousand females aged between 12 and 20 years, or 447 for a thousand females aged 15. The 1872 figure is approximately 229 per thousand males aged 15, and 331 per thousand females aged 15. The rise of proportion over fifty years must reflect the endeavours of parish priests and bishops, in a generation when other influences were beginning to work against them. Manifestly the increase per cent kept pace with the increase per cent of the population.

By 1911 the females confirmed exceeded the males by more than forty thousand. The doctrine that 'religion is for women' appeared quite late in the Victorian age; or at least, the lament that the churches contain far more women than men did not become frequent until the last twenty years, still more the last decade, of the century. You can find a few such laments as early as the sixties, but only by the eighties were they frequently asking the question, why so few full-grown men were found in church. That they realised the

[1] *Facts and Figures*, 3,54; 1,24.
[2] G, 92, 209, from Year-Books; cf. *Facts and Figures*, 3, 55; 1, 25.

comparative absence of men may be connected with the agricultural troubles of a few years earlier, and the rapid or even sudden break in the custom whereby farm labourers attended the country church. But it was not only seen in the countryside. They observed that not so many men were found among the congregations of London churches. The number of confirmations show that, however it was remarked during the last decades of the century, it represented an earlier truth about the sexes, if they or their parents were faithful churchgoers. For, though the absolute numbers rose, the ratio between the sexes of confirmed was in 1911 almost exactly that of 1872.

At York in 1901—

   in every 100 Anglicans were 35 men and 65 women.
   in every 100 Nonconformists were 49 men and 51 women.
   in every 100 Roman Catholics were 41 men and 59 women.
   In every 100 at the Salvation Army services were 46 men
      and 54 women.

More baptisms; more confirmations; and, though it is not possible to find statistics sufficiently reliable of communions, far more communions. This was what gave the later Victorians their sense of belonging to a religious revival, a steady progress of Christianity in the world. For such an increase of practice was found not only in the established church, but among the Roman Catholics and among several of the nonconformist denominations. Men wrote articles on the progress of nonconformity. And when to the sense of home advance was added the knowledge of missionary strides in India or Africa or China, some of the later Victorians came to rejoice in a tide of Christian advance; so that they could sing, with a confidence not possible to their successors, the hymn written by A. C. Ainger in 1894, a hymn which could only have been written towards the end of the Victorian age:

God is working his purpose out as year succeeds to year,
God is working his purpose out and the time is drawing near;
Nearer and nearer draws the time, the time that shall surely be,
When the earth shall be filled with the glory of God as the
   waters cover the sea.

The world was in progress. Civilisation spread over the primitive peoples of the world. The Victorians owed much to secular dogmas of progress. But to the Christian no progress was progress, and no civilisation was civilised, unless it was moral. They saw savages becoming educated men, barbarous superstitions expelled by Christian doctrine and by European intelligence. At home they saw less to encourage, but still much to encourage. Despite science and religion, Biblical criticism, urbanisation, secularisation, materialism, country churches declining, they believed into the nineties that they were part of a religious expansion. And the statistics modestly justified their belief. It was easier to count the new buildings than the new occupants of those buildings, and so far as more bricks and mortar were evidence of more Christianity, the evidence was overwhelming.

'It is well known', said Archbishop Benson of Canterbury in 1891,[1] 'that throughout the country the number of those who attend church has largely increased and is still increasing.' Whether the statistics of attendance bore out the archbishop's claim must be further considered. But that it was 'well known' need not be doubted. There can be no question, it was asserted in 1886, that the church has gained immensely in influence during the last twenty years. This was so widely assumed that when the first voices warned against it they caused comment and even alarm. Early in 1900 the warden of Radley said that he believed *the tide of religious revival* to be at last receding.[2] And in 1902 Bishop Talbot of Rochester caused still more comment by a sermon to the Church Congress at Northampton, which talked of a declining zeal, of a feeling of discouragement among the churches. 'There is a sense that we are not on the flow of the tide, and perhaps feel its ebb.' The Boer war gave a shock to the idea of general progress, and may have helped to open the eyes of churchmen to see that their faith outran the facts. But the statistics do not at once show a marked alteration of pattern to warrant such a sense of discouragement. It may be that the sense of an ebb tide owed more to a realisation that their hopes were pitched higher than could be achieved. Or it may be that a greater knowledge of the statistics, especially of worshippers, made men see how little was done, how much was still to do. The sense of ebb might also be due to a circumstance not reflected in the statistics: the alleged decline in the social status of the clergy.

The only government census of religion was that by Horace

---

[1] G, 91, 1769.   [2] G, 86, 1516; G. 1900, 189.

Mann in 1851, based upon counting those who attended church on a particular Sunday. The census was much criticised, but may be used as a guide. In preparation for several later censuses of the nation, men proposed that the census should contain a census of religion. But any proposal caused religious argument in Parliament, which the government wisely sought to avoid. Only government had money and resources to hold a national census of religion. But government refrained, and the enumeration was therefore left to a variety of unofficial efforts. These unofficial censuses could not hope to cover the country. They must be content either with a single denomination, or with a single area. The amateurs differed in method and reliability but, like Horace Mann, they may be taken as useful guides.

The enumerators of a denomination were the officials of that denomination, depended on help less organised than the enumerators of an area, and usually had to manage with returns that were incomplete. Roman Catholics did not attempt to count until the end of the century, and even in the twentieth century found it impossible to persuade parishes or dioceses to adopt a uniform system for making returns. The amount of 'estimate' was larger in counting the denomination than in counting those who attended church in a single city. When they applied the estimates to other denominations than their own, guesswork began to rule. On the other hand, those who counted a single city counted the churches on a single Sunday. No one could adequately correlate attendance at church on a single haphazard Sunday to the total of Christian worship and practice in that city. Surveyors of an area were almost always Protestant nonconformists. Sometimes, but not always, they had ulterior purposes in counting. It was a rough instrument. But these efforts helped the planners of that age, and helped the historian. Students are endeavouring to use these counts to gain reliable conclusions, and at present all inferences are tentative.

The figures were collected on no uniform plan. Usually Sunday schools were included, sometimes not. Some percentages were calculated on the assumption that one-quarter of the attendants attended only one service. Probably more than a quarter attended only one service, and, if so, the percentage of attendants would rise. Without trusting the figures far, we can make broad inferences.

v.c.–8 *a*

Here is a list, after amateur nonconformist censuses, of a variety of cities, taken during 1881:[1]

Place	Population	Total Attendances	Attendance per cent of population (after allowance for twicers)
Liverpool	552,425	146,256	19·9
Sheffield	284,410	87,771	23
Bristol	206,000	109,452	40
Bradford	194,467	70,338	27·1
Nottingham	188,000	60,615	24·2
Hull	153,000	63,138	31
Portsmouth	125,112	68,324	41
Leicester	122,650	53,183	32·5
Bolton	108,963	35,373	24·3
Derby	81,000	30,868	28·6
Wolverhampton	75,738	26,214	26
Burnley	63,502	20,415	24·1
Southampton	60,235	30,324	39
Stockport	68,000	12,000	20·3
Bath	57,790	35,885	52
Northampton	51,226	21,934	32
Ipswich	49,655	29,201	44·1
Coventry	45,116	27,537	45
Warrington	40,960	12,476	22·8
Stockton	40,000	14,681	27·5
Gloucester	36,310	18,395	50·7
Rotherham	35,115	11,215	31·9
Darlington	33,104	7,521	23
Hastings	31,250	21,958	52·7
Scarborough	30,484	19,557	48·1

Average percentage, 37·93. Though the optimistic Horace Mann reckoned that 58 per cent of the country *ought* to attend church, there was little wrong with the Victorian churches if the average percentage of the population that attended church or chapel was nearly 38 per cent. If the figures were correct.

So large a minority of the population attended chapel or church on Sunday that it is no wonder if the churches were a powerful force in Victorian society and politics. Secondly, until

[1] Summarised by C. S. Miall in a letter to *Daily News*: cf. G, 82, 20. The final figures of Andrew Mearns vary but not significantly.

about 1885 the churches and chapels nearly kept pace with the rising population. They were not gaining on it, but they lost little. And, in face of the rapid increase of people and growth of towns, the feat is evidence of extraordinary endeavour in pastoral care and in building new churches.

Each denomination except the Church of England and the Roman Catholics issued statistics of membership either annually or every few years. No means is possible of checking how reliable such figures are, but again they may be taken as rough guides. It must be remembered that the number of attendants was larger than the number of members. Among the Methodists it was much larger, perhaps twice.

An Anglican tried in 1886 to use the various returns of denominations and estimate their progress for the ten years from 1875 to 1885. He produced the following table:[1]

	Members 1875	Members 1885	Increase per cent.
Congregationalists	366,090	418,100	14
Wesleyan Methodists	358,062	413,163	15
Baptists	263,729	310,818	$17\frac{3}{4}$
Primitive Methodists	169,720	191,098	$12\frac{1}{2}$
Calvinistic Methodists (Wales)	101,575	124,505	$22\frac{1}{2}$
United Methodist Free Churches	62,379	67,081	$7\frac{1}{2}$
Presbyterian Church in England	40,440	58,423	44
Methodist New Connexion	22,833	28,032	$22\frac{3}{4}$
Bible Christians	18,324	23,455	28
Friends	14,638	15,219	$3\frac{3}{4}$
	1,417,790	1,649,894	$16\frac{1}{3}$

A net increase of 232,104 in ten years

In the same period the population of England and Wales increased by $14\frac{1}{3}$ per cent. Therefore nonconformity did more than keep up with the population. The 44 per cent increase in Presbyterians was no doubt due to Scotsmen coming south. But that increase was not a large proportion of the whole. The important increases were among Baptists, Congregationalists, and Methodists both Wesleyan and Primitive.

[1] G, 86, 699. Areas in 1851 and 1881 not quite the same. 1851 included Sunday schools and 1881 did not.

The Anglican statistician asked himself why the Baptists advanced, and answered that Spurgeon gave them a marvellous impetus. He also attributed something (as did every enquirer who investigated the subject) to the consistent endeavour of the nonconformist denominations to provide Sunday schools for the children.

	1875	1885	Increase per cent.
Wesleyan Methodists	701,871	862,279	21
Baptists	372,242	467,930	25
Primitive Methodists	316,985	405,389	28

These figures are much less reliable than the figures of members. But it was a truth which they reported. An Anglican Sunday school (except in Lancashire and the West Riding and other parts of the north) depended on the vicar. Some Anglican Sunday schools were excellent. Some vicars were incapable of organising a good Sunday school, and others preferred not to separate the children from adult worship. Many Anglican parents sent their children to nonconformist Sunday schools.

This increase of nonconformity was not spread evenly over the country. In 1886 the Wesleyan Methodists attempted to analyse the rates of growth or decline in different areas. In London and neighbourhood they found the very high increase of 59.9 per cent over seventeen years, and attributed it largely to the building of sixty-odd new chapels after a gift of £75,000 by Sir Francis Lycett. As the iron industry developed at Barrow-in-Furness, so grew the Methodists in Cumberland (50 per cent in seventeen years). Liverpool, Bristol, Manchester, Nottingham, Derby came next. But in Lincolnshire or rural Yorkshire the increase was 3 to 4 per cent, and in Cornwall (where the county was emptying, not slowly) a marked decrease.

The 1881 nonconformist census selected fourteen towns, Liverpool, Sheffield, Newcastle and Gateshead, Bristol, Bradford, Nottingham, Hull, Portsmouth, Leicester, Bolton, Derby, Wolverhampton, Southampton. In these towns, of the total attendance

Church of England	37·03
Nonconformists	55·21
Roman Catholics	7·73

(percentages of total attendants)

Bristol[1]

	1851	1881	(counted by Western Daily Press)
Church of England	23·60	22·83	
Independents	8·79	6·12	
Baptists	4·58	4·62	
Wesleyans	3·16	4·31	
Roman Catholics	3·29	1·66	
Salvation Army	—	5·35	

percentage of population

The percentage of worshippers to the rising population had not changed greatly over the thirty years. A slight rise in total, but a slight fall without the intervention of the Salvation Army. The denominational pattern ran fairly consistently across these big or middle-sized towns, and similar results are reached whether we take a percentage of the populations or a percentage of the counted attenders. In the big towns of the north, except perhaps in Manchester and Liverpool, the total number of Anglican worshippers was usually lower, sometimes much lower, than the total number of nonconformist worshippers. In the home counties and in resorts like Scarborough or Bath the proportions were usually reversed. This result was reached by counting those who attended church. But if the different method was adopted of asking men what church they belonged to, the Anglican (and in Lancashire the Roman Catholic) numbers rose sharply. In 1881 an Anglican statistical expert at Liverpool organised a census on this alternative method. The number of Anglicans was much larger than by the other method. The statistician calculated slightly more than half the number of Anglicans to be 'non-attendants'[2] and that the real proportion of Anglican attendants was about 26 per cent. Ten years later the *Liverpool Daily Post* organised a counting of the morning services and calculated Anglicans at two-fifths of the attendants. But counting only a main service inevitably inflated the proportion of Anglicans to all worshippers. And the *Liverpool Daily Post* counted only churches and omitted mission rooms. The census showed that especially in northern cities a sizeable fraction of those who

[1] G, 81, 1591.
[2] G, 82, 393; for material on Liverpool see R. B. Walker, 'Religious changes in Liverpool in the nineteenth century', JEH, xix, 2 (1968) 195ff.

worshipped God worshipped in little rooms and little meetings not
with elaborate liturgies or famous preachers or consecrate dbuildings.

Since these censuses usually counted attendants, they seldom
threw light upon those who rejected Christianity. The Liverpool
census of profession (i.e. not of attendance) in 1881 produced the
result that 0·6 per cent of the population professed to be not Anglican
not Roman Catholic not dissenting. They were classified as 'religion
unknown', and doubtless included Lascar seamen and oriental
religions as well as a few Englishmen who rejected Christianity.
At almost the same date a census of profession in St. Matthew's near
Victoria Docks, East London, where the inhabitants were dockers
or railway men, produced an astonishingly different result.[1] 622
families inhabiting 439 houses were visited; total souls, 2,696. Of
this sample 67·28 were Anglicans, 16·24 Protestant dissenters, 4·78
Roman Catholics, and 11.7 were described as 'Nothingarians'—
that is, 62 families out of the whole number. The nothingarians
were more than twice the number of the Roman Catholics. It looks
as though the secularist movement in the age of Bradlaugh pene-
trated the docks efficiently. (Contrast a rural diocese—the visitation
records of the diocese of Lincoln for 1886 produced only one
instance of unbelief.) One similar piece of evidence from about the
same date raised the percentage of nothingarians a little higher.
About 1883 a man went out and asked for the 'religious views' of
the first 200 male adults whom he met and classified 13 per cent
as 'unbelievers'. Twenty years later in 1903 he repeated the same
experiment, and classified 28 per cent as 'unbelievers'.[2] But we
cannot trust these figures unless we knew where he asked the
questions, how he framed them, and how the questioned framed
their replies.

Such creatures as nothingarians were seldom recognised by
censuses except by silence. The burial board at Kidderminster (1882)
suffered trouble about atheistic addresses at certain funerals in the
public cemetery.[3] The amateur census at Kidderminster recorded no
such persons, but a low proportion of attendants at worship to the
total population.

As late as 1906 a parliamentary paper gave the religious profession
of the 21,580 prisoners[4] and the figures may be thought to say

[1] G, 82, 560.   [2] Do We believe? 1905, 87.
[3] G, 82, 344.   [4] PP, 1906, xcix, 893.

something about the religious affiliations (but not attendance at church) of labouring men. Church of England, 16,089; Roman Catholic, 4,397; Wesleyans 352; Jews, 257; Baptists, 132. No other denomination had as many as 100. Atheists, 22; 'no religion', 26; not ascertained (delirium tremens), 1. Bishop Fraser of Manchester[1] received a census from three parishes. Parish A had 1,233 families, and 904 families or 73 per cent went nowhere. One only out of the 904 avowed atheism. Parish B had 1,803 families and 40 per cent went nowhere. Parish C had 1,719 houses, and twenty-six families made 'no pretence to Christian belief' while 707 families had the most nominal attachment to their denomination. These figures were still very respectable from the point of view of the churches. But in 1898 Bishop Moorhouse conducted a visitation of his two northern archdeaconries of Lancaster and Blackburn, and was disquieted at the result.[2] It was clear to him that places of worship, whether churches or chapels, were not nearly so well attended as twenty years earlier. He attributed the fall not to avowed infidelity but to amusements and the quest for material prosperity.

Those who abstained from attending church were far more numerous than those who professed not to have a religion. And as a corollary the social influence of the churches cannot be judged by the number of actual attendants. We shall see that in some towns nearly every child attended Sunday school.

In Bacup (1883) Beatrice Potter lived in the house of a dissenter and so saw the town through dissenting spectacles. But she was sure that religious feelings still held the working man—and yet heard the more religious of them agree that 'the younger generation are looking elsewhere for subjects of thought and feeling'.[3] She found faith 'absorbing' their nature, claiming 'as its own all the energy unused in the actual struggle for existence'. All social life depended on the chapels and the co-operative—(the parish church had not an effective pastor)—and so the control of private morality was stern, and to escape this control a man must leave Bacup.

We have a church census of York, in March 1901. York was neither a typical country town nor a typical cathedral town of the smaller kind, for it contained a larger colony of Irish than was

---

[1] *Charge*, 1880, 24.
[2] *Charge* in Preston parish church on 24 January 1899, 7–9.
[3] *My Apprenticeship*[2], 139–40.

usual in such a town, and the railway and cocoa and brewing offered more industrial employment than was common in a small cathedral town. The Quaker Seebohm Rowntree organised the church census as part of his enquiry into the social conditions of the city, afterwards published under the title *Poverty: a study of town life*. The census was not organised exactly. It omitted early services, counted only the two main services, and failed to include a large mission service then being conducted in York theatre, on the ground that it was temporary. But with the aid of his enumerators he proved (after allowing for twicers) that something between one-third and one-quarter of the adults (over 16) of York went to church or chapel; between 28 and 32 per cent of the adult population.[1]

Of the total attendants, the percentages by denominations, averaging over two consecutive Sundays, read: 43 per cent Church of England, 38 per cent Nonconformist, 14 per cent Roman Catholic, 5 per cent Salvation Army and mission services.

The figures available to us are still miscellaneous, and much more local enquiry is needed. But we may make the following inferences from such figures as we find.

1. All churches were powerful in the north; but the Church of England was relatively weaker in the north than in the south.

2. The bigger the city, the sooner a decline in religious practice began to be observed.

3. Until the last fifteen years of the century, the churches succeeded marvellously in their endeavours to keep pace with the rising population. After 1886, though the leaders of most churches had just as powerful a feeling of advance, the figures show that the churches failed markedly to keep pace with the rise in people; and more, that in towns where the population was still rising, the number of attendants at church began to decline. We may guess at some obvious causes; the bigger the town the bigger the problem, and the easier the wastage; intellectual unsettlement of the age may have begun to affect the young; and we remember Beatrice Potter's judgment on Bacup in 1883, that despite the extraordinary religious-ness of the town, the young people directed their interests to other and secular ends. But during the last two decades of the century it became more obvious than ever before that the working man of

---

[1] *Poverty*, 344–8.

the big towns, with few exceptions, did not think of attending
church or chapel.

The religion of London was unique because the size and social
circumstance of London were unique. From the statistics of London
we cannot usefully make inferences to any other city or county of
England.

After Mann in 1851, two censuses of London were organised.
Both were organised by dissenting newspapers. In 1886 William
Robertson Nicoll started the *British Weekly* and at once conducted
an enquiry, which was amateur like most of the local censuses.
Robertson Nicoll entrusted the work to Major Colquhoun, who
had counted a smaller area in Glasgow. They used several thousand
enumerators to count everyone who attended church or chapel on
24 October 1886. In response to the argument that they counted
only the main churches, they took a census of missions and halls
on the last Sunday in November 1887, but with Horace Mann's
method, that is, the managers of the mission made a return.

In 1902 the *Daily News*, owned by the Quaker George Cadbury
and favouring disestablishment, arranged a far more systematic and
reliable count of attendances. The organisation was placed under
Richard Mudie-Smith, who published the results in a book of 1904,
The Religious Life of London. The method varied from the previous
censuses, which counted the worshippers in all the churches on a
single Sunday. Charges had been heard that as the single day was
known, a whip went out to adherents. Mudie-Smith therefore
counted one group of parishes on one Sunday and the next group
on another, so that he conducted the whole count over several
months. Thus he was able to keep a comparatively small and
experienced staff of workers. He selected 400 men, mostly pensioners
from the army and navy, paid them and put them under careful
supervision. He was also able to make allowance for those who
attended twice, for the weather, and for other random circumstances which eluded the method of the two earlier enquiries.
Mudie-Smith claimed his census to be the first 'scientific' census.
His men investigated every street to find missions or chapels or
rooms not to be found in any list official or unofficial. Strangely, he
took no account of early services (before 9.30 a.m.) except in the

Anglican churches of only nine boroughs, on the ground that 'many' of those who attended came again later in the morning; sampled afternoon and weekday services, but took no account of hospitals, workhouses or prisons. He attempted the first crude test of 'twicers' by handing slips (in selected churches) to worshippers coming out of a morning service, and asking them to return them if they came back in the evening. Of his predecessors he formed a much higher opinion of Robertson Nicoll than of Mann. The 1851 census he came to believe almost worthless. He allowed, however, one of his colleagues to criticise even Robertson Nicoll for 'a hurried and somewhat insufficient' numbering.

In addition to these three censuses of 1851, 1886, 1902–3, the sociologist Charles Booth included seven volumes on religion in his monumental *Life and Labour in London*. Between 1898 and 1900 he and his staff surveyed London parish by parish, church by church, chapel by chapel. The whole is more impressionistic than the almost contemporary figures of Mudie-Smith. The impressions are often valuable, and make the volumes indispensable to the student of London religion during the last Victorian decade.

The most important news disclosed by these censuses was the difference between the 1851–86 age and the 1886–1902 age. Comparisons between Mann's census and Robertson Nicoll's census are by no means easy to make reliable. But on the whole the churches seemed to be more or less keeping pace relatively to the rise in population. Between 1886 and 1902 they were not. So far from keeping pace, they declined. They declined not only in relation to the rising population, but absolutely. And the established church lost more than any other denomination.

	Population of London	Total worshippers
1886	(1881) 3,816,483	1,167,312
1901	4,536,541	1,003,361

The *British Weekly* census was taken on a bright autumn Sunday. The *Daily News* included winter and foggy nights.

Between 1886 and 1901 the Londoner developed the new habit of getting out of London for the weekend.

The increase in population misrepresents. This increase is in part an immigration of foreigners, so that (for example) large parts of

Whitechapel became a Jewish quarter. It did not follow (so it was argued) that the Anglicans ceased going to Anglican churches. It only meant that they moved out of the London area.

	Anglicans	Nonconformists
1886	535,715⎫ excluding	369,349
1901	396,196⎭ missions	363,882

In Anglican churches, if the statistics were right, only three persons attended where four attended fifteen years before. In 1886 the Church of England had still a big majority in London. Not so in 1902.

The statistics confirmed the feeling of those like the Bishop of Rochester, who sensed it before they saw the statistics, that the churches were at last on an ebb-tide.[1]

The poorer the area, on the whole, the worse attended the churches. Hackney was a parish less crowded than Hackney Wick and its churches flourished more. The only church to flourish in Hackney Wick was the Roman Catholic, which suggested a population part-Irish and part-Italian.[2] Shoreditch was one of the most crowded parishes in London, and was next to the bottom in church attendance: 1 person to 16 of population in the morning, 1 to 11 in the evening, the men being markedly absent.

Masterman[3] summed up the verdict of the census on South London:

1. the poor (unless Roman Catholic, or a few Primitive Methodists, Baptists, adherents of the Salvation Army, etc.) do not go to church.

---

[1] Totals of each denomination for London (Mudie-Smith, 271):

Church of England	396,196 (+ 33,626 missions)
Baptists	98,635 (+ 9820 missions)
Congregationalists	91,828 (+ 13,707 missions)
Roman Catholics	93,572
Wesleyan Methodists	72,830 (+ 5,309 missions)
Presbyterians	22,921 (+ 1857 missions)
Salvation Army	22,402
Brethren	16,812
Primitive Methodists	13,481
Unitarians	3,599
Catholic Apostolic Church	3,232
Friends	2,987

[2] Mudie-Smith, 27.   [3] Mudie-Smith, 201.

2. the working man does not go to church.
3. the tradesmen and middle class of the poorer boroughs are active, mainly in the larger nonconformist chapels, especially Baptists.
4. residents in suburbs support liberally all forms of organised religion.

Until the nineties the word *suburban* had a well-to-do air. The new working-class suburbs had a more shifting population, and were almost entirely inhabited by young married couples with tiny children. Everyone testified that work in this kind of suburb was particularly difficult and unrewarding; that it was difficult to build churches or maintain them; that it was a sphere which had not the romance of the slum and did not attract many good ministers; that the people tended to be materialists; that the parishioners did nothing in the parish but sleep; that some of them were quite out of reach of church or dissent.

By 1900 quite a number of working men had already moved further out, and lived in 'suburbs'. Church attendance was lowest of all where the working man thus moved. Tottenham had fewer than Poplar or Stepney or Deptford. Places like Edmonton or Leyton were dormitories for London workers, without industry of their own. In all these workers' suburbs the nonconformists were in the majority. At the opposite end, in Richmond or Carshalton, the Church of England was in a big majority.

The working man was more likely to go to church or chapel if he lived in a partially middle-class district. Stoke Newington contained a large population of working men. But one in three of the whole population went to church or chapel, almost certainly because a majority of the population was not working class but lower middle class.[1] Influenced by their neighbours, they went to church.

In West London therefore the figures were far higher, though Fulham (counted under unfavourable conditions) was lower even than Shoreditch. St. Marylebone had over 26 per cent of worshippers to population, Westminster (which still contained many dwellings of the poor) over 22 per cent, Kensington over 20 per cent.[2] And the total results, in a manner, were not disheartening. Mudie-Smith

---

[1] Mudie-Smith, 129. No estimate for twicers.
[2] Mudie-Smith, 88–89. After allowing for twicers.

made them sound disheartening because like Horace Mann he wanted to stir the churches to endeavour. The figures gave the Anglicans matter for self-examination. But in all London, including Greater London, of those who could physically attend church or chapel one in five persons worshipped somewhere. In Greater London the best area was Barnet, 1 worshipper to 1·66 population. The worst was Tottenham, 1 worshipper to 6·06 population. While complaints resounded that working men did not come to church, 47,282 men attended church in the East End, as against 61,301 women.[1] Deduct 700 men more or less compulsory in workhouse chapels, and 8,000 Jewish men in synagogues, and estimate for twicers, and the men were reduced to about 22,000 for all East London. It was not much, but its proportion to the women was much larger than would have been gathered from the complaints that religion is for women; and it made no allowance for the proportion of men who must work on Sunday.

The tremendous efforts of their fathers to build enough churches, in the hope that the churches would be filled, left them with too many churches. What they saw was not the amount of church-going but the quarter-full churches almost side by side in some half-inhabited street like the Gray's Inn Road. That devoted Anglican layman and future statesman, C. F. G. Masterman, lived in South London among a people, none of whom he thought went to church. He supposed that the break-up of faith, and destructive criticism of the Bible, had helped to make them hostile or indifferent. He guessed that the active Christian population of South London might be as low as one per cent and was not higher than four per cent. Therefore he was astonished when the census proved to him that in his area one man in every six, and one woman in every five, attended some church or chapel on Sunday.[2]

Masterman inferred that the churches were maintained by the middle class, the grocers and tradesmen, who still lived scattered among the parishes to the south of the river. He did not believe that the poor ever went to church. Whenever he went into a church or chapel in the area, he saw no sign of poverty. He found the poor in only two places: in the Bermondsey mission where H. T. Meakin filled a large hall, and in the Roman Catholic cathedral of Southwark where the poor were so numerous that the incense was no ritual

[1] Mudie-Smith, 18, 36.   [2] Masterman, in Mudie-Smith, 195.

necessity. He proved the point to himself by comparing the working-class district of Walworth with the 'suburban' district of Dulwich and Sydenham. In Walworth the percentage of worshippers to population was 6·5; in Dulwich and Sydenham, 30·6.[1] Probably 30·6 underestimated the suburb, for some of its inhabitants would travel to churches outside their parishes. Scrape off, said Masterman, 'a layer of middle-class houses from the main streets of Walworth' and 'you would probably diminish your church attendance by at least two-thirds'.

Astonished and gratified by the number who went to church, Masterman was yet gloomy. Such efforts, money, devotion, heroism, were poured out upon the poor streets of London, and to no avail. 'If the works done in South London today, one is inclined to assert, had been done in Sodom and Gomorrah, they would have repented in sackcloth and ashes.' South London showed no such signs. It was just passive. Every variety of churchman beat in vain against this wall of indifference.

Further south, in the suburbs, there were parishes where almost the entire population seemed to go to church on Sunday.

2. NUMBER OF CHURCHES

In the big towns everyone could find space. You went into a suburb or a slum some way from any church, and opened a room for Sunday worship, in a shack, a living-room, a conservatory. Then the children collected and you had a Sunday school, and if you had children you were soon in touch with their parents and had a congregation. Then you persuaded the congregation to work towards a temporary church, and afterwards a permanent church. Meanwhile organisations for young people, or for welfare towards the old or poor or sick, were generated by the impetus of the new congregation. This was long the method of nonconformist expansion and after Peel's act of 1843 it became the principal method of Anglican expansion; not the only method, for bishops also planned new churches at diocesan level, and created new parishes from above as well as from below. The Roman Catholic priest opened a room where he could find a few Roman Catholics. The Anglican always assumed that he would find a majority of Anglicans where-

---

[1] Masterman, in Mudie-Smith, 197–8.

ever he opened a room. The nonconformist did not need to look for members of his denomination before he opened a room, for he rightly assumed that he would find people willing to join. The method produced the rapid multiplication of places of worship so characteristic of Victorian England. Bishop Jackson of London said in 1877 that the sub-division of parishes was proceeding with such rapidity that no man went to bed at night knowing whose parish he might wake up in.[1] Churches and chapels in Camberwell: 1851, 26; 1902–3, 156;[2] Ripon diocese (still with Leeds and Bradford and Huddersfield): 1832–5, 4 churches consecrated; 1867–71, 42 churches consecrated.[3] Examples of these new creations are plentiful.

In 1866 Bishop Sumner of Winchester appointed a missionary curate to serve a district parish of Blenheim Grove in Camberwell, and bought a site for the church (£750) with a diocesan loan, and a grant of £1,000. A letter was sent to every house in the district explaining what was happening, and asking for help. The curate furnished a semi-detached house for services, and held the first service in August 1866. It was attended by a lot of children and 25 adults. Within eighteen months they established a school and a mission, and then they collected nearly £7,000 for a church by 1872, when the new church of All Saints was consecrated (population 4,891). The stipend was formed from an endowment of £34 a year plus pew rents.[4] Indeed the chief argument against those who wished to abolish all pew rents was that it would make expansion impossible.

Here is a parallel case in nonconformity. The Congregationalist R. H. Smith, formerly apprentice to a printer, opened a room in his house at Surbiton, then built a room in the garden, then built a small church, and his successor Mackennal built Surbiton Park church. Later Smith went (1865–81) to Gospel Oak Fields, a new housing estate near Hampstead Heath, threw together two rooms of his house and a conservatory, and then his congregation built Gospel Oak chapel with money from the London Chapels Building Society and gifts from Samuel Morley and others; later still they added a schoolroom. In almost all such cases the Sunday school was the nucleus round which the new congregation was built.[5]

---

[1] CCR, 1877, 307.　　　　　　　[2] Dyos, 156–7.
[3] CCR, 1872, 20–1. Ripon diocese was created in 1836.
[4] Dyos, 161–2.　　　　　[5] For Smith, CYB, 1885, 227.

In these new town parishes the Church of England at last developed the responsibility of its laity like the nonconformists. They needed the interest and active help of the general laity, and not only of magnates and squires and patrons. Hobson took charge of St. Nathaniel's, West Derby in Liverpool, and conducted his first service in a cellar with four people. Seventeen years later he conducted services for 4,000 people; and the feat was accomplished by using 200 helpers and by training working men to conduct open-air missions.[1]

The Roman Catholics could not expand their parishes in this way. For it required laymen even to teach religion, and their system did not yet countenance such a development. In consequence Roman Catholic parishes were rare, and had rare congregations. In North London (1902) were 15 parishes with an average attendance of 1,053 at each church, in an area where the Wesleyans had 29 churches and an average attendance of 541, 40 Congregationalist churches with an average attendance of 526, 50 Baptist churches with an average attendance of 442, and 180 Anglican churches with an average attendance of 400.[2] These vast Roman Catholic congregations had the advantage that they looked so powerful and made possible great corporate acts of worship. They kept a group of priests together; and some Anglicans kept protesting that their system of division into many weak units was an error, and that a vast parish with ten priests was better than the same area divided into ten districts, each with one priest. But the Roman Catholics were not always content with these arrangements. They were able to maintain it because their people were willing to travel longer distances, partly because it was sin not to attend mass, and partly because Irishmen found in the mass a link with their home and nation as well as their religion. The experience of Anglican parishes in the northern industrial cities showed that where they retained vast districts they merely lost people to nonconformist chapels. Above all the system of sub-division, however it might be criticised for creating weak units (and it was impossible beforehand to predict whether the unit would be weak), drew an ever-increasing number of laymen to take responsibility.

The expansion and sub-division is recorded for the Church of England in the money spent on building churches. Between 1840

---

[1] CCR, 1888, 640–1.   [2] Mudie-Smith, 152.

and 1876 the Anglicans alone built in England and Wales 1,727 new churches and rebuilt or restored 7,144 old churches and cathedrals, at a total cost of £25,548,703. The new churches were chiefly in the dioceses of Winchester (294) especially in South London, Manchester (193), Ripon (182), Lichfield (169), Durham (154), Oxford (145), and York (127).[1]

The Anglicans stood in a privileged situation, in that some of their money did not need to come from the pockets of their worshippers. The Ecclesiastical Commissioners or Queen Anne's Bounty helped, as did the surviving endowment in the hands of the Church Building Commission. Until their abolition in 1868 church rates helped with the repair of a few town churches. But the figures show that these sources from endowment, or even from public funds, were tiny compared with the total cost. Diocese of London: cost, £2,708,613. From private sources: £2,536,629.

Meanwhile other denominations increased their places of worship. The Roman Catholics had 798 churches or chapels in 1861 and 1,536 in 1901, but the number is not reliable because even in 1901 many of the places recorded as churches had still no weekly service. The Congregationalists, however, had 2,236 churches or chapels in 1861 and 4,579 in 1901, the Baptists claimed 1,150 churches or chapels in 1860 and 6,313 in 1901; but in independency the loose union with a central organisation influenced the figures.

The nonconformist town churches showed their equality, and their municipal importance, by their architecture. John Angell James wrote in 1860 that dissent, which used to be the religion of barns, was becoming 'infected with the ambition of becoming the religion of cathedrals'.[2] Albion church at Ashton-under-Lyme cost £50,000 (1897), Joseph Parker's City Temple (classical 1874) £80,000. The little country chapels were still cheap, but the urban nonconformists were no longer afraid of decorated pulpits or even of stained glass. Christ Church, Westminster Bridge, was given a central lantern supported on foliated capitals. They were willing to seek the celebrated artists of the day. The windows at Albion church were designed by William Morris and Burne-Jones.

Matthew Arnold's superior tone about the lack of taste in non-conformity was sometimes justified by the productions of this phase. But in less grand places the people did not object because they

[1] PP, 1876, lviii, 553.   [2] Dale, *Life of J. A. James*, 560.

made what they could make for themselves, and planned it as they liked. Often they used local labour, and eschewed the architect or large contractor, and they might have a carpenter or metal-worker or small builder among their own people, and they might paint or furnish it for themselves.[1] The result was not perfect in taste, but it was their own.

Some of their people had wealth on the new scale—the Wills family of Bristol, Sir Francis Crossley and carpets at Halifax, Sir Titus Salt and alpaca at Saltaire, Samuel Morley and his hosiery— still simple and God-fearing men, but munificent.

The architect afforded a problem to the designers, how to com- bine the almost compulsory Gothic with a place where everyone could hear the word. A Congregationalist of 1878 blamed the early Gothic chapel-makers because they were likely to make the preacher almost inaudible. But he still wanted Gothic, for it aspired to heaven and looked like a church. He said that he was stopped in front of a large classical Congregational church and was asked 'What is it?' 'Is it a town-hall?' 'Is it a railway-station?' When Mansfield College (Congregationalist) was built in Oxford by Basil Champneys, it was a little Gothic jewel, such as a high Anglican of the Camden Society might have envied.[2]

In the last twenty years of the century the standard of Roman Catholic churches built, and especially the furniture inside those churches, was no longer cheap like the little sheds forced upon them in the age of Irish immigration. Organs, altars, communion rails, sanctuary lamps were of better workmanship. A fair number of the churches and chapels were still unconsecrated because they were in debt, but money was no longer quite so short. The outward symbol of this ability at last to build well and expensively was Westminster cathedral. The laity wanted a memorial to Cardinal Wiseman, who longed for a great church in London. But Manning had no desire to spend money on a great church when so much else needed doing, and quite disconcerted a meeting to raise funds for the cathedral by talking of the needs of 20,000 uncared-for Catholic children in London.[3] He thought of it as a plan for Cloud-Cuckoo Land. 'Could I leave 20,000 children without education, and drain my friends and my flock to pile up stones and bricks?' It was a strength to the

---

[1] John Betjeman, *Architectural Review*, lxxxviii, December 1940, 161–74; Moir, *History Today* 1963, 389.   [2] Cf. Horton Davies, iv, 56.   [3] Purcell, ii, 354–5.

denomination that neither of its two famous men cared, as Manning once wrote to Newman, for *decorations*.[1] The site was purchased in 1868 for £36,500, and changed in 1883 for another £20,000, so that the acquisition exhausted the effort for money, and Manning did not encourage further effort. When he died, Archbishop Vaughan began to build. He laid the foundation stone in 1895 but was dead in June 1903 before it opened.

The other prominent symbol was the Brompton Oratory, where Manning opened the new church in 1884. But these great churches must not obscure the constant shortage of funds under which the Roman Catholics still laboured, as their effort to build schools and churches always outran their means.

3. NUMBER OF MINISTERS

For many Anglicans the ideal of a town pastor was Walter Hook, who as vicar of Leeds changed the Christian feeling and the ecclesiastical complexion of that town. When Hook was asked how a vicar worked a populous parish he gave a simple reply. The vicar should hire curates. The curates should go out and persuade a lot of laymen to help them. The vicar had better not try to tell the curates or the lay workers what to do but leave it to their individual genius. The vicar need do nothing but reserve the right to say no to suggestions. It was, however, essential that the vicar should know what the Church of England was about.[2]

This modesty concealed the truth that the modern urban parish could no longer be worked like a country parish of tradition where the incumbent directed every activity. It was work for a team. The first consideration therefore was to find men and women; in Hook's simple terms, to find the right clergy and enough of them, and to find the laymen and laywomen and give them what needed to be done.

In all the main denominations the number of full-time ministers rose markedly during the last twenty years of the reign. Counting all from Roman Catholic priests to (paid) local preachers of non-

[1] Manning to Newman, 4 June 1865. Ward, *Newman*, ii, 89. Manning was referring to the honour of a titular bishopric, which he had been trying to secure for Newman.
[2] CCR, 1863, 181.

conformity, we find just over 36,000 men in 1881, and twenty years later just on 45,000 men, an increase in twenty years of about nine thousand. This can be broken down into groups thus.[1]

	1881	1891	1901
Clergymen	21,663	24,232	25,235
Roman Catholic priests	2,089	2,511	2,849
Nonconformist ministers	9,374	10,057	11,572
Local preachers etc. male	2,965	5,119	5,293
female	1,660	4,194	4,803

Contrast this with the number of people to each Anglican clergyman.[2]

	Number of Clergy	Number of Laymen to each Clergyman
1841	14,613	1,101
1851	17,621	1,024
1861	19,195	1,054
1871	20,694	1,097
1881	21,663	1,194
1891	24,232	

Notice the large increase of clergymen during the forties. It was probably due in part to the age of the Oxford Movement; in part to the pluralities act of 1838, which by limiting pluralities increased the number of men needed; in part to the new parishes and new churches in the movement for church extension; and the special provisions for paying new clergymen made by the Church Pastoral-Aid Society or the Additional Curates Society. The Ripon diocese, with Leeds and Bradford and Huddersfield still within it, had 297 incumbents and 76 curates when it was created in 1836. In 1872 it had 462 incumbents and 245 curates; so that in thirty-six years the number of incumbents rose by more than 50 per cent and the number of curates by more than 300 per cent.[3]

The general increase between 1861 and 1871 looks slower. In the

---

[1] Census 1901, pp, 1904, cviii, app. A, 264. Monks and nuns to be added.

[2] G, 73, 1243; 85, 1327. The number of clergy stated in the national census was 2000 or so less than the number who appeared in the clergy lists, for if a clergyman described himself (e.g.) as a schoolmaster, he was entered only as a schoolmaster for the national return.   [3] CCR, 1872, 20–21.

sixties sounded the first cries that good men will not take orders because they cannot believe what they are expected to teach. But the slowing of advance was probably less slow than the bald statistics suggested. For in the late sixties fellows of colleges at Oxford or Cambridge ceased so automatically to take orders in order to retain their fellowships. And about the same period schoolmasters no longer felt the same need to take holy orders in order to perform their work effectively or to command the confidence of parents. This was not true of the headmasters of great schools, who must be ordained men until the end of the century. (There was a stir when in 1903 Marlborough appointed as headmaster a layman, Frank Fletcher, without expectation that he would afterwards take orders.) In the sixties the teaching profession, apart from holy orders, was created, and this trend diminished the number of those ordained. Yet the schoolmaster-parson or don-parson might in his retiring years seek a parish and so help the parochial system of the Church of England. The smaller number of clerical schoolmasters had eventual consequences in the parishes.

When it is said that in 1871 there were 1,097 laymen to each clergyman, it must not be thought that every 1,100 laymen had a clergyman. This was the national average. But many country clergymen were serving 150 laymen in deep country. And the diocese of Manchester averaged 4,000 to each parish, with some very populous parishes. The figures of slow increase of laity to each clergyman concealed a much more rapid increase of laity to each clergyman in many big towns.

The Bath and Plymouth Church Congresses of 1873 and 1876 were the first to discuss how to increase the number of ordinands. The debates aroused no interest and were attended by a handful. The generosity which built new churches and founded new parishes created new openings for curates. The principal of St. Aidan's College, Birkenhead (W. Saumarez Smith), received 59 applications for curates in 1873 and each year thereafter the number of applications rose.

The tradition of the Church of England required a 'learned', or at least an educated, or at least an upper middle class, ministry. In short, it demanded Latin and Greek and a university degree. The great body of Anglicans assumed that it was one main strength of the Church of England that their clergymen were gentlemen. This was the admiration of Taine when he visited England.[1] They were expected to take their place in gentle society. Few Anglicans of the seventies wished for a ministry from 'the lower ranks of society', 'like the dissenters'. The weightiest men urged that the standard must not be lowered. It was better to have fewer and educated than more and uneducated. The suggestion kept being made that the ministry of the Church of England should be thrown open to those of 'lower social rank', and kept being resisted. Hurrell Froude might call it the *gentleman-heresy*, but the idea of a clergyman was united with the idea of a gentleman. Bishop Tait of London, who did as much as his predecessor for church extension in that diocese, nevertheless attacked the theory of clergymen 'of a more homely type' in his charge of 1858. 'There may come a time', said Professor Stubbs of Oxford, 'when, the doctrinal teaching of the Church remaining and retaining its hold on the classes of society that it now affects, it may still be so bad a speculation to bring up sons for the clerical office, that candidates must be sought in a lower grade; and that very large sphere and those many ways of usefulness which are now utilised by the clergy, as leaders of country society, and prominently interested in all social movements, must be given up; their sole means of influence being the sacerdotal, their spiritual or ministerial influence. I do not think it desirable that such a time should be hastened.' Samuel Wilberforce remarked, on the doctrine that poorer classes supply the best clergy for the poor, that all experience proved the contrary.[2]

As late as 1873 three dioceses were said still to refuse ordinands without degrees.

From time to time protests were raised against this doctrine. The bestowal of the extended franchise by the Reform act of 1867 caused thought about the gulf between the parson and the working man. When the Conservatives lost the seat at Christchurch in the election of 1868, Lord Malmesbury wrote to Disraeli that 'the church cannot hold its own with the new electors if it does not institute a class like the *bas clergé* in Roman Catholic countries. They [i.e. the labourers] have no sympathy with *gentlemen* parsons.'[3] Less politically and more religiously, heads of theological colleges like

---

[1] *Notes on England,* 159.
[2] CCR, 1872, 307; Wilberforce, *Essays,* 2, 94; from QR July 1867.
[3] Hughenden Papers, B/XX/HS/157.

Ashwell of Chichester[1] demanded variety of sources for clergymen. He had known 'the clever scholarly Oxford honour-man startled at finding a companion fresh from a London counting-house able to initiate him' into dealing with roughs or holding an audience at a mission service. But the plan to widen the range needed only a statistical argument. The number of clergymen now needed could not be supplied by the universities. And even while this debate continued in the seventies (and it continued to the end of the century and after) the statistics show that the number without university degrees increased. It increased very slowly. In 1879 about one in six of the Anglican clergy had no degree:

Total clergymen (in Crockford): 23,612.
Cambridge, 8,615. Oxford, 7,682. Dublin, 1,761.
Durham, 655. London, 176. No return, 1,640.

So just over 19,000 out of 23,612 clergymen had degrees.[2] In the seventies and eighties about 72 to 75 per cent, at a rough calculation of deacons ordained, possessed a university degree.

We must not forget, however, that the degrees of all five universities mentioned above varied in their quality and attainment. The Victorians themselves did not forget it. 'Oxford and Cambridge degrees . . .', said the chancellor of Truro cathedral in 1897, 'do not always imply what may be termed a good education. [3] What the figures prove is that Anglican clergymen came from the homes of the upper middle class. The parishes were unanimous in supposing that they were given a second-rate man if they were given a curate without a degree. The chairman of one theological college said ruefully that 'the title of B.A. without much knowledge of divinity is more esteemed in the world than a good knowledge of divinity without the title of B.A'.[4] And this is one reason why the Anglicans were slower than any other denomination in providing money to train men who could not afford their own training. They were accustomed to men who could afford their training. A Wesleyan, a Presbyterian, a Roman Catholic, had the expenses of his training for the ministry largely found. It did not become easy for Anglicans who could not afford it until the end of the

[1] CCR, 1873, 135–6.   [2] G, 79, 384.   [3] CCR, 1897, 400.
[4] Dean Howson of Chester, CCR, 1873, 130.

century or beginning of the twentieth century.[1]

The later Victorians debated much why more men did not come forward to take holy orders. They were inclined to diagnose thus. At the beginning of the reign a gentleman could only earn his living in the army, the navy, the church, the law, and perhaps the civil service. Now commerce was opened even to the sons of gentlemen. The civil service made greater demands. The commitments of empire drew good men overseas. The profession of teaching, whether in school or university, no longer required holy orders. And meanwhile the value of clerical stipends did not keep pace with the stipends of other professions. The profession, *qua* profession, was not so 'attractive'.

They talked also of the unsettlement of belief. Most of them laid little stress upon it. Some of those more experienced in the matter (Randall Davidson, Henry Scott Holland) believed that intellectual difficulties were a cause of shrinking from orders in 1860 but not in 1900. Not everyone agreed. But everyone agreed that they were less important than the general trend of society.

They were also staffing the missions overseas. By 1897 there were overseas 92 bishops and 4,225 clergy. Not all of these were of European race, and some were provided by the colonies themselves. It is not possible to say how many of these bishops and clergy came from England, but the number is certainly high. The missions were at once a strength to the church at home and a drain upon its best men.[2]

Yet the figures of ordination remained steady. The Victorians were disappointed that they did not rise faster than they did, fast enough to keep pace with the rising population. Only in the last years of the reign did the steady rise become a steady fall. 1901 was the first year for nearly thirty years when the number fell below 600. And meanwhile the number of incumbencies and curacies rapidly increased, and the population more rapidly still.

[1] The Ordination Candidates Fund was founded in the seventies. It had an income of about £2,000 a year by 1883, and in that year helped 33 candidates out of 95 applicants. The London Clerical Education Aid Society was founded in 1877 and helped 152 candidates by 1883. Canterbury diocese formed a fund by resolution of the diocesan conference in 1877, Carlisle diocese in 1874. The Bishop of Bedford's fund, for work in East London, began to help ordinands in 1882. All the grants were small. *C of E YB*, 1883, 2ff. Several of the theological colleges had small bursaries or exhibitions.
[2] Figures given by Worlledge, CCR, 1897, 399.

Church of England deacons ordained :[1]

1872	582	1890	746
1875	610	1891	745
1878	665	1896	704
1881	713	1897	652
1886	814	1900	650
1889	777	1901	569

During the seventies and early eighties the increase of ministry kept pace with the increase of population. The number of deacons ordained in each year rose, almost steadily.

The year 1886 was the maximum. Contemporary evidence shows that the churches were far more conscious of anti-Christian pressure in the early eighties than ten or fifteen years later. In the early eighties cries about the poverty of the clergy became louder. It is possible that Tithe did more than Doubt to turn the scale downward.

Throughout the period of rise and after, we detect no diminution in the quality of the men. The only test possible (however inadequate) is the percentage with Oxford and Cambridge degrees. This percentage remained steady. Of the deacons ordained between 1877 (when careful attention started to be paid to these matters) and 1901, the percentage of Oxford and Cambridge men remained constant, usually between 55 and 58 per cent, occasionally falling almost to 50 per cent, occasionally rising as high as 63 per cent. The numbers of Oxford and Cambridge men seeking orders therefore rose, though nothing like so sharply as the numbers of undergraduates in the two universities rose. And when the numbers began to decline after 1885, the number of Oxford and Cambridge ordinands did not decline more than the others; probably a second little pointer that intellectual disturbance at the universities was not (at first) contributing formidably to the change of direction.

The dioceses did not share the graduates equally. Durham, before Lightfoot became its bishop (1879), was well known as a diocese to which few graduates went. The diocese of Ripon (Bickersteth) was also a cause of comment. Conversely Worcester's deacons were

---

[1] Burnside's figures. These figures, like most Victorian figures, should not be treated as exact. One set of figures was collected, by H. T. Armfield of the Salisbury diocese, who analysed newspaper returns. Another set was collected by Canon Burnside, editor from 1883 of the Church of England Year Book, by application to bishops' secretaries. The two sets of figures disagree. After 1893, only Burnside's existed. Cf. also G, 06, 1849.

V.C.–9

nearly all graduates. A diocese like Ely seldom had a deacon who
was not a graduate of Cambridge. The north-west complained that
they were not getting their fair share of graduates. Someone calculated in 1880 that one-third of the curates in the diocese of Liverpool did not hold a degree; and that in the Manchester diocese 221
clergymen out of 788 held no degree; and this though Trinity
College, Dublin, gave more of its graduates to Lancashire than to
other areas of England. Even so, more than half the clergy in the
diocese of Manchester still held degrees from Oxford or Cambridge.[1]

The old ideal of the country parish, presided over by some quiet
man of learning and of sanctity, began during the seventies to look
uncomfortable in the town parish. You take a gentleman's son,
educate him excellently in Latin and Greek and cricket, send him to
Oxford, let him read widely, and then set him down in the middle of
Salford single-handed—to do what? Some of the duties were the
same as in Hursley, prepare sermons, teach in school, prepare children for confirmation, minister to the sick. But the classes in the
school were much larger, individual care less possible, the sick were
in great hospitals, the organisations were more numerous, Sunday
schools, night schools, clubs, charities, guilds, Bible classes. The task,
said one head of a theological college (Ashwell of Chichester)[2] 'is
as absurd as expecting a soldier to act as an officer of engineers in
the morning, of cavalry in the afternoon, besides getting through a
paymaster's work in the evening, and lecturing on strategy once
or twice a week besides'. The great town parish, it was clear, could
not do with a solitary incumbent, or incumbent and curate. It
needed a staff.

Therefore the sources of Anglican ministry became steadily more
varied during the last thirty years of the century. But it was a slow
process, and did not proceed without the regret of the old-
fashioned that the identity of *clergyman* was being prised apart from
the idea of *gentleman*. In 1880 Bishop Harold Browne of Winchester confessed his sorrow and alarm at the growing rudeness
and roughness of the English people—'and especially among the
clergy'.[3] Twelve years later the old and retired Dean Goulburn

---

[1] G, 80, 945. Cambridge usually supplied a few more deacons each year than
Oxford. But in 1883–5 the Oxford numbers were larger. In the twenty-nine years
between 1872 and 1900 Cambridge supplied just under 400 more deacons than
Oxford, an average of about 13 to 14 more men each year.
[2] CCR, 1873, 135.   [3] CCR, 1880, 364.

compared the English clergyman now with the clergyman of his younger days. He confessed that they work harder but they have 'sadly deteriorated' in breeding. He attributed this, not only to the admission into the ministry of men of a lower social grade, but also to the pressure and hurry of modern life.[1] The ministry of the Church of England, more than the ministry of other denominations, kept a measure of its social flavour and influence, with the advantages in nation and country and middle class, and the partial disadvantage in industrial society and among working men.

The *Catholic Directory* recorded the increase of priests in England and Wales: 1860: 1,077; 1880: 1,946; 1900: 2,856. Many of the bishops lived on stipends barely sufficient for their public responsibilities, stipends like £425 to £500. In 1863 the stipends in the diocese of Leeds varied from £25 to £50, with maintenance and official expenses paid, but even this could be achieved only if the priests collected money from house to house at weekends, and these collections were a grievance to the clergy.

Near the end of his life Manning reckoned the Catholics of the land at more than a million, but out of that number only 200,000 were English, and of those a proportion had Irish sympathies.[2] He reckoned (17 July 1890) that the state of priesthood was as important to the social gulf as the poverty of the people. The priests were often of Irish background, often of working class origins. While liberal Anglicans demanded that the Anglican ministry open its doors to men from lower strata of society, Manning believed that the Roman Catholic Church could not flourish until it had more priests from higher strata of society. For until it had such priests the priesthood would be 'confined to the sacristy' and unable to mix in the civil life of the country.

But Manning was far from being guilty of what after Hurrell Froude he called the fine gentleman heresy. He was the last man to suppose that the old aristocrat's chaplain was the proper priest for the new Catholic parishes. Anglican clergymen he knew to be educated and wishing to share in and to promote the civil life of the people.

---

[1] Goulburn, *Burgon*, ii, 361–2. H. H. Kelly founded the Society of the Sacred Mission in 1891 for the purpose of giving a free training for ordination, 'with no half-baked gentility'. But his Society trained men for the missions overseas until after 1900. Cf. Kelly, *No Pious Person*, 1960.

[2] Purcell, ii, 775; Beck, 266.

The habit of mind formed by the penal laws, a habit which survived the disappearance of the laws, so alienated the Catholics from public life that they 'have been tempted to think that patriotism is hardly reconcilable with Catholic fidelity'. And the Irish majority were not yet assimilated to the English tradition. When Manning was at Bayswater he asked his people to sign a petition to Parliament, and left it at the school for signatures. A young Irishman ruined it by upsetting the ink-bottle over it in protest against Parliament. 'We have a million of people, priests, and faithful of Irish blood, faith, and civilisation in England, and they are not only alienated from our laws and legislature, but would upset the ink-bottle over the statute book. So long as this habit of mind lasts we shall never have a civil priesthood; and so long as our priesthood is not civil it will be confined to the sacristy as in France, not by a hostile public opinion, but by our own incapacity to mix in the civil life of the country.'[1]

The old division between English Catholic and Irish Catholic still made for awkwardness between priest and bishop. The divide between priest and bishop was greater among the Roman Catholics than among the Anglicans, for it was partly a social division. Most priests were Irish, most bishops were English. Only three of the Roman Catholic bishops during the reign of Queen Victoria were of Irish birth, and all three presided over northern sees.[2] The bishop needed to be an Englishman if he would exercise influence with the middle class and in his city. He needed also, if possible, some private money. Few Irish priests had the means which would enable them to perform the bishop's duty on the exiguous stipend.[3]

They could seldom get priests of a higher rank except from converts or (better) the sons of a convert parent, like the Vaughan brothers. Some converts were married, and some felt no vocation to the Roman priesthood, and those who sought ordination sometimes found it a suffering to be a Roman priest working among their former people. 'God knows what it has cost me to be a priest', wrote Manning, 'and to do the work of a priest, and to bear the name of a priest, here in the midst of kindred and old friends, and the world in which I lived before.'[4] When Newman considered the

[1] Purcell, ii, 774–5.
[2] Chadwick of Hexham and Newcastle, 1866–82; O'Reilly of Liverpool, 1873–94; Lacy of Middlesbrough, 1879–1929; Beck, 188.
[3] Beck, 290.
[4] Manning to Robert Wilberforce, 1 April 1856; Purcell, ii, 46.

erection of a hostel or Oratory at Oxford, he had to overcome a
shrinking from meeting old acquaintances in the street of his
university—'How could I mix again with Oxford men?'[1] 'I should
be a stranger in my dearest home.'[2]

Manning's main endeavour within his church was to raise the
standard of the priesthood. He was confronted with a situation
which the Anglican archdeacon still strong in him, as well as his
Christian soul, wholly disapproved, that the 'secular' clergy were
regarded by the faithful, and worse still regarded themselves, as on a
lower level than the monks. Wiseman encouraged the religious
orders, the laity preferred the religious as confessors or counsellors.
Some of the religious were less well qualified than the secular, but
laymen took it for granted that they were not. Manning believed that
the effect was to encourage the secular clergy not to aspire but to be
content to pass souls onwards as too difficult for them, to assume
that they were not capable of preaching good sermons or conducting
retreats. He sought to obliterate the distinction where he could. The
secular clergy, who were hitherto known as in other countries by
the title of *Mr.*, should henceforth be called *Father*, not without
murmurs from some of them. He applied to Rome that in official
documents the secular clergy should no longer be called *secular* but
pastoral, and was refused, for Rome found the name harmless and
traditional. He stopped using the phrase in his own public utterances.
Towards the end of his life he argued that the priesthood is the first
and chief of all religious orders, the only such order founded by
Christ. He removed from his seminaries the use of a text book by
the Jesuit theologian Gury which declared that 'the priest is higher
in honour, the monk higher in perfection', and wrote that the
proposition was erroneous and offensive to pious ears and materially
heretical,[3] because it was putting a state of life instituted by the
church above a state of life instituted by Christ. And throughout his
archiepiscopate he acted without enthusiasm towards the religious
orders, especially the Jesuits. He much encouraged the use of the
Bible, and tried to persuade his priests that it was not wrong to
co-operate in social endeavour with Anglicans and dissenters. He
wished them to eschew a narrow attitude towards Christians of other

[1] Newman to Hope-Scott, 29 August 1864: Wilfrid Ward, *Newman*, ii, 52.
[2] Newman to Pusey, 29 April 1866: Ward, *Newman*, ii, 122.
[3] Purcell, ii, 763–5, 784–8.

persuasions, and not to rely upon their status or their privilege of celebrating mass, nor to magnify their office. He summoned his priests to a diocesan synod each year, not without murmurs from some of them. He encouraged them to give missions and conduct retreats, so that they might discover themselves to possess the power which they did not think themselves to possess. He wanted them to adopt a more missionary spirit, to realise that England was lost to the faith and that they had a duty to others besides their faithful. 'What is the good of preaching on the Immaculate Conception to people who do not believe in the Incarnation? or on the Church to those who do not believe in Christianity?'[1] He wanted open-air preaching, instruction outside churches, hymns in the street instead of the rosary. He disapproved of other bishops who were discouraged by the low level of their secular clergy and therefore turned to the religious for a difficult task. In every way he persuaded his men out of the sacristy. His best and most influential book was entitled *The Eternal Priesthood* (1883) in which he sought to give a theological and devotional ground for these ideas. Manning, powerful offspring of the Oxford Movement, tried to do for the clergy of the Church of Rome what that entire movement sought to do for the clergy of the Church of England.

The Roman Catholic, Anglican and Wesleyan Methodist ministers on the whole became more priestly during this age. In bustling unquiet times they felt the need for separation and otherworldliness, and the outward signs showed it. Roman Catholic clergy became more uniform in dress, dog-collar and black suit; Anglican clergy followed the example, though more slowly as Tractarian innovation quietly became expected of everyone, even evangelicals; and Wesleyans also followed, though still more slowly. In contrast Congregationalist and Baptist ministers became more like laymen. They reacted against priestliness and professionalism. Robertson Nicoll, who became editor of the most distinguished nonconformist journal in 1886, thereafter became steadily more lay and at last accepted a knighthood. Sylvester Horne, brilliant preacher among young Congregational ministers, accepted a Liberal seat in Parliament. David Lloyd resigned a pastorate at Lymington because of ill-health, joined a bank and rose to be manager, and while acting as local preacher on Sunday reorganised the finances of the local

---

[1] Purcell, ii, 791.

Congregational churches.[1] The Congregationalists and Baptists had less sense than the Methodists and Presbyterians of the ministry as set apart. Like Spurgeon and Dale, they abandoned the Genevan gown. Some chapels, especially in the north, ceased to have forms of ordination when a man was inducted to his ministry. The term *ordination* was not quite liked by some communities, who preferred *recognition*, and the laying-on of hands was often disused. Until about 1870 they restricted the celebration of the Lord's Supper to ordained ministers, and continued to prefer that custom, but more and more admitted with Dale that any layman could celebrate. An ex-Congregationalist minister felt that some took so low a view of his vocation that they regarded him as an employee to administer church affairs.[2] And where the layman was confessed to be able to preach and to administer the sacraments, such views were intelligible.

Here are two extremes, this-worldly and other-worldly, of the Victorian ministry. The Congregationalist pastor, R. W. Dale of Birmingham, eschewed the Reverend, would not wear black like the clergy, abandoned the white tie, started to smoke a pipe, even grew a moustache (at which some protested in the newspapers); was one of the political leaders of Birmingham Liberalism and weighty in the councils of the Liberal party; and became one of the profound divines and preachers of the Victorian churches. Kenelm Vaughan, brother of the future cardinal, was a priest such as the Roman Catholic community of an earlier generation could not have produced; and those who have studied the family attribute something to the Welsh evangelicalism of the mother before she was a convert. He founded an order of expiation which was impossible because it aimed to combine active missionary endeavour with a life of severe asceticism and perpetual adoration; lived a hermit life in a back garden in Chelsea or at Hatfield; devoted much time to encouraging the study of the Bible among simple laity, after a controversy in which the Roman Church was accused of hindering the study of the Bible; wandered through South America distributing copies of the New Testament, and there were rumours that he exorcised devils; collected fragments from every abbey or shrine suppressed at the dissolution and made an altar from them;

[1] CYB, 1885, 209–11. For an alive portrait of life as a Wesleyan pastor, see F. W. Macdonald, *Reminiscences*, (1912).
[2] R. J. Campbell, *A Spiritual Pilgrimage*, 36.

devoted his life to prayer, and used to sleep in a coffin or on his funeral bier.[1]

Whatever the increase in supply of ministers in all denominations, and the variety of social strata from which they came, and the variety of modes in which they conceived their vocation, the work could not be done without other means than professionals. Some believed for a short time that the bicycle, by increasing the mobility of the clergyman in a large town, would enable him to cover more ground and shepherd more people. The prediction was right. The bicycle did for the pastor of Birmingham what the pony did many years before for the pastor of Cumbrian valleys. But it was soon clear that the bicycle also made the people move elsewhere. They lived further away; and the young men in the choir were too often found away on bicycles on Sundays, especially during the summer months.

The only further source of agents was the laity.

In the Baptist denomination the number of lay preachers rose faster than the ministers (1891: ministers 1,767, lay preachers 3,784; 1901: ministers 1,852, lay preachers 5,032). Of the Wesleyan Methodists this is probably true also. The Roman Catholics hardly used the laity.

The Church of England had long used district visitors, Scripture readers, Bible-women, in the poor parishes. A vicar divided the parish into areas, assigned a woman to each area, and the women visited all the houses and brought back reports, for alms, education, need in sickness. The evangelical Church Pastoral-Aid Society, so suspect at first, provided money for lay workers from the beginning of the reign, and during the sixties and seventies came at last into its own as the model for other organisations.

The London diocese first established a 'lay helpers' association' in 1865, and this kind of work received the formal approval of the bishops at a Lambeth meeting on Ascension day 1866. As part of this work 'lay readers' were commissioned to act as missioners in sheds and houses, but the growth both of the order of lay readers, and of what they were allowed or expected to do, was slow. Laymen were most used as teachers in the Sunday schools.

In 1818 about 4 per cent of the population attended Sunday

---

[1] *Letters of Herbert, Cardinal Vaughan*; F. A. MacNutt, *A Papal Chamberlain*, 1936; *Remembered in Blessing* (memories of the Vaughan family), 1955.

schools. Seventy years later about 20 per cent of the population attended. In 1888 about three children out of four attended Sunday school in England and Wales. And among the children who failed to go were included most children of the upper and middle classes, whose parents did not think Sunday schools suitable for their children. Though Victorian working men did not go to church often, they or their wives sent their children in multitudes. The Sunday schools reached their climax in the seventies and eighties. Some believed them to be the most important and effective of the religious influences upon the English population.

In origin they were far more nonconformist than Anglican. In the earlier half of the century many Anglican parishes did not have Sunday schools. As late as the sixties some old-fashioned clergymen objected to them and said that they were nowhere authorised by the Prayer Book and therefore not part of the system of the Church of England. As they came around to the idea of Sunday schools, they might join a catechism to the afternoon service, or they might create a proper Sunday school like that of the chapel.

In 1887 the denominations divided the children thus[1] (these are the numbers on the books—attendants were said to be between 60 and 70 per cent):

Church of England	2,222,000
Wesleyans	825,000
Congregationalists	686,000
Baptists	426,000
Primitive Methodists	369,000
Others, (about)	700,000

In the following year, of the 680 parishes in the diocese of Norwich, only 48 had no Sunday school.[2]

'I don't believe', John Bright was reported as saying, 'that all the statesmen in existence—I don't believe all the efforts they have ever made—have tended so much to the greatness and true happiness, the security and glory of this country, as have the efforts of Sunday school teachers.'[3] Not everyone accepted these friendly judgments. The chaplain at Leeds gaol found that 230 out of 282 male prisoners had attended Sunday school. But everyone agreed that something happened; that as a wounded soldier lay dying on the field, or the

[1] PP, 1888, xxxv, 320.   [2] CCR, 1888, 366.
[3] CCR, 1894, 393; 1888, 363.

V.C.–9 a

old woman in the hospital, some experience or memory of the religion of childhood would often come back. In towns like Accrington or Huddersfield hardly a child failed to attend. In Birmingham about 1887 they calculated that 26,000 of the children on the books of elementary schools were not to be found in Sunday schools. In London the gap was still wider. In the deanery of Fulham at that time they found that 30 per cent of the boys and 11 per cent of the girls who attended church day-schools did not attend Sunday schools; at St. James' Westminster it was 28 per cent of the boys and 15 per cent of the girls.[1]

Most of them were inefficient, especially before 1870. Originally they taught the three Rs as well as Scripture. The teachers were almost wholly untrained during the first half of the century. As lately as 1873 the words 'Sunday school teacher' were said to conjure up the idea of a 'half-educated, narrow-minded, somewhat self-conceited, and yet easily taken-in class of young persons, to which a man of superior parts would not condescend to belong'.[2] Throughout the century they suffered from a famine of male teachers of sufficient education. There were complaints that teachers attended irregularly, or supposed that they did the parson a favour, or imagined that it was very good of them to be doing it. Bishop Fraser of Manchester said that Anglican Sunday schools were a disgrace to the Church of England; and a curate in Salford reported that they were either an 'orderly conversazione' or a 'disorderly bear-garden'.[3] Yet there were confessed to be many good Sunday schools. Three lord chancellors in succession—Hatherley, Cairns, Selborne—taught in Sunday school. At Cambridge the Jesus Lane Sunday school was the most famous in the Church of England. In Lent 1877 its staff, of undergraduates and a few dons including four Fellows of Trinity College, numbered 160.[4]

All denominations had central societies or institutes which attempted to raise standards. They circulated literature, attempted to secure a syllabus, sought means of training teachers. It was not easy. In the diocese of Norwich (1888) out of 621 parishes which made

[1] CCR, 1888, 366.   [2] CCR, 1873, 424: Eugene Stock speaking.
[3] CCR, 1894, 384; 1888, 380.
[4] Harford-Macdonald, Moule, 114; Jones-Appleton, A History of the Jesus Lane Sunday School, 1877. It was in King Street 1833–67; then in Paradise Street. The difficulty of vacations was great. One Sunday there would be 100 teachers, the next, ten, cf. Jones-Appleton, 132.

returns, only 251 used a syllabus. The S.P.C.K. made grants for renting rooms, and for Bibles and picture books. The National Society sought to publish useful tracts. 'I would rather *muddle on*', said the vicar of St. John's, Cardiff, 'in the old-fashioned common-sense friendly way, than I would go in for so-called organisation.'[1] The education act of 1870 raised teaching standards everywhere, and indirectly in Sunday schools.

The development of the day schools held out to masters and mistresses higher ideals of teaching, not achieved often in day schools and still less often in Sunday schools, but spreading a knowledge of teaching method. The day schools provided for the Sunday schools children with less ignorance of the Bible, with a habit of discipline, with an ability to read more easily. Many Sunday school teachers remained irretrievably amateur, but the equipment for assisting them was much extended during the seventies and eighties. The day school teacher sometimes gave model classes for the benefit of the Sunday school teachers. Where there was an Anglican school, the classes were often held in that school, and many incumbents preferred not to hold them in church. Methodists preferred not to hold their Sunday schools in the chapel, but usually did so for lack of other accommodation. The denominational schools, in employing a teacher, commonly required him or her to teach in the Sunday school. In the country he or she was also organist and choir-trainer.

Despite fears of their decline, the Sunday schools remained strong after 1870. Parents were strongly attached to them by ties of affection, for in them many had learnt to read and write. Some bishops, especially Woodford of Ely, elevated the office of teacher into a minor order in the church, with a diocesan admission for the especially qualified and a certificate. By 1893, however, the diocese of Ely had only 650 'diocesan teachers' of whom 66 were at one town parish in Cambridge.[2]

In most parts of the country the leaving of day school was the signal for leaving the Sunday school. But in Lancashire, and parts of the West Riding, young people usually continued in Sunday school until they were married, and often remained after marriage. Wesleyan Methodists had a tradition of remaining longer and in

[1] CCR, 1888, 369, 382.
[2] The organisers experienced the difficulty that some older teachers were not willing to work for the certificate, and others were not willing to become communicants, CCR, 1894, 386; Ely diocesan calendar, 1893, 180; 1894, 180.

1888 one witness estimated that more than a quarter of the Wesleyan Methodists at Sunday schools were over the age of 15.[1]

The Lancashire Sunday school was not a group of children taught by young girls. It was an adult Bible class containing working men who remained there till death. Of 1,000 members of the Rochdale Sunday schools in 1889, 170 were over 21 years. Many of these schools went back to times when the hierarchy of the church was slothful or infrequent, and had been founded by laymen apart from the vicar of the parish. Their constitution was therefore independent. They elected representatives and ran themselves, choosing their teachers and their choirmasters. As the Church of England organised itself better in the north, friction grew between these strong republics and able new incumbents. The vicar was disturbed to have no control over the choice of his own teachers, and especially if the Sunday school chose men or women who were not communicants, or who did not even bother to attend church. A new vicar in the diocese of Wakefield suggested to the choir that in future the members of the choir ought to belong to the Church of England. 'Our notion', he was told, 'has been that to qualify a boy or man for the choir he must have a good treble, alto, tenor or bass voice, and must read music well; but whether he is a Liberal or Conservative, or a churchman or nonconformist doesn't seem to us to be here or there'.[2] In a Yorkshire village the choristers were the village singers. They sang in the parish church almost as much because it was a village institution as because it was a church institution. To be a teacher in such a Sunday school was a natural way of leading a Christian life. Cecil Hook, vicar of All Souls in Leeds, said that if he spoke seriously to a parishioner about his godless life, he 'many times' heard the reply, 'Well, I don't mind trying to be better—I'll come and teach a bit in your Sunday school.'[3]

The size was considerable. In 1878 St. Paul's in Manchester had 1,865 children on the books of its Sunday school, and 163 teachers of whom only two or three were said not to have been pupils in the school. Reports of these northern numbers caused discouragement in the south. When Kennion went to be vicar of All Saints, Bradford he found a Sunday school of 700 and when he resigned six years later he left a Sunday school of 1700.[4]

---

[1] PP, 1888, xxxv, 325.   [2] G, 96, 757.
[3] CCR, 1878, 474.   [4] CCR, 1878, 461, 469; 1898, 361.

The Sunday school at Stockport in Cheshire claimed to be the largest in England. It dated from the end of the eighteenth century, and near the end of the nineteenth century had about 5,000 members. The constitution, by custom though not by rule, excluded the Anglican or Free Church ministers from any part in the management. The teachers gave instruction in the Christian religion which their critics called undenominational. They probably did not realise it to be undenominational until they were told that it was. It was attacked for stamping on Stockport Christianity an unsacramental and latitudinarian character. It was fair criticism that men who remained in the Sunday school felt less the need of a church. And yet it was a powerful force in Stockport, not least because working men felt that it belonged to them and they to it.[1]

There were clashes between new reforming vicars and old Sunday schools. Their music was more hearty than devotional. They detached themselves remarkably from the life of the church and the movements of contemporary religion. They did not always seek confirmation, and often disregarded communion. The *Year Book* of the Church of England calculated that in 1885 there were 168,734 members of Sunday schools over the age of 14.[2] Most of these would be in Lancashire. But of these thousands, only 48,680 were communicants. The schools were strong corporations in parishes where the clergy and ministers felt that they needed to lead. One vicar described himself ruefully as chaplain to his Sunday school.[3] Yet the vicar, if he were wise, cherished his Sunday school and swallowed his private picture of a well-organised parish. These schools were truly religious, and full of horny-handed men. No gulf existed between them and the working population. The Sunday school anniversary in a Lancashire or West Riding town became the social event of the year, with massed choirs, and concord between church and dissent, congregations joining to go out upon a neighbouring hill in their hundreds and sing hymns lustily.

In the seventies and eighties something similar happened in Birmingham and the Potteries. The children learnt to read and write in government schools, the adults must catch up. At Wednesbury (1886) was a non-denominational class of 600 men which met at 7.30 a.m. and learnt the three Rs and Scripture; at Darlaston a class of

---

[1] Cf. G, 99, 1695. [2] *C of E YB*, 1885, 499.
[3] J. M. Wilson, *Autobiography*, 182–3.

400; at a third parish nearby, a class of 500 to 600. A lady at Blackburn conducted a class of 160 to 170 men whose average age was 40.
These Bible classes often contained more than divinity. The young
Tom Mann, who was a practising member of the Church of England,
attended a Bible class conducted by a Quaker. Looking back he was
grateful to his old teacher. The lessons which he thought to have
learnt are not mentioned as Biblical. 'He . . . helped me in the matter
of correct pronunciation, clear articulation, and insistence upon
knowing the root origin of words, with a proper care in the use of
the right words to convey ideas. He encouraged the class systematically to use a good dictionary . . .'[1] The mid-Victorian age was a
time of vast adult Bible classes. Working men would not go inside
a church. Offer them a Bible class and their attitude was often
different. Handley Moule used to conduct a large class for the railway
workers in the second-class waiting-room at Cambridge station.

The Sunday school anniversary flourished in many other places
besides the north and north midlands. Even in Sheringham, then
still a little fishing village, which contained two Methodist chapels, a
Salvation Army contingent, and a church room in which the
Church of England held services, the men took poles and sails from
their vessels to the Skelding hills (now the golf course) and made a
large tent; all the children of the villages round paraded with new
frocks through the streets singing hymns and collecting at doors,
until they reached the hills, where they had tea and then ran races.[2]

4. THE ATTITUDE OF THE WORKING MAN

On the afternoon of 24 May 1883 there was an interview between
Beatrice Potter, afterwards Beatrice Webb, and Eleanor Marx,
daughter of Karl Marx, in the refreshment room of the British
Museum.[3] They argued over the rightness of ridiculing Christianity.
'We think the Christian religion', said Eleanor Marx, 'an immoral
illusion, and we wish to use any argument to persuade the people
that it is false. Ridicule appeals to the people we have to deal with,
with much greater force than any amount of serious logical argument. . . . We want to make them (the working classes) disregard the

[1] CCR, 1886, 262; 1878, 461; T. Mann, *Memoirs* (ed. 1967), 7.
[2] S. Craske, *History of Old Sheringham* (unpublished), 45; my thanks to the author.
[3] B. Webb, *My Apprenticeship*[2], 258-9.

mythical next world and live for this world, and insist on having what will make it pleasant to them.' Beatrice Potter found it useless, she wrote, to argue with one who had no idea of the beauty of the Christian religion, and read the gospels as the gospel of damnation.

These middle-class Marxist assailants of the churches in the eighties had little enough influence; less influence than was possessed by the old and cruder deist pamphleteers of two generations before. There was just a moment when it looked as though the working classes might go secularist and anti-Christian, and it was about the time that Eleanor Marx met Beatrice Potter in the refreshment room of the British Museum. The business of getting Charles Bradlaugh into Parliament went on from 1880 to 1886. The objection to Bradlaugh was that he was a professed atheist, and that members of Parliament by the constitution of the country must be Christians or Jews. The effort to get Bradlaugh a seat looked for the moment as though it might identify the interest of the working man with an overthrow of the Christian constitution of the country. Never was the secularist movement, as they called themselves, so strong in England as it was during the eighties. Never before or since did so many 'halls of science' or 'ethical societies' spring up with the object of replacing the churches and of educating men out of the need to go to church.

It did not last, this sense that the working man was on the point of going secularist. It might have been so in parts of London, especially East London. But the typical working man was a midlander or nor-therner and lived in some great Yorkshire or Lancashire or Midland centre of industry. He was more likely to be vaguely nonconformist, if not very vaguely Anglican, than he was to be atheist. If he was a working-class politician, he was likely to despise the middle-class anti-Christian intellectuals who sought to theorise on his behalf. Old Will Crooks used to dismiss the intellectuals of his party in the say-ing, 'They've got no backs to their 'eads'.[1] An experienced manager of working men's meetings gave advice to a would-be political speaker thus: 'We want no Karl Marx and surplus values and that sort of stuff. Make it plain and simple. Tha' can put in a long word now and then so as to make them think tha' knaws a lot, but keep it simple, and then when tha'rt coming to t' finishing up tha' mun put a bit of *Come to Jesus* in like Philip does.'[2] The Philip, who was

[1] G. K. Chesterton, *Autobiog.*, 126.   [2] Snowden's *Autobiog.*, i, 32.

there held up as a model, was Philip Snowden, the future Labour chancellor of the exchequer. And Snowden was usually sure that he was a Socialist because he was first a chapelgoer.

In 1893 the police were told of a threat of riot in a Yorkshire mining village during the lock-out. A large detachment of police found a long procession of miners marching to a meeting at the Methodist chapel, and singing O *God our help in ages past* as they went.[1] A Socialist lecturer, touring the country about 1895, found Scriptural texts adorning the walls of nearly every bedroom where he was given hospitality.[2]

The worker, if politically conscious, was more likely to continue the old Chartist tradition. Some of the old Chartists were never sure whether they attacked the churches because they were Christian, or whether they attacked the churches because the churches betrayed Christianity by permitting such poverty and class structure. But the second attitude was commoner than the first. There were many working-class secularists and free-thinkers. But almost all the early Labour leaders, if they were working class, had a religious element in their Socialism. And some of them, like George Lansbury, a deeply Christian man as well as a deeply Socialist mind, did not easily distinguish their Christianity from their Socialism.

The churches, they believed, needed altering drastically. That was to make them like the sort of churches that Christ meant them to be. But we must not underestimate the bitterness of the working-class assault upon the churches, even when conducted by men with religious feelings. Keir Hardie was a man with a religious sense. But his Christmas message to the churches in 1897 can hardly be paralleled for its ferocity: 'When I think of the thousands of white-livered poltroons who will take the Christ's name in vain, and yet not see his image being crucified in every hungry child, I cannot think of peace. . . . A holocaust of every church building in Christendom tonight would be an act of sweet savour in the sight of him whose name is supposed to be worshipped within their walls. . . . We have no right to a merry Christmas which so many of our fellows cannot share.'

At the end of February 1887 Socialist workmen paraded with banners at St. Paul's cathedral. They sent a message to the archbishop requesting a sermon on the text 'Let him that stole steal no

[1] Snowden's *Autobiog.*, i, 63.   [2] Thompson, *Blatchford*, 183.

more, but rather let him labour'. They issued a statement that 'Modern Christianity is essentially a middle-class creed'. There was some disturbance in church. The canon-in-residence did not take the requested text, but one less suited to the mind of the congregation: 'The rich and poor meet together; the Lord is the maker of them all', Proverbs xxii, 2.[1]

Mrs. Lynn Linton, the daughter of a Cumbrian parson, turned away from Christian faith. She married an ex-Chartist in 1858 but the marriage was not a success and she became a novelist of deism and social reform. Like so many of her kind she looked with hope at the Paris Commune of 1870. In 1872 she published an anonymous novel called *The True History of Joshua Davidson, Christian and Communist*. It had six editions by 1874 and the author's name was known. Some regarded it as a blasphemous parody of the life of Jesus.

She asked herself the question, what would happen to Jesus if he walked the streets and fields of England in the eighteen-seventies? He would be a working man. His accent would be provincial. He would attack capitalists, economists, sabbatarians and bishops. His home would be in the east end among roughs and gaol-birds, and he would denounce the luxury of the west end as once he denounced Dives. His faith would be accused of unorthodoxy. He would not be crucified nor beheaded, but the entire press would conspire to damn him. He would work to destroy caste in society, and show that Christianity is Communism. He would be more a politician than a theologian, teaching men to work for the kingdom of heaven on earth. Joshua Davidson used to say, 'You can't make a man a saint in mind when you keep him like a beast in body'; and 'higher wages, better food, better lodgment, and better education will do more to make men real Christians than all the churches ever built'.[2] He crossed the Channel to help the Paris Communists and minister heroically to the sick and wounded at the barricades. Back in England he went to a town of the provinces to lecture in the town hall on how Christ and the apostles were Communists. Led by a clergyman the audience rushed the platform, beat the lecturer, and kicked him on the head so that he died. The novel was a sophisticated version of the old Chartist, and new Labour, claim that Christ was on the side of the worker against the churches.

[1] G, 87, 337.
[2] *Joshua Davidson* 224–5; cf. G. S. Layard, *Mrs. Lynn Linton*, 1901, 180ff.

The leaders of the working men nearly all had a nonconformist background. Several of them were Scottish by race, from Ramsay MacDonald and Keir Hardie downwards. If they were Irish, they had at least an exiguous connexion with Roman Catholicism. In the great strike of the late eighties, which took a stride in turning Labour men away from their reliance on the Liberal party, it was the Roman Catholic Cardinal Manning who could help mediate in the strike, not the Bishop of London; for many of the dockers were Irish. George Lansbury was the exception in being brought up an Anglican. But Lansbury was the exception that proved the rule, by the nature of his religious upbringing in the seventies. Most Sundays his mother took the children to the parish church. But if the children were particularly bad she felt that they needed stronger medicine than that administered in the established church, and would take them round to a small Primitive Methodist chapel in Banner Lane, where they were sure to hear about hell.[1]

The working men never quite understood what the churches were doing in their midst. Despite an undercurrent of distrust for the institution, they often respected the individuals and were grateful. But they never quite knew what they were about. The representatives of the church were half-suspected of being agents of the Conservative party, or moral policemen in mufti, or enthusiasts odd in their intelligence and activity.

On 21 January 1867 a meeting of working men was held at the London coffee-house, Edward Miall in the chair. Why do not working men go to church?[2] A cabinetmaker complained that ministers did not concern themselves with the social questions which concerned working men. Working men felt that clergymen separated themselves from the rest of the world. Religion seemed to have nothing to do with their daily life. The dissenting chapels seemed to them like shops where religion was served across the counter. An engineer said that their hours were so long on weekdays that they could do nothing but take fresh air and exercise on Sundays. It was not right to call working men atheists and deists because they did not go to church. Another engineer said that ministers despised working men. Another said that the church was rotten to the core, that bishops received £10,000 a year while their curates starved. A tailor thought the clergy to be so highly educated that no one

[1] Lansbury, *My Life*, 28.   [2] G, 67, 113.

could understand what they said. A plasterer talked of the confusion caused by the controversy of religion and science. 'Professor Huxley would say one thing, and a clergyman would say another—which was the working man to believe?' A porter talked of the drinking customs of the country, and how ministers were seldom seen in the houses of the poor. Dr. J. C. Miller said that clergymen were not all (as was supposed) Tories. An 'ex-scavenger' talked of sermons which sent to sleep. Mr. Beales said that the working class were against the rulers of this country, and regarded the clergy as part of the ruling class.

Bishop Walsham How had a meeting in Hackney Wick on hindrances to going to church. The men's hindrances were very simple. 'They said they were very tired in a morning, and they liked a walk in the afternoon.'[1]

Winnington-Ingram reported from East London that the principal belief of the working man was a sense of injustice and that he was inclined to classify the churches among the causes of that injustice. Ingram himself suffered nothing more than epidemic questioning about Cain's wife. Some working men thought religion to be an unpractical affair. By 1893 they used the word *sky-pilot* as a contemptuous description of a minister. In Adderley's novel *Stephen Remarx* working men laughed at a mate who went to church every Sunday 'like a little girl, to listen to a sky-pilot yarning about the stars and the cherrybims'.[2] They suspected the parson of being an idle fellow. Nothing is commoner in the working men's meetings at Church Congress than for a bishop or a dean or a canon to claim that he *also* was a working man. Some labourers were once rash enough to ask John Clifford what he knew about hard work seeing that he was a parson. Clifford was not a suitable target, for he rose in wrath and told them of his youth in a factory in the days before factory acts, and how at the age of nine he was sometimes made to work sixteen or even twenty hours in a day.[3]

An experienced observer in Poplar (1898)[4] wrote that the inhabitants were indifferent to religion. This was not because they were atheist. You could hardly find an atheist. You found everywhere a vague belief in God and vague aspirations after humanity. They had no sense of sin. When they said that they had never done anything wrong they meant that they had not been arrested. The only things

[1] CCR, 1885, 396.   [2] *Remarx*, 55, 66.
[3] Marchant, *Clifford*, 79.   [4] Arthur Chandler, G, 98, 1978.

which they cared about were the barest physical needs. It was not a religious apathy but a universal apathy. Athletic clubs and socialist clubs fared as ill as religious clubs. The attitude to religion rested not upon hostility but upon a total slackness.

This was the opinion of an individual. Much other evidence suggests that though the working men might be indifferent, an undercurrent of inarticulate hostility to the churches ran through the working-class movement. But all the evidence supports the view that apathy was much commoner than enmity. The poor were not interested in the churches, but were hardly interested in anything. The days when some came to church were New Year's Day and a harvest festival. The attendance at harvest festivals was extraordinary for most of them could never have seen a harvest, and perhaps had some memory from the history of their once-rural family.

Perceptive people already recognised that caste, or the custom of the tribe, had something to do with it. A respectable grocer might be a very sincere worshipper; but even if his worship was formal, he had few temptations not to go to church, for he was a respectable grocer, and going to church was part of his way of life. The disreputable navvy, on the contrary, found it difficult to go to church even if he possessed worshipping instincts. The act seemed outside his way of life. It was not an act which his group performed. He would feel as incompatible in church as if he suddenly appeared among his friends in a top-hat and morning-coat.

If the working man—or especially if his wife—were got into church he might be persuaded at first to come in his only clothes. But before long he felt the need to put on a better suit. He did not feel reverent in his working clothes. The social pressure towards decency can almost be chronicled in one or two parishes. At the squalid parish of All Saints in Newcastle-on-Tyne the vicar persuaded the working population to come as they were, and the women came with their heads covered in shawls. Five years later the large church was still full but the women were all wearing bonnets. The churchwarden said that 'they can afford bonnets now, but they are the same heads'. It may be doubted whether the five years between 1882 and 1887 brought such prosperity to Newcastle as to justify the churchwarden. They wore bonnets because some had bonnets and the others felt ashamed to be in shawls.[1]

[1] CCR, 1887, 99.

In the winter of 1881–2 the vicar of a country town found several hundreds of unemployed. The ground was under snow, and he organised them to clear the roads of the drifts, himself wielding a shovel, and raised a public subscription to pay them for the work. They were grateful to him, and decided to show their gratitude by attending church one Sunday evening. They came and overflowed every pew and quite dismayed the regulars. But they came only that once, to say thank you. It did not occur to them to make it a custom.[1]

The Victorian working man, however, was courteous to clergymen and ministers. A clergyman who laboured among 12,000 people in the poorest area of Manchester told his bishop that he hardly entered a house but was received kindly and courteously.[2] Louts could be guilty of rudeness or violence, as when a dignitary in gaiters was driven off a working site in the West end, or *no popery* was shouted after two Roman Catholic nuns, or Anglo-Catholic ritualists were disturbed in church, or Protestant tub-preachers were pelted at street corners, or the Salvation Army processions were assaulted. These were not typical of the Victorian labourer. We may chronicle his general courtesy by the fact that no procession at a Church Congress needed the protection of police from angry unemployed until the year 1908.

5. THE TOWN CHURCH AND SOCIAL ACTION

All churches knew that the consequences of expanding cities concerned them. Their daily work and their Sunday worship were affected by prostitution, drunkenness, poverty, overcrowding. They stood there to minister to suffering. Just as Bishop Tait of London went down to St. George's-in-the-East during the plague of cholera and was remembered so gratefully by the people that a street was named after him, so the Victorians observed a large overlap between the leaders in programmes to raise society and the practice of the Christian religion. Dr. Barnardo began as an Irish revivalist and missioner to children, and his first home (Stepney 1870) sprang out of his East London juvenile mission. Barnardo's work was characteristic of most social action among the Victorian churches. They met the suffering of children as they met cholera. Their first concern was not how to prevent cholera but how to help the sufferers. Barnardo

[1] CCR, 1888, 135.   [2] CCR, 1873, 349.

was not concerned with the conditions of society which made
children sleep under tarpaulins, but the children themselves, and how
they were to find homes, and be employed and civilised.

To this kind of social action most congregations in most towns
contributed something. The working-class critic of Christianity
abused the ministers or their people for disregarding the plight of
men and women in this world because they concerned themselves
with another world. No charge could be less well-founded. Much of
what was done to relieve the poor was done by religious men and
women, and a lot of it by men or women who represented a church
in doing it.[1]

And yet even in the nineties eminent churchmen as well as
firebrands accused the churches of complacency and lethargy. The
ordinary pastor of the country parish, or of the town parish, or of
the nonconformist chapel, hardly believed that *qua* pastor he was
responsible for the state of society corporately, as well as for the
plight of individuals under his care; otherwise than as citizen he had
a vote to choose a government. What was sometimes called the
'lethargy' of the Victorian churches was lethargy in the sense that on
such a matter a doctor or a lawyer might be 'lethargic', who got on
with the work before him and did not raise his eyes to problems
outside his immediate task. The work before many pastors included
a lot of poor folk and suffering folk, and most of those responsible
worked well to do what they could. The social reformers among the
churches sought to persuade the leaders of their churches, whether
laymen or ministry, that they had a responsibility, not only as citizens
but as churchmen, to adopt programmes of social reform which
could only be achieved by political action.

Still the churches laboured under the reproach of articulate working men that they did too little, that their ministers were sky-pilots.
George Lansbury remembered how in the cholera plague of 1866 he
was taught at church that God used these plagues as a way to trans-
plant his beloved to heaven,[2] and all his life resented this mode of
comfort. James Adderley wrote a novel about a socialist Anglican
priest, *Stephen Remarx*, who received a letter (p. 134) thus: 'You
seem to me to completely misunderstand your duties as a minister.
. . . Your business is to lead men to be content with their wages, and

---

[1] See among many examples the considerable collection in K. Heasman, *Evangelicals in Action*, 1962.   [2] *My Life*, 27.

to look forward to a brighter land hereafter.' Despite the caricature *Remarx* sounds in places like autobiography. And pastors in the slums must sometimes have preached like that. Their business was not to foster greed or covetousness, even among persons in whom greed was hardly a sin, especially when no good could come to the person in whom it was fostered. The doctrine that suffering should be accepted with resignation was easily perverted or misheard to mean that the conditions of society were unalterable. Even the greatest preacher in England, H. P. Liddon, was denounced by the journal *Christian Socialist* for preaching in St. Paul's cathedral on being content with one's lot.[1]

The common charge of the atheist that the churches were indifferent to this world because they busied themselves with the next was refuted by the extraordinary social action and sometimes heroism of otherworldly men and women. It was true that a lot of social endeavour sprang from a desire to convert, as Booth's revivalism led him to the succour of the down-and-out, and Barnardo's revivalism to the succour of the destitute child. And this aspect of Christian action led to another charge, or another form of the same charge. The Christians believe that if men are converted all will be well, or at least all will be much better, with society. It was true. Christians believed that, and continued to act as though they believed it. They thought that men would be less drunken, women better wives and mothers, children more honest, work more diligent. They had evidence to show that this sometimes happened. And they made little profession that men could be made better by act of Parliament.

Or they sometimes argued that men could not be made better by act of Parliament. But they did not act as though they always believed it. With regard to Sunday, for example, they continued to press for laws which would enable the working man to have a day of rest, and would preserve the quietness of the English Sunday. Faced with the rising incidence of drunkenness, they wanted legislation to restrain the hours of drinking or to tax the liquor or to diminish the number of licences; and some of them wanted the law of local option, by which a majority of ratepayers could prohibit all public houses in the area. Everybody saw that you could better the individual by amending laws. The question, then, was not of the principle but of its application. When Christians said that you could not make men

[1] *Christian Socialist*, June 1884, 5.

better by act of Parliament, they sometimes meant that some
proposed change in the law would not have this effect.

The political rights of the labouring man and the socialist ideal of
economic structure came into a different category from the effort to
reform society by legislation. Some devout men believed that the
churches as such had nothing to do with political or economic
programmes. Other devout men, though fewer, believed that a
Christian structure of society could not be achieved without support
for the political and economic aspirations of the labourer. The
question became controversial in the middle of the seventies. The
managers of the Plymouth Church Congress in 1876 kept the
subject of labour off the agenda because it led to fierce statements at
previous congresses.

The memory of Frederick Denison Maurice was powerful as the
churches faced the development of industrial society. It was something if a Christian treated socialism with sympathy. But he might
be treating it with sympathy because he was a socialist by habit and
heredity, or because he was sympathetic by nature, not because he was
a Christian. Among Christian Socialists some were Christian as
well as socialist, as a man might be Christian as well as interested in
maps. The two attitudes occupied the same mind but the one did not
derive from the other. No such charge could be levelled against
Maurice. Whatever doubts might be expressed about his socialism,
no one could doubt that he called himself a socialist because he was
a Christian. He was through and through a theologian whose
theology of the world led him to socialist utterances. He was not a
socialist as well as a Christian, but a socialist because he was a
Christian. The nonconformist leader R. W. Dale of Birmingham,
said that many nonconformists owed to Maurice the change from
the view that political activity lay outside the province of Christian
life.[1]

In the seventies some students of the New Testament began to
interpret *the kingdom of God* in a sense less otherworldly than in
traditional Christian explanation. On 22 February 1876 Matthew
Arnold delivered a lecture to the London clergy at Sion College,
contending that in the original gospel *the kingdom of God* meant the
kingdom of God on earth. This is not surprising, for Arnold was not
always a reliable interpreter of the texts of the New Testament.

[1] Dale, *Fellowship with Christ*, 201.

What was surprising was the way in which he carried his audience. Bishop Piers Claughton rose to protest. He said that the *kingdom of God* did not mean what Arnold said that it meant. Then clergyman after clergyman rose to speak for Arnold and against Claughton.[1] In the eighties the theologians started writing books on the social impact of Christianity, but the scene at Arnold's lecture shows that before that time the younger clergy of London moved towards what would later be described as the social gospel.

By the eighties, the question of Christianity and socialism touched the churches. Some socialists, probably a majority of socialists, claimed that the new political and economic programme for society was the only Christian programme in the circumstances of the age, and that all good Christians ought to support it. And a small number of able and devoted clergymen agreed with them. Those who loosely called themselves Christian Socialists represented a wide variety of opinion, some of it deeply Christian and hardly socialist, some of it deeply socialist and hardly Christian, with diverse shades between the two. They were all agreed that the conditions of society were morally intolerable and therefore that every religious man ought to wish to change them towards the direction recommended by the Labour leaders of the working men. They were not agreed that the right method of furthering their moral end was to vote Labour (after Labour candidates began to contest elections), for such a vote could only weaken the Liberal party which some of them still saw as the only hope of winning power for their social policy.

The early socialists were divided about religion.

If they were middle class, they were often rebels against their background, and were usually against religion and did not believe in God and attacked churches in their journals. They regarded religion as a mistake, if not as superstitious, and its organised expression as a piece of hypocrisy in favour of the upper and middle classes. Some English socialists, especially Hyndman and Belfort Bax, expressed this belief in fierce language. They regarded Christian Socialism as a contradiction in terms.

If they were middle class and Christian men as well as socialists, they were often Anglo-Catholic curates in the slums, or among the most intelligent and independent of nonconformist pastors.

[1] Matthew Arnold's Letters, ed. Russell, ii, 147–8; address in *Macmillan's Mag.*, April 1876.

If the working man practised Christianity he often belonged to the Primitive Methodists or to one of the congregation of extreme Independents. If he were Irish, his Roman Catholicism might be part of his nationality. If he were Scottish, presbyterianism might be part of his nationality. Or he might come from an area or parish where the Church of England was powerful among the poor, or had been touched by a revivalist mission sponsored by another of the old denominations. Almost all the early Labour leaders, if they were working class, had a religious element in their Socialism. 'I claim for Socialism', wrote Keir Hardie, 'that it is the embodiment of Christianity in our industrial system.'[1]

A little discount must be made for political utility. Socialists were accused of atheism. The behaviour of the German and French socialists encouraged the accusation, and several leading English socialists were atheists or agnostics—Aveling, Hyndman, Belfort Bax, Blatchford, William Morris—and propagated their creed in public journals. At the Blackburn election of 1900 agents thought it worth while to issue a handbill against the socialist candidate, *Down with Atheism, Socialism and Anarchy*, though the socialist happened to be a Methodist.[2] The early Socialists were indeed inclined to lay stress upon the religious or ethical inspiration of their movement, more stress, perhaps, than could easily be justified by a cold examination of the facts. Such a stress denied the still dangerous charge, and appealed to the better instincts in middle-class opponents. But though they were inclined to stress it, they were far from inventing it out of nothing.

Lansbury was rare among the leaders in being a member of the Church of England. Several were of Scottish background, though seldom from the established Church of Scotland. The early Labour party did not usually attract nonconformist ministers, with a few eminent exceptions. It attracted more Anglican priests, for the Anglican priest was independent. The nonconformist minister depended on his congregation, and if the congregation were of mixed class—and most nonconformist congregations were not working class but lower middle class—he could not introduce his politics into his church. Like the Chartists, their successors were often as hostile to chapel as to church. But if the Labour party did not

[1] *British Weekly*, 18 January 1894; Pelling, *Labour Party*, 148.
[2] Snowden's *Autobiog.*, i, 101–2.

attract ministers, it attracted laymen, especially local preachers, drawn towards socialism by its ethic for society.

It is possible, though as yet far from certain, that the churches suffered by the new political consciousness of the worker. A local preacher of (say) Keighley in Yorkshire in past years found his social and ethical sense of mission in his chapel. With his political club or union or co-operative his energy and idealism went into a different kind of organisation. That this happened with some is evident. Tom Mann was an evangelist in the temperance cause before he was a Labour leader, and his autobiography shows that something like this movement of ethical endeavour from church to politics occurred in his career. If the rule is generalised, it might be argued, and it has indeed been claimed, that the rise of the local political societies for working men distracted them from the chapel or the church. There may be some truth in the generalisation, but it needs more enquiry before it can be called evidence. Some who worked hard for a trade union contiued to work hard for churches.

Priests or pastors who ministered to labouring men in slums usually began to share their sympathies and opinions. And the London slums attracted curates of intelligence. In the late seventies and early eighties the doctrine that socialism was authentic Christianity began to be heard from a few clergymen or nonconformist ministers on platforms, and occasionally in pulpits. Thomas Hancock preached a celebrated sermon of 1887 with the title *The Banner of Christ in the hands of the Socialists*. In the offices of the English Church Union, after a lecture on Christian Socialism, a curious debate arose to reveal the extraordinary atmosphere of the age (December 1883). It was thus reported,[1] 'The Reverend Stewart Headlam said that he would rather see socialism established in this country than what was called Christianity or supernaturalism. . . .' All could work for the revaluation of the land and a progressively heavy tax on large incomes.

'Mr. Andreas Scheu, as a man who had no reverence for religion, urged the separation of Socialism and Christianity, because people thought Christianity was producing the effect which was really due to Socialism.

'Mr. Hubert Bland dwelt on the value of joining the word Christian to Socialism as a mere piece of worldly wisdom, since it

[1] G, 83, 1834.

enabled them to push their teachings into otherwise inaccessible quarters.

'Mr. J. C. Wright attacked the bishops . . . in violent language as "the true living devils of society" . . .

'Mr. H. C. Williams, as a Christian, dwelt on the irreconcilability of Christianity with socialism.

'Mr. Layman said the best socialist teaching was to be found in the church catechism.'

This extraordinary difference of opinion ran through the working class as well as the middle class. The leaders of the workers were at least agreed that socialism was a *moral* force of power. Whether it was Christian or anti-Christian they were not agreed. On the one hand they appealed to that vague idealism which most workers associated with religion. On the other hand they had affinities with the secularist lecturer, denouncing priestcraft from his platform. In 1891 John Trevor, a Unitarian minister of Manchester, founded a Labour church to harness these religious aspirations to the Labour movement, and the little movement (about fifty-four congregations at its largest) found it not always easy to determine when an address was a sermon or a speech.

The attitude of the churches to this claim that socialism was the Christian programme varied as widely as could be predicted. A Baptist minister in Forest Hill was said to have denounced socialism as the mad dream of wicked men.[1] Dean Goulburn of Norwich, a conservative by nature, was reported to have said in a sermon that socialism 'ought rather to be called anti-socialism, inasmuch as it strikes at the divinely appointed constitution of the social fabric'. But when such remarks were made, not everyone understood what socialism intended, except vaguely that it seemed to encourage class hatred by teaching the poor to see the rich as their enemies and exploiters. The term socialism was open to various interpretations, and the word did not at once sound with the associations of brotherly love. Until the middle eighties, and the London riots, many church-men pooh-poohed the movement as a passing wave of ideas. On 21 December 1883 the *Church Times* entitled one of its leaders *Socialism, Christian and otherwise*, and declared the movement to be only a communistic ripple on the surface of public opinion.

The question of the kinship (or otherwise) of Christianity with

[1] *Christian Socialist*, April 1887, 53.

socialism stood before the churches in 1883 and the following years. In that year Samuel Barnett, vicar of St. Jude's, Whitechapel, avowed himself a Christian Socialist in the columns of the *Nineteenth Century*, though his measures were timid in the eyes of the Christian Socialists proper. Others were beginning to contend that socialism could not be Christian because it must tend to decline in moral standards. Parents who save help their children: parents who do not save are to have their children looked after by the state: therefore, sooner or later, goes the incentive to work, saving, thrift and self-respect. And still others contended that this claim of socialism to morality could not stand when it was compared with Christianity. Christians indeed, said a member of Parliament,[1] were the true socialists, but in a sense quite other than that intended by the socialists. Who did most in hospitals, temperance, emigration, co-operative societies, national insurance, housing, education? The Christians endeavoured to do their duty by humble service to their neighbour. The socialist merely preached political revolution.

Many members of the Victorian middle class thought that virtue usually led to prosperity and sin often led to poverty. They could see before their eyes how in the expanding economy of the age an industrious and honest man could make his way in the world; and when they investigated the predicament of the destitute they too often found it derived, at least in part, from someone's drunkenness or gambling or extravagance. And every social worker in East London could point to the connexion between alcoholism in a father and the rags of his children. Much experience of relief seemed to show that mere doles were a palliative but not a cure, and that men must be helped to self-respect by earning for themselves, and learn to stand upon their own feet. What Stewart Headlam said was an extreme reaction against the doctrine that sin produces poverty. If sin, then the sin of the rich and not the poor. Society produces poverty, and the system must be changed. Headlam fiercely attacked Archbishop Benson of Canterbury for implying that sin caused poverty.[2]

---

[1] CCR, 1887, 165ff.

[2] *Church Reformer*, iii, 121; June 1884. Four years later Headlam ridiculed the third Lambeth Conference, which made sympathetic remarks about the socialist movement but committed the report to the statement, 'After all the best help is self-help.' 'However,' wrote Headlam, the bishops 'are at least awake' (*Church Reformer*, 1888, 200). The *Church Reformer* collapsed, because of its tiny circulation, absence of advertisements and chronic shortage of money, in December 1895. It was the organ of the

Meanwhile another group adopted the name of *Christian Socialist* for its journal. It was a 1*d.* a month and first appeared in June 1883. J. L. Joynes was the son of an Eton master and himself formerly an Eton master. Joynes was humanely convinced that he should take the name of which Maurice and Kingsley were proud, and became (after a brief stage of editorials by committee) the first editor of the *Christian Socialist*. He saw signs that the choice ahead for the nation lay between social disruption and social reform. To the Christian he would advocate social reform, to the Socialist he would show that no act of Parliament could make the world happy; and he would exclude all class hatred and class prejudice from the journal. 'In our view Christianity and Socialism are almost interchangeable terms' (November 1883). For several months the journal had an excellent circulation. But in January 1884 the non-Christian Socialists founded *Justice*, which helped to diminish the circulation by supplying part of the need. Thenceforward the journal struggled. In 1887 it was taken over by another small group, undenominational, partly Scottish, more woolly in intelligence, also calling themselves *Christian Socialist*, but less religious than social, and the journal collapsed at the end of 1891. It was never a very theoretical journal; always more lay than clerical; never attempting to emulate Frederick Denison Maurice in profundity; but in its earlier years under Joynes a sensible contribution to the great argument. The group was always under fire from both sides. Non-Christian Socialists thought it fatal to identify a political programme with religious opinions which some men might not believe, even though the political programme appealed to a moral view of the world.[1]

In June 1889 Henry Scott Holland founded the Christian Social Union and secured Bishop Westcott as its first president. It had 2,600 members by 1897.

Headlam and his friends attacked the Christian Social Union as wishy-washy, and in some respects they had reason. Westcott lived in a world of vast opaque statements and did not like to define. But the Union allowed men, who wanted to see what moral force

---

Guild of St. Matthew, founded by Headlam in 1877 and always small (200 members after thirteen years). By socialism Headlam always meant the ideas of Henry George on land nationalisation.

[1] Aveling, in *Today*, January 1884; Karl Pearson, *The Moral Basis of Socialism*, 1887. Joynes went abroad for his health till the summer of 1885; decided to be a doctor; broke down while in training and died 1893. Bax, *Reminiscences*, 103–4.

socialism offered, to study with sympathy and without the necessity to label themselves a friend of Headlam or an extreme Anglo-Catholic. Holland was profound, and hesitant, but not in the least wishy-washy, and in 1896 started the *Commonwealth*, which was his personal journal, and contained some of the best writing of all the Christian Socialist movement. Charles Gore, a strong member of the Oxford branch from its early days, thought that in the long run the Christian Social Union succeeded in altering the official attitude of church leaders. Bishops Westcott and Moorhouse could rightly raise an abstract and ideal socialism into a Christian ordering of society. The testing question was whether such ordering of society would be promoted by the nationalisation of the means of production. To a Stewart Headlam the lofty language of a Westcott appeared to be too lofty to be useful. To Westcott the political advocacy of a Headlam appeared to confuse an eternal moral principle with a temporary and expedient programme of politicians.

Among the clergy and ministers of the left—whether they were radical by temperament, or slum-pastors moved by the poverty of their people, or evangelists bridging the gulf between themselves and the working man—the social gospel reached its Victorian culmination about 1891, 1892, 1893. At a Congregationalist meeting in Southport the orator Ben Tillett said that it was the churches, and not Parliament, which had the duty of emancipating the people from vile conditions. A Congregational minister said that in the present day they must 'preach a gospel' of fair wages and a just distribution of wealth.[1] The rector of St. George's Southwark, Thory Gardiner, who worked hand in hand with Tom Mann on municipal reform of the L.C.C., tried to persuade Mann to be ordained and become his curate, on the ground that they did the same work, and said the same kind of thing, inside church as well as outside.[2] A rumour that Mann was to be ordained reached the newspapers. And Mann seems to have taken the suggestion seriously. A newspaper correspondent roused the ire of Charles Marson by suggesting that if Mann were ordained he would be the solitary socialist parson in the church. Marson replied with a picture of 'seven and seventy' determined socialist priests in the Guild of St. Matthew and a large nursery, full of socialists 'cutting their teeth',

[1] G, 91, 1725.
[2] T. Mann, *Memoirs*, 1967 ed., 86, 91–2.

in the Christian Social Union; 'and the still greater fact remains that
the church herself is a socialist body'.[1]

One great cleavage of doctrine divided the two schools of
Christian Socialists: their attitude to the state.

The rebellious curates, like Headlam and Arthur Stanton, hated
the establishment. They wanted the church more 'democratic', and
believed this to be impossible so long as the Church of England was
by law established. A not so rebellious incumbent, like Llewelyn
Davies, though a disciple of Maurice, wanted drastic modifications
in the establishment for similar reasons.

But Maurice had valued the establishment for social reasons. He
did not wish the church to shut itself inside its private life. He wished
the church to be the religious and moral organ of the nation, and its
national duty meant more to him than its ecclesiastical duty. During
the later years of the century the disciples of Maurice usually made
the same link between the national duty of the church and its drive
towards social welfare. This school of Christian Socialists talked of
the need for the church to go out into the world, to engage in politics,
to be (in the right sense) worldly. Maurice never identified nation
with church, though at times he seemed to come close. His disciple
W. H. Fremantle harked back to Dr. Arnold and identified the two.
In 1883 he gave the Bampton lectures at Oxford, on *The World as
the subject of Redemption: being an attempt to set forth the functions of the
Church as designed to embrace the whole Race of Mankind*. The lectures
were published two years later and fell dead. But an American
publisher took them up, the Americans adopted them as part of the
social gospel and when Fremantle printed a second edition in 1895
the English found them to be a fundamental work of the Christian
Socialist movement. The church is the whole community of
Christian people tending to embrace the whole world, for Christianity is to be identified with goodness. Its business is not to save
individuals from the world so much as to save the world. It cannot
do this as a sect or number of sects because it is too weak. And if it
tries, it removes the Christian name from the effort of nation and
government towards social welfare, and separates it as 'secular' or
something lower. The whole of organised society is God's dwelling
place. Like Arnold, Fremantle trusted that diffused, inarticulate,

---

[1] C. W. Marson to *Westminster Gazette*, 5 October 1893; Mann, *Memoirs* (1967
ed.), 94–95.

embryo, half-conscious faith of a whole people, and believed that history led the churches to define their idea of faith and of church membership too narrowly. This was a more diffused idea of the church than Maurice could have followed. It claimed even more vigorously than Maurice the sovereignty of Christianity over society. But the Christianity held to be thus sovereign was a less dogmatic religion than that of Maurice. The merit of Fremantle was social concern, the demerit that his picture of society and the world was so optimistic as to be utopian.

By the late nineties nearly every denomination had its socialist society or its minority of leaders who were content to be called socialist: a Quaker Socialist society (1898), Roman Catholic Socialist societies in Leeds and Glasgow, a Swedenborgian Socialist society in London; the Baptist John Clifford founded the Christian Socialist League in 1894 (it became the Christian Social Brotherhood in 1898),[1] R. J. Campbell among the Congregationalists. If they were Tractarians they ransacked the fathers of the early church and found justification, as in the *magnificat* or the sermon on the mount, for a social gospel.

During the late eighties and nineties we find a new complaint: that clergymen and ministers do not preach the gospel any longer because they preach instead on fair wages. Some working-class congregations wanted sermons on the social gospel. Not only working-class. The Christian Socialist H. C. Shuttleworth and his curate Thomas Hancock preached a social gospel in St. Nicholas, Cole Abbey, in London, and thereby filled a hitherto empty church. At the other end of the country and social scale, a dissenting minister in Lancashire said, as early as November 1883, that the congregation more and more wanted social and political subjects treated in the pulpit, and 'it was very difficult for a minister, now, to please'. He was a man whom Beatrice Potter[2] admired, a man of the people, chosen by the people to lead them. Three years later she went back to the same chapel and found a new minister, a college man, shabby-genteel, 'more of a politician than a preacher'. He had a certain influence over the people 'through his gift of the gab'; but they half-unconsciously felt that the 'real thing' was passing, and there were 'na more plain men as *feel* the word of Christ'.

[1] P.d'A. Jones, 28–29. See also the accounts in S. Mayor and K. S. Inglis.
[2] *My Apprenticeship*, 138.

V.C.–10

The pulpit, it had been agreed, was no place for politics. But we have already seen how in moments of national crisis this good rule broke down, where a political judgment was believed to touch a moral issue. The entire social question could be seen as at once political and moral. And yet, like the Lancashire folk and their minister, most congregations wanted to hear of God and of Christ, of Scripture and of parable, and felt deprived if they heard only of wages or prostitution. A citizen of Bristol expressed it in epigrammatic vexation after hearing a sermon of Samuel Barnett: 'We come to church to be comforted, whereas you seem to think it proper to make us uncomfortable.'[1] The chairman of the Congregational Union in 1894 delivered a warning address entitled *The Secularization of the Pulpit*.[2] The churchwarden of Manchester cathedral denounced his dean, John Oakley, as a political dean.[3]

The same Christian critics of the Christian Socialists fastened, in part, upon the idea of freedom. Granted that the nationalisation of property would reduce the poverty of a lot of people, would it be consistent with that freedom in the state which was also a precious possession with moral consequences? Bishop Magee of Peterborough, who was a conservative, compared the Christian Socialists with the puritans, attempting to make England moral by law. Was it really contended that Christ's word could be taken to deal with the economic relations of men in the sense of deciding political questions? The duty of the church was to infuse charity into the mind of the labourer and of the capitalist, and to stand up for the oppressed; so that men 'would do from love what the state could not justly require or compel them to do by law'. Some interpreted or misinterpreted Magee's speech to mean that Christianity was concerned only with the individual, and must not interfere with economics or politics.[4]

The articulate critic was the young Oxonian Herbert Hensley Henson, who experienced London while head of Oxford House in 1888, and then London-over-the-border as vicar of Barking, where the works at Beckton supplied the city with gas. His ability was exceptional, his temperament rebellious, his person angular. His suffragan bishop regarded him as the *enfant terrible* of the diocese. All his life he believed in the law that the market must control

[1] *Life of Barnett*, ii, 213.   [2] *CYB*, 1895, 19–33 ; S. Mayor, 67–68.
[3] *Manchester Guardian*, 28–29 April, 1 May 1886.   [4] *Times*, 26 October 1889.

wages. All his life he attacked Christian Socialists for woolliness of thought, and for being chaplains of King Demos; clergymen blessing the political power of the new age as their predecessors blessed King Henry VIII.

Henson had no doubt that preachers who preached politics or socialist measures abused their pulpits, that the Bible warranted no one form of government or social order, and that Christ taught a kingdom not of this world. Christianity was to inspire men's hearts with the desire to better their fellow-men, and therefore society. But its mode was inward, and gradual, it could never baptise a political programme which it had no sound means of valuing. The church makes good citizens because it makes good men. The Christian Socialist pastor is controversial, but Christ's pastor is peaceful and pastoral. One is the apologist of men's discontent, the other is the apostle of social harmony. He confessed the self-devotion of many Christian Socialist priests. 'The self-abandonment of their personal lives compensates for the errors of their social creed.'[1]

And yet such was the atmosphere of the nineties that the Christian Socialists were justly able to accuse Henson of inconsistency. He denied them the right to use their pulpits to promote social reform. They found in his sermons a grudging admission of the rightfulness of trade unions, a denunciation of excessive rents and scoundrel landlords, an advocacy of better hospitals and perhaps of a system of pensions, or of security against sudden loss of employment. Nothing (he said) afflicted him more, with a sense half of fear and half of guilt, than the sight of unemployed men.

Where the strike became a weapon which could devastate the country and the homes of the worker, bishops sometimes offered themselves, or were persuaded to be, arbitrators. Their status in these matters was nothing, in theory, to do with their place in the argument about Christianity and Socialism, but the status of any eminent man likely to be fair-minded and able to appeal to the better side of either party. But in practice arbitration, in any case the most delicate and unrewarding of tasks, could only be successfully undertaken by bishops whom working men already looked on as their friends, for the word *bishop* was still associated for many of them with the counter-revolution. At a meeting of the Guild of St. Matthew a speaker referred to a Frenchman as 'bishop and democrat'. 'That's

[1] Henson to the clergy of Barking, 29 January 1896: G, 96, 283.

nonsense', said a secularist, 'for it stands to reason that if a man's a bishop he can't be a democrat, and if a man's a democrat he oughtn't to be a bishop; so there's an end of it.'[1] In these circumstances a bishop needed to be publicly known before he could intervene. Ever since Arch and the horsepond affair, it would have been no use if the gentle Bishop Ellicott of Gloucester offered himself as an arbitrator.

In the seventies the bishop whose personality came over to the worker was Fraser of Manchester. As soon as he was consecrated he started to conduct services in mills and factories during the dinner-hour, and concerned himself with the bargemen on the canals and the dustmen. He rapidly won their affections. But even Fraser could do little enough in a crisis. By request he arbitrated between the house-painters and their employers in two successive conflicts. In April 1878 the owners of cotton-mills, faced with slump, demanded a 10 per cent reduction in wages, refused to accept less than 10 per cent, and locked out strikers. The mill-hands rioted through the streets of North Lancashire and the army was called in. Bishop Fraser was one of those who tried to persuade the men to accept the reduction for three months in the hopes of a turn of trade, but without success. He tried to persuade the masters to lessen the reduction to $7\frac{1}{2}$ per cent, but without success. After nine weeks the strikers surrendered. Fraser did not believe himself suited to arbitrate, and his impartial good sense lost him some of the popularity which his care for the operative brought him. No Anglican bishop did more to make his diocese feel the social force of Christianity in an industrialised area.

Cardinal Manning, whose flock contained many Irish labourers and therefore some of the poorest labourers in England, identified himself with the cause of the worker. He was the only prelate except Fraser to support Joseph Arch, and his public activity was not popular among his English constituents. He served on the royal commission on the housing of the poor, and did what he could to encourage emigration. In an article of 1887, during the worst of the distress, he published an article in the *American Quarterly Review* to the effect that man had a natural right to life and food and that since this right prevailed even over laws of property, a starving man did not steal if he took sufficient food from his neighbour.[3]

---

[1] *Church Reformer*, iii, 124.   [2] G, 78, 702, 849; G, 80, 1325.
[3] Manning's social activity is well described in V. A. McClelland, 129ff.

In 1889 the dockers of the Port of London went on strike, and four-fifths of them were Irishmen. In the fourth week the directors planned to bring over foreign labour, and Manning feared bloodshed. To try to reconcile the opponents, a committee was set up which contained the lord mayor and Manning and Bishop Temple of London and three other laymen. When negotiations broke down, Temple went away on holiday to Wales, believing that nothing more could be done. But Manning went on and on imperturbably, and at last secured a compromise.

In 1892 Bishop Westcott of Durham intervened in the Durham coal strike at just the moment when the battle reached an intolerable impasse. He did not propose a solution. He simply invited both sides to meet at his house, and began the meeting by appealing to both sides for concession. The meeting broke the impasse.

'The clergy', Bishop Creighton charged the diocese of Peterborough,[1] 'are, as a rule, from the mere nature of their vocations, the class in the community which is least versed in business affairs. They are little suited as a body to decide economic questions'. In 1895 the employees of the boot-and-shoe trade at Northampton and Leicester went on strike. Creighton was begged to intervene, but knew better. 'Intervention, unless it is welcomed, would only spoil the future chance, and would count as fussy interference'. He went about behind the scenes urging moderation and passing information, but 'it is entirely a matter for expert opinion, and good intentions avail little'.

When Frederick Temple became Archbishop of Canterbury, it was as though the seal was set upon the acceptability of the doctrine of evolution among Christian men. It was also as though the seal was set upon acceptability of the social gospel. He visited labourers and told them that he would like them, if it were possible, to become partners in their business. In 1900 he told a deputation of trade societies that he was friendly to a proposal (by Charles Booth) that the state should pay a pension of 5s. a week to everyone over the age of 65 years. But (he would not have been a Victorian if he had not added) if the labouring class was to be helped, they must also help themselves by economy and self-restraint; and he drew their particular attention to drink and early marriages. He explained to

---

[1] *Life*, ii, 119–32.

the deputation how hard it would be to persuade the country to adopt the plan.

6. REVIVAL

The Methodists, especially the Primitive Methodists, had a time-honoured way of reaching out towards the working man, by preaching in the open air and revival missions. In the bigger cities, as a good man could gather a little congregation by simply opening a room, so he could gather at least a temporary congregation by standing at a corner or in a park and talking about God. In the fifties Anglican evangelicals began to look towards these methods. When Tait was Bishop of London, he surprised everyone by going himself to preach in the open air in a working-class district, and founded the London diocesan home mission, under which clergy preached in the open air or held mission services in rooms or schools.

In 1859 a revival in northern Ireland achieved extraordinary results in the way of conversions. In England the movement had smaller consequence in converts at the moment. But it gave a sudden new stimulus to everyone who believed in the methods of old-fashioned revival, and persuaded others, who hitherto could not believe in them at all, to give them a trial. It happened to coincide with the sixties when it was clear that the working man of the big towns could not be got inside the churches by the usual services. Evangelicals of the Church of England began to organise more frequent parochial missions. Wesleyans renewed their tradition of revivalist preaching. During these years East London was invaded by revivalists who took up their stance at street-corners, in parks, sheds, halls, tents, theatres. Backed by philanthropists like Lord Shaftesbury or the Congregationalist Samuel Morley, various organisations were created to minister to this need. Few could get the poor into church. But it was discovered that the poor would listen in great numbers provided that they were not asked to enter a church. Anyone with conviction and humour and aggressiveness could gain a hearing. A group called the East London Special Services committee sought to co-ordinate the efforts and employ evangelists. The mode of evangelism was given a new impetus after 1874–5, when the American D. L. Moody, with Sankey to sing solos for him, conducted a powerful tour of revival, preaching a very simple gospel of salvation through God's love, and organising the 'after-meeting' or 'enquiry-room', with a system new to England, and seeking to supplement and not compete with the churches.

The remarkable new development of the sixties was the acceptance by some high Anglicans of the evangelical methods of parochial missions. A growing number of their best people would organise a week's preaching in their parish, with an evangelistic call as powerful as any in the more usual circumstances. Hay Aitken and Richard Twiss were the most famous missioners of this new movement. The ideal was baptised when bishops began to use a canonry to release a 'canon-missioner' from all other parochial responsibilities and allow him freedom to travel in evangelistic preaching. The most delightful and famous among Anglican canon-evangelists was George Body, who became a canon of Durham in 1883, and specialised in missions among the miners.

In the first half of the century the Primitive Methodists succeeded, as no other denomination (except the Roman Catholics with the Irish and some Anglican congregations) in touching the poor or very poor. In the second half of the century the Primitives continued some of this work. But their working men prospered, and became more middle class. As the decades passed the social atmosphere of the Primitive chapel began to resemble that of the Wesleyan chapel; and yet till the end of the century they were nearer to the poor, and were always more rural, whereas the Wesleyans remained more largely urban.

The most remarkable revivalist of the age appeared among the radical Methodists.

William Booth was born into the Church of England at Sneinton, Nottingham, in 1829. As a boy he started to worship with the Methodists. In 1844 he was converted by Methodist revival, and two years later, partly because he heard the American evangelist James Caughey, he became a street preacher in his spare time. In 1849 he went to London in the quest for work. There he was caught up indirectly with the Methodist calamity of those years, and in 1852 became a minister of the Wesleyan Reformers at Spalding in Lincolnshire. For the remainder of his life he retained an almost physical sense of divine presence and peace of heart, a vivid conviction of hell and Satan and salvation, and a belief in the manifestations of revival.

In London he met Catherine Mumford, a masterful and able girl whose mother was turned out of house for marrying a Methodist lay-preacher. They married in 1855. She supplied a certain knowledge of the world and of books, and a wider sense of religion than he had yet met. She had links with the Methodist New Connexion, and in 1854 persuaded him to join it. From 1855, the year in which he married her, he was a travelling evangelist of the Methodist New Connexion. He began to gather celebrity as a revivalist preacher. A mission to Staffordshire in January and February 1855 brought great crowds and a denominational fame. As minister at Bethesda chapel in Gateshead in 1858 he turned a congregation of 120 into a congregation of 1500.

His methods were extreme. He would play any honourable trick, perform any antic, to win attention. His colleagues were not sure that his methods were right. And in Gateshead Mrs. Booth, who believed in the equality of women, proved herself to have gifts of revival as powerful as those of her husband. While she brought up eight children and lived in uncomfortable accommodation, this astonishing woman led revivals all over the country. She appeared alone among the prostitutes or the drunks. They both knew that evangelism, revival, was their vocation, not a steady ministry to a chapel or a circuit. When Conference of 1861, by a majority, refused Booth leave to become a travelling evangelist, he resigned and drifted out of the Methodist New Connexion. He and his wife became private evangelists, wherever chapels or mission-stations would let them into the pulpit or rostrum. He began to move away from preaching inside chapels to preaching in the open, or to hiring a hall. Then the East London committee began to use him, preaching in parks, or on street-corners.

The authorities discouraged meetings in the parks.

The Society of Friends had a burial ground in Whitechapel, closed for burials. They now allowed a tent of the East London Special Services committee to be erected in this burial ground. The committee summoned William Booth to preach in this tent. The Salvation Army looks back for its origin to the tent in the Quaker cemetery at Whitechapel.

If a preacher brought a poor drunkard to the penitent's bench and conversion, what could he do with him? Send him into a church? The chances of getting him into a church or chapel were tiny.

Therefore he must be enlisted in an open-air religious society where the poor felt at home. The convert must also prove his conversion by standing out and speaking in the alley. By 1868 Booth controlled thirteen preaching stations. He could get an audience in almost any East London street almost any hour; get it by hymns if not by speech, by antics if not by hymns. He began to show that he could organise. In 1872 he appeared before the public with a pamphlet called *How to reach the Masses with the Gospel*.

In 1870 Booth fixed a constitution. It was a liberal Methodist constitution, with Conference as the supreme authority. But it was distinguished from Methodism, first, by the general superintendent, who held his office for life under the control of Conference, but could be removed if Conference *unanimously* declared him incapacitated; secondly, by the equality of women, equal not only in the work but in the government; and thirdly by the obligation on all office-holders (but not yet all members) to be teetotal.

The constitution did not work. The general superintendent was effective, Conference ineffective. It was composed of a miscellany of itinerant evangelists or new converts, not many educated. The interminable discussions became intolerable to Booth's young men like George Railton. They looked to Booth, not to Conference, for leadership. As the war metaphor grew upon them, as they encountered persecution in the streets, they demanded a more powerful, more military, command.

In 1875 Booth fixed the articles of faith, the terms under which the property was held, by a deed in chancery. The articles contain, in addition to evangelical faith, the old Methodist doctrine of entire sanctification (article 10). There was still an annual Conference. But Booth might set aside all decisions of Conference which he thought contrary to the laws or objects of the Christian Mission. He had the power to appoint his successor as general superintendent. Conference was given a number of rules for action, but Booth (though not his successor as general superintendent) might overrule them all. This great power did not content them. The deed was annulled in 1878, and replaced by another deed. This gave Booth control over all moneys and property. The provision disappeared that a unanimous Conference could depose him. Conference was not mentioned in the deed of 1878. There was only a general meeting, which was recorded to approve the deed. No one objected to this constitution.

V.C.–10 *a*

In the age of persecution and of rapid expansion and quick decisions, the Christian Mission believed it necessary to have a head who could act unchecked.

By 1876 the numbers were recorded as 2,455. There was some doubt whether these numbers were not exaggerated.[1]

They were liable to be pelted with mud or stones or worse. What the villagers of forty years before did to the Ranters, their sons in East London did to the ritualists in churches and to evangelists in the street. One of Booth's evangelists, Elijah Cadman, was formerly a Primitive Methodist preacher. Cadman introduced Booth to methods more remarkable than any yet used. He was a member of a Hallelujah band, who wore red shirts. In 1876 Booth appointed him as a preacher at Hackney.

Booth's proper title was general superintendent of the mission. His colleagues referred to him as 'the General' for short. Cadman pretended to assume that Booth was General in the Lord's war against wickedness. He habitually used military metaphors. He signed his reports to Booth *Yours in the King's Army*. He called himself Captain. In a mission to Whitby of November 1877 he plastered the town with placards of War in Whitby, demanding recruits for the Hallelujah army.

The annual meeting of August 1878 was called Our War Congress. Across the platform ran a great painted sign, *Salvation Army*. They had a battle-song, and the evangelists began to be called field officers. In October 1879 Booth was called for the first time the General of the Salvation Army, when a notice to Coventry declared that he would publicly enter the town at the head of the 25th (Coventry) Corps. In the next year the new name was endorsed on the deed. The paper which he published became *The War Cry* on 27 December 1879.

The military metaphor was not the property of the revivalists in East London. Since the Epistle to the Ephesians wrote of the shield of faith, such language was at home in Christian poetry. But several of the most famous battle-hymns are of the sixties. *Stand up, stand up for Jesus* was written for the American revival in Philadelphia during 1858. *Fight the good fight*, by the Anglican J. S. B. Monsell, was of 1863. In 1864 the Anglican curate Sabine Baring-Gould published the greatest of them all, *Onward Christian soldiers*, for Sunday school

[1] Sandall, i, 188.

children at Horbury Bridge near Wakefield; though at first it was sung to an adaptation of Haydn, and did not receive Arthur Sullivan's marching tune till 1871.

In September 1878 the Army had 91 officers, of whom 41 were women.[1] The women were often the more effective. They were an odder sight and therefore drew larger crowds. They also came from more educated homes, and in marriage there was a problem of alliance between the rougher men and gentler women. In 1879 a girl called Kate Shepherd conducted a mission of astounding success in the Upper Rhondda valley.

In the moment when Booth adopted the name of an army, the military drama began to grow. The chain of command became more authoritarian. The brass music was a straight inheritance from the old Hallelujah bands. Mrs. Booth presented the Coventry corps with the first flag in 1878. Hitherto the evangelists went out in top-hat and frock-coat. The military Cadman demanded 'a suit of clothes that would let everyone know I meant war to the teeth and salvation for the world.'[2] George Railton argued at first that uniform would be a barrier between evangelist and people, but in November 1878 they decided to adopt uniforms. Cadman and Railton began to wear old scraps of cast-off uniform, helmets or caps. At first the uniform was a simple artisan's blue jersey, with *Salvation Army* or a motto embroidered across the chest. The Hallelujah band had worn red shirts. In 1882 the jersey became a red jersey with words embroidered in yellow. It served all the purposes of a Franciscan habit. It enabled the poor convert, who shrank from a top-hat or frock-coat as he shrank from a chapel, to go out preaching in something which he could afford. By 1882–3 the wearing of uniform was becoming universal, and Booth strenuously encouraged it. Mrs. Booth selected the Hallelujah bonnet for the girls. The women kept privately adding decorations—braid or trimmings.

The first officer to be called major was he who was in charge of the north-east in February 1879. The rank of colonel appeared by 1886.[3]

The brass bands were originally formed to blow down opposition. At Salisbury young roughs gathered to drown the hymn-singing with popular songs, and the Salvation captain (August 1878) persuaded four Methodist performers to bring their brass and defeat

---

[1] Sandall, ii, 6.   [2] Sandall, ii, 38, 43.   [3] Sandall, ii, 49–52.

the enemy. The innovation disturbed some of the Army leaders but was rapidly adopted elsewhere. The flutes and violins had left the galleries of the parish churches and now appeared in the streets, with the necessary addition of instruments which could make enough noise for the open air. The harmonium was suspect because it was churchy. The hymns were soon called songs, and not hymns, to avoid the same association of ideas. At Mansfield in 1881 the captain bought a tambourine in a pawnbroker's shop, and soon women with tambourines were joyful in the processions. Booth at first forbade choirs with parts, as too churchy. But experience showed that they had great possibilities, and before 1886 they were well established. At first their 'songs' were old revivalist hymns, but soon they wrote their own. The tunes had a swing and a rollick. Booth at first doubted the use of music-hall tunes. Even when he began to allow them, several of his supporters protested violently at the profanation. When the Clapton Congress hall was opened in 1882, the audience sang the chorus again and again, beating time with clapping and waving handkerchiefs.

The officers were on the whole of the lower middle class. Converted drunks who became officers were rare. Most of the officers were young men and women. Some were converts from another church who found no outlet for evangelism in that church. Frederick Tucker, who brought the Salvation Army into India, resigned from the Indian Civil Service. Adelaide Cox was the daughter of an Anglican vicar. Elwin Oliphant was an Anglican curate. David Lamb was apprentice to an Aberdeen chemist. William Stevens was a prosperous jeweller at Worthing who sold the jewellery and gave the money to the Army. Mildred Duff was a Norfolk débutante. Bernard Shaw's character in the play *Major Barbara* (November 1905) was not typical but not unique.

The Army could not do without a seminary. Railton suspected all forms of training as bound to produce 'parsons'. The first training consisted only of evening meetings for a year followed by apprentice-work at a station for a year, that the future officer might not be divided from men. In 1880 the Booths' old home at Hackney was turned into a training home for thirty women, and later the same year another house in Hackney became a training home for men. 'Some friends', wrote Booth, 'have been a little afraid that we are in danger of departing from the simplicity of the movement, and going off on college lines. They must come and see us, and their fears will at once vanish.' The homes needed to teach reading, writing and spelling, and even personal habits, in addition to the usual curriculum in a Christian seminary. Early in 1882 the recruits began to sign pledges called 'articles of war', and at the same time teetotalism was made a condition of membership. The halls were soon called barracks. The phrase 'promoted to glory' to mean 'died' is first found in December 1882.[1] The word Salvationist was first found in 1882 among critics, but was soon adopted by the members of the Army as convenient.

Anglicans were repelled from the 'vulgarisation' of religion as near blasphemy, and many others could not see how religion and rowdiness could marry. General Booth was attacked for pretending to military ranks, Queen Victoria disliked the uniforms and the ranks, the publicans hated the teetotalism, young thugs, called the Skeleton Army, broke up the meetings. They continued to gather converts; usually from the lower middle class already Christian, but sometimes from human beings so low in the scale that no other church could get down to them. They were gospel-makers, cheery, happy, unquenchable. Educated men were often friendly. They watched the Salvation Army in the cities with that same detached respect with which some of their fathers in the country watched the Primitive Methodists in the villages. If these methods could reach the vice of the slums, they deserved a blessing.

The Salvation Army forfeited much sympathy by insisting on marching or trumpeting or meeting whatever the police decreed. They were accused of causing obstruction or of provoking to riot. In many towns the police refused them adequate protection because they resisted orders. Several Salvationists did a few days in prison for disobedience to the police. Local magistrates were often hostile. The Army discovered a powerful protector in the ex-Tractarian Lord Chief Justice, Coleridge, who gave a judgment vindicating their liberty and protection against decisions by magistrates.

1878, 50 corps, 88 officers; 1883, 528 corps in Britain, 1,340 officers in Britain; 1886, 1,006 corps in Britain, 2,260 officers in Britain.

At the beginning of the century Bishop Law of Chester defined the duty of a Bishop of Calcutta as 'to stop the wild progress of enthusiasm'. The new cities of the nineteenth century, and the land

---

[1] Sandall, ii, 68, 340.

of free religion, made this sober attitude old-fashioned. The world needed extraordinary efforts if it were to be Christianised. The church must draw attention to itself. The Roman Catholic hierarchy must make a noise in the world, Anglican ritualists must draw men in by the strangeness or beauty of their rites, dissenting preachers must be Spurgeons and make the crowds listen, chapels must be grander, outside the chapels text or wayside pulpit must remind the passer-by, tracts must be distributed. The Salvation Army was an extreme variety of wayside pulpit. Its fervour was not easy, in those early years, to distinguish from fanaticism.

In the earliest years, between 1878 and 1881, it was not clear whither this movement would lead. The Methodists, seeing it as an unusual form of Methodism, befriended it. The Wesleyan Conference of 1880 invited Booth to address it. Many Anglican vicars praised its work. Between 1880 and 1884 they often invited the Army to attend service and, with choir and surplice, would march to church at the head of the procession. The Church of England looked back with penitence upon the Methodist losses of the previous century, and was determined that, if possible, no want of sympathy should prevent alliance. The Anglicans were sensitive to Macaulay's charge that the Roman Church was able to find a home for the Franciscans but they found no place for the Methodists. Was it a new sect, or simply an agent for evangelism? Was it parody of religion, or could it be used by the churches? Booth said, the second. As yet it had no credit whatever for that social endeavour which won the respect of the modern world. Was it just another passing fervour, like the ranters and the Hallelujah bands, or was it working true revolution among the poor? Some devout men felt their inmost being repelled, almost to blasphemy, by religion made a spectacle to mobs. Churchmen in villages were shattered to hear the children shouting sacred language in their games to the tune of *Champagne Charlie* or *Over the garden wall*. Others declared that a true catholic would seize upon the enthusiasm and direct it. At least the poor would have religion, and if they had it in a form open to criticism that, declared the headmaster of Clifton (J. M. Wilson) was caused by the long failure of educated pastors.[1] In some towns—Nottingham, Northallerton, Newcastle-upon-Tyne, Middlesborough, Bristol, Coventry—the Army attended Anglican services by invitation.

[1] G, 82, 385.

Bishop Walsham How preached to them in June 1883 at St. Faith's Stoke Newington, and two years later in St. John's, Bethnal Green. Bishop Durnford of Chichester warned his diocesan conference in October 1882 not to look at them with contempt or dislike, 'lest haply we be found to fight against God'.[1] Bishop Lightfoot of Durham, in a charge to the clergy of 14 December 1882, criticised and yet praised the Army, and recommended his clergy to study their books.[2] Mrs. Booth declared to a packed and cheery meeting in the corn exchange at Oxford that she had received many beautiful letters from clergymen who found their flocks stirred by the Army to a deeper spirituality. Bishop Benson of Truro told his rural deans that the voice of the Salvation Army was the voice of the masses against secularism.[3]

The Anglican bishops were forced to consider the question by a sudden act of that strong individualist, Archbishop Thomson of York. In March 1882, 400 members of the Army in York were allowed to attend the early celebration of holy communion at St. Paul's church, Holgate. More than one vicar in York and outside it believed that this was profanation of the sacrament. More than one vicar approved. Fifty members attended a communion at Northallerton. 'Why', asked General Booth, speaking about the Salisbury riots in their new Congress hall at Clapton, 'Why did not my brother the bishop and his clergy put themselves at the head of the Army, and then there would be no more of this persecution?' Might there be alliance between the Army and the established church? When their doctrines were examined the Salvationists were found to teach two very simple truths also taught by the Church of England, those of sin and redemption. Archbishop Thomson wrote directly to General Booth, asking for discussions (18 April 1882).

On 12 May 1882 the bishops of the Canterbury Convocation appointed a committee to consider how far the Army could be attached to the Church of England. The committee appointed by the bishops never reported. It went so far as to send out a questionnaire to clergy and others, about the methods, effects, and risks of the Army. A meeting was held between Bishop Benson of Truro and Professor Westcott on one side and William Booth on the other.[4]

[1] Sandall, ii, 137–40.   [2] Lightfoot, *Primary Charge*, 1882, 67–77.
[3] G, 82, 416–17.
[4] G, 82, 441, 495, 761; letter printed by H. Begbie, ii, 9–10; Questionnaire in Benson Papers, 1883, S. 168A.

The committee was then overtaken by events. Twelve months after it was appointed, opinion swung so unfavourably to the Army that the old talk of 'attachment' to the church looked wild.

The Salvation Army began by being afraid of work for society. They saved the drunks by conversion, not by relief nor by medicine. Booth at first condemned 'mere' relief of the poor. But as the Army spread across the world, its agents neither distinguished nor wished to distinguish. A major in Melbourne opened the first home for the care of discharged prisoners, a major in Glasgow opened a home to rescue prostitutes, the Army opened a London home for prostitutes in 1884. In 1886 the London division organised a 'post' in slum London (furniture, two old bedsteads, and three broken chairs), whence two Salvationists could visit, help the 'deserving poor' and nurse the sick; and six months later they manned six posts.

As the work among London prostitutes developed, the Army began to discover how girls were trapped into it. Bramwell Booth, William's son and chief of staff, engaged in the attempt to 'buy' a little girl of thirteen called Eliza Armstrong, to prove to the public how it could be done. The articles of W. T. Stead on the case, in the *Pall Mall Gazette*, led to violent controversy and Stead's imprisonment. But the case of Eliza Armstrong identified the Salvation Army in the public mind. They not only converted drunks, but aimed to raise the lowest human beings from the depths of degradation. From this moment the Army rapidly developed its social relief. Their aim was no longer 'the deserving poor', but the poor: tramps, destitute men sleeping wrapt in newspaper under bridges, harlots, unemployed, discharged prisoners, deserted wives, the waifs of night life in cities. They opened the first depôt for food and shelter at Limehouse in 1888. Among the fish-stalls and potato-scraps and braziers and beer-taps and barrow-boys, where the Roman mass or the Anglican liturgy or the Congregational sermon were but a dream, the Army was strange but somehow at home. In 1890 Booth published his only famous book: *In Darkest England and the Way Out*. It was partly written by Stead. Darkest Africa? There was jungle in England, a tenth of the people living below the level of human beings. Booth produced a scheme of emigration, and demanded money. The public did not give him the £30,000 a year which he asked, but they gave him a total of £100,000 odd, not without controversy whether it was right to give money to utopian schemes organised by an uncontrolled authority.

By the end of the reign the Salvation Army was no longer in the ranting epoch. In June 1904 King Edward VII received Booth at Buckingham Palace. In 1905 Booth was given the freedom of the city of London, in 1907 the honorary degree of doctor of laws from Oxford university. It is a sign of the road travelled by Victorian society and religion. It is impossible to imagine what Oxford would have said to a proposal for an honorary degree to any of Booth's religious ancestors half a century before. The once-Anglican university was now willing to encourage all service to church and state, from whatever quarter. The most revivalist of sects was now willing to allow that a Christian had other duties to his neighbour apart from his duty to convert him. Yet in Booth's lonely old age (he lived until 1912) he sometimes wondered whether he had been right to allow the Army to divert its energies from conversion.[1]

The idea was seen to work. It was imitated in more staid denominations. H. A. Colvile was one of Booth's officers who left him because he could not reconcile his Christian mind to no sacraments. Bishop Maclagan of Lichfield, who was conservative, nevertheless made him the head of a Lichfield diocesan mission, and during the eighties he established centres of evangelism in the Pottery towns, and a small training home for his evangelists, who wore when on duty a brown cassock and a girdle. In St. Ann's parish in Nottingham there were a 'captain' and a 'lieutenant' who went out with a brass band to preach in the open and lead working people to a service with plenty of hymns at a mission-room.[2] The vicars of several parishes formed such bodies. A Church Salvation Army under a 'general' appeared at Wallingford in Berkshire. The vicar of Holy Trinity at Richmond issued members cards for a Church Gospel Army, and soon had ten captains under him, each with five to ten men.[3] At Bedminster by Bristol was a Church Mission Army, at St. Aldate's in Oxford a second Church Salvation Army.

In North Kensington there was a Church Militant Mission, enduring rotten eggs and the Skeleton Army with amusement, and run by one of the most remarkable and enchanting curates of the

---

[1] Begbie, ii, 88.   [2] CCR, 1886, 265; 1888, 629.
[3] George Surft to Tait, 23 January 1882; Evan Hopkins to Tait, 7 July 1882: Tait Papers 1882, A3.

Victorian age, Wilson Carlile. He was an evangelical with a belief in the methods of revival, a total loyalty to the parish system of his church, an absence of fanaticism, and a sense of humour.

Carlile slowly unified the groups of various parishes into the Church Army, which began its work under that name with a mission to Walworth in December 1882. Confined to parishes where the incumbent would let them in, the Church Army could not hope to rival the Salvation Army in expansive power. Carlile played the cornet loudly but badly in the slums of Westminster, and a crowd soon collected at the oddity of a clergyman with a cornet. In April 1883 he started a weekly paper called *The Battleaxe* but the name was soon made more sober as the *Church Army Gazette*. He did not at once become an institution. At the Carlisle Church Congress of 1884 he was almost howled off the platform because he urged that laymen should be allowed to lead prayers inside churches.[1] At the Congress a year later he was received with friendliness. He tramped hundreds of miles round the country persuading suspicious priests to allow the Church Army into their borders. By January 1885 he had forty-five evangelists and 4,000–5,000 active members, many of them converts. Bishop Mackarness of Oxford was a great stay and in February 1885 persuaded the bishops of his Convocation to a unanimous vote of approval. Lightfoot of Durham publicly backed it, and Fraser of Manchester. The name Army met much Anglican reproach, and for a time Carlile considered whether to drop it. Mackarness and Fraser advised him to keep it, and the name remained. But it steadily lost its military aura, and turned into an important instrument for training lay evangelists for parish work. A training house was created, first in Oxford and after 1885 in London where groups of fifteen or twenty men at a time lived in a house over a shop in the Edgware Road, studied the Bible and Prayer Book, and practised preaching in Hyde Park or among the slums. The movement was strongest in Lancashire, which produced about a third of the officers. All officers were required, like those of the Salvation Army, to be teetotal and not to smoke. By 30 June 1905 the Church Army had 1,034 trained workers. They earned in 1889 19s. a week; 5s. extra if married; 1s. extra for each child up to three; 2s. 6d. extra if the rent was more than 5s., and many hundreds of 'soldiers' were evangelists in their spare time after mill or mine

[1] E. Rowan, *Wilson Carlile and the Church Army*, 1905, 190, 196, 204, 224.

or shop. They adopted the plan of sending horse-drawn vans, or caravans, usually inscribed with texts in great capitals, round the villages. By the end of the reign about fifty of these vans were touring the English countryside.[1]

Missions were said not to be useful in country parishes, though Hay Aitken once preached a remarkable mission among several remote parishes of the Cumberland hills. Some Anglican clergymen were never reconciled to such missionary methods. Harry Jones, of St. George's-in-the-East, who knew as much about East London evangelism as any Anglican incumbent, continued all his life to dislike parochial missions. He could not give a clear reason. He confessed to an indefinable aversion. The methods stuck in his throat: 'insistent domestic visitation', 'importunate religious pressure', 'exceptional strain', 'whipping up' attendances—such was the language he used. He confessed that they could do good, but not that they were his way of doing good.[2]

7. THE SCHOOL

For the Church of England and the Roman Catholics, the day school was thought to be a necessary organisation in every parish properly organised; partly because the church had the duty to educate, and partly because it could thus secure education in the precepts and doctrines of the Christian religion.

Forster's act of 1870 created the national system of education because the religious schools could not cover the country. It provided board schools where the voluntary schools were inadequate or did not exist. For the first time in English history it allowed schools which did not teach religion of any kind to receive grants, for between 1833 and 1870 a school which received grants must teach either religion according to the denomination of the school or the Bible in the authorised version. And as the government inspector was no longer to inspect the religious instruction, the state seemed to stand a little further away from the religious instruction of the young.

This standing further away did not mean that the state was under pressure to become neutral between the Christian religion and other

[1] Rowan, 365.
[2] *Fifty Years*, 104. He publicly protested against the great London mission of 1874.

religions or none. Nearly everyone wanted the children taught religion because nearly everyone identified religion with morality. The Forster act provided that school boards could order religious teaching provided, under the famous Cowper-Temple clause, it was not teaching of the formulas distinctive of a particular denomination; made the conscience clause compulsory, and all religious teaching, even in denominational schools, to be at the beginning or end of other instruction so that the parent could easily withdraw the child on grounds of conscience; and enacted that where a school board did not teach religion, it must teach morality. Few intellectuals could conceive how it was possible to teach morals to children except in a religious context.

Forster declared in the House of Commons[1] that the enormous majority of the country—and he included 'all' the members of the Commons—agreed 'that the standard of right and wrong is based on religion, and that when you go against religion you strike a blow against morality'. Here is an exchange between the chairman of the Cross Commission and a witness from the London school board.[2]

... Must they not be taught religion?—I do not know about the religion; I should do my very best to moralise and civilise them.

Can you moralise them and civilise them without having religion at the bottom of it?—I should ... gather them into Sunday schools on Sundays.

... Would you not teach them religion, which is the basis of all moral teaching?—I should teach them to love one another.

Would you not go a great deal higher than that?—I am inclined to think that a scheme has yet to be devised that can influence these children religiously.

Later R. W. Dale asked the same witness:

Should we be able to give any real reverence to God himself if we had not an independent knowledge of morals apart from God?—I should think not.

The secretary of the National Society, Duncan, could not distinguish between moral and religious teaching. Matthew Arnold, who was consulted in his capacity as inspector of schools, admitted that he had seen no successful teaching in morals which was not also

[1] Hansard, cic, 1938, 14 March 1870.
[2] Mark Wilks, PP, 1887, xxx, 241, q. 48,822-7; 48,959.

teaching in religion, but he did not see why some way to teach morals apart from religion might not be discovered.[1]

In the few places where religion was excluded from the school, the teaching of morality was usually regarded as worthless, especially because no one knew how to do it. But some witnesses held that, though almost worthless, it was better than nothing.

Few school boards outside Wales decided against religious teaching.

Radical nonconformists did not wish the state to teach religion. Edward Miall and the *Nonconformist* wanted schools in which religion was not taught. Spurgeon and Samuel Morley wanted schools which taught 'undenominational' religion. The nonconformists were divided. But a secular system was impossible, politically and practically. Forster tried to imagine excluding the Bible from schools by act of Parliament, and knew it to be a proposal intolerable either to Parliament or to the general public. The religious dissenters who disliked religious teaching in schools took a different ground. They did not deny that morality was based upon religion. But they believed that religion should be, and could be, taught only by religious men. Further, they believed that to teach the Bible like a 'secular subject' lowered it in the eyes of the child, and that reverence would be lost. 'Religion', said Dr. Crosskey of Birmingham, 'cannot be taught in a school like grammar or arithmetic; the children associating it with their ordinary lessons will never feel its power; the Bible suffers by being made a class book like a grammar, and the giving of information about the Bible is confounded with religious teaching.' Visitors were disturbed to see children standing apart to be caned because they could not answer rightly on the history of Joseph.[2] But on many school boards the nonconformists aided the Anglicans and Roman Catholics in securing the teaching of 'undenominational' religion.

What was this undenominational religion? At one extreme Canon Gregory of St. Paul's cathedral believed that the government asked teachers to propagate a mingle-mangle or compromise. 'I thought', he said ferociously to one witness, 'the great recommendation of your system of religious teaching was that it was one in which nobody believed?'[3]

[1] PP, 1888, xxxv, 137.   [2] PP, 1888, xxxv, 146–7, 318, 322; cf. q. 41,123–5.
[3] PP, 1887, xxx, 252, q. 49,166.

At the other extreme Lord Norton (8 May 1888) proposed to the
Cross Commission 'that there is a common ground of simple
Christian truths, free from any special dogmata, on which all
Christians agree, which it is the bounden duty of a Christian nation
to make a part of national school instruction' (Ayes, 1: noes 13).[1]
Some said that board school religion was worthless; others said, 'no
good but better than nothing'. In Birmingham a teacher was
observed reading the Bible to 300 children, many inattentive and
uninterested.[2] Parents, it was widely agreed, valued religious instruction for their children even when themselves not markedly
religious.

The Cross Commission of enquiry (1886-8) had little doubt that
the religious instruction in voluntary schools was on average better
than the religious instruction in board schools, but the religious
instruction in board schools, *when sufficient time was granted*, was
good. And because the board schools slowly began to collect the
better teachers, the religious teaching in board schools was sometimes better, because more competent, than in voluntary schools. In
voluntary schools, however, the religious teaching was frequently
conducted not by the schoolmaster but by the clergyman, who was
usually a more educated man than the teachers in the school, but
might not have those gifts in experience which enabled him to
instruct a too large class in an elementary school.

The school boards were often excellent, and their syllabuses
admirable. The school board elections, in great cities, resurrected a
shadow of those vanished parochial contests over church rate. But
only a shadow. The elections were conducted according to a system
with transferable votes, which ensured the representation of minori-
ties; and therefore few majorities on school boards in the great cities
could be sure of continuous power. Rochdale produced a Roman
Catholic priest at the head of the first poll for a school board.[3] Most
school boards were elected to provide schools, and not as a means
of continuing a party campaign in the town. David Vaughan, the
vicar of St. Martin's, Leicester, became the chairman of the Leicester
school board, and after stormy meetings for three years refused to
serve again; yet men looked back upon his fairness as the source of
harmony in Leicester between board school and voluntary school.

[1] PP, 1888, xxxv, 487.   [2] PP, 1887, xxx, 103.
[3] Bright to Forster, 5 March 1871: Reid, *Life of Forster*, i, 527.

The first London school board was a group of distinguished men, with Lord Lawrence of India as its chairman. It decided for the reading of the Bible with instruction. Its years were troubled, however, because Canon Gregory and others attacked its building programme as unnecessary and harmful to the voluntary schools, especially in the borough of Finsbury. Manchester school board had a majority strong for religious instruction. The first Birmingham school board decided in the same sense; but its members were chosen by prudent tactics under the system of transferable votes, and the second election of 1873 gave R. W. Dale the leadership of a majority. They abolished religious instruction, and formed a Religious Education Society to provide voluntary teaching in the schools outside school hours. The plan for such voluntary teaching collapsed after six years, and a 'concordat' of 1879 established Bible reading for quarter of an hour at the beginning of the morning. The worst awkwardness of the school board era came from sudden changes in the majority on the board. The 'moderates', that is, those befriending religious education, captured Leeds in 1879 and brought in a strong syllabus of religious teaching. Three years later their opponents regained the control and undid what was done. In 1893 Athelstan Riley caused the London board to issue a circular strengthening the religious instruction, and three thousand teachers asked to be exempted from the duty of teaching religion. The 'moderates' won the election of 1894, though with a smaller majority, and the circular was quietly dropped.[1] Birkenhead strenuously acted to keep out the school board by covering the town with denominational schools. When the town was threatened with a school board in 1882, the people raised £17,000 to thwart it. Preston, Lancaster and Darwen were among towns which had no boards by 1886. Stockport dissolved its school board in 1879, amid protests, for the majority were afraid of unnecessary expenditure on board schools to the detriment of voluntary schools. Burnley, a largely nonconformist town, was nevertheless in favour of the voluntary system, and its board (1886) contained a Roman Catholic priest and two clergymen of the Church of England as well as the Baptist minister. Huddersfield had a strong school board and no religious instruction, but solemn worship at beginning and end.[2]

[1] Cruickshank, 63–4; A. W. W. Dale, *Life of R. W. Dale*, (1899), 475ff.
[2] PP, 1887, 116, 155, 178, 200ff, 231ff; 1888, xxxv, 139.

Forster's system brought competition between the board schools and the 'voluntary' schools, which the voluntary schools were likely to lose because they could not draw upon the rates. The standard of education rose rapidly, and with it the cost of equipping schools and paying teachers. The maintenance of the voluntary schools required great new sums of money, and only two denominations believed in the system sufficiently, or suspected undenominational religion sufficiently, to make the attempt: the Church of England and the Roman Catholics. The figures show it:[1]

Denominational Schools	Church of England	Roman Catholics	Wesleyan	British
1878:	10,910	693	572	1,436
1885:	11,794	850	554	1,387
increase %	9	22·6	−3	−3·4

Either the nonconformists knew that they could not raise the money or they were content with the religious instruction given in board schools. Some Anglicans were content with the board schools and believed that the church made a mistake in not throwing all its resources into the national system. Some experts in education believed this rivalry to be healthy for the country. Each system raised its standards to keep pace with or outpace the other, and therefore standards rose more rapidly than in a single national system.

The denominational schools found it difficult to keep their quality to the level of the board schools. They were often older and their buildings more dilapidated and their classrooms smaller. In 1887 the denominational schools of Huddersfield averaged 1 square yard per child, the Roman Catholic school of St. Patrick's had only 0·52 square yards, while the board schools of Huddersfield averaged 4·8 square yards per child, and the largest of them at Almondbury had 8·1 square yards. The merit grants awarded to Huddersfield during 1886 show that the board schools achieved 66·6 per cent excellent and 33·3 per cent good, while the denominational schools achieved 27 per cent excellent and 66 per cent good and 7 per cent fair.[2] Worcester held an enquiry into stipends elsewhere and produced this result:[3]

	Masters	Mistresses	Asst. Males	Asst. Females
Church of England	£120	£70	£68	£45
Board Schools	£148	£101	£99	£75

[1] Adamson, 364.   [2] PP, 1887, xxx, 706–7.   [3] PP, 1887, xxx, 642.

The figure did an injustice to the Church of England schools because so many of them were country schools, and rural expenses, as well as rural pay, were lower than town expenses and pay. Yet they show why teachers drifted from church schools to board schools. Average salary of principal teacher (1886):[1]

In Roman Catholic schools	£111 11 11
In Church of England schools	£120 3 3
In board schools	£148 3 9

Beware again of the circumstances that most board schools were in towns. But so were Roman Catholic schools. If however the average teacher in a denominational school had lower expenses, he probably must also teach (especially if he were a Roman Catholic) a larger class of children.

In London the voluntary schools retained a faint repute of superiority. Parents of a slightly higher social grade preferred them, if possible. In Huddersfield, where the buildings of the voluntary schools were deplorable, playgrounds muddy, sanitation primitive, class-rooms ill-ventilated, and obsolete stoves giving forth fumes as well as heat, the reverse was true, and the voluntary schools generally educated a slightly lower class than the board schools. But geography played some part, for the board schools were mostly in the town and the voluntary schools mostly outlying. In Leicester the alliance between board schools and voluntary schools was harmonious, and the voluntary schools reached an excellent standard.

In Edgbaston the Anglican school was started because the local high school for girls taught no or little religion. The new school was filled almost at once because (it was argued) parents wanted their children to be taught religion.[2]

The voluntary schools continued to rise till 1890 when they numbered 14,479 and thereafter declined. The task of raising money was too great. Each child educated cost 25s. 5d. in 1870 and 36s. 8¼d. in 1880 (that is, 34s. 7¾d. in voluntary schools and 41s. 11¾d. in board schools) and 39s. 5d. in 1886 (that is, 36s. 4½d. in voluntary schools and 44s. 11¾d. in board schools). The country spent, in all, about £1½ million on schools in 1870; more than £6¾ million in 1886. Voluntary subscriptions rose from £418,839 in 1870 to £742,597 in 1886, but it looked stationary. In 1870 there were over

[1] PP, 1887, xxx, 294.   [2] PP, 1887, xxx, 106, 146–52, 169.

12½ thousand of certificated teachers in England and Wales, in 1886 over 42 thousand.[1] But though the number of voluntary schools rose, they did not maintain their relative place in the system of education. In the country they maintained their supremacy, in the towns they lost ground steadily. The rise in numbers of children was nevertheless remarkable. In 1886 far more English children were receiving definite religious instruction than at any earlier date in English history:[2]

Church of England:	1870	6,382 schools	Average atten.	844,334
	1886	11,864 schools	Average atten.	1,634,354
Roman Catholic:	1870	350 schools	Average atten.	66,066
	1886	892 schools	Average atten.	180,701

This conclusion assumed that Church of England schools were teaching Church of England doctrine. But, the Church of England being tolerant and comprehensive, the teaching of some Church of England schools differed little from the religious teaching in many board schools.

By the middle eighties everyone saw that the voluntary schools could not compete much longer unless they received more aid from the state, and it became an anxious question how they could receive such aid without making concessions towards an undenominational system. The majority of the Cross commission of 1888 recommended a limited payment from the rates, but not even all the denominational leaders wanted it. Archbishop Manning, a member of the Cross commission, wanted it but he was not typical of the Roman Catholic leaders. Archbishop Benson of Canterbury was no friend to accepting aid from the rates. Such men could not see how you could accept money from the rates without receiving representatives of the ratepayers among the school managers. They believed that money from the rates must mean a weakening of control by a church over its schools. Not till Benson was succeeded at Canterbury by Temple in 1896 did rate-aid become acceptable to Anglicans. An act of 1897 permitted aid to poor schools. Balfour's controversial act of 1902 provided for payment from the rates for all schools and in exchange caused the local authority to be represented among the school managers, and among the teachers only the head teacher could be appointed by reason of his or her religious denomination.

[1] PP, 1888, xxxv, 72.   [2] PP, 1888, xxxv, 316.

The denominations, and especially the Church of England, continued to exercise influence through the training colleges. The figures for 1886 were:

	Students	%
Church of England	2,210	67·5
Undenominational	147	4·5
British	515	15·7
Wesleyan	227	7
Roman Catholic	173	5·3

Thus, though 47·3 per cent of children attended board schools, only 19·8 per cent of the students were at undenominational colleges.[1] These colleges practised no conscience clause, and their friends did not believe that they could do so without destroying the common religious life.

The Ragged School Union was founded in 1844. The ragged schools, established in slum areas by Lord Shaftesbury and others, for the purpose of instructing poor children in the three Rs and in the Bible, were 132 in number during 1870, with a total attendance of 23,132. They really aimed at taking waifs off the streets. The creation of board schools, and the quickened efforts of the denominations, made them unnecessary. Standards were lower and discipline worse. During the fifteen years after 1870 they sank to 24, with a total attendance of 3,062, and only 7 of these schools qualified to receive grants. The London school board took over many of the buildings by request; and buildings which were not taken over were sometimes used as night schools or Sunday schools. But the night schools, which also sought to educate waifs, declined for the same reasons as the ragged schools.

The rapid development of education, while it killed ragged schools, transformed night schools, and strongly influenced Sunday schools, had other important consequences for the churches. The teachers became a profession; and whereas Dr. Thomas Arnold thought that a teacher ought to be a clergyman partly because the people had confidence in a teacher only if he was a clergyman, such a proposition was already obsolescent before 1870, though traces of the heritage could still be seen, especially in public schools. But most important was the new power of the printed word. When everyone

[1] PP, 1888, xxxv, 310.

could read (everyone could not yet read) the sermon must change its function from that imagined by early Victorian theorists, who conceived it as the one regular instructor of the parish. It placed books in the hand of every worshipper and so influenced the modes of ritual and congregational worship, and allowing spectacular innovations in usage, for when a man could hardly read he could join only in what he knew already. Above all it made nearly everyone the reader of a newspaper, especially (among the working classes) a Sunday newspaper.

8. RITUAL

Some Anglican clergy believed that one important way to approach the working man was by a more elaborate ritual. The poor learnt more by the eye than by the intellect. Ashton Oxenden, whose tracts and sermons were much used in country parishes, looked back upon his early days of clerical work as a time when you did not need to wonder whether you were high church or low church, for you were simply a clergyman of the Church of England. But as he got older, life became more complex. For he needed to take position, whether he would follow this custom or that custom, if he visited another church. Oxenden's memory exaggerated the absence of difference in his earlier years. But it was true in good part. The customs of different parish churches began to divide more widely, especially after 1865, and a man accustomed to the usages of one church might more frequently feel a strangeness if he entered another church. This difference of custom was mostly due to more ceremony in those churches touched by the high church movement. But not only. Evening communions, which were disliked by many Anglican clergymen and laymen and repugnant to some high churchmen, became much commoner after 1865 (London churches with evening communion: 1869, 65; 1874, 179; 1879, 262; 1882, 285).[1]

Pastoral need was the chief reason for all these changes. The incumbent of St. Margaret's, Brighton, introduced evening communion on one Sunday in the month, and was asked by a critic why. He simply replied that he tried it as an experiment and found it succeeded marvellously.[2] And so, in different circumstances, reported

[1] Mackeson's *Guide to the Churches of London and its Suburbs*, 1866-94.
[2] PP, 1867, xx, 820. The incumbent was Edmund Clay.

high churchmen who used some ceremonies to which their people were not accustomed. One man was criticised for inviting the congregation to come forward to receive their communion with the words, 'Behold the Lamb of God . . .'; for such words were not to be found in the Prayer Book, and were therefore illegal. He took the view that this was a more reverent mode of drawing the attention of the congregation than that which prevailed in the church of his upbringing; where the vicar would beckon to the people with the words, 'Dear people, you can come up now.'[1]

By its nature liturgy could never be static, for all the innate conservatism created by hallowed associations. The evangelical and Tractarian movements and the whole Victorian quest for reverence, elevated the Book of Common Prayer as a vehicle for worship. They sought to make its use more congregational, and more evangelistic, to prevent it resembling a dialogue between parson and clerk, to help the simple worshipper, slowly being educated, no longer to sit in dumb respectful silence on the parish bench, to use it effectively, not only where the congregation was familiar with it, but in mission halls of cities where the people were rather an assembly than a congregation, and were familiar with no forms of worship whatsoever.

In the Victorian age few wanted a revised Prayer Book. The high churchmen, without whose assent no revision was possible, were convinced that revision merely meant an act of Parliament to alter rubrics against them and to make the Church of England less comprehensive. Pusey near his death said, 'Our only safeguard, under God, is to keep our Prayer Book as it is.'[2] And many of those who did not regard it as protection, were attached to it in their hearts and would not countenance change. The introduction to the marriage service had brutal language about the purpose of marriage and man's carnal appetites. Gentle Victorian ladies sometimes disliked the language as indelicate, and clergymen were known to use their discretion in omitting words. But the first year in which I find a serious proposal to alter the phrases was the year 1902.[3] This was not because the Victorians had a sub-Christian doctrine of marriage. But the Prayer Book was a possession to them almost like the authorised version. Shakespeare was sometimes indelicate, but however you might bowdlerise him for children, you did not think of redrafting.

[1] E. R. Wilberforce, in PP, 1906, xxxiv, 178.   [2] CCR, 1888, 297.
[3] But see Jasper, 14, 51, 85.

It was all the worship that the Anglicans had and was all the worship that most of them wanted to have.[1] But in the rich varieties of Victorian religious life, these same formulas must be used in many different contexts.

The development of ritual was caused by (1) the taste of the age, (2) the widespread belief that this was the way to draw in working people, (3) the growing congregationalism of town parishes, and (4) the strong Anglican desire for due obedience to authority.

We need only remember what happened to the furniture of the Victorian drawing-room to understand what happened to the interior of Victorian churches. The taste of the middle-class house-wife liked her room to be well-furnished, even elaborately furnished, with strong simple chairs or settees but with many little ornaments on tables or in cases. A Victorian drawing-room gives a later generation a sense of clutter, and the same is true of the furnishing of many Victorian churches. They liked colour, perhaps frescoes on the walls, mosaic in the pavement, coloured hangings at the altar, carved re-redos behind the altar. It was natural that religious sentiment should desire to ornament churches in conformity with the better taste of the generation. And the dress or posture of those conducting services was closely related to the total impression made by the furnishing of the church. For example: when bishops wore cassocks, they normally wore black cassocks. But violet or purple cassocks had not been unknown, for the evangelical Bishop Ryder of Lichfield and Coventry preferred to wear violet. In 1868 it was noted that three bishops followed Ryder's custom: Sumner of Winchester, Wilberforce of Oxford, and Ellicott of Gloucester and Bristol, of whom Sumner and Ellicott were far from being high churchmen. Or again, Bishop Hamilton of Salisbury used a pastoral staff. He was the first of the Tractarian bishops, and therefore the use caused comment. But about 1867 at least three bishops accepted gifts of such staffs, Lonsdale of Lichfield (ruefully, for he was not fond of ceremony), Claughton of Rochester, and Wilberforce of Oxford who was in trouble for the usage. The laity liked the symbol. They desired that their bishops should carry such an instrument of office when performing duty in church, and gave them to more and more bishops. A bishop was hesitant to accept lest he give offence, but

---

[1] The Act of Uniformity amendment act 1872 provided for shortened forms of morning and evening prayer, but only allowed them to be used on weekdays.

usually preferred not to refuse lest he give offence. Lightfoot of Durham refused a staff at first and accepted it later. The laity found it a historic and meaningful symbol. Such little changes, as purple cassocks and pastoral staffs, are typical of the way in which the usages became more elaborate, because they felt appropriate to the aesthetic judgment of many lay worshippers. A majority of bishops were not eager to carry staffs and a majority of bishops ended by carrying staffs. This was the truth in the assertion (only true in part) that ritual development owed more to laity than to clergy. Samuel Wilberforce visited Manchester and was told that in that city laymen were showing a love for ritual; and wrote to the Archbishop of Canterbury to say that, 'There is, I believe, in the English mind a great move towards a higher ritual.'[1]

There was evidence that the town labourer was attracted to churches where the ritual was more elaborate. The evidence was not plentiful because the town labourer was not attracted to churches at all. But some evidence showed, first, that the labourer was repelled from the old bald liturgy because it was dull and uncongregational; and secondly, that he came in noticeably larger numbers where he found ornament and colour and movement. In the argument over architecture and ornament of Roman Catholic churches, Pugin pleaded for magnificence since thus the labourer would be taken out of his dreary slum environment and taught by eye and ear. In the sixties some Anglican pastors argued the same. St. Barnabas, Pimlico, famous as a ritualistic church (though in 1867 it had no incense, nor vestments, nor wafer-bread), attracted a great many poor worshippers, not to the morning service but to the early communion on Sunday and to evening prayer on Sunday; and had an attendance at *weekday* evening service of 100 to 150.[2] It was so crowded with the poor that they separated the sexes, and justified the introduction of another custom. St. Alban's, Holborn, under A. H. Mackonochie became in the late sixties the most notorious of the ritualistic churches, The parish had many Roman Catholics, including a large number of Irish immigrants. One of the churchwardens, by trade a stationer, said that he agreed with the elaboration because he saw its impact upon the poor (again, not at the high service at 11 a.m. but early on Sunday morning and on weekdays).

[1] Ashwell-Wilberforce, iii, 189, and note; Wilberforce to Longley, 16 December 1865.   [2] PP, 1867, xx, 754.

'I was not a high churchman', he said, 'before I joined. I joined it as a moderate man, but all these things have been forced upon me. Over and over again clergymen of great eminence have said to me, "If you want to stir up the lowest classes, you must have this kind of services".'[1] This opinion kept being offered. You ought to have more ceremonious services because more of the poor will come if you do. Not everyone agreed. The Church Association employed an agent to count the poor at St. Alban's, Holborn, and he reported eight persons of the working class in a full church on Sunday morning and ten persons of the working class on Sunday evening;[2] and on Wednesday evening eight poor men in a congregation of eighty-odd. Nevertheless, men of much experience maintained the opinion. And their opinion was reinforced by a measure of identification between the use of such ceremonial and the work of a few among the best pastors in London, like Charles Lowder at St. Peter's, London Docks, whom the poor came to revere. It was also reinforced by the curious origin of the Church of England Working Men's Society which started as a group of men determined to protect St. Alban's, Holborn, from its assailants.

Thirty-five years later the census-makers surveyed London and asked whether Anglo-Catholic churches were more successful among the working men. They found that it was true only in occasional parishes. Roman Catholics mainly held the poor, but did they hold them because the priests were ceremonious or because the poor were Irish? A few Anglo-Catholic churches held the poor though they were not Irish (St. Peter's, London Docks, in 1902: attendants in morning, 884, of whom 584 were children under fifteen). The census-makers confessed that such churches succeeded with working men, but argued that it was due not to the ritual but to the quality of priests who used the ritual. Mackonochie, Lowder, Dolling, Stanton, Suckling, Russell, Wainright, came through to the imaginations of the poor. Charles Booth the sociologist believed that of all Anglicans the high churchmen were more successful among the poor, not because of their mode of worship, but because their lives were more evidently self-denying, their enthusiasm more forceful. 'At a little distance', wrote Booth sympathetically (vii, 51), 'it is easy to feel contempt for imitations of Rome, to laugh at church millinery, or scoff at "men in coloured garments sprawling before the altar". But

---

[1] PP, 1867, xx, 838.   [2] PP, 1867, xx, 842.

coming close, we find beneath all this a true spirit of religion, and as such it is undoubtedly recognised by the people, even by those who care nothing for the doctrines, and to whom the ceremonial is idle show. . . . Nowhere in London can such devout behaviour and such apparent intensity of religious feeling be seen as in the congregations which gather in the high church.' Yet Booth did not think that in the end such services could win the world of men.

Another intelligent observer, C. F. G. Masterman, believed that the working man accepted elaborate ceremonial with resignation, and found the ornaments and the processions inexplicable; that he did not mind what they did in church, for he respected them because they went down and lived among the poor and demanded justice for the working man.[1] A working man from an Anglo-Catholic parish told Charles Booth (vii, 35) that they would fight for their parson against Protestant agitators and interrupters, but did not care whether the parson 'stands on his head or his heels before the altar'. This was not the evidence offered in the earlier days of the revival of ceremonies. In the sixties it was almost an axiom that only a more elaborate service fitted the needs of the urban poor.

Some observers attributed a part in this development to the way in which the parish system developed in towns. In London, and in a few other big cities, some congregations were always gathered from far and wide and not simply from residents in the parish, according to the power or reputation of the preacher. But the old parish church of a town, or of a place within London like Stepney or Whitechapel, still meant something to the inhabitants, even if they were non-conformists. Under the various church building acts, and the drive for church extension, the Church of England divided the old parish into districts of 4,000 or 5,000 people, and built new churches for them. But the new church was unknown to the people of the districts, they had no sense of historical association with it; and many of them were surprised if they were told what parish they now belonged to. The old parish church still had a measure of geographical meaning in relation to the inhabitants of the district, whereas the new church had as little geographical meaning as a nonconformist chapel. The new vicar gathered a congregation. But this congregation might come from within or without the parish. Harry Jones, the excellent incumbent who raised up St. George's-in-the-East after its

[1] Mudie-Smith, 216.

nadir, noticed that nearly all the ritual controversies took place over district churches. There the incumbent gathered laymen, the laymen were like-minded and came there because they were like-minded. Almost the only case of an old parish church with a ritual controversy was St. George's-in-the-East itself, and the battle there was so embittered because the congregation was more miscellaneous. Harry Jones exaggerated the importance of this, but there was at least a truth in the argument.[1]

With a few important exceptions, country churches hardly ever had ritual troubles until near the end of the century—though of course many country parishes argued whether the psalms should be chanted or the choir should be in surplices. The church was the parish church. The influence of a miscellaneous population, and the incumbent's pastoral need, combined to make for moderation.

A touch of the same congregationalism which Harry Jones observed in London can occasionally be seen in a country town. At Durham, St. Nicholas was low and St. Oswald was high. Many in St. Nicholas went to St. Oswald and vice versa, and the vicar of St. Oswald (J. B. Dykes) claimed that no one had a practical grievance.[2] At Frome W. J. E. Bennett, with five curates, had elaborate ceremonies because he had evidence that they drew the poor. The church held about 1,000 and was full on Sunday evening and about half-full on Sunday morning and had twenty communicants every day. He had no prayers except from the Prayer Book and no incense and no reservation of the sacrament because he thought that the Church of England did not permit them though he wanted it to permit them. But in Frome there were two other churches and each of the three followed different usages, which might be called high and moderate and low. Bennett and the other two incumbents therefore came to an agreement. Any parishioner of any of the three parishes might attend whichever church satisfied him. They agreed that each clergyman could visit 'his' sick even if they lived in the parish of one of the others. Bennett did not think that his own usages were the sole usages possible for good clergymen in the Church of England. He did not think uniformity at all services of the Church of England to be in the least desirable. Indeed, he declared, he thought the Act of Uniformity 'the cause of the whole

---

[1] Cf. H. Jones, *East and West London*, 51–59.
[2] *Life of J. B. Dykes*, 118, 312.

of the misfortunes of our church'[1] and would have liked to see it repealed.

Not only was the Church of England becoming more varied in its customs, but a few of its members began to think it good that it should so become. And part of the cause was the growth of the towns, which made each parish less important as geography and more important as a congregation, and therefore allowed each worshipper to choose.

Deep in the historic consciousness of the clergy of the Church of England—dependent no doubt on the history of their church during the seventeenth century—was a strong desire to find and obey lawful authority. This desire was strengthened by the Oxford Movement. And lawful authority seemed to demand more ceremony than they were then using: especially at the time of holy communion, lighted candles on the altar and the traditional vestments of the celebrant. For these were ordered by the ornaments rubric of the Prayer Book. That no one lit candles or wore vestments showed only with what laxity the church behaved. In the early sixties several churches introduced vestments, and in most of those churches no one objected. In several churches, like Frome (1865) or St. Matthias, Stoke Newington (1865), the vestments were gifts from some of the laity to the vicar. In other churches, as in Wymering (1864), they could be said to be gifts from the laity, but in fact the vicar caused the gift to himself. Any substantial change might cause disturbance of mind among some worshippers. But more people were disturbed by the introduction of chants for the psalms, as happened in the fifties and sixties, than were disturbed by vestments. One of Keble's former curates, who was vicar of St. Matthias, Stoke Newington (C. J. Le Geyt), said that he had never had a protest, and that all the lay pressure upon him favoured more elaborate ceremonial. Even some bishops who had no use for ceremony themselves could not see harm in whatever ceremonies within reason a parish wanted. On 23 June 1865 Bishop Sumner of Winchester sanctioned the use of incense on five festivals a year at Christ Church, Clapham. When afterwards incense became a centre of controversy, people found it hard to believe that so evangelical a bishop could have sanctioned so unevangelical a usage and attacked the letter as a forgery.[2]

Here, for comparison, is the practice of two very different London

[1] PP, 1867, xx, 816.   [2] PP, 1906, xxxiv, 156.

churches about 1867: Islington, a church with a famous evangelical tradition, where the vicar was Daniel Wilson, and St. Andrew's, Wells Street, the first district church created under Peel's building act, where the vicar was Benjamin Webb, a Tractarian and formerly one of the founders of the Cambridge Camden Society. St. Andrew's was famous as a church of elaborate ritual.

Islington: surplice scarf and hood for prayers; black gown and cassock for preaching. No change in ritual for ninety-five years except that the previous vicar (Daniel Wilson senior) introduced holy communion on Sundays at 8 a.m., but so few (30–40) came that it was now altered to evening and got 120 communicants. The Athanasian creed was always read according to the rubric. He wore no vestments at all when baptising or communicating in a private house. There was disturbance in the parish when Bishop Blomfield required preaching in the surplice and the offertory, but Daniel Wilson remonstrated with the bishop, and he did not insist.

St. Andrew's, Wells Street: had offertory, flowers, mixed chalice, coloured altar frontals, cross and candlesticks. But the candles were only lit when light was needed. No vestments. Members of the congregation offered Webb vestments but he refused. Why no vestments, he was asked, if the rubric orders it? 'My congregation have no desire for it, so far as I know. It is a matter of Christian charity, expediency and prudence only with me.' The church held 250 and was always full and he needed a second Sunday morning service as overflow. He had a professional paid choir, aided by volunteers, about 140 communicants on a Sunday (500–600 at a festival), holy communion every Wednesday and sometimes on Friday. The congregation joined in the singing, 'too much sometimes'.[1] He always used the Athanasian creed according to the rubric. No one had ever protested against his ceremonial. Webb thought that it would be fatal to restrict by law the present liberty of the Church of England. Like Bennett at Frome, he was no advocate of strict uniformity.

St. Andrew's, Wells Street, St. Alban's, Holborn, St. Barnabas, Pimlico, St. Peter's, London Docks, St. Matthias, Stoke Newington, were all district churches. All five began their life as churches with an elaborate service, nobody needed to go, nobody could be disturbed by sudden changes of old custom. All five were carved from old

[1] PP, 1867, xx, 737–45, 765–73.

parish churches, three of which had a very plain service. All five believed that they offered better worship for everyone and attracted more poor among their worshippers by adopting this elaboration. All five got working men among their worshippers, though fewer at Holborn and at Wells Street. All five were supported by strong bodies of like-minded laymen, except that one churchwarden at St. Alban's, Hubbard, who gave the church, disapproved of the incense and vestments there used. When middle-class or upper-class visitors entered these churches, their attitudes varied. Some were horrified at popery; some found the effect theatrical and distasteful; and some were exalted. Dykes the musician first attended such a church on a visit to Brighton. 'I felt a strange mixture—delight and sorrow through all—delight at seeing such a *glorious* service in the Church of England, and such signs of life!—and sorrow at comparing all this with our shortcomings in the north. . . . I have never enjoyed any services so much in my life. They have moved me more than I can tell; I found myself constantly in tears.'[1]

For though the ritualistic churches began by aiming at the working man, they succeeded especially among the middle class. In the sixties their leaders talked much of the artisan's interest in high worship. Over thirty years later a religious census of South London proved what was not expected, that the middle class, believed to be puritan by tradition and conservative by habit, attended them in large numbers. Across South London, from St. Stephen's Lewisham (1,443 attendants) to St. Peter's West Norwood (1,429 attendants) ran a belt of high Anglican churches, most of them flourishing. Evidently the movement nourished the devotional and aesthetic instinct of the educated more than it attracted the interest of the uneducated. The same appeal to the educated is proved by the kind of nonconformist church which experimented in more formal ceremonials and prayers and music at the same period. But lest we think of it as solely middle class, here is one of the lesser known ritualist churches, St. Katherine's Rotherhithe. It started in 1880 as a mission tent among the dockers, and sailors, and prostitutes, and workers at Peak Frean, in the midst of row upon row of little houses. With the help of Bishop Thorold of Rochester they finished the church in 1882, and it started as a ritualistic church, so that the congregation which gathered never knew another form of worship. Twenty years later (vicar, E. M.

---

[1] *Life of J. B. Dykes*, 98: Easter 1864, St. Paul's, Brighton.

O'Hara Lee) it had a guild of men with 127 communicants, some of whom once expelled the Protestant agitator Kensit by force from the parish, a large men's institute, a large institute for boys of 15–18 years, a gymnasium twice a week, a Sunday school with 600 boys on the books (attendance from 57 to 76 per cent), a temperance society with 270 adult members, an orchestra of young men, a military band for use at outdoor services, clubs for cricket and football, and a penny bank. When the next vicar (at the request of the bishop as the congregation believed) dropped the use of candles in procession and incense, the congregation twice petitioned for their restoration.[1]

To themselves the ritualists seemed to be adopting customs harmless, edifying, devotional and warranted by the authority of the Church of England. Before long these usages met the Protestant feeling of the country, and became a focus of a political and legal debate which outlasted the century.

In the eye of reason the problem was small. Out of the London churches of which information was accessible in Mackeson's *Guide*:

	1869	1874	1879	1882
Number of churches	588	745	864	903
Choir in surplices	114	265	375	476
Vestments	14	30	33	37
Incense	8	14	13	10
Candles on altar	not known	not known	43	45
Eastward position of celebrant	not known	74	214	270

The early problem, then, was how to stop ten or so churches in London, and a few more elsewhere, from using incense; and from fourteen to forty churches in London, and more elsewhere, from using vestments—if it were first agreed that it was necessary to stop them whether they offended members of the congregation or not.

But the later problem was more extended and more insoluble. Public controversy over ritual, and the needs of the age, increased the number of churches with the more elaborate ceremonial.[2]

[1] In the same way when at last a vicar came to Frome who wanted to undo what Bennett had done he ran into fierce opposition from the congregation, PP, 1906, xxxiv, 18–19, 215.

[2] PP, 1906, xxxiv, 100; *Tourists Church Guide*, 1902. The *Tourists Church Guide* was first published by a clerk in the employment of the English Church Union. It was taken over by an official of the Union, Colonel Hardy, who loved statistics, until the Union discovered that it was useful as a guide also to brawlers.

	1882	1888	1894	1901
Number of churches ('mostly' in England and Wales)	2,581	3,776	5,957	8,689
Vestments	336	599	1,370	2,158
Incense	9	89	250	393
Candles on altar	581	1,136	2,707	4,765
Eastward position	1,662	2,690	5,057	7,397

Most of the churches with vestments and/or incense lay in the south of England. Northern bishops agreed that their northern peoples were not attracted. Westcott of Durham thought that, with the exception of the clergy, 'the Oxford Movement had nothing more than an academic hold at any time over the north of England', and Bishop Eden of Wakefield assented.[1]

This problem had already a history, entangled with fear of popery and of Irish immigrants, of papal aggression and of Puseyites. It was charged emotionally, both for those who wanted ceremony and for those who did not. The simple way, it might be thought, was to test in the courts whether this or that practice, which offended the visitor or the parishioner, was lawful in the Church of England. On this ground a few bishops, and many low churchmen, and some who were not low churchmen, were content if one of the ritualist clergymen, like Mackonochie of St. Alban's, Holborn, was prosecuted in the courts. In November 1865 Protestant churchmen formed the Church Association, with the object of resisting innovations in ceremonial by legal action. And for the first ten or twelve years devout and high-minded evangelicals believed in the policy of taking clergymen to court as the only effective way of determining what was the law of the Church of England.

This way, which looked simple and harmless, was neither simple nor harmless. On the one side the Protestant laity of the country were not satisfied with its results. On the other side the alleged culprits were not willing to recognise the authority of the church in the court of final appeal to which the case must go.

The Protestant tradition of the country ran deep in the people's mind. Any innovation of usage was coming to be suspect. The epidemical difficulty of this whole controversy consisted in the formularies of the Church of England being broader and more comprehensive than a lot of laymen wanted them to be. Bishops were

[1] PP, 1906, xxxiv, 79.

often sent charges against clergymen who did nothing but what the Prayer Book decreed. When a Hampshire incumbent appeared in his cassock in the road, the squire (a very troublesome squire) was horrified and protested that 'from his peculiar clothes down to his heels, you could not distinguish whether he had a coat and trowzers on'.[1] When a religious brotherhood wearing a habit appeared in public a retired admiral wrote about 'phantoms', and how the pleasant roads were darkened, 'by these associations of the Inquisition'.[2]

When the clergyman at Kirkley in East Anglia paused in the service for private prayer, it appeared in the record of a spy as 'he appeared to be engaged in secret devotions over the elements'.[3] The formularies of the Church of England were not at all compatible with the formularies of the Church of Rome. But they permitted voluntary confession. They permitted (if they did not order) vestments. They did not condemn the teaching of a real presence in the sacrament. The mind of the Protestant laity could not be satisfied with such comprehensiveness. An appeal to the courts merely showed what liberty was possible within the formularies. Therefore, if they were to be satisfied, they wanted to alter the law by a new act of Parliament. They were concerned with purity of doctrine. And some of them believed in a high church conspiracy to turn the Church of England into a Roman Catholic Church. The Church Association declared that it aimed 'to counteract the efforts now being made to pervert' the teaching of the Church of England 'on essential points of the Christian faith, or assimilate her services to those of the Church of Rome'. What were the limits of the Church of England? Were they what was laid down, or were they what was popularly assumed to be laid down? As Lord Shaftesbury was reported to have said, 'If the rubrics allow it—well then, away with the rubrics.'[4]

Queen Victoria, essentially a broadminded person, nevertheless felt the same; that the Church of England could not be allowed to remain with its existing breadth. In her retreat at Balmoral she came to love the presbyterian services in the little church at Crathie. On 2 November 1873, attending the communion, she could not forbear

---

[1] PP, 1867, xx, 799; the incumbent was George Nugee.
[2] PP, 1867, xx, 857: Admiral Sir Lucius Curtis, Bart.
[3] PP, 1906, xxxiv, 247.   [4] *Life of J. B. Dykes*, 312.

to join and stepped quietly among the communicants. Some of the congregation did not observe her, so humbly and unobtrusively was it done. When strict English churchmen expressed their displeasure, a few of them in terms which were less than understanding, she decided that the Church of England was being ruined. She had hardly met a ritualist, but from her retreats at Balmoral or Osborne her imagination inflated their power and made her fearful. Ten days after the Crathie communion she wrote to Dean Stanley. 'She thinks a *complete Reformation* is what we want. But if *that* is *impossible*, the archbishop should have the *power* given him, by *Parliament*, to *stop all* these ritualistic practices, dressings, bowings, etc., and everything of that kind, and *above all*, *all* attempts at *confession*.'[1] In short, though she knew it not, she wanted a new kind of high commission or star chamber to prevent clergymen from actions which hitherto the law was not known to forbid. The queen represented a widespread feeling in the country, that if the law of the Church of England was found to be so comprehensive, that law must be narrowed. Where orders could be given, they were given. In June 1865 the war department ordered army chaplains to use a surplice.[2]

This desire to keep the Church of England pure in doctrine complicated the work of the Church Association. They declared their especial wish to counter 'the idolatrous adoration of the elements in the Lord's Supper'. Nothing could be further from the minds of Mackonochie or Bennett, or all those who held with Pusey on the meaning of the sacrament, than idolatrous adoration. Some of those who introduced vestments said that they found a doctrinal significance in them and wished to emphasise the sacrificial nature of the sacrament. Others who introduced them saw no doctrinal significance, and introduced them because the laity asked and the Prayer Book ordered or allowed.

For there was a real grievance, which was partly concealed in being taken up into a national campaign. A new district church, where the eclectic congregation never knew anything else, was one thing. An old parish church, with prevailing customs, was another. And if vestments (for example) were legal for Mackonochie, they were legal for every vicar in the country who decided to put them on, whether his congregation was disturbed or not. It was reported

---

[1] Queen Victoria to Dean Stanley, 13 November 1873; *Letters of Queen Victoria*, II, ii, 290–1.   [2] Hansard, clxxx, 731.

that at Northmoor Green in Somerset (population 800) when the vicar started wearing vestments, the congregation sank to three,[1] and on a Good Friday morning tipsy interrupters threw eggs at the priest's back. A layman might have worshipped at, even been a churchwarden in, a church all his life and suddenly find an innovation which he thought to be shocking. For thirty-eight years Andrew Adams was a member of the choir at Headington, and left nine months after a new vicar introduced vestments, incense and other changes.[2] A sidesman served at Haggerston for forty years and at last left because he could not bear the last changes.

The village church showed how the authority of the layman faded and left the clergyman in sole charge. The layman as a citizen had no longer constitutional power because church rates were abolished; and the layman as churchman was not yet given constitutional power because no one knew how to give it. The town parish, and indeed the nation, witnessed the same weakening of lay authority; in the town parish for the same reasons as in the village, in the nation because Parliament could no longer legislate for the church without the assent of Convocation (the Public Worship Regulation act of 1874 was the last such act) and yet the church had no other effective legislature. We enter the most clerical age of English life, clerical in the sense that the parson had more individual power in his parish church than ever before or after. The symbolic limits of this 'clerical' age may be dated to begin with the abolition of church rates in 1868, and to end with the parochial church councils measure of 1921. These limits are symbolic because long before 1868 the individuality of the Anglican parish and parson was safeguarded by the patronage system and the freehold; and long after 1921 the parochial church council could influence a troublesome parson only by staying away from his church. But the dates represent an important period of sovereignty within the parish church, and of a constitution which on its better side allowed experiments in worship of momentous value to the devotions of the Church of England, and on its worse side allowed the exceptional and petty dictatorships in which a parson drove away his congregation by novel ceremonies.

The ritualists could not accept the system of courts as settling the issues. If Parliament made vestments illegal by an act, they would disobey, for in their eyes a non-Anglican Parliament had no more

[1] PP, 1867, xx, 827; *Times*, 22 April 1867.   [2] PP, 1906, xxxiii, 1028.

right than the emperor of Japan to determine their clothes in church. The highest court of appeal was the judicial committee of the privy council. And since the Gorham case, and the case over *Essays and Reviews*, the high church party, or many of them, regarded the judicial committee as a state court which did not bind the church. The ornaments rubric of the Prayer Book ordered vestments. If the judicial committee declared vestments illegal, the authority of the church must be preferred to the authority of the state and the Prayer Book must be obeyed. And they were supported in this viewpoint by many moderate Anglicans who had no especial liking for ceremonies, but could not see why Parliament or any other body should restrict the liberty of the Church of England and narrow its comprehensiveness. The evangelicals, and indeed everyone with a pastoral sense, had as much reason to fear a rigid conformity as the high churchmen. Gladstone poured scorn on the bill of 1874 as designed to make the clergy 'march, like the Guards, in the same uniform, with the same step, and to the same word of command'.[1] In refusing to recognise the authority of the judicial committee they were not only a few unusual or truculent men. They were vocally supported by canons of St. Paul's cathedral and professors of divinity, and silently sustained by the sympathies of a handful of bishops. Their excesses did not command the assent of serious and sober men. Their resistance to the cure of such excesses received that assent.

The opposition to the ritualists was formidable enough to menace the established church. It was fanned by the occasional folly, such as the inexperienced enthusiast was liable to perpetrate, as when the vicar of Haydock in Lancashire carried a pig's head in procession at the harvest festival;[2] yet when Hugh Price Hughes, the eminent Methodist, who experimented in ceremonial permissible within his own denomination, made the mistake of having live sheep bleating under the pulpit during a harvest service, no one took the matter up in Parliament. It was fanned by graver feelings; the steady belief that the high churchmen conspired to make England Roman Catholic, in an age when *no popery* was still powerful in emotion; and above all, by the use which political enemies of the established church could make of the controversy.

[1] Hansard, ccxx, 1874, 1381.
[2] *Times*, 12 and 21 September 1868; *Life of H. P. Hughes*, 241.

The worst passions over ritual were raised in 1867–74 and in 1899–1903 (interrupted by the Boer War). The first of these dates coincided with the agitation over Irish disestablishment, the embittered controversies over the place of the Church of England in national education, and the *no popery* aroused by the Vatican Council. The second coincided with debates over Welsh disestablishment and Irish home rule, and above all the agony over the place of the established church in the Balfour education bill. In the political controversies across the floor of the House of Commons the state of the Church of England was a fair argument, and the dispute over ceremonies became a make-weight within larger and more momentous disputes.

The speakers could get carried away and magnify shadows, and give the world the impression that the difficulty was not how to prevent a small number of persons from unusually dramatic acts in church, but how to save the Church of England from overthrowing the Reformation. Lord Shaftesbury said in the House of Lords[1] that 'the very fate of the Church of England is trembling in the balance'. It happened not to be true that the fate of the Church of England was trembling in the balance. But it was true, or in part true, that Shaftesbury spoke for the Protestant feeling of the country. Even the two archbishops told a Protestant deputation in June 1873 that the church was in danger from a *considerable minority* of clergy and laity who desired to subvert the principles of the Reformation.

The bishops were anxious to prevent Parliament passing any act to regulate what went on inside churches, because they knew that it would not be obeyed and might cause schism. Therefore they normally side-tracked attempts at legislation into commissions or committee; the earlier disputes into the ritual commission of 1867–70; the disputes of 1877–82 into the ecclesiastical courts commission of 1881–3; the disputes of 1899–1903 into the royal commission on ecclesiastical discipline of 1903–6. The one act which passed Parliament was the Public Worship Regulation act of 1874, advocated by most of the bishops as better than other possible bills which would pass if this did not.[2] It cannot be said that any of these

---

[1] Hansard, cxcii, 1868, 333.
[2] For the Public Worship Regulation act, see P. T. Marsh, *The Victorian Church in Decline*, 159ff. In the eyes of the bishops it was a better bill than other possible bills wanted by the queen or some of the laity because it did not alter the law of worship but only (and not very significantly) the machinery for enforcing it. Archbishop Tait

endeavours slowed or speeded the development of ceremonial, but they saved the Church of England by preventing precipitate action based upon emotion or prejudice.

There is no evidence that the occasional judgments of the judicial committee, and the occasional debates in parliament, had a marked influence upon the changes of custom in worship; though the tone of some of the debates with their attendant publicity may have acted as a spur to brawlers in churches. Disraeli described the Public Worship Regulation act as intended to put down ritualism, but the statistics show that the increase in the criticised practices continued without a pause. The judicial committee condemned vestments (with dubious and controverted reasons) in 1871 and 1877 but the statistics show that the condemnations made no difference whatever. The important consequence, as we shall see, was the development in the authority of the bishop, as the guide of the clergy amid disagreements, as the maintainer of a reasonable measure of agreement in modes of worship, and as the safeguard for a reasonable liberty in liturgical experiment.[1]

The nonconformists likewise were less afraid than their fathers of liturgy. They struggled, sometimes with success, to improve their music. A few advocated surpliced choirs or wanted more ministers to hold university degrees. Thomas Binney at the King's Weigh House was the earliest leader to work for good chants. The advocates of liturgical prayer met strong resistance from those who feared formalism and loss of liberty. Old Wesleyan congregations continued to use the altered Anglican liturgy to their contentment, and

---

shared some of the blame with Disraeli for representing it to the general public as a bill to put down ritualism. But he had the defence that in wanting the bill he carried with him nearly all the other bishops. The bill shortened the procedure before the case reached the provincial court; amalgamated the two provincial courts of York and Canterbury under one judge; protected the clergy a little more by giving the bishops no right to suspend while the suit was in progress; and made a certain provision for costs. But the act did not abolish the procedure under the Church Discipline act of 1840 which thus became an alternative procedure.

[1] Some new ritual customs observed before the end of the century: kneeling during the reading of the epistle; kneeling down individually after giving money at the offertory; wiping the chalice with a cloth, on medical grounds. But at Bitton near Bristol a cloth was used throughout the reign. The curate of St. Giles, Cambridge, used a cloth during the fifties. Perhaps more important was the revival by Lord Radstock of unction for the sick. Selwyn of Lichfield was the first to use Christian names when confirming.

their example influenced others. Chapels which adopted set prayers (without eschewing extempore) found it a relief both to the minister and themselves. With their extended education they were more sensitive about improprieties, or rambling, or repetition in extempore prayer. In January 1887 the presbyterian church at Hampstead introduced prayers from the Prayer Book, and the innovation was approved. At the same time a Baptist minister in Manchester argued to his colleagues in favour of reading prayers, especially the use of a general confession and thanksgiving. Less frightened by formality, they perceived the congregational nature of much in liturgical worship, and wished to diminish that dominance of the minister in worship which was more appropriate to a less educated people. A Methodist chapel in Southwark, which used the liturgy, voted to drop the use when they found their numbers dwindling. As a result of this decision many of the congregation left, and they had a difficult discussion on whether to restore it. Methodists, whose Sunday schools were excellent, began to hanker after some form of confirmation. Hugh Price Hughes was a high church Methodist, in the sense of wanting liturgy and solemnity in Methodist services. He held a retreat, and founded a small Methodist sisterhood, and even planned a kind of monastic brotherhood. Oddities were seen to be oddities and discarded, and more enrichment, more liberty, less formalism, and a more congregational service were the consequences. These changes made a difference to the general tradition of free church worship, and yet its form continued to be the old free form of hymns and prayers and sermon. There were three stages: first, the minister supplementing his extempore prayers by reading prayers; second, a printed sheet or sheets so that the people might join with the minister; and finally, at the end of the century or after, a denominational commendation for forms of prayers. Newman Hall printed a form of Congregational service in the early sixties. John Hunter printed services with responses for Salem Chapel in York, and after 1882, when they were published as *Devotional Services*, they were adopted or adapted in many other churches.[1] He stated his intention to be variety, to save public prayer 'from becoming a one-man utterance'. *Devotional Services* has been described as the first dignified Congregational liturgy in English, modern and yet not afraid to draw upon the Catholic tradition. Even if ministers did not use such forms,

[1] Horton Davies, iv, 65, 69, 221ff; L. S. Hunter, 48, 912.

they were likely to take more trouble in preparing 'extempore' prayer.

The King's Weigh House started a good choir, and a good choir produced anthems. The Wesleyan chapel at Blackheath in 1885 had Tallis's responses and chanted canticles. Thomas Binney tried to interest readers in the liturgical heritage of the Protestant churches of the Reformation. At first he was like Dale and Spurgeon in preferring lay costume, lest the minister seem priestly or professional. But later he decided that a distinctive dress was right and took to a gown and cassock and bands ('I confess I don't like to see a man go into a pulpit as an auctioneer goes into his rostrum, or as a lecturer ascends his platform')[1] and preferred kneeling as a posture for praying. He introduced the chanting of psalms, not metrical. He began to argue for the use of the Christian Year.

The use of unfermented wine is first found about 1873 as part of the temperance campaign, the use of separate cups at the Lord's Supper, on medical grounds, not until after the turn of the century.

Resistance to innovation was not rare. Presbyterians found difficulty over admitting organs. Two congregations, at Liverpool and Warrington, introduced organs and found themselves condemned by synod after synod, until at last (1870) the convenience and beauty of the organ gained the day. But as late as 1882 61 Presbyterian congregations in England (out of 279 who replied) had no musical instrument with their worship and 218 used mainly metrical psalms and not hymns. The desire among Wesleyans or Congregationalists did not escape criticism from members of their denominations who compare these innovations with those of the Anglican ritualist.[2]

The desire for liturgical form did not lead to development of sacramental life. Baptism was usually regarded as a kind of dedication, the Lord's Supper as a memorial. The roots of nonconformist life lay in the little democratic chapel with its lay preachers, and therefore the innovations of Londoners, whether liturgical or sacramental, passed for the most part over their heads. Free church worship retained a strong continuity through the century, powerful in its directness, reality and simplicity. They might build cathedrals, but never forgot the upper room.

[1] Horton Davies, iv, 225, 235.   [2] Horton Davies, iv, 107, 251.

CHAPTER VI

THE BISHOP AND DIOCESE

I. THE PATRONAGE OF THE CROWN

NOTHING could dissuade the queen from the belief that she was 'head' of the Church of England. From childhood she was accustomed to it. Her servants in the palace accepted it among themselves. She had a sense of responsibility for its welfare, and especially in that matter which concerned her prerogative, the choice of its leaders. She kept herself informed on matters concerning the Church of England, knew most of the leading clergy and enjoyed conversations about them, their books, their preaching and their churchmanship. She welcomed opinions, and in such circumstances was easy to talk to, and persuaded her advisers to say rather what they thought than what they supposed her to want.

Her first adviser was always the Dean of Windsor, since by his common sense Gerald Wellesley gained such influence with herself and her husband. He was never known to the public, but when Archbishop Tait of Canterbury was wrongly believed to be dying, Gladstone resolved to nominate Wellesley as his successor and obtained the queen's leave.[1] The queen recognised that the prime minister must initiate the nomination, and that she could only exclude from particular posts, or suggest names for general consideration. But over the deaneries of Windsor and Westminster, and to some extent over the canonries of those royal peculiars, she claimed a special interest. Prime ministers recognised these special interests though they did not always welcome her mode of expressing them. Gladstone gave way to her when he wanted Edwin Palmer to be Dean of Westminster and she wanted G. G. Bradley. She offered a canonry of Windsor without asking the prime minister, then Disraeli, and the prime minister took it as a command. Therefore

---

[1] Gladstone to the Duchess of Wellington, 24 September 1882; Stratfieldsaye Papers.

when Dean Wellesley died in 1882, she made[1] direct offer of the deanery of Windsor to Canon Connor of Winchester cathedral not even using the prime minister as an intermediary. It was not a very good choice, for Connor was not well suited to be the queen's private adviser.[2] This direct exercise of crown patronage was not acceptable to Gladstone. He challenged her right, and insisted that it was his constitutional duty to advise before nomination, even with the deans and canons of Windsor. The queen conceded the theory, but continued to get her way in practice. When Connor died after only a few months as Dean of Windsor, she wanted Randall Davidson, who was only thirty-five years old. Gladstone said that he was too young. But, he afterwards wrote, he was 'estopped by the heavy artillery she was pleased to bring into the field, which reduced my little point to dust and ashes'.

With the aid first of Wellesley and then of Davidson, she knew something about the subject before the suggestion of a prime minister reached her. If a post was vacant she would ask the dean of Windsor to describe the sort of man who ought to fill it. Sometimes she asked for suggestions of names, but Davidson at least did not encourage her in naming individuals lest she seemed to trespass upon the function of the prime minister. She sometimes suggested names to the prime minister, but rather as persons generally worthy than as persons fit for a particular post. She had a shrewd sense of the kind of men who were wanted, and the different needs of Manchester compared with Wells.

When the prime minister suggested a name she telegraphed it (in code) to the dean for his opinion, and often received a long memorandum.

Some prime ministers did not like the influence exerted upon her by deans of Windsor. In her early days without the aid of the Prince Consort, she argued with Palmerston over the matter and won. The argument added a new phrase to constitutional history. In April 1864 Palmerston baldly submitted for the see of Peterborough, in succession to Dr. Davys, the name of Dr. Jeune. The queen objected to Dr. Jeune, on the reasonable ground that he had lately become Dean of Lincoln, and suggested two other names. Palmerston suspected this of being unconstitutional influence. 'He regrets to find', he wrote to her on 29 April, 'that your Majesty has some objections

---

[1] *Letters of Queen Victoria*, II, iii, 227, 236; 188; 341–6; 421; II, ii, 440–5.
[2] Bell, *Davidson*, 76.

to Dr. Jeune's appointment, and a Preference for other Persons not
named by Viscount Palmerston. . . . Other persons, if they had the
duty of advising your Majesty might . . . in the crowd find others
who might in many respects be equally fit, but the responsibility of
advising your Majesty must rest with somebody, and it happens to
rest with the first Lord of the Treasury.' Dr. Jeune was appointed.
But early in July, the same year 1864, the queen wrote asking that
more than one name should be submitted to her for the rectory of
St. Margaret's Westminster. 'Although', Palmerston wrote on 5
July, 'this in some degree implies a Reference of a Recommendation
by one of your Majesty's responsible advisers to the judgment of
your Majesty's irresponsible advisers in such matters, Viscount
Palmerston, would submit the names . . .' and he submitted two
names. The queen did not submit quietly to the rebuke. The queen
'is much surprised at the tone of Lord Palmerston's remarks, for he
can never pretend that the Sovereign has not the right, as everyone
else has, to ask anyone she chooses about any person who is recommended. . . . The Queen makes it a rule, as the Prince did, to make
enquiries in various quarters . . .' (7 July 1864).

Prime ministers continued not quite to like these 'irresponsible
advisers', though no one after Palmerston protested. They kept
silent upon the subject, as though they were not supposed to know
these advisers to exist. The only prime minister who openly talked of
the communications between the queen and Randall Davidson was
Lord Rosebery. 'He', said Davidson, 'made no bones about it.'[1]

The older and more experienced she grew, the more formidable
she became. During the last thirty years of her life and especially in
the last twenty, she did not hesitate to veto nominations which she
thought, after advice, to be bad. She was sometimes persuaded by
her advisers into accepting nominations which she did not like, and
which could not be said to be good, but which could not clearly be
argued to be bad.[2] When the queen tried to exercise a veto, the most
pertinacious of her prime ministers was Gladstone, the least pertinacious Lord Salisbury.

In this capacity the queen became an important safeguard to the
interests of the Church of England. She was a kind of jury, of perfect
integrity and unpalatable frankness, before whom prime ministers
must justify their nominations. An ignorant prime minister found

[1] Bell, 165.   [2] Cf. Davidson's memorandum in Bell, 164–5.

that the queen was better informed than he, and speedily diminished his ignorance if he wanted to carry his point. An informed prime minister still needed to explain himself if he were proposing some-body unusual or unknown. Disraeli was the most ignorant of her prime ministers, though he respected the Church of England even more perhaps than he respected the Christian religion. When arguing with the queen, he would send out cries for help to his secretary. 'Ecclesiastical affairs rage here', he once wrote from Balmoral. 'Send me Crockford's directory. I must be armed'; or again, 'Send me down tomorrow the clergy list. I don't know the names and descriptions of the persons I am recommending for deaneries and mitres.'[1] Disraeli resembled Palmerston in this, that his chief adviser in this was not a clergyman but an eminent evangelical layman, Lord Cairns. The best informed of her prime ministers was Gladstone, who had a wide acquaintance among the clergy, kept his reading abreast of the theologians, and was as concerned as any good layman for the wel-fare of the Church of England. Gladstone took as his secretary E. W. Hamilton, son of Bishop Hamilton of Salisbury. Hamilton was the first example of those secretaries who made it a special duty to keep the prime minister informed on ecclesiastical affairs.

The queen's influence had other consequences. It slowly brought the Archbishop of Canterbury more and more into taking a direct part in the system. Formerly prime ministers consulted archbishops as they thought fit, and sometimes informed them only as a matter of courtesy. Such absence of consultation continued, but became less frequent. For if the queen doubted, she was likely to ask what the Archbishop of Canterbury thought about the name that was being suggested. And if the queen firmly objected to a name, even the strongest of prime ministers did not quite like to carry it without the backing of the Archbishop of Canterbury. Gladstone wanted Liddon to be a bishop, and the queen believed that Liddon would be a calamity as a bishop. Even Gladstone felt that he could not nominate Liddon against so severe an opinion unless he had the support of Archbishop Benson of Canterbury. And when he found that the archbishop thought the queen nearer to being in the right, he spent some time in arguing to the archbishop why he was right, and at last brought him over to say that he would support the nomination.

This influence of the archbishop varied according to the time and

[1] Monypenny-Buckle, v, 58.

the man and the prime minister. When Davidson himself became archbishop, it became a permanent feature of the system. But many anticipations may be observed in the last decades of Queen Victoria's reign, and were in the first instance due to the queen's interest and information.

The queen also helped to move the reason for the choice further away from politics. Taught by her husband, she long disliked merely political appointments in the church, and had the effect of bringing to bear the influences of two men, the Dean of Windsor and the Archbishop of Canterbury, who equally disliked political appointments. Other reasons for the non-political bishop helped them. Palmerston had already tried to choose bishops who were good for the pastoral work of the church, without concerning himself much over their politics. After 1872 the ballot meant that a man's political party need not be known. And bishops were not now so important to prime ministers either as votes or as political levers. Disraeli wrote to Lord Derby in 1868 that 'Bishoprics, once so much prized, are really graceless patronage now; they bring no power'.[1] Yet Disraeli was the last prime minister to be perfectly open, at least in conversation, that his ecclesiastical patronage was politically important. 'Another deanery!' he wrote to his secretary at a time of political crisis, when a dean died. 'The Lord of Hosts is with us!'[2] He was sensitive to the circumstance that many members of the Church of England voted Conservative, and still wished his ecclesiastical policy to fortify his party. Dean Wellesley said: 'He regards the church as the great state engine of the Conservatives.'[3] Disraeli wanted Conservative clergymen and nothing but Conservative clergymen. So long as he was in power there was danger that the political and party aspect of a bishop, which the queen and Lord Palmerston had been trying to remove, would reappear in a form as bad almost as in the days of Lord Melbourne.

Gladstone made sure that some clergymen of the Liberal party were made bishops. So long as there were two great parties in the state, it was indeed desirable that those parties should be represented among the bishops. On the other hand Disraeli, as one who cared less than Gladstone for those things, was often ready to content the

[1] Monypenny-Buckle, v, 73.
[2] Disraeli to Corry, 9 October 1868: Hughenden Papers, B/XX/D/105.
[3] Wellesley to Queen Victoria, 30 January 1875: Blake, 507.

queen on matters of less importance. More than once he accepted direct suggestions from her. And one of these was of the highest importance. In 1868 he wanted several others before Tait for Archbishop, and pressed one of them, Ellicott of Gloucester and Bristol, upon her. He had arguments against Tait, especially that he was an enthusiast, and that no Archbishop of Canterbury ought to be an enthusiast. At last he gave way, and nominated Tait, though Tait was more liberal in politics than he wished. He was so kind to the queen in these matters that she preferred his conduct to that of Gladstone. That was not the view of Dean Wellesley. And yet it was a stage of constitutional history when a prime minister nominated as Archbishop of Canterbury a man whose politics he did not quite like.

Among the nominations of Gladstone were members of the Liberal party, like Frederick Temple; and one, Mackarness of Oxford (1869), was even described as a Radical. Partly perhaps for this reason, one or two of Gladstone's men were exceptional in their influence among working men. Fraser of Manchester (1870) was the bishop who above all others exerted power among the working men and not only because in Lancashire more than any other county the Church of England was a church of the working classes. But Gladstone's nominations became less political after the first year or two of his ministry.

Benson used to point out with pride that he became Bishop of Truro under Disraeli and Archbishop of Canterbury under Gladstone. He regarded himself as a living proof that political motives ceased to guide the choice of bishops. Gladstone indeed, provided that he could have some Liberal bishops, was very willing to have Conservatives if they were good men. Both the bishops whom Gladstone sent in succession to the see of Lincoln (Christopher Wordsworth, 1869, Edward King, 1885) were staunch and life-long adherents of the Tory party.

Lord Salisbury, when he took Disraeli's place, followed Gladstone rather than Disraeli. Frederick Temple was made Bishop of Exeter (1869) because Gladstone needed him in that moment of crisis as a strong member of the Liberal party. Gladstone nominated him for London (1885), not so much because he was a Liberal in politics as because he was liberal in divinity. Salisbury, not without qualms, named the old man for the archbishopric just because of his stature. Salisbury also nominated Westcott to Durham (1890) and E. S.

Talbot to Rochester (1895) though both men were far from being Conservatives.

It may be said that after Disraeli's death (1881) politics almost ceased to count in the choice of bishops, at least until the earliest years of the twentieth century. But to this rule there is one great exception: the nomination of John Percival to the see of Hereford in 1895.

Percival, headmaster of Rugby, wrote a letter to the *Times* (printed 4 May 1894) denouncing the bishops for their hostility to Welsh disestablishment. In January 1895 Lord Rosebery shocked the queen by wanting to nominate Percival to the see of Hereford. The queen, who had been moderate about Irish disestablishment, was not moderate about Welsh disestablishment. She determined to veto Percival 'as she will on no account appoint a Disestablisher'[1] and asked Davidson how to do it. Davidson replied advising that an absolute refusal was impossible, and that the queen could only raise the doubt whether such a prelate could be acceptable to the clergy of the diocese. Rosebery persisted; the diocese contained thirteen Welsh parishes, and he would never appoint a clergyman who favoured establishment. Davidson held that the queen could not resist indefinitely, partly because Percival was a good man, and partly because to say 'I won't have anyone in favour of Welsh disestablishment' would be like saying 'I will only have bishops from one political party.' So Percival was consecrated; and the queen was right in one of her doubts, for he never became quite acceptable to the clergy of the Hereford diocese.

The case of Percival led to an important argument between queen and prime minister. The queen accused Rosebery of being markedly political in his appointments. Not only the new Bishop of Hereford, but new deans of Hereford, Durham, Ripon and Winchester, and new canons at Westminster and Canterbury, were all members of the Liberal party. Rosebery hardly denied the charge. But he attacked her sharply, saying that she reserved her criticisms for the appointments made by a Liberal prime minister. To this the queen had a crisp reply. She needed only to point to her previous record. The last Conservative prime minister had nominated Dr. Westcott, and at least three other prelates not of the Conservative party (Creighton, Perowne, Davidson).[2] This argument shows how the

---

[1] *Letters of Queen Victoria*, III, ii, 468.
[2] *Letters of Queen Victoria*, III, ii, 498; Bell, *Davidson*, 242ff.

idea of choosing a bishop for political reasons became disreputable, and in part thanks to the queen.

This had the effect of freeing the bishop from the need to vote on controversial matters of politics. Shortly after the end of the reign, the bishops were corporately attacked, in an old-fashioned manner, as always likely to vote on the Conservative side. Davidson, then archbishop, had no difficulty in showing from voting records the inaccuracy of the charge. Under Salisbury's administration he voted against the government eight times out of eleven, and on two of the other occasions some Liberals voted with the government.[1] Where the political issue concerned Irish or Welsh disestablishment, or some kindred subject, the bishops were generally found to vote for the Conservative party. Where the issue concerned a social question, as more often towards the end of the century, they were usually found voting with the Liberal party.

The queen exerted further influences on the choice of bishops. She disliked evangelical names or high church names, as she regarded both parties as extremists. She longed for moderate men. Following her husband, she longed for learned men, whom she was also likely to identify with moderate men. She sometimes undervalued pastoral gifts.

Nothing could be less just than the comparison of a dissenter in 1898, who said of someone that 'he was as ill-read as a bishop'.[2]

In Stubbs, Creighton and Lightfoot, the English bench had three of the leaders of European scholarship. The queen's policy of promoting learned men failed under Lord John Russell because the men were not available. The Church of England now profited from the development of European scholarship and the reform of the English universities.

Whether or not the policy were right, the queen could take much credit for it. Disraeli had no interest in scholarship. Salisbury was certainly no enthusiast for Creighton, and Westcott would never have been a bishop if the queen had not pressed his name again and again. She got him his bishopric dead against the reluctance of Salisbury, who was a Conservative prime minister and rightly suspected Westcott of being half a Socialist and of not being earthbound.

[1] Hansard, clxxiv, 1907, 4.
[2] W. Robertson Nicoll of Henry Drummond, Darlow, Life of Nicoll, 163.

The queen was less good about pastoral men. When the name of the evangelical Champneys, one of the best slum pastors of the century, was suggested to her as a possible dean of St. Paul's, she dismissed him with absurd injustice, as 'an insignificant low churchman'.[1] Like her ideals of liturgy, her ideals of pastoral care were formed in the thirties and did not keep pace with the times. She was oddly suspicious of clergymen who tried to do good to the poor. When the Dean of Windsor visited one of her coachmen in his illness, she did not quite like it.[2] She advised Davidson not to visit too much. Archbishop Benson wrote in his diary (28 February 1885), 'The Queen, says Davidson, can't understand why the clergy should go fussing about the poor or servants. . . . The servants are very good people—why can't they be let alone?' She suspected visiting the sick, or instructing the poor, of being 'clerical' or even 'sacerdotal'.

Thus she was less equipped to choose pastors if they were not also learned. During the years after Palmerston, she appointed many excellent pastors. But they were suggested to her by others. She did not guide the church towards this kind of excellence, as she guided it towards scholarship and towards freedom from political entanglement.

She approved neither of evangelicals nor of Tractarians. When Davidson became her adviser he was formally instructed that neither of these categories was to be promoted. She wanted moderate churchmen. 'It is by such appointments alone', she told Disraeli in 1874, 'that we can hope to strengthen the very tottering fabric of the established church. The extreme evangelical school do the established church as much harm as the high church.'[3] In the circumstances of the day she would have excluded half the best men in the Church of England if she had been able to carry out so consistent a policy, unhampered by Disraeli or Gladstone or Salisbury.

Palmerston nominated several evangelicals. For the thirty-six years of the reign after his death, only five leading evangelicals were nominated to bishoprics. Disraeli, who for political reasons favoured evangelicals because they were also low churchmen, made a few evangelical deans or canons.[4] When men complained that the

[1] *Letters of Queen Victoria*, II, i, 539.   [2] Bell, *Davidson*, 90.

[3] *Letters of Queen Victoria*, II, ii, 342.

[4] Thorold of Rochester (1877) was Disraeli's only evangelical bishop. Gladstone nominated J. C. Ryle to the new see of Liverpool in 1880, perhaps in fulfilment of an expectation already created by Disraeli. In 1885 Gladstone, with three simultaneous

evangelical party was not receiving its proper share of crown patronage, Davidson replied that it was difficult to find suitable evangelicals. 'The younger generation', he wrote in 1890, 'is not overstocked ...'[1]

The Tractarians had not received any crown patronage before 1865; for the only Tractarian bishop, W. K. Hamilton of Salisbury, came quietly to the see because the queen did not know him to be Tractarian. The leading Tractarian of all those who remained Anglican, John Keble, died in 1866 without having received any hint of preferment from his little country parish, not even an honorary canonry. Thus the great change of the later years was the opening of crown patronage to the Tractarians. Thereby the devotional and pastoral force within the Oxford Movement began at last to dominate a main part of the Church of England.

Pusey was properly left in his Christ Church hermitage. But after him all the younger Tractarian leaders were given office.

William Bright, tutor of University College, Oxford: professor of ecclesiastical history, Oxford, 1868 (Disraeli)

George Moberly, till 1866 headmaster of Winchester, long excluded: Bishop of Salisbury, 1869 (Gladstone)

Samuel Wilberforce, Bishop of Oxford: not quite a Tractarian, but regarded by many Tractarians as their chief on the bench: Bishop of Winchester, 1869 (Gladstone)

H. P. Liddon, Pusey's faithful disciple: canon of St. Paul's, 1870 (Gladstone)

R. W. Church, Newman's intimate: dean of St. Paul's, 1871 (Gladstone)

J. B. Mozley, former Tractarian editor: regius professor at Oxford, 1871 (Gladstone)

J. R. Woodford, vicar of Leeds: Bishop of Ely, 1873 (Gladstone)

E. King, Principal of Cuddesdon: professor of pastoral theology, Oxford, 1873 (Gladstone)

(Disraeli prime minister, 1874–80)

G. H. Wilkinson, London vicar: Bishop of Truro, 1883 (Gladstone)

---

vacancies, consciously chose an evangelical, a high churchman, and a broad churchman; and by this impartiality E. H. Bickersteth became Bishop of Exeter. All three were good bishops. The queen was content, especially with Thorold. Perowne of Worcester and Moule of Durham were nominated by Salisbury.

[1] Davidson to F. Gell, 11 March 1890; Bell, 178.

H. Scott Holland, student at Christ Church: canon of St. Paul's, 1884 (Gladstone)

W. Stubbs, historian: Bishop of Chester, 1884 (Gladstone): of Oxford, 1888 (Salisbury)

E. King (as above), Bishop of Lincoln, 1885 (Gladstone)

E. S. Talbot, Bishop of Rochester, 1895 (Salisbury)

The table shows what a difference was made to the Church of England by the arrival of a prime minister who was a disciple of the Oxford Movement.

This acceptance of Tractarians helped the Church of England. They had felt the long exclusion of their leaders from office as a sign of disfavour and distrust, as though they must be near Roman Catholics and not loyal to their church. Their energies were now turned into the main stream of Anglican life and development. They had the most powerful preacher of the day in Liddon of St. Paul's; the most respected of all Victorian clergymen for wisdom and breadth of mind, R. W. Church as Dean of St. Paul's; the two most sensitive Anglican theologians of the age, James Mozley and Henry Scott Holland; the most eminent historian of the English constitution and of establishment, Stubbs; the first stable religious order of men in the Cowley Fathers, founded by R. M. Benson in 1865 and widely approved by the end of the seventies;[1] and two saintly bishops in Woodford and Edward King. By 1885 the Oxford Movement was at last attaining the summit of its influence in the Church of England.

The queen could not resist this new development because Gladstone was irresistible and because good men, even great men, could not for ever be excluded on the ground that they were very high churchmen. She was never in danger that one of them would be suggested for either of the archbishoprics. But one of them she did help to exclude from an English bishopric, H. P. Liddon.

Even before Pusey's death Liddon was the leader of the Tractarian party, in the public eye. His sermons commanded congregations of 2,000 and more, in his turn at St. Paul's. He stood out as the defender

---

[1] The community of St. Paul was founded in 1889, originally for work among seafarers. It was at Alton from 1895. The Community of the Resurrection was founded by Charles Gore at Pusey House in 1892, and was at Mirfield from 1898. The Society of the Divine Compassion was founded by J. G. Adderley at Plaistow in 1894. There were two half-attempts at a Benedictine community, by Ignatius Lyne from 1863 and by Ailred Carlyle from 1896 but neither attempt was stable.

of orthodoxy against the Biblical critics, especially against the Germans. In private life he was delightful. And yet he seemed so extreme. He fought so hard for all the outworks. He told Archbishop Tait that he would resign his clerical office even if they reduced the number of occasions on which the Athanasian creed was recited in church. After he determined that Archbishop Tait was not to be trusted, he refused to go to meetings or services where the archbishop presided. He was full of melancholy about the future of the Church of England, and especially the future of the university of Oxford, and his public gloom did nothing to strengthen religion in either church or university.

Many who guessed the inside story were inclined to blame the queen. But Liddon helped because he could not reconcile himself to the idea. Gladstone wanted to put his name forward to the queen in January 1885, and Liddon begged that his name might not go forward. It is clear from his diary that, moved because his friend King accepted Lincoln, he would have been ready to accept Salisbury that summer, but it was not offered to him. There is as yet no evidence that the queen had anything to do with this absence of an offer, though one high church newspaper, the *Guardian*, held her responsible and came near to rebuking her.[1] Three years later there was talk of the see of Oxford, but nothing happened, for the queen said that he might 'ruin and taint' all the young men, like Pusey.[2] Finally in the last months of Liddon's life Lord Salisbury persuaded the queen that Liddon ought to be offered the see of St. Albans, though no one expected him to accept. He refused, and was dead that autumn.

The queen liked broad churchmen. Her ideal clergyman was Dean Stanley who was broadest of the broad. But she made no attempt to insert the new liberal divinity into the bench, merely because it was liberal. She was pleased when Temple became Bishop of Exeter and London, not particularly pleased when he became Archbishop of Canterbury. She went for learned men and expected them to be liberal, and knew too little theology to worry her head over what was liberal divinity in the technical sense. She wanted Kingsley to be canon of Westminster. James Moorhouse was a very liberal divine and became (1886) Bishop of Manchester, but the queen seems to have known nothing about his divinity. William Boyd Carpenter was another very liberal divine and became Bishop of

[1] G, 85, 1205.   [2] *Letters of Queen Victoria*, III, i, 427.

Ripon (1884) but the queen valued him rather as a moving preacher and courteous pastor than as a theologian—which was the right way to value him. When the queen died, the liberal divines on the bench numbered five or six.[1] But she had not pushed for this school of theology, except so far as she was right in her belief that learning went together with liberality. She was a little indignant with Lord Salisbury when he accused her of pushing, lest it be thought 'that we were rationalising the church. A very extraordinary idea I must say.'[2] Curiously, of all her prime ministers Salisbury was the most antipathetic to broad churchmen. He had a masculine religion, an aversion to metaphysics, an affection of soul for the sacramental teaching of the high churchmen and a dislike of 'pigeon-holing' in religion. And of all her prime ministers Rosebery promoted the largest number of broad churchmen. But the queen and Davidson seem to have believed that he promoted them not because they were liberal in divinity but because they also happened to be Liberal in politics.

The queen's exercise of patronage was valuable to the Church of England. The system worked well. Her veto excluded the occasional folly or eccentricity of a prime minister. She was a formidable barrier for the sake of the interests of the Church of England as she saw them. Occasionally prime ministers were indignant at her interference, like Palmerston. Occasionally they lamented at the trouble caused them.[3] The system was not without trials to those working it. But it evidently worked well, for it produced a bench of bishops more eminent in wisdom, learning, personality and holiness of life, than the Church of England had hitherto seen.

It might have been expected that there would be protests against a system under which the prime minister exercised so powerful an influence in the choice of leaders for the church. And some men objected. The slum-priest Charles Lowder believed it an anomaly. Colin Lindsay, the first head of the English Church Union, declared publicly that of all men the prime minister was the most unfit to be entrusted with this duty.[4] (It happened to be the age of Palmerston when he was speaking.) A few church reformers, almost invariably

---

[1] Temple, Moorhouse, Boyd Carpenter, Westcott, Ridding, H. E. Ryle ?
[2] The Queen to Archbishop Benson, 1890: *Letters of Queen Victoria*, III, i, 635.
[3] Cf. Stephenson, *Life of E. S. Talbot*, 95.
[4] CCR, 1861, 64; 1876, 68.

strong high churchmen, or strong broad churchmen, protested against the system. But they were never representative, and never commanded more than a little support among either clergy or laity. The striking evidence of willingness in the Church of England to accept the system was its ready application to bishoprics newly founded and endowed by private subscription. Most Anglicans could conceive no other system that would be acceptable. They observed systems of election working in some of the colonial churches, but did not wish to reproduce them in England.

They were content, partly because all Victorian prime ministers were members of the Church of England, and three of them were devout members (new criticism developed when a non-Anglican, A. J. Balfour, who was a Scottish presbyterian, became prime minister in 1902); partly because most Anglicans valued the union between church and state and regarded the system as part of that union; and partly because in relation to democratic prime ministers the church was seen to have important safeguards.

A bishop-designate must be elected by the chapter and consecrated by other bishops. The second safeguard made little difference. Eight bishops, including men of weight like Wordsworth of Lincoln and Selwyn of Lichfield and Magee of Peterborough, formally protested against the consecration of Temple to the see of Exeter, and it made no more difference than the still larger protest against Hampden earlier in the century. The real safeguard was election by the dean and chapter. For although a prime minister did not need that election in law, and although a refusal to elect would make the chapter liable to the penalties of praemunire, no one could conceive praemunire being applied; and if a chapter refused, and the prime minister simply appointed by letters patent, the situation of the bishop in his diocese would have been more than uncomfortable. It was not in the public interest, nor in the interests of a political party, that its head should cause scandal by an act of patronage. Public opinion, as well as the queen, was a safeguard to the church. From time to time members of a chapter abstained from voting for the nominated man. At Exeter the sub-dean and five prebendaries voted in a strong minority against Temple. At Lincoln in 1885 the Archdeacon of Lincoln and the dean abstained from appearing at the election of Edward King, but perhaps the dean abstained because he was ill.[1] From time to

---

[1] Lincoln Dean and Chapter Minutes, 20 March 1885.

time laymen thought the election to be dangerous and proposed a bill in Parliament to abolish the *congé d'élire* and with it the election. The leaders of the church preferred to keep the election. On one such occasion they appealed to Gladstone for his advice, as one who had been responsible. Gladstone told them that in his experience the *congé d'élire* was a safeguard to the church, and that prime ministers, being aware of the need that bishops-designate should be elected, felt a check to their freedom. Gladstone thought it a salutary check, and did not want it abolished.

2. INCREASE OF BISHOPS

The clergy felt that there ought to be more bishops.

Some bishops—Wilberforce of Oxford, Denison of Salisbury, Lonsdale of Lichfield, and others—did more than their predecessors and raised the expectation of what a bishop could do. He could look after his ordinands better, make their ordination a solemn occasion in the cathedral,[1] go to a parish church to institute its incumbent instead of instituting him at a brief ceremony at his house, get to know many of his clergy and their work, become a leader of his diocese at public meetings, take part in parochial endeavours, even lead a week of missionary preaching. The old clergy had not expected to know the bishop, but the younger clergy hoped to know a little of him and were not content with a bishop who was only a voice behind a legal secretary. They thought of him as a leader whom they would like to consult, and from whom they might receive not only admonition if they offended, but encouragement and stimulus.

The most important occasions for the parish were confirmations. Men of long experience contrasted the reverence of the smaller confirmations begun by Bishop Denison with the vast irreverent crowded confirmations of an earlier day. Mackarness had seen a multitude surging round the doors of St. Paul's while the pickpockets

---

[1] Philpott of Worcester (died 1892) seems to have been the last of the old-fashioned bishops about ordination. About 1856 Wilberforce started to make a present to ordinands of the New Testament or the Bible according to whether they were being ordained deacon or priest, with a personal inscription. Before this it had been placed in the hands at the service but afterwards returned to the archdeacon. But even Wilberforce does not seem to have presented them regularly until the late sixties, for he gave none at the Advent ordination of 1865, and there was at least one Bible short at the Advent ordination of 1866. Selwyn always gave them at Lichfield from 1868, and in 1870 the Bishops of Ely, Carlisle and Rochester gave them.

worked, and could remember standing at the door of a cathedral in the provinces (probably Exeter) as he listened to relatives who charged the church and the bishops of the scandal of keeping them out while their children or godchildren were confirmed; and he had explained to them 'the hard necessity, and ... that it must be so until the number of bishops, scarce adequate those centuries ago, could be increased'.[1] In Lancashire vast confirmations, with occasional irreverence, continued at least until the end of the eighties.

The movement for more bishops was strongest where the illness or incapacity of the bishop coincided with reason for local patriotism. Cornwall was different in race and religious tradition from Devon, and its western parish was nearly 150 miles from Exeter. Ancient Bishop Phillpotts was of the old tradition, never moved round Cornwall with frequency, and in the sixties became immobile and at last bed-ridden. Bishop Trower, formerly of Gibraltar, was sub-dean and helped with confirmations, the family of Phillpotts (especially his archdeacon son) ran the administration. Cornwall had a strong local patriotism at a time when even Devonshire had hardly a bishop. Newcastle was another town with a local patriotism and a Bishop of Durham (Charles Baring) who till his death in 1879 was of the old tradition in his manner of administration. The West Riding wanted another bishop partly because Bishop Bickersteth of Ripon in his last few years could not act because of ill-health and they were almost without a bishop. In the year 1868 every diocesan bishop from Land's End to South London was too ill to work—Phillpotts of Exeter, Auckland of Bath and Wells, Hamilton of Salisbury, and Sumner of Winchester. There was already talk of a need to divide Winchester as well as Exeter.

Archbishop Longley approached the government for a bishop in Cornwall and was told by the home secretary that modern means of communication rendered an additional bishop unnecessary. It was obvious to nearly everyone but the home secretary that if the Church of England was episcopal Cornwall needed a bishop. But the laymen and some of the clergy were hard to convince. For years Bishop Baring of Durham resisted the desire to cut off Newcastle, and his arguments were respectable. What was the cost? Bishop Selwyn of Lichfield, from his experience in New Zealand, thought that England could have bishops on the cheap at £600 a year. But the English

[1] CCR, 1864, 21.

bishops had £4,000 a year or more, and all but one were peers of Parliament. The laity were accustomed to refer to the schemes for numerous bishops by the contemptuous phrase of Sydney Smith, *gig-bishops*. If you created new bishops, you must create bishops as England was accustomed to them, or England would not regard them as bishops. Bishop Baring of Durham believed that Northumberland needed its £100,000 in parishes and their men, not in a bishop and his palace. Would the cost end with a bishop? The new diocese would need a cathedral, a dean, canons, more archdeacons, a new centre of administration. If you had money, it must go to help objects more urgent than new dioceses.

The fact was, that the Church of England could not carry on without more bishops. Bishop Baring was at last convinced. The parish pastors baptised more babies and brought more young people to confirmation. The number of persons confirmed, especially in the great cities, rose rapidly. Colonial bishops, retired to England through ill-health or other reasons, helped in several dioceses. Bishop Chapman, formerly of Colombo, helped in the diocese of Bath and Wells. Trower, formerly of Gibraltar, helped in Exeter and other dioceses. Selwyn at Lichfield had two of his former New Zealand colleagues to help him. In 1867 Bishop Anderson, formerly of Rupert's Land and now a canon of St. Paul's, was formally appointed assistant bishop to the Bishop of London for the purpose of confirmation. 'Bishops', said Christopher Wordsworth as early as 1864,[1] 'are all over-worked', and he wanted to double their numbers. Four years later the Lower House of Convocation resolved that the use of ex-colonial bishops was to be deplored, first because it postponed reform, secondly because it tended to encourage resignation of colonial sees, and thirdly that if a man resigned a colonial see it made a presumption that he ought not to be performing episcopal functions in England.[2] They wanted suffragan bishops.

An act of Henry VIII permitted suffragan bishops, and they existed in England during the rest of the sixteenth century. The bishop of the diocese was to nominate two names to the crown and the crown should choose one. During the later sixties the plea for suffragans as more regular than ex-colonials grew stronger; and in the crisis over the election of Frederick Temple to the see of Exeter, Gladstone's government issued a declaration to the Archbishop of Canterbury,

---

[1] *Chron. Convoc.*, 1864, 1504.   [2] *Chron. Convoc.*, 1868, 1584.

only a few days before the election and with the obvious intention of conciliating churchmen, that in suitable cases they would not refuse to consider the appointment of suffragan bishops under the act of Henry VIII. Accordingly two suffragans were created in 1870, Bishop Parry of Dover to help the Archbishop, and Bishop Henry Mackenzie of Nottingham to help the Bishop of Lincoln (this second thanks to the generosity of Christopher Wordsworth). The first full ordination by a suffragan was held at Southwell minster in 1878.

Were they after all creating two grades of bishop? How should a suffragan sign himself? Bishop Mackenzie of Nottingham was almost at once in trouble for signing himself (as was alleged) Henry Nottingham. Should you address a suffragan as *my Lord* upon envelopes or at meetings? Some held that a bishop was called *my Lord* because he was a peer of the realm, others held (and more truly) that it had nothing to do with the House of Lords, and was a title applicable to all bishops. The need to have titles according to the act of Henry VIII led to unusual situations, especially that the two suffragans of London were the Bishops of Bedford and Marlborough, though they had nothing to do with either Bedford or Marlborough. Gladstone publicly declared that the crown was free to choose either of the two names, but in practice the crown steadily selected the first name as a matter of form, so that the diocesan bishop in fact chose his suffragan; until 1888 when Temple of London chose Archdeacon Sandford of Exeter for his suffragan and was astonished when the crown chose the second name (R. C. Billing, rector of Spitalfields) whom Temple had not even thought to inform beforehand.[1]

Most people believed that the suffragans came as a necessary relief to the diocesans. But there were two opinions even on this. Wordsworth of Lincoln thought that suffragans made the people more conscious of what a bishop was for and so increased the work of diocesans. But the common view was expressed by Archbishop Tait's coachman, who was reported as saying, 'We had a hard time of it some years ago . . . but since we've taken Mr. Parry into the business we've done better.'[2]

In 1879 Walsham How became suffragan to Bishop Jackson of

[1] *Life of Temple*, ii, 28. The anachronism of the see towns was remedied by the suffragans nomination act 1888, 51 & 52 Vic., cap. 56, allowing any towns designated by order in council.
[2] CCR, 1876, 54; Walsham How, *Lighter Moments*, 112.

V.C.—12

London, though all his experience lay in the country. He was not a good preacher, and so tiny in stature that vergers needed to provide a platform inside the pulpit to enable the congregation to see him. Everything else about him was delectable, and his books were read in thousands as aids to devotion or the parish worker. He was afterwards said to be worth a hundred curates, as he pulled together the work of the church in East London. Walsham How set the office of suffragan bishop in the national consciousness, as pastor and leader in his own right. But Jackson allowed him to be the effective diocesan of that part of London, and never interfered. When the stronger Temple succeeded Jackson, and would not countenance the same arrangements, Walsham How soon accepted the new see of Wakefield (1888).[1]

But ex-colonial bishops continued to be needed as assistants, often in dioceses where there was already a suffragan.

Disraeli's home secretary Richard Assheton Cross, a practical and honest churchman, at last carried through Parliament bills to increase the number of dioceses—St. Albans, Truro, Liverpool, Wakefield, Southwell and Newcastle-on-Tyne.[2] All these sees extended the principle of 1847 that the number of bishops in the House of Lords remained the same, and that each bishop except those of the senior five sees should attain his seat by seniority. Archbishop Tait had qualms about so extending the principle, not without reason, for

---

[1] How publicly denied that Temple's arrival caused his departure. But *Lives* of How and Temple prove that something was behind the story. Walsham How, with Temple's advice and agreement, refused Durham in 1890. He died in 1897. His memory was preserved for those who had not known the delightful little man by the hymn *For all the saints*.

[2] St. Albans contained Essex and Hertfordshire thus relieving Rochester of these counties and instead giving Rochester eastern and mid-Surrey, so taking south London out of Winchester diocese (act of Parliament 1875, first bishop 1877); Truro for Cornwall (act of Parliament 1876, first bishop 1877); Liverpool, Wakefield, Southwell and Newcastle-on-Tyne (act of Parliament, thanks to Cross, in 1878, first Bishop of Liverpool 1880, Newcastle 1882, Southwell 1884, Wakefield 1888). The money for St. Albans was found chiefly by selling the Bishop of Winchester's town house in St. James's Square; for Truro, from a gift by the Cornish Lady Rolle. Cf. P. T. Marsh, 201ff. The Cornish diocese transformed the church in Cornwall, for the diocese had a natural unity. Neither St. Albans nor the new Rochester had any natural unity and never elicited much loyalty, so that their frontiers must later be redrawn; Liverpool and Northumberland had a natural unity and were successful; Wakefield had no natural unity but became a success thanks to the extraordinary personality of its first bishop, little Walsham How; Southwell had rather less success because Derbyshire did not easily marry Nottinghamshire.

some more 'junior' bishops had sometimes more to give in the Lords than some 'senior' bishops, who perhaps had no wish whatever to serve there. Bristol was separated again from Gloucester to make two dioceses—act of Parliament, 1884, first bishop of restored Bristol, 1897.[1]

Here are the approximate figures of mileage for one bishop, Boyd Carpenter of Ripon. In 1886 he travelled about 12,000 miles, in 1895 13,481 miles, in 1903 16,255 miles. His sermons and addresses remained steady at about 190 in a year. The letters which he wrote rose steadily in number each year; for example, 1895, 4,936 and in 1903, 6,809.[2] This steady rise can be shown from the work of other bishops of that age and proves (if any proof were needed) that the bishop of 1890 was far closer to his clergy and laity than the bishop of 1850 could be or was expected to be.

3. THE BISHOP'S VETO

The bishop was brought into closer relation with his clergy because he confirmed in their churches, went to their churches to institute them, and ministered to them when they were sick in body or in mind. After 1882 he became important to them in another way —as the source of authoritative advice on the mode of worship. This happened through the controversy over ritual.

Ashton Oxenden, as we saw, observed and perhaps exaggerated the change between his youth and old age, from the time when you never needed to think how to conduct a service because you always conducted it the same way, to the time when you had to think what was the usage in the church where you officiated and to decide whether to adopt that usage. As the customs of churches varied more through the experiments or innovations of the age, more advice or direction was needed from the bishop, for he represented both the law of the church and the law of the land. But circumstances slowly compelled the bishops from a legal attitude to a pastoral attitude in this matter of worship. They ceased to think of themselves as judges, set to secure order and decency in the parishes

[1] Southwark was attempted, but not successfully created as a new diocese till 1905.
[2] *Life of Boyd Carpenter*, 61; CCR, 1886, 152. This activity needed fitness. The bishops' resignation act of 1869 allowed the infirm to resign (previously they needed an act of Parliament) and the incumbents' resignation act of 1871 followed: in both cases the arrangements for dividing the stipend between the pensioner and the new holder caused a difficulty.

under their charge, and came to think of themselves as fathers, intent on helping the parish to the best way of worship. This change of attitude arose first through a constitutional development.

In 1874 Parliament passed the Public Worship Regulation act to correct irregularity of ritual in the Church of England. The act did not change the law of ritual but tried to improve the ecclesiastical courts. It had no sufficient effect, for some clergymen refused to plead before the courts or to obey court orders. During the next years five clergymen were imprisoned for contempt of court.[1]

There were fewer than might have been, but for the action of bishops in using their veto. Archbishop Tait vetoed the prosecution at Wolverhampton after a partial submission, and vetoed an attempt to prosecute (1878) Charles Lowder at St. Peter's, London Docks, without exacting any submission whatever. Tait began to prefer allowing vestments to risking contempt of court and imprisonment.

The veto was becoming a necessity to peace. Prosecutions must at all costs be stopped. They could not be stopped by legislation, for the only laws which Parliament would grant would be laws likely to drive high churchmen into further intransigence. They could not be stopped by altering courts, because most informed lay people were satisfied with the judicial committee as an impartial body of eminent lawyers.[2] They could not be stopped by persuasion, because the

[1] Arthur Tooth of Hatcham, 22 January 1877 to 17 February 1877; Thomas Pelham Dale of St. Vedast's, Foster Lane, in the city of London, 30 October 1880 to 24 December 1880; R. W. Enraght of Bordesley, Birmingham, 27 November 1880 to 17 January 1881; S. F. Green, of St. John's, Miles Platting, Manchester, 19 March 1881 to 4 November 1882, much the longest imprisonment. They did not know how to get Green out. Bell Cox of St. Margaret's Liverpool, 5–21 May 1887.

[2] After the Gorham case Gladstone argued that the judicial committee would be better (because more obviously lay and not a 'church court') if the bishops, who were added to it by the church discipline act of 1840, were not members. Bishop Wilberforce was strongly for this view. In 1873, on a bill to reform the supreme court, Gladstone and Wilberforce prompted an amendment to make the court of final appeal also the court of final appeal in ecclesiastical causes. The amendment passed the Commons and had the effect of ejecting the bishops from the judicial committee. Archbishop Tait did not like it, and secured a further amendment in the Lords that the bishops should sit as assessors but not as judges. The act became law in 1873, and this form of the court for ecclesiastical appeals was preserved when the Appellate Jurisdiction act was passed in 1876. The change made no difference whatever to the course of events.

The prevailing discontent of clergy with the judicial committee produced a strong ecclesiastical courts commission 1881–3. The minutes of evidence (PP, 1883, xxiv, 1) are valuable (for the historian very valuable, because Stubbs uncovered much important information) but no one acted on the recommendations. The judicial committee only ceased to be the final court of appeal in ecclesiastical cases in 1963. Cf. P. T. Marsh, 129ff, 274; M. D. Stephen, in *Historical Journal* ix, 2, (1966), 191–200.

Church Association was determined to prosecute in order to keep popery out of the Church of England. Therefore they could only be stopped by using the power of veto so consistently that no one could prosecute. This plan had the defect that it must vastly increase the area of comprehension and tolerance in the Church of England. It would mean that the bishops allowed practices within the church believed by some to be 'Romanising'. It would mean that the bishops would lay themselves open to public attack as protecting evil-doers within the established church. It would mean that the bishops might lay themselves open to prosecution instead of their clergy. They preferred all these results to allowing imprisonments of honest or misguided men.

In 1882, in consequence of a long series of troubles with Mackonochie at St. Alban's, Holborn, the dying Tait persuaded Mackonochie at last to resign. But Tait and Bishop Jackson of London had already agreed to veto; not just to veto a particular prosecution, but steadily to veto. It was a courageous act, and a large-minded act coming from a low churchman like Tait who had as little sympathy with the 'offenders' as any bishop on the bench.

A fifth clergyman was imprisoned, Bell Cox of Liverpool in 1887, because the evangelical Bishop J. C. Ryle of Liverpool conceived that he had no right to veto. The exception proved the rule. No other prosecutions were permitted during the reign of Queen Victoria.[1] The known intention to veto averted far more suits than were vetoed formally.

This decision to stop prosecution gave liberty.[2]

---

[1] Tait declared his policy, in effect, to Convocation on 8 February 1881, as a general attitude though allowing exceptions in extreme cases. He always conceived it, there is no doubt, as an interim measure. He was challenged in the House of Lords on the point, and denied that the bishops had agreed consistently to veto, Hansard, cclxiv, 1881, 1504; nevertheless everyone believed in the intention as an interim pacification.

Presentations under the Public Worship Regulation act, 1875–98: 23 (London diocese 6, Lichfield 5, Exeter and Hereford 2 each, Bristol, Carlisle, Manchester, Oxford, Peterborough, Rochester, Salisbury, Worcester one each).

Uses of veto, 17:

Cases where prosecution was allowed: 6

Bishops who vetoed: Tait of Canterbury, Temple while at Exeter and later at London, Ellicott of Gloucester and Bristol (case of Randall at All Saints, Clifton), Harvey Goodwin of Carlisle, Magee of Peterborough, Bickersteth of Exeter, Moberly of Salisbury. Thus all schools were represented. The evangelical Bickersteth gave as his sole reason for veto, that 'in the present state of the law I fear that prosecutions in the courts on such matters of ritual only aggravate the evils they are intended to suppress'. PP, 1899, lxxiii, 941.

[2] G, 03, 370.

	1882 *(London only)*	*1898–9* *(England)*	*1901–2* *(England)*
Churches with incense	10	381	393
Churches with perpetual reservation	almost certainly less than 12	?	71

This growth of liberty, or break in uniformity, rendered the bishops unpopular with some Parliamentarians. But it greatly developed what was called the bishop's *jus liturgicum*. Since so many had no confidence in decisions by the courts, the law of worship was uncertain. Conscientious men would therefore go to the bishop and ask his leave for some innovation, secure in the knowledge that his veto was the final arbiter of what was right. This large development of the bishop's discretionary powers in the realm of worship was the most important Victorian innovation in the authority of the bishop, and markedly affected his relation to some of his clergy. It had the advantage that he was enabled to treat problems of parish worship more from a pastoral than from a legal point of view; the disadvantage that if a clergyman turned rebel, the bishop was conscious of protecting illegality, because he could do nothing but refuse to license curates or to confirm at that church, and then good Christian souls suffered more than the rebel clergyman.

But first it had to be established that the veto was absolute. The Church Association was determined to prove that it was not; for if they failed to deny that the veto could be used merely for the sake of avoiding scandal, they failed to stop the spread of ritual innovation in the Church of England.

4. THE ATTACK UPON THE BISHOPS

Thomas Thellusson Carter, vicar of Clewer, was among the best of the Tractarian clergy, gentle, ethereal, not at all angular. No one could call him an awkward or truculent ritualist. With the good will of nearly all his parishioners, who loved him, he wore vestments, mixed wine with water, used the sign of the cross in blessing the congregation and lighted candles on the altar, allowed *O Lamb of God* to be sung after the consecration, and elevated the bread and wine in what was described as 'an unauthorised manner'. A doctor of medicine named Julius, a parishioner (though he lived as much in Egypt as at Clewer), said that he was driven away from his church by these acts, and applied to Bishop Mackarness of Oxford that he might prosecute. Mackarness wrote (10 August 1878) that the recent failures of such legal proceedings had 'a tendency to cover all persons concerned in them with ridicule, and to bring on the church itself some contempt'. He did not at first veto the suit, but replied that he had not made up his mind what to do. Julius treated this as a veto and sued. The bishop refused counsel and conducted his own argument in court. He defended himself and the veto with force. He supposed a curate playing cricket for the village and drinking too much. Must he issue a legal enquiry merely because there was an undoubted legal offence against the laws ecclesiastical, just because a parishioner complained? He would not so blame a young man. He would shift him to another parish where he would behave more honourably and serve usefully. The law must intend such exercises of discretion by a bishop even where manifest offences had been committed. The bishop also said that he was not prepared to bear the ruinous costs which would fall upon a bishop if a suit went forward. The idea of old Carter committed to prison, after so long a life of loyal service to his church and his people, was an idea which he could not countenance.

In March 1879 the queen's bench court, presided over by Lord Chief Justice Cockburn, shattered everyone by holding that the bishop could be compelled to allow a prosecution of Carter. He had no discretion whatever. Such a judgment, if upheld, would have transformed the Church of England.

Bishop Mackarness appealed, and now consented to be represented by lawyers. In May 1879 the court of appeal and in March 1880 the House of Lords allowed the appeal.

For a few months Mackarness was the bishop most popular among the clergy of the Church of England. He was greeted with ovations at public meetings. The moment the case was ended in his favour, conscientious Carter insisted on resigning the parish of Clewer. There is little doubt that this decision in Julius v. Mackarness encouraged Tait and the bishops to their policy of vetoing ritual cases.

Mackarness was opposed to the ritualists. It was important that the man who established the right of veto could not be charged with protecting ritualists merely because he was a ritualist. Nor was he a bishop who despised the judicial committee, or intended to scorn the verdict of courts. He manifestly protected Carter on the purest motive of pastoral care.

In 1883 the chapter of St. Paul's invited G. F. Bodley to design a new high altar. Bodley succeeded Street and Butterfield as the architect who understood the worshipping aspirations of the Oxford Movement. And as the simplicity of early Tractarian worship was enriched, so the architect felt as appropriate an elaboration which would not have been acceptable to John Keble, or to his brother for whom Bodley designed his first aisle. In his later years he began to favour designs of a lavish medievalism. For St. Paul's he now designed an elaborate reredos in marble, with a crucifixion in the centre. Liddon at first did not like it and asked for something simpler. But Bodley was never conscious of his clients' wishes, and soon Liddon came to think this dignity appropriate. Work began in August 1886 and the reredos was dedicated on St. Paul's day (25 January) 1888. It was the largest crucifix to appear in an Anglican church since the Reformation.

The unaccustomed splendour disturbed minds. The Church Association wished to remove the 'images' and could only do so by prosecuting the dean and chapter under the Public Worship Regulation act. Bishop Temple of London vetoed the suit. The Church Association then applied for a mandamus to compel Temple to allow the suit. The queen's bench under Lord Coleridge held in June 1889 by majority that Parliament could not have intended any such absolute right of veto, because it gave an irresponsible power to the bishop. He accused Temple of treating it as 'a matter of no importance' that a statue of the Virgin should be erected at the east end of St. Paul's cathedral. He was less than just in supposing that Temple thought the matter of no importance. Temple thought that litigation was more disastrous for the church than a splendid reredos even when it offended the consciences of some worshippers. He appealed. On 17 December 1889 the court of appeal unanimously reversed the judgment. A second suit was instituted against Temple on the plea of additional evidence: that the reredos was not only likely to cause superstitious practices but had actually done so. The suitors gained nothing, and in July 1891 the House of Lords ruled unanimously that Bishop Temple could not be compelled to allow either suit. Even if a bishop thought that a law was being broken, he might still refuse leave to prosecute considering the general circumstances; and the general circumstances include the undesirable nature of litigation on such a subject.

This vindication of the veto was of the first importance. Its existtence lessened the danger that the tensions of the establishment would end in schism, averted strife in many parishes, secured the Church of England from a measure of public scandal, stopped conscientious clergymen from being imprisoned, and became the anchor of Anglican liberty and comprehensiveness. And yet it was an interim solution, or rather a manner of putting the solution away into the future, when men's minds could treat the problem of variety in worship with less emotion.

The Church Association believed in a conspiracy to introduce popish practices into their Protestant church, and bishops prevented them from prosecuting ritualists. In 1888 they therefore attempted the new plan of prosecuting a bishop, not for misusing his veto, but for his own ritual irregularities. They chose unfavourable ground. They selected the saintliest bishop on the bench, Edward King of Lincoln. The case centred upon his conduct in the parish church of St. Peter-at-Gowts in the city of Lincoln, where he was not responsible directly for the ritual but conformed to what he found there. And the practices of which he was accused were not those mainly in controversy, like incense, vestments, statues. They were little acts, hardly noticed by many: the eastward position, lighted candles on the altar, mixing water with wine, allowing O Lamb of God to be sung, using the sign of the cross at absolution and blessing, cleansing the vessels during the service. The Church Association could hardly have chosen weaker ground. King was loved in his diocese by evangelicals as by high churchmen, by Methodists and members of the Salvation Army. But he was suspect, for his elevation was the signal for rejoicing by Tractarians. He was the first to wear a mitre in public ministrations, was not afraid of ritual acts or garments not hitherto seen among Anglican bishops, and went down to Holy Trinity Church at Gainsborough, which was in the habit of using vestments at holy communion, and wore them himself, the first English diocesan bishop to do so since the Reformation. And yet he

V.C.—12 a

was no ritualist, in any narrow sense of the word.

Perhaps Archbishop Benson would have been wise to veto the case and so discover whether he had a veto if a bishop were prosecuted. But he saw a chance to escape the difficulty that some refused obedience to secular courts. The archbishop had a court. Its last precedent (Lucy *v.* Bishop of St. David's 1699) was dubious. But the judicial committee decided that he had jurisdiction, and he therefore heard the case in his own court. The spectacle of an archbishop in the library of Lambeth Palace deciding amid wigs and legal paraphernalia which side of the holy table one of his bishops should be standing, was not edifying. Benson (judgment, 21 November 1890) forbad the sign of the cross at blessing and absolution, and mixing the wine with water during service, but allowed the eastward position during the service, provided that the manual acts be visible to the people. He acquitted the bishop on the other charges.

The Church Association appealed to the judicial committee, which Bishop King would not recognise. On 2 August 1892 the judicial committee upheld the archbishop's judgment, with one minor exception.[1]

The evangelical party was more damaged by the case of Read *v.* the Bishop of Lincoln than by any other circumstance in the entire controversy over ritual, even the imprisonments of clergymen. This was unjust. Almost all evangelicals now disapproved the policy of prosecution. But the Church Association proceeded in the name of evangelical truth, and the evangelicals suffered. The committee of the Church Association saw the judgment in Read *v.* the Bishop of Lincoln as a rout.

Frustrated in the law-courts, Protestant fanatics turned to direct action. Their fears were rising. The case of the Bishop of Lincoln, and the security of veto, caused rapid increase in liturgical innovation. In 1894 they were disturbed when Lord Halifax, the president of the English Church Union, visited the pope at Rome and organised discussions on the Catholic validity of Anglican orders. The negotiations came to nothing, for the Pope ended by condemning Anglican orders. But they were shocking to Protestant Anglicans.

---

[1] The exception laid stress upon the circumstance that with regard to lighted candles King simply conformed to the ritual of St. Peter-at-Gowts, and was thus far exempted of responsibility. Thus Benson believed the lighted candles legal. The judicial committee believed them (probably) illegal, but that the incumbent and not the bishop was responsible.

The agitators began to disturb and rabble at services, as of old at St. Barnabas, Pimlico, or at St. George's-in-the-East. In January 1897 the secretary of the Protestant Truth Society, John Kensit, publicly objected at the Bow confirmation of the new Bishop of London, the historian Mandell Creighton; first because he wore a mitre, and secondly because he failed to banish erroneous (Tractarian) doctrine while he was Bishop of Peterborough. With the protest Kensit began a campaign of public interruption at ritualist churches, mostly in London.

In those years 1898–9 the English public, not usually friendly to agitators, was willing to give Kensit a hearing; partly because of the recent negotiations between Lord Halifax and the Pope, partly because of the interest of newspapers in rare ritual, and partly because of an astonishing book which appeared in 1897, entitled *The Secret History of the Oxford Movement*. The author was Walter Walsh, assistant editor of the evangelical newspaper *The English Churchman*.[2] Walsh collected papers of some good and some dubious groups on the extreme fringe of the Anglo-Catholic movement, and published them. They were used to accuse Anglo-Catholics of an excess of direction and effeminacy and the religion of the sacristy and Romanising and secrecy and bad faith—it was a *no popery* book, yet with the power that the material, however bizarre, was in small part authentic, the unveiling of an Anglo-Catholic underworld. The English nation asked whether there was indeed a conspiracy to turn the Church of England into a popish church. The campaign of 1898–9 against popery in the Church of England was the worst of the century after the riots over papal aggression in 1850–2.

For the attack, which began with a few fanatics under Kensit molesting elaborate services in London, was turned into a parliamentary question. The benefices bill, then under debate in the House of Commons, allowed Sir William Harcourt to assail the conspiracy, the lawlessness of the clergy, the inaction of the bishops. Once aroused, Harcourt carried the campaign forward with zeal and with the regret of his colleagues. The campaign of 1898 to 1899 was caused by Halifax, Kensit, Walsh, Harcourt, acting upon a genuine and uneasy feeling in the country that many Anglican clergymen were becoming popish and were acting in bad faith. As once Newman's honour was suspected by Kingsley, the honour of the entire high church party was now impeached. In the novel *Red Pottage* by

Mary Cholmondeley (1899) the main character, plainly identifiable in opinion with the authoress, condemned a clergyman for lacking the sense of honour found among ordinary men. In those years there was an unusual fear of underhand conduct, casuistry, shiftiness. He who would understand this phenomenon must read *The Secret History of the Oxford Movement*.

The difficulty was always to distinguish what was lawful from what was popularly supposed to be lawful. Many Protestants in England were disturbed by the practice of confession. But the Prayer Book provided for confession. Thus the campaign was either to alter the Church of England, or to attack some forms of teaching about confession. Often those who attacked Anglican clergymen for 'disloyalty' were only men who wanted the Church of England to be other than it was. Archbishop Temple of Canterbury, in a charge of exceptional courage in 1898, declared outspokenly that confession and prayers for the dead and the doctrine of the real presence were lawful, but certainly not compulsory, in the Church of England. The charge did not content Sir William Harcourt, still less Kensit, and the label of 'disloyalty' continued to be pinned to high church clergymen, even by Bishop Percival of Hereford. The English Church Union, headed by Lord Halifax, did not help the high church party when Halifax adopted a very defiant posture—he and his men would disobey the bishops whatever they ordered if it were uncatholic.

Still the bishops would allow no one to prosecute. Incense became more common, reservation rapidly more common. The two archbishops met at Lambeth in 1899–1900 and declared that incense and reservation were illegal in the Church of England. A number of extreme clergymen conformed to these judgments, especially that on incense. But was a declaration by archbishops equal to determination in a properly constituted court? It had no authority over the defiant. And it could not determine whether these practices were legal or not. The only way to discover was by prosecution, which the bishops would not allow. Archbishop Temple was particularly resolute against prosecution, and subjected to much blame. But the bishops knew that those who were prosecuted would refuse to recognise the supreme court to which the case would go.

The extremists could not be stopped by moral authority. And indeed not everyone thought it necessary to stop them. They could not be stopped in the courts, unless the bishop lost his power of veto.

Therefore Parliament must act, either to abolish the bishops' veto, or to bring in new laws for the church. The bishops were confronted therefore with a new danger to the unity of their church in that Sir William Harcourt and his men would do what Lord Shaftesbury for so long failed to do, attempt to rule the Church of England without asking the Church of England. Even the *Times* came on 17 September 1898 to threaten that Parliament must do for the church what it could not do for itself. A church discipline bill of 1899 won ominous support in the House of Commons. The bill was stern. It made it illegal for clergymen to describe the holy communion as the mass, or to enjoin regular confession, almost ruled that men must only do what the Prayer Book orders and never what it omits, and abolished the veto.[1]

New names came into existence at this period: 'central churchmen', 'moderate churchmen', to represent men who were old-fashioned high churchmen but would no longer accept the title of high churchmen lest they be identified with extremists.

It must be remembered once more that the problem was still tiny, by any objective standard. In 1902, out of 39 churches in the London diocese with incense, only six incumbents refused to accept the regulations of Bishop Winnington-Ingram. In 1903 the number of churches in London with continuous reservation was still only twelve. In the diocese of Winchester in 1899 seven churches used incense, and several of the seven stopped after the archbishops' ruling.[2]

A bill to abolish the veto passed a second reading in the Commons during 1903. No fewer than a hundred members of Parliament waited upon the new Archbishop of Canterbury, Davidson, a month after he took office in 1903, to persuade him to act. Such was the effect of the extreme ritualists and of Halifax, Harcourt, Walsh, Kensit and the campaign of 1898–9. It was impossible to imagine any other moment of church history, except those few years, when a hundred members of the House of Commons would have waited

[1] PP, 1899, i, 205. The proposer 'ventured to say the mass was illegal in the Church of England and therefore any reference to it must be illegal', Hansard, 4th series, lxxi, 240. Balfour pointed out the oddness of forbidding the use of the word mass while you did not forbid the teaching of transubstantiation, ibid. 290, and that the bill would forbid (e.g.) harvest thanksgivings. It nevertheless collected 156 affirmative votes.

[2] G, 02, 770; 03, 145; Bell, *Davidson*, 341. But it was more in the whole country. See for 1901–2 on page 350.

upon the Archbishop of Canterbury to demand that he repress a few ceremonies used in a few churches. Protestant votes were still powerful at elections, especially in the north of England. Dissenting votes were much troubled over state support of church schools, and took unusual interest in the ceremonies of the Church of England.

So continued the quest for ritual order in the Church of England. Everyone who had responsibility in that age was permanently marked by this experience. It led to the Royal Commission on Ecclesiastical Discipline of 1904–6, the quest for a new prayer book, the debates in the Commons of 1927–8. It turned the eyes of the Church of England towards the inner organisation of the church, at a time when their leaders needed to look outwards. It unbalanced the quest for new modes of worship adapted to new generations, and for the proper autonomy of the Church of England within the establishment. It was one heritage of the Victorian engagement over church and state. Though some of its expressions were trivial or fanatical, it was no trivial argument. The argument was necessary to the inward cohesion of the religious society.

Whatever may be thought of the wisdom of Archbishop Benson's court, before which Edward King appeared, or of the ruling by two archbishops on incense and reservation, these were the two important symbols of a change which had come over the Anglican episcopate. They claimed to be trusted on matters of common worship where the early Victorian bishop would have conceived no such claim as possible. And being pastors of quality, they were largely trusted, and to the benefit of the established church. In an impossible thicket of law, they helped the congregations to adjust their worship to the needs of new times while they maintained the ideal of general loyalty to the Prayer Book.[1]

---

[1] Bishop Fraser of Manchester refused on ritual grounds to institute the patron's nominee to Miles Platting (after S. F. Green's removal) and was sued in the courts but won (P. T. Marsh, 284). Bishop Percival of Hereford twice refused to institute to parishes clergymen whose record was 'ritualistic' and so risked being taken to court by the patron but got his way. PP, 1906, xxxiv, 292. His example was later followed by Knox of Manchester. There were probably other examples which never became public but these refusals were certainly infrequent. For a difficult case between a rebel priest, who happened to be a fine pastor of the poor, and his bishop, see the affair of Robert Dolling at Landport, in Osborne, *Dolling*; Bell, *Davidson*, 263ff.

5. THE QUEST FOR AUTONOMY

The bishop was more diocesan, the cathedral more diocesan. The clergy and still more the laity were made conscious of the diocese by the diocesan conference.

Most of those who struggled to revive Convocation in the forties and fifties were prominent in a campaign to revive 'diocesan synods' in the fifties and sixties. Those who wanted this usually meant an assembly of the clergy of the diocese round their bishop, receiving and approving his proposals, giving him their advice in council. There was an element of theory in the proposals and the manner of making them. There was also an atmosphere of 'church defence' against dissenters or politicians. They did not usually want an assembly which included laymen. The clergy wanted diocesan synods as a way of reducing their sense of isolation. The wish was part of that discontent with the remoteness of bishops which was common in that age. A ruridecanal meeting at Frant (August 1863) paid tribute to the high quality of the bishops and then said that 'there is an impassable gulf at present between the bishops and the other clergy, and between both these and the laity'.[1] Bishop Wilberforce, who was not at all distant among bishops, said that he 'by no means felt so isolated as the bishops had been represented as being'. Therefore some people, like Archdeacon Emery, father of the Church Congresses, always wanted laymen in the synod. Emery was willing to concede that the word synod meant a meeting of clergy, and to use such words as diocesan *conference*, or *convention*, or *meeting*, to describe what he wanted. Archdeacon Denison[2] denounced the name diocesan conference as rubbish. Whatever the name, laymen must somehow be brought into the authoritative organs of the church in some way other than by membership of Parliament. Few were willing to add them to Convocation. Therefore diocesan conferences were the only means available. 'My Lord,' George Trevor told Archbishop Thomson of York who disapproved of such meetings, 'the diocesan synod is the bishop's lungs.'[3] The ordinary Anglican layman usually suspected what was proposed. 'What does all this mean', wrote the queen to Dean Wellesley, 'about the revival of diocesan synods?'[4]

[1] CCR, 1863, 245, 259; Cf. G, 63,881.   [2] CCR, 1869, 47–49.
[3] CCR, 1866, 233.
[4] 31 October 1863, Stratfieldsaye Papers. On 21 April 1864 the Lower House of

The real impetus came from Harold Browne who began consulting and planning from the moment he became Bishop of Ely. He encouraged meetings of clergy and laity of the rural deaneries, and when these were working successfully caused them to elect a lay representative to a diocesan conference. Thus the first English diocesan conference, held in the south transept of Ely cathedral in 1866, was small: bishop, dean and archdeacons and canons, proctors in convocation, and one layman for each rural deanery. They voted by houses. Browne secured a better meeting by holding conferences in each of his four archdeaconries, where up to four laymen were allowed from each parish. Two years later, Selwyn of Lichfield, accustomed to a synodical system in New Zealand, started introducing it into the diocese of Lichfield which, despite controversy, became the second English diocese to have a diocesan conference.

The misgivings were many. Were these organisers creating machinery for the sake of machinery? Would it not give a platform for cranks and partisans? Would it not increase the power of the laymen which through Parliament and patronage was already as great as in any church of Christendom? Selwyn tried to call his meeting a diocesan synod and was sharply forced to turn it into a 'conference'. But those who tried it were pleased. The laymen, especially of the little country parishes, were brought for the first time into touch with the central working of the diocese, and forced to consider important matters of policy in a general context. That the new machinery was needed is evident from Browne's astonishing doubts about what he was doing. 'I had certainly some little misgiving as to how the clergy would feel when brought face to face with the laity, and how the laity would feel when brought in like manner into public contact with the clergy.'[1]

By 1882 all the dioceses but three had diocesan conferences. The three exceptions were London, where Bishop Jackson thought the diocese too large to confer seriously; Llandaff, where Bishop Ollivant was too old; and Worcester, where Bishop Philpott did not believe in any such machinery.

The Church of England never accepted the proposition, dear to

---

Convocation asked for diocesan conferences. They renewed the request on 25 February 1869.

[1] Speech to the Ely diocesan conference 1869; CCR, 1869, 32.

Sir William Harcourt, that Parliament could rule it as it liked. ('The Church', said Sir Andrew Lusk from his place in Parliament, 'is a department of the state for the management of which the House is responsible.')[1] Though composed of English citizens, it owed a loyalty to God above the loyalty which it owed to Caesar, in doctrine, worship, pastoral care. The doctrine and worship of the church were approved in 1661–2 by Convocation before they were approved by Parliament. Since the day when Lord Grey abolished ten Irish bishoprics and caused Keble's assize sermon, parliamentary leaders from Lord Melbourne onwards recognised that they should not legislate for the Church of England without the consent of a majority of the bishops who sat in the House of Lords.

The Convocation of Canterbury was again active since 1851, the Convocation of York since 1860. Parliamentarians were slow to confess that Convocation had any right to be consulted on church matters. In the long debates over *Essays and Reviews* or Colenso, and again over the Athanasian creed during the early seventies, Convocation had not achieved a high reputation among those who sat in Parliament. They found it a body unrepresentative even of the clergy, and backward-looking. So great an ecclesiastic as Archbishop Tait shared the common parliamentary opinion that Convocation had no constitutional right to be consulted, and that it would be a pity if such a right became established. Many members of Convocation desired to amend their mode of representation and were refused permission by government. And yet they achieved the right to be consulted. They were first cited in the preamble to an act of Parliament when the act of uniformity was amended in 1872. The fate of the Public Worship Regulation act of 1874, carried though without proper consultation, convinced everyone but the unreasonable that it was expedient, even if not necessary, to allow Convocation to debate any law proposed for the church.

Thus Convocation added a new problem in the debate over reform of the constitution. The Church of England must be consulted before church measures became law. That now meant, allowing Convocation to discuss. Yet everyone, even the friends of Convocation, confessed that it was not satisfactory for the purpose. Its opinion must be asked. And its opinion, when given, was not respected.

[1] Hansard, ccxli, 1878, 1029.

Until 1874 many good Anglicans, probably a large majority of those who thought upon these matters, still regarded crown, lords and commons as the lay voice of the Church of England. After 1874 this view was still common, but less common. During that year the debates on the Public Worship Regulation bill convinced many more people that the House of Commons was an unsuitable assembly to debate the doctrine and worship of the Church of England. Many of the speakers in those debates spoke excellently. But others, and not least the Conservative prime minister, either spoke in ignorance and prejudice, or spoke with one eye upon the ignorance and prejudice of their constituents.

The Church of England was not content to be governed only by its clergymen, though it confessed that bishops and priests had a proper and prominent part in that government. It was not content to be governed by Parliament, though it confessed that the nation had an interest in the established church. Therefore a new mode of government was neceassry. Somehow Anglican laymen who were interested in the church because it was the church of Christ and not only because it was the church of the establishment, must be associated with the government of the Church of England.

This idea became more familiar, partly because of experience in the colonial churches, partly because of diocesan conferences, and partly because of Church Congresses.

The Church Congress was afterwards said to have been invented at Cambridge in November 1861, when a few guests, few enough for the senior proctor to invite to his rooms, met in the hall of King's College. The little meeting became a Congress at Oxford in 1862, open to the public, with papers and discussions by clergy and laity. They took the meetings of the British Association as their model, an annual meeting at some big town, presided over by the bishop of the diocese. At Oxford they only allowed ladies into the galleries, but from 1863 they allowed ladies into all meetings, though it was not the custom for ladies to speak in debate. The bishop was always prominent in the chair. They could not hold the Congress at Birmingham in 1867 because the bishop (Philpott) would not have them. They had difficulty about holding it at Norwich in 1865 because Bishop Pelham doubted. The meeting originally grew from the needs of church defence and therefore had aggressive moments. But it became the national sounding board of church opinion. From all over England men came to see the famous churchmen of their age, Denison or Wilberforce or Halifax.

After about 1886 they became less important, in the sense that the celebrated men ceased to go unless they were invited to read a paper. And after that year other opportunities were open to laymen who wanted to make a contribution to the welfare or thought of the Church of England. It was still a display of strength. But it ceased to have the importance of the earlier years as experience on the road towards autonomy. It also became less important because it slowly became less exciting, less hot. At the Manchester Congress of 1863, with working men present in great numbers, the debates were often noisy and even unseemly, with groups of partisans applauding or dissenting in the hall. By 1886 the Congresses were agreed to be more edifying and more boring. In the last decade of the century they were freely declared to have had their day.

It became more edifying because it became more representative. Wilberforce was prominent in its origins, and for some years evangelicals refused to attend. At the 1862 meeting critical references to evangelicals were loudly applauded by the audience. If the Congress was to represent the Church of England its managers needed more tact. But evangelicals started to go. There was party trouble at the Leeds Congress of 1872 when a man who said that he was a member of the Church Association was howled down. Evangelicals argued among themselves whether they should attend. Dean Close said that the Congress at York (1866) was the first he attended and the last he would attend. Despite much that was pleasant, he felt that he had no business to be in that atmosphere of cloudy confused misty compromise.[1] The Congress at Croydon in 1877 was the first attended by the Archbishop of Canterbury. Its coming was awaited with anxiety lest it display rather division than strength, but all passed excellently. J. C. Ryle and other leaders urged evangelicals to take part. The meeting was important to the national life of the church, and it was their duty to be there. They formed a committee for protecting evangelical interests at Church Congresses. 'I might compare Congress', Ryle once told a large audience there, 'to the ships which King Solomon sent to Tarshish, which brought back not only gold and silver and ivory, but apes and peacocks too.'[2]

[1] G, 78, 956.
[2] CCR, 1878, 579. Numbers: Bristol, 1864: about 2,000; Nottingham, 1871: 3,205; Leeds, 1872: 5,138; Brighton, 1874: 4,935; Brighton, 1901: 2,897.

In its heyday the Congress did much for Anglican life. It was the only place where clergy and laity spoke on equal terms about the main matters then of concern. They brought together all opinions within the church, and therefore promoted understanding. Their platforms gave scope to the best minds of the day. It was a place where men were 'discovered'. Walsham How was an obscure country clergyman who went to the Congress at Wolverhampton in 1867 and made such a speech that henceforth he was a marked man. Edward King went from Cuddesdon to the Leeds Congress of 1872 and made a devotional speech which at once raised him among the three or four leaders of the Tractarian movement. Some even hoped that the Congress would grow to be a national synod of the Church of England. The minutes and reports of the Congress give the historian excellent evidence of the changing state of opinion on subjects of the day.

In 1885 the Convocation of Canterbury accepted a house of laity with a proviso (regretted by the bishops) that the lay house should not be consulted on matters of faith and doctrine. A lay house of the Convocation of Canterbury met for the first time on 16 February 1886. It was unrepresentative. Most of the leading laity could not think what it would do and did not take part. A question about it, or against it, was asked in the House of Commons. Archbishop Thomson of York was against it, and York Convocation had no house of laity till 1892.[1]

Towards 1890, a year or two after the House of Laity first met, we hear talk of someone called an 'ecclesiastical layman'. The laymen were being brought into church affairs as never before. They became servers and readers as well as churchwardens or sidesmen, and in national councils or congresses they contributed as much as experts among the ordained. In truth such laymen always existed. Gladstone or Shaftesbury were such. But in the old days the layman influenced church affairs from his place in Parliament, or his leadership in society, or by his duty as squire or patron. Laymen like Lord Salisbury or Sir Richard Assheton Cross continued in that way, but now the layman began to exert influence through the organs of the church. A man like Lord Halifax influenced the history of the Church

[1] Hansard, cccii, 1886, 1195. Thomson died, and Magee summoned the laity but died, so Maclagan first presided over the York Laity.

of England far more by his presidency of the English Church Union than from his seat in the House of Lords. Opponents of the high churchmen sometimes attacked them for turning 'church laity' into a kind of separate class. The ecclesiastical layman *par excellence* was seen in Earl Beauchamp, a friend of Liddon, who was active everywhere in defending the rights of the church. Such men were said by enemies to be more ecclesiastical than the ecclesiastics. Certainly some of them were the least ready of all men to compromise. But otherwise the charge had no relation to anything that mattered. They were men of public spirit and energy, willing to give time to unpalatable subjects for the sake of their church, and without them the Church of England could not have reorganised itself to encounter the twentieth century.[1]

[1] Archbishop Benson, aided by Stubbs, tried to amalgamate the two Convocations and houses of laity into a single assembly. Then the established church would have the structure of a representative system—parish council, diocesan conference, national assembly. To this end the foundation stone of Church House was laid in 1891, not without criticism for waste of money. Benson and Temple both believed that the separateness of the Convocations and House of Laity harmed the Church of England. From 1896 it was established that all the houses could 'unofficially' meet together. Meanwhile the Church Reform League, of which the principal spokesman was Charles Gore, adopted a plan, first suggested as long ago as 1874, that the (still hypothetical) national assembly of the church should legislate for the church by sending measures direct to the crown for royal assent. The 'Representative Church Council', consisting of the two Convocations and the two houses of laity, met for the first time in July 1904. The bishops discovered in Arthur Balfour a statesman who, perhaps because he was a Scottish presbyterian, believed in due autonomy for the Church of England. He surprised the bishops by being the first eminent politician publicly to respect Convocation. A Scot (Aberdeen) did most to restore Convocation and another Scot did much to create a national assembly. The Representative Church Council did not, as was hoped, replace the Convocations, for many members of the Convocations refused to be assimilated. The new council existed side by side with the old organs of debate. The Enabling Act of 1919 named it the National Assembly of the Church of England, and gave it the special powers of presenting measures for royal assent provided that they were reported on favourably by an ecclesiastical committee of both houses and a motion that they should be so presented was carried in both houses of Parliament.

At the same time, and for the same reasons, the Wesleyan Methodists introduced laymen into Conference. In 1878 laymen were admitted to the Conference despite John Wesley's first deed, but only by a compromise (comparable with the compromise reached by the Church of England in the division of authority between Convocations and Representative Church Council). The representative session of ministers plus laymen met after the pastoral session of ministers only, so that ministers made up their minds before the agenda reached the laymen. In 1889–90 Dr. Rigg and the conservative ministers conceded the 'sandwich compromise' whereby the representative session met between two meetings of the pastoral session. The representative session was allowed to meet first from 1901. But the ministers continued to elect the president of Conference. Cf. *Life of Hugh Price Hughes*, 527–8.

6. THE CATHEDRAL

In the first thirty years of the reign, Victorian churchmen reformed the town parish and the country parish. But the cathedrals were still under attack. They were more popular than in the days when a Bishop of London saw little use for St. Paul's cathedral. But in 1870 their utility was still doubted, and there was even talk once again of sweeping all away.

All were great corporations reaching back into the Middle Ages, touched by the Reformation, abolished by the Long Parliament, restored with Charles II, and touched drastically by the act of 1840 which removed many of their endowments and left most of them with only four canons. Some of them had statutes unaltered since the Reformation, but none had the power of making new statutes for themselves, except Lichfield, where since the middle ages the dean and chapter claimed and exercised the right to make statutes with the consent of the bishop. They all catered for the tourist on week-days and for at least a small congregation of the musical on Sundays. Otherwise they varied in statutes, function and effectiveness. St. David's had been restored but was sixteen miles from the nearest railway station, and Ely was a magnificent church in a little country town. Norwich and Bristol and York were like great city churches, ministering to a busy population. Manchester was the old parish church, to which the people were much attached, and its services drew nearly four thousand of them every Sunday, and its clergy baptised 3,300 babies and married 2,500 couples a year. Oxford was also a college chapel. Carlisle had its nave cut off and used as a parish church. Bristol was hardly the seat of a bishop, who now resided at Gloucester. Ripon and Manchester were old collegiate churches turned by the nineteenth century in *o cathedrals. The nave of Bangor was cut off and used as a parish church and the cathedral clergy had no control over the parish services. The fruitless cathedrals report of 1852 was blamed by the seventies because it suggested a common framework for all the cathedrals, and they had realised how each cathedral needed separate treatment.

The prominent feature of nearly all the cathedrals in 1870 was their poverty. The act of 1840 left them with a dean at £1,000 and canons at £500, unless they were Welsh, when the act made the strange assumption that Welsh deans needed only £700 and Welsh canons

THE CATHEDRAL   367

only £350, or unless they were members of some great chapter like
that of Durham. With regard to the general income, an act of 1868
ratified schemes whereby they handed estates to the Ecclesiastical
Commissioners, who would give them a steady annual income, until
such time as they restored estates which would bring an equivalent
rent. The object of this double transfer was to get rid of the system of
tenure under which cathedral lands were held, the old system of
leases let at low rates but renewable by fines. Thus some cathedrals
had not handed over their estates, some had commuted their estates
for an annual income, and some had received back estates to produce
the equivalent of the annual income. By 1880, and the age of the
agricultural depression, those cathedrals were managing best who
commuted and were receiving a fixed sum from the Ecclesiastical
Commissioners. They alone had a guaranteed income, while all the
others were receiving less than the estates had been expected to
produce. York commuted in 1852, ten years later received back
lands calculated to bring them £4,410, and in the depression received nothing like that sum. Nearly every cathedral in the country
was in difficulty during the eighties. Canterbury gave back 20 per
cent of its rents in 1880, and the next year permanently reduced its
rents by £1,467. 14s.[1] Winchester wondered for a time how to stay
open. No cathedral could repair its fabric from its fabric fund. And
while the money fell, the expenses rose. The salary of the organist
or the vergers needed to keep pace with the times. And the demand
that cathedrals should do better work and more work meant need for
more money, without which they could not do more. Every friend of
cathedrals still hated the act of 1840 for taking away too much. It was
called the cathedral-crushing act. More than one attempt was made to
get Parliament to allow or compel the Ecclesiastical Commissioners
to give to the cathedrals more of what had once been their own
money. 'The nut has been cracked and the kernel removed,' replied
a canon of York to the question what should be done with cathedrals,
'and the only question now remaining is, what is the best arrangement of shells.'[2] In the early nineties the dean and canons of Winchester, Salisbury and Gloucester drew half their proper stipends.

Chester, for example, laboured under peculiar, but not exceptional
difficulties.[3] Its statutes were of 1544 and unrevised. Richly endowed

[1] PP, 1884-5, xxi, 457.   [2] PP, 1884-5, xxi, 450.
[3] Compare with Chichester in Lowther Clarke, *Chichester Cathedral*, 10.

in 1541, its property was much diminished by alienations under Queen Elizabeth, and it struggled ever since. They had no fund at all for the fabric. The choirboys lived in a tumbledown house to receive what only generosity could call education. 'I am compelled', said the organist, 'to accept boys of mean parentage and poor quality of voice . Parts of the cathedral itself were almost in a state of ruin. Between that year and 1883, thanks chiefly to the energy of Dean Howson, they raised £75,000 and persuaded the Commissioners to contribute £15,000. They could not finish it, and the chapter house continued in dilapidation. The choir had six men and twelve boys, which was a little better than the choir of one or two other cathedrals. But the lay clerks were paid miserable stipends (£25 and 2s. 6d. a day for two services; but the senior was also the headmaster of the choristers at £70) and no one knew whether they could be dismissed if the voice failed. The close contained only one house for a canon, which each of the four canons therefore occupied in turn for his residence of three months, and otherwise lived on the benefice which he also held.

Another sign of poverty was the predicament of some deans. Dean G. H. S. Johnson of Wells, limited by the act of 1840 to £1,000 a year, was to live in a lovely and expensive house which needed five or six servants and a gardener. The chapter saw the dean's stipend to be so mean that they paid an extra £200 from their general fund. In 1858 the Commissioners recommended that the income be £1,500 but Lord Derby did not approve, and then the stipend depressed the dean and became public concern in Somerset, even a matter for embarrassing discussion at a diocesan conference. In 1860 the salary of the Dean of York became even more embarrassing, for it was discussed in Parliament. 'I never knew the sense of being really poor', said Dean Burgon of Chichester, 'until I came hither.'[1]

The rising costs, apart from fabric, and due to rising stipends or rising standards of choir, may be seen at Bristol.[2]

And Bristol allowed its standards to rise more slowly than nearly all the others. 'Our service', said one of the canons in 1883, 'is far less helpful to my devotion than that of many other cathedrals that I visit', and some critical visitors agreed with him.[3] When Charles Kingsley pictured a cathedral service, not everyone thought it

---

[1] PP, 1860, liii, 237; 1884–5, xxi, 368.   [2] PP, 1883, xxi, 201.
[3] J. P. Norris in PP, 1883, xxi, 210.

Bristol cathedral

		£			£
1850	6 lay clerks	249	1879	9 lay clerks	540
	6 choristers	24		18 choristers	44
	1 organist	100		1 organist	200
	1 verger	20		1 verger	20
	1 schoolmaster	60		1 schoolmaster	120
					+ house £50
(in all)		——	(in all)		————
	24 people at £794			39 people at £1838	

caricature: 'The organ droned sadly in its iron cage to a few musical
amateurs. The scanty service rattled in the vast building like a dried
kernel too small for its shell. The place breathed imbecility and
unreality, and sleepy life in death, while the whole nineteenth
century went roaring on its way outside.' Dr. Cumming the
presbyterian saw the sights of Lincoln cathedral and said to a canon,
'You can make no use of it. You are like two or three peas rattling
up and down in a dry pod. It is much too big for you.'[1]

An observer of Chichester cathedral said that in some of the
arrangements was something 'pinched and poverty-stricken'. One
important proof of scanty money was the condition of the cathedral
libraries, some of which housed irreplaceable books and incunabula.
In 1879 a large piece of marble became detached from a capital and
crashed down on the bookcases in the Exeter library, and about the
same time they discovered that valuable books were covered in
mildew and that the incunabula were perishing. An expert reported
in 1880 that as many as twenty-one of the cathedral libraries did not
come up to indispensable standards.[2]

St. Paul's library was put into order by Sparrow Simpson after
1861. The Lambeth library, which had benefited from S. R. Maitland,
was specially assisted by the Ecclesiastical Commissioners. But at
first they assisted it so meanly (£150 a year for everything) that
Archbishop Longley made public protest, and at last secured a better
arrangement, under which the line of distinguished librarians con-
tined with William Stubbs and J. R. Green.

Here is a report on one exceptional case of 1853. Llandaff cathedral
was a parish church. It had no residentiary canons, no organ, no choir.
It had no dean until 1843, and he soon fell ill, and the management

[1] CCR, 1880, 393.   [2] PP, 1884-5, xxi, 339, 374.

was in the hands of a senior vicar aged 81. The west end was in ruin. They were half-restoring the nave but the work stood still for lack of money, and the only place for either parish or cathedral services was a small chapel at the east end. The only instrument of music was a violoncello from which the melody was scratched by an old man with trembling hands. The best that could be said was that Bishop Ollivant preached there 'not infrequently'.[1] This was quite exceptional, and serves only to remind us of the heroism of a man like C. J. Vaughan later in the century, consenting despite criticism of his Englishness to become dean of Llandaff and build upon such ramshackle foundations.

If Llandaff was unusual, it was true that many cathedrals, even in 1870, had poor choirs, poor choir school, non-resident canons, some dilapidation in their buildings; and meanwhile faced a public demand for more devotional services and better music and pastoral activity, a demand which could not be met without more money. There were important exceptions. The choir of Ely in the middle sixties was claimed as one of the best choirs in the country. At the same time Elvey raised the music of St. George's Windsor to a standard which was thought to be better than the music at any cathedral. Meanwhile they raised considerable sums to repair and restore their fabrics. Gloucester restored its choir after 1870 at a cost of £15,000. Dean Bickersteth repaired the west front of Lichfield. At Peterborough, Gilbert Scott renewed the roof of the north aisle and built buttresses to under-pin the north wall. At Wells between 1869 and 1876 they restored the west front and levelled the cathedral green at a cost of £13,000. In truth they nearly all did major works of repair or renovation during this age. It was calculated that during the ten years after 1874, the English cathedrals had some £643,298 spent on them. Salisbury spent £42,000 odd, York £27,000 odd, of which nearly £11,000 came from income and the remainder from donations.[2] Lord Grimthorpe was supposed to have spent a quarter of a million of his own money on his dictatorial restoration of St. Albans abbey. And still the need to spend and spend continued, solely to maintain such historic fabrics. 'In order to keep cathedral works going,' said Harvey Goodwin sadly, 'the dean must beg.'[3] In Septem-

---

[1] PP, 1854, xxv, 585; *Musical Times*, November 1878, 594; Scholes, 527.
[2] CCR, 1894, 33; PP, 1884-5, xxi, 497-8.
[3] 'Recollections of a Dean', in *Essays* ed. Howson, 21.

ber 1891 a writer in the *Contemporary Review* proposed that the only solution was to nationalise the cathedrals, but then he wanted to use the deaneries of Norwich and Canterbury for eminent writers or scientists. In 1899 Lord Wemyss proposed that they be made historic monuments, and that the state should protect their restoration and furnishing. The authorities of the church felt discomfort at such suggestions. They looked at France where the state maintained cathedrals, and did not admire what they saw. They preferred to carry the heavy but glorious burden.

The dean could mar a cathedral, but it was not always the case that he could make it. In most cathedrals all the canons were non-resident, and in nearly all cathedrals one or two were non-resident. At York and Chester and Bristol and Llandaff and Ripon only one canon could reside at a time because they had only the one canon's house to occupy, and occupied it in turn. Bangor had no houses for residentiaries. Three of the old canons' houses at Manchester had been swept away for street improvements, and the other two were let as shops.[1] As late as 1880 Chichester had two houses, one of which was always occupied by the principal of the theological college, and the other was claimed permanently by the senior canon, thus leaving the others with the need to lodge in the city when in residence.[2] A canon who held a benefice for nine months and a stall for three months could not regard the cathedral as his main duty. His three months seemed more like an interlude in his proper work. If the canon held a benefice in or near the cathedral city, he could take a frequent interest in the cathedral. But this was not always what happened. Of the four canons of Carlisle in 1869, one lived in Northumberland, another in Hertfordshire, a third in Devonshire, and only one lived within fifty miles of Carlisle.[3] Of the four canons of Norwich in 1869 one (Sedgwick) was the professor of geology at Cambridge, another (Robinson) was the Master of St. Catharine's College at Cambridge, a third was the rector of St. Giles-in-the-Fields in London, and the fourth was an ex-professor of the East India College, still much concerned with military examinations on behalf of the government.[4]

At Exeter, conversely, all four canons resided in Exeter and without parishes.[5] But whether the canons were near or far, they much

[1] PP, 1884–5, xxi, 303.   [2] PP, 1884–5, xxi, 367.
[3] PP, 1871, lv, 201.   [4] PP, 1871, lv, 227.   [5] PP, 1871, lv, 214.

depended on the dean, who resided for at least eight months. The
much abused act of 1840 compelled the dean to reside.

Cities varied in their attitude to hardly resident canons. Norwich
was proud of its visitors, especially Adam Sedgwick. Carlisle complained that the canons bore no part in the work of the city and
were useless to its social life, and disliked the chapter as isolated
from the life of the place.[1]

Cathedrals also varied in the power which ancient statutes gave to
the dean. Policy depended on the dean, because he almost alone was
continuous in supervision, but the canons could, though they often
did not, obstruct whatever policy a dean wished to advocate. At
Bristol the canons could not make the dean do what they were
unanimous in wanting. They were agreed in wishing for a weekly
sacrament in the middle of Sunday morning but could not get the
dean to consent. At Canterbury could be found the opposite
situation, where Dean Alford wanted to do things and felt himself to
be so frustrated that he recommended to the archbishop the abolition
of canons. 'At present', wrote Alford,[2] 'that office [of dean] is, in
many of our cathedrals, practically useless; the dean, while nominally
the head of the cathedral body, is almost without employment, and
absolutely without power to act.' Old Bishop Maltby of Durham
thought the dean's office to be so much a sinecure that he recommended the lessening of his residence to four months, and then he
would be enabled 'greatly to increase his usefulness' by taking
charge of a parish.[3]

Even at Ely in 1869 the dean had power only to preach three
times a year in the pulpit of his own cathedral. In 1880 they argued
in the close at Peterborough over the respective powers of dean and
canons. In that year the dean and canons of Chichester, where the
dean was Burgon who had strong ideas on every subject, were at
loggerheads over the same point in the constitution. 'I am bound
to say', wrote Bishop Durnford of Chichester, 'that the existing
relations between the dean and his canons are highly unsatisfactory
and call for a decisive remedy.'[4] In the eighties Dean Purey-Cust of
York steadily recorded a protest in the chapter minutes against the

---

[1] So Francis Close said, PP, 1871, lv, 201.

[2] PP, 1871, lv, 198. Cf. also Alford's article on the subject in *Contemp. Review*, xii,
1869, 38. The canons of Canterbury made it clear that they did not share the views of
the article.

[3] PP, 1854, xxv, 561.   [4] PP, 1871, lv, 211; 1884–5, xxi, 279, 366.

presence of one of his canons.[1] The cathedrals found themselves, sometimes eagerly and sometimes less willingly, in the midst of a movement to reform cathedrals, which like all reforming movements placed a strain upon a constitution unaccustomed to such external pressure.

But though the powers of dean might be hedged, most developments of cathedral life grew from his initiative. Sometimes, as with R. W. Church at St. Paul's, he was blest in being given canons of like mind. Occasionally ancient statutes gave him an authority which enabled him to ride over his chapter. Still more occasionally a powerful dean rode over his chapter whatever the statutes said. Therefore a cathedral often changed when a new dean appeared. It is possible even to name the dean in whose reign several of the cathedrals entered the modern world. Ely (perhaps the earliest), Harvey Goodwin (1858–69); St. Paul's, R. W. Church (1871–90); York, Duncombe (1858–80); Durham, Lake (1869–94); Wells, Plumptre (1881–91); Norwich, Goulburn (1866–89); Lichfield, Bickersteth (1875–92). Some who transformed most vigorously did not always carry their canons with them but went ahead. At York Duncombe exercised almost a personal rule. At Durham Lake, who believed that if the dean was to do good against conservatism he must have authority like that of the headmaster of a school or the vicar of a great parish, went so far as to secure a legal opinion on the dean's powers, to his comfort; and five years later the canons took a legal opinion on the same question, which confirmed the dean's authority.[2]

However opinion varied on the purpose of a cathedral, nearly everyone agreed that the prime duty of the cathedral was *opus dei*, the daily worship of God in a form as beautiful as they could achieve.

The principal difficulty of the dean and chapter, even before they were asked by public opinion to do more than they were doing, was the choir. This difficulty had three separate parts: the boys, adult male singers called in most cathedrals lay clerks, and the clergy whose duty was to sing services, called in some cathedrals minor canons and in other cathedrals priest-vicars. The organist was not usually a difficulty. The work attracted able musicians, and the problem for poor cathedrals was to find a stipend adequate to the work; and sometimes less poor cathedrals had a problem (as with Philip Armes

---

[1] York, Dean and Chapter acts, 3 January 1883. [2] PP, 1884–5, xxi, 91.

at Durham) if the organist needed a holiday. (But some cathedrals, as Salisbury, had an assistant organist.) One or two cathedrals had a small problem over the constitutional position of the organist. At Lichfield for example he was a lay vicar-choral.

St. Paul's cathedral found it easy to find enough boys and men for its choir. But many cathedrals before 1870 had tiny choirs. When Duncombe arrived to be dean of York, the choir consisted of three men and five boys on each side, and this was below what responsible musicians called starvation-rate. About 1833 York had eight men and eight boys. About 1853 the boys were increased to ten, and the organist (Camidge) persuaded the dean and chapter to reduce the singing men from eight to six, and use the money thus saved to pay eight supernumeraries at 10s. a year, the supernumeraries to sing at two Sunday services and one weekday, and attend a choir practice. Duncombe gave the chapter £2,000 to endow the singing men. By 1867 York moved to six men and seven or eight boys on each side.[1] Salisbury in 1884 had three men and seven boys on each side. In 1850 Bristol had only six choirboys, and thirty years later they had eighteen. On 6 February 1880 seventeen of the cathedral organists, headed by Stainer, met at the chapter house of St. Paul's and agreed (with ten absentees also agreeing) (1) that no choir should be less than twenty boys and twelve men; (2) that boys should be boarded in school, and (3) that, because of the increase in demand for music, the organist should be freed from the necessity of earning a living by teaching, and that therefore his stipend should be not less than £400 and a house.[2] Durham, which always had good music despite a choir too small in the earlier years for the space, suffered from the disadvantages that the statutes made no provision for a choir practice, and the adult singers so resented and resisted if required to attend, that they could only be got to practise if the sweet-natured precentor and hymn writer J. B. Dykes went round and begged them to attend as a personal favour.[3] When Bridge went to Westminster abbey (1875), his plan for regular rehearsals was opposed by a choirman of near seventy, who said that on his appointment 'he undertook to obey the laudable customs of the abbey, and he did not find that the laudable customs of the abbey included any rehearsals'. At Westminster abbey a number of men had acquired the right to creep out

---

[1] PP, 1854, xxv, 683; York Dean and Chapter acts, 3 August 1860; PP, 1867, xx 777.   [2] PP, 1884-5, xxi, 243.   [3] PP, 1854, xxv, 685.

before the sermon to earn a stipend by singing at the Chapel Royal.[1]

The choirboys could not be improved except by good schooling. Miss Maria Hackett, who died in 1874, devoted more than fifty years of her life to bettering the condition and happiness of the choirboys, learnt the statutes of cathedrals, went round visiting her charges and raising public opinion. The cathedrals needed to make the choir school the kind of school which would attract parents who wanted their children properly educated. The schools varied widely. At Chester and Salisbury the choir school was disgraceful. At St. Paul's it was reasonable, and the chapter secured an eccentric and celibate Tractarian priest, Albert Barff, who proved to be a most effective headmaster. Exeter choristers' school opened in 1869 as a purely private venture of the choirmaster, and failed to make ends meet because parents refused to send children to a cathedral school, thinking that it was meant only for choirboys. The schools at Canterbury and Durham were regarded as excellent places of education. This kind of reform cost a lot of money, but it had the merit not only of securing good music but of reviving the cathedral's ancient function of promoting good education. Through the sixties and seventies and eighties the cathedrals strengthened both their choir schools and their general schools. The Endowed Schools act of 1869 caused the standards of similar schools to be a matter of public interest, and therefore had an influence on cathedral schools. They needed to raise much fresh money for the purpose. For where, as with many cathedrals, the school dated in its present form from the Reformation, the schoolmaster had been assigned a stipend which remained more stationary than those of the canons, despite the fall in the value of money; and when the cathedral estates were commuted with the Ecclesiastical Commissioners, they were commuted as though the chapter needed to pay obsolete stipends.[2] In some cathedrals the choir school was earlier removed from the historic foundation. At Ely the choir school and the King's School used to be the same. But the choirboys were often out of school for rehearsals

---

[1] F. Bridge, *A Westminster Pilgrim*, 73–4.

[2] *Essays*, ed. Howson, 293. An act of Parliament in 1866 had a clause (section 18) permitting the Ecclesiastical Commissioners to use cathedral money for the benefit of the cathedral school. The Commissioners made enquiry of the cathedral schools, and were evidently alarmed by the result, for on 17 March 1869 they announced that they could not take action under the provisions of the statute. The Endowed Schools act of 1869 (section 27) had a similar but stronger clause authorising the Ecclesiastical Commissioners to make such provision.

or services, and the inconvenience led to a separation and a new choir school on the opposite side of the cathedral from the King's School.[1] Some chapters preferred to move in the opposite direction. Since they had a good grammar school, they incorporated into it the separate choir school—a still more expensive mode of proceeding. Most people agreed that this was the right way to go. The ideal of a reformer like Sir Frederick Gore Ouseley was Magdalen College School, Oxford, where the choir school was the nucleus of a general school.

The devotional life of a choirboy left something to be desired. In a few cathedrals the examples of some of the men singers during the service was irreverent. In 1870 most cathedrals had no prayers in the vestry before or after service. Hereford had such prayers but was regarded as unusual. Chester adopted the practice about 1869, Lincoln about 1871, St. Paul's in 1872, and so the custom spread. Norwich (by 1871) started a new rite by admitting a chorister with a little form of prayers, an address by the dean, and an investiture with the surplice. The standard of reverence in the choirs rose markedly during the seventies.

The lay vicar in the choir might or might not have security of tenure. At Salisbury and York he could be dismissed, at Wells and Durham and Winchester he was appointed for life. At St. Paul's he had a freehold tenure. Even in cathedrals where he was not appointed for life, they did not always like to dismiss him when his voice failed (or for other reasons) because he had no pension and no other means of support. Probably two or three lay vicars in every choir were singing when their voice had failed. Evidence was given in 1883 that of the nine lay vicars at Winchester two or three 'manage to mar all the music of our services, and they cannot be removed'. At Wells we hear talk of 'numerous cases of grossly irreverent conduct during divine service' even as late as the early eighties. Bishop Frederick Temple regarded the college of vicars at Exeter as a serious hindrance to the music.[2] To the end of the century many cathedrals did not know how to get rid of singers who needed to be superannuated. The minutes of the chapter at St. Paul's contain a minute of 1901: 'News was received of the death of Mr. Charles Lockey who was admitted to the vicars-choral in 1844 but owing to the loss of his voice has been represented by deputy since 1859.'[3]

[1] Essays, ed. Howson, 293.
[2] PP, 1883, xxi, 269; 1884–5, xxi, 54, 335.   [3] Matthews-Atkins, 274.

Wells was especially interesting in constitution because of the nature of the college of vicars-choral. It was a cathedral of the old foundation (that is, a secular and not a monastic cathedral during the Middle Ages, and therefore with no break in its continuity at the dissolution of the monasteries). The nine cathedrals of the old foundation (York, London, Chichester, Exeter, Hereford, Lichfield, Lincoln, Salisbury and Wells) still had medieval corporations of vicars-choral or minor canons, usually with their own traditions and property, sometimes with customs and names dear to the historian. The existence of these corporations made, or could make, music more independent of the dean and chapter than probably the music ought to be. At St. Paul's, for example, the minor canon was responsible to his college, not to the dean and chapter. The chapter required the college to provide the statutory duty, and the college must see that the duty be provided.

Wells had the most remarkable of these corporations under a charter of 1591, though being itself much older than 1591. By statute there must be not less than fourteen vicars-choral, but by long custom there were only eleven. In 1874 the chapter raised the number with difficulty, and compensation to the existing incumbents, to fourteen. Since the income of the vicars-choral was not sufficient to maintain a man (the separate endowment being commuted for £880 in 1866), they had other work. If they were laymen, they worked for shops or had trades in the town. If they were clergymen they were called priest-vicars and held benefices in the diocese. Hence the college of vicars-choral suffered from a wide gulf, socially and educationally, between these members who were clergymen and those who were not. Probably in the old days this would not have been so, but the standard of education among clergymen had risen. This gulf had the unfortunate consequence of making some lay members aggressive of their rights. Their conduct inside the cathedral was apt to assert an equality with the priest-vicars and they were inclined to take liberties. And yet their security was such that they could hardly be touched. Dean Johnson of Wells complained that about 1874 his services 'suffered greatly from the non-attendance and insubordination of some members of the body of vicars. One member . . . absented himself from his place in the choir more than five hundred times in one year, in spite of the remonstrances of the dean and chapter . . . Another . . . has been forbidden, on account

V.C.–13

of misconduct and insubordination, to appear in . . . the cathedral; and for some years past has drawn his full income without discharging any duty.'[1]

We must not get these matters out of perspective. However they looked to those inside, these stresses did not often appear on the outside. Out of this constitution the organist at Wells succeeded in performing music which the public greatly liked. The cathedral body was respected in Somerset, and its services were valued. If there was to be criticism, the public was more likely to criticise the standard of preaching than the standard of music.

Yet perhaps the public was not unaware of the problem raised by the corporation of vicars-choral. For when Charles Dickens wrote his last unfinished melodrama, *The Mystery of Edwin Drood*, he set the plot in the cathedral at Cloisterham, where the service is cold and the procession undignified and the surplices dirty, and Jasper the blackguard opium-smoker is the leader of the choir. Harvey Goodwin thought it worth telling the world that this portrait bore no relation whatever to a real cathedral, and nevertheless did not doubt that some readers would believe it.[2] He confessed (1871) that lay singers were still a weak place in some cathedrals, and yet testified that in his own experience some of them were the worthiest members of the whole cathedral body.

A cathedral commission of 1879–85 recommended the dissolution of all these corporations and the transfer of their estates to the dean and chapter.

St. Paul's was also unique. For the minor canons were a corporation, and the vicars-choral another corporation. The act of 1840 looked as though it might suppress the college of minor canons. But no one knew whether it did, and Dean Copleston assumed that it did not, and no one challenged it, and so the college continued. When Liddon became a canon in 1870, and Church became dean in 1871, their reforming drive used this legal doubt. They wanted the minor canon to be responsible to the dean and chapter, and to control absolutely his appointment, to limit the freehold tenure, and to control the seventeen benefices on which the minor canons had a claim. To the alarm of the minor canons they went to Parliament and secured an act of 1875 which, with a subsequent order in council of

---

[1] PP, 1883, xxi, 254–5.
[2] Recollections of a Dean' in *Essays*, ed. Howson, 5, 16.

1876, gave them all that they wished. The minor canon ceased to be able to hold a benefice with his minor canonry. He was made to retire at 55, with the right to a pension for life. 'He is to be a chanting machine', lamented one of the older minor canons, 'without affections and without feelings.'[1] The reform was necessary to the general reformation of St. Paul's.

Meanwhile much discussion continued on the purpose of cathedrals. But whatever view was taken in the discussion, nearly everyone agreed that the system of four residentiary canons who were non-resident most of the time was a bad system. The Earl of Harrowby doubted in 1865 whether the cathedral could ever be made useful to the church. Some proposed that all deans and canons should be abolished and the cathedral be run by chaplains under the bishop,[2] but such a drastic solution was entirely unacceptable to most members of the Church of England, who were proud of their cathedrals and wanted them preserved. Some, who wanted more bishops, thought that it would be good to make every dean a bishop. When the first two suffragan bishops were appointed in the southern province, they were given canonries. Some wanted the chapter cut from four canons to two. Some wanted to compel all the canons to resign their benefices and reside. But it was not easy to see the reason in making the canons of St. David's reside at St. David's where there was nothing to do, nor was it sensible to make the canons reside at any cathedral unless they would have enough work to do. Nor were all good men agreed that canons should be made to reside nine months in the close, wherever the close. And yet it felt wrong that even in 1869 Bishop Phillpotts of Exeter was also a 'residentiary' canon of Durham cathedral.

Some thought that the comparative absence of occupation had an adverse effect on appointments. The corrupt old days were gone, and bishops or the crown appointed the best men whom they could see. But how should you define *best* when there was not much to do? Best for what? So they sometimes chose a man because he had private means, or because he was poor, or because it would be politic to recognise him; and not because he was fit for the work, whatever it might be, that he was chosen to do. In the minority of cathedrals where the crown appointed the canons, some were chosen

---

[1] W. H. Milman in PP, 1883, xxi, 131.
[2] CCR, 1865, 97–8. Cf. J. C. Ryle, *Church Reform*, 1870, iii, 9 ff.

by the prime minister and some by the lord chancellor. Even so late as the sixties, there were those who argued that the prime minister did better than the lord chancellor. For he had an interest in public opinion, he was responsible before this world, at the lowest he did not wish to harm his party. The lord chancellor was not so responsible. In 1869 Dean Law of Gloucester, where as in Bristol the canons were all nominated by the lord chancellor, overstated the matter thus to the archbishops: 'In the case of this church there is scarcely an instance of a lord chancellor making appointment except in favour of some relative, personal friend, or at the request of some influential personage.'[1] And Dean Law was himself the son of a previous bishop. Bishop Monk of Gloucester and Bristol could not remember an occasion when a clergyman from his diocese was preferred to a stall in either of his cathedrals.[2]

The historian Professor Freeman, who did more to illuminate the history of cathedrals than anyone else in the nineteenth century, put the point less unjustly. It was rare to choose a man because he was 'fit'—since no one knew what fitness meant in this work. On the whole the appointments turn out well. Yet they would be better if they were appointments to definite duties and required definite qualifications.[3]

Dean Goulburn of Norwich, who was a man of deep spiritual feeling, argued persuasively that the proper use of cathedrals was simply worship, and therefore that their closes should be harbours of quiet for study and meditation, retreats where men could forget the pressures of the age and open their minds to the things of the spirit. In those days there was not a retreat-house in the Church of England, though Tractarian clergy were beginning to use retreats at a theological college like Cuddesdon or a religious house like Cowley. But this attractive plan might do for St. David's. It was inappropriate for St. Paul's or even for Norwich, and Harvey Goodwin, who had already set Ely on other lines, rejected it as inadequate to justify cathedrals. Dean Francis Close of Carlisle used stronger language, and attacked Goulburn's plan as picturesque and as ancient drapery.[4]

The example of holding great nave services, set by Westminster abbey and St. Paul's cathedral, was followed in several cathedrals. These services were valued and attracted large crowds. Ely had a

[1] PP, 1871, lv, 215.   [2] PP, 1854, xxv, 577.
[3] Essays, ed. Howson, 160.   [4] PP, 1871, lv, 202.

population of 5,000 to 6,000 and under the octagon of the cathedral
on every Sunday evening of 1872 were gathered, it was estimated,
some 1,200 or 1,300 worshippers.[1] They could not be popular
services in the manner of Spurgeon, because cathedrals were
unsuited to the form. Their worship needed to be simple, and yet
with dignity and without aggression. Duncombe said that the
working class loved the choral service held in the nave at York, but
that they did not come only to hear the music, and that the service
was 'a strong religious act'.[2] (Duncombe himself knew nothing
whatever about music.) At York in 1867 they got not less than 2,000
to their nave service at 7.30 p.m. and sometimes they got 3,000.

Not everyone approved of these nave services. Winchester refused
to have them because they might empty the parish churches of the
town. Goulburn did not start an evening service for the poor in
Norwich; and when Dean Lefroy started it, and filled the nave with
working people, some in Norwich did not quite like it and thought
that the cathedral was being turned upside down.[3]

At York Duncombe reckoned that nine-tenths of the working
people who came to the nave services never went to any other
church. This was not the opinion of all in York. Archdeacon Hey
believed that they drew worshippers from the parish churches.
Canon George Trevor was an incumbent in York during the twenty
years after 1847. When he arrived, the cathedral services were cold
and dull and lifeless, and his church services flourished and were
crowded. When Duncombe came, the cathedral filled and Trevor's
church emptied. So in 1867 'I was thoroughly beaten', and he
accepted a country living.[4] Duncombe denied the cause and effect
to be necessary.[5]

The nave service at St. Paul's cathedral became with Liddon's
preaching one of the great services of England. Not less than 2,000
attended, sometimes up to 6,000.

The existence of the nave services probably raised the standards of
cathedral preaching. For they now provided vast congregations and
needed able preachers, and men who knew that they possessed
the unpredictable quality would be readier to accept work in the
cathedral. The standard of preaching at Worcester in 1886, with

[1] Harvey Goodwin, Recollections of a Dean, in *Essays*, ed. Howson, 28.
[2] PP, 1867, xx, 777.   [3] PP, 1884–5, xxi, 54; CCR, 1894, 57.
[4] PP, 1884–5, xxi, 444–5.   [5] CCR, 1869, 241.

Knox Little and Creighton among the canons, was as high as any church of the country. Close went to be dean of Carlisle and McNeile to be dean of Ripon, though it was almost a burial of their preaching gifts.

In the crisis of the thirties some canons, especially Pusey, argued that the cathedrals ought to be centres of theological study. In pursuance of this ideal theological colleges were found at Chichester and Wells and later Lichfield (1857), Salisbury (1861), Exeter (1861) and Gloucester (1868). Many disapproved the schemes. A canon of Canterbury proposed to Archbishop Howley a theological college at Canterbury but was discouraged.[1] The ideal was still alive in the sixties and seventies, but gathered less enthusiasm. It also gathered criticism. Francis Close, who wanted cathedrals to become like parish churches, asked whether they were to be made 'intellectual hospitals for the reception of decayed scholars, and used-up literates?'[2] In the cities where theological colleges were founded, the dean and chapter took little or no notice of them. The college at Wells occupied some buildings of the corporation of vicars-choral, but otherwise had nothing whatever to do with the chapter. ('Study and research', said Dean Johnson of Wells, 'are scarcely feasible. There is no sufficient library, no learned society, and the air is depressing and unfavourable to exertion.'[3]) The chapter at Wells, after thirteen years, chose the first head of the theological college, Pinder, to be a residentiary canon, but were careful to make it plain that they did so because of his personal excellence and not at all because they intended to countenance his college.[4] The plan of more theological colleges kept being suggested, and that one canonry should be reserved for its head, but little was done. Even the cathedral commission of 1883 suggested, for example, that one of the canons of Chester should be head of a theological college (meaning St. Aidan's at Birkenhead). Not as much was done as might have been expected because in the seventies the founders of theological colleges began to look to the universities. But two of the best of the 'cathedral' theological colleges were founded in this epoch: Scholae Cancellariae (1874) by Bishop Wordsworth at Lincoln (the name betrays his interest in continuity with medieval statutes) and Ely

---

[1] PP, 1854, xxv, 247. [2] PP, 1871, lv, 202. [3] PP, 1883, xxi, 252.
[4] PP, 1854, xxv, 613. The chapter elected residentiary canons from the prebendaries. The act of 1840 brought the system to an end but it continued so long as a canon continued who held office before 1840.

Theological College by Bishop Woodford in 1876. Wordsworth regarded the universities as places from which after 1871 it was better to keep away. 'Now they were driven from the universities', said Wordsworth in a speech at Cambridge, 'they would have to look to the cathedrals, which would become the fortresses of the church.'[1]

The theological college and the chapter had little to do with each other, before the foundations of the seventies, because the college was essentially the bishop's college. Cuddesdon indeed had been founded nowhere near the chapter, but seven miles away opposite the front gate of the bishop's palace. This circumstance was a sign of what was soon seen to be the great weakness of the cathedrals. They had nothing to do with the bishop. The bishop might have certain rights in the cathedrals, like holding ordinations or preaching on certain days. But there it ended. The cathedral was hardly part of the diocese and was not part of the diocesan system. 'The cathedral', wrote Prebendary Perry of Lincoln, '. . . is in no true sense the mother church of the diocese. Rather it resembles an extraneous ornament or decorative addition to the diocesan edifice.'[2] And therefore nearly all the reformers of the sixties and seventies, with Harvey Goodwin at their head, wanted to integrate the cathedral into the diocesan machinery.

The gap between diocese and chapter was wide before 1840. Some observers believed that the act of 1840 made it wider; partly in state of mind, because the chapters did not approve of bishops who joined the Whig plan to reform them by taking away their money; and partly by the consequences of abolishing so many (382) cathedral offices. These 382 prebends or offices were perhaps trivial and useless. But they linked 382 people, in some tangible manner, to the cathedral. It was true that the bishop could make men honorary canons, and the prebends continued as titles. But almost everywhere the honorary canonries were purely honorary. After the man was admitted he had no more to do with the cathedral than before. In the

[1] Harvey Goodwin started the plan to found a college at Ely. He went to Bishop Turton. 'He was very kind and civil, but he requested him to allow him to die and get out of the way before he took any action in the matter.' Goodwin's speech at Cambridge, reported in *Cambridge Independent Press*, 4 June 1881, p. 7. Goodwin strongly pleaded for it in his letter to the archbishops of 1869, PP, 1871, lv, 212. If there are to be theological colleges in cathedral closes, what more suitable place than Ely, so linked with the university of Cambridge? 'It might be regarded as an outlying college of the university.' For Wordsworth's contrary view see *Cambridge Independent Press*, ibid.   [2] PP, 1884–5, xxi, 412.

cathedrals of the old foundation, especially at York, the honorary prebendary had more right, for he might share (for example) in the election of the bishop. Many reformers wanted to give the honorary canons a say in the chapter, that is, to make the constitution of the cathedral of the new foundation resemble those of the old foundation. The commission of 1879–85 recommended that this be done by act of Parliament.

The new deans and new bishops of the later half of the century, at varying speeds according to a variety of men, sought to diminish the gap. But it was slow work; partly because of custom, and partly because residentiary canons who were mostly non-resident could not be free to do diocesan work. Bishop Philpott of Worcester had so little to do with his chapter that as late as 1886 one of the canons was astonished at being invited to be his examining chaplain.[1] But by then it was a survival, for Philpott was the most old-fashioned bishop on the bench. And Worcester, like certain other cathedrals (Canterbury, London, Bristol, Gloucester, Norwich) had this constitutional oddity, that the bishop or archbishop appointed none of the canons residentiary. These cathedrals were often grateful that appointments by crown or lord chancellor brought other than diocesan interests into the choice of persons. But when the bishop chose none of the canons, the interests of the diocese were not, or were felt by the clergy to be not adequately represented. Some bishops, who lived in remote places, moved or wanted to move into their cathedral town. Phillpotts lived outside Torquay, Temple moved into Exeter. King moved from Riseholme, four miles north of Lincoln, to the old palace south of the minster. Stubbs wanted to move from Cuddesdon into Oxford and would not forgive the Ecclesiastical Commissioners because they prevented him. Thorold of Winchester wanted to move out of Farnham Castle but historical memories were too strong for him. The biggest of these moves was the removal by Temple of the archbishop's country house, by the sale of Addington Park, to Canterbury. Their motive, however, was not to make the cathedral more diocesan, but the bishop more diocesan.

What the leading reformers wanted was, first, to make the canons reside like the dean for eight months instead of three; therefore to provide canons' houses in those few closes where only one existed; therefore to prevent canons holding other benefices. They did not

[1] *Life of Creighton*, i, 352–3.

wish canons not to hold any other work in the church. They were content that Oxford or Durham canons should be professors, that one canon of St. Paul's (Liddon) should also be a professor at Oxford and another canon of St. Paul's (Lightfoot) should also be a professor at Cambridge, that suffragan bishops or archdeacons should hold canonries in the diocese where they worked. But the remaining canonries they wished to be used in diocesan work. A diocesan committee at Gloucester, for example, recommended that one canon should be a diocesan missioner; another should be lecturer in theology at the theological college; a third should take charge of religious education in the diocese.[1] The habit of mind quickly became so dominant, that warnings were uttered against making cathedrals too diocesan. The railway helped most cathedrals but St. David's to become centres of their diocese. They reserved side-chapels for private prayer (St. Paul's first made provision for private prayer late in 1870); organised lectures in the chapter-house; gathered the organisations of a modern diocese, school-teachers, missioners, temperance workers; made themselves more available to requests from parishes in the diocese; held missions and quiet days; and, though never a formal council of the bishop as some reformers wanted them to be, made themselves auxiliaries to the bishop at his request. In 1853 only twelve cathedrals had a weekly celebration of the holy communion. Thirty years later this looked quite different. They emptied their side-chapels of junk and furnished them as chapels; not without delay on account of scruples that it was un-Anglican to have more than one altar in a church. York was the first to have a choral celebration, in 1866.

Harvey Goodwin succeeded in making Ely into a force in the diocese, even though his bishop (Browne) sometimes wished that the cathedral was sited at Cambridge. He even used a transept, curtained off, for the first diocesan conference (1866) not without a little criticism that the cathedral was secularised if used for a public meeting. The climax of the Ely revival was the service commemorating the twelve hundredth anniversary of the foundation, when the cathedral was crowded from the altar to the west door, and Bishop Magee of Peterborough preached to 6,000 folk in a voice which could be heard at the far end of the nave.

The cathedral building could be taken to the heart. Harvey

[1] PP, 1884–5, xxi, 213.

Goodwin was not ashamed to confess that after begging for it and watching every crack with anxiety, he was in love with Ely cathedral.[1] More remarkable perhaps was the affection of Benjamin Jowett who had never been a canon.

The world saw St. Paul's cathedral as the supreme example of change for the better. For though Sydney Smith did much for it, and Archdeacon Hale did something, and Dean Milman did something, it was famous before 1870 for an old-world disorganisation. Its music and choir were slovenly, though Goss was a fine musician, because he had no idea how to control a choir and because some of the singing men took little notice of anyone. The choir never rehearsed, except for special occasions. The architecture induced a chill which the lack of reverence within did little to warm. Its prebendaries were at legal war with the residentiary canons over their rights and in 1867 won in court the right to join in electing a proctor. One or two of its officers survived from days before the Whig reforms of the thirties, like Precentor Belli, brother-in-law to Archbishop Howley, who died in 1886 aged 94 but had only appeared two or three times in the cathedral during many years. Only the library was beginning to be organised by the first of the new type of scholarly cathedral librarian, Sparrow Simpson, appointed under Milman in 1861.

Reform needed money and men. It got the money when in 1872 the chapter agreed to a commutation of estates with the Ecclesiastical Commissioners, and this recovery of a stable income was necessary to what followed. A remarkable series of appointments gave it the most distinguished and harmonious chapter in the Church of England; Gregory as canon (by Disraeli 1868), a foursquare Tory high churchman who devoted his life to the cathedral and its organisation; Liddon as canon (Gladstone, 1870), so that St. Paul's with its poor acoustics became the most famous house of preaching in England; Church as dean (Gladstone, 1871, after Hook refused); Lightfoot as canon (1871). Liddon got hold of Stainer to succeed Goss as organist (stipend, but whole time, £400, instead of Goss's £250 to be supplemented by outside work), and Stainer was not only an even better musician than Goss but an organist of the first rank and a devout man. Stainer suffered many difficulties in his endeavour to secure choir practices, eliminate bad voices, and get

---

[1] Recollections of a Dean, in *Essays*, ed. Howson, 3.

regular attendance, and at one point the voluntary choir for Sunday evenings resigned in a body. The music became more beautiful, the behaviour of the choir more reverent, the preaching better, the services more attractive and numerous. A chapel for private prayer, 1870; vestry prayers, 1872; choirboys began to wear cassocks under surplices, 1872; men began to wear cassocks under surplices, 1873; passion music in holy week, 1873 (not without overcoming scruples in Dean Church); choristers moved to new school, 1875; holy communion every day, 1877; three hours devotion, 1878; preaching every weekday in Lent, 1882.[1] The cathedral gained a reputation for high churchmanship, because its most prominent canon was the leader of the high church party after Pusey's death, because its dean was an old Tractarian, and because some of their activities followed the ideals of the high church party. They suffered the law-suit over thereredos and three disturbing incidents from brawlers. They expected disturbance at the first three hours devotion, but did not get it. But they were not in the narrow sense ritualistic, for they did not even wear copes or coloured stoles until 1897.

In the eighties and nineties men who spoke on cathedrals often held up the new St. Paul's as a model of what the cathedral ought to be.

The reform of the cathedrals engendered not only stress in the chapters but an occasional conflict with the public. The ritual innovations, moderate though they were, caused a few scenes of brawling at St. Paul's. That great service for charity children, which filled St. Paul's with wooden stands for weeks on end, was dismantled in 1877 not without regret. The worst clash came at Worcester. The three choirs festival of music had a warm place in the affection of the three counties and beyond their borders, had continued unimpeded since the eighteenth century, and produced good money for the poor children of clergy in the three dioceses. Its stands, sometimes constructed even over the altar, its secularity, the atmosphere of a concert hall imported into the cathedral, offended reformers. In 1875 the dean and chapter of Worcester unanimously

[1] Attendances in 1878: Dean Church, 380; Gregory, 324; Liddon (also professor at Oxford), 184; Lightfoot (also professor at Cambridge, 180; Claughton (also arch-deacon and assistant bishop), 160. PP, 1883, xxi, 110. The first provision for private prayer was a little grudging—in the choir between noon and 3 p.m. on weekdays, on application to a verger. G, 70, 819. The reform of St. Paul's has been studied by G. L. Prestige, *St. Paul's in its Glory* and Atkins in Matthews-Atkins, 250ff.

determined to change it. They refused to give the cathedral to the musicians unless all music should be part of a service and admission was free to the poor. This stand caused a storm in the diocese and the local press, and for two or three years Worcester had the most unpopular dean and chapter in England, and the festival of 1875 had to be held only with organ and choir. But Gloucester and Hereford continued almost unchanged, Bishop Philpott of Worcester refused to support his chapter, and in 1878, when the turn of Worcester came again, the chapter gave way on the understanding that the oratorio should be a service and that the hideous structures should not be erected. The affair did them no good in Worcester, but it made for reverence at the three choirs festivals in all three cathedrals.

The popular impression of cathedrals was long in fading. When Westcott became a canon of Peterborough he wrote to his wife the first day: 'Faith is omnipotent even in a cathedral town.'[1] When Creighton went to see Worcester cathedral, he horrified the courteous canon who greeted him by saying that he had been offered a canonry, and wished to know 'whether the members of the chapter quarrelled; because if so, nothing would induce him to come'.[2] A parish priest of 1895 thought that still the cathedrals were used as places of honourable retirement.[3] Indeed among their functions honourable part-retirement continued to find an occasional place, with the approval of all.

Some of the new canons, like some of the old, were unmusical, and one witness gave public evidence that during the anthem at Oxford one canon read the psalms and another the thirty-nine articles. Dean Stanley was notorious at Westminster abbey for his inability to care about the music.[4]

The cathedral commission of 1879 to 1885, first under Tait and then under Harvey Goodwin, made recommendations to further these reforming ideals, and brought bills to Parliament. They wanted a standing commission empowered to give, and alter, statutes for each cathedral according to circumstances. But it was slow work, for the bills never got through Parliament. At bottom the act of 1840 needed amending if the cathedrals were to flourish, and to tamper with the act of 1840 might mean tampering with that modest

---

[1] Letter of 1869 from Westcott in Selwyn College MSS.
[2] *Life of Creighton*, i, 310.   [3] CCR, 1895, 611.
[4] CCR, 1894, 52–3; F. Bridge, 72.

prosperity of parochial life which depended on the use of cathedral endowments in parishes.[1] In 1873 Beresford Hope secured the passing of a cathedrals act which permitted re-endowment of canonries where money was provided by private benefaction, in order that a canon might have a specific function, provided that the existing chapter, the bishop and the queen in council, agreed. The cathedrals managed by collecting money, by drawing crowds to special services, by wise deans and wise bishops, and by that mellow tradition and musical worship which made them so historic a part of English religious life. Men commented that thirty years before they had been one of the weakest parts of English religious life and now were one of the strongest.

The reformers were so busy trying to find work for the old cathedrals that they could hardly imagine anyone wanting to found a new one. 'We may as well expect another Iliad from a Greek poet', wrote Harvey Goodwin in 1872, 'as another cathedral from an English architect.'[2] They reckoned without the historic sensibility and civic pride of the English laity.

New dioceses were founded; Southwell was chosen because like Ripon and Manchester it had an ancient cathedral church. The first bishop, George Ridding, was thus provided with a cathedral for his diocese whether he wanted it or not. He was totally puzzled by the question what to do with it. What is the good, he asked, of a cathedral in a village? Is it not better to change?[3] However, it had an endowment to maintain its daily worship.

The first bishop of Truro was E. W. Benson, a man of strongly antiquarian tastes who was much interested in the history of cathedrals and who as canon of Lincoln was the chief agent of Bishop Wordsworth in doing what he could to make the cathedral more diocesan.[4] He could not conceive a diocese without a cathedral

---

[1] Between 1840 and 31 October 1898 the Commissioners endowed and augmented about 5,800 benefices, and this with grants for parsonages made grants of above £817,290 per annum equivalent to a capital sum of about £24,584,500; of which a greater part came from the money which before 1840 belonged to cathedrals. Cf. PP, 1899, xix, 250.

[2] Recollections of a Dean, in *Essays*, ed. Howson, 7.　　　　[3] CCR, 1885, 250.

[4] Wordsworth called his greater chapter together to consider with them what should be the future of the cathedral, CCR, 1873, 340. Nothing much was done till W. J. Butler became the dean in 1885. Cf. Chadwick, *Edward King*, 23–24. Dean Blakesley used drily to block Benson's plans. And yet Arthur Benson as a boy found

church nor a bishop without a chair. But though his enthusiasm was indispensable, the enthusiasm of Cornishmen almost equalled it. They wanted their bishop, and now wanted their cathedral. By this date the diocesan function of cathedrals had developed so strongly that a diocese looked amorphous without a cathedral. So Truro cathedral was founded, out of a tiny and dilapidated parish church of St. Mary's with its choir. Here the bishop remained uniquely the dean until such time as a dean might be appointed, but a dean never was appointed. The foresight of Henry Phillpotts of Exeter had retained an extra canonry in 1840 in order that it might become a canonry of a Cornish see.

The founding of new sees was seen as a partial reversal of the act of 1840. That act abolished many resident canonries. The number of resident canonries now grew again, but the canons who occupied them were more resident than those who had been suppressed.

The struggle of Truro to create a cathedral stirred interest and sympathy everywhere, for men imagined that such a work was not of the modern age, and thus their sympathy contributed to the feeling that each new diocese should have a cathedral and a chapter.

When the sees of Wakefield and Liverpool and Newcastle were founded, their bishops were too busy with other things, and Ryle of Liverpool was well known as one who thought the historic system of cathedrals to be a survival and a mistake. Though under pressure from the laity, he would take no action to secure a cathedral for

---

much beauty in the cathedral of Blakesley's time. Cf. A. C. Benson, *The Trefoil*, 116, 140ff.

Truro cathedral was instantly short of money, with heavy expenses, little income, a debt, and no houses for residentiaries. The south aisle was still reserved for the parish church. The statutes followed the modern axioms in providing for a canon missioner to the diocese, and indeed the formation of an order of preachers in the diocese under his headship. Benson founded a theological college which lasted 1877–1900. Henry Phillpotts left a lot of money for a theological college at Exeter, and such a college existed during his last years, for he greatly admired the college at Wells. But after his death the project languished, and Exeter used the money instead to keep students at Oxford an extra year to study theology. Truro felt this diversion of the intention of Phillpotts to be a grievance, and tried but failed to get the money for its own college. The entire organisation was founded on (1) an Exeter canonry of £1,000 from Phillpotts's prudence, which they divided into two canonries; (2) a private gift from Benson to make a canon-missioner at £100 a year; (3) a gift of £800 a year which Temple of Exeter gave from his stipend when the see was founded; and (4) the stipend of the rector of St. Mary's (under £100 a year) who continued as sub-dean. In 1894 Truro cathedral had about £1,200 a year, and Exeter had over £11,000. All else had to come from gifts in an area with no industry and a diminishing population. Cf. CCR, 1894, 37–49.

Liverpool when he needed so much money to extend the ordinary work of the diocese. The diocese of Bristol was re-created in 1897 but already had an ancient cathedral. Newcastle, Wakefield, Liverpool and St. Albans remained parish churches with a vicar or rector and curates. St. Albans was a very special case because the diocese, without any other natural unity, was founded round the old dilapidated abbey as a suitable cathedral. No provision was made for a dean and chapter. The restoration therefore fell into the hands of the powerful layman Lord Grimthorpe, whose restoration included the most systematic destruction of medieval work in any English restoration, but who could do what he liked because he supplied nearly all the money from his pocket and because no dean nor chapter existed to influence his decisions.

Here is a little contrast at Manchester between the old world and the new.

Canon Wray of Manchester,[1] who died in 1867, could remember the days before Bonaparte, and was old-fashioned. 'He disliked hymns, evening services and, above all, extempore preaching.' He was always careful to keep 5 November as a holy day. He never walked to church, like his dean, 'but always drove thither in a roomy carriage and pair, with footmen in dark blue liveries. In the chapter house he bowed to the dean, and addressed him as *Sir*, extending his full hand to the canons, and two fingers to the non-capitular members; when a curate approached him, he had to be content with one finger.' He used to dine the neighbouring curates with excellent wine, and exhort them 'to be thankful for present mercies', and remind them that 'although they must not all expect prizes in the church, they need not remain curates all the days of their lives, for even the Archbishop of Canterbury was once a curate'. In his duties he was regular and taught weekly in the Sunday school, and men revered him as the good old canon. He gave the ancient communicants a Christmas dinner of beef and plum pudding, and gave the schoolchildren hot cross buns on Good Friday, and willed money to buy good worsted stockings each year for eight poor men and eight poor women who usually attended service at the cathedral. He claimed to have baptised more babies, and married more couples, than any other clergyman of the Church of England. He felt able to preach in 1863 a sermon which he had preached in 1803, but then his

[1] Huntington, *Random Recollections*, 283ff.

sermons were not audible. 'He loved the Old Church, its worship, its people, its customs.'

Only fourteen years after Canon Wray died, John Oakley became dean of Manchester.[1] He was a well-to-do priest, formerly president of the Oxford union, whom Tait persuaded to accept the slum parish of St. Saviour's, Hoxton. Over fifteen years he transformed the parish, becoming a Christian Socialist in the process, a lover of Maurice as well as of Pusey and Keble, making his politics part of his religion, taking the chair at meetings between clergy and representatives of the trades unions, and exhausting his restless spirit. In 1881 Gladstone made him Dean of Carlisle, presumably for a rest; but he caused joy and consternation by behaving not at all like a dean of Carlisle, shaking hands with the vergers, travelling third class on the railway, singing in the choral society as a member of the chorus, inviting labourers to meet their employers in his drawing-rooms, not merely advocating public baths but swimming in them, seldom wearing gaiters or aprons, attempting to make the cathedral 'popular', importing evergreens at Christmas and flowers at Easter, and starting a Sunday evening service. He was a little incongruous in Carlisle and after only two years Gladstone transferred him to Manchester, where he was not at once welcome even to the bishop because, ever at the side of rebels, he publicly defended the conduct of the imprisoned Lancashire ritualist Green. He was never quite accepted in Manchester by some who had the welfare of the cathedral at heart, but was among the best of all the Christian Socialist pastors, and when he died his family received a resolution of sympathy from the gasworkers' union, whose strike he had lately backed. His was a nimble, agitated mind, always on the side of the underdog, always turning after the latest idea, unable to suffer fools, rapid in speech and deeply compassionate. He wore himself out and died at the age of 56.

Westminster abbey had a special function, that of national sanctuary. Its monuments and tombs and history made so interesting a spectacle that it was sometimes hard for Christian prayer and worship amid the crowds and sightseers. Under the deans of the second half of the century it failed to achieve the place which St. Paul's achieved in the affections of the Church of England. It had

[1] *Manchester Guardian*, 11 June 1890.

no daily communion till 1901, and St. Faith's chapel was used as a store till 1895. And yet it moved, though more slowly, in the same direction. Its revival of worship was delayed because the commutation of estates was postponed till 1888, and during the eighties they were affected by the poverty of agriculture. They could not replace the aged Turle by the effective Frederick Bridge as organist till 1882. While at St. Paul's the canons were predominantly high churchmen, at the abbey they were predominantly broad churchmen as was appropriate to a society so identified with the name of Dean Stanley —Kingsley, Farrar, Basil Wilberforce, Westcott, Henson. (But Gore was canon 1894–1902.) And Stanley's enterprise, however disapproved by some, caused the abbey to make innovations which no ordinary cathedral dared. We have seen how the abbey started those nave services which were afterwards so important in the cathedral revival. The abbey first (1871) accepted passion music as suitable.

Stanley was almost incapable of administering those details which composed the reform of a great church, and which so engaged a Gregory at St. Paul's and a Duncombe at York. These changes were slowly achieved rather by the canons than by the dean, and the chapter was still guilty of one or two misjudgments. But Stanley was perfectly appropriate to his office. This disciple of Arnold thought of the Church of England as the religious face of the nation, and the stones of the abbey spoke to him of the Christian state through the centuries. He was succeeded by another disciple of Arnold in G. G. Bradley, dean from 1882 to 1902.

The only problem which need here concern us, because no diocesan cathedral except St. Paul's needed to attend to it, was the problem of burials, monuments, tombs, busts. By the end of the eighteenth century the abbey was already crowded with tombs and monuments, for to be buried there a person could be rich instead of distinguished. The dean and chapter had never been precise over the quality of life in those whose bodies or memorials they admitted. The chapter in the nineteenth century, aware that it had little space, became acutely conscious of the need to limit the memorials to those of a truly national eminence, and to exclude persons whom it was hardly fitting to commemorate in so great a Christian sanctuary.

On the second ground they refused twice to admit a statue of Lord Byron. But the tradition of the abbey never enquired too closely. When Lord Palmerston died, Lord John Russell curtly telegraphed to Dean Stanley that the funeral would take place in the abbey on Friday, and Stanley, though he had the office of deciding, regarded this telegram as an intervention by government which removed from him the responsibility; this intervention was publicly criticised on moral grounds. Dean Bradley at once assented to the request for Darwin's interment and with general approval, though he did not avoid all criticism, and later by telegram to Venice offered interment for Browning. Dean Armitage Robinson refused a memorial to Herbert Spencer, but on the ground that he was not eminent enough in his contribution to philosophy. There was an interesting discussion of the proposal to bury George Eliot in the abbey. Livingstone was buried in the presence of a crowd, Dickens at his own wish in the presence of a handful of mourners.

But the difficulty of deciding on national eminence was great. When a man died, his friends usually believed in his eminence, but it was not always certain that posterity would confirm the verdict, and yet the dean must decide instantaneously. Stanley did not want to allow Sir Rowland Hill into the abbey, but allowed himself to be overruled by strong representations.[1]

Stanley used to lay much stress on the need for a requisition, especially from the secretary of state of the department related to the dead man's sphere of eminence. But he could not quite keep his own rules, for he consented to Charles Dickens without any such request, and once offered burial for the American George Peabody because he had been a benefactor to London. There was argument over a proposal that Longfellow be buried in the abbey. But the great controversy, debated even in Parliament, concerned a statue in the abbey to the Prince Imperial, son of Louis Napoleon, who died fighting in the Zulu war, for Queen Victoria wished for it, and anonymous letters threatened dynamite if it were erected, and at last the House of Commons passed a resolution against it. The debates produced widely opposite views, from those who protested against any interference by the Commons in a sacred place, and those who contended that it was the 'national Walhalla', as one member put it, over which the representatives of the nation should rightly exert influence. The Commons included in its resolution an assertion of

[1] PP, 1890–1, xliv, 656; cf. also Stancliffe in *Hist. of Westminster Abbey*, ed. E. Carpenter, 303.

'the national character' of the abbey, but did not accept a suggestion that no monuments might be erected without leave from the first commissioner of works.[1]

Various schemes were put forward to extend the space for monuments. The difficulties were great when monuments were placed in sites otherwise inappropriate, and when a medallion to W. E. Forster had to be placed so high that no one could read an inscription. Some objected that they had to have standing statues because there was no room for recumbent statues. Gilbert Scott produced a scheme for a *campo santo* in 1853, and again in 1863, and various other schemes were put forward, for building at the west end, or near poet's corner, or in the cloister, or in St. Margaret's church, and men wondered whether to persuade St. Paul's to accept more national monuments but were much discouraged by Canon Gregory,[2] and wondered whether to remove old monuments of no importance but were much discouraged by antiquaries. From 1860 they used windows as a means of commemoration, the first to officers killed in the Indian mutiny. All the schemes foundered on expense, and left the same difficulty for the twentieth century.

The art of stained glass started the reign as a poor medievalism and had not the technique or equipment to attain the results which it sought; but after the researches of Charles Winston and W. E. Chance, the production of 'antique' glass from 1863 onwards allowed the artists to attempt far less crude mosaics; and the art attained its Victorian zenith, not with the aesthetic innovations of William Morris and Edward Burne-Jones, but in the Tractarian artist Charles Eamer Kempe, who had only been deterred from taking holy orders by reason of a distressing stutter, and who was first brought to fame by his decoration of Castle Howard chapel in 1872. His windows appeared in several cathedrals (Wakefield, Gloucester, Southwell, St. Paul's, Lichfield), he restored the windows of King's College Chapel, Cambridge, and some of his fairest work may be found in parish churches. But Kempe was but first among several fine artists, of whom Henry Holiday, and the partners J. R. Clayton and Alfred Bell, were perhaps the foremost.

[1] The Prince Imperial's statue was suspected of being a political act against the French republic; or it was feared that some Frenchmen might so regard it. Hansard ccxlix, 1879, 531; ccliv, 1880, 699.   [2] Cf. PP, 1890-1, xliv, 602-3.

9. CATHEDRAL MUSIC AND PARISH MUSIC

Samuel Sebastian Wesley was the organist who did most to advance the music of cathedrals. He went from Hereford cathedral to Exeter cathedral, then to serve Hook at Leeds parish church and then again to Winchester cathedral and finally to Gloucester cathedral, trying to improve taste and standards, making better music available, and forming at last the opinion that deans and canons and precentors had better be removed because they interfered with good music. He was widely regarded as the best organist of his day.

Music needed to serve two incompatible purposes. As educated worshippers wished the language of their prayers cast into suitable language that would not jar them by slang or by pretentiousness, and would sometimes uplift them by its poetry or rhythm, they wished the music to be the most beautiful that they could create. And some of them, especially the musicians, could hardly understand any other point of view. Stainer once compared bad singing by a congregation to the same congregation assisting with pots of paint to bedaub the walls of the church as a crude form of decoration.[1] He thought that a voice which sounded like a bee in a bottle ought to keep silence for the sake of others during the musical part of the worship.

At the opposite extreme churchgoers knew that they wanted to sing because religion caused them to want to sing praises, and did not care whether the music was by Bach or Handel so long as they could sing. In the earlier Victorian age country and town churches, in the endeavour to make the service more congenial, tried to imitate cathedral music. In big towns this could be (though it was not always) very successful, in little villages it could be (though it was not always) unsuccessful. Later Victorian congregations reacted somewhat against this imitation of cathedrals. Men wanted to sing, regarded anthems with suspicion, and did not quite approve music suitable to the choir but not suitable to the people. They reacted somewhat because choirs got better and as they got better they naturally became ambitious. Part singing was not common among ordinary parish choirs, even in 1868. It became steadily more common, and so the choir ceased to be confined to leading the people in unison. Some reacted for similar reasons against the early Victorian drive to

[1] CCR, 94, 532.

put the choir in the chancel, on the ground that the choir in the chancel was isolated from the people.

Meanwhile far better music was available. The house of Novello played a distinguished part in making available better church music. Alfred Novello was an excellent manager as well as a good musician, and understood mass-production with the modern methods of printing. Between 1846 and 1859 he brought down the cost of the score of the *Messiah* from 6s. to 1s. 4d.[1] Choirs were able to sing because they could buy enough copies of what was good to sing. And when Stainer took the view that no one should be allowed to sing badly, he did not take the extreme view that all church music should be of the highest taste. He wanted to defend the anthem as one of the glories of English church services, but was well aware that congregations sometimes needed music that was popular. Austere musicians accused the romantic composers of hymn-tunes like J. B. Dykes (as with his tune for *Lead kindly light*) of weakness and sentimentality, as if taste was being debased for the sake of the common people—'we are giving to God what is not good enough for man'.[2] Stainer warmly defended Dykes, for he saw that a hymn tune was not only a melody but an instrument of evangelism. And it was agreed that if musicians insisted only on the highest music in churches, the result must be a break between the churches and the musician's art.

The austere point of view reached its climax in the Yattendon Hymnal (1899), where the poet Robert Bridges attempted a hymn-book where neither words nor music would fall below the highest taste, and in the preface to its notes confessed disarmingly that some tunes could not be sung by a congregation. It was agreed that the hymn might not only be good music but music which the people wanted to sing. Not every organist was quite reconciled to Arthur Sullivan's tune to *Onward, Christian Soldiers*. And yet even Liddon, who personally disliked all the modern part of *Hymns ancient and modern*, believed that hymns did more than anything to keep religion alive among the masses.[3]

An enquiry of 1872 showed that in one Worcestershire town thirteen different hymn-books were in use, and in another town twelve. In that year it was calculated that some 3,500 Anglican churches did

[1] Scholes, 752.   [2] G, oo, 1532, Hadow.
[3] Liddon to Holland, 9 January 1887; Paget, *Holland*, 145.

not use one of the three best known hymn-books. Two decades later a similar enquiry produced astonishingly different results. The return of 1894 showed that 13,280 churches or chapels out of 13,659 used one of the three main hymn-books and only 379 used others. The three books conquered on merit and convenience.[1]

From time to time proposals were made that the Church of England should have an authorised hymn-book. It was odd that everything in church should be controlled except the words of the hymns which on some worshippers had more influence than any other words; and those who understood that the law of prayer was the law of belief sometimes feared lest error be introduced into the faith by the use of words which became familiar and so beloved. By the end of the century the three chief hymn-books were almost universal.

They were (1) *Hymns Ancient and Modern* (1861, appendix 1868, revised edition 1875, supplement 1889); by 1882 used in twenty-one cathedrals and most London churches and by authority in the army and navy; of moderate Tractarian inspiration; dominant before the end of the century. The principal founder was Sir Henry Williams Baker, vicar of Monkland in Herefordshire. Keble took a close interest. New music principally by Dykes, Ouseley and W. H. Monk.

(2) *The Hymnal Companion to the Book of Common Prayer*, 1870, edited by the evangelical E. H. Bickersteth, based on the *Psalms and Hymns* of 1858.

(3) *Church Hymns*, S.P.C.K., 1870. About 250 hymns were common to all three collections.

They could not amalgamate these hymn-books into a single authorised hymn-book because scruples were still felt over some of the words, and the new comprehensiveness of the Church of England was nowhere demonstrated more clearly than in 1894 when the Lower House of Convocation accepted a motion implying that the church was (at present) better off with its varieties to suit different schools.

Until after 1860 the cathedrals used the anthems of the old English composers or foreign composers. In the fifties the influence of Spohr and Mendelssohn became very marked, and its romantic sentiment filled the mood of the expanding taste in church music, so that the

[1] *Chron. Convoc.* 1894, April, 145–6. For hymody see M. Frost, *Historical Companion to Hymns A. & M.*, 1962; and Julian.

English composers like J. B. Dykes or Joseph Barnby or Arthur Sullivan, and later Stainer, wrote rich and emotional anthems. In the eighties, with changing taste, the reaction began against 'sentimentality' or at least towards sobriety, represented especially by Stanford. Between 1870 and 1900 far more church music was composed in England than at any previous epoch. Meanwhile the romantic mid-Victorian age gave the English churches a new treasure in Christmas carols. Novello first advertised Christmas music and hymns in 1850.[1] In December 1853 Thomas Helmore published *Carols for Christmastide, set to ancient melodies*, in which John Mason Neale wrote or arranged the words. But it does not appear that the Christmas carol became domiciled in the churches until after the publication by H. R. Bramley of *Christmas Carols, Old and New*, 1867. From about this date carol services, or at least the use of carols, spread rapidly from church to church.[2] The carol service of nine lessons was invented at Truro by Bishop Benson.[3]

While he was at Leeds, Wesley, who disliked plainsong, prepared a pointed psalter for the use of parish choirs, but parish choirs were not yet universally ready to chant psalms.

In 1878 Novello published *The Cathedral Psalter*, and parish churches largely adopted it. In the Peterborough diocese (1897) 219 out of 356 churches used it, but all the others used one pointed psalter or another.[4]

Alfred Novello, being himself of Italian Roman Catholic descent, made methods of plainsong known during the forties, but the book which most high Anglican choirs used was Thomas Helmore's *Manual of Plainsong* (1849), for Helmore tried out plainsong in St. Mark's college at Chelsea and at Holy Trinity, Brompton.

The Gregorian movement met opponents who regarded it as high church, and opponents like Wesley who thought it a reversion to primitive music or even barbaric music. For a time it advanced into parish churches, especially in the fifties and sixties, but congregations found it too difficult and soon there was reaction. In the eighties its use was probably less common than in the sixties. Only seven churches

---

[1] Scholes, 559.
[2] Scholes, 560; Bramley published a second series in 1870. Cf. also Richard Chope, *Carols for use in church* (1868–76) and Woodward's *Cowley Carol Book* (1900). Cummings's adaptation of the Mendelssohn tune for *Hark the Herald Angels sing* conquered from 1867. Scholes, 561.
[3] *Life of Benson*, i, 484.   [4] Scholes, 551.

of the Peterborough diocese in 1897 used Gregorian chants.[1]

When the old barrel organ was removed, the new organ was often a simple instrument and exhausting to play for very long. Even the organ at Bristol cathedral in the nineties was regarded by musicians as primitive. Country organs were pumped by hand, as are many still, but St. Paul's cathedral had eight organ blowers as lately as 1864. The first electric organs were built in 1868–9 for Christ Church, Camberwell and for St. Michael's, Cornhill. As late as February 1873 an 'experienced' organ-blower advertised in the *Musical Times* for a situation 'in cathedral or church'. The hydraulic or electrical organ became quickly common. In the middle years of the reign the profession of organist was overstocked, to judge by the number of applications in answer to advertisements. Though the pay was small, it was a useful supplement to the salary of weekdays. Some Victorian organists held country churches in plurality. In 1866 John Warriner was organist to two churches in Minehead and two in Dunster, and in 1901 George Havelock of Doncaster was organist of six country churches, using pupils as his assistants.[2]

[1] The Gregorian Association was founded in 1871, (the London association held annual festivals in St. Paul's cathedral); the Plainsong and Medieval Music Society in 1888. Scholes, 554–5.
[2] Scholes, 576, 583, 587, 603.

CHAPTER VII

THE ROMAN CATHOLICS

THE Roman Catholics increased their numbers steadily during the second half of the century. The rate of increase is at present impossible to determine. It is certain that it was much slower than during the twenty years before 1850, as fewer Irish immigrants came in to England and Wales. The Roman Catholics never regained the extraordinary sense of confidence and hope which the years, and the statistics of, 1844–54 bred in them. For ten years even the absolute numbers of Roman Catholic marriages declined (1864: 8,659; 1869: 7,231; 1874: 8,179).

The statistics of clergy and chapels show that the original towns of Irish immigrants remained the chief centres of Catholic population for the rest of the century. London, Liverpool and Birmingham contained most flourishing congregations. The diocese of Northampton, which contained East Anglia, and the dioceses of Clifton and Plymouth in the west country, contained the smallest number of priests and churches. Outside the three great cities, growth was most visible in South Wales and in Yorkshire, where the see of Beverley was divided (1878) into the two sees of Leeds and Middlesborough, thus supporting those bishops of 1851 who preferred sees in modern cities to sees with historic titles.[1] In 1882 a diocese was created for Portsmouth out of the diocese of Southwark. In 1895 Menevia was separated from Newport and two years later was made a separate diocese. England and Wales were thus divided between fifteen dioceses.

The census of 1881 analysed the distribution of the Irish; negligible in the country, a big minority in Liverpool (12·8 per cent of the population), Manchester and Salford (7·5 per cent). In all towns with over 50,000 inhabitants, the average Irish-born population numbered 3·3 per cent, in all the rest of the country 1·5 per cent. But these

[1] The see of Hexham became the see of Hexham and Newcastle as early as 1861; Beck, 187.

figures listed only persons born in Ireland and failed to represent the full measure of Irish immigration. In Ireland Roman Catholicism was primarily a religion of the countryside, in England almost exclusively a religion of the cities. The Irish labourer still caused the anti-popery riot of the working men for social and non-religious reasons, but less often. The last serious no-popery riot of this kind occurred in Birmingham in June 1867 when a no-popery lecturer named Murphy was besieged in his hall by the Irish, and a Protestant mob then sacked the streets in the Irish quarter.

The *Daily News* census of 1902 made the Roman Catholic attendants in London to be 93,572 or about the same as the Congregationalists and rather less than a quarter of the Anglicans.[1] The census of 1886 made the total 54,315, and therefore the *Daily News* showed an increase of nearly 40,000 in sixteen years. A Salford census of December 1875 showed 116,504 people at all services.[2] Since the churches were few in proportion to the population, some churches had great congregations. They held the poor better than most denominations, partly because their poor were Irish (or in London sometimes Italian) and the religion of the once foreign poor was the expression and the memory of their national inheritance. In North London at the 1902 census there were only fifteen Roman Catholic churches with an average attendance of 1,053.

The estimates of total Catholic population in the *Directory* cannot be regarded as based on accurate information. But as estimates, they moved from 700,000 in 1840 to a million and a half at the end of the century. Among these were many Irishmen who said that they were Catholics if they were asked, but who had ceased to have any but a nominal connexion with their church. The total Catholic population at Cardiff was reckoned at 9,800 in 1861, and those who practised their Easter duties were reckoned at 2,500,[3] but to this number must be added children. Therefore the number of those who practised their religion was high in relation to the number of those who said that they belonged, perhaps as many as half.

The Roman Catholic community tended to put out prickles against its environment. For it mostly consisted of working men who felt half-foreigners and knew that they were disliked; and where it did not consist of Irish, it consisted either of old-fashioned recusant

---

[1] Mudie-Smith, 271.
[2] *Letters of Cardinal Vaughan to Lady Herbert*, 274.   [3] Hickey, 91.

aristocrats with a long tradition of quiet separateness, or of a small number of converts from other churches who knew themselves disapproved as converts by the main body of society. The men among whom this attitude appeared least were either the hereditary English Catholics or such converts as remained laymen after their conversion and continued to live a useful life accepted by society; Hope-Scott, Renouf, Coventry Patmore.

The Irish community kept to itself for three-quarters of the century. They were of a lower social stratum and suspect to the English or Welsh workers, and therefore intermarriage between Catholic and non-Catholic was rare until towards the end of the third quarter of the century. After 1875 English names become more common in Roman Catholic marriage registers, and the problem of mixed marriages faced the church authorities. They had long tried to insist on a promise, to be taken by a Protestant husband before a marriage with a Roman Catholic, that the children should be brought up Roman Catholic; and this demand caused controversy, especially when the courts held it not to be a legally binding contract. Manning resisted mixed marriages so far as he could. For even though the promise was faithfully kept, the children entered a new environment on one side of their family, with new friends and new modes of thought. From the social point of view nothing could be more desirable than that the Irish should be more assimilated into their new environment than they were; and yet Manning could see how assimilation weakened not only their Irishness but the simplicity of their inherited faith.

The old aristocratic strain was important to English Catholicism. The *Catholic Year Book of* 1900 included a list, forty-one in number, of Catholic peers of Great Britain and Ireland, and a list, fifty-four in number, of Catholic baronets, and another list of twenty-eight knights. They included the Duke of Norfolk and the Marquises (both converts) of Bute and Ripon, the Earls of Denbigh (convert), Abingdon, Ashburnham, Mexborough and Gainsborough, Viscount Llandaff (created 1895), Lords Mowbray, Vaux of Harrowden, Braye, North, Petre, Arundell of Wardour, Dormer, Stafford, Clifford of Chudleigh, de Freyne, Howard of Glossop, Acton, Emly (convert), Morris, Brampton (convert); the lord chief justice of England, Russell of Killowen, was a catholic. This list was not printed in the *Directory* till 1861. The chief Catholic seats lay in the north, in Northumberland and Durham, Lancashire and North Yorkshire.

The importance of the old families was still visible in the importance of private chapels as supplements to parochial churches. This carried the penalty that private chapels were not usually well-sited for the population, and that if the estate passed the chapel could collapse. In 1899 a Protestant bought the estate of Weston Underwood, which had a chapel, school and priest's house, and they could find no way of maintaining worship except by building a new chapel in Olney more than a mile away.[1] When the great house of Alton Towers passed from a Catholic Lord Shrewsbury to a Protestant, it made a Catholic visitor melancholy to find a turnstile at the gate.[2]

The alliance between a small minority of the English gentry, who usually voted Tory, and a crowd of working men who looked to the Liberal party, continued to make for stress throughout the century. It meant that the chief English laymen did not always have a high regard for their priests, and that they suspected Archbishop Manning because he was bold enough to see that his true duty lay primarily with the working man. Cardinal Wiseman had placed the Roman Catholics of England on the map and had made the nation aware of them as an element important in British life. Manning wanted his people to take their part in the life of the nation. He felt how his change of allegiance removed him from the main stream of national life. He wrote that in the first years after his conversion he was as exiled from public life as if he had been an alien, like 'a dead man out of mind' and the sense of being up against society, men thought, made him for a time stiff in manner and difficult to know,[3] and therefore unpopular with other Roman Catholics.

When Lord Shaftesbury's *Life* was published, Manning ruefully contrasted Shaftesbury's unique record of public service with his own. 'It makes me feel that my life has been wasted. . . . His whole life was spent in working for the English people. So I began in a little, and then have spent my life in working for the Irish occupation in England.' Speaking of dockers, he once talked 'not only of my own men but also of the Englishmen'. He kept repeating the saying about Irish occupation.[4] But not with bitterness. The Irish were now a

[1] *Catholic Year Book, 1900*, 152.   [2] Roskell, *Amherst*, 316–17.
[3] Purcell, ii, 79, 680.   [4] Cf. Purcell, ii, 604, 677–8, 801.

permanent fact of English life, and he came to believe that he could never have worked for England as he had if he had remained in the Church of England, for Anglicanism would have fettered him.

Manning's power and status among the Roman Catholics of England, and upon the English who were not Roman Catholics, really rested upon this power of sympathy with the demands of the Irish. It might have been expected that the ex-archdeacon of Chichester would not have befriended the Irish. Others among the ex-Anglican converts preferred the Roman Catholic Church to be allied to the Tory party. Manning openly backed Irish claims, first to disestablishment and then to home rule. He was an unusual kind of authoritarian radical, who acquired his radicalism as a superlative Anglican pastor among the labourers of Sussex. He despised the House of Commons and cared passionately for the social causes, housing, wages, prostitution, temperance, education; always upon the side of the labourer. His social endeavours thrust Roman Catholicism at last into the public life of England, more evidently and more constructively than the various Roman Catholic parliamentarians or public servants, and the question placed a political strain upon the Catholic body.

To the end of his life Manning regarded it as a sign of the social ostracism of Roman Catholics that such a tiny handful could get into Parliament. The 1885 election produced eighty-three Roman Catholic members of whom seventy-nine were Irish and one Scottish. In 1894 the House of Commons contained five English Roman Catholics, including Russell the attorney-general, but one of the five was T. P. O'Connor who sat for a Liverpool constituency. John Pope Hennessy (M.P. 1859) and a few others sat as Conservatives. Nevertheless the strong force of Irish members, while they helped to make Catholics unpopular, gave the denomination a political weight which it could not otherwise have achieved. This weight was momentous in the development of national education, and probably helped to change the atmosphere. When Lord Ripon became a Roman Catholic, the *Times* published an extraordinary leader (5 September 1874) that a statesman who becomes a Roman Catholic forfeits the confidence of the English people, that Ripon had renounced his moral and mental freedom, and that the act could only be seen as a sign of fatal demoralisation. Six years later, when Ripon became viceroy of India, the press was calm. And by the end of the century newspapers like the *Times* and the *Spectator* treated Roman Catholics with respect.

Ripon's office in India was a sign of the way in which a few Englishmen, though they were Catholics, began to appear in public life. Sir John Acton was elevated to the peerage in 1869. In 1886 Lord Llandaff became home secretary in Lord Salisbury's government, the first Roman Catholic to become a cabinet minister. Sir William Shee was the first to become a judge. In 1866 Roman Catholic members of the House of Commons ceased to have to take the offensive oath to maintain the Church of England and profess their loyalty, as laid down by the emancipation act.

In 1862 Parliament voted £550 for Roman Catholic chaplains in seven prisons. Four years later the reformatory and industrial schools acts allowed Roman Catholic delinquents and destitute to be housed in denominational institutions, aided by the rates.[1] Two years after that an act allowed a Roman Catholic minister to visit Roman Catholics in workhouses, not if they asked for him, but unless they objected. They could appoint chaplains to the army and navy, though the number of chaplains in the middle years of the century were small in relation to the numbers of Irish soldiers in the army and navy. In 1871 the ecclesiastical titles act was repealed, though chiefly for the sake of Anglican bishops in Ireland. On Easter Sunday of 1899, at St. Peter's, Hatton Garden, the sacrament was carried in solemn procession through the streets for the first time outside the Church of England since the Reformation. It has been argued that the social plight was sufficient to prevent some converts from making their way in the world as far as their merits warranted; that, for example, Hope-Scott, though he became an eminent railway lawyer, would have risen higher but for his conversion. It is not easy to find evidence in support of this speculation.

The relation of the queen to the Roman Catholics marked by its change the partial change in the English people. In May 1887 Cardinal Howard at Rome asked whether an envoy from the Pope would be acceptable at the queen's jubilee and was told that the queen was gratified. That November she sent the Duke of Norfolk on a mission to the Vatican to assure the Pope of

---

[1] Beck, 371; 29 & 30 Vic. 117, 118; Hansard, clxvi, 1862, 1032. A proposal to vote money for prison chaplains was negatived in 1854.

her 'sincere friendship and unfeigned respect and esteem'.[1]

The Prince of Wales was friendlier. He became attached to one of the Vaughan brothers, Bernard the popular preacher, and when at Cannes used to attend Vaughan's sermons. There is a story, said to be reliable, that when as Edward VII he was to undergo an operation, he made Bernard Vaughan stay in the next room while the operation was performed.[2] He became the first reigning sovereign since the Reformation to visit the Pope.

Yet they continued unpopular, not as individuals but as a denomination. With the lower middle class and artisans, the old strand of no-popery was strong, though more displayed in badgering Anglican ritualists than against Roman Catholics. This feeling was fed by Irish labour and Sinn Fein and occasional murder. The educated English did not admire the ultramontane devotion which spread over the Roman Catholics of England and squeezed the old and austere tradition of English Catholicism. They did not admire the syllabus of errors (1864) wherein Pope Pius IX condemned reconciliation between papacy and the modern world. They did not admire the definition of papal infallibility in 1870, and regarded it as a setback to all the churches. They were friendly to Bismarck in his assault upon the Catholic clergy of Germany.

As early as 1867 Manning wrote that the hostility was still hostility but it was a more civilised hostility.[3] Roman policy did little in the way of seeking to diminish the hostility, for the curia had a feeling that it needed to fight against modern society. In 1896 Pope Leo XIII, after some of his men half-encouraged the Anglican Lord Halifax to get the matter considered as a way towards reconciliation, condemned Anglican orders as null and void. Manning and then Vaughan were both stern on the rules for mixed marriages. The ultramontane was definite in his dogma. R. H. Hutton, who admired and liked W. G. Ward, wondered at Ward's death whether his theological beliefs were now more or less definite than a few days before, and imputed that they had just become less definite.[4] The ultramontanes had no use for Biblical criticism, and thought that the Church of England in permitting it was becoming apostate from the faith. Manning publicly accused the established church of

---

[1] PP, 1890, lxxxi, 761, 775; cf. Hansard, cccxlviii, 525, 548ff. The needs of Malta were again in question.

[2] Martindale, B. Vaughan, 63–64; Macnutt, A Papal Chamberlain, 253.

[3] The Reunion of Christendom, 12.   [4] Hutton, Contemp. Th. and Th., ii, 220.

encouraging all the modern aberrations. The gradual lessening of the world's hostility was not due to Roman softness towards the world.

The English were not in sympathy with some forms of devotion which they found; the association of St. Antony's miraculous brief with its headquarters at Nottingham; the pilgrimages to Lourdes or to Paray-le-Monial; the devotion to the Sacred Heart, which spread widely among English Roman Catholics during the nineties, encouraged by Pope Leo XIII. On 29 June 1893 the cardinal and his bishops solemnly dedicated England and Wales to Our Lady and to St. Peter. The poet Coventry Patmore, who had been a devout high Anglican and became a Roman Catholic partly to marry his second wife, made four pilgrimages to Lourdes. He wanted to strengthen his soul, to seek inspiration for his poetry, to help the lameness of a daughter and the half-blindness of a son.[1] Among various little groups the doctrine of indulgences was made to mean more than it had meant to Roman Catholics in England since Luther's protest. The sacrament of the altar was the centre and strength of all this devotion, and the poet, Gerard Manley Hopkins, became a Roman Catholic (1866) partly because thus his intelligence could hold the doctrine of the sacrament which was necessary to his moral being. In the late nineties 'many' Catholics were said to wear the Carmelite scapular in the diminutive form, because our Lady promised a good and pious death to those who wore it. Some of their people, even a bishop like Amherst of Northampton, had still a faith in holy wells or apparitions. They were inclined with a scholarly ingenuity to defend the authenticity of texts of the Bible (like 1 John 5 verse 7, or the angel of the Bethesda pool, or the eunuch's baptismal creed) which the rest of the scholarly world was agreed in dropping. Of all the Anglican champions they were inclined most to admire J. W. Burgon. Bishop Clifford of Clifton caused a sensation in 1880 when he publicly abandoned the historical truth of the first chapter of Genesis. But the atmosphere of simplicity was not of the credulous but of the childlike. And a sophisticated leader like Manning preferred to have it so. He saw the strength of simple faith in the little isolated community of the English past, and was afraid of the perils of acclimatisation in the modern world, and therefore preferred them to be isolated though they were no longer a little denomination, in order that the values inherited from the past could be preserved.

[1] Champneys, *Patmore*, I, 288.

The communities of religious, both male and female, steadily grew in number, until in 1900 Westminster had 33 male and 49 female, Birmingham 22 male and 42 female, Clifton 17 male and 14 female, Hexham 17 male and 35 female, Leeds 7 male and 27 female. The old conflict of jurisdiction between bishops and religious was brought to a head when the Jesuit provincial opened a school in Manchester without asking leave from Bishop Vaughan of Salford, and the case was settled by Rome in *Romanos Pontifices* of 1881, which gave the bishops almost everything that they wanted and was an important decree in making the pastoral system more orderly.

The Benedictines came to Buckfast in 1882 and to Farnborough in 1883–8, the Carthusians came to Parkminster in 1873 and were enclosed ten years later.[1] Probably one important cause of growing respect among the public was the work of the orders in hospitals and in the care of the old. In the late eighties we find English Protestants referring with reverence to the work of Father Damien in his leper settlement at Molokar, and this was before Damien's death in 1889 and the consequent *Lives*.

A Catholic publisher complained, as late as 1890, that Roman Catholics did not read books.[2] And yet their educated clergy and laity had a rare breadth of knowledge and sometimes a unique expertise in antiquarian lore. The learned journals run by English Roman Catholics were admirable in their surveys of literature. The community felt part of an international community, and its news and its historical scholarship always had a European flavour. The two most eminent scholars at the end of the century, Acton and Friedrich von Hügel, were both in part of non-English extraction. Journals like the *Month* (1864) and the *Downside Review* (1880) were of high quality in literary criticism and Catholic history, always had a European slant and were strongly interested in the history of the Roman Catholic past in England and the continuity of the great Roman Catholic families. They concerned themselves little with Biblical studies, and tended to reaction in their attitudes towards new scientific theories, but with the exception of these blind spots they were marked by a humane breadth and depth derived partly from the cherishing of the recusant past and partly from the consciousness of a European inheritance.

They still hoped that one day England would turn to them but not

[1] Beck, 453, 468.   [2] Kegan Paul, *Memories*, 293.

with the naïve and excited hopefulness of the forties, and the Anglican ritualists rather depressed than cheered them. In the *Dublin Review* of 1884 (ii, 65) Mivart wrote a daring article asking why their progress was so slow and why the expectations of 1850 had not been fulfilled, despite the growing number of churches and chapels and convents. He diagnosed four main reasons: (1) assimilation of the Catholics into the rest of the community, especially through mixed marriages, (2) the movement of the general world away from religion instead of (as in the forties) towards it, (3) the aggressive behaviour of the ultramontanes on the continent, (4) the great revival of church life in the Church of England; so that whereas in the forties they competed with bald irreverence, they now competed with a liturgical life richer and more reverent than their own. He doubted whether the Italianate movement in English Catholicism had been wise, and wanted a return to the English tradition of Catholicism, perhaps with some services in the English language. Mivart's article was not popular, but it produced a list of Roman Catholic churches where the liturgy was confessed to be beautiful.[1] Too much use of the vernacular would have been repudiated by the community as a whole. But converts especially saw the value of vernacular prayers, and in 1888 Manning and the bishops sanctioned a manual of such prayers for congregational use.

Because of the Irish they were later than other denominations in making their singing congregational. St. Marie's at Sheffield and St. Charles in Ogle Street, London, were regarded as exceptional churches (1884) because they tried to persuade the congregation to join with the choir in singing the creed;[2] and a number of organists were still said not to like harmony. Unaccompanied singing was more common than in other churches. They first produced a hymn book sufficient to 'rival' *Hymns Ancient and Modern* in the year 1881, when Burns and Oates published *The Parochial Hymnbook* edited by Father Police; and three years later Burns and Oates published *Annus Sanctus*, the first part (the only part to appear) of hymns for the ecclesiastical year, which was by some confessed to be the best collection of Catholic hymns. It was no coincidence that the editor was an ex-Anglican ritualist, Orby Shipley. As the converts did

---

[1] They were Downside and Belmont, St. Chad's at Birmingham, St. Marie's, Sheffield, the Jesuit church of the Holy Name in Manchester, the Benedictine church in Seel Street, Liverpool, and in London the Oratory, the Jesuit church at Farm Street, and St. Charles, Ogle Street.   [2] DR, 1884, ii, 80.

something to encourage vernacular prayers, so they did something to encourage hymn-singing and congregational worship. And yet Shipley's principles of selection were narrow. He would admit only medieval Latin hymns, and English translations only by persons who died as Roman Catholics, whether or not they were Catholics when they made the translation. He regarded unity of faith in writer and in user as essential. Thus he excluded nearly all the hymns popular among English Protestants.

This talk of slow progress or even recession, though at first disreputable, was given a justification when Bishop Vaughan of Salford issued an enquiry (1885) into the state of Roman Catholics in Manchester and found leakage; so that the word leakage became fashionable, and was discussed in the *Tablet* and the *Month*. In 1893 they took a census of the Archdiocese of Westminster, and found that many young people of both sexes were lost to the church between the ages of fourteen and twenty-one years. Many names once on a church register were no longer found on any register, even when allowance was made for re-emigration to America. The enquirers diagnosed simply 'London life and labour' and the cardinal started a Catholic social union which had eleven clubs in the slums by 1900.[1] Evidently the Roman Catholics, like the Anglicans, experienced the general ebb of religion during the nineties.

Meanwhile another portrait of English Catholicism began to affect the public favourably: in the person of Newman.

In 1861–3 Newman was at the low ebb of his fortunes. His university at Dublin failed. His project for an English Bible was discouraged by authority. An article, 'On consulting the faithful in matters of doctrine', printed in the *Rambler* for 1859, was delated to Rome by the Bishop of Newport on a charge of unsoundness. He had a sense of not being in sympathy with the powers ruling his church, a certain sense that his life was more fruitful while he was an Anglican. Rumours circulated about him, that he was about to return to the Church of England, and forced him to sharp public denials.

At the end of 1863 the editor of *Macmillan's Magazine* sent to Kingsley for review the 7th and 8th volumes of Froude's *History of England*; that Froude who had once been a disciple of Newman, had revolted against him, and had turned himself into a historian of the

---

[1] *Catholic Year Book, 1900*, 332.

England of the Reformation. In reviewing these volumes in the January (1864) number of *Macmillan*, Kingsley attributed the demoralisation of Europe to the belief that the Pope's dictate was the creator of right and wrong, and portrayed the heap of lies piling up since the first monk forged the first charter of the first monastery.

'Truth, for its own sake, has never been a virtue with the Roman clergy. Father Newman informs us that it need not, and on the whole ought not to be; that cunning is the weapon which heaven has given to the saints wherewith to withstand the brute male force of the wicked world, which marries and is given in marriage.'

This personal attack led to an unsatisfactory exchange of letters between Newman and Kingsley. Kingsley made a public apology, but Newman was advised by his lawyer friends Badeley and Mr. Serjeant Bellasis that the apology was insufficient, and that it would be good to 'expose' Kingsley in a pamphlet.[1]

Kingsley's answering pamphlet, *What then does Dr. Newman mean?*, contended that Newman's late Anglican sermons, though preached before the author was a Roman Catholic, were in doctrine and in spirit Roman Catholic sermons[2]; and thus it gave Newman the chance which he above all men was fitted to seize. It called in question not merely the technicalities of his moral teaching, which would have interested few men, but the honesty of his Anglican career.

It was simple for Newman to show that he was treated unfairly. He was a man of cleverer mind than his opponent, more subtle, more poetic, more complicated, and above all a trained dialectician and logician, trained by Whately while he had been a young fellow of Oriel. The contest was not an equal contest; and if that had been all, Newman could doubtless have knocked Kingsley to the ground with a devastating pamphlet and the controversy would have only an ephemeral importance. But there was more than this; Kingsley called into doubt Newman's career as an Anglican, questioned his faithfulness to the Church of England while he had been a member of the Church of England. To reply to Kingsley meant, if the matter was to be raised above logomachy, a reconsideration of his whole career as an Anglican and of his endeavours as the leader of the Oxford Movement.

---

[1] Badeley to Newman, 1 February 1864; Oratory MSS.
[2] 'I call the man who preached that sermon a Protestant? I should have sooner called him a Buddhist.' (*Apol.*, ed. Svaglic, 399).

Many a man would have shrunk, and have satisfied himself with the little unanswerable pamphlet. But not Newman. During these last years he brooded much over the past, sadly contemplating his career. Newman was not a man pursuing some long project of scholarship and turning reluctantly aside to think about his past and defend it. Kingsley struck at the centre of his interest, the subject over which he meditated and which fascinated him. Some men are inevitable autobiographers, because by nature egotistical; and some men are reluctant autobiographers, because they feel that something must be said and yet that in a measure it is egotistical to say it. Newman, in a curious manner, was in both these categories; without being in the least a selfish man he was intensely interested in the growth and development of his own mind, and to that extent was an inevitable autobiographer. We now know how many little drafts of auto-biographical writings he made for his private satisfaction. But he would never have published these fragments, because he would have thought it wrong to do so. He was, in 1863, an autobiographer manqué.[1] And then Kingsley, without knowing what he was doing, demanded a defence of the Anglican career, and so opened the door to the offering of these meditations to the British public. Newman was forced to publish an autobiography, though it was so contrary to the ideal of reserve which he long ago learnt from Keble; not only for his own sake, but as a public duty; a duty to clear the name of the Catholic priesthood of England from the imputation and slander:

'I must, I said, give the true key to my whole life; I must show what I am that it may be seen what I am not, and that the phantom may be extinguished which gibbers instead of me. I wish to be known as a living man, and not as a scarecrow which is dressed up in my clothes.'[2]

As a source for the history of the Oxford Movement the *Apologia* had defects but Newman did not intend it to be such but only to describe the course of his own opinions. He overcame the notorious difficulty of describing changing opinion by a large reliance upon contemporary letters, of which he was a hoarder, and by consulting old Tractarian friends like Copeland and Rogers, Church and Keble. He must convince the public of his sincerity because it was his sincerity which was challenged, and the book is manifestly truthful.

[1] Cf. Newman to Keble, 27 April 1864; Ward, ii, 22.
[2] *Apologia* ed. Svaglic, 406.

Perhaps he was inclined to a touch of unconscious misrepresentation by portraying a more unbroken continuity between his new opinions and his old than was quite in accordance with the facts, and therefore looked for the seed of his new opinions further back in his career than a critic might approve. But he retained so strong a conviction of continuity in his personal history, and wished to show how he could be at once a loyal member of the Church of England and a Tractarian leader and yet be led step by step into the Church of Rome; the continuity which the *Apologia* beautifully marked by the choice of Hurrell Froude's breviary as a kccpsake after his death in 1836, a breviary which, he recorded, he still had on his table and used constantly 'to this day'. 'I was not conscious to myself, on my conversion, of any difference of thought or of temper from what I had before.'[1] This feeling of continuity is well explained[2] as a sign that to Newman dogmas of faith were always expressions of attitudes or feelings less articulate and more profound. Newman was less interested in the various articles of a creed than in the atmosphere, the cast, the inmost breathing of the mind. And this makes part of the fascination of the *Apologia*. He could not show what he thought without also showing what he was.

This sense of continuity made an overwhelming impression upon Anglicans because to many of them it was unexpected. 'The Newman whom they had known since 1845 was an enemy of the Church of England; a Newman with the disease of repudiating his past; a Newman who printed sharp statements against Anglicans in books and in newspapers. The Newman whom they found in the *Apologia* appeared a being transformed. . . . He seemed to be grateful for what he owed to his Anglican past. He learned his Catholicism within the Church of England and was willing to say so. Anglican critics thought him marvellously generous. "It is with pleasure that I pay tribute to the memory of . . ."—the attitude seemed new and extraordinary in Roman Catholic writing. Whately's generous heart, "my dear and true friend Dr. Pusey", the holiness of Keble and "his religious teaching so deep, so pure, so beautiful", the genius of Hurrell Froude, the large mind and true sensibility of Hugh James Rose—Anglican hearts suddenly rose to this retrospective generosity. It seemed to them unique among converts to the Church of Rome.

---

[1] *Apol.*, Everyman ed., 215; cf. the change in Svaglic, 214.
[2] By W. E. Houghton, *The Art of Newman's Apologia*, 38.

It was possible, then, to become a Roman Catholic and not to trample upon the body to which you once owed your highest ideals. The book came upon some Anglicans with shattering effect—warmth instead of ice, generosity instead of narrowness, affection where they looked for a sneer.'[1]

As the years went by, the *Apologia* helped to make Protestant Englishmen understand that Roman Catholic priests might be human and English and large-hearted. Richard Holt Hutton, who helped to establish the reputation of the *Apologia* by his reviews in the *Spectator*, believed to the end of his life that no single book had done more to this end. Such an influence affected only the educated; but to alter the attitude of the educated was in the long run the surest way to diminish popular prejudice.[2]

The contents of the *Apologia* were somewhat changed in successive editions with a view to meeting important critics. He made the principal alterations for the second edition, 1865, when the title was changed to *History of my religious opinions*. By these alterations and change of title he aimed to leave Kingsley behind, to remove the occasion of writing and lift the book above the controversy which produced it. Some epigrams against Kingsley were more cheap than worthy. Fenton Hort[3] found the *Apologia* 'sickening to read, from the cruelty and insolence with which he trampled on his assailant'. Even Newman's friend, Rogers, said that he had the feeling of seeing a man horsewhipped after you thought that he had been done with.[4] This was not the only difficulty felt by readers. Edward Denison could not finish the book because he was vexed with Newman's 'morbid scruples'.[5] Even his old curate, Copeland, regretted from time to time that such a heavy toil should be spent upon Kingsley.[6] So in the second edition Kingsley vanished and became 'a popular writer', and the autobiography no longer needed an excuse for its writing.

The extra material in editions after 1865 was nearly all added in the form of notes. The more important of these notes were intended to improve the book in the eyes of its Roman Catholic critics. For while

---

[1] *Anglican Initiatives in Christian Unity*, ed. E. G. W. Bill, 82–83.
[2] Perhaps even Kingsley helped to elicit this side of Newman's affection; for in his pamphlet he called Newman a priest who had rounded upon his mother-church with contumely and slander. *What then does Dr. Newman mean?*, Svaglic, 365.
[3] *Life of Hort*, ii, 424.
[4] Rogers to Newman, undated but 1864, Apologia MSS, Oratory.
[5] *Life of Edward Denison*, 14.
[6] Copeland to Newman, 1 May 1864, Apologia MSS, Oratory.

most were grateful for the book, and while Newman quite cleared
the dust from his reputation among them, ultramontanes like
Manning and Vaughan disliked the liberal touches in the book, and
that sense of continuity which the Anglicans found so remarkable. A
writer in Rome regarded the *Apologia* as additional evidence that
Newman must not be allowed to go back to Oxford. Such men
doubted whether it could be right to ascribe so much even of partial
truth to the Church of England. 'He had ceased writing, and a good
riddance', said Monsignor Talbot unkindly—'why did he ever begin
again?'[1] Friendly Bishop Moriarty, in congratulating Newman,
said that he had heard critics speaking of one sentence in which
Newman seemed to imply that he would not go out of his way to
bring an Anglican into the Roman Catholic Church.[2] The convert
T. W. Allies, who as a layman was doing a great work in Catholic
elementary education, told Acton that Newman had never really
been a Catholic.[3] Newman therefore made adjustments to his
language to show, what no ordinary reader of the *Apologia* ever
doubted, his complete loyalty to the Church of Rome.

Newman's book did more than clear himself of the charge that he
did not care for truth. It helped in a more momentous undertaking,
that of persuading Protestants that the Roman Catholic Church
cared for truth.

The ultramontanes appeared to set the authority of the church
above truth. If the doctrine of the church and the results of human
enquiry disagreed, then human enquiry must give way. This year of
1864 was the year of the Pope's syllabus of errors, and of argument
over infallibility and Galileo. In the atmosphere of doubt and
incipient agnosticism created by the studies of historians and
scientists, the Church of Rome stood unyielding. And though this
unbudgeable picture of authority attracted hesitant souls, it repelled
more, and among them Roman Catholics like Acton who were
determined that the scientific and historical intelligence must be
confessed to be sovereign in its own sphere.

Newman was not in the least a liberal Catholic like Acton. Though
they worked together for a time in the affair of the *Rambler*, when
Acton and his group produced the most intelligent Roman Catholic

---

[1] Ward, *Newman*, ii, 400, 544.
[2] Moriarty to Newman, 6 September 1864; Apologia MSS, Oratory.
[3] Acton to Döllinger, 5 August 1866; Conzemius, i, 438.

writing of the century,[1] they moved steadily further apart, until by the seventies there was a chasm between their minds. The definition of infallibility, which Newman thought inopportune and Acton thought untrue, discouraged all the more liberal minds. Young Edmund Bishop, who learnt from Acton his vocation as a lay scholar in the service of the church, half-decided to give up religious scholarship, as the church did not desire this from laymen, and was advised by two priests 'not to mind but to go on'.[2] He cultivated patience and what he called 'personal indifference'. Richard Simpson, once so lively a collaborator with Acton in the *Rambler*, gave his last years to the study of Shakespeare.

The question whether a man could be at once a good Catholic and a good Englishman was brought excitedly before the nation by Gladstone, in consequence of the Vatican decrees.

The Vatican Council of 1870 defined papal infallibility in a manner bound to cause unsettlement of mind in all the western Catholic groups. For it met in the shadow of the Italian revolution, and was dispersed by the Italian occupation of Rome, and men's attitude to the Pope and his doctrine was entangled with their attitude to the Pope and his maltreatment. The atmosphere which surrounded the definition was charged not only with controversy but with emotion. Moreover the definition was fought at every stage by a powerful minority; and though the minority succeeded in limiting the exercise of infallibility to occasions when the Pope spoke on faith and morals to all the churches, the council still seemed to attribute infallibility to the Pope when he spoke formally on such matters, even though he did not possess the substantial agreement of the Roman Catholic Church; and attributed to the Pope a universal jurisdiction, which pointed towards a larger exercise of direct rule by Rome in administering the church in the various countries. Nearly all the European and American churches suffered internal stress, and in Germany Döllinger and other Catholic professors refused to submit and led towards their excommunication and a total breach with Rome. In England Archbishop Manning was well-known to be an advocate of the definition and a few intelligent non-Catholics like Odo Russell, the English agent in Rome, thought that the doctrine must be defined if papal authority was not to be

[1] For the *Rambler*, etc., see Altholtz, *The Liberal Catholic Movement in England*, 1962.
[2] Abercrombie, 31, 44–5.

V.C.–14 a

destroyed. But several eminent Catholic leaders were identified with the resistance. Bishop Ullathorne of Birmingham was prominent among the minority who believed the doctrine but thought its definition inopportune. Newman was marked for the same opinion, since a fierce private letter to Ullathorne during the council was published to his embarrassment. Newman also believed in infallibility, but did not see what good purpose was served by narrowing the liberty of opinion. For a short time there spread a foolish rumour that he would soon join Döllinger.[1] And the greatest layman in England, Lord Acton, was not only friend and pupil of Döllinger, but led extreme resistance to the definition, which he was known to disbelieve. The course of the council, the group of journalists like Tom Mozley in Rome, the letters from Rome written (partly by Acton) under the name Quirinus and intended to deter the definition, left England with no friendly picture of the council. Men feared or expected that England would see excommunications like Germany.

The unsettlement of Catholic minds troubled Roman authority, and the Vatican did what it could to allay fears by sanctioning private interpretations of a minimising character, and being silent when the Swiss bishops issued a statement which limited the effect of the decree. Newman was helped in his private consultations by the approved statement of Fessler, formerly secretary-general of the Vatican Council, who published a book *On True and False Infallibility*, which much limited the possible area of infallibility.[2]

Acton argued that the definition must make Catholics disloyal members of society because they must then 'profess a false system of morality' and 'repudiate literary and scientific sincerity'. He injected these ideas into his friend Gladstone, who believed ultramontanism to be in the proper sense anti-social. Gladstone was shocked at the definition. 'The whole proceeding has been monstrous, and it will hereafter become one of the laughing-stocks of history. The fanaticism of the Middle Ages is really sober compared with that of the nineteenth century.'

In 1874, Gladstone, beaten at the general election, retired from the

---

[1] *Letter to the Duke of Norfolk,*[4] 107.

[2] Ambrose St. John undertook an English translation of Fessler but died before he could complete it, Ward, *Newman*, ii, 373, 409, 556. Newman was attacked by J. M. Capes, who ceased for the time to be a Catholic, for not having believed infallibility and forcing his mind to accept it; and had an easy and just answer.

leadership of the Liberal party, and felt himself free for his old theological interests of church and state. In September he visited Döllinger at Munich, and 'it makes my blood run cold to think of *his* being excommunicated in his venerable . . . old age'.[1] He came back from Munich and wrote the boiling pamphlet *The Vatican decrees in their bearing on civil allegiance: a political expostulation.* Acton tried vainly to stop him from publishing.[2] The pamphlet denied with all his unique vehemence that after the Vatican decrees logical Roman Catholics could be loyal in their civil allegiance. It sold nearly 150,000 copies in two months. After twenty replies including one from Manning, Gladstone answered his critics in a second pamphlet, *Vaticanism* (1875), which was corrected in proof by both Acton and Döllinger. To have an ex-prime minister writing pamphlets is not necessarily a disadvantage to a religious denomination, especially if he is emotional and overstates his case. Gladstone compelled more liberal minds among the Roman Catholics to assert that what he said was either a platitude which applied to all religious men—that sometimes they must render to God before Caesar—or was simply untrue. At one extreme Manning's reply was so strong as to confirm men in their evil opinion. At the other extreme Acton's reply was so outspokenly anti-Roman as to bring him near to excommunication. An ultramontane reply would not do because it repelled. An Actonian reply would not do because everyone knew that the Roman Catholic authorities repudiated it. Therefore the most important answer was that of Newman in a *Letter to the Duke of Norfolk* (1875). It was gentle, moderate, honest, and loyal to Rome. It denounced progress, liberalism and democracy, and said that Catholicism was the only divine form of religion. It declared Döllinger to be utterly wrong and argued for papal infallibility. It freely confessed that some Catholics had themselves to thank for having alienated minds like Gladstone, by 'wild words and overbearing deeds', and by flourishing the claims of the Pope defiantly in the face of England. It contained an eloquent chapter in praise of the sovereign conscience, ending with a sentence which became famous. 'If I am obliged to bring religion into after-dinner toasts (which indeed does not seem quite the thing) I shall drink—to the Pope if you please—still, to Conscience first, and to the Pope afterwards.' It raised the possibility

[1] Morley, ii, 88–90.
[2] Acton to Simpson, 4 November 1874; Gasquet, *Acton*, 358.

that the council, being interrupted, might later be corrected.[1] It strictly limited the exercise of infallibility, and declared that the decree made no real increase in papal authority. It suggested that so far from strengthening the Pope's general authority in Europe, the council had perhaps weakened it. The pamphlet was welcomed by all the moderate English Catholics. It was also welcomed by Manning, despite 'inaccurate' expressions and a sentence which might be understood as hostile to himself. Manning discouraged Propaganda when it asked whether the second part of the pamphlet ought not to be censured by Rome.[2] Propaganda continued to worry that sentences in the pamphlet were heretical.

It could not escape public attention that the two great English converts were divided. They had each made their divergence plain, over universities, the temporal power of the Pope, the definition of infallibility and its interpretation. England found the disagreement notorious, and some Roman Catholics jested that they should adopt the beginning of the Anglican catechism ('What is your name? N or M?') to identify which leader they followed. Since Manning was unpopular (that is, with educated men, for with the working classes he was on the way to becoming the most popular clergyman in England) and Newman was popular, but Manning had the power, the notorious cleavage began to harm the church in England. Here was the one Roman Catholic to whom Protestants listened, and it was too easy for these Protestants to dismiss his words as contrary to the mind of the church. To some leading English Catholics it became an important matter of policy that Rome should be seen to approve Newman. They exerted themselves to secure for him high honour from Rome. In 1879 the new Pope Leo XIII, to whom the Duke of Norfolk first suggested the plan,[3] overcame opposition in the curia and the reluctance of Manning, and made Newman a cardinal. Educated Protestant England was glad, and accepted it as an honour justly conferred upon a great Englishman.

This was no small tribute to the change of attitude wrought by Newman. He was the first Englishman to win non-Catholic applause for becoming a cardinal. The *Guardian*, still the leading journal of the Church of England, invited subscriptions for his portrait.[4] Why this feeling, the editor of the *Guardian* asked his readers? Was it possible

---

[1] *Letter to the Duke of Norfolk*[4], 74, 114.   [2] Butler, *Ullathorne*, ii, 101–2.
[3] Ward, *Newman*, ii, 436.   [4] *Guardian*, 79, 436, 700.

that there exist affinities subtler than the legacies of schism? Even Acton, who was infuriated by Newman's refusal to undertake historical enquiry when making judgements on past historical questions, and by a certain credulity towards ecclesiastical miracles, and who called him the splendid Sophist,[1] regarded him as among the greatest as well as among the most intelligent of his English contemporaries. Newman himself found the honour to be a kind of unsought self-justification, second only to the *Apologia*. 'All the stories', he told Dean Church, 'which have gone about of my being a half Catholic, a Liberal Catholic, under a cloud, not to be trusted, are now at an end.'[2] The same national feelings were kindled, eleven years later, when Newman died.

Newman owed part of his national stature to one hymn, for *The Dream of Gerontius* (published 1865) was not national until Elgar gave it music in 1900. *Lead kindly light* was written in 1833 while he was becalmed in the straits of Bonifacio between Sardinia and Corsica, and was included among the Tractarian *Lyra Apostolica*. In 1865 J. B. Dykes of Durham gave it a memorable tune (which came into his head while he walked in the Strand), often accused of emotion or even of sentimentality, but capturing the affection of every congregation allowed to use it. The hymn became one of the four or five most popular among the Victorians, though the author of the words never heard it as a hymn, for he became a Roman Catholic before it reached Anglican hymnody and died before it reached Roman Catholic hymnody. So essential to hymn books was it that Bickersteth, the editor of the evangelical hymn book, included it with the addition of a less effective verse of his own composition. Out of the exchange of letters after this embarrassing predicament Newman came with honour, and the extra verse was later dropped. Probably this was the most beloved of Victorian hymns, the favourite of Archbishop Tait, said at the death-bed of Queen Victoria. Newman was very modest, and attributed its acclaim rather to Dykes than to himself.

Newman was not a Liberal Catholic like Acton. He shared the general feeling of Catholics in his age and was devoted to Popes though not to their advisers. Retired from the world though he might be, his voice counted in the religious history of the age, for he once

[1] Figgis-Laurence, i, 59; Acton to Gladstone, 14 August 1890.
[2] Newman to Church, 11 March 1879; Ward, *Newman*, ii, 452.

led a movement which changed the Church of England. In the second half of the century many Anglicans, not always high church-men, saw what good the Tractarians had done and were proud of their work as part of the heritage of English religion. After the *Apologia*, and perceiving the generosity of Newman's memories, they were able to claim him also as part of that heritage. He had taught them, though they were still Protestants, to sympathise with and understand a wider and more catholic tradition. Because Newman was still powerful in the Church of England though no longer a member, he was even more powerful in the English Roman Catholic community, for he was almost the solitary voice which would be heard with respect by anyone outside. He could not influence the policy at Propaganda or Westminster, even after he was a cardinal. But without being a liberal, he retained a hesitant, academic, questing, non-scholastic habit of mind which attracted Catholic liberals everywhere. When Döllinger heard that Newman was cardinal, he said that it only showed how Rome had not read Newman's writings, and that if the books were written in French or Italian or Latin, many of them would have been placed on the index of prohibited books.[1] Manning and Vaughan were a little nervous at Newman becoming a cardinal, lest his ideas be thus thought to be approved. Rome made Newman a cardinal not because of his books but because of his influence in England. Yet the honour could not help increasing the influence of the books. In an ultramontane age Newman stood for moderation, and a certain recognition of the rights of criticism. Though he was not learned nor free nor out-spoken like Acton, no one did more to prevent ultramontanes from closing their minds to the modern world and its opinions.

[1] Döllinger to Michelis, 1 May 1879: *Briefe und Erklärungen von Döllinger über die Vatikanischen Decrete*, 1890, 109; *Month*, 1903, i, 345; cf. *Times*, 17 May 1879, and Newman's answer, *Times*, 10 June 1879.

CHAPTER VIII

SECULARISATION

THOUGH modern historians first began systematically to apply the idea of 'secularisation' to the nineteenth century, the Victorians used it from the seventies onwards. The difficulty is to form any precise idea of what is meant by the imprecise word. That it represents truth is hardly to be doubted, but what truth is not so easy to define.

Many more people went to church in 1901 than in 1837, but fewer people in relation to the population. The number of people who did not go to church was far larger in 1901 than in 1837. That made a difference to the atmosphere of Sunday, and to the sense of obligation which men felt about churchgoing. And transport made non-worshippers more obvious: bicycle-rides for the young, the golf club for the middle-aged. In 1895 golfers were said to give a little scandal in country towns by arriving at the station just when folk were on their way to church.

Clergymen in 1901, though by no means all, were willing to go to the theatre. Devout Christians were not merely willing to read good novels, but sometimes thought it a duty to do so. Changes like these tell nothing about the power of Christianity in the country, and were as much changes in fashion as the change from shaven chins to beards. The country was less Calvinist, and believed little in hell, had its uncertainties about the Bible and traditional dogma. But it felt itself to be still very Christian, without knowing in what precise formulas Christianity consisted. 'Secularisation' could mean that public life was more 'secular'; that is, influenced less, or not at all, by religion. Evidence that public life was more secular in this sense is hard to find. The law of divorce was still based upon the text of the New Testament. And some claimed that the standards of public life were higher, because more subject to religious opinion, than in an earlier generation.

Some nonconformists, like John Clifford, suffered from qualms that you could not keep public life pure by campaigns, because a campaign was a blunt instrument which must judge the outside of men. Despite such qualms nonconformists were resolved that public life should be seen to follow Christian standards of morality. 'The nonconformist conscience' was a phrase coined by enemies at the fall of Parnell and gladly accepted by the Methodist minister Hugh Price Hughes. But this conscience was not particularly nonconformist. It was powerful in politics because it represented a wide and inarticulate feeling in the nation. Gladstone could appeal to it against Italian prisons or Turkish massacres, and plenty of Anglicans had what in others might be called a nonconformist conscience.

From 1886 atheists could sit in the House of Commons. It will not however do to think that the atmosphere of that House changed markedly. The early Victorian House knew men like Roebuck whose effect was quite as 'secular' as that of the few professed atheists like Bradlaugh. We should not exaggerate the Biblical knowledge of the mid-Victorian M.P., for when John Bright used a Biblical reference to create a political phrase, talking of the cave of Adullam, many members of Parliament did not know where the cave of Adullam was to be found. And until after the end of the reign unscrupulous electioneers still found atheism a useful word to hurl against a parliamentary candidate if they thought that it would stick. The statesmen continued to be humane Christian men. There is no question that England was more 'secular' in 1901 than in 1837. But compare the cabinet of 1837 with the cabinet of 1901: the prime minister of 1837 was a gay unitarian with a cynical air, he of 1901 a devout Anglican modestly influenced by the Oxford Movement. The colonial secretary of 1837 (Glenelg) was an earnest evangelical, he of 1901 (Joseph Chamberlain) a unitarian who would on occasion be flippant about religion. The leader of the House of Commons in 1837 (Lord John Russell) was a latitudinarian, he of 1901 (Balfour) a Scottish presbyterian who was a Christian philosopher of the first rank. The foreign secretary of 1901 (Lansdowne) was a quiet Anglican but he of 1837 (Palmerston) would not count among the devout. The chancellor of the exchequer in 1837 (Spring Rice) was more religious than he of 1901 (Hicks Beach) but it was no sharp contrast. At the leadership of the nation we cannot say that the last years of the reign were any less Christian than the first.

The Victorians successfully retained (for the most part) the highest standard of integrity in public life, and more evidently in the later

Victorian age than the earlier. Ministers like Gladstone, statesmen like Lyttelton or Carnarvon or W. H. Smith, lawyers like Hatherley and Cairns and Selborne, administrators like Blachford, parliamentarians like John Bright—conditioned public life far more than the reports of high society.

England as a whole was more 'secular' in atmosphere. For the big town was always and inevitably more 'secular' than the village, and in 1837 England was a land of villages, in 1901 a land of towns. The working man of the towns was more detached from religious institutions, by sentiment as well as by physical circumstances. In 1837 he was partly uneducated, almost wholly unorganised, and politically powerless, whereas in 1901 he was literate, organised, and powerful.

I. THE PRESS

Some things were more secular, others less. The air of Sunday in the city was a little more religious, in the country a little less so. The press as a whole, though with exceptions, encouraged a detached attitude towards religion. If we try to define 'secularisation', we need to pay much attention to the atmosphere, and to the selling needs, of the press. The abolition of taxes on newspapers between 1853 and 1861, and then the elementary education act of 1870, made the last thirty years of the reign the time of flowering for the modern press. Thackray Bunce, who was a good Anglican layman and the editor of the *Birmingham Daily Post*, confessed that the press, by the nature of its work, dealt with religion as if from outside.[1] Yet the *Times*, the *Spectator*, and the great provincial newspapers headed by the *Manchester Guardian*, continued to deal in religious matters with a sense of responsibility and a lot of accurate information, even (at times) in theological matters. The *Manchester Guardian* printed a long, technical, and expert review of *Lux Mundi*.

The upper and middle class of 1901 knew the Bible less well than the same classes in 1837. The working man knew it, in general, better, for now he could read, and though he did not read it, he had been taught about it in Sunday school. And some who knew the Bible less, knew other things more—*Hark the herald angels sing*, or *Abide with me*, or *Lead kindly light*. The sense of obligation to go to church had partly gone, and he who went to church might find open spaces

[1] CCR, 1893, 512.

in the pews which chilled him, but his soul would be more likely than in 1837 to be touched by the beauty of the liturgy or the warmth of the congregational singing.

In the middle eighties the churches became more fully aware of the power of the press, and the extent to which printed literature reached the homes of the newly educated. The nonconformists were quicker than the Anglicans to perceive the importance of the press. The clergy of the Church of England continued to believe that wise men kept their names out of newspapers. They were slow or reluctant to use the opportunities for information offered by the press, finding it difficult at first to distinguish influence from self-advertising. A meeting at the Portsmouth Church Congress of 1885 to consider the question was thinly attended. It was thought to be a considerable feat to get lectures which answered Bradlaugh printed in the *Kentish Mercury* (circulation 16,000 plus). The London secular press did not usually publish sermons, except that the *Pall Mall Gazette* sometimes printed summaries of Liddon's sermons.

From time to time they tried to found a national daily of a specially religious tone, but never succeeded. Some of the professionally Christian journals were not narrowly ecclesiastical. Such papers as the *Church Times* (1863), the *Rock* (1868), the *Record* (1828) always looked to a fairly small professional market, but the *Guardian* (1846) or the *British Weekley* (1886) were among the best of the weeklies for intelligent men. Probably the widest circulations of any specially religious newspapers were achieved by the *Christian World* (1857), which under the editorship of James Clarke (1859) became the organ of the free churches and reached a circulation at best of about 120,000,[1] and the monthly *Good Words*, with a circulation of about 130,000, edited by presbyterians who collected some of the eminent writers in the country from Gladstone downwards. But if they could not compete in the national field, they made remarkable new departures in the local field. The parish magazine became viable after printing and paper became cheap and education became universal. The Anglican clergyman J. Erskine Clarke in the sixties edited a variety of papers (*Chatterbox, Children's Prize*) but the most important was *The Parish Magazine* (1859 onwards); for from this initiative sprang local parish magazines. Clarke's publication was adopted by parishes with the addition of local advertisements and some local

[1] Darlow, *Life of W. Robertson Nicoll*, 57ff.

matter. St. Mark's, Kensington, was using Clarke in this way by January 1865, for a copy is in the British Museum. Scarborough had a magazine by 1869. At an exhibition of parish magazines held at Cambridge in 1942 the earliest exhibit came from the remote Cumberland village of Plumpton, 1876.[1] By 1885 the Anglican parish clergy were said to make an almost universal practice of publishing their own monthly magazine, but there was exaggeration in the claim. Already the covers of magazines were an art, as they intended to lie interestingly on tables. The parish of Forest Gate circulated about 6,000 copies a year between 1875 and 1885.[2] Eight years later the total circulation of parish magazines was said to be about a million and a half.

2. DISESTABLISHMENT

State recognition of religion was removed from one area of the united kingdom and was soon to be removed from another; if by state recognition was meant a formal link in law between the government and a particular church. Few claimed that these proceedings made the society more 'secularised'.

An established church could marry with democracy only if it was not a grievance to an important minority in the nation. In Ireland it was offensive to a majority. After the extension of the franchise by the second reform act of 1867 it was only a question of political timing when the Irish Church would be disestablished, and after the further extension of the franchise by the reform act of 1884 the campaign for Welsh disestablishment became practical. In England the minority was not small, but after 1871 the grievances were few. In Scotland the minority was large, but the grievances were hardly visible to the eye of sensible men.

Ever since Catholic emancipation sympathetic treatment of the Roman Catholics in Ireland was a necessity of good government in England. In the difficulty of governing Ireland at all, the influence of Catholic priests with their flocks was believed with reason to be important to the conduct of the Irish as citizens of Great Britain.

---

[1] Alan Webster, *Theology*, xlvii, July 1943, 156.
[2] CCR, 1885, 356, 364. The earlier parish magazine in a big London area was a less ecclesiastical production. The British Museum repository possesses (e.g.) the *Parochial Chronicle*, a weekly newspaper for the metropolitan area, 10 April–29 May 1852; the *Parochial Gazette*, of St. Marylebone, 8 May–10 June 1837; the *Vestryman and Metropolitan Parochial Gazette*, 7 June–2 August 1834.

Therefore no government after 1829 could simply support the established Church of Ireland against its critics. Peel's dealings over Maynooth showed how even a Conservative government must seek to do what it could for the Roman Catholic church in Ireland. Most Conservatives, and some Whigs, preferred to maintain Protestant ascendancy because only then could they see a probability of maintaining the union between England and Ireland. But it ceased to be sensible or prudent to emphasise this ascendancy. Sometimes, even to moderate statesmen, ascendancy looked like a survival of the past which made more difficult the government of Ireland. Though most men in Parliament would have preferred Protestant ascendancy undisturbed, the disestablished Catholic bishops of Ireland wielded more influence at Westminster than the established Protestant bishops of Ireland.

To the Irish the Protestant establishment was offensive as a badge of English conquest. By removing the establishment the government could cure no practical evil, except by using some money to other ends. But it would remove a stigma identified with English ascendancy. Though Roman Catholic doctrine expected state establishment of religion, the Catholic leaders of Ireland accepted the plan to disendow the Protestant church. In 1864 several Roman Catholic bishops joined in founding the National Association, which among other ends aimed at the disendowment of the Church of Ireland by constitutional means. They did not ask that Anglican money be given to Roman Catholics. Since emancipation and before, the possibility of 'concurrent endowment' in Ireland, or of establishing Roman Catholics and perhaps Presbyterians as well as Anglicans in Ireland, looked attractive to some Whig and some Conservative leaders. In the debates over Irish disestablishment such a proposal was supported even by one Roman Catholic bishop in Ireland, Moriarty of Kerry, and by several eminent moderates of the Church of England. In the course of the debate the plan became almost accepted by the leaders of the Conservative party. When it looked as though the only way to preserve the established church was to establish other churches, the Conservatives for a moment backed concurrent endowment. Even Gladstone's original draft bill to disestablish the Church of Ireland had traces of this idea. It would have preserved the idea that the state should encourage and approve religion, and should not be seen to be neutral. It would have ensured that any endowments taken from the Church of Ireland should be given to religious purposes not too remote from those purposes for which they were first given. But it had the single objection, that it was impossible. The Englishmen whose votes were necessary to disestablishment would not countenance it for a moment. The Liberal party depended in part upon the nonconformists, who would never give money to the Church of Rome, partly because they were hostile to popery and partly because they disapproved of giving state money to churches. To gain disestablishment Roman Catholic Irishmen must join with English dissenters otherwise hostile to Catholicism. Such an alliance could never agree on a plan to strengthen rather than to abolish establishment in Ireland. Therefore the Irish Roman Catholic bishops were wise in refusing to ask for concurrent endowment. And Archbishop Manning was wise in publicly demanding religious equality and privately urging Rome to disapprove any scheme for concurrent endowment.

The defenders of the Irish Church were nearly all the Conservative party; nearly all Ulster; Englishmen with land in Ireland; perhaps two-thirds of the clergy of the Church of England;[1] some Anglicans afraid that an attack upon Irish establishment must be followed by an attack upon English establishment; some English Protestants afraid of Roman Catholicism. But they were weaker than their numbers. Their fundamental weaknesses were first, that the election of 1868, the earliest under the new franchise, produced a great Liberal majority, of a more radical mood than any government for more than thirty years; secondly, that Gladstone succeeded in uniting the Liberal party, and forcing the resignation of the Tory government, on the issue of Irish disestablishment, and therefore that question was suddenly the political issue of the hour; and thirdly, that the Conservatives had little enough confidence at that time in their leader Disraeli. He seemed so weak on the issue of Ireland, and when he was not weak he was rallying the support of *no popery*, which was unwelcome to many moderate churchmen in the Conservative party.

They were also weakened because the high Anglicans, formerly stalwart in defending establishment, were in no mood to use vigour in defending. They had seen the judicial committee of the privy council trampling, as some of them believed, upon the faith of the

[1] So R. W. Church guessed, *Life*, 180.

Church of England. Men like Pusey, or Liddon, or C. J. Vaughan, or Roundell Palmer, were not so enamoured of establishment as to think that the Irish Church could not well do without it. And in this conviction they were fortified by the extraordinary circumstance that the leader of the disestablishing party was a devout and revered Tractarian. In the past, Gladstone had little communication with dissenters, or sympathy for their demands. About 1865 he began to enter into friendship with leading protestant dissenters. He used to go to the house of the minister Newman Hall, and there meet nonconformist pastors of eminence. So he came to know a great dissenter of the past like Thomas Binney, and a great nonconformist of the future like R. W. Dale of Birmingham. Yet Gladstone never really understood the dissenters. He loved Keble, and *The Imitation of Christ*, and the letters of St. Bernard.[1] He was an altogether new type of Liberal leader. By the standards of the past it was incongruous to have a Liberal prime minister who was a high churchman. To the end of his life he regarded Laud as a martyr, and that was once a shibboleth among a select band of high Tories. Nowhere in writings or speeches would he allow praise to Cromwell or the Puritans, to whom the dissenters looked for their ancestry. Yet this Tractarian was nearer in theology to dissenters than the older Whigs. The Whigs often sat loosely to Christian doctrine. His predecessor as Liberal prime minister, Russell, preferred Christianity to be undogmatic. Gladstone resembled the leading dissenters at least this far, that he thought undogmatic Christianity to be worthless.

Dr. Pusey had little in common with Newman Hall. But Tractarians shared with dissenters a determination to prevent the church from being a department of the state, and to insist upon the independent life of the church in worship and doctrine.

Part of Gladstone's new attitude to Ireland was simply a sense of justice; part, a sensitivity to political winds; and part, a desire to strengthen the Church of England. What was so extraordinary about him was his steady churchmanship at a time when most steady churchmen regarded him as pursuing a course destructive of the church. It was the old notion of Peel: strengthen the Church of England by abandoning whatever trappings may be seen to be indefensible and so to weaken action. He found his eldest son in a mood to concede nothing and defend everything. He wrote to him: 'I am convinced

[1] Morley i, 575, 613.

that the only hope of making it possible for her to discharge her high office as stewardess of divine truth, is to deal tenderly and gently with all the points at which her external privileges *grate* upon the feelings and interests of that unhappily large portion of the community who have almost ceased in any sense to care for her.' When he carried the bill of 1868 which at last abolished compulsory church rate, he appeared to dissenters as the author of a tardy act of justice. To himself he appeared rather as one who removed the highest obstacle to the proper influence of the Church of England in many parishes. 'The whole of my public life with respect to matters ecclesiastical, for the last twenty years or more', he wrote to Bishop Wilberforce of Oxford in 1863, 'has been a continuing effort, though a very weak one, to extricate the church in some degree from entangled relations without shock or violence.'[1] He took office with a religious sense of responsibility. A few enemies believed him a blasphemer; a few friends believed him possessed of divine vocation. He did not doubt the vocation, and approached his task with reverence. He sometimes felt it odd that he, a life-long and convinced Anglican, should be heading what he called his three corps, Scottish presbyterians and Welsh or English nonconformists and Irish Roman Catholics.[2] But if he sensed the oddity, he doubted not for a moment either the propriety or his mission. He felt no incompatibility within. If he helped to pacify Ireland, he also strengthened his own church, by clearing it of a just accusation.

The bill to disestablish the Irish Church was the work of Gladstone's pen, and as able a piece of administrative drafting as appeared in the nineteenth century. A comparison with Welsh disestablishment fifty years later, carried through with muddle and necessary retractation, shows how coherent and skilful was the Irish plan. This is the more remarkable in the absence of precedent. Gladstone sought information about other episcopal churches which were not established, as in Canada and Scotland and America. He knew of the important precedent of disendowment in Canada, where the Canadian act, depriving the Anglican clergy of the land known as clergy reserves, preserved the life interests of the clergy but allowed them to commute their interests into capital terms which thereafter were paid to them by the church authority in the form of stipends.

[1] Morley, i, 593.
[2] Gladstone to Bishop Hinds, 31 December 1868; Morley, i, 669.

To separate justly church and state when the union was so historic and therefore so complex would have been hard enough. To separate justly when the Conservatives believed it injustice to take any money away from the Church of Ireland, and the nonconformists believed it injustice to leave any money with the Church of Ireland, required powers of political leadership and administrative capacity seldom united in one mind.

The Church of Ireland was thus disestablished from 1 January 1871, with compensation to existing office holders and (thanks to the resistance of the House of Lords) a reasonable assistance in money from the endowments to enable the disendowed church to proceed.[1]

Once it was done, it moved the Church of England little. Archbishop Tait, who endured great strain between securing good terms and persuading the Conservatives not to throw it out altogether in the Lords, went down for the weekend afterwards to preach at Herne Bay, and was relieved to find that scarcely anyone thought about the Irish church. Dr. Pusey took part in every controversy important in his eyes, and was known at the time to favour Gladstone's policy, yet his vast biography does not mention the disestablishment of the Irish Church. The world had moved on since 1833 when a proposal to abolish ten bishoprics caused Keble to preach the most famous of assize sermons. A number of Anglicans were thankful that their church was 'cleansed'. Liberals headed by Frederick Temple wanted it, Tractarians like R. W. Church and W. F. Hook thought it right. But the only bishop to vote for the second reading was Thirlwall of St. David's, and the sixteen bishops who voted against were more representative of the Church of England. Like all Irish acts it failed to bring conciliation and in a few months the relations between the Irish and the government were as bad as ever. But Manning and the Roman Catholics continued to be

---

The disestablished church received the churches free, and the manses on very favourable terms; half a million pounds in lieu of private gifts; 12% bonus on top of the commutation of vested interests by office holders. The Irish bishops in the House of Lords, even those already sitting, lost their seats. For financial circumstances see Hugh Shearman's 'Irish church finance after the disestablishment' in H. A. Cronne and others, *Essays in British and Irish history in honour of J. E. Todd*, 1949. The English governments used the money from the Irish church for intermediate education, pensions for teachers, relief of distress, the royal university of Ireland, sea fisheries, seed potatoes, congested districts board and agricultural and technical instruction. The act also ended the Maynooth grant and the Irish regium donum by giving a capital sum in lieu.

pleased that a 'stigma' was removed. The bill left the disestablished Irish church with formidable tensions in reconstruction.

The act forced the repeal of the ecclesiastical titles act of 1851, which penalised the use of territorial titles by bishops not of the established church unless they were Scottish. For disestablishment thereby rendered the titles of Irish Anglican bishops illegal. If the titles of Anglican bishops in Ireland were to be made legal, the titles of Roman Catholics bishops must be permitted to be as legal. The repeal of the ecclesiastical titles act was carried through Parliament in 1871.

Thus, for the first time, one part of Great Britain existed without an established church. It did not seem quite such a novelty as it otherwise might have seemed because in South Africa and Canada and Australia men saw parts of the empire without any established church. But that it should happen in Great Britain looked to some like the probable start of a new era in the relations of church and state. For a few years the Irish Church act encouraged Welshmen who wanted to disestablish the church in Wales, Scotsmen who wanted to disestablish the Church of Scotland, nonconformists who wanted disestablishment in England, liberationists who wanted disestablishment everywhere.

During the middle years of the nineteenth century the Welsh language and nonconformist religion joined to beget a more lively sense of Welsh nationality. When all English laws applied to Wales as to Yorkshire, it was natural that the Church of England should be established in Wales. But here was a law which slowly began to appear 'alien' because a large majority of the Welsh-speaking Welsh dissented (by 1853) from the established religion. Nonconformity helped to make Wales articulate. The new Welsh-speaking newspapers in the middle years of the century were without exception nonconformist. The Welsh looked up to nonconformist ministers as their first 'national' leaders, in Parliament and especially in public opinion. Their chapel and their Sunday school became, as nowhere else in Britain, the centre of social life in the villages and little towns among the hills and mines.

The Anglican bishops in Wales were Englishmen and were sometimes blamed by Welsh pamphleteers for being out of touch with the people. No bishop in Wales had spoken Welsh from birth since the reign of Queen Anne.[1] The argument for appointing Englishmen as bishops to Wales was not trivial. The gentry of Wales were English-speaking. If the work was open to anyone, whether English or Welsh, there were many more suitable men. The bishop must be respected by the upper class. If the prime minister confined his nomination to Welsh speakers, he might simply be appointing less qualified people—so argued Lord Melbourne on one occasion. Educated Welshmen were proud of the national stature of Bishop Copleston of Llandaff and Bishop Thirlwall of St. David's. Yet it made still more impression in Wales when Copleston took trouble to see that persons who spoke Welsh were appointed to his parishes. He even attacked the lord chancellor's exercise of patronage because it offended his rules.[2] It made an impression when Thirlwall was the first bishop in Wales for centuries who learnt the language, preached in Welsh, and conducted confirmations in Welsh.

Despite Thirlwall and Copleston, and the respect which they achieved, the Welsh people regarded their English bishops with a distant detachment. Lady Llanover told Gladstone that Thirlwall was very learned, but as a Welsh bishop he might as well be in New Zealand.[3] The Roman Catholics of Ireland regarded English Protestant bishops as part of the English conquest. The dissenters of Wales did not so express their attitude, nor did they feel it like the Irish. But a shadow of that feeling towards the English people affected their attitude to bishops, and therefore to the Church of England in Wales. The leading Welsh clergy were educated at Jesus College, Oxford. But some good Welsh speakers still preferred in 1850 to opt for the dissenting ministry. If they chose the established church, they would not be likely to receive work worthy of their talents.[3]

The flowering of dissent was due to causes more pastoral than an inarticulate semi-nationalism which thought the established church to be unWelsh because English.

The population moved. The great age of industry came upon South Wales. English immigrants moved in, Welsh labourers from

[1] K. O. O. Morgan, 7: Thirlwall and Campbell of Bangor (1859–90) learnt Welsh as adults. Campbell was much liked by nonconformists as well as churchmen. For Melbourne's opinion, see Melbourne to Bishop Copleston of Llandaff, 15 September 1840, MP.

[2] K. O. O. Morgan, 33; from Add. MSS 44424, 166–71.

[3] Edwards, *Memories*, 137.

the farms moved south. The flexible organisation of independency was better suited to this movement than the parochial system of the established church. Moreover in South Wales the provision of the established church was as weak as anywhere in Britain. In the north of Wales the livings were respectable and the clergy reasonably provided. In South Wales the average income of the clergy was lower than the average income of any English diocese. The machinery of establishment never adapted itself easily to large movements of population. In the villages of the south the number of churches grew too slowly for the people. The average income of each beneficed clergyman in the diocese of St. David's was £137, on an average of three years ending 31 December 1831.[1] In that diocese 86 livings had an income of less than £75 a year. Only 110 houses were fit to live in, that is one house in every four benefices. In short, the established church in South Wales was more starved of funds than the established church in any other part of Great Britain, just at the time when the tide of immigrants flowed into the ports and mines of Monmouthshire and Glamorgan.

Anglican clergy were expected to be gentry. Welsh-speakers were seldom gentry. Therefore either the Anglicans must cause their clergy to learn Welsh, or they must use as their clergy less educated persons. Since these clergy could look forward in the south to a scanty maintenance and a dilapidated dwelling, they were not performing the function attributed, not without reason, to the English clergy in Ireland, of being a resident man of education in every parish. Though they were men of the people only the exceptional were influential among the people. St. David's College in Lampeter did something to train those who could not go to Jesus College in Oxford. But in its earliest years Lampeter was starved of money, could not award the B.A. degree till 1865, and was a meagre institution. It nevertheless secured some remarkable men on its staff, like Rowland Williams and Harold Browne. Its starvation and its inadequacy lasted until the seventies, when Principal F. J. Jayne began to turn it into a reasonable place of education and training for the ministry. In the seventies the Welsh church could be seen to advance rapidly, in communicants, enthusiasm and efficiency. It shared the rising standards of the Victorian church revival. In 1870 Gladstone appointed the first Welsh-speaking bishop, Joshua Hughes, to the

[1] Phillips, 195-6.

vacant see of St. Asaph. Cardiff had one church in 1861 and thirty-eight in 1906. Swansea had two churches in 1831 and thirty-four in 1906.

In 1886 Gladstone announced his conversion to home rule in Ireland. The attempt to give home rule spurred nationalism in Wales, and the serious campaign for Welsh disestablishment began.

The first steps towards disestablishment in Wales were heralded by a tithe war of 1888–90. There were no murders, as in the war in Ireland half a century before, but it divided Welsh society, so that hitherto kindly Welshmen would pass their clergyman with a scowl and a mutter.[1] The refusal of tithe led to scenes at auctions, and to the near starvation of some clergymen. The clergy were saved by the coming of a tithe act of 1891, transferring payment of tithe from tenant to landlord; and the temperature in Wales dropped. But those years of tithe war were the bitterest years. Thomas Gee recommended the people of Wales not to show loyalty to Queen Victoria when she visited Wales in August 1889, because she was the 'head' of the 'alien church'.[2] At the general election of 1892 the Liberal candidates in Wales placed disestablishment at the front of their programme, and received strong support from the ministers and deacons of many chapels. The power of nonconformity was shown by the board schools. Two hundred and forty-two schools out of about three hundred schools had no religious teaching at all, or read the Bible only without comment.[3] In 1895 the House of Commons carried the second reading of a disestablishing bill on severe terms of disendowment, but the government of Lord Rosebery fell.[4]

Successful disestablishment of the Irish Church inevitably produced motions in the House of Commons to disestablish the English Church. Edward Miall proposed and comfortably lost such motions in 1871, 1872, 1873. He collected, respectively, 89, 94 and 61 votes.

---

[1] Edwards, *Memories*, 129.   [2] K. O. O. Morgan, 87.
[3] Edwards, *Handbook*, 32.
[4] The Welsh church was finally disestablished by an act of May 1914 being amended by an act of August 1919. It cost about £48,000 a year out of (1910) £268,558. The Welsh church was separated from the province of Canterbury. A. G. Edwards of St. Asaph was enthroned as Archbishop of Wales on 1 June 1920. It was a more muddled process than Irish disestablishment, but the muddle was partly due to the war of 1914, and it came out not too unreasonably in the end. The money taken from the church went to help the University of Wales and educational or cultural or welfare schemes managed by Welsh county councils.

This was not Conservative versus Liberal with many Liberal abstentions. In 1873 Miall would have been defeated by about two to one if not a single Conservative had voted.

The members of the Church of England valued establishment chiefly because many of them could hardly conceive the Church of England without it. To some of them disestablishment looked like disembodiment, so inextricably was the history of the church bound with the history of the nation. They therefore felt a certain insecurity, so long as the Irish Roman Catholic members sat at Westminster and so long as the Welsh members had a motive for their campaign to disestablish. A mild sense of insecurity lasted from 1871 till 1914. The most insecure elections were the general elections of 1880 and 1885, when some men even talked of a 'disestablishment crisis'. In those elections nonconformist support was felt to be vital to the political successes of the Liberal party, and therefore many Liberal candidates brought the possibility of disestablishment into their speeches. Gladstone himself always discountenanced any suggestion that the Liberal party wanted English disestablishment. But some nonconformists claimed (though with more enthusiasm than exactness) that they brought Gladstone to power in 1880. In May 1880 the Liberation Society and the Protestant dissenting deputies gave a dinner at Cannon Street Hotel to the 'friends of religious equality' who had been elected to the new parliament. The dinner was attended by 174 M.P.s and the chairman, Henry Richard, declared that there were more than 100 nonconformist M.P.s. The summer of 1880 was a time when conservative churchmen told each other that there was no cause for disquiet; and when men so remind themselves they mean the opposite. The conversion of Gladstone to Irish home rule in 1886 gravely weakened the Liberal party and incidentally destroyed much of the political power of nonconformity. But in the earlier eighties reappeared the prediction which no one had made since the early thirties, namely that the establishment could not have long to run. Bishop Ryle told the Liverpool diocesan conference of 1883 that he did not see how the establishment could last more than a few years.[1] Englishmen sometimes needed reminding that the church would continue to be the church whatever its relation to the state.

During the campaign for Welsh disestablishment an occasional

[1] G, 83, 1722.

attack spilt over into demanding total disestablishment. In 1897 Samuel Smith almost repeated Miall's best feat by gaining 86 votes for such a motion, but without serious debate. Welsh members by then realised that their hope lay in a separate Welsh measure, and that a demand for a wider measure merely frustrated what they wanted.

Whether or not the consequences of Irish and Welsh disestablishment increased the trend towards a less Christian tone in general society, or 'secularisation', is a matter only of speculation. But unlike the French separation between church and state, they cannot be used as evidence of a growing 'secularity'. For most of the supporters of disestablishment in both Wales and Ireland hoped to increase the effectiveness of the churches in those countries. Disestablishment was mostly conceived, or at least defended, as a step towards more Christianity and not towards less.

The nonconformist campaign for disestablishment was a sign of the strength of Victorian Christianity. For the nonconformists were not afraid that if they weakened establishment they would weaken Christianity. Their attitude changed markedly after 1914, when Christianity was weakened by war and when popular habits were altered by the use of the motor-car. Then some of their leaders began to value a recognition of religion by the state as a bulwark to the practice of their own religion as well as the Anglican. But in the reign of Queen Victoria such an attitude was rare, and its rarity witnesses to a certain confidence about Christianity in England.

Rebel Anglo-Catholic curates—Arthur Stanton, Mackonochie, Bryan King—argued for disestablishment but were exceptional among the Anglican clergy. The principal rub was the divorce act of 1857 which compelled a clergyman to remarry the innocent party in a divorce suit and to lend his church for a remarriage of the guilty party. The divorce rate rose steadily in the eighties and nineties, and the press reported the proceedings with alacrity. In the middle of the nineties a demonstrating priest, Father Black, took to interrupting the marriages of divorced persons in London churches, by conduct more conscientious than Christian. Bishop Temple of London even felt obliged to withdraw the subject of divorce from the agenda of his diocesan conference in 1896 lest it cause an explosion. Biblical criticism made the argument sterner—the single case where the advance of knowledge affected contemporary practice—by showing that the exceptive clause in St. Matthew, permitting divorce on the ground of adultery, was perhaps not an original saying of Christ. Bishop Edward King of Lincoln disagreed with almost the entire group of high churchmen; arguing after long meditation that though the church must at all costs maintain the binding nature of the marriage vow, the final and overriding consideration was charity and pastoral care. The Victorians did not change the law.

3. THE UNIVERSITIES

Two ideals of a university struggled for the mastery, and the new won a sweeping victory but with compromise in the endeavour to preserve what was best in the old or to satisfy the adherents of the old.

The acts of 1854 and 1856 opened the education and lower degrees at Oxford and Cambridge to members of any religion or none, and reserved the government of the university and its colleges to members of the Church of England. The same acts and their consequences made competition almost the sole gateway to scholarships and fellowships.

The old university gave a liberal education to the upper and upper-middle classes, among them the future clergy of the Church of England. Its government was in the hands of clergymen, like almost all great educational institutions in the middle of the century. Its object was to educate the young in virtue as well as in knowledge. It advanced knowledge, but more as a by-product of its activity in education than as an end. Newman began the most celebrated of Victorian lectures on the university by declaring that the university is a place of teaching universal knowledge. 'This implies that its object is, on the one hand, intellectual, not moral; and on the other, that it is the diffusion and extension of knowledge rather than the advancement.'[1] Though it advanced knowledge, and though Oxford possessed in the Bodleian Library one of the great international institutions of the academic community, it hardly advanced it more than the occupants of rural parsonages, or than private men who wrote. Of course the occupants of parsonages always, and the private men often, learnt how to advance knowledge while they studied at the university. The university wanted culture for the sake of culture. It was not yet entangled with a need to serve the nation more

[1] *The Scope and Nature of University Education* (1859), Preface.

directly (for educating the upper classes and the clergy was a sufficient mode of serving the nation) or to respond to the hazy ideas of
education formed by a wider constituency of parents. 'Though the
university cannot help begetting a few professors, its true function is
the nurturing of citizens, of gentlemen, of Christians. By its mathematical discipline it trains them in logic, by its physics it opens to
them the order and beauty of creation, by its studies in ancient
history and literature it brings them into converse with minds of philosophic power and literary imagination, by its religious teaching and
pastoral care it fosters the virtue without which no state can stand.'[1]

'The fact', said the Oxford university commissioners of 1850
(page 94), 'that so few books of profound research emanate from the
university of Oxford materially impairs its character as a seat of
learning, and consequently its hold on the respect of the nation. The
presence of men eminent in various departments of knowledge
would impart a dignity and stability to the whole institution . . .
whilst from within it would tend above all other means to guard the
university from being absorbed, as it has been of late years, by the
agitations of theological controversy.' More professors, less power to
college tutors. The commissioners underestimated the amount of
learning available in Oxford and were wrong in thinking that
professors were less likely to engage in controversy than college
tutors. They were right in thinking that Oxford needed more men
engaged on fundamental work, and that the informed public was
beginning to criticise Oxford on this score.

In modern words, therefore, the university must engage more in
research and less in elementary teaching. Extremists said that the
advancement of learning, in this modern sense, ought to be the sole
aim of the university. Men not extremists wanted a wider front of
advance; more history, more natural science, more philosophy, more
economics, and perhaps more modern literature. A marriage between
such an ideal and the ideal of providing a liberal education for the
upper classes, especially for clergymen, had discomforts.

Men who valued the old university for its religious and pastoral
care—they included big men, like Newman or Sedgwick or
Christopher Wordsworth and probably they included most men
who had been educated at the old university—feared the new
theorists as men who wanted to turn the endowments of an ancient

[1] Chadwick, *Westcott and the University*, 3.

and Christian institution into something different for their own ends. The new men wanted men appointed as fellows only for intellectual reasons. The old men wanted fellows who would educate in virtue as well as knowledge, and therefore thought it proper to take account of character as well as intellectual record. For the new men the rules of celibacy and religious profession merely hampered Oxford and Cambridge in their proper endeavour to encourage the advancement of knowledge. They wanted fellowships open to all comers of any religion or none; no obligation on any fellow to be ordained except so far as an ordained man was needed in colleges to conduct the services in the chapel; no obligation to remain unmarried (but not all the liberals wished celibacy to end). Thus the fellowship would become a lay career for life instead of a stage in the clerical way to a country benefice.

In neither Oxford nor Cambridge did the new men possess a majority. At Oxford the conservative majority grew during the sixties. The universities would not have changed their structure so radically if left alone by the outside world. But the old dissenting drive to open the universities, which achieved a partial success in the fifties, turned the internal and local argument into an external and national argument.

The internal argument was warm at Oxford, quieter at Cambridge. The Earl of Powis asked a Cambridge tutor, 'To what do you attribute the comparative freedom of Cambridge from strong religious partisanship or extreme religious movement?'[1] The tutor gave reasons for the difference which the historian may doubt, but he did not question that Cambridge suffered less strife than Oxford. The defenders of old Oxford, determined to preserve religion and morality, judged a man not exclusively but partly by his religious opinions, and under the Oxford constitution had much chance of exercising their judgment. Eight other professors besides the professor of poetry were elected by an open poll of Convocation. As the poetry chair was the focus of theological argument in the clash of the Tractarian movement, so the election to the Sanskrit chair in 1860, and to the chair of political economy in 1868, showed signs that the constituency judged a candidate more by his religious opinions, which they could understand, than by his scholarship, of which they knew nothing. Mark Pattison wrote: 'It has always been

[1] PP, 1871, ix, 147.

assumed that university appointments should be made with a reference to the interests of the church, or those interests as interpreted by
one of the parties in the church.'[1] He denounced the assumption as a
false standard which perverted the judgment of men and things. But
the defenders of old Oxford did not see why it was a false standard.
The university was an institution of the church as well as of the state.
It was therefore not only natural but right that appointments should
be made in the interests of the church, and any other course would
betray conduct improper in the trustees of church endowments.

The longest struggle was fought over Jowett's stipend, where the
increment above £40 was blocked because of Jowett's opinions on
religion, until in 1865 Christ Church agreed to provide it. Probably
nothing did more to embitter the Oxford minority than this stipend.
And the leaders of the Oxford liberals were as anticlerical as their
chief opponents were clerical. Goldwin Smith was naturally fierce,
Mark Pattison grew to be fierce. And on their side the churchmen
suffered from the rigidity with which they applied their principles
and from the personalities of one or two of their most trenchant
writers. A party which had J. W. Burgon contending for it in
university politics was likely to stir animosity among the enemy.

The air at Cambridge was calmer.

Some conservatives were inclined to exaggerate the beauty of the
past Christian university. Only thirty years before Sir Charles
Wetherell argued in a court of law that the letters B.A. marked a
Christian as well as an educated gentleman. Mark Pattison declared
the letters B.A. to have only a social value. 'They are an evidence
that a youth has been able to afford not only the money, but . . . the
time, to live three years among gentlemen, doing nothing, as a
gentleman should.'[2] Certainly the ideals and the practice of the old
university did not always agree, though in this it was not unique
among institutions. Though many of the fellows were clergymen,
some of them were clergymen like Pattison and exercised influence
in ways which were not at all ecclesiastical; though all undergraduates must pass an examination in divinity, the examination was not
highly regarded; though the colleges had chapels with compulsory
attendance, not everyone believed that religion was well served by
them, and one Oxford observer said in 1871 that he attributed no
religious value to them and believed compulsory attendance to be an

---

[1] Pattison, *Suggestions*, 226.   [2] Pattison, *Suggestions*, 236.

irreligious influence.[1] The strongest religious influences, though exerted by fellows of colleges, were exerted rather apart from colleges, though not apart from the status of those fellows in the university; men like Charles Simeon and later Westcott and Handley Moule at Cambridge, or like Liddon and Edward King at Oxford.

The memories of graduates seized upon those features of their university which made it so intimate and happy a society, and sometimes focussed their affections upon the constitution now under attack. But their affectionate idealism was shaken in 1882 when Tom Mozley published his *Reminiscences of Oriel College and the Oxford Movement*. These were two volumes of gossip and anecdote of the thirties and just before, garrulous and readable and inaccurate, presenting a portrait of the university of those days which no man with eyes could admire, the more because Mozley evidently had no intention of denigrating the university of his youth.[2]

In 1871 Gladstone's government carried the universities tests act, opening all degrees and offices (except those tied to holy orders) to men of any religion or none, at the universities and colleges of Oxford, Cambridge and Durham. The act recognised the old rights of the church in these universities, first, by affecting only colleges then existing, and therefore allowing the possibility of denominational colleges provided that they became part of the university after 1871, and secondly by obliging all those existing colleges to maintain the services of the Church of England in their chapels and to provide religious instruction for undergraduates who were members of the Church of England.

Some members of the universities, like some Conservative members of Parliament, opposed this bill and regretted it when it became law. They were convinced that to make the colleges non-denominational was also to make them secular, and that (whatever the act might say) a college under the new conditions could not provide effective instruction in religion if its members were of any religion or none. This feeling led to the founding of Keble College at Oxford (1870) and Selwyn College, Cambridge (1879–82). The founders of

---

[1] C. Appleton, in PP, 1871, ix, 290.

[2] Mozley's *Reminiscences* affected the judgment of historians who wrote about the Oxford Movement and occasionally misled them. I have tried to amend the most important portrait by an article, 'The Limitations of Keble' in *Theology*, lxvii, 1964, 46ff.

these colleges wished to preserve a Christian college in a university which they believed to be going non-Christian, and supposed that they could only preserve them as Christian if they preserved them as denominational.

But many good Anglican divines, and several bishops, believed that the act was right. They saw that a constitution was effective only if public opinion in the university supported it generally. At Cambridge Lightfoot wanted the tests removed for the sake of the Christian religion. The young men saw a good man refused a post, or refusing to take a post, out of scruples of conscience, and 'it begets a sort of sympathy with his non-belief'.[1] In the early seventies prophets of gloom were wont to denounce Oxford as lost to the Christian religion, and undoubtedly Oxford colleges contained more argumentative agnostics during those years than any city outside London. But wise men saw that the abolition of tests had not created these agnostics, and that the sharpness of the argument partly arose out of a constitution which included the tests. For prophets of gloom were already denouncing Oxford before the tests were abolished. Bishop Mackarness of Oxford, whose charge of 1875 was regarded as the most outspoken and damaging utterance against Oxford irreligion, already said something not unlike it in the debate on the tests.[2] But Mackarness was one of those who wanted the bill to pass. Several other bishops, headed by the two archbishops and by Frederick Temple of Exeter and Fraser of Manchester, wanted the bill to pass. In former days tests served their purpose. Now they did nothing but damage the cause of religion.

Meanwhile the universities wanted to improve themselves, and were expected by the informed public to improve themselves, as places of academic study. They were less efficient than they might be because they were limited in their choice of staff, many of whom must be unmarried and in holy orders. A correspondent of the *Times* said that already some colleges found it very difficult to 'man the lecture-rooms'.[3] As the secondary schooling of the country advanced during these years, and as the universities widened their curriculum and adopted new courses, the colleges could not do their traditional work of teaching unless they removed the restrictions. In Cambridge,

---

[1] PP, 1871, ix, 183. Probably Lightfoot had the case of Henry Sidgwick in mind.
[2] Hansard, cciii (14 July 1870), 214.
[3] *Times*, 26 December 1871; Winstanley, *Later Victorian Cambridge*, 264.

unlike Oxford, the chief source of argument was the inability of colleges to elect to fellowships their most intelligent students if they happened to be dissenters (especially Michael Foster the physiologist, and two or three excellent mathematicians).

Thus the demand to abolish clerical fellowships was only part of a wider reform of the universities begun when a Conservative government appointed a commission of 1877. But the tests act largely placed the security for continued religious colleges on the existence of these clerical fellowships. Gladstone seems to have reconciled himself to the 1871 act by the knowledge that the fellow-ships existed as a further security. The commission was empowered to make statutes for each college, and therefore was assigned three extra commissioners to be elected by each college and to take part in the voting when the commission discussed the affairs of that college. On this provision for three college commissioners Liddon made a remark which illustrated how Oxford had changed. 'Twenty years ago such a provision would have secured the religious character of nine colleges out of ten. In the present circumstances of Oxford it was fatal.'[1]

The commission was far from being an anti-Christian commission. One of the commissioners was Lightfoot, another was Bishop Philpott of Worcester, who had been a good head of a Cambridge college, was renowned for conservatism in ecclesiastical affairs, and often presided at the commission in the absence of the chairman. Philpott did not believe in the alleged security provided by clerical fellowships, and several other bishops thought with him. There was a lot of Christian feeling against men who were encouraged to take orders in order to secure or to retain their stipend, and most of the Church of England did not regret the disappearance of many of the clerical fellowships.

The campaign to be rid of clerical fellowships became a struggle in the universities, especially at Oxford, and therefore generated a certain fear of 'clericalism' among the lay fellows of colleges. When a young and brilliant Fellow of Merton, Mandell Creighton, decided to take orders, he was sure that his colleagues must think him either a knave or a fool. The tests left the legacy of an opinion that men took orders for their private advantage, and Liddon claimed to have heard it argued that 'the intention to take orders is of itself so

[1] CQR, 1881, 221. For Liddon's authorship, see J. O. Johnston, 253.

decisive a proof of intellectual inferiority as to dispense with the necessity of an examination'.[1] This view must have been unusual, for Liddon was fond of selecting the provocative utterance, but laymen who elected a new member of their academic society had sometimes a feeling that too many clergymen might be a disadvantage. Bishop Mackarness even talked in Parliament of Oxford colleges where a devout Christian would not be elected to a Fellowship, and pessimistic Liddon expected before long that colleges would turn their chapels into libraries, or museums, or lecture-rooms.[2]

To a man who lived through the changes as a fellow, the university after must have seemed surprisingly like the university before. Some who came back after an interval noticed and felt the difference. Edward King graduated from Oxford in 1851, and twenty-two years later returned to Christ Church as a professor. He did not admire the religious arrangements under Provost Hawkins during his undergraduate days, but in some respects the college was more like a seminary mingled with some hunting men than a modern college, and to one of its dons, Charles Marriott, he felt that he owed his soul. At Christ Church the hunting men and the ordinands might still be found, but not the air of a seminary. King came of a religious family and his career hitherto was passed in circumstances where his faith was unchallenged. He found the Oxford of 1873 to be at first a strain, indeed always a strain. It disturbed him that any day he might find himself sitting next to a man who disbelieved the axioms on which his life rested. It was a relief to this side of him when he was taken out of Oxford into the country parishes of Lincolnshire, and found himself again moving where men accepted the same axioms as himself. He warned the undergraduates of 1881 against the temptation to despair of Christianity, and we cannot imagine an Oxford religious leader uttering the same warning twenty years before. The historian F. Y. Powell of Christ Church never in his life attended a service in the cathedral, and was almost certainly the first student of the college to achieve this record.[3]

Meanwhile conflict between the old world and the new would still occur. At the level of the university it could bring votes on whether the university should award an honorary degree to Darwin (opposition withdrawn, but Darwin did not come), or have Stanley as

[1] CQR, 1881, 224.
[2] Hansard, cciii, 214; CQR, 1881, 232.   [3] Cf. Elton, Powell, i, 15.

select preacher, or elect Matthew Arnold as professor of poetry, or send a greeting to the Germans commemorating Luther. At this level the worst clash came over Jowett's proposal (1883) to appoint a dissenter, R. F. Horton of New College, to examine in the paper on 'Rudiments of Faith and Religion', which included the thirty-nine articles (placet 155, non-placet 576, and painful—'A ridiculous force', said Scott Holland, 'to have turned out for so small an occasion.'[1]) At the level of the college the division was more secret and personal, for it still concerned the choice of men. The tests act ruled that in existing colleges religious views might not be considered in choosing fellows or university officers. But what of other offices in college? The most painful case arose over a tutor at Christ Church. R. W. Macan published a book radical enough in divinity. In 1882 his office fell due for renewal. The college was still confessed to be a house of religion and dying Pusey could not bring himself to allow that such a man was possible in an office responsible towards undergraduates.[2] He came from his bed to the last meeting which he ever attended, to testify that if they re-elected Macan it would proclaim religion to be at last no part of their system, and carried a sufficient majority. The refusal to re-elect Macan divided the college distressingly for several years. Such a breach was a suffering due to the age of transition.

During the seventies, therefore, Oxford and Cambridge divines felt the need to reassure the world about religion in those universities. The regius professor of divinity at Oxford, William Ince, assured the public more than once that Oxford teachers were not aggressive even when they were infidel. Edward King, regius professor of moral and pastoral theology, gave a moving assurance in the same sense. At Cambridge Westcott published a striking and influential little book to the same end, entitled *The Religious Office of the Universities* (1873). Not everything which he argued in that book would have been acceptable to his Oxford colleagues, who had a stronger sense of the duty of Christian teachers to pass on the teaching of the Church of England. A Liddon would have said 'that the first religious duty of the university was to transmit the known doctrines of the Christian religion. Westcott said that the first religious duty of the university

---

[1] Paget, *Holland*, 110.
[2] Cf. especially Pusey to Liddon, 10 June 1882, Pusey House MSS; and his speech at the meeting appended.

was to study man and his world, in science and in history, and so
to inspire the student with the sense of their sovereign grandeur.'[1]
Westcott had a wider, and perhaps nobler, idea of the religious
office of the university. But he sometimes laid himself open to the
criticism of Oxford realists that his expressions were too misty to be
useful.

However differently the comfort was expressed at the two
universities, these reassurances were given. The Bishop of Ely, who
never ordained anyone but graduates, took the trouble to consult the
Cambridge professors on whether recent changes forced him to alter
this policy. They replied that nothing in the conditions of the
university gave a reason for change.[2] Possibly the general public
would have taken little notice of these assurances if they found them
to be untrue, if religion in Oxford or Cambridge started to dis-
appear, if dons used their academic opportunities to propagate anti-
Christian opinions among their pupils. The predictions of Liddon
remained unfulfilled during the Victorian age. The number of
ordinands declined relatively as the numbers of undergraduates rose,
but did not decline absolutely until the end of the century; and they
had been high, so that (for example) four-ninths of those who
graduated from Brasenose during the ten years to 1880 were
ordained.[3] A lot of young men in the university were religious, and
now had ways of expressing their religion unhampered by an
archaic constitution. Many capable observers believed that the two
universities, regarded less as institutions than as groups of men, were
more religious in 1884 than before 1871.[4] The college chapels began
to be affected by the worshipping movements of the day. (Oriel
College: earlier part of reign, sacrament once a term; before 1872,
twice a term; October 1894, four a term; October 1896, every
Sunday.[5]) At Cambridge over 150 undergraduates taught in the
Jesus Lane Sunday School during Lent 1877.[6] Religious societies

[1] Chadwick, *Westcott and the University*, 29.
[2] CQR, 1881, 201. This confidence was marked by the founding of new theological colleges in the precincts of the older universities; St. Stephen's House (1876) and
Wycliffe Hall (1877) at Oxford, Ridley Hall (opened 1881) and the Clergy Training
School (1881), from 1902 called Westcott House, at Cambridge.
[3] J. Wordsworth, *The Church and the Universities*, 13.
[4] So, for example, W. D. Maclagan, G 84, 903; and Westcott at the laying of the
foundation stone of Selwyn College.
[5] L. R. Phelps to G. W. E. Russell, 30 September 1912, Lincolnshire Archives.
[6] Harford-Macdonald, 114.

flourished as never before—the Confraternity of the Holy Trinity, the Christian Union, the Church Society at Cambridge.[1] Lay heads of houses felt a duty, like their clerical predecessors, to attend their college chapel. And a few men possessed a powerful religious influence over the undergraduates. Edward King, though he was a professor at Oxford, was not very academic. But he was one of the holiest men of the Oxford Movement as well as one of the most likeable, and sensible men said that nothing like his influence with undergraduates had been seen since the days of Newman. At Oxford the friendlier atmosphere of the eighties was in part due to the friendlier tone of the philosophers, and Mark Pattison, who did not like the change, ascribed much consequence to the work of T. H. Green.[2]

At the end of the century some thought Oxford and Cambridge to be less religious than they seemed to be in the eighties. The larger number of secular dons contained some devout men and some anti-Christians, but mostly consisted of men who got on with their work and thought about religion not at all. Among the young dons at Trinity and King's was found a group of brilliant intellectual agnostics comparable to Oxford groups of an earlier decade, but a phenomenon relatively new to Cambridge.

The universities of Oxford, Cambridge and Durham inherited from their trust deeds, and from the tests act of 1871, the duty of instructing their Anglican undergraduates in the doctrine and worship of the Church of England. And yet the universities could not help but become more neutral in their attitudes, even while they attempted to fulfil that duty. When in 1867 William Stubbs delivered his inaugural lecture as regius professor of modern history at Oxford, he did not blush to see in historical study a growing perception of the workings of God in the world, and of his overruling providence. So religious an utterance from the professor of history did not go without comment even then. So religious a lecture from such an officer on such an occasion would have seemed inappropriate only twenty years later. If it behoved atheists, in their courtesy or their loyalty to a historic institution, to refrain from pushing their atheism at the Christian young, it behoved Christians

[1] See F. Meyrick, *Memories*, 173–5; F. L. Cross, *Darwell Stone*, 13–14; *Journals and Papers of G. M. Hopkins*, 305–6; G 1907, 833; J. C. Pollock, *A Cambridge Movement*, 1953.
[2] Pattison, *Memoirs*, 167.

in equity to refrain from pushing their Christianity at the atheist young; provided always that the members of the Church of England might be instructed, and that a man might give his opinions fairly to anyone who consulted him.

The social and religious enthusiasm at the older universities during the eighties was shown by the growth of 'settlements' or boys' clubs in the slums of London. Some older men who were educated at Oxford or Cambridge during the fifties found it extraordinary when they heard that teams of undergraduates went down to the east or south London for the purpose of helping to convert or educate or relieve the poor. As communities of undergraduates Oxford and Cambridge were hardly more 'secular' in 1900 than in 1860, and some evidence tends to the contrary conclusion.

Thus the thirty years before the end of the reign saw the universities, as groups of men, more religious if anything than before though also more lay in tone; as institutions, made neutral in religion except for the historic connexions with the Church of England; and as places of academic enquiry, far more detached in their study of religion.

This was observed most plainly in the faculties of theology.

Many of the reformers wanted theology to be among the new subjects of study, as the universities widened their curricula, and this desire agreed with the desire of the divines to make their syllabus and their studies more profound. An honours school of theology was founded at Oxford in 1870, a theological tripos at Cambridge in 1871 (first examination, January 1874). Hitherto the study of religion among undergraduates was seen as twofold, to give them all a rudimentary knowledge of Christian doctrine, and to prepare the ordinands for holy orders. Neither of these activities promoted 'scientific' theology, as the jargon phrase was now coming to be used. 'Theology', wrote Mark Pattison in 1868, 'has not begun to exist as a science among us', and he feared that in the state of national opinion it would continue to occupy 'its present degraded position of an extraneous appendage tacked on to the fag-end of every examination in every other subject'.[1] This verdict did scant justice to those who then lectured on divinity. Younger men like Lightfoot and Hort and John Wordsworth were doing work of the first importance. But Pattison's verdict had a pretext. In 1871 Cambridge

---

[1] *Suggestions*, 320.

reformed its higher degrees in divinity, hitherto acquired by anyone who could print a few sermons and pay the fee.

The faculties of theology inherited the duty of teaching the ordinands of the Church of England, and if they failed to perform that duty they would hardly find pupils. For this purpose they must teach religion as well as theology. Yet if they were to gain the respect of their colleagues in the university they must become (or at least thought sometimes that they must become) drily academic, and seek to squeeze the last drop of religion out of their theology. And if they were to teach the growing number of nonconformists who came forward, they must not be denominational.

It was easy to make the curriculum 'scientific' and the standards high, and both universities achieved this during the seventies. It was less easy to attract to the subject undergraduates capable of profiting from these standards. At Oxford the new school of theology gained a doubtful reputation among undergraduates, because they suspected it to mean more work and less reward than the school of Greats,[1] and tutors sometimes discouraged men from taking the course. Able ordinands went for Greats and left theological honours to those who would doubtfully profit from so severe a discipline. The professors of theology complained that they were not getting many good men. At the same time one professor not of theology complained the opposite. 'The waste of power here at Oxford is fearful', wrote Max Müller to Tyndall on 26 March 1881. 'I have known dozens of young men who might have done any amount of solid scientific work, and who dwindle away into judges or bishops.'[2]

The easiest way to make theology scientific was to make it historical. And it happened to be the age when theology needed to adopt the new knowledge offered by study of manuscripts and the opening of archives. Under Lightfoot, Westcott and Hort theology at Cambridge became dominated by textual criticism and ecclesiastical history. In Oxford this dominance was less marked, but no one at Oxford quite secured the academic reverence which Cambridge accorded to Lightfoot, whose personal interests were far more historical than theological. At both universities the new divines approached their work with an attitude different from that of their predecessors. Pusey was first a canon and second a professor, for his duty in the church was paramount and his duty to the university a

[1] CQR, 1881, 238. [2] *Life of Max Müller*, ii, 99.

part of that larger duty. His successor Driver was first a professor and then a canon, for his paramount duty was the advancement of knowledge, which his place in the church allowed and encouraged him to do.

From time to time individual professors tried to set the clock back. Neither Liddon nor King at Oxford accepted the new theory of what a theological faculty should be doing. In 1899 the evangelical Handley Moule declared in his inaugural lecture as Norrisian professor at Cambridge that his duty was religious, in its application of Scripture to living problems,[1] and this kind of utterance was often welcomed by observers. It never sounded so inappropriate as Stubbs's profession of faith began to sound in the faculty of history. But the faculty of divinity, if not by an inter-denominational character then by the necessity of scientific enquiry, moved quickly in the same direction. The mark of it was the founding in 1899, by both faculties jointly, of their journal for the scientific study of divinity, the *Journal of Theological Studies*, which from the first maintained high standards of scholarship. It was also marked by an entire absence of opposition, in either university, to the founding of further chairs in divinity. In 1881 the old Rochester canonry, which used to endow the provost of Oriel when he must be in holy orders, was first used to endow a new chair, the Oriel professorship of the Interpretation of Holy Scripture. In 1889 the canonry at Ely, which used to endow the Cambridge professor of Greek when he must be in holy orders, was first used to endow a new chair, the Ely professorship of divinity. In 1882 Emmanuel College generously founded the Dixie professorship of ecclesiastical history, though the chair was primarily assigned to the faculty of history and not of divinity. At Cambridge the chair of ecclesiastical history and probably (for men doubted the words of the statute) the Norrisian chair of divinity could be held by laymen. The first layman to become a professor of divinity was F. C. Burkitt at Cambridge in 1905; the first nonconformist to be a professor of divinity at one of the older universities, C. H. Dodd at Cambridge in 1935.

The tests act of 1871 carefully refrained from opening the theological faculties or the higher degrees to non-Anglicans in order to preserve the historic duty of training Anglican ordinands. Cambridge was quicker than Oxford to change. At Cambridge the non-

[1] Harford-Macdonald, 153.

conformist Moulton worked in close harmony and friendship with Hort, and in 1884 a nonconformist first examined in the theological tripos.

The faculty at Oxford was more suspicious that its traditional responsibilities would be weakened by the opening of its degrees. Yet nonconformist divinity became stronger in Oxford than in Cambridge. In 1889 Mansfield College opened for the training of Congregationalist ministers and in 1888 the Unitarian Manchester College moved to Oxford. In 1895 negotiations between the faculty and the hebdomadal board broke down because the board wanted degrees in theory to be awarded solely on academic grounds and the faculty of theology could not accept. The Cambridge degrees of bachelor and doctor of divinity were opened to any candidate in 1915, the Oxford degrees in 1920.

In 1886 Ffoulkes of St. Mary's delated Fletcher of Carfax for heresy in a sermon.[1] This was the last occasion when such a sermon was delated within the university.[2]

The Roman Catholic authorities refused to allow the faithful to send their children to the now open Oxford and Cambridge. Nonconformist leaders felt uneasy at seeing the children of their faithful going to the old, still part-Anglican and now part-doubting universities and turning into Anglicans or agnostics. But nonconformity soon began to play an integral and beneficent part in the religious life of the universities, and nonconformists on the whole were grateful for the better opportunities of higher education which were thus opened to their young. The fears felt by nonconformist leaders were felt tenfold by Roman Catholic leaders. A few not very loyal Catholic laymen of the upper classes sent their children to the universities, but acted against official policy. In consequence the upper forms of Roman Catholic schools languished without aim.

There was no theoretical absurdity in attempting to create a Roman Catholic university. Such universities existed in Catholic countries, as at Louvain or Milan. But they could also exist in

[1] Macan, *Religious Changes*, 25, 46; *Times*, 7 February 1887.
[2] A return of 1886 shows the approximate number attending the lectures of divinity professors: Oxford: Ince (regius), 91, 51, 122; Heurtley (very old), 7, 19, 16; Paget (moral and pastoral), 59, 104; Bright (church history), 19, 30, 31; Hatch, 50, 3; Sanday, 47, 6; Cheyne just elected. Cambridge: Westcott (regius), 300–350, 30–60, 10–20; Hort (austere lecturer), 11, 9; Swainson 23, 4; Creighton (church history), 40–60. PP 1886, li, 523.

democratic non-Catholic lands where a government tolerated all
religion. In 1889 Pope Leo XIII erected the Catholic university of
America at Washington into a papal university. In theory a university of this kind, with constitutional safeguards for Roman Catholic
teaching, could be created in England. And if it were created, so
argued men like Ward or Herbert Vaughan or Manning, it would
safeguard the faith of young Catholics and not expose them to the
Anglican or agnostic temptation of Oxford and Cambridge. The
vision created Prior Park which ended in burdensome debts; caused
Wiseman to talk of making Oscott into a university;[1] created the
university of Dublin, where Newman struggled for a few years
during the fifties, and which despite his good management foundered
on the suspicions of Irish bishops and the reluctance of English
Catholics to send their children across the sea; and finally created a
Catholic university in Kensington (1874–82), which rapidly foundered through an ill-chosen rector and a similar lack of support.

For though the theory was sensible, the means did not exist. Such
a university must become a reputable rival of ancient universities. It
required money, libraries, laboratories, on a scale far beyond the
scanty means of the Catholic community of England. It also required
staff. Newman was the single Roman Catholic in England whose
name might attract an adequate staff. He succeeded in drawing to
Dublin a group of professors sufficient to make certain faculties
weighty. Even though Manning, suspecting Newman's freedom of
mind, excluded him from all part in the Catholic university at
Kensington, that university collected two or three men of eminence.
This was not enough to prevent the university from collapsing, with
a little ridicule and a little scandal. If Newman failed in Dublin,
Manning without Newman could not succeed in London. But
Manning worked for many years under an illusion of hopefulness.
He thought that foreigners could compensate for a scarcity of English. In a famous article in the *Dublin Review* (July 1863), he said
that the Society of Jesus alone could supply professors equipped to
hold the chairs in arts, literature and science.[2]

Roman Catholics could get non-resident degrees by affiliating
their colleges to London university.[3] This was the least satisfactory

---

[1] Ward, *Newman*, ii, 50.   [2] DR, 1863, July, 158; cf. Beck, 296.
[3] Cf. H. Tristram, 'London University and Catholic Education', in DR, 1936,
October, 269.

mode of securing a university degree. The English ideal of a university contained the belief that mere information was not the sole object of the university.

For forty years after the law allowed Roman Catholics to take degrees at Oxford and Cambridge, the bishops (at least corporately) refused to allow them to take advantage of those degrees. The bishops were not familiar with Oxford and Cambridge and feared what they imagined. Every Anglican bishop of an English diocese during the reign (but two[1]) was educated at Oxford or Cambridge. Only three of the Roman Catholic bishops were so educated, all converts, Manning and Coffin at Oxford, Brownlow at Cambridge. And about Oxford Manning shared the despair of Liddon. Behind the bishops stood Propaganda in Rome, which knew still less of the place held by universities in English society.

The English upper classes had the habit of sending their sons to Oxford or Cambridge. And some Catholics belonged to the English upper classes. If they were lax, even mildly lax, they started to send their sons and took no notice of their bishops. The bishops never sought to discipline anyone who thus transgressed.

From early in the sixties, therefore, liberal-minded Catholics, priests and laymen, sought to secure a provision for Catholic students at Oxford. If Catholics were sent to Oxford, they argued, it would be better that they should not need to join colleges but should live more securely within a Catholic hall. In 1864 a hundred laymen sent petitions to Rome in support of such a hall at Oxford. Manning and Ward, both Oxford men, could not see that a Catholic hall made a difference. Nor could Dalgairns, or several among the converts formerly round Newman. If the Catholics were at Oxford they would be influenced by the university even if they did not reside in a college with an Anglican chapel. In 1864–5 Manning and Propaganda prevented Newman from establishing an Oratory to act as a chaplaincy to Catholic students. In 1866–7 Propaganda was persuaded to sanction such a foundation in Oxford, and for a moment Newman talked excitedly of the prospect perhaps of a second Oxford Movement, perhaps of bringing in Mark Pattison, certainly of strengthening the Christian cause against Oxford sceptics.[2] He agreed with the

[1] Magee of Peterborough and York, and Bardsley of Carlisle; both from Trinity College, Dublin.
[2] Conversation with Father William Neville: Ward, Newman, ii, 138.

directors of policy that a Catholic university would be better, and that Oxford would be full of peril, but everywhere that a young Catholic might go was equally full of peril and 'you cannot keep young men under glass cases'. Then he discovered that though Propaganda sanctioned the Oratory at Oxford, it did so only under the strong persuasion, indeed condition, that Newman should not himself reside there. They were afraid that Newman's presence would encourage Roman Catholics to go to Oxford. They were right. Also they did not trust Newman, for in the sixties extreme ultramontanes ruled Roman policy, and some of them eyed Newman as a minimising Catholic and as one who might become a centre of disaffection. When Newman discovered that he must not go, he withdrew all plans for an Oratory at Oxford, and for the second time resold land which he had bought in preparation. Some people, even one or two intimate friends, thought that he was being sensitive. But there was no purpose in starting an Oratory at Oxford without Newman, and Hope-Scott, who himself thought Newman sensitive, withdrew a generous subscription when he found that Newman was not to go.[1]

On 6 August 1867 Propaganda issued a rescript declaring that any Catholic who went to Oxford or Cambridge would commit the sin of exposing himself to a proximate occasion of mortal sin.[2] At Advent 1867 the bishops, as required by Propaganda, issued pastoral letters explaining this doctrine to their clergy and people: 'it is next to impossible to discover circumstances in which Catholics could without sin attend non-Catholic universities'. Catholics continued to go to Oxford and Cambridge. Some asked and received dispensation or permission from their bishops, some did not ask. Nothing convinced the bishops or Propaganda that it was desirable. A private enquiry into the question was instituted. How impartial was the enquiry is not known, but the evidence that appeared was discouraging. A priest who worked two years in the Oxford mission said that a large proportion of Roman Catholic undergraduates slowly ceased to practise their religion, and some graduate converts were recorded as saying that to send the young to Oxford would be to shake the very foundations of their belief.[3]

---

[1] Ward, *Newman*, ii, 136, 141.
[2] Beck, 295–9; Guy, *Synods of Westminster*, i, 254; ii, 330.
[3] Wilson, *Hedley*, 238–9.

About 47 Roman Catholics matriculated at Oxford between 1867 and 1887, over 100 between 1887 and 1894. It is not certain that many Catholics who wished to go were prevented by the ban. Bishop Brown of Newport said that there was only one family in his diocese which the rescript of Propaganda in 1867 could affect.[1]

In 1878 Pope Pius IX was succeeded by Pope Leo XIII and the atmosphere changed. And Oxford and Cambridge seemed friendlier to religion between 1885 and 1895, friendlier at least than Oxford seemed between 1865 and 1885. Many leading laymen, from the Duke of Norfolk downwards, now wanted the change. Newman wanted it and several of the leading clergy, headed by Bishop Hedley of Newport. Hedley's arguments afford evidence of the difference in religious atmosphere between 1871 and 1881. Confessing the 'rationalism' and 'infidelity' among the dons and undergraduates, he yet argued that it was not aggressive and that there was a very large amount of religious seriousness especially at Oxford, and 'no one is mocked or insulted for religious opinions'; and a 'preponderating class' of learned Anglicans engaged with unbelief and not in controversy with Roman Catholics.[2] A decade later a petition of the Catholic laity said that the atmosphere of the universities was now different, that the 'hostile infidelity' which earlier marked them had 'died down'; that Catholic books were used in the Oxford school of history, and 'no one was obliged to study philosophy'.[3] This Catholic evidence is important for the widespread belief that as a place of religious education Oxford was better in 1890 than twenty-five years before. In 1867 even Newman, who preferred a Catholic university but knew it to be a dream, and wanted Roman Catholics at Oxford, wrote in a private letter of 'the scepticism and infidelity which too notoriously prevail there just now'.[4]

For several years Propaganda refused to change its policy, and there is every reason to think that Manning was in part responsible. As late as 1887 Manning wrote a memorandum of his conviction 'that no Catholic parents ought to send their sons to the national universities; that no Catholic can be there without danger to faith and morals; and that to engraft ourselves on the un-Catholic and anti-Catholic intellectual culture of England would have two effects—the one that

[1] Beck, 304.   [2] Wilson, *Hedley*, 234.
[3] Evennett, in Beck, 307–8.
[4] Newman to Canon Jenkins, 12 December 1867: Ward, *Newman*, ii, 199.

the Catholic Church would abandon all future effort to form its own university, and the other, that our higher laity would be like the laity in France, Catholic in name, but indifferent, lax, and liberalistic'.[1]

Manning died in 1892 and his successor Vaughan agreed with him. But the situation was already absurd. In February 1893 Baron Anatole von Hügel, who was curator of the archaeological museum at Cambridge, dressed himself in a Cambridge gown and hood and presented to the Pope an address and a gift from the Catholics of Cambridge university; persons not supposed by the Pope to exist lawfully. Vaughan made last soundings on the possibility of founding a Catholic university, but the laymen would not back him. In May 1894 he caused the cancellation, at some inconvenience, of a summer-course at Oxford for Catholic teachers in elementary schools, on the ground that it would indirectly encourage 'mixed' education.[2] The laity were roused. The Duke of Norfolk gathered a petition, lay and clerical, to the bishops. That summer Vaughan was at last convinced. Four or five bishops still resisted the change. On 4 January 1895 the majority of bishops decided to petition Rome to remove the ban. Propaganda (26 March) and Pope Leo (2 April) at once consented. Rome tried to insist that Catholic undergraduates must attend lectures by Catholics on philosophy, history and religion. The ruling was not practicable, but the English bishops appointed special Catholic chaplains to the university. Several bishops preferred to make it clear that they were allowing, but not encouraging, Catholic young men to run the risks of the ancient universities. Bishop Riddell of Northampton 'hoped against hope' that Catholics at Cambridge university would 'pass through the ordeal unscathed'.[3]

The religious orders had been wanting to take advantage. Almost at once (1896) the Jesuits founded the hall at Oxford which is now Campion Hall; and soon the Benedictines of Ampleforth founded (1897–9) a hall which is now St. Benet's Hall.

At Cambridge was founded St. Edmund's House (1896).

The dissenting bishops appealed to Rome against priests or ordinands thus being sent to non-Catholic universities. Rome (5 June 1896) ruled in favour of the permission, on condition that students should keep ecclesiastical discipline.

---

[1] Purcell, ii, 349.
[2] Beck, 307 (Evennett); M. S. Parry, *The Month*, March 1933, 215; cf. Evennett in DR, April 1946.   [3] Beck, 312.

No Roman Catholic priest or ordinand was allowed to study in the schools of theology. It was a weakness to the new schools of theology that such strong religious forces refused to participate. By their origins, and their place in the university and the modern world, the faculties tended to be interdenominational and to have affinities with the divinity of broad churchmen; more evidently so in Cambridge than in Oxford, for in Oxford the faculty remained more evidently Anglican. At one side the Roman Catholics felt unable to participate because they questioned the axioms on which the divines worked; though their scholars, especially the Benedictine Cuthbert Butler at Cambridge, made contributions to historical and textual scholarship which added to the prowess of the university. At the other side some evangelical leaders in the Church of England discouraged their young men from the academic study of theology, for they also questioned the axioms on which the academics worked.

The Roman Catholics were at once accepted and taken for granted in the universities, but one or two incidents marked the transition. In 1877 Trinity College, Oxford, pleased and surprised many by electing Newman to an honorary fellowship; and when two years later he became a cardinal, Oxford was proud of one of her sons. But afterwards a plan for a statue of Newman ran into hot opposition despite a list of subscribers which included nonconformists. When St. Edmund's House was founded at Cambridge, its proposers wished to have it recognised as a public hostel of the university, and the plan was voted down by an opposition which may have included some prejudice. A year later the Roman Catholic authorities refused to allow a seminarist to put the weight against Cambridge though he was the best putter at Oxford.[1] These were little signs of an age of transition.

King's College, London, was another Anglican foundation, but during the eighties came under the difficulty of paying its way. In 1884 the department of general literature and science had a staff of twenty-three for thirty-nine students.[2] They were hit by the establishment of the Victoria university (Manchester, Liverpool and Leeds) in 1880, and then by the university of Wales in 1893; while their theological department was hit by the establishment of other Anglican theological colleges, especially by Ridley Hall in 1881. The

[1] G, 99, 360.   [2] Hearnshaw, 354ff.

expenses of laboratories steadily increased while the income from fees steadily fell. An appeal to the church for money to preserve the college from secularisation brought in £25,000 which was pitifully inadequate, and showed only that lay churchmen were not interested in preserving the strictly Anglican nature of the college. They must close their doors or accept public money.

In 1889 Parliament began voting money to the provincial university colleges, and for five years King's College received £1,700 a year of public money. But in 1893 (16 September) Liberals in the House of Commons demanded that the grant to a denominational college be withdrawn, and in 1894 the government decided to withdraw it. When the Conservatives returned to power next year they renewed the grant, but with a private warning that they could not do it for ever unless the college altered its religious requirements.

Meanwhile growing numbers in the late nineties lessened the difficulty over money. But they needed more laboratories and more professors, and to find Anglican professors of science at a stipend which attracted reasonable men got beyond the power of the principal. Further appeals for money brought little, and all wise men saw that the college could not do its work without grants from central or local government. The professors themselves were unanimous in wishing the tests to go, and in 1898 an act of Parliament allowed commissioners to reconstruct London university in such a way as to make the tests look more of an anachronism. The council of King's College therefore carried by majority (13 June 1902) a motion to remove all religious tests except in the faculty of theology, and in the following year an act of Parliament gave effect to the resolution.

The new civic colleges made little impact upon the churches during the Victorian age. From their foundation they all had a clause (or its equivalent) forbidding religious tests in the choice of either teachers or pupils. This clause was not directed against religion, but against sectarian religion. They wished to prevent denominational debates, not to diminish the influence of the Christian religion. In a city where denominational hostilities were possible, like Liverpool, this clause was made a legal bar. In Owens College (1851) which later became (1880) the Manchester constituent of the Victoria university, nearly all the original trustees were devout nonconformists, the first principal A. J. Scott was formerly a presbyterian minister, and the attitude of the managers had no 'secular' tang like the Benthamite tang of University College, London. The original trustees recommended that Owens College should give optional teaching in religion, and nearly all the original professors of science considered that by their studies they advanced the knowledge of the creator through his creation. This friendly attitude at Manchester was important because with the aid of exceptional scholars and strong local backing the college took the lead among the civic colleges of the later Victorian age. Both its last two Victorian principals, A. W. Ward the historian, who was an Anglican, and Arthur Hopkinson, who was a nonconformist, worked for a theological faculty. In 1890 the proposal for degrees in theology was put to the Victoria university, and revived again in 1900. But Liverpool in its special circumstances was barred by law, and the principal of Leeds, Nathan Bodington, believed it undesirable to use denominational colleges in a theological faculty. Therefore Manchester did not found its theological faculty until 1904 as the Victoria university split up and its three colleges became independent universities.

These university colleges were founded with two aims not easily compatible; to open the education of a traditional university to a wider population, and to train technicians in an industrial city. Their managers could only unite these two aspirations into a single university worthy of the name if they could persuade society that applied science was a pursuit worthy of the epithet academic. Since all these university colleges had strong schools of applied science, and one or two of them sprang out of colleges of science or medicine, their success slowly began to effect a change in the public idea of a university education, and to shift the balance away from the ideal of a classical education.

This shift may have slowly affected the relations between religion and the universities, but in the present state of knowledge it is impossible to point to evidence of such an effect.

Few Anglican leaders outside the civic universities took much notice of the civic universities. They were engaged in preserving their heritage at Oxford and Cambridge, and their experience in the schools made them suspect the interdenominational theology which was the only theology possible in a civic university. But several liberal churchmen were important to the movement. Jowett and John Percival and Dean Elliot of Bristol did most to found the university college at Bristol, and Jowett did as much as anyone to

secure government money (1889) for the university colleges. The
vicar of St. Mary's at Nottingham, F. Morse, and the Congregationalist J. B. Paton were powerful in the foundation of the university
college at Nottingham (1881). At Owens College the first principal
A. J. Scott was a friend and disciple of Frederick Denison Maurice.
At Nottingham the second principal was a Cambridge clergyman,
J. E. Symes, a remarkable disciple of Maurice, often in trouble with
the city magnates for his advocacy of socialism and other unpopular
opinions.

4. THE AUTONOMY OF LITERATURE

The conflict between science and religion during the thirty years
after 1860 showed physical science claiming its independence of all
evidence but the physical, and in return restricting its own function
to the physical.

Though not a science, history dealt in a body of information which
needed to be treated scientifically. The great historians of the earlier
part of the reign were men of literature. Carlyle lived by his pen,
Macaulay was a politician, J. R. Green a Christian Socialist parson,
Arnold a headmaster, Milman a dean. In the later Victorian age the
tradition survived, for Creighton and Stubbs wrote and studied in
country parsonages, and Hodgkin was a Quaker banker. But the
new history was written by professional historians like Lightfoot or
Freeman or Stubbs or Gardiner or Maitland, whose work was their
history and who aimed to contribute rather to the knowledge of
society than 'literature'. And yet the change was only a more explicit
recognition of what was already explicit, namely that a man must
try to tell the truth (if he could find it) just because it was the truth.

The Victorian public never accepted the doctrine of art for art's
sake. To the end of the century most of them retained the doctrine
of Ruskin that all art is praise. But the attitude perceptibly changed.
Nearly all the novelists of the earlier part of the century believed
that they wrote novels as a way of conveying a moral or religious
message—Charles Kingsley and *The Water Babies*, Elizabeth Sewell,
and above all Charlotte Yonge, to whom the sole intention of writing
was a moral intention, and yet the result was at times very nearly
great art. Many of these writers could only justify to themselves
the time spent in writing such books if the books were intended in

some way to do good. But no creative writer could rest in such a position, because in true creativity that which was being created always ran away with its creator and became an end in itself, far transcending the purpose with which the author might have set out, or deceived himself that he set out. In this sense all the great writing of the nineteenth century, however moralist, became writing for 'its own sake'; and in this sense, too, there was nothing whatever new in the idea (as opposed to the expression) of Pater and the aesthetic movement.

But, in a manner, the cry *art for art's sake* did not need to be said until the Victorians entered their age of intellectual turmoil. For to the earlier Victorians God was so clearly the end, and he was for his own sake. In art they touched something beautiful and all beauty was a divine gift. Then the insecurity of faith in the sixties and seventies prevented some of them from justifying their art by an otherworldly reference. The justification of art must be in this world, in its impact upon society; as Matthew Arnold in *The Study of Poetry* conceived poetry as providing the principles of living, focussing the better aspirations of mankind, allowing poets almost to be the spiritual directors of society. Where art had to be justified as useful to society, it was inevitable that the *end-in-itself* school should start calling aloud; and perhaps exaggerate, and declare that art was not in the least useful to anyone. In this way the cry of *art for art's sake* was a new variety of otherworldliness, without reference to the divine. And it was one sign that literature had lost or was losing an agreed framework, a harmonious philosophy of the world.

Let us compare the Oxford professors of poetry at the beginning and end of the reign. They were very different men, but their different attitudes to poetry suggest a difference not only in themselves but in their audiences; even apart from the contrast that the one lectured in Latin and the other in English.

For John Keble poetry was a gift of God to express the outpourings and aspirations of a man's overflowing heart. The object of the poet, so far as he has an object beyond the fine expression of his own sacred feelings, is to be the minister and interpreter of nature to other men; and a Byron, who could have served this high vocation, turned away and ceased to be a true poet when he wrote of his own voluptuousness. Thus poetry is an end in itself; and yet it is the prelude or gateway to religion, for the poet is to express his feelings of truth, and the deepest and most powerful of all such feelings is religion. Though it is itself a lovely experience, God gave it as a minister to religion, like some high-born lady to wait upon a queen.

A. C. Bradley entitled his inaugural lecture in 1901 *Poetry for Poetry's Sake*. It was a delightful and subtle lecture concerned to meet the criticism launched against *art for art's sake*, when adopted by Oscar Wilde and others, that they were not concerned with what a man said but only with how he said it. In poetry, form and substance are inseparable, and the experience of the unity has an intrinsic worth. Poetry might also serve other purposes, like culture or religion or the poet's peace of mind or pocket. But the considerations of these ends, as part of the experience, 'tends to lower poetic value', for the nature of poetry 'is to be a world by itself, independent, complete, autonomous; and to possess it fully you must enter that world, conform to its laws, and ignore for the time the beliefs, aims, and particular conditions which belong to you in the other world of reality' (p. 8). Poetry gives its unique satisfaction as religion or philosophy each gives its unique satisfaction. It may be a matter of doubt whether Bradley succeeded in defending this doctrine of poetry against the charge that the religious experience of Tennyson's *Crossing the Bar* was then separated from the poetic experience of the same poem, which he admitted to be an absurdity. But there is no doubt that the doctrine, so attractively set forth, met wide acceptance. Autonomy was a conception powerful in science, history, poetry, art and the novel.

The novelists and poets of the later Victorian age spoke differently from those of the earlier. Dickens and Thackeray were succeeded by George Eliot and Hardy and Gissing and Meredith, Wordsworth and Tennyson and Browning were succeeded by Swinburne and Matthew Arnold. The generations were not so far apart as the recital of their names seems to suggest, but the principal difference seems to lie in the partial loss of an agreed framework of philosophy. Most Victorians held to the framework to the end of the reign. They always read Dickens much more than Hardy, and Tennyson much more than Matthew Arnold.

It was rather a change of fashion than of 'secularity', though a change partly due to the moral power of writers like Dickens or George Eliot, which finally made the reading of novels respectable. By the eighties statistics showed that more than half the books taken out of public libraries were books of fiction. Augustus Jessopp was brought up to think that reading novels was a sinful waste of time. By the eighties he did not think so in the least, and believed that the tone of all that literature had been lifted during his life. The moral theologian Edward King made a point of including a few good novels among his reading so as to deepen his understanding of human beings. Not everyone thought the same when French publishers started sending translations of Zola's novels into England. When Zola came to England in 1893 he received a triumphal reception in which reputable newspapers took part, and the reception caused cries of pain that so 'corrupting' a writer could be welcomed by responsible men.

As literature broadened, the question came before publishers whether they should publish works of a tendency with which they disagreed. In the earlier Victorian age non-Christian writers had to find publishers more or less of their own opinions. It would be interesting to know more of the slow change in publishing habits, until the day when a Christian publisher would publish a non-Christian book and vice versa. One stage in the process can be marked. Kegan Paul, who was at that time a positivist, went into partnership as a publisher with Trench who was the son of Archbishop Trench of Dublin. About 1878 or 1879 the partners were confronted with the question whether they could accept manuscripts against religion or of an agnostic trend. They consulted the archbishop. He is reported to have advised 'that the day was long past in which the questions discussed in these books could be shelved; that our attitude should be that when they were treated in a reverent and serious spirit we should by no means refuse to publish works of a free-thinking or agnostic type; but that we should sternly reject any that were merely flippant and written for the sake of destruction'. The partners acted on this advice.[1]

This trend was perceived by contemporaries. In 1882 W. H. Fremantle published *The Gospel of the Secular Life*, confessing that science and art and politics were now 'secular' and therefore pushed Christianity into a corner of human life; and the book tried to stem this cleavage between sacred and secular by claiming every area of life as sacred, every excellence as religious even when it was unaware of religion, every corner of the world as indwelt by the spirit of God.

[1] Kegan Paul, *Memories*, 291.

5. VICTORIAN RELIGION

If society was more secular, religious men were not less religious.

To think of 'Victorian religion' is to think of an infinite diversity, from Annie Besant to John Stuart Mill, from Cardinal Manning to William Booth. Or, to the contrary, Victorian religion was almost universally Christianity, and as such was not the religion only of the Victorian age, and part of what is said about it might also be said about the eighteenth century.

The most marked character in Victorian religion is the sense of vocation, and this sense carried with it a powerful sense of the sacredness of time and the sin of wasting it. They were servants of God, under his eye, and their hands found plenty to do in his cause, in mission, social reform, commerce, administration, empire, evangelism, ministry to the sick. Life therefore was earnest enough to prevent them from writing lightly of morality or its religious aspect. It marked a new age at the end of the century when G. K. Chesterton began to write seriously of religion with the quips and paradoxes which rose from the gaiety of a bubbling nature. In a Pusey the sense of responsibility before God's judgment could be so aweful as almost to overwhelm. A hymn based upon an ancient Byzantine idea but really written by John Mason Neale spoke of the Christian soul surrounded by the prowling hosts of Midian, and stirred it to smite in the name of the Lord of hosts. All the great military hymns sprang out of the sixties and the seventies, because they suited the mind of Victorian ethics. Despite Spurgeon and other mighty nonconformist preachers, Calvinism declined steadily, even among the evangelicals of the Church of England. For all their powerful sense of election to a divine purpose, men had less assurance of faith, and more of an Arminian sense of working out their salvation. The doctrine of justification by faith alone was little prominent in later Victorian preaching, even if we allow for the desire of preachers not to state old faith in old words.

> Come, labour on!
> No time for rest, till glows the western sky.
>   (Jane L. Borthwick, 1859–63)

Despite the immense Victorian popularity of Mendelssohn's aria *Rest in the Lord*, and despite the natural optimism of an age of progress, their religion was *in via,* their favourite hymns called upon their maker out of darkness—*Lead, kindly light* or *Abide with me* or *Guide me, O thou great redeemer.*[1] It was curious that while Calvinism declined, the classical book of English Calvinism advanced in national esteem. John Bunyan's *Pilgrim's Progress* started the century as a book which had almost but not quite escaped the reputation of being a book for the kitchen and servant's hall and cottage. The Oxford Movement did not like the theology of the book, Archdeacon Froude would not have a copy in the house and John Mason Neale committed the solecism of publishing a corrected version. But as the hard lines of separated systems became more blurred the parable became a treasure not only of the nonconformists and the lower classes but of the English people, until in 1874 the Duke of Bedford gave a statue of Bunyan to the town, with a generous speech by Dean Stanley which represented Bunyan as more of a broad churchman than history could quite confirm. For Stanley was right thus far, that the English people ceased to be disturbed by the theology with which they might not agree and gloried in the penetrating ethical power and beauty of the book. And it fitted that aspect of Victorian religion which was canonised in *Abide with me,* the pilgrim struggling through the valley of the shadow of death. Though the belief in real demons faded before the century began, and was revived or kept in being only by the religious antiquarian, they were still conscious of the powers of darkness, replacing the demons of legend with the demons of the subconscious or the demonic processes of society. The idea of pilgrimage was found elsewhere than in Bunyan. Neale's *O happy band of pilgrims* (1862) and Baring-Gould's translated hymn *Through the night of dark and sorrow onward goes the pilgrim band* (1867) gained steadily in popularity. Often they saw themselves as on the way, less often as in possession. And like the soul, so the church was too plainly seen to be *in via—*

> Though with a scornful wonder
> Men see her sore opprest,
> By schisms rent asunder
> By heresies distrest,

---

[1] The great *Cwm Rhondda* tune of *Guide me, O thou great redeemer* was not written by John Hughes till 1905. I have not observed the saying 'Englishmen are by nature Pelagians' until just after the end of the century.

Yet saints their watch are keeping,
Their cry goes up, 'How long?'
And soon the night of weeping
Shall be the morn of song.

(S. J. Stone, 1866; said to have been written
with Colenso and Gray in mind)

With this feeling of struggle and pilgrimage so characteristic of medieval piety, was joined the inseparable quality of medieval piety, the contemplation of heaven. Neale reintroduced Abelard's *O quanta qualia*, but it never became popular like his translation of part of another medieval hymn *Jerusalem the golden*. And with this vision of a new Jerusalem went the religious drive to mend society. The social gospel created new emphasis in Christian devotion during the later part of the century:

When comes the promised time
That war shall be no more,
And lust, oppression, crime
Shall flee thy face before?

(Hensley, 1867)

The historical consciousness, which helped to create the Catholic movements in the Church of England and the free churches, was represented in devotion by an awareness of the history of the church. They were willing to recognise Christian sanctity among those with whose doctrines they disagreed. Father Damien on his leper settlement helped to inspire Protestants, Livingstone helped to inspire Catholics. The reputation of St. Francis of Assisi rose steadily among later Victorian Protestants, first by Mrs. Oliphant's life in 1870 and finally when the enchanting life by Paul Sabatier was translated in 1894 and set the seal on a long-growing reputation.

The repute of St. Francis and Damien fitted another trend of Victorian devotion, which intellectually touched the quest for the historical Jesus. They were more conscious of Jesus the man. They therefore realised the possibility of a literal, i.e. a human, imitation of him in his humanity. *The Imitation of Christ* was a book which sold in increasing numbers, and the idea of imitation became prominent in sermons. One of the most widely read books of devotion at the end of the century was entitled *In His Steps*, by the American

Charles M. Sheldon (1897), in which an imaginary pastor persuaded members of his congregation to vow a literal imitation of Jesus for one year, with agonising results in an industrial society. Holman Hunt's *Light of the World* (1853), given by its purchaser to the chapel of Keble College, was reproduced on an enormous scale to be hung in homes, the human suffering Christ, crowned with thorns and knocking at the door.

The stronger sense of the church created a series of devotions to the Holy Spirit. The hymnody of the Spirit was hitherto almost confined to the *Veni creator* and ordination. It was not a subject which drew the evangelical hymn-writers. Though the devotions of the spirit were part of a renewed affection for the church and a concern for its corporate inspiration, they reached their height in one individualistic hymn, *Come down, O Love divine*, which the Tractarian R. F. Littledale translated (1867) from the late medieval Italian, and so created a Christian poem more inspired than its original.

The intellectual difficulties of the nineteenth century were little reflected in devotion.[1] They were the property of the discursive reason and not of the religious apprehension. That humane scholar Edwin Hatch privately printed (1878) a little book entitled *Between doubt and prayer*, but his most celebrated hymn (*Breathe on me, breath of God*) contained more assurance of faith than many famous Arminian hymns. Though the theology of the later Victorians moved a little away from the atonement towards the incarnation, we might err in attributing to this the marvellous flowering of Christmas carols and Christmas poetry which was one of the Victorian gifts to the Christian heritage. Perhaps it is a little more significant that none of the famous hymns of the passion or hymns for Easter came after 1862. The passion hymn most beloved of the Victorians, *There is a green hill*, dated from 1848.

Liberal divinity helped men to receive the inheritance of the centuries. They were willing to put tolerable meanings on words which in their original sense they could not share. The older translations of *The Imitation of Christ* used by Protestants omitted or altered the chapters on eucharistic devotion as erroneous and perilous to uninstructed readers. By the end of the century the accuracy of the text

---

[1] We have seen that *The Church's one foundation* was influenced by Colenso. We cannot tell whether the formulation of *Lord, thy word abideth* (H. W. Baker, 1860) was influenced by the feeling that in the age of *Essays and Reviews* some thought that the Bible was not quite what it was once.

was seen to be preferable, and readers were assumed to be instructed enough to look after themselves, and the error did not seem after all so heinous. Men sometimes preferred poetry to exact doctrine if they must choose. They remembered how Bishop Blomfield once corrected the text of a hymn-book and succeeded in removing the poetry with the blemishes. When the editors of *Hymns Ancient and Modern* added a supplement (1889) which contained Baxter's hymn *Ye holy angels bright*, a reviewer hailed this addition as a mistake, for faith in the properties of angels was more agnostic, and men thought the hymn too archaic for modern taste. But unlike the reviewer the people loved it, and the people had better taste than the reviewers. Hymns were a part of Christian democracy. They were accepted or rejected by popular acclamation. If editors omitted favourite hymns from their book, either because they suspected the theology or because they regarded the poetry as unrefined, they lost their public. But the innate sense of congregations and their ministers knew in outline what they wanted from theology, and over the years discarded the tasteless or absurd or ultra-sentimental hymns.

Partly because the devotions were popular, and partly because theology was complicated as it engaged with contemporary doubt, their religion valued almost above everything simplicity, the childlike. Mrs. Alexander wrote *There is a green hill* for little children, but it became a hymn for all ages. Christina Rossetti wrote *In the bleak midwinter* about 1870. It was not known as a hymn until the twentieth century. But the simplicity of the poetess perfectly fitted the later Victorian mood. It was quieter, more poetic, more content with the legendary, less concerned to preach, happy to experience without being able to frame it in words, willing that the prayer of it should speak for them while the discursive reason was silent. Edward King, theologically instructed among Victorian bishops, formerly a professor of moral theology, revering the last of the Tractarian systematisers in James Mozley, defending the use of the Athanasian creed in church, came at last to think that books of prayer expressed his theology even better than the books of theologians. Though the creed might be firm, they saw it in a context of worship, and the best late-Victorian defences of creeds put them into the realm of prayer as well as the realm of doctrine. The best Victorian credal hymns were written by J. H. Newman (as *Firmly I believe and truly* or *Praise to the holiest in the height*), but one such was St. Patrick's breastplate, of which the version that became popular was translated by Mrs. Alexander in 1889. (The breastplate however was not widely known in England until the twentieth century.) The other leading Roman Catholic writer of hymns after Newman, F. W. Faber, abstained almost altogether from such credal hymnody.

The theologians justified their activity by appealing not to external nature but to the inner evidence of religious and moral experience. The worshipper valued hymns because they spoke to his soul and less because they spoke to his head. In the last quarter of the century, therefore, we find an interest in that which in a Catholic context is called *mysticism*. It did not become an instructed movement, influential among the churches, until W. R. Inge's Bampton lectures of 1899. But for twenty years before, we find new traces of interest in the medieval formulations. Pusey sought to draw Protestants to value the saints or devotional writers of the Counter-Reformation, and the school steadily drew upon this group of writers. While the interest in mystical language was confined to high churchmen outside the Roman Catholic church—and until the last quarter of the century was not prominent inside the Roman Catholic church—some evangelical language, especially of the Keswick school, needed only a little translation to be turned into a form of Catholic mysticism. The central idea of General Gordon's Biblical faith was that of indwelling.

Evangelical piety remained Biblical and puritan. It had nothing to do with Biblical criticism, and remained conservative against doctrines of evolution or folk-lore in Genesis. It retained a strong doctrine of justification by faith alone, and encouraged men to find the assurance of salvation in the belief that the converted man could never be allowed to fall from grace. But it was not Calvinistic, unless the word is used loosely. Moody's gospel in the revival of 1874–5 was a simple direct gospel of God's love and conversion, and was suspect to some old-fashioned evangelicals because it hinted at neglect of dogmatic systems for the sake of friendship with a person. The Keswick conventions became an annual meeting from 1875, teaching a strong perfectionism and a gospel more of indwelling than of exterior atonement. And though Keswick was at first disliked by the evangelical leaders and generated extravagances which justified their dislike, the movement captured Handley Moule (1884–1886) who became the most eminent Anglican evangelical after

Bishop Ryle, whose mind had a mystical interest in indwelling, and whose devotional books fostered a piety at once evangelical and Catholic. No Calvinist after Spurgeon became a leader of English religion. The congregations loved the Reformation hymns of assurance like *A safe stronghold*, or the Calvinist hymns of faith alone like *Rock of Ages*, or the greatest of all Calvinist hymns of assurance in *Glorious things of thee are spoken*. But their generation was no longer creative of hymns like these. They used them gladly while they put their own meanings.

The Victorians covered industrial England and its suburbs with churches and chapels. Wherever the population spread they succeeded in putting a spire or a church room within reach. That would have been impossible if the endeavour had been merely from upper class to lower. They succeeded in the feat because the people felt a moral and social need of religion, at least so far that within any new community or suburb could be found groups willing and eager to make a church, and sometimes several churches. Whether or not the citizens attended those churches or chapels, the Victorians preserved a country which was powerfully influenced by Christian ideas and continued to accept the Christian ethic as the highest known to men.

ABBREVIATIONS

Add. MSS	British Museum additional manuscripts
BL	Bodleian Library
CCR	Church Congress Reports
Chron. Convoc.	Chronicle of the Convocation of Canterbury
CQR	Church Quarterly Review
CT	Church Times
CUL	Cambridge University Library
CYB	Congregational Year Book
DNB	Dictionary of National Biography
DR	Dublin Review
G [1]	Guardian
HJ	Historical Journal
PP	Parliamentary Papers
QR	Quarterly Review
R	Record
YB	Year Book

[1] If the date is not cited, the first figure after G is the year. Thus G, 59, 207 means *Guardian*, 1859, page 207.

BIBLIOGRAPHY

This is not a comprehensive list of relevant books. It is intended to make the use of the footnotes easy.

The place of publication is London except where otherwise stated.

Abbott, E. A. *The Kernel and the Husk*, 1886.

Abbott, E., and Campbell, L. *The Life and Letters of Benjamin Jowett*, 2 vols., 1897.

Abercrombie, N. J. *The Life and Work of Edmund Bishop*, 1959.

Acton, Lord. *Selections from the Correspondence of the first Lord Acton*, ed. J. A. Figgis and R. V. Laurence, I., 1917; *Letters to Mary Gladstone*, ed. with introd. memoir by Herbert Paul, 2nd ed., 1913.

Adamson, J. W. *English Education, 1789–1902*, Cambridge, 1930.

Adamson, W. *The Life of Joseph Parker*, 1902.

Adderley, J. G. *In Slums and Society*, 1916; *Stephen Remarx*, 1893.

Addison, W. G. *J. R. Green*, 1946.

Ainger, Alfred. *Life and Letters of Alfred Ainger*, ed. Edith Sichel, 1906.

Alington, Cyril, *A Dean's Apology*, 1952.

Altholtz, J. L., *The Liberal Catholic Movement in England: the 'Rambler' and its Contributors, 1848–64*, 1962.

Anson, P. F., *The Call of the Cloister*, 2nd ed. by A. W. Campbell, 1964; *Fashions in Church Furnishings, 1840–1940*, 2nd ed., 1965.

Arch, Joseph; the story of his life, 2nd ed., 1898.

Argyll, Eighth Duke of. *Autobiography and Memoirs*, ed. by the Dowager Duchess, 2 vols., 1906.

Armytage, W. H. G. *A. J. Mundella, 1825–97; the Liberal background to the Labour movement*, 1951.

Arnold, Matthew, *Letters, 1848–1888*, ed. G. W. E. Russell, 2 vols., 1901.

Ashwell, A. R., and Wilberforce, R. G. *The Life of Samuel Wilberforce*, 3 vols., 1880–1883 (2nd ed. of vol. 3).

Atkinson, J. C. *Forty Years in a Moorland Parish*, 1891.

Atkinson, T. D. *English and Welsh Cathedrals*, 1912.

Atlay, J. B., *Sir Henry Wentworth Acland, Bart.: A Memoir*, 1903.

Atlay, J. B. *The Life of E. R. Wilberforce*, 1912.

Bailey, E. B. *Charles Lyell*, 1962.

Baillie, A. V., and Bolitho, H. *A Victorian dean: a memoir of Arthur Stanley*, 1930.

Balgarvie, Robert. *Sir Titus Salt, Bart.*, 1877.

Barnett, Henrietta Octavia. *Canon Barnett: his life, work, friends*, 2 vols., 1918.

Barrett, C. K. *Westcott as commentator*, Cambridge, 1959.

Bateman, C. T. *R. J. Campbell, pastor of the City Temple*, 1903.

Battiscombe, G. *Charlotte Mary Yonge*, 1943.

Battiscombe, G., and Laski, M. (edd.). *A chaplet for Charlotte Yonge*, 1965.

Bax, Ernest Belfort. *Reminiscences and Reflexions of a Mid and Late Victorian*, 1918.

Beck, G. A. (ed.). *The English Catholics, 1850–1950*, 1950.

Beeching, H. C. *Pages from a Private Diary*, new ed., 1903.

Begbie, H. *Life of William Booth*, 2 vols., 1920.

Bell, G. K. A. *Randall Davidson, Archbishop of Canterbury*, 3rd ed., 1952.

Bennett, Frank. *Chester Cathedral*, Chester, 1925.

Benson, A. C. *Diary*, ed. P. Lubbock, 1926; *The House of Quiet: an autobiography*, 1910; *The Leaves of the Tree*, 1911; *Life of Edward White Benson, sometime Archbishop of Canterbury*, 2 vols., 1899.

Besant, Sir Walter. *Autobiography*, 1902.

Best, G. F. A. *Bishop Westcott and the miners*, 1967.

Bettany, F. G. *Stewart Headlam: a biography*, 1926.

Bill, E. G. W. (ed.). *Anglican Initiatives in Christian Unity*, 1967.

Binney, Thomas. *A memorial to the late Thomas Binney*, ed. J. Stoughton, 1874.

Blaikie, W. G. *David Brown: a memoir*, 1898.

Blake, R. N. W. *Disraeli*, 1966.

Blakiston, N. (ed.). *The Roman Question: Letters of Odo Russell*, 1962.

Bonney, T. G. *Memories of a long life*, Cambridge, 1921.

Booth, Charles. *Life and Labour of the people of London*, Series 1–3, 17 vols., 1902–3.

Booth, M. *Charles Booth: a memoir*, 1918.

Boreham, F. W. *My Pilgrimage: an autobiography*, 1940.

Bowen, Desmond. *The Idea of the Victorian Church*, Montreal, 1968.

Bowen, W. E. *Edward Bowen: a memoir*, 1902; *Contemporary ritualism: a volume of evidence*, 1902.

Boyd Carpenter. *See* Carpenter, W. Boyd.

Bradley, G. G. *Recollections of A. P. Stanley*, 1883.

Bridge, J. F. *A Westminster Pilgrim*, 1919.

Bright, William. *Selected Letters*, ed. by B. J. Kidd, 1903.

Bromley, J. *The Man of Ten Talents: a portrait of R. C. Trench, 1807–86*.

Brooke, Stopford, A. *Life and Letters of F. W. Robertson*, 2 vols., 1865.

Brown, A. W. *The Metaphysical Society. Victorian minds in crisis, 1869–1880*, New York, 1947.

Browne, G. F. *The Recollections of a Bishop*, 1915.

Bullock, C. *Near the Throne: F. R. Havergal*, new ed., 1902.

Bullock, F. W. B. *The History of Ridley Hall, Cambridge*, 2 vols., Cambridge, 1941–53; *A History of Training for the Ministry, 1800–1874*, St. Leonards-on-Sea, 1955.

Bumpus, J. S. *A History of English Cathedral Music 1549–1889*, 2 vols., 1908.

Brown, C. K. F. *A History of the English Clergy, 1800–1900*, 1953.

Budd, Susan. 'The Loss of faith: reasons for unbelief among members of the secular movement in England', in *Past and Present*, xxxvi (April, 1967), 106–125.

Burt, Thomas. *An Autobiography*, 1924.

Butler, E. C. *The Life and Times of Bishop Ullathorne*, 2 vols., 1926.

Butler, J. R. M. *H. M. Butler, Master of Trinity College, Cambridge*, 1925.

Byrt, G. W. *John Clifford, a fighting Free Churchman*, 1947.

Campbell, R. J. *A spiritual pilgrimage*, 1916.

Carpenter, E. F. (ed.). *A House of Kings: the history of Westminster Abbey*, 1966.

Carpenter, S. C. *Winnington-Ingram*, 1949.

Carpenter, W. Boyd. *Some Pages of my Life*, 1911; *Further Pages of my Life*, 1916; *The Permanent Elements of Religion*, 1889.

Cecil, Lady Gwendolen. *Life of Robert, Marquis of Salisbury*, 4 vols., 1921–32.

Chadwick, Henry. *The Vindication of Christianity in Westcott's thought*, Cambridge, 1961.

Chadwick, Owen. *Edward King, Bishop of Lincoln*, Lincoln, 1968; *Westcott and the University*, Cambridge, 1963.

Chambers, E. K. *Matthew Arnold, a study*, Oxford, 1947.

Champneys, Basil. *Memoirs and Correspondence of Conventry Patmore*, 2 vols., 1900.

Charteris, E. E. *The Life and Letters of Sir E. Gosse*, 1931.

Chesterton, G. K. *Autobiography*, 1936.

Church, R. W. *Life and Letters* : ed. M. C. Church, 1895.

The Church, the census and the people. By a priest of the Church of England, 1882.

Clark, H. W. *A History of English Nonconformity*, 2 vols., 1911–13.

Clarke, B. F. L. *Church builders of the nineteenth century*, rev. ed., 1969.

Clarke, W. K. Lowther. *Chichester cathedral in the nineteenth century*, Chichester, 1959; *A History of the S.P.C.K.*, 1959.

Clayton, J. *Father Dolling: a memoir*, 1902.

Clifford, W. K. *Lectures and essays*, ed. by Leslie Stephen and Frederick Pollock, 3rd ed., 1901, 2 vols.

Cobbe, F. P. *Life, By Herself*, 2nd ed., 1904.

Coleridge, A. D. *Reminiscences*, ed. J. A. Fuller-Maitland, 1921.

Coleridge, C. R. *C. M. Yonge: her life and letters*, 1903.

Compton, Berdmore. *E. M. Goulburn: a memoir*, 1899.

Conzemius, V. *J. J. I. Döllinger: Briefwechsel, 1850–90*, Munich, 1963–.

Coombs, Joyce. *George and Mary Sumner, their life and times*, 1966; *Judgment on Hatcham*, 1969.

Cornish, F. Warre. *The English Church in the nineteenth century*, 2 vols., 1910; *Sunningwell*, Westminster, 1899.

Cox, G. W. *The Life of J. W. Colenso, Bishop of Natal*, 2 vols., 1888.

Creighton, L. *Life and Letters of Mandell Creighton*, 2 vols., 1904.

Cross, Colin. *Philip Snowden*, 1966.

Courtney, W. L. *The Diary of a Churchgoer*, 1904.

Cowie, L. W. in *The City of York* (*Victoria County History, Yorkshire*, ed. P. M. Tillott, 1961), 353ff.

Cross, F. L. *Darwell Stone*, Westminster, 1943.

Cruickshank, M. *Church and State in English Education: 1870 to the present day*, 1963.

Currie, Robert. *Methodism Divided*, 1968.

Dale, H. Pelham. *Life and Letters of Thomas Pelham Dale*, 2 vols., 1894.

Dale, R. W. *Life of John Angell James*, 2nd ed., 1861.

Dark, S. *Mackay of All Saints*, 1937.

Darlow, T. H. *William Robertson Nicoll: Life and Letters*, 1925.

Darwin, Charles. *Autobiography, 1809–82, with marginal omissions restored*, ed. N. Barlow, 1958; *Darwin and Henslow, the growth of an idea: letters 1831–1860*, ed. N. Barlow, 1967; *Life and Letters*, including an autobiographical chapter, ed. by F. Darwin, 3 vols., 1887; *More Letters*, ed. F. Darwin and A. C. Seward, 2 vols., 1903.

Daubeny, C. G. B. *Miscellanies*, 2 vols., Oxford, 1867.

Davies, D. Horton M. *Worship and Theology in England*, 1963–.

Davidson, R. T., and Benham, W. *Life of A. C. Tait, Archbishop of Canterbury*, 2 vols., 1891.

Davidson, S. *Autobiography*, 1899.

Davies, E. T. *Religion in the industrial revolution in South Wales*, Cardiff, 1965.

Dawson, A. *Joseph Parker*, 1901.

Dawson, E. C. *James Hannington*, 1887.

De Morgan, S. E. *Memoirs of Augustus de Morgan*, 1882; *Reminiscences*, ed. M. A. de Morgan, 1895.

Denison, Edward. *Letters and other writings of the late Edward Denison*, ed. Sir Baldwyn Leighton, 1875.

Diggle, J. W. *The Lancashire Life of Bishop Fraser*, 3rd ed., 1889.

Do we believe? A correspondence in the *Daily Telegraph*, 1904. Introd. by W. L. Courtney, 1905.

Dolling, R. W. R. *Ten Years in a Portsmouth Slum*, 1896.

Donaldson, A. B. *The Bishopric of Truro: the first twenty-five years, 1877–1902*, 1902; *R. W. Church*, 1905; *H. P. Liddon*, 1905.

Dorling, W. *Memoirs of Dora Greenwell*, 1885.

Drew, Mary. *Diaries and Letters*, ed. L. Masterman, 1930.

Duncan, D. *The Life and Letters of Herbert Spencer*, 1908.

Dykes, J. B. *Life and Letters*, ed. J. T. Fowler, 1897.

Dyos, H. J. *Victorian Suburb: a study of the growth of Camberwell*, Leicester, 1961.

Eden, G. R., and Macdonald, F. C. *Lightfoot of Durham*, 1932.

Edwards, A. G. *A Handbook on Welsh Church Defence*, 3rd ed., 1895.

Eiseley, L. C. *Darwin's Century*, 1959.

Ellegård, Alvar. *Darwin and the general reader*, Göteborg, 1958.

Elliott-Binns, L. E. *English Thought 1860–1900: the theological aspect*, 1956.

Ellman, E. B. *Recollections of a Sussex Parson*, 1912.

Elton, Oliver. *F. Y. Powell: A life, and a selection from his letters and occasional writings*, 2 vols., Oxford, 1906.

Eve, A. S., and Creasey, C. H. *Life and work of John Tyndall*, 1945.

Facts and Figures about the Church of England, 1, 1959; 3, 1965.

Fairchild, H. N. *Religious Trends in English Poetry*. New York, 1939–.

Farrar, Reginald. *The Life of F. W. Farrar*, new ed., 1905.

Figgis, J. N., and Laurence, R. V. (ed.). *Selections from the Correspondence of the first Lord Acton*, vol. 1, 1917.

Fleming, D. H. *J. W. Draper and the religion of Science*, Philadelphia, 1950.

Fox, Adam. *Dean Inge*, 1960.

Frost, M. (ed.). *Historical Companion to Hymns Ancient and Modern*, 1962.

Fullerton, W. Y. *F. B. Meyer: a biography*, 1929.

Gardiner, A. G. *The Life of Sir William Harcourt*, 2 vols., 1923.

Gasquet, F. A. (ed.). *Lord Acton and his circle*, 1906.

Glover, Willis Borders. *Evangelical nonconformists and higher criticism in the nineteenth century*, 1954.

Gooch, G. P. *Life of Lord Courtney*, 1920.

Gosse, E. W. *The Life of P. H. Gosse*, 1890; *Father and Son: a study of two temperaments*, 1907.

Gott, John. *Letters of Bishop Gott*, ed. A. J. Worlledge, 1919.

Goulburn, E. M. *John William Burgon*, 2 vols., 1892.

Graham, E. *The Harrow Life of H. M. Butler, D.D.*, 1920.

Grant, Brewin. *The dissenting world*, 2nd ed., 1869.

Grant, J. W. *Free Churchmanship in England, 1870–1940, with special reference to Congregationalism*, 1955.

Graves, R. P. *Life of Sir W. R. Hamilton*, 3 vols., Dublin, 1882–.

Gray, Asa. *Darwiniana*, ed. A. H. Dupree, Cambridge, Mass., 1963.

Gray, C. N. (ed.). *Life of Robert Gray*, by H. L. Lear, 2 vols., 1876.

Green, J. R., *Letters of*, ed. L. Stephen, 1901.

Green, V. H. H. *Oxford Common Room: a study of Lincoln College and Mark Pattison*, 1957.

Greenslade, S. L. (ed.). *The Cambridge History of the Bible*, vol. 2, Cambridge, 1963.

Gregory, Robert. *Robert Gregory, 1819–1911; being the autobiography of Robert Gregory, Dean of St. Paul's*, ed. W. H. Hutton, 1912.

Grosskurth, Phyllis. *John Addington Symonds*, 1964.

Guedalla, P. *The Queen and Mr. Gladstone, 1845–98*, 2 vols., 1933.

Guy, R. E. *The Synods in English: being the text of the four Synods of Westminster, translated into English*, 1886.

Hadden, R. H. *Reminiscences of William Rogers*, 1888.

Haight, G. S. *George Eliot*, Oxford, 1968.

Hare, Humphrey. *Swinburne: a biographical approach*, 1949.

Harford, J. B., and Macdonald, F. C. *H. C. G. Moule, Bishop of Durham*, 1922.

Harris, J. Rendel. *The Life of F. W. Crossley*, 2nd ed., 1899.

Hatch, Edwin. *Memorials*, ed. by his brother, 1890.

Haw, G. (ed.). *Christianity and the Working Classes*, 1906.

Hearnshaw, F. J. C. *The centenary history of King's College, London, 1828–1928*, 1929.

Heasman, K. *Army of the Church*, 1968; *Evangelicals in Action*, 1962.

Heath, F. G. *The English Peasantry*, 1874; *British Rural Life and Labour*, 1911.

Helmore, F. *Memoir of the Rev. Thomas Helmore*, 1891.

Hemphill, S. *A History of the Revised Version of the New Testament*, 1906.

Henson, H. Hensley (ed.). *A Memoir of Sir William Anson*, Oxford, 1920.

Herford, C. H. *P. H. Wicksteed*, 1931.

Heygate, W. E. *Anecdotes of an old Parson*, 1892.

Hickey, J. *Urban Catholics*, 1967.

Himmelfarb, G. *Darwin and the Darwinian Revolution*, 1959; *Victorian Minds*, 1968.

Hinchliff, P. B. *The Anglican Church in South Africa*, 1963; *J. W. Colenso, Bishop of Natal*, 1964.

Hirst, F. W. *Early Life and Letters of John Morley*, 2 vols., 1927.

Hodder, Edwin. *The Life of Samuel Morley*, 3rd ed., 1887.

Hogben, John. *Richard Holt Hutton of the 'Spectator'*, 2nd ed., Edinburgh, 1900.

Hole, C. *Then and Now*, 1901.

Holland, H. S. *A Forty Years' Friendship: letters to Mary Drew*, ed. S. L. Ollard, 1919.

Hood, E. Paxton. *Thomas Binney*, 1874.

Hooykaas, R. *The Principle of Uniformity in Geology, Biology, and Theology*, Leyden, 1963.

Hopkins, A. B. *Elizabeth Gaskell, her life and Work*, 1952.

Hopkins, G. M. *Journals and Papers*, ed. H. House and G. Storey, 1959.

Horne, C. S. *Nonconformity in the Nineteenth Century*, 1905.

Hort, A. F. *Life and Letters of F. J. A. Hort*, 2 vols., 1896.

Horton, R. F. *An autobiography*, 1918.

Horton Davies. *See* Davies, D. Horton M.

Houghton, W. E. *The Victorian Frame of Mind, 1830–70*, New Haven, 1957; *The art of Newman's Apologia*, New Haven, 1945.

How, F. D. *Archbishop Maclagan*, 1911; *Bishop Walsham How: a memoir*, 1898; *A memoir of Bishop Sir Lovelace Tomlinson Stamer*, 1910; *The Rev. T. M. B. Bulkeley-Owen. A memoir*, 1914.

How, W. Walsham. *Lighter Moments*, ed. F. D. How, 1900.

Howson, J. S. (ed.). *Essays on cathedrals*, 1872.

Hughes, Dorothea Price. *The Life of Hugh Price Hughes*, 4th ed., 1905.

Hughes, Thomas. *James Fraser, second Bishop of Manchester. A Memoir*, new ed., 1888.

Hunter, L. S. *John Hunter*, 1921.

Hunter, W. W. *Life of B. H. Hodgson*, 1896.

Huntington, G. *Random Recollections of some noted bishops, divines and worthies of the 'Old Church' of Manchester*, 1893.

Hutton, R. H. *Aspects of religious and scientific thought*, ed. E. M. Roscoe, 1899; *Criticisms on Contemporary Thought and Thinkers*, 2 vols., 1894.

Hutton, W. H. *William Stubbs, Bishop of Oxford, 1825–1901*, 1906.

Huxley, Leonard. *Life and Letters of T. H. Huxley*, 3 vols., 1903; *Life and Letters of Sir J. D. Hooker*, 1918.

Huxley, T. H. *Collected Essays*, 1896.

Hyde, H. M. *A Victorian Historian: private letters of W. E. H. Lecky, 1859–78*, 1947.

Ideas and Beliefs of the Victorians: an historic revaluation of the Victorian age, 1949.

Illingworth, J. R. *The Life and Work of J. R. Illingworth, as portrayed by his letters*, ed. by his wife, 1917.

Inglis, K. S. *Churches and the Working Classes in Victorian England*, 1963; 'English Nonconformity and Social Reform, 1880-1900' in *Past and Present*, vol. iv, 1958–9.

Jacks, L. P. *Life and Letters of Stopford Brooke*, 2 vols., 1917.

Jasper, R. C. D. *Prayer Book Revision in England, 1800–1900*, 1954.

Jessopp, Augustus. *Arcady: for better for worse*, 1887; *The Trials of a Country Parson*, 1890.

Johnston, J. O. *Life and Letters of H. P. Liddon*, 1904.

Jones, C. A., and Appleton, R. *A History of the Jesus Lane Sunday School*, Cambridge, 1877.

Jones, Harry. *East and West London*, 1875; *Fifty Years*, 1895.

Jones, J. D. *Three Score Years and Ten*, 1940.

Jones, Sir Lawrence Evelyn. *A Victorian Boyhood*, 1955; *An Edwardian Youth*, 1956.

Jones, P. d'A. *The Christian Socialist Revival, 1877–1914*, Princeton, 1968.

Jowett, B. *Letters*, ed. E. Abbott and L. Campbell, 1899.

Julian, John. *A dictionary of hymnology*, revised ed., 1907.

Kegan Paul. *See* Paul.

Keith, Arthur. *Darwin Revalued*, 1955.

Kelly, H. H. *No pious person: autobiographical recollections*, ed. by G. Every, 1960.

Kent, J. H. S. *From Darwin to Blatchford; the role of Darwinism in Christian apologetics, 1875–1910*, 1966.

Kilvert's Diary, ed. W. Plomer, 2nd ed., 3 vols., 1961.

King, E. *The Love and Wisdom of God*, ed. B. W. Randolph, 1910.

Kirk-Smith, H. *William Thomson, Archbishop of York*, 1958.

Kitchin, G. W. *E. H. Browne, Bishop of Winchester. A memoir*, 1895; *Ruskin in Oxford, and other studies*, 1904.

Knox, E. A. *Reminiscences of an Octogenarian, 1847–1934*, 1935.

Knox, W. L., and Vidler, A. R. *The development of modern Catholicism*, 1933.

Langley, A. S. *Birmingham Baptists, Past and Present*, 1939.

Lansbury, Edgar. *George Lansbury, my father*, rev. ed., 1934.

Lansbury, George. *My Life*, 1928.

Layard, G. S. *Mrs Lynn Linton*, 1901.

Lecky, E. *A memoir of W. E. H. Lecky*, 1909.

Lee, A. A. *A Happy Warrior: Thomas Yates, D.D.*, 1938.

Lennox, Cuthbert. *Henry Drummond*, 3rd ed., 1901.

Lerry, George. *A. G. Edwards*, 1940.

Leslie, Shane. *Memoir of J. E. C. Bodley*, 1930; *Cardinal Gasquet; a memoir*, 1953; *Cardinal Manning, his life and labours*, Dublin, 1953.

Lidgett, J. Scott. *Reminiscences*, 1928.

Bishop Lightfoot. Reprinted from the *Quarterly Review*, London, 1894.

Lonsdale, M. *Sister Dora: a biography*, 1880.

Luke, W. B. *Sir Wilfrid Lawson*, 1900.

Lyell, Sir Charles. *Life, letters and journals*, ed. by his sister-in-law, 2 vols., 1881.

Lyons, A. N. *Robert Blatchford*, 1910.

Lyttelton, E. S. *Alfred Lyttelton*, 1917.

Lyttelton, W. H. *The Life of Man after Death*, 4th ed., 1893. With preface by E. S. Talbot and In Memoriam by Lady F. Cavendish.

Macan, R. W. *Religious Changes in Oxford during the last fifty years*, revised ed., Oxford, 1918.

McClelland, V. A. *Cardinal Manning: his public life and influence, 1865–92*, 1962.

McCormack, Arthur. *Cardinal Vaughan*, 1966.

Macdonald, F. W. *The Life of W. M. Punshon*, 3rd ed., 1888; *Reminiscences of my early ministry*, 1912.

Macfadyen, D. *Alexander Mackennal. Life and Letters*, 1905.

V.C.–17

McKnight, W. H. E. *Recollections and Letters*, ed. E. I. Thomson, 1907.

Maclagan, W. D. *The Church and the People*, 1882.

Maclean, C. M. *Mark Rutherford: a biography of William Hale White*, 1955.

MacNutt, F. A. *A Papal Chamberlain*, 1936.

Maison, Margaret Mary. *Search your soul, Eustace: a survey of the religious mind in the Victorian age*, 1961.

Maitland, F. W. *The Life and Letters of Leslie Stephen*, 1906.

Major, H. D. A. *The Life and Letters of William Boyd Carpenter*, 1925.

Malan, S. C. *Solomon Caesar Malan; memorials of his life and writings*, 1897.

Mallet, Marie. *Life with Queen Victoria: Marie Mallet's letters from court, 1887–1901*, ed. by V. Mallet, 1968.

Mallock, W. H. *Atheism and the value of life*, 1884.

Mann, Tom. *Memoirs*, 1923.

Marchant, Sir James. *Dr John Clifford*, 1924; *A. R. Wallace: Letters and Reminiscences*, 2 vols., 1916.

Mare, M. L., and Percival, A. C. *Victorian best-seller: the world of Charlotte M. Yonge*, 1947.

Marlowe, John. *Late Victorian: the life of Sir Arnold Talbot Wilson*, 1967.

Marsh, P. T. *The Victorian Church in Decline*, 1969.

Marson, C. L. *Huppim and Muppim*, etc., with a memoir by H. S. Holland, 1915.

Martin, E. W. *The secret people: English village life after 1750*, 1954.

Martindale, C. C. *Bernard Vaughan, S.J.*, 1923.

Masterman, Lucy. *C. F. G. Masterman*, 1939.

Matheson, P. E. *The Life of Hastings Rashdall*, 1928.

Mathew, David. *Lord Acton*, 1968.

Matthews, W. R., and Atkins, W. M. (ed.). *A history of St Paul's Cathedral and the men associated with it*, 1957.

Max Müller, Friedrich. *Auld Lang Syne*, 2 vols., 1898–9; *My Autobiography*, 1901. *The Life and Letters of F. Max Müller*, ed. by his wife, 2 vols., 1902.

Mayor, J. E. B. *Charles Cardale Babington*, Cambridge, 1895; *Twelve Cambridge Sermons*, ed. with memoir by H. F. Stewart.

Mayor, S. *The Churches and the Labour Movement*, 1967.

Meacham, S. 'The Church in the Victorian City' in *Victorian Studies*, March 1968, 359ff.

Mearns, Andrew. *The statistics of attendance at public worship*, 1882.

Merivale, Charles. *Autobiography of Dean Merivale, with selections from his correspondence*, ed. J. A. Merivale, 1899.

Meyrick, F. *Memories of Life at Oxford, and experiences in Italy, Greece, Turkey, Germany, Spain, and elsewhere*, 1905.

Miall, C. S. *Henry Richard MP*, 1889.

Monypenny, W. F., and Buckle, G. E. *The Life of Benjamin Disraeli, Earl of Beaconsfield*, new ed., 2 vols., 1929.

Morgan, K. O. O. *Wales in British Politics 1868–1922*, Cardiff, 1963.

Morley, John (Viscount). *On Compromise*, new ed., 1886; *Recollections*, 2 vols., 1917; *The Life of William Ewart Gladstone*, 2 vols., 1908.

Morris, M. C. F. *Yorkshire Reminiscences*, Oxford, 1922.

Moule, H. C. G. *The Evangelical School in the Church of England*, 1901.

W. F. Moulton, a memoir, 1899.

Mudie-Smith, Richard. *The Religious Life of London*, 1904.

Muggeridge, K., and Adam, R. *Beatrice Webb*, 1967.

Müller, Max. *See* Max Müller.

Neill, S. C. *The Interpretation of the New Testament, 1861–1961*, Oxford, 1966.

Nethercot, A. H. *The first five lives of Annie Besant*, 1961.

Nettleship, R. L. *Memoir of T. H. Green*, 1906.

Nias, John. *Flame from an Oxford Cloister: the Life and writings of P. N. Waggett*, 1961.

Osborne, Lord Sidney Godolphin. *The Letters of S. G. O. published in* The Times *1844–1888*, ed. Arnold White, 2 vols., 1891.

Osborne, C. E. *The Life of Father Dolling*, 1903.

Otter, J. L. *Nathaniel Woodard*, 1925.

Overton, J. H. *John Hannah*, 1890.

Overton, J. H., and Wordsworth, E. *Christopher Wordsworth, 1807–85*, new ed., 1890.

Oxenden, Ashton. *The History of my Life*, 1891.

Paget, E. K. *Henry Luke Paget*, 1939.

Paget, Sir James. *Memoirs and Letters*, ed. Stephen Paget, 3rd ed., 1903.

Paget, S. (ed.). *H. S. Holland. Memoirs and Letters*, 1921.

Paget, S., and Crum, J. M. C. *Francis Paget, Bishop of Oxford*, 1912.

Parker, Joseph. *Paterson's Parish: a lifetime among the dissenters*, 1898; *A preacher's life. An autobiography and an album*, 1899.

Pattison, Dora. *See* Lonsdale, M.

Pattison, Mark. *Memoirs*, 1885; *Suggestions on academical organisation, with especial reference to Oxford*, Edinburgh, 1868.

Paul, C. Kegan. *Memories*, 1899.

Peake, L. S. *A. S. Peake; a memoir*, 1930.

Pearson, C. H. Ed. W. Stebbing, 1900.

Pearson, Karl. *The Life, Letters and Labours of Francis Galton*, 4 vols., Cambridge, 1914–30.

Peel, A., and Marriott, J. A. R. *R. F. Horton*, 1937.

Peel, Albert (ed.). *Letters to a Victorian editor, H. Allon, editor of the British Quarterly Review*, 1929.

Peel, A. *The Life of Alexander Stewart*, 1948.

Pelling, Henry. *The origins of the Labour party, 1880–1900*, 2nd ed., Oxford, 1965.

Pelling, H. M. 'Religion and the Nineteenth Century British Working Class' in *Past and Present*, XXVII, 1964, 128–133.

Perkins, Jocelyn. *Westminster Abbey: its worship and ornaments*, 2 vols., 1938–40.

Perowne, J. J. S. *Report of the Commissioners appointed by the Lord Bishop of Worcester to inquire into the needs and resources of the Church in the rural deaneries of Birmingham and Northfield*, Birmingham, 1898.

Phillips, Sir Thomas. *Wales*, 1849.

Picht, W. *Toynbee Hall and the English Settlement Movement*, 1914.

Pick, J. A. *G. M. Hopkins, priest and poet*, 2nd ed., 1966.

Pike, G. H. *Dr Parker and his friends*, 1907.

Pollock, J. C. *A Cambridge Movement*, 1953; *The Keswick Story*, 1964; *Moody without Sankey*, 1963.

Porritt, Arthur. *J. D. Jones of Bournemouth*, 1942.

The Position of the Agricultural Labourer in the past and in the future. By an Agricultural Labourer, 1885.

Postgate, R. W. *The Life of George Lansbury*, 1951.

Potter, Beatrice. *See* Webb, Beatrice.

Prestige, G. L. *The Life of Charles Gore*, 1935; *St. Paul's in its glory, 1831–1911*, 1955.

Prothero, G. W. *A memoir of Henry Bradshaw*, 1888.

Prothero, R. E. *The Life and Correspondence of A. P. Stanley*, 2 vols., 1893.

Purcell, E. S. *Life of Cardinal Manning*, 2nd ed., 2 vols., 1896.

Pusey, E. B. *Spiritual Letters*, ed. J. O. Johnston and W. C. E. Newbolt, new ed., 1901.

Ramsey, A. M. *From Gore to Temple*, 1960.

Reid, T. Wemyss. *Life of W. E. Forster*, 4th ed., 2 vols., 1888.

Reynolds, J. S. *Canon Christopher of St. Aldate's*, 1968.

Richter, M. *The Politics of Conscience*, 1964.

Rickards, E. C. *Bishop Moorhouse*, 1920; *Felicia Skene of Oxford. A Memoir*, 1902.

Robson, R. (ed.). *Ideas and institutions of Victorian Britain: essays in honour of G. Kitson Clark*, 1967.

Rogers, J. Guinness. *An Autobiography*, 1903.

Romanes, Ethel. *Charlotte Mary Yonge*, 1908.

Romanes, G. J. *Life and letters*, written and ed. by his wife, new ed., 1896.

Roskell, M. F. *Memoirs of F. K. Amherst, Bishop of Northampton*, 1903.

Rothblatt, S. *The Revolution of the Dons; Cambridge and society in Victorian England*, 1968.

Rowan, E. *Wilson Carlile and the Church Army*, 1905.

Rowntree, B. S. *Poverty: a study of town life*, new ed., 1922.

Rupp, E. G. *Thomas Jackson, Methodist patriarch*, 1954.

Russell, G. W. E. *Edward King, sixtieth Bishop of Lincoln*, 3rd. ed., 1912; (ed.) *Sir Wilfrid Lawson. A Memoir*, 1909; *Dr. Liddon*, 1905; (ed.) *H. C. Shuttleworth. A Memoir*, 1903; *Lady Victoria Buxton*, 1919; *Fifteen chapters of Autobiography*, 1915; *Collections and recollections*, series 1–2, 1909; *Arthur Stanton: a memoir*, 1917; *Selected essays on Literary Subjects*, 1914; *Basil Wilberforce: a memoir*, 1917.

Sandall, R., and Wiggins, A. R. *A history of the Salvation Army*, 1947–.

Sanday, W. *Divine Overruling*, Edinburgh, 1920.

Sayce, A. H. *Reminiscences*, 1923.

Scholes, P. A. *The mirror of music, 1844–1944: a century of musical life in Britain as reflected in the pages of the Musical Times*, 2 vols., 1947.

Selbie, W. B. *The life of A. M. Fairbairn*, 1914; (ed.) *The life of Charles Sylvester Horne*, 1920.

Selley, Ernest. *Village Trade Unions in two centuries*, 1919.

Simeon, A. B. *A short memoir of Thomas Chamberlain*, 1892.

Simey, T. S., and M. B. *Charles Booth, social scientist*, Oxford, 1960.

Simpson, J. Y. *Henry Drummond*, Edinburgh, 1901.

Smellie, A. *Evan Henry Hopkins*, 1920.

Smith, B. A. *Dean Church*, 1958.

Smith, G. Adam. *The Life of Henry Drummond*, 1899.

Smith, G. B. *The life and speeches of John Bright*, 2 vols., 1881.

Smith, P. Vernon. *The Law of Churchwardens and Sidesmen in the Twentieth Century*, 1903.

Smith, Warren Sylvester. *The London Heretics, 1870–1914*, 1967.

Snead-Cox, J. G. *The life of Cardinal Vaughan*, 2 vols., 1910.

Snowden, Philip. *An Autobiography*, 2 vols., 1934.

Sparrow, J. H. A. *Mark Pattison and the Idea of a University*, Cambridge, 1967.

Stephen, Leslie. *An Agnostic's Apology, and other essays*, 1893, 2nd ed., 1903.

Stephen, M. D. 'Gladstone and the composition of the final court in ecclesiastical causes, 1850–1873', in *Historical Journal* IX, 2 (1966), 191–200.

Stephens, W. R. W. *The Life and Letters of E. A. Freeman*, 2 vols., 1895.

Stephenson, A. M. G. *The First Lambeth Conference 1867*, 1967.

Stephenson, G. E. S. *Talbot, 1844–1934*, 1936.

Stevens, T. P. *Father Adderley*, 1943.

Stevenson, Lionel (ed.). *Victorian Fiction: a guide to research*, Cambridge, Mass., 1964.

Stewart, W. *James Keir Hardie: a biography*, new ed., 1925.

Stirling, A. M. W. *The Richmond Papers*, 1926.

Stokes, Sir George G. *Memoir and Scientific Correspondence*, ed. J. Larmor, 2 vols., Cambridge, 1907.

Stranks, C. J. *Dean Hook*, 1954.

Street, A. E. *Memoir of George Edmund Street*, 1888.

Stubbs, C. W. *The land of the labourers*, 1884.

H. B. Swete: a Remembrance, 1918.

Swinburne, A. C. *Letters*, ed. C. Y. Lang, 6 vols., New Haven, 1959–62.

Taine, Hippolyte Adolphe. *Notes on England*, ed. by E. Hyams, 1957.

Temple, Frederick. *The Relations between Religion and Science*, 1884; *Memoirs of Archbishop Temple*. By Seven Friends. Ed. by E. G. Sandford, 2 vols., 1906.

Temple, W. *Life of Bishop Percival*, 1921.

Tennyson, Alfred, 1st Baron. A memoir by his son, 2 vols., 1897.

Thompson, L. V. *Robert Blatchford: portrait of an Englishman*, 1951.

Thomson, E. H. *William Thomson, Archbishop of York: Life and Letters*, 1919.

Thring, Edward. *Life, diary and letters*, 2 vols., 1898.

Tillyard, A. I. *A History of University Reform from 1800 to the present time*, Cambridge, 1913.

Tollemache, L. A. *Recollections of Pattison*, 1885.

Torr, Dona. *Tom Mann and his times*, I, 1956.

Trench, M. *Charles Lowder*, 1881; *James Skinner, a memoir*, new ed., 1884; (ed.) *Letters and Memorials of R. C. Trench*, 2 vols., 1888.

Trevelyan, G. M. *Grey of Fallodon*, 1937; *An Autobiography and other Essays*, 1949.

Trevelyan, J. P. *The Life of Mrs. Humphry Ward*, 1923.

Trevor, John. *My Quest for God*, 1897.

Trevor, Meriol. *Newman, Light in winter*, 1962.

Trilling, Lionel. *Matthew Arnold*, 1939.

Tuckwell, *W. Reminiscences of Oxford*, 2nd ed., 1907; *Reminiscences of a radical parson*, 1905.

Unbelief in Christian England. By a Mission Priest, 1904.

Unwin, George, and Telford, John. *M. G. Pearse*, 1930.

Vaughan, D. J. *Questions of the Day*, 1894.

Vaughan, Herbert, Cardinal. *Letters to Lady Herbert of Lea*, ed. S. Leslie, 1942.

Victoria, Queen, The Letters of, ed. G. E. Buckle, 2nd series (1862–85), 3 vols.; 3rd series (1886–1901), 3 vols., 1930–32.

Vidler, A. R. *F. D. Maurice and others*, 1966.

Wagner, D. O. *The Church of England and social reform since 1854*, New York, 1930.

Wake, Joan. *A Northamptonshire Rector: The Life of Henry Isham Longden*, Northampton, 1943.

Wallace, A. R. *My Life*, 2 vols., 1905.

Walpole, Spencer. *The History of Twenty-Five Years (1856–80)*, 4 vols., 1904–08.

Ward, E. M. *Memories of Ninety Years*, 1924.

Ward, Maisie. *Gilbert Keith Chesterton*, 1944; *Return to Chesterton*, 1952; *The Wilfrid Wards and the Transition*, 2 vols., 1934–38.

Ward, Mary Augusta, Mrs. Humphry. *A Writer's Recollections*, 1918.

Ward, Wilfrid. *The Life of John Henry, Cardinal Newman*, 2 vols., 1912.

Watson, Aaron. *Life of Thomas Burt*, 1908.

Watson, E. W. *Life of John Wordsworth*, 1915.

Webb, Beatrice. *My Apprenticeship*, 2nd ed., 1946.

Webb, C. C. J. *A study of religious thought in England from 1850*, Oxford, 1933.

White, A. D. *Autobiography*, New York, 1905.

White, W. Hale. *The autobiography of Mark Rutherford, dissenting minister*, 1881.

Wickham, E. R. *Church and People in an industrial city*, 1957.

Williams-Ellis, M. A. N. *Darwin's moon; a biography of A. R. Wallace*, 1966.

Williamson, D. *Alexander Maclaren*, 1910.

Wills, Alfred. *A treatise on the powers and duties of parish vestries in ecclesiastical matters*, 1855.

Wilson, J. A. *The Life of Bishop Hedley*, 1930.

Wilson, J. M. An Autobiography, ed. A. T. and J. S.Wilson, 1932.

Wilson, J. M. *Six Lectures on Pastoral Theology*, 1903.

Winnington-Ingram, A. F. *Work in Great Cities*, 1896.

Winstanley, D. A. *Later Victorian Cambridge*, Cambridge, 1947.

Woodham-Smith, Cecil. *Florence Nightingale*, 1950.

Woods, C. E. *Archdeacon Wilberforce: his ideals and teaching*, 1917.

Wordsworth, J. *The Church and the Universities*, Oxford, 1880; *The one religion*, Oxford, 1881.

Yeo, S., and others. *For Christ and People: Studies of four socialist priests and prophets of the Church of England between 1870 and 1930.* (Thomas Hancock, Stewart Headlam, Charles Marson, Conrad Noel.)

Yonge, C. M. *Musings over John Keble's 'Christian Year' and 'Lyra Innocentium', with recollections of John Keble*, Oxford and London, 1871; *John Keble's Parishes*, 1898; *Old Times at Otterbourne*, 2nd ed., Winchester, 1891.

INDEX

Abbott, Edwin A., 65, 137–9, 148
Aberdeen, 4th Earl of, 365
Abide with me, 177, 467
Abingdon, 7th Earl of, 403
Accrington, 95, 258
act of uniformity, 314–15
act of uniformity amendment act (1872), 310, 361
Acton, Sir John (later Lord Acton), 71, 403, 406, 409, 416–18
Adderley, J. G., 150, 167, 267, 270, 338
Addington Park, sold, 384
Addis, W. E., 127
Additional Curates Society, 244
advowsons, 208 ff.
agnosticism, 122 ff., 127, 181, 184
agricultural unions, 154 ff.
Ainger, A. C., 223
Ainon (Rhondda), 184
Aitken, W. Hay, 287, 299
Albert, Prince Consort, 329–30
Alexander, Mrs. C. F., 469–71
Alford, Henry (Dean of Canterbury 1857–71), 372
Alington, Cyril, 130
Allen, John, Congregational pastor, 182
Allen, John (Archdeacon of Salop), 186, 203
Allies, T. W., 416
Allison, Falkner, 165
Almondbury, Yorks, 304
Alton Towers, 404
Amberley, Viscount, 115–16
Amherst, F. K. (R.C. Bishop of Northampton 1858–79), 404, 408
Amiel, H. F., 141
Ampleforth, 458
Amport, Hants, 214
Anderson, David, Bishop of Rupert's Land 1849–64, 344
Anderson, Sir Robert, 74
Andover, Hants, 214
Andrewes, Lancelot, 108
Anglican orders, condemned by Pope, 354, 407
Annus Sanctus, 410
anthems, 396 ff.
anthropology and religion, 33 ff.
Apologia pro vita sua (Newman), 411 ff.

apostles' creed, 147–8
Apostolicae curae (bull of 13 September 1896 condemning Anglican orders), 354, 407
Appleton, Charles, 68, 442–3
Arch, Joseph, 155–7, 284
Archko Volume, The, 42
Argyll, 8th Duke of, 19, 34, 64
Armes, Philip, organist, 373
Armfield, H. T., 249
Arnold, Matthew (1822–88); and *Essays and Reviews*, 89; *Literature and Dogma*, admired by Swinburne, 118; criticised by Hutton, 124–5; not influential as theologian, 129; influence on Mrs. Humphry Ward, 141; criticises dissenting architecture, 241; lecture on the Kingdom of God, 272–3; consulted on teaching of morality in schools, 300–1; professor of poetry at Oxford, 447; *The Study of Poetry*, 463; 464
Arnold, Dr. Thomas (headmaster of Rugby), 141, 164, 280, 307, 393, 462
Arnold, Thomas, the younger, 127, 141
art for art's sake, 118–19, 463
articles, thirty-nine. *See* subscription
Arundell of Wardour, Lord, 403
Ascott-under-Wychwood, 156
Ashburnham, 5th Earl of, 403
Ashburton, Devon, 198
Ashill, Norfolk, 177
Ashton-under-Lyme, 241
Ashwell, A. R., 247, 250
Athanasian creed, 130, 132, 138, 150, 316, 339, 361, 470
atheists, 125–7, 205, 231, 266–8, 424. *See* Bradlaugh
Atkinson, J. C., 180–1, 186
Atlay, James (Bishop of Hereford 1868–1894), 88, 193
Authorised Version of the Bible, 43 ff., 172
Aveling, Edward, 274, 278
Awdry, W., 214

Bacon, Francis, 19
Bacup, Lancs., 231–2
Bad Squire, The, 151

489